Accounting
Information
Systems

a cycle approach

Second Edition

Leonard A. Robinson
University of Alabama in Birmingham

James R. Davis
Clemson University

C. Wayne Alderman
Auburn University

HARPER & ROW, PUBLISHERS, New York
Cambridge, Philadelphia, San Francisco,
London, Mexico City, São Paulo, Singapore, Sydney
1817

Sponsoring Editor: Peter Coveney
Project Editor: Eleanor Castellano
Text Design: Hudson River Studio
Cover Design: Hudson River Studio
Text Art: Fineline Illustrations, Inc.
Production: Willie Lane
Compositor: ComCom Division of Haddon Craftsmen, Inc.
Printer and Binder: R. R. Donnelley & Sons Company

Accounting Information Systems: A Cycle Approach, Second Edition

Copyright © 1986 by Harper & Row, Publishers, Inc.

Library of Congress Cataloging-in-Publication Data

Robinson, Leonard A., 1920–
    Accounting information systems.

    Includes bibliographies and index.
    1. Accounting—Data processing.   2. Information
storage and retrieval systems—Accounting.   I. Davis,
James Richard, 1947–   . II. Alderman, C. Wayne.
III. Title.
HF5679.R55 1986   657'.028'5   85-21905
ISBN 0-06-045515-2   87 88 9 8 7 6 5 4 3
International Edition
ISBN 0-06-350613-0   87 88 89 9   8 7 6 5 4 3 2 1

CONTENTS

⬛ Controls and Auditing   **149**

▌◗▌Information Systems Analysis and Design   **211**

I ▪ The Conversion Cycle   345

I▪▪The Administrative Cycle   **507**

■ ■Appendixes   **573**

PREFACE

The emergence of the study of information systems in university accounting curricula is evidenced by two historical facts. Less than twenty years ago, the schools offering courses in accounting information systems could be counted on the fingers of one hand. Today, all AACSB (American Assembly of Collegiate Schools of Business) accredited accounting programs are required to offer at least exposure to information systems. In many schools, however, a course in information systems is considered prerequisite to the senior-level auditing course. During the last five years alone, about a dozen new texts entitled *Accounting Information Systems* were introduced by publishers. That number approximates the entire number that was previously in print.

In our first edition, we emphasized the modern "cycle" approach to transaction flow analysis, which, especially at that time, was on the very cutting edge of auditing philosophy. Having talked to many educators since that time and having participated in numerous seminars and discussion groups on the subject, we are more convinced than ever that this approach is "on target." We have consistently taken the view that the study of accounting information systems in university accounting programs is comparable to the study of anatomy in a medical curriculum. Students are better able to localize their concentration and accept a higher degree of topical specificity when they can perceive its role and purpose in the larger context.

More than ever before, and increasingly in the future, accountants (public, academic, managerial, and governmental) must accept the responsibility and the burden of assuring the reliability of financial information processing systems. General acceptance of accounting products demands that of our profession.

Based on the enthusiastic reception of our first edition, we continue with renewed confidence the primary objectives of this book: (1) a thorough introduction to basic information systems theory, (2) a firm working knowledge of systems analysis and design techniques, and (3) an exposure to the several fundamental accounting information systems inherent in most business firms. Rather than permitting computer hardware and software to dominate the presentations, we include a "measured" amount of technology needed to update and augment a presumed minimum level of student competence in this area. Students enrolled in accounting information systems courses that use this text should have completed at least one course in EDP hardware and language before qualifying to enroll in accounting information systems. This assumption permits us to focus on financial information flow patterns, the need for adequate systems controls, risks inherent in control weaknesses, and refined systems output to support management decision processes. We observe these topics in a variety of systems configurations (both EDP and manual) needed to produce the desired results.

Organization. The overall structure of the book remains essentially unchanged. Following a brief introduction in Section A, information systems concepts and procedures are discussed in Section B. A separate chapter specifically addressing microcomputers has been added to this section (Chapter 5). Systems controls and auditing are again contained in Section C. Section D begins to direct the reader's attention more precisely to information systems analysis and design theory, ending with an overview of the whole accounting information systems network cast in four operating cycles: spending, conversion (production), revenue, and administrative. Sections E, F, G, and H cover the several accounting information subsystems that are, after all, the only justification for writing an *accounting* information systems book.

Nine chapters covering twelve major subsystems constitute the four cycles that comprise the modern approach to auditing. In writing these chapters, we relied heavily on staff auditing procedures followed by several of the national accounting firms.

The final part, Section I, contains four appendixes. Appendixes A and B cover specialized information systems in banking and hospital institutions. Appendixes C and D present comprehensive "real-world" cases for student analysis.

Each chapter is followed by a set of review questions and a number of "situational" cases and problems, some taken from the actual business environment and others adapted from professional certification examinations. All have been selected to provide an in-depth understanding of the material presented in the respective chapters. Beginning with Chapter 10, the last two problems at the end of each chapter suggest student assignments on the two comprehensive cases in Appendixes C and D. A solutions manual covering all questions, problems, and cases is available.

New to this edition. In response to adopters and reviewers, we have either added or expanded the following:

- Chapter 5, mentioned above, is a brand new chapter on microcomputers and small business systems.
- Chapter 13, covering production control systems, includes a production system configuration.
- A new Comprehensive Case (Appendix D: Bubbling Stone Beverage Company) presents an additional opportunity for student analysis.
- Additional end-of-chapter problems provide much more material for student review.
- Terms discussed in the chapters are now included at the end of early chapters.
- The expanded glossary now includes terms that bring the student up to date with the current business environment.
- A brand new Casebook is available that provides twelve additional cases and that can be used as a supplement to this book or to any other text. It comes with its own solutions manual.

We express appreciation to Touche Ross Foundation, Ernst & Whinney, Arthur Andersen, Coopers & Lybrand, the American Institute of Certified Public Accountants, the Financial Executives Institute, the Institute of Internal Auditors, and the Institute of Management Accounting for their permission to use problems and questions from professional examination materials, and various in-house publications. We are especially grateful to Russell Manufacturing Company, Lockheed, West-Point Pepperell Company, Sewell Manufacturing Company, Georgia Power Company, Toms Foods, Inc., Uniroyal, Ampex, Vermont-American, Vulcan Materials, Moore Handley Hardware, Golden Flake, U.S. Pipe and Foundry, and other companies that cooperated by allowing us to observe operating systems that contributed materially to the content of this text.

Finally, we are indebted to those of you throughout the country, and in New Zealand and Singapore, who adopted this book and so generously shared your comments and suggestions. We sincerely hope that this edition reflects the changes and improvements you wanted. Your continued interest and suggestions are most welcome.

We accept full responsibility for all errors.

Leonard A. Robinson
James R. Davis
C. Wayne Alderman

SECTION

INTRODUCTION

CHAPTER ONE

An Introduction to Accounting Information Systems

Accounting is more than simply recording, summarizing, and reporting the financial aspects of business operations. It transcends these routine and practical functions by encompassing the organization, the delegated responsibilities, the processing functions, and the expected outputs that we think of as the *system*. The system is in fact the "anatomy" of accounting. Its domain encompasses the entire financial dimensions of business operations including the flow of financial intelligence throughout the entire organization—and beyond.

There is often a tendency to teach accounting in the traditional approach with rigid topical specialization. Accounting curricula tend to emphasize basic accounting methodology, theory, cost allocation methods, taxation, public-sector accounting, and auditing almost as if they were independent, self-contained disciplines. There are, of course, separate and substantial bodies of knowledge and practice associated with each of these topical areas. In the instruction process, however, the interrelations among the various accounting "specialties" are too often minimized or ignored. This practice tends to negate the concept of the integral, unified nature of accounting.

The integration of the topical areas of accounting and the related functional activities may be accomplished through an in-depth study of accounting information systems (AIS). In this way the basic functional activities and their interrelations may be more readily perceived and the means for accomplishing the fundamental goals of accounting more easily understood. Succinctly, the principal aim of this book is to bring the topical areas, the functional activities, and modern electronic data processing into focus as a fully integrated system—the accounting information system.

ACCOUNTING INFORMATION SYSTEMS DEFINED

Webster defines a system as "an organized set of . . . principles intended to explain the . . . working of a systematic whole; an organized or established procedure (of operation); a manner of classifying, symbolizing, or schematizing; harmonious arrangement, or pattern, bringing order out of confusion."[1] Cast in a business environment, we may conclude that the system is an orderly approach to accomplishing organizational goals.

An engineer may use the term *system* to indicate design, symmetry, pattern, circuitry, physical flow of forces, and the like. Electronics professionals who design and build computer hardware use the term to describe not only circuitry but components and computer hardware configurations as well.

Financial management, on the other hand, is apt to allude to organization, procedure, decision processes, functional operations, and cost and information flows when using the term *system*. We shall characterize this latter perspective as management information systems (MIS), placing accounting information systems within this more pervasive concept as a subsystem, or series of subsystems. The relationship between the AIS and MIS will be discussed in greater detail later in this chapter.

Accounting information systems encompass the processes and procedures by which an organization's financial information is received, registered, recorded, handled, processed, stored, reported, and ultimately disposed of. Accountants have been historically conditioned to visualize a transaction processing model such as the one illustrated in Figure 1.1. This concept emphasizes only the recording, summarizing, and reporting phases of the accounting information system. The physical document-handling activities are by far the more visible aspects of accounting information systems, spanning the spectrum from document creation to permanent filing. These processes are uniquely adapted to such isolated subsystems as payroll, inventory, purchasing, and accounts payable.

In a similar but greatly simplified manner, accountants may view the major organizational functions of a manufacturing company as shown in Figure 1.2 and from this perspective discern the kind of accounting treatments needed to serve these functions. These are typically areas of high transaction volumes and often require special techniques and designs to accommodate management's information needs and control requirements.

OBJECTIVES OF ACCOUNTING INFORMATION

Accounting products, financial statements, are prepared for two separate user groups, each with different interests, needs, and points of view. One group is external to the corporate body in an operational sense and is concerned principally with the financial strength and performance of the business. The other group is internal management and focuses primarily on (1) organizational planning through the use of budgets and (2) data refined for use in control and decision making. Thus we may expect to observe information systems designed to produce financial information for general use and tailored to communicate specifically with outsiders. These are often called financial accounting systems. Others, called managerial accounting systems, uniquely serve management's need to (1) control operations and make responsibility assignments and (2) effectively plan the organization's financial activities through operations budgets.

Financial Accounting Systems

Generally accepted accounting principles (GAAP) have evolved over the years mainly through the coordinating efforts of the Accounting Principles Board (APB) of the AICPA, replaced in 1972 by the Financial Accounting Standards Board (FASB). These principles govern the accounting treatment for the broad spectrum of financial transactions and the content and format of published financial information. Generally, they provide uniform-

TRADITIONAL ACCOUNTING SYSTEMS.

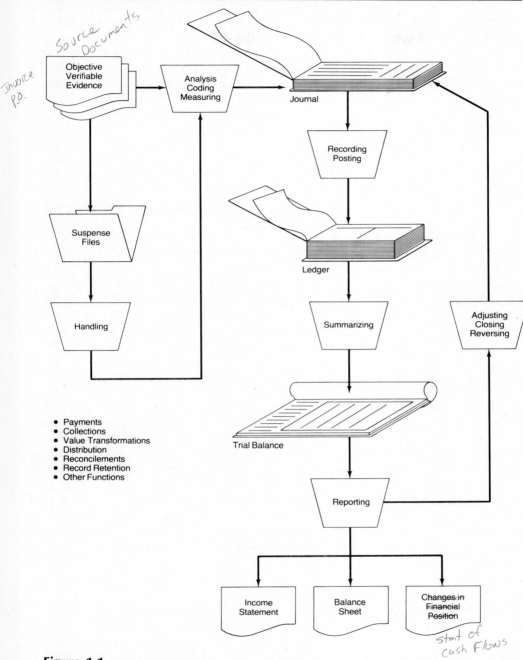

Figure 1.1

THE MANAGEMENT INFORMATION SYSTEM (AN ACCOUNTING PERSPECTIVE).

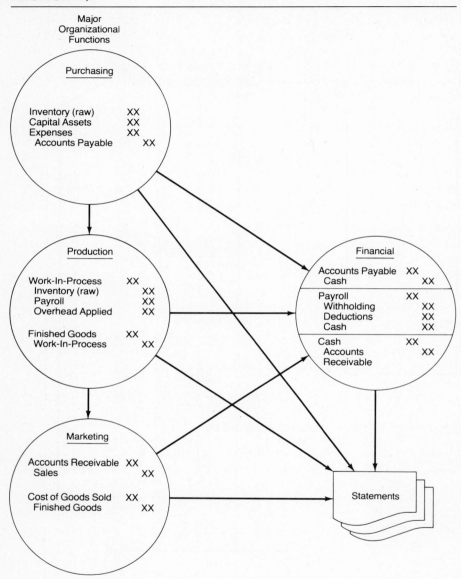

Figure 1.2

ity of reporting within the required financial statements (income statement, balance sheet, and statement of changes in financial position).

The systems that serve these needs are structured to provide transaction audit trails, guarantee the inclusion of all legitimate transactions, and provide current general ledger account balances, all of which are processed and maintained under carefully contrived internal control procedures. Societal elements that rely on financial reporting include current (and potential) stockholders, federal and state taxing authorities, banks and other financial intermediaries, labor unions, and management itself.

Managerial Accounting Systems

Managers need financial information for at least three fundamental purposes: (1) effective planning and the subsequent analysis of deviations from operating plans, (2) activation and direction of daily operations, and (3) problem solving and intelligent decision making.

No less than eight major differences between financial and managerial accounting have been identified:[2]

1. The system focuses on providing financial data for internal (management) uses.
2. Management information needs are relatively more oriented to the *future* than to the past.
3. Management accounting is *not* governed by generally accepted accounting principles.
4. The system emphasizes relevance and flexibility of data, in contrast to financial accounting.
5. Relatively more emphasis is placed on nonmonetary data, often at the expense of financial precision.
6. Managerial accounting focuses more on organizational divisions (segments) than on the entity as a whole.
7. The system draws heavily from other disciplines (economics, quantitative methods, etc.)
8. Managerial accounting is not mandatory.

The cost accounting system is the most visible of *managerial* information systems, assisting management in two important control functions. By using standard costs as a "benchmark," management is able to make a comparison with actual costs to ascertain areas of production inefficiency possibly requiring corrective action. Timely reporting of unfavorable production cost variances then permits the assignment of responsibility for poor performance. In effect, "responsibility accounting" personalizes the accounting system by monitoring performance (typically costs) from a personal control point of view rather than from an institutional standpoint.[3]

Budgeting Systems

It is almost unthinkable in the modern business world to enter a new operational period without a financial plan. Such a plan is commonly referred to as a "budget." Budgets reflect management's best estimates of its financial operations during an ensuing accounting period. They may be static, flexible (variable), short range, long range, and even continuous (perpetual) in nature.

Normally, a budget system will include and effect all subunits within an organization. Its success as an operational "road map" will be determined largely by the manner in which it is developed. The most successful method of budget construction is "bottom-up" in approach. Managers with responsibility for cost control centers will prepare their respective budget estimates. Such estimates are then refined and incorporated in larger budgets at successively higher levels of responsibility until an *overall* budget is eventually achieved. A budget forced on operating managers from "top-down" is likely to generate more excuses for failure than it will increase productivity.

The process of budgeting depends, of course, on historical data generated by the various accounting subsystems. Such data will be embellished and refined based on management's perceptions of social, political, and economic events impending, or expected to occur, during the upcoming period. Modeling and simulation techniques often yield interesting alternatives for management's considerations. The end product of the budgeting process is the full range of the pro forma operating statements by which management can see the effect of its operating strategies.

ACCOUNTING INFORMATION SYSTEMS IN TRANSITION

The recent increased interest in the information systems area is precipitated not by changes in the basic functions of accounting but by the dramatic changes in the business environment over the past several decades. Certainly, business must continue to be flexible and responsive to social and economic pressures if the free enterprise system is to survive. Thus we may expect continued, and perhaps even geometric, expansion in future business techniques and operating procedures.

Economic and Political Influences

Since the turn of the century the accounting profession has witnessed substantial changes in practice. Rapid economic and political events, beginning about the time of the Industrial Revolution and increasing in tempo to the present time, have substantially altered the accountant's functions and responsibilities. The pressure for independence has significantly redirected the original owner/client relationship, forcing the accountant into a ubiquitous role as financial police officer for government(s), financial custodian and advisor for the owner/client, producer and interpreter of financial indicators for analysts and brokers, certifier of financial strength and integrity for lenders in the money markets, and guarantor of financial fidelity on behalf of the investing public. Additionally, a growing national conscience relative to multinational business operations, a societal demand for some form of social accounting, and procedural changes imposed by the incursion of electronic data processing into accounting information systems have all complicated and magnified the judgment and disclosure problems of accountants. A chronology of events and their influence on accounting is shown in Figure 1.3.

Information Systems Evolution

Business transactions have been recorded since very early times. Indeed, the ancient Assyrians recorded business transactions on clay tablets, some of which survive to this day. The practice of accounting grew out of the need for financial history, the visual evidence of wealth and its distribution. Financial history is no less important than politi-

CHRONOLOGY OF ACCOUNTING EVENTS.

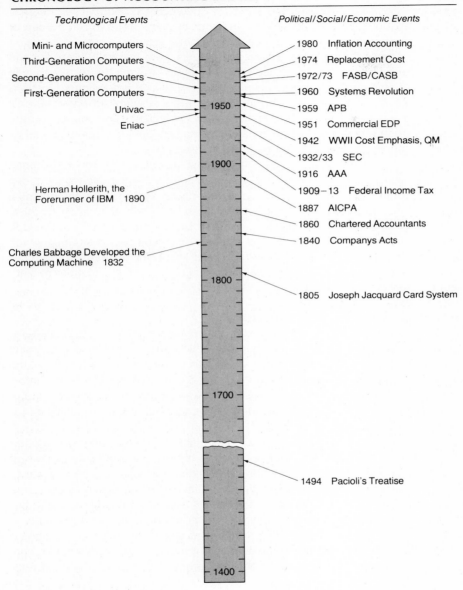

Technological Events   *Political/Social/Economic Events*

Mini- and Microcomputers

Third-Generation Computers

Second-Generation Computers

First-Generation Computers

Univac

Eniac

1980   Inflation Accounting

1974   Replacement Cost

1972/73   FASB/CASB

1960   Systems Revolution

1959   APB

1951   Commercial EDP

1942   WWII Cost Emphasis, QM

1932/33   SEC

1916   AAA

1909–13   Federal Income Tax

1887   AICPA

1860   Chartered Accountants

1840   Companys Acts

1805   Joseph Jacquard Card System

Herman Hollerith, the Forerunner of IBM   1890

Charles Babbage Developed the Computing Machine   1832

1950

1900

1800

1700

1400

1494   Pacioli's Treatise

Figure 1.3

cal, social, and economic history. Sales tickets, purchase orders, financial contracts and agreements, invoices, and receiving and shipping documents constitute only a small portion of the vast body of documentary evidence of business history. The burden of such evidence increases in direct proportion to economic growth.

Until modern times, business transaction documents were manually prepared and recorded. The sheer physical burden of such records tended to limit the system to only the most essential elements of business activity. Further, the record-keeping functions tended to become decentralized with business expansion, resulting in organizational separation for many accounting functions in the interest of efficiency and control. In spite of the abundance of business information, meaningful management information could be extracted only with some difficulty and had limited usefulness.

Beginning with the invention of the "computing machine" by the Englishman Charles Babbage in 1832, and aided by the previous creation of the punched card idea by Joseph Jacquard in France to control weaving patterns on textile looms, the potential for ameliorating the data processing burden was born. The first adaptation of these principles to mass data processing was accomplished by Herman Hollerith in the U.S. Census Bureau around 1890. There followed a period of several decades during which many companies converted their manual systems over to electric accounting machines (EAM) utilizing punched cards. Full-scale adaptation of commercial applications to electronic data processing (EDP) was begun by the mid-twentieth century.

The Impact of Advancing Technology

Perhaps the most profound external pressure placed on accounting information systems resulted from the adoption of EDP techniques. A new and powerful data processing organization (function) emerged, usurping, at least to a certain extent, many of the functions and operations previously performed by accountants. A new breed of "information systems specialists," often more oriented toward mathematics and computer languages than toward accounting applications, began to assume the responsibility for information systems analysis and design.

The ability to process huge volumes of raw data quickly and efficiently by computer with relatively error-free results began to reverse the trend toward decentralization of accounting information systems. As accounting information flows have turned "inward" toward a more centralized and independent data handling and processing concept, some of the traditional control features based on the formal organization structure have become ineffective. Such controls were designed to meter information and documents as they flowed across organizational lines and promoted accuracy while discouraging collusion and fraud. In an EDP environment the accountant must rethink traditional internal control solutions and reshape them around the data processing center, where information converges from all sources.

Indeed, in today's business environment the accountant must assume a more positive role in the analysis and design of information systems if integrity of the systems and their products is to be maintained. The importance of a general understanding of and appreciation for computers in the accountant's repertoire of professional skills is emphasized in the report of the Committee on Accounting Education, American Accounting Association and Computer Education Sub-Committee, American Institute of Certified

Public Accountants. The report emphasizes that accounting graduates are certain to be involved in the use of computers, whether in corporations or in public accounting. They should therefore begin their careers not in awe of computerized accounting systems, but with a firm grasp of the benefits and drawbacks of their use.[4]

Pros and Cons of Computerization

Computer systems owe much of their acceptance in business to the increased speed and efficiency that they provide for data processing and reporting. Without the computer, most large, complex organizations would slowly suffocate under increasing paperwork. Computers have helped management cope with the increasing problem of paper handling not only by speeding up the process, but also by eliminating some of the paper needs through the storage of data in elaborately constructed data bases and files where they can be retrieved when needed.

A second advantage of computers is the cost reduction per transaction they provide even though the initial investment is often large. This large initial investment is generally offset by continual cost reductions related to record keeping, the ability to handle large increases in volume (if properly planned), and the processing of data that permit other essential activities to be implemented or improved in the system. Also, cost reductions may occur from the greater efficiency of a computerized system over human processing. Such cost savings result from a reduction of accuracy tests, increased efficiency of tasks by both internal and external auditors, and fewer error corrections. The actual processing costs per transaction in recent years have been further reduced for companies that have kept pace with the changes in technology. For example, recent studies show that current costs are only 2 percent of comparable 1965 costs to process the same volume of data through normal routines.

Another major advantage is in data handling. Large volumes of financial transactions require efficient storage, computation, retrieval, and auditability. Computer systems are much more efficient in such applications than are manual systems, especially with data calculations. This advantage can be viewed as a substantial increase in the manageability of data.

The shift in emphasis at most managerial levels from data manipulation to data evaluation and control represents another advantage of computerization. The increased accuracy, efficiency, and timeliness of reporting can be most helpful in improving the decision-making activities of management.

The preceding advantages are very real in most organizations, but several potential disadvantages do exist. First, in small and medium-size organizations the initial costs can be prohibitive. If a company needs the advantage of a computer but cannot afford to purchase one, several alternatives are available, including time sharing and service bureaus. Second, a company should be aware of the time required to plan, install, test, and implement a computer properly. Depending on the amount and degree of organizational change, the implementation of a new system may take from a few months to several years. Third, organizational placement of the department, employee training, and reassignment of employees can be disruptive and require skillful leadership. Fourth, even after a computer is installed, acceptance by employees, clients, creditors, and auditors may be slow and troublesome.

An organization's leaders must avoid a myopic concentration on only the advantages of EDP in its decision to install or change a computerized information system. In placing the pros and cons in perspective, management must consider factors such as (1) its position in both the industry and the community, (2) size, (3) growth pattern, and (4) willingness to change.

Once computerization has been accepted by an organization, its accountants (especially) must begin to educate themselves in EDP concepts, computer systems terminology, controls necessary in an automated system, the changing relationships with other organizational departments, new ways of performing accounting tasks, and the new role of auditors with computerized systems. A major objective of this text is devoted to acquainting accountants with these aspects of computerized accounting information systems.

DATA PROCESSING AND INFORMATION SYSTEMS

Although modern, sophisticated accounting information systems are the products of the marriage of two separate disciplines, accounting and electronic data processing, these disciplines evolved independently of each other and from completely different origins.

Data processing focuses largely on the incredible ability of computers to ingest vast quantities of raw data, to manipulate the data in an almost unlimited variety of ways, and to report the results quickly and accurately. Consider, for example, a major oil company with several million credit card holders. The number of transactions resulting from the use of these cards for 1 month (a standard billing period) would present an imponderable burden for human processors. The same transaction-volume problem is encountered by a large aerospace/missiles manufacturing firm that maintains perpetual inventory accounts on an average cost basis for 75,000 inventory items, not to mention the distribution of related inventory issues to thousands of open in-process work orders. The central points of interest in electronic data processing are obviously in the computer hardware (physical components) and the software (programming) that gives it impetus and guidance.

In contrast, *information systems* concentrate on the orderly and controlled transformation of raw transaction data into useful information to fulfill the decision-making needs of management. Interest focuses on the origination of the data, the data's authenticity and legitimacy, the controlled steps of the data-to-information process, the protection of the documents and records involved, and the utility of the end product.

The synergistic combination of accounting and electronic data processing has given status to accounting information systems and has concomitantly created a new area of knowledge. Today the complete union of the two disciplines is an accomplished fact. Accounting functions have been fully automated in thousands of business firms. The recent introduction of mini- and microcomputers extends the feasibility of automation to the relatively small business firm. Today, and to an even greater extent in the future, accountants must have the ability to think "automation" to successfully engage in any of the various areas of accounting practice on a broad scale.

Nevertheless, the use of a computer may *not* be essential in a given information system. The computer in this instance is viewed simply as a very sophisticated, powerful tool that can possibly facilitate the operation of an accounting information system. There are undoubtedly many small, low-volume, special-purpose information systems for which computer adaptation may be impractical. This book will direct attention to specific accounting information systems and discuss EDP as a technique for accomplishing their purposes.

Data Base, Information, and Organizational Relationships

The data base of any organization contains information for daily operations and is considered a basic tool of planning. The input of data for any system is generated throughout the organization for utilization anywhere within the organization. Chapter Four develops the concept of data control wherein all data belong to the organization, and the users and applications are assigned to given data. The data base management system (DBMS) has developed to control this new concept of data utilization through the application of specialized software. As the concept is developed in Chapter Four the elements of DBMS are explained and the role of the accountant defined. Although the philosophy of DBMS varies, there are certain concepts that apply to any type of system. As shown in Figure 1.4, the relationship of the data base to the organizational functions or subsystems is basic, but the role of the data base in each of the subsystems can be substantially different. Likewise, with different organizations there is a myriad of philoso-

BASIC DATA BASE RELATIONSHIPS.

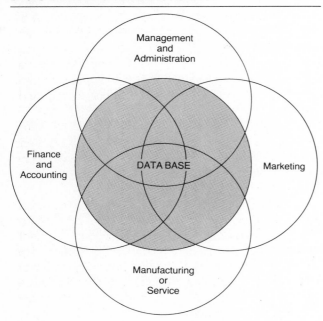

Management
and
Administration

Finance
and
Accounting

DATA BASE

Marketing

Manufacturing
or
Service

Figure 1.4

phies that can be developed and employed. Figure 1.4 illustrates the overlap of data within the organization; the overlay of functions represent the data that the different functions share with each other.

Electronic Funds Transfer Systems

Electronic funds transfer (EFT) systems represent another technological advance in information systems. Unlike traditional systems in which data are recorded and transferred via paper documents, EFT systems record, transfer, and deliver financial information to the users by electronic means. When an EFT system is utilized, not only are inefficiencies in the cumbersome processing of paper documents eliminated, but in addition, financial data are recorded and financial information is generated more quickly.

Today EFT systems are most widely used by financial institutions to process a variety of transactions such as withdrawal of funds, acceptance of deposits and payments, and verification of balances. By processing this information more quickly, an EFT system generates convenience for the user and economies for the financial institution. EFT systems are discussed in detail in Chapter Four.

Minicomputers

Although the storage of minicomputers may be quite large, they are small in size compared to large-scale computers. Most of these computers have all the external processing capabilities of large computers. These include reading punch cards, producing punch cards, printing, controlling input/output terminals, and interrelating with other computers.

Minicomputers often use preprogrammed tapes or disks that can be inserted when a particular function needs processing. The most popular programs for minicomputers are payroll, inventory, and cash-related functions.

The continued popularity of minicomputers has resulted in a management philosophy shift from centralization to decentralization. This concept is known as *distributed processing*. This type of system uses the decentralized concept to serve remote locations, diverse operations, and real-time applications. However, the centralized concept of shared data files is used when control and efficiency can be improved. The minicomputer makes such configurations feasible for the smaller organization that has only one large computer. Large organizations may use combinations of large and minicomputers to achieve the same results on a more complex scale.

Microcomputers

To meet the demands of specialized processing needs and small computer users, manufacturers now offer small systems known as *microcomputers,* or *microprocessors.* These systems can be used as components of large computer systems, for stand-alone applications such as order entry or inventory control, for home applications, and for automated financial systems of small businesses. Microcomputers come with preprogrammed disks or cassettes for most applications. The most popular application of microcomputers is the handling of a specific function within a business. The function may be a general accounting activity such as accounts payable or a specific application such as recording and keeping track of the direct-labor hours worked on all jobs in the manufacturing plant.

Microcomputer popularity is growing rapidly because of their comparatively favorable costs. Such systems provide the small business with the opportunity to begin electronic processing without having to use service bureaus or time sharing. Such systems are frequently found in medical offices, bookstores, and small banks. A complete analysis of microcomputer systems and applications is presented in Chapter Five.

INFORMATION SYSTEMS AND DECISION MAKING

In recent years the term *decision support systems,* or DSS, has become synonymous with computerized information systems. Strictly speaking, a DSS is a systematic means for supplying management with all available information essential for sound decision making. To simply equate DSS with computerized information systems, without imposing certain qualifying conditions, is technically incorrect. Observe the diagram in Figure 1.5, which illustrates the type and nature of information needed by management to make intelligent financial decisions.

At the left-hand side of the continuum there are standard transaction-oriented accounting information systems adapted to computer processing. As previously noted, such systems are designed to prepare and maintain requisite business records and to report operating results periodically for particular organizational units. In many cases these systems served low level operating decision needs. During the monthly billing cycle, for example, seriously delinquent accounts could be pulled for possible collection follow-up, or perhaps for bad debt write-offs. On the whole, however, such systems were not designed to provide management with a comprehensive picture of future operations.

On the right-hand side of the continuum there are those information systems providing full decision information for responsible managers. *Full* information should *not* be confused with volume of reports. A wheelbarrow loaded with daily reports would overwhelm even the most conscientious manager. Rather, the necessary information must be presented in a usable form and include the minimum content to maximize usefulness to the manager. Individual systems may be rated on the continuum based on

THE SPECTRUM OF MANAGEMENT INFORMATION NEEDS.

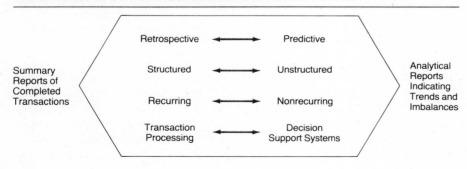

Figure 1.5

the amount and nature of the information needed by the decision makers in the organization.

Individual managers ordinarily need several different types of reports to assess accurately the operation of their organizational unit(s). These reports would include status reports, activity reports, management exception reports, and analytical reports. Each of these report categories portrays a separate and distinct facet of unit operations. Together they complement each other and provide a relatively complete summary of current operations. Let us examine each type of report and its characteristics. Traditionally, accounting information systems have provided the status information needed by management, but formal exception and analytical reporting are of relatively recent origin, particularly as a by-product of computerized accounting information systems.

Status Reports

Status reports define the condition of a particular system (organizational unit) at a point in time. A corporate balance sheet, for example, describes the financial condition of a business firm at the close of business on a certain date. Inventory status reports show item quantities on hand at that date. Other examples might include unfilled customer orders, open purchase commitments, and a bank reconciliation at the end of the month.

Status reports, of course, are accurate only on their preparation date. As transactions continue to occur, they become "dated" and become limited in usefulness. Ironically, the length of their effectiveness varies inversely with the volume of systems activity whereas management's need for the reported data varies directly with volume.

Activity Reports

Activity or transaction reports describe what has taken place within a given operating system during a specified period of time. A corporate income statement, for example, summarizes revenues and categorizes expenditures in determining the net profits of a business firm for a defined period of time. Inventory receipts and disbursements reports, periodic sales reports, and the payroll check register are other examples of activity reports.

Responsible managers cannot allow themselves to become intimately involved in the routine activities of their organizational units. Therefore, activity reports and listings constitute an essential link between status reports and, when combined with preestablished standards and budgets, provide excellent documentation of organizational activity and vitality. When well designed and timely, they become important control media.

Management Exception Reports

Management exception reports are analyses of selected items that exceed established quality or quantity parameters and may therefore suggest managerial attention. Conditions and circumstances that caused these items to fall outside acceptable limits often require special investigation and remedial action. Examples of such accounting reports include an aged analysis of accounts receivable over 90 days, checks outstanding for more than 90 days, overshipments from suppliers exceeding acceptable dollar limits, and production cost variances.

Because managers are typically held accountable for the operations of their organizational units, they are vitally interested in all instances of operational malfunction, particularly those that appear to be repetitious or indicative of potential trouble or breakdown in the system. Defensively, lower- and middle-level managers feel the need to correct malfunctions at the earliest possible moment to avoid criticism from superiors.

Analytical Reports

Analytical reports are usually designed to examine or highlight particular trends, directions, conditions, and relationships in the operation of an organizational unit. Their purpose is to provide managers with a clearer understanding of departmental behavior for better planning and control. A report analyzing the payment habits of customers, for example, could be of great value to the credit manager of a business firm. A forecast of cash requirements based on accounts receivable, accounts payable, and payroll is essential to the efficient management of the firm's quick assets.

Since analytical reports examine unique operating relationships, a substantial volume of business transaction data collected over an extended period of time is usually required for their preparation. Computerized information systems have the ability for specialized processing of voluminous data using modeling and simulation. With such capabilities, users must make sure that such refinement of discretionary information is worth the costs of creating it.

Behavioral Considerations

Sociologists and industrial psychologists have made it abundantly clear over the years that severe changes in the work environment can cause negative reactions from employees on whom the ultimate success of a system may ultimately depend. Whether because of resentment, disagreement, failure to visualize the change in its overall perspective, or just plain fear of personal obsolescence, accounting information systems modifications may be adversely impacted by employee frustration and resentment.

The accountant's primary task is to design reliable financial information systems from which authorized user needs are satisfied. He or she is first a "processor," then a "communicator." Although accountants need not be professional "behaviorists," they certainly should be aware of the fact that information systems are *operated* by people and that the output is *used* by people. Both operator and user perceptions of accounting products can be greatly, and profitably, enhanced by eliciting their input, opinion, and cooperation in systems design and change.

Quantitative Methods

Although quantitative tools and models can in no way be considered accounting information systems in and of themselves, their use in the refinement of financial information can provide effective input for management decision processes. Typical examples of quantitative methods (QM) in practical use are: (1) regression analysis applied to historical (recorded) data for forecasting purposes, (2) use of economic order quantity (EOQ) to refurbish depleted inventories, and (3) simulation to test the impact of a series of decision options. A good working knowledge of these and other tools, such as linear programming, PERT, correlation analysis, and queuing theory, add tremendous significance and facility to accounting products.

COMMONALITIES IN INFORMATION SYSTEMS

Information systems are said to be "isomorphic" because they all have basic characteristics that are generally identical, although in specific detail they may appear to be widely dissimilar. In a like manner, their purposes appear to be the same in the sense that they are dynamic, and as such they are continuously subjected to exogenous stimuli (input). They are required to identify, analyze, measure, and act upon (process) those stimuli and to produce a product or result (output) in partial fulfillment of the objective of the system. The system automatically produces its own endogenous stimuli (feedback) by which it modifies future systems processing. Of course, accounting information systems are specifically designed to accomplish a desired purpose. It follows, therefore, that the foregoing functions cannot be left to chance but must operate under the aegis of some predesigned regulating features (controls).

Figure 1.6 characterizes the information system reduced to its simplest form—a transaction processing model. Viewed more closely, the five *system characteristics* of input, output, process, controls, and feedback may be translated into more familiar business terms. The following sections define and discuss each of these characteristics.

EXAMPLES OF SYSTEMS CHARACTERISTICS EXPRESSED IN ACCOUNTING TERMS.

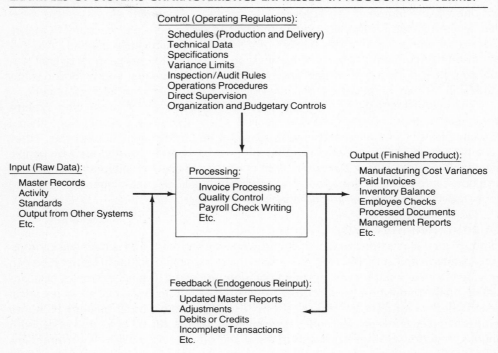

Figure 1.6

Inputs

Accounting information systems are fed by business activity. Input items are thus the representations of documents and contracts that constitute the "objective, verifiable evidence" of consummated business transactions. Characteristically, these input elements are consumed in the processing cycle as data are converted into information. Replenishment is, of course, implied. A reduction in the flow of input diminishes systems efficiency and effectiveness; more importantly, however, it signifies a general diminution in the tempo of the business itself, which may be a far more alarming situation. As we look more closely at individual subsystems in the following chapters, the input elements familiar to accountants will become more obvious in their own particular spheres of influence.

Outputs

Information is the product of the refinement of raw data. The operation of a dynamic process therefore creates certain *visual* or electronic evidences of successful processing. Ideally, such evidence will signify consummated business transactions, but realistically it may also include processing exceptions that prevented conclusion of some transactions. No distinction is made between output elements routinely expected or desired and those created as by-products of the operation of a dynamic system. Both are almost certain to appear. In fact, unexpected and unwanted by-product information often serves a more useful purpose than the more boring, voluminous evidence of completed transactions. For example, an abnormal variation between actual and standard product costs could be the stimulus for desired changes in the production process, yet variances barely within an acceptable tolerance may allow an inefficient operation to go undetected. Similarly, in accounts payable consistent vendor overshipments or overbillings may continue unnoticed if they fall within established limits of acceptance. An exceptionally large violation of the procurement contract, on the other hand, would yield a by-product exception report that should stimulate buyer action to discipline the vendor.

Generally speaking, outputs from accounting information systems take the following forms:

1. Audit trails in the form of activity lists and backup files.
2. Expected products that the systems were designed to yield, such as accounting statements, inventory balances, payroll checks and withholding statements, vendor checks and remittance advices, and production cost and status reports.
3. Updated master files of open (active) records which constitute an input into subsequent processing cycles.
4. Data conditioned for input into other related subsystems.
5. Processing exceptions designed to elicit external responses affecting future systems processing.

The Process

In order to describe the process, the processor must first be identified. The accounting process has historically been defined as identifying, classifying, sorting, recording, storing, summarizing, and reporting the results of business transactions. Although these elements are inherent in all accounting systems, computer processing techniques and manual methods are quite dissimilar. The processor is the environment within which the process occurs, and the process encompasses all the systemic elements and operations that contribute to the data transformation sequence. For our purposes, the process can be spoken of synonymously with the processor and the application programs since all systems discussed in the following chapters contemplate the use of large-scale electronic data processing equipment. The computer programs that actually guide and sequentially perform each action essential to the data transformation are indeed the forces that replace the manual processors.

Controls

The function of control can be defined as the "regulation of the process" to assure a predictable output of uniform quality. Controls regulate the flow of data, prescribe operating logic, establish parameters and tolerances, and generally structure the procedures and processes by which the data transformation is accomplished.

To the accountant, control literally means inviolable operating rules. If a system is to maintain integrity, procedures must be rigidly interpreted and consistently applied. Such interpretations should be found in the computer programs and operating procedures of a system.

Feedback

Theoretically, the term *feedback* is commonly used to denote the modification of the processing activity based on measurements of the output stream, as compared to some predetermined standard. In practical business terms, this means a constant stream of uncompleted business transactions and adjustments to other input records affecting future processing. Examples would be automatically generated adjustments and exception reporting of inefficient operations requiring management's attention.

SYSTEM DEVELOPMENT

To satisfy management's desire for decision efficiency, information systems must operate successfully, some even outside the formal organization structure (the grapevine, e.g.). Informal information systems are flexible, ubiquitous, and difficult to define; yet they provide a useful and valuable organizational function. Their weaknesses lie in the reliability of the input sources and the tendency for the output to become embellished and distorted by the process, a circumstance reflecting the absence of controls so conspicuous in formal systems.

Other special systems include the communications network that links two or more related subsystems; the organizational system that depicts, but does not necessarily control, the formal chain of command; the management information system that tends to encompass the whole decision-making process, including the several systems that feed information to it; the data processing system that alludes to the electronic or electromechanical technology facilitating the flow and transformation of data; and, finally, the several "operating" information systems that perform the record-keeping requirements so essential to the decision-making process.

Some of these systems change as readily and as spontaneously as they originate. Others must be created, often laboriously and painfully. Accounting information systems fall in the latter category and are the accountant's major concern. A brief discussion of the creation and development of an accounting information system is presented in this section. A more thorough review of systems analysis and design is presented in Chapter Eight.

Usually a rethinking of the whole systems philosophy is necessary to establish and give permanence to the most efficient and effective flow patterns and processes and to purge the systems of archaic, costly, and clumsy traditions. Such a philosophy requires a total commitment from top management and a clear and unmistakable delegation of authority to those entrusted with the development and implementation of EDP information systems throughout the entire organization.

Systems Analysis

Systems analysis begins with an in-depth study of the individual information subsystems and a sound grasp of the organizational and operational concepts. Although being careful to evaluate and preserve the desirable characteristics of the existing system, the analyst should incorporate only those elements necessary for the efficient operation of the new system. To avoid seriously delimiting the potential of the new system, analysts must constantly seek new and better ways.

As is true in almost any research and development effort, the project should be approached with a definite strategy in mind. The following steps should yield effective solutions for the accounting information systems analyst.

First, the objectives of the system must be verified or established. Frequently one may find a number of "subsidiary" objectives underlying the primary goal(s). For example, the paramount objective of an accounts payable system may be to liquidate the firm's legal liability to trade creditors in such a manner as to minimize risk and maximize cash discounts earned on purchases. Subsidiary to this major goal one might assume subgoals such as (1) maintenance of current unpaid liability, (2) maintenance of an approved vendor master file, and (3) preparation of long-, medium-, and short-range forecasts of cash needs.

Creation of an overall plan for implementing computerized data processing systems is a critical first step in developing accounting information systems. A feasibility study is usually conducted. This investigation identifies all information system goals and objectives, determines possible adaptation to EDP techniques, assesses their success potential, and assigns a priority to their implementation. The plan also considers the computer configuration required to accomplish the job and estimates a cost/benefit relationship associated with implementation.

Through interviews with people directly involved in the existing or proposed systems and by close observation of ongoing activities, a schematic diagram of the information flow pattern and specific operations performed at various points along the flow can be developed. Careful study of these flowcharts often yields rich opportunities for improvement in time and cost. Management must acknowledge the inadequacies of existing methodology before a new philosophy of improvement can be embraced. A completed feasibility plan is typically presented to a management steering committee for its approval.

Next, all critical business documents and their sources must be identified. Accountants are conditioned to look for documented evidence to verify each business transaction. The systems analyst must not only identify these instruments, but he or she needs to define carefully their content, function, distribution, and handling as well.

The analyst must discern the flow patterns of these documents and establish the natural boundaries of the system and its interfaces with other systems. Full advantage should be taken of opportunities to capture automatically in machine-sensible form all the raw data that the system requires. In the process of improving this aspect of the system, redundancies should be minimized.

A detailed description of the *functions* of the system should be prepared. The product of this step may well be a narrative statement of detailed operating procedures. Included among the functions might be (1) methods of data verification, control, and audit; (2) the process of matching interdependent documents; and (3) decisions and actions taken in response to certain conditions found in the documents.

Following the descriptions, the critical factors of success must be determined. Almost every system depends on some special condition or characteristic for maximum effectiveness and efficiency. These factors are sometimes in conflict between major interfacing systems. Management must therefore decide the issue in the interest of overall corporate benefit to the possible detriment of one of the systems involved.

Systems Design

The management reports must be evaluated next. Ironically, managers sometimes ask for a great deal more than sound decision making requires because of a lack of understanding of the system's capabilities. Generally, the more relevant and refined a report is, the more useful and effective it is to the decision maker. Systems analysts should tailor management reports to the purposes they serve and should assume responsibility for extracting, refining, and formatting that information in the most economical and effective presentation. Of course, in all cases the systems analyst should seek the input of appropriate management personnel.

Adequate and effective controls must be incorporated into the system. Perhaps no single aspect of information systems design strikes more clearly at the heart of an accountant's concern than the problem of maintaining control in the midst of change. Every major change and technological advance throughout the history of accounting has introduced new control problems. As data processing and communications techniques continue in this refining process and as traditional business documents diminish and perhaps even disappear, control problems become a paramount concern.

Also, alternative configurations of system components should be recommended. To design the "ideal" information system without an awareness of the hardware and software required to operate it would be naive. Systems analysts must remain abreast of the technology in data processing facilities and recommend the equipment best suited to the job, commensurate with the lowest possible cost. All of the foregoing should be documented to show the controls surrounding the system and the involvement of those related to the changes.

Implementation

Finally, the system is reviewed and approved by management, and implementation begins. This requirement includes the conversion of data base files where necessary. A test period is usually conducted, during which the new system parallels the old one and close comparisons of outputs and effectiveness are made. Following a successful parallel period, the final changeover to the new system is authorized. A planned program of systems review should be implemented to keep the system properly attuned to the organization's goals and objectives.

SYSTEM INTERRELATIONSHIPS

As has already been indicated, the various information systems of an organization can seldom stand alone. Rather, they interrelate in a seemingly complicated way as they depend on each other for input supply. The output stream of one subsystem often provides an essential input for another subsystem. For example, the payroll system depends on the production system for time and job cards, whereas the production system looks to the cost system for labor cost distribution and labor variance analysis. These systems relationships, when graphically portrayed, give the impression of a network of subsystems as shown in Figure 1.7.

The primary examples of the system interrelationships related to accounting are shown in Figure 1.8. Beginning with Chapter Ten, each of these accounting functions is discussed as it relates to one of the four major cycles as described in Chapter Nine. Instead of independently discussing the primary accounting functions, we have assigned each of them to a cycle and related its role to the cycle and to the organization as a whole.

INTERSYSTEM RELATIONSHIPS.

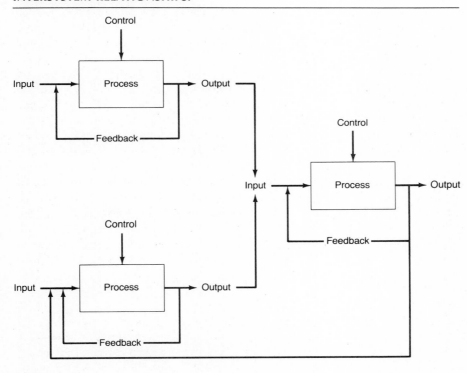

Figure 1.7

FUNCTIONAL RELATIONSHIPS.

	Functional Relationships										
	Accounts Payable	Billings & Collections	Cash	Inventory	Marketing	Payroll	Production	Purchasing	Receiving	Shipping	Vendors Customers Banks and Other Internal Systems
Accounts Payable			✓	✓		✓		✓	✓		✓
Billings & Collection			✓	✓	✓					✓	✓
Cash	✓	✓				✓					✓
Inventory	✓	✓			✓		✓	✓	✓	✓	
Marketing		✓		✓						✓	✓
Payroll	✓		✓				✓				✓
Production				✓		✓					
Purchasing	✓			✓					✓		✓
Receiving	✓			✓				✓			✓
Shipping		✓		✓	✓						✓
Total Major System Interfaces	5	4	3	7	3	3	2	3	3	3	8

Figure 1.8

The *spending cycle* includes procurement, receiving and inspection, and accounts payable, all of which are related to the function of exchanging cash for convertible resources, expenses, and capital assets. The spending cycle interfaces with the *conversion cycle* at the raw materials inventory point. The conversion cycle includes production, payroll, and both raw materials and finished goods inventory—all of which are involved in the transformation of raw materials into finished products. The *revenue cycle* interfaces with the conversion cycles at the finished goods inventory point. This cycle includes marketing, shipping, and billings and collection. In a manner exactly opposite to the spending cycle, systems in the revenue cycle are involved in exchanging finished goods for cash. Finally, the *administrative cycle* includes the controlled inflow and outflow of cash, the acquisition, depreciation, and disposition of capital assets, and the maintenance of the general ledger accounts. This cycle interfaces with all other cycles.

SUMMARY

A knowledge of accounting information systems concepts is important for students of accounting because of the complex nature of today's financial environment. The traditional accounting functions are only part of the accounting information system, and to understand the role of accounting in the organization, one should consider many other aspects, such as the decision processes, human relations, and data processing technology. The information system feeds the vital components of the organization, providing inputs, outputs, and controls. Propelled by sound financial management decisions, the system is stimulated by external transactions that are converted into refined financial inputs, which in turn result in sound financial decisions.

Such systems must be accurate, dependable, automatic, and spontaneous. To the accountant, such systems must be clearly observable, definable, predictable, controllable, and readily modifiable under proper authority. This text concentrates on presenting the techniques necessary to develop accounting information systems that contain these characteristics.

NOTES

[1] *Webster's New Collegiate Dictionary* (Springfield, Mass.: G. & C. Merriam Company, 1978), p. 1184.

[2] Garrison, Ray H. *Managerial Accounting,* 4th ed. (Plano, Tex.: Business Publications, Inc., 1985). pp. 15–18.

[3] Morse, Wayne J., James R. Davis, and Al L. Hartgraves *Management Accounting,* Reading, Mass.: Addison-Wesley Publishing Co., 1984, pp 253–256.

[4] Committee on Accounting Education, American Accounting Association, and Computer Education Sub-Committee, AICPA, "Inclusion of EDP in an Undergraduate Auditing Curriculum: Some Possible Approaches," *The Accounting Review,* 49 (October 1974): 863.

SELECTED REFERENCES

Burch, J. G., Jr., F. Strater, and G. Grudnitski. *Information Systems: Theory and Practice,* 3rd ed. New York: John Wiley & Sons, 1984.

Committee on Accounting Education, American Accounting Association, and Computer Education Subcommittee, American Institute of Certified Public Accountants. "Inclusion of EDP in an Undergraduate Auditing Curriculum: Some Possible Approaches," *The Accounting Review,* 49 (October 1974): 859–864.

Committee on Management Information Systems, American Accounting Association. "Report of the Committee," *The Accounting Review,* Supplement to Vol. 49 (1974): 140–155.

Davis, Gordon B. "Computer Curriculum for Accountants and Auditors—Present and Prospective," *Education for Expounding Computer Curriculums.* New York: American Institute of Certified Public Accountants, 1976, pp. 12–21.

Firmin, Peter A. "The Potential of Accounting as a Management Information System," *Management International Review* (February 1966): 45–55.

Garrison, Ray H. *Managerial Accounting,* 4th ed. Plano, Tex., Business Publications, Inc., 1985.

Institute of Internal Auditors, "The Changing Management Information Systems Environment," *Systems Auditability and Control* (1977): 11–19.

Moore, Michael R. "Undergraduate Computer Curriculum Requirements for Entering Staff in Accounting and Auditing," *Education for Expanding Computer Curriculums.* New York: American Institute of Certified Public Accountants, 1976.

Morse, Wayne J., James R. Davis, and Al L. Hartgraves, *Management Accounting,* Reading, Mass.: Addison-Wesley Publishing Company, 1984.

Murdick, R. G., and J. E. Ross. *Information Systems for Modern Management,* 3rd ed. Englewood Cliffs, N.J.: Prentice-Hall, Inc., 1980.

Sanders, D. H. *Computers in Business: An Introduction,* 4th ed. New York: McGraw-Hill Book Co., 1979.

Senn, James A., *Information Systems in Management.* 2nd ed. Belmont, Calif.: Wadsworth Publishing Co., 1982.

Ullman, Arthur A., "Triumphs of Minicomputers Have Only Begun," *Management Focus* (Peat Marwick Mitchell & Company, May–June 1980): 8–13.

Vanecek, M. T., R. F. Zant, and C. S. Guynes, "Distributed Data Processing: A New 'Tool' for Accountants," *Journal of Accountancy* (October 1980): 75–83.

QUESTIONS

1. Explain or define the following terms:

System	Decision support systems	Budgeting
Data processing	Status report	Financial accounting
Information systems	Activity report	Managerial accounting
Minicomputers	Exception report	Responsibility accounting
Microcomputers	Analytical report	Feedback

2. What is an information system?
3. Differentiate between MIS and AIS.
4. Has the rapid development of data processing techniques changed the basic functions and objectives of accounting? The systems design? How?
5. Describe some of the pressures placed on the accounting information systems by the following events:
   a. Federal income tax laws
   b. The Securities and Exchange law
   c. Commercial adaptation of EDP
6. How has the accountant's responsibility changed in the last 150 years?
7. Differentiate between data processing and information systems.
8. What basic types of information does management need to accurately assess corporate operations?
9. How has the usefulness of management decision information improved over the past 50 years?

10. What common characteristics exemplify all accounting information systems?
11. Information is the product of the refinement of raw data. Explain.
12. Classify and discuss the normal outputs of accounting information systems.
13. Controls have been defined as the "regulation of the process." Explain the role of controls in accounting systems.
14. What is systems analysis?
15. In converting a manually operated information system to computer processing methods, what pitfalls face the systems analyst?
16. Describe an approach, or strategy, that you feel would produce the most acceptable design of an information system such as payroll.
17. If an accountant is assured within reason that the input data to a given system are accurate and complete and that computer center security is inviolable, why should he or she be concerned with computer processing controls and logic?
18. What responsibility should the accountant (internal and external) assume in the design, development, installation, and regular operation of accounting information systems?

PROBLEMS

19. Relevant Body of Knowledge

The following five topics are part of the relevant body of knowledge for CPAs having fieldwork or immediate supervisory responsibility in audits involving a computer:

a. Electronic data processing (EDP) equipment and its capabilities
b. Organization and management of the data processing function
c. Characteristics of computer based systems
d. Fundamentals of computer programming
e. Computer center operations

CPAs who are responsible for computer audits should possess certain general knowledge with respect to each of these five topics. For example, on the subject of EDP equipment and its capabilities, the auditor should have a general understanding of computer equipment and should be familiar with the uses and capabilities of the central processor and the peripheral equipment. *(AICPA adapted)*

Required:

For each of the topics, describe the general knowledge that should be possessed by:

a. CPAs who are responsible for computer audits.
b. Managerial accountants working with computerized systems.
c. Internal auditors working in companies with large computer systems.

20. Systems Concepts

For each pair of concepts listed here, explain the difference between the two concepts. Identify, when necessary, the importance of each concept to accounting information systems.

a. Data and information
b. Classifying and sorting
c. Communicating and reporting
d. Feasibility and economic efficiency
e. Transaction processing and decision support systems
f. Exception reports and analytical reports

21. Systems Applications

Thorne Services Company is a business consulting firm that has a professional staff of 50 people who perform financial, tax, and legal consulting for all types of businesses. They have many clients in the textile and fishing industries where they spend most of their time. Approximately 40 percent of their clients are in other various types of business, including a few governmental agencies. Jack Thorne, the president, is interested in computerizing the company and would like to know whether anything other than the traditional accounting functions can be placed on the computer. Many of Thorne's clients have elaborate computer systems for keeping track of inventory, work-in-process, and finished goods, and he wants to know how such computerization could be applied to his service-oriented company.

Required:

a. Discuss the types of computer applications that could be used in service-oriented businesses.
b. What types of nontraditional applications would be useful in Thorne Services Company?

22. Systems Survey and Analysis

Business organizations are required to modify or replace a portion or all of their financial information system in order to keep pace with their growth and to take advantage of improved information technology. The process involved in modifying or replacing an information system, especially if computer equipment is involved, requires a substantial commitment of time and resources. When an organization undertakes a change in its information system, a series of steps or phases is taken. The steps or phases included in a systems study are:

a. Survey of the existing system
b. Analysis of information collected in the survey and development of recommendations for corrective action
c. Design of a new or modified system
d. Equipment study and acquisition
e. Implementation of a new or modified system

These steps or phases tend to overlap rather than be separate and distinct. In addition, the effort required in each step or phase varies from one systems change to another depending on factors such as extent of the changes or the need for different equipment. *(IMA adapted)*

Required:

a. Explain the purpose and reasons for surveying an organization's existing system during a systems study.

b. Identify and explain the general activities and techniques that are commonly used during the systems survey and analysis phases of a systems study conducted for a financial information system.

c. The system survey and system analysis phases of a financial information systems study are often carried out by a project team composed of a systems analyst, a management accountant, and other persons in the company who would be knowledgeable and helpful in the systems study. What would be the role of the management accountant in these phases of a financial information systems study?

B

INFORMATION SYSTEMS CONCEPTS AND PROCEDURES

CHAPTER TWO

Systems Tools and Techniques

To begin the study of accounting information systems, one must learn the basic tools and techniques of systems development and design. This chapter examines the concepts that are considered the most important in the body of knowledge for accounting information systems. Although these concepts are frequently covered in information systems texts, their analysis with an accounting emphasis often provides additional insights. The material in this chapter is continually referred to and used in the remainder of the book, and the topics covered here also frequently appear on the various professional examinations in accounting.

Flowcharting is one of the basic functions that must be performed in systems development. It is a basic tool of information systems and is the first function discussed in this chapter. A system can also be analyzed in other ways, particularly with decision tables and questionnaires. Although decision tables are often considered a subcategory of flowcharting, a separate section defines and explains their use.

Document design is another important basic function that must be examined. Because accountants use both input and output documents, they are very concerned with this area. Document design, like flowcharting, is part of the initial planning phase of systems development.

For accounting, the coding techniques to be used in the system are also very important. Coding, as distinguished from programming, is the aspect of the system that identifies all the elements of a system—from the simplest (a customer account code) to the most complex (a secret product code for remote transmissions). Accountants are normally concerned with any codes that relate to the financial activities of an organization.

With the increasing size and complexity of information systems, analysts and designers have had to develop or adapt new ways of analyzing, designing, implementing, testing, and adjusting information systems functions. In addition to flowcharting, decision tables, and coding schemes, analysts and designers also need scheduling charts and techniques and simulation models to assist them in their role of information systems development. Although these topics are used more by analysts than by accountants, they are nonetheless necessary for a complete understanding of information systems.

FLOWCHARTING

Flowcharting is used in two broad areas: developing new systems and evaluating existing systems. In new systems, flowcharting serves as a map of what is to be created. Understanding a current system is a time-consuming and often difficult problem of systems design and analysis. For any system, old or new, flowcharts provide pictorial information that is often difficult to communicate through language narratives alone. Although there are various types of flowcharts, they all possess several *general advantages* over narrative descriptions.

Flowcharts make it easier to describe any type of system that has sequential processes, especially large, complex ones. An experienced analyst can readily see the flows, strengths, and weaknesses of a system by simply studying its flowcharts. Strengths and weaknesses frequently are hidden in narrative descriptions but become obvious when the system is flowcharted. Flowcharts facilitate making changes during the planning and design stages because sections, decisions, or other elements can be substituted and redrawn more easily than a narrative description can be rewritten. Also, they are very convenient for anyone analyzing a system.

The preceding advantages apply to the four basic types of flowcharts discussed in the following sections. The proper documentation files of an existing computer system should include all four types of flowcharts.

Systems Flowcharts

The systems flowchart provides a logical diagram of how a system operates. Properly prepared, it illustrates the flow of data in the correct perspective. This is accomplished by interrelating all elements of a system, including the inputs, outputs, processing steps, constraints, controls, and data storage. Because there is no standardized sequence of elements, each system can be designed in any format that meets the needs of users.

The systems flowchart serves to organize these elements during systems design. It illustrates (1) the system in a step-by-step fashion, (2) the conversion from input through processing to output, and (3) which functions are manual, mechanized, and computerized. Because the systems flowchart is both an analytical and a design tool of information systems, it has many uses in the organization.

For the systems analysts, it is easier to describe the functions of a system using systems flowcharts than one using simple narrative descriptions. The various elements that interact to produce the desired outputs are distinctly separated on a systems flowchart. Analysts using the document should have a clear understanding of the major elements found in the system and how they interact. Since analysts are generally the experts in systems flowcharting, they can readily utilize them for systems evaluations. Their familiarity with many different types of systems permits them to pinpoint strengths and weaknesses of a given systems function by studying its systems flowchart. In systems evaluations, analysts use systems flowcharts to locate errors and control weaknesses and inefficient data flows. Also, analysts can easily simulate changes in a system by flowcharting specific sections and evaluating the changes on the total system.

Because management must have control over the various functions of an organization, the systems flowchart can be a useful tool in communicating the critical aspects of the different functions to those responsible for the operation of the functions. Management also uses systems flowcharts to evaluate the separation of functions for control purposes. When systems changes are made management can use "before" and "after" flowcharts to evaluate the need for the changes. Systems flowcharts can communicate to management whether their directives are being properly implemented; if not, the specific areas of failure can be easily detected.

Information systems personnel uses systems flowcharts as overall guidelines in programming a system for the computer. The systems flowchart provides the programmer with a technical perspective of the system. This includes the types and quantity of inputs and outputs, processing components, logic, types of data storage, and user accessibility. Because the systems flowchart is a major source of information for the preparation of the program flowchart (discussed later), it should be filed, along with the other documents in the programming department, for reference and justification if programmers are accused of improperly programming a systems function.

User departments are on the receiving end of the communication link provided by systems flowcharts. After management decides to correct, add to, or modify a systems function, the departments involved with the changes should periodically review what is being proposed by the systems analysts. Because the users probably provided the analysts with general descriptions of the changes being made, the analysts are obligated to the users for approval of their changes. The system flowchart is a tool generally understood by most users, especially accountants.

Files Before a flowchart illustration can be presented the principal file concepts used must be defined. These file concepts are primarily related to computer applications but may be applied to manual situations. There are two primary categories of files: master and transaction.

Master files are the permanent records of a specific application; examples are payroll, general ledger, and accounts receivable. They are normally updated as transactions are processed and carry current balances or year-to-date totals. For computer systems, these files are usually kept on disk, drums, or magnetic tape. They may also include history files that store the recent transactions used to update the master file. History files vary with their relevant uses.

Transaction files are the data used to update records in the master files. They may be in the form of punched cards, source documents, magnetic tapes, or terminal inputs. These files update the master file by adding, deleting, and changing data. Examples include: a week's payroll records, a batch of accounts payable vouchers, daily sales invoices, and receiving reports from the warehouse.

After studying Figure 2.1, one should easily be able to follow the situations presented in the following sections. Although Figure 2.1 is not all-inclusive, it uses the most common symbols as published by the American National Standards Institute (ANSI). The two illustrations demonstrate the use of most of the symbols.

FLOWCHART SYMBOLS.

NAME	SYMBOL	DESCRIPTION
Input/Output		For general use, denoting data entering the system or information generated from the system. Used when specific media are not stated or else vary. Also used to represent accounting journals and ledgers, and the manual recording of such.
Manual Operation		A manual operation or one that requires an operator.
Keying Operation		Shows operations such as keying in data through a cash register that is connected to the computer.
Punched Card		An input of data on cards or an output of information on cards.
Magnetic Tape		An input or output medium or a means of secondary storage.
Document		A printed document or report. Used to show either input or output.
Processing		The performing of the primary operations of a program by the computer, CPU.
Auxiliary Operation		Off-line equipment used to perform basic functions such as sorting.
On-Line Keyboard		Represents terminals used as input/output devices.
On-Line Storage		Connected directly to computer and represents such devices as disks and drums.

Figure 2.1

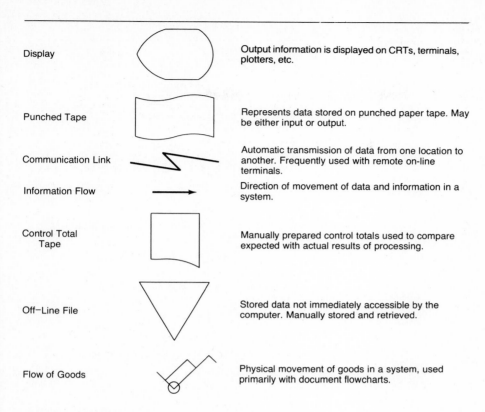

Display		Output information is displayed on CRTs, terminals, plotters, etc.
Punched Tape		Represents data stored on punched paper tape. May be either input or output.
Communication Link		Automatic transmission of data from one location to another. Frequently used with remote on-line terminals.
Information Flow		Direction of movement of data and information in a system.
Control Total Tape		Manually prepared control totals used to compare expected with actual results of processing.
Off–Line File		Stored data not immediately accessible by the computer. Manually stored and retrieved.
Flow of Goods		Physical movement of goods in a system, used primarily with document flowcharts.

Figure 2.1 (cont'd)

Illustration A   A simple accounts payable system is shown in Figure 2.2. This system is initiated by a completed file of source documents from a purchase transaction. The files for each week's completed transactions are batched and keypunched. After the cards are verified, they are sorted according to vendor number and converted to tape for processing. This tape and the accounts payable master file are the inputs for the processing run. The output includes an updated master file, a weekly report, a set of checks, and a check register that contains the details of each check, such as purchase order numbers paid, discounts taken, and vendor code. The details of the controls for such a process are explained in Chapter Six.

Illustration B   The flowchart of a retail organization's inventory system is presented in Figure 2.3. Each store is capable of transmitting every sales transaction from the cash register to the computer center. The inventory master file is on-line during store and warehouse operating hours. The receiving department enters each shipment into the terminal upon acceptance by the inspector. Inventory control has access capabilities to the inventory files to update the system for returns and allowances, making corrections, and testing item balances against periodic physical inventory counts.

ACCOUNTS PAYABLE SYSTEMS FLOWCHART.

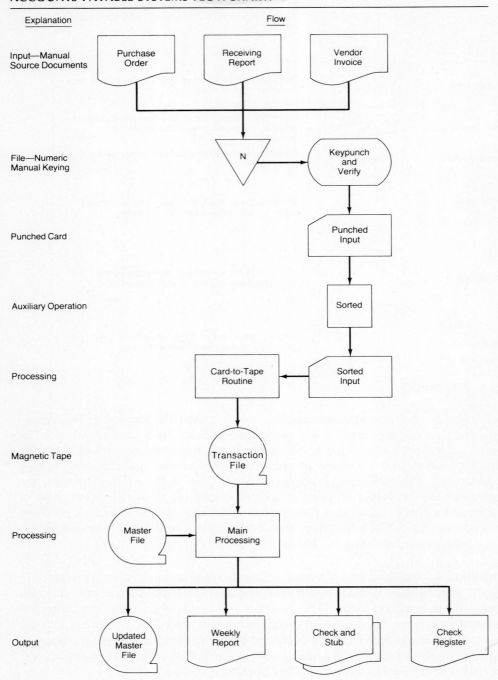

Explanation

Flow

Input—Manual Source Documents

Purchase Order

Receiving Report

Vendor Invoice

File—Numeric Manual Keying

N

Keypunch and Verify

Punched Card

Punched Input

Auxiliary Operation

Sorted

Processing

Card-to-Tape Routine

Sorted Input

Magnetic Tape

Transaction File

Processing

Master File

Main Processing

Output

Updated Master File

Weekly Report

Check and Stub

Check Register

Figure 2.2

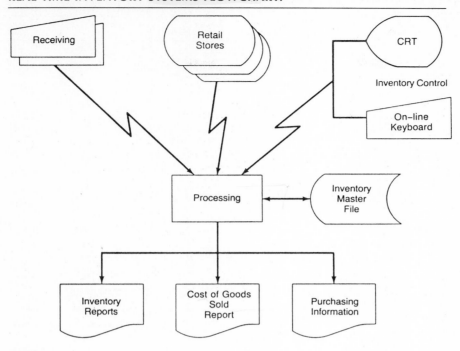

Figure 2.3

The output of the system includes periodic inventory status reports, monthly cost of goods sold statements, and periodic purchasing information for inventory replacement. The purchasing system is initiated primarily by this output, which is its input authorization for ordering.

Other systems flowcharts may combine batch and on-line processing and may be much more complex than those illustrated in this chapter. More examples of systems flowcharts can be found in the procedures chapters, which illustrate all the major accounting subsystems discussed in this text.

Document Flowcharts

The systems analyst uses a document flowchart to trace the flow of documents and reports for that function through the system from origination to destination. Not to be confused with the systems flowchart, the document flowchart does not detail the procedures and processing steps. The emphasis is instead on document flow from one department to another. As shown in Figure 2.4, the flowchart is divided into the various elements necessary for a particular function. A document flowchart is not designed around one document but around a major function, such as sales or accounts payable.

The document flowchart uses the same symbols as shown in Figure 2.1, except that

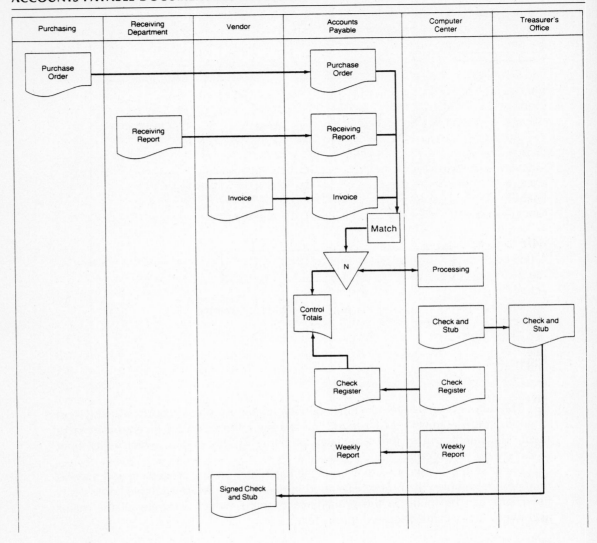

Figure 2.4

it does not have a need for several of them because it is not concerned with the processing steps of a given systems function. Figure 2.2, the accounts payable illustration in the last section, is used as an example of a systems flowchart. The basic differences between systems and document flowcharts can be seen by comparing Figures 2.2 and 2.4.

The document flow for accounts payable begins when purchasing sends copies of the purchase orders to the accounts payable department, where they are filed numerically. Next, the receiving department sends the receiving reports, which are also filed by purchase order number. When accounts payable receives the invoice from the vendor, it is matched with the related copies of the purchase order and receiving report and filed by purchase order number until the next processing run. Before each processing run, accounts payable prepares control totals to ensure the accuracy of the check preparation. After the batch is processed, the reports are sent to accounts payable for storage, and the checks are sent to the treasurer's office for signature.

For the proper design of a systems function, both the document and systems flowcharts are necessary. The role of each is vital in the development and evaluation of any function, and the completed system should have finalized flowcharts on file for reference, updating, and auditor evaluations. Document flowcharts are particularly useful in analyzing the control procedures of a system, and, when designed with employee function headings, they can provide evidence of the extent of separation of duties.

Micro Document Charts

A flowchart closely related to document flowcharts is the micro document chart. After the necessary document flowcharts have been drawn for a system or a function, the actual flow of the multicopied documents must be verified. This ensures that there are no unnecessary copies, duplication of efforts, or gaps in the audit trail. Figure 2.5 illustrates a micro document chart for a sales invoice of a wholesale grocer. The sales department creates a five-part invoice upon receiving an order by telephone or from a salesperson. The first copy of the invoice goes to accounts receivable for billing purposes and monthly statements. Shipping receives a copy to be used as the authorization for creating a packing slip or a bill of lading. The warehouse also receives a copy of the invoice, which initiates the order-pulling process. The last copy is sent to the customer after shipment of the goods or it may be included with the goods in a local delivery.

In contrast to the document flowchart, the microchart emphasizes where forms go rather than where and how they originate and the various steps they take. These charts may also be used to evaluate separation of duties, a very important control feature when handling such documents as payables vouchers, sales invoices, and purchase orders.

Program Flowcharts

The flowcharts and charts mentioned earlier relate to the flow of documents, data, and information through a system or a function of the organization but do not illustrate the actual processing steps of the computer. These flowcharts and charts also relate to either manual or computerized systems. For the systems or functions that are going to be placed on the computer, another type of flowchart is necessary—the program flowchart. The program flowchart illustrates the logic of a given computer program and is usually detailed as to the type of instructions needed within the program. Programmers often need these flowcharts before they write the computer programs because they aid in the logic flows and show precisely where the steps and activities of the program should take place.

SALES INVOICE MICRO DOCUMENT CHART.

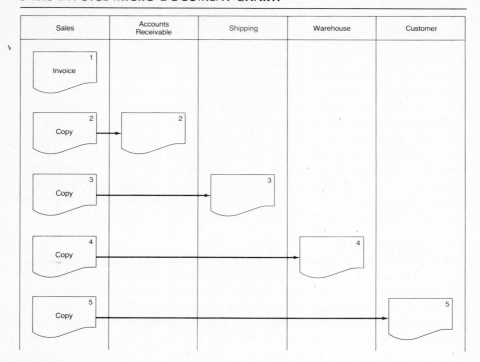

Sales	Accounts Receivable	Shipping	Warehouse	Customer

Figure 2.5

Program flowcharts vary as much as systems flowcharts and use most of the same flowcharting symbols. Figure 2.6 illustrates the symbols unique to program flowcharts. The primary symbol in program flowcharting is the decision symbol. This symbol represents alternative actions that must be taken by the program as it processes the incoming data. The function compares the data to preset conditions and transfers the flow to the direction indicated by the decision response—for example, a yes or no decision, a larger-than or equal-to decision, or a new-account or old-account decision.

Because program flowcharts are primarily constructed by programmers and not by accountants, such flowcharting is not developed in great detail in this text. Figure 2.7 illustrates a simple program flowchart to update the cash balance in the general ledger. Sales clerks receive cash and make cash refunds. As each transaction is registered by the clerk, an activity card is generated. This card is processed at the end of each day. Figure 2.7 shows the card being read by the computer and three decisions being made. First, is the card for a cash receipt? If it is, the program adds the amount to cash; if not, it subtracts from cash. The second decision relates to the last record being processed. If it is not the end of the cards, another record is read; if it is the last card, the cash balance

SYMBOLS UNIQUE TO PROGRAM FLOWCHARTS.

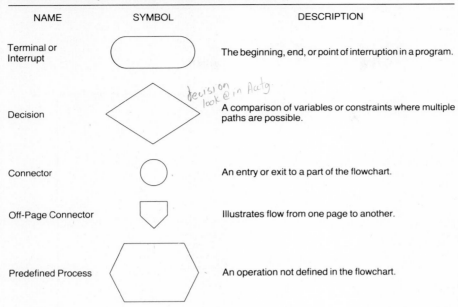

NAME	SYMBOL	DESCRIPTION
Terminal or Interrupt		The beginning, end, or point of interruption in a program.
Decision		A comparison of variables or constraints where multiple paths are possible.
Connector		An entry or exit to a part of the flowchart.
Off-Page Connector		Illustrates flow from one page to another.
Predefined Process		An operation not defined in the flowchart.

decision look @ in Actg.

Figure 2.6

is computed. The last decision relates to the end of week. If the process is a weekday run, only the cash balance is computed and printed out. If the process is coded as a closing run, the cash balance and weekly summary are printed.

DECISION TABLES

A systems analysis and design technique that makes use of the logical data flows and decision alternatives found in flowcharts is the decision table. This is a representation of the logic of an activity that illustrates the possible combinations of alternatives available in a systems function. Decision tables are very useful in systems where numerous alternatives are interrelated. Because one decision alternative may have a multiple effect on other alternative decision modes, overlooking a given alternative is possible when flowcharting a system. In this respect the decision table can be a backup control feature for the flowchart of the given system. Decision tables are mathematically precise because they are constructed in such a way as to ensure that every possible combination of activities is included.

The four sections of a table are conditions, condition entries, actions, and action entries. As shown in Figure 2.8, the table is divided into the four quadrants for ease of development and understanding by the user. The conditions represent the decisions in

PROGRAM FLOWCHART.

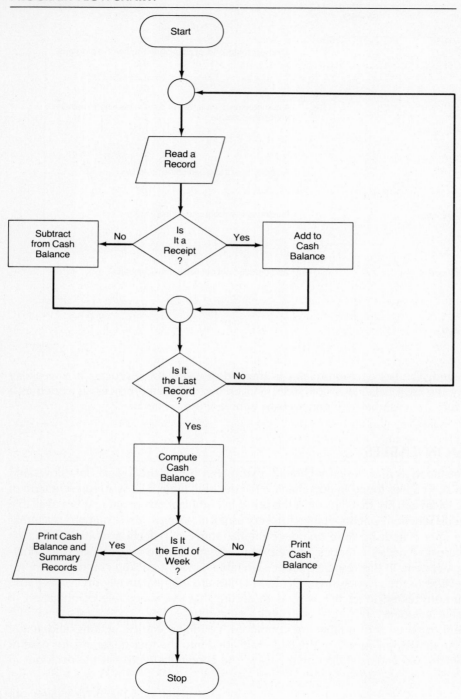

Figure 2.7

DECISION TABLE.

Conditions					
End of Cards	No	No	Yes	Yes	Condition
Cash Receipt	No	Yes			Entries
End of Week	No	No	No	Yes	

Actions					
Add to Balance		X			Action
Subtract from Balance	X				Entries
Compute Balance			X	X	
Print Balance Only			X		
Print Report				X	
Repeat Table	X	X			
Stop			X	X	

Figure 2.8

the system, the actions represent the alternatives that can be made given the particular set of characteristics found in the condition entries, and the condition entries represent the binomial expressions of the decisions (e.g., yes or no, or positive or negative).

To provide a simple and understandable situation, the facts related to the program flowchart of the previous section are used to develop the decision table in Figure 2.8. Because the conditions are binomial, there are eight (2^3) possible condition entries resulting from the three decisions found in the program flowchart of Figure 2.7. First, the program needs to know if the end of the input records have been reached. A yes or no condition entry satisfies this decision. Next, the program needs to know how cash is affected. The third condition concerns the run status, daily or end of week.

The actions to be taken by the program are clearly stated in the action quadrant of the table. The only action not on the program flowchart is "repeat table," which instructs the reading of another card and the asking of the same questions over again. After all the conditions and entries have been placed on the left of the table, the user must determine all the combinations possible for the system. For very complicated systems the computer can be used to verify the possibilities. For the illustration in Figure 2.8 only the relevant combinations are listed. As an example, if the last record is "no," there is no need to ask if it is the end of the week (see Figure 2.7 for proof). When the other conditions are eliminated by the answer to a previous condition, a "blank" is placed in the position. For this program only four of the eight condition entries are relevant.

The action entries of a given action are represented by an X if the set of conditions apply and by a blank space if there is no impact. Referring to Figure 2.8, if the set of conditions is "no," "yes," "no," the following actions should take place—add to the balance, and repeat the table. If the set of conditions is "yes," "blank," "no," then the program should compute the balance, print out the balance, and stop.

Decision tables cannot replace flowcharts for analysis purposes. They are generally used to supplement flowcharts and verify that all the alternatives have been considered. They are additional documentation for the system and aid in the understanding of the system, particularly by auditors and nonsystems analysts, such as accountants, who must understand their own operations. One disadvantage of decision tables must be noted. They do not provide the user with the sequence of processing, and this can be confusing when the program is large with many complex decision alternative interrelationships.

DOCUMENT DESIGN

All documents should be designed with the user in mind, whether an input user, processing user, or output user. Because most economic transactions require documents, it is important for the accountant to be involved with the creation and design of the documents that relate to accounting either as input, processing, or output. When asked to aid in the design of documents, the accountant must give careful consideration to the needs of the preparers and users in order for the communication link to be effective. If either preparer or user has difficulty with the form, the communication process will be hampered.

There are several considerations in determining the characteristics of a given form. Because most of these are self-explanatory, the following list will not be discussed in detail. To ascertain whether a form is adequate for the projected needs, the designer must consider the following:

1. The users and their needs must be known.
2. The number of users or uses must be known to determine the proper number of copies needed. Color can be used effectively for multicopied documents.
3. The source of each form must be easily identified by the user.
4. The form must be legible and intelligible so that the important items are readily found and the overall content is understandable.
5. Storage requirements must be known to determine the type and quality of paper or other medium needed.
6. Order or sequence of preparation or use should be known. For example, data should be placed on the form in the order that it is to be keypunched.
7. All fixed data should be printed on the form to minimize user effort when filling out the form.
8. There should be clear instructions for filling out the form.
9. Adequate space should be allowed to make the input readable.
10. Shaded areas can be used to indicate where users fill out their appropriate sections.
11. All forms should be prenumbered if possible. This usually assists in internal control.

Once the needs for a document have been analyzed, the actual format of the document must be constructed. Most documents have two types of data: fixed, or preprinted, and variable. The document in Figure 2.9 shows fixed data with variable data yet to be completed.

Most documents are similar to formal business letters in that they have organized parts. The *introduction* should be at the top of the document and contain the title, company name, date, and other necessary items. The *main body* of the form presents the primary information to be communicated by the form. For ease of preparation and

SAMPLE DOCUMENT.

FORM CUBO 209A
WITH ORDER COPY
REV 7/81

DIRECT PURCHASE VOUCHER

**THIS VOUCHER IS AUTHORIZED FOR PROCUREMENT OF
EQUIPMENT, SUPPLIES AND SERVICES OF $100 OR LESS.**

control feture

CLEMSON
UNIVERSITY

No. _____

DATE:

VENDOR:

**INVOICE IN TRIPLICATE
AND SHIP TO:**

CHECK NO.

ACCOUNT NUMBER(S)	VENDOR NUMBER	INVOICE DATE	INVOICE NUMBER	AMOUNT TO BE PAID

ITEM NO.	QUANTITY	UNIT OF MEASURE	DESCRIPTION	UNIT PRICE	AMOUNT

**ALL SALES SUBJECT TO S.C. SALES
TAX UNLESS OTHERWISE SPECIFIED.**

control

SIGNATURE OF PURCHASER

Figure 2.9

readability, the body should be outlined with lines, boxes, or columns with their arrangements in a logical order of understandability. The *conclusion* of the form appears at the bottom with summary information, balances, authorization lines, and receipt dates. The last element found on most forms is that of *instructions* which generally explain how to fill out the form and what to do with the form once it is completed. The form reproduced in Figure 2.9 had its instructions on the back.

One of the most important outputs of computerized systems is the printed material. Although not often thought of as a document, most computer output is in a report format for information users. Accountants must give equal consideration to the design of manual forms and computerized output. The most critical factors in computerized output are usually readability of important items, number of required copies, and sequence of information. These factors must be considered for both printed output and CRT uses.

Document design is an important step in the design phase of systems implementation, whether for a manual or computerized system. Documents control the flow of input and output within an organization and to and from its related environment. So important are documents and forms in some organizations that document management programs control the design of all documents and forms. These programs provide for document standardization when needed, prevent different documents from being similar and confusing to users, and control all changes in documents. This activity also serves as the document control unit, ordering and distributing documents and forms as necessary.

CODING CONSIDERATIONS

A code is a system of arbitrary symbols used to represent something else, usually a word, a group of words, a set of numbers, or a combination of items. In accounting, codes are generally necessary to facilitate the handling and transcription of data and information. Inserting a six-digit code for an inventory transaction along with the number of added or deleted units is much more efficient than writing out the name of the inventory item, description, and unit amount. In computerized systems the efficiency of both input and processing is improved. Most computer systems are geared to process data by using coded transactions of certain fields, thereby eliminating the need for the computer to read an entire record every time there is a change in the record. Although many coding schemes have been developed in the past, most of them have the common element of minimizing the space needed to store a maximum amount of data. In computerized systems this is important because of storage limitations, costs and the amount of data that can be placed on most input devices.

Codes may be numeric, alphabetic, or alphanumeric. In constructing the code for a set of items, one should consider several general characteristics. These include:

1. Flexibility should be maintained for expansion of new items without getting the new items out of order.
2. A code order sequence should be maintained so that other users understand the item placement. For example, the first item in a set should not be numbered 100 and the last item numbered 001. Whether the code is numeric or some other character variation, the order of the code should fit some logical pattern of the items being coded.

3. Each code must be a unique modifier of the item it represents. No code is used twice in a given scheme.
4. The code should be standardized to decrease confusion among users.
5. Long codes, over five digits should be divided for ease of human use.
6. The code should be kept as short as possible. This facilitates transcription and general understandability. For computerized systems it also saves space, which in return reduces expenses.
7. The code should be adaptable for all uses, computers, macroprocessors, people, and other possible applications.
8. The code should have a basic meaning to human users. This means that when human users see an inventory code for raw materials, they know that it is for raw materials and not accounts payable, or vice versa. Codes should have some general distinguishing characteristic that allows human users to categorize or identify an item quickly. Also, when reports are generated, the program should convert the codes to human readable terms; for example, inventory code 45 converts to "sheet plastic."

Although every coding scheme cannot follow all of the preceding characteristics, most of the items have some application in a system's coding scheme.

In computerized systems everything must be coded in order to be accepted by the computer. Because of the diversity found in some types of codes, the following discussion relates to the coding techniques generally adaptable to accounting systems and subsystems. In accounting, the coding system must be designed to record and classify incoming data in the most efficient manner possible and to provide information to a variety of users.

Chart of Accounts

The primary type of coding that accountants encounter is the assigning of numbers to the accounts found in the financial systems—that is, general ledger accounts, subsidiary accounts, and other related accounts. These account codes are usually referred to as the *uniform coded chart of accounts* and each organization will have its own coding scheme. The codes usually begin with the basic accounts of the organization and may be listed as follows:

Code	Basic Accounts
001–099	Current Assets
100–199	Plant and Equipment
200–299	Other Fixed Assets
300–399	Current Liabilities
400–499	Long-term Liabilities
500–599	Other Liabilities
600–699	Capital Stock Accounts
700–799	Retained Earnings
800–999	Income Statement Accounts

Next, the basic groups are divided into the major general ledger accounts of the organization. For different types of organizations, the details of the basic accounts vary, but the following is a realistic example of part of the basic account code breakdown.

Code	Account
001–099	Current Assets
001	Cash, First National Bank
002	Cash, City National Bank
038	Prepaid Insurance, Fire and Home Insurance Co.
049	Prepaid Interest, State Savings Association
087	Raw Material Inventory
800–999	Income Statement Accounts
800	Sales Revenue, Products
801	Sales Returns and Allowances
802	Sales Revenue, Other
856	Depreciation Expense, Plants
891	Sales Commissions
903	Payroll Expense
934	Supplies, Office

After all the basic accounts have been assigned, the organization may add suffixes or prefixes to denote such characteristics as divisions, plants, cost centers, profit centers, or departments. For example, a large organization may desire quarterly plant income statements that can be prepared from the data sent to the home office. To keep the data segregated by plant, the organization can add a prefix to each set of incoming financial data.

Code	Plant
10	Atlanta
20	Boston
30	London
40	Los Angeles
50	Montreal

Therefore, when data arrive at the home office, the two-digit location code indicates where the data came from and the system is able to account for it by plant. A particular piece of equipment from Montreal might be coded 50–137; the same piece of equipment in Boston could be coded 20–137.

For organizations with a very large number of basic and subsidiary accounts, the basic data code may contain a suffix. Suppose the preceding company wanted to keep the equipment by department within each plant. A general suffix code may be established as follows:

Code	Department
111	General Office
211	Plant Office
311	Engineering
411	Warehouse
511	Department A
611	Department B
711	Shipping Department

The equipment in the Montreal plant might be located in the shipping department and would therefore be coded 50–137–711. Because of multiple users and their various needs, the output of a given program might show the equipment as item number 137 or as item 50–137 or as item 50–137–711. The same type of illustration could be made for an expense item on the income statement, a particular account receivable under current assets for the Atlanta plant, or a cash account in a particular bank in London under current assets for the London plant.

Instead of numbering everything in sequence, these illustrations have used the *block code* concept (sometimes called "Group" or "Hierarchical" codes). Although the items may be assigned sequentially within each block, the major item classifications are blocked for easy identification (prefix 10 is always Atlanta) and flexibility of adding more elements. In a block code the position of a set of code elements (the three-digit suffix) always has a special meaning, whereas sequence codes have no assigned meaning to the various code positions.

Classification Codes

There are certain functions in most organizations that need a coding scheme for detailed analysis or segregation. The two most common areas are payroll and inventory. Many organizations require the payroll system to furnish items such as departmental expenses, direct labor, indirect labor, supervisors' salaries, and sales commissions. To keep track of all the different labor classifications, most payroll systems develop elaborate coding schemes.

Assume that the previous company has a payroll coding scheme that applies to all its plants so that each plant and the home office can classify its own payroll by established categories. The reports can also be combined so that company-wide payroll analysis can be performed. The following four-digit code could be used by the company.

CODE

X X X X

Digits 1 and 2 Labor Classification	Digit 3 Qualification Status	Digit 4 Pay Period
01 Direct Labor	0 Entry Level	0 Weekly
02 Indirect Labor	1 Junior Level	1 Biweekly
03 Plant Supervision	2 Intermediate Level	2 Semimonthly
04 Office Supervision	3 Senior Level	3 Monthly
05 Office Clerk		
06 Sales Salaries		
07 Sales Commissions		

The payroll code is large enough to permit the company to expand its systems without redesigning the code. For an employee who works in Los Angeles in the warehouse, is paid biweekly, and is new on the job, the complete payroll code would be 40–411–903–0201. The last four digits are for payroll and can be used alone or with any of the other code sections.

Such code schemes are often known as *significant-digit codes* because each digit, or set of digits, has a special meaning to the users. With this type of code the input user can assign new entries to the code by looking at the coding scheme. Also, all users quickly become familiar with the code and do not need to look up every item when they are working with the payroll account.

The weakness of such a code is its inability to distinguish between employees for payroll tax purposes, personnel needs, and the budget requirements. However, this type of code may be used with the employee's social security number to provide individual identification.

Additional subsidiary accounts that frequently need codes of their own are accounts receivable, accounts payable, and inventory. These code schemes are generally similar to the preceding payroll code in that they contain certain account characteristics. A popular type of scheme with these accounts is the *partial-sequence code.* The accounts are put in alphabetical order and blocked into groups, and each account within a group is numbered according to its order in the alphabet. Only the original items will be in alphabetical order because as new items are added they are sequenced after the last item. For example, in a four-digit code the first two digits represent the letters of the alphabet; for example, A = 01, B = 02, C = 03, and so forth. The other two digits represent the initial alphabetical listing of the accounts and all additional accounts. So if the original account names were Caldwell, Caylor, Cole, and Curtis, they would be coded in 0301, 0302, 0303, and 0304, respectively. The next account that the company received that started with the letter C would be coded 0305 regardless of its alphabetical place in the list. This accounts for the labeling of the code as a partial sequence; only the original list is in sequence by alphabet.

Code Functions

For most systems the coding scheme provides two primary functions. First, it defines all data items with unambiguous identifications. The coding scheme should be developed so that different classifications of items do not have the same numbering; for example, inventory item numbers should be different from accounts payable item numbers. Second, coding schemes add meaning to the items from the perspective of most users, and this assists in assigning inputs, retrieval requests, and file changes when using items in a coding scheme.

Designing correct coding schemes is one of the most important functions the accountant can perform in helping the systems analyst design the accounting information system. Coding schemes must be designed with all aspects of the organization in mind, with the growth potential of the organization taken into account, and with the primary users having input into the scheme.

SCHEDULING CHARTS

Most organizational planning and development projects require some type of activities schedule. Such a schedule should be provided to management in systems analysis and design operations. Most basic time and schedule charts define the activities to be undertaken, the amount of time for each activity, and the dates of each activity. A schedule of this type assists management in planning around disruptions to keep the related operations ongoing and under control.

The most popular scheduling chart is the Gantt chart, or some modification of it. Figure 2.10 illustrates a modified Gantt chart that shows the activities of the analysis and design operations and when they are to be conducted; the progression of each activity can be noted at each evaluation date. The current evaluation date on Project 138 is April 1. As of that date, the estimated completion percentage is indicated by marking the bar for each activity. Notice that Activity 3 is on schedule, Activities 1 and 2 are behind schedule, and Activity 4 is ahead of schedule.

By utilizing such a model, management can monitor the activities of the tasks being undertaken and can take appropriate action when needed. As the different activities progress, resources can be shifted away from those that are ahead of schedule and added to those that are behind schedule, or assigned to other projects or tasks. The use of Gantt

ANALYSIS AND DESIGN ACTIVITY CHART.

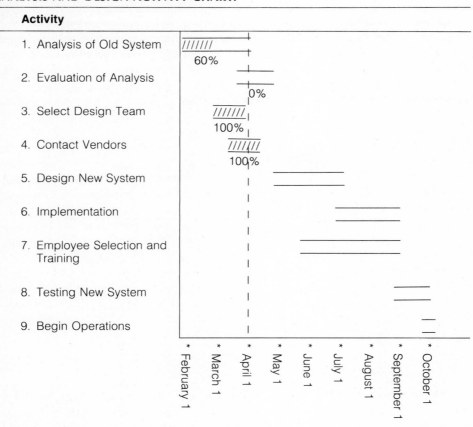

Figure 2.10

Systems Tools and Techniques **53**

charts alone furnishes management with all the information it needs about the timing of a project. However, projects that are lengthy or complicated often require more analysis than the simple timing of the activities. It is often important for management to know something about the relationships of the activities to each other. This requires network analysis.

PERT/CPM

Program Evaluation and Review Technique (PERT) and the Critical Path Method (CPM) are primarily scheduling techniques that relate the activities of a project to each other in terms of time and dependency. PERT and CPM are similar in that they use the same type of network structure to represent a project under consideration; see Figure 2.11. The two concepts may be used together, although PERT is considered probabalistic, whereas CPM is deterministic and node-oriented.

    PERT and CPM provide management, analysts, and designers with a clear perspective of the relationships between the activities and events of the project and provide a means of evaluating potential problems with the activities on each path. The *activities* in a PERT or CPM network represent the tasks that must be conducted and performed in a project. The *events* are points in time that mark the completion of given activities. In Figure 2.11 the activities are represented by the letters and the events by the numbers

PERT NETWORK FOR INSTALLING PAYROLL SYSTEM.

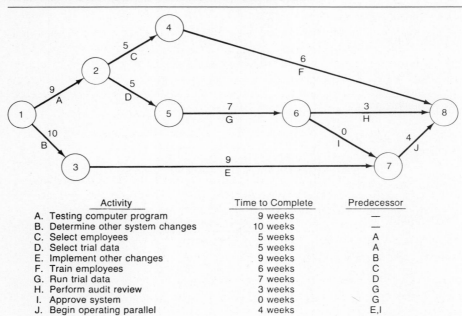

Activity	Time to Complete	Predecessor
A. Testing computer program	9 weeks	—
B. Determine other system changes	10 weeks	—
C. Select employees	5 weeks	A
D. Select trial data	5 weeks	A
E. Implement other changes	9 weeks	B
F. Train employees	6 weeks	C
G. Run trial data	7 weeks	D
H. Perform audit review	3 weeks	G
I. Approve system	0 weeks	G
J. Begin operating parallel	4 weeks	E,I

Figure 2.11

in the circles. Number 1 represents the event "Start" and Number 3 represents the completion of Activity B. Before the network can be completed, the designer must be able to define the relationships between all of the activities and events. Each path may be expressed in terms of activities or events. Once the relationships are determined, the time element must be inserted into the network in order to permit the use of the CPM.

After the estimated times have been included in the network, it is usually necessary to determine the time that the total project is going to take. This is accomplished by computing the critical path for the network. The critical path is the longest time path through the network. Slack time is the time difference between the critical path(s) and other paths through the network. The path times are computed by adding the estimated times of each of the activities on a given path. In Figure 2.11 the path ADGIJ is found to be the longest and therefore the critical path for the network. Assuming a timely progression, the project can be completed in 25 periods.

This section has provided a basic introduction to PERT/CPM. There are many modifications of these models, and additional information can be found in operations research texts. Such modifications as probability estimates for each activity can be applied to the network, and cost estimates for the various times of each activity can be determined. The concept of PERT/Cost provides for selecting alternatives based on both the time and cost of each activity.

SIMULATION

Simulation is an operations research technique that uses a given model to represent a systems function or project and is constructed in such a manner that it can be manipulated and studied in order to understand the response of the function or project or given stimuli. This concept allows analysts and designers to find out what will happen in a system even before installation. This technique can save time otherwise spent in experimenting with the system and can prevent the embarrassment of implementing a system that does not properly operate and function according to plans. Some of the other reasons for using simulation are as follows:

1. Errors and weaknesses can often be found in a system by testing it in a controlled environment.
2. Special high-level programming languages have been developed to aid in writing computer programs for simulation experiments. This saves time for the designer.
3. Because simulation is used frequently in management training programs, it is familiar to those who will be working with the designers in developing a new system.
4. Since most systems work today deals with the computer, the computer itself can assist in the simulation process by setting aside part of the computer operation to simulate the new systems.

As a basic tool of systems design, simulation can help to organize complex situations involving multiple data and information relationships. Anytime the systems designer does not understand the relationship between two or more variables, a simulation model can put the relationships in a better perspective by providing sample outputs from given sample inputs.

SUMMARY

Before the various aspects of accounting information systems can be understood, the fundamentals of information systems must be considered. This chapter has provided many of the fundamentals considered necessary for an introductory course in accounting information systems. Of the areas presented, flowcharting is the most important because accountants, auditors, and systems analysts in accounting must use flowcharts in the design, evaluation, and understanding of accounting systems. Decision tables, related to flowcharts in the analysis and design stages, assist in assuring that the logic of a program or system is sound, correct, and complete. The scheduling charts are also very beneficial when conducting the design and implementation phases of the systems life cycle.

Two areas that accountants should always be concerned with are document design and coding. These areas affect the daily affairs of accountants and their systems. Often the systems analyst must consult with the accountant in order to design a document properly because the accountant is the primary user, in either the input or output process.

In today's complex information systems the accountant is only one of many users of systems tools and techniques. Accountants should be aware of the various tools and techniques and their proper use and application. The basic benefits that are provided for accounting users include improved control, reduced costs, and greater data utilization.

SELECTED REFERENCES

Halton, John B., and Bill Bryan. "Structured Top-Down Flowcharting," *Datamation* (May 1975): 80–84.

Li, David H. "Control Flowcharting: An Introduction," *The Internal Auditor* (June 1983): 26–29.

Mize, B. Jay, Jr. "Flowcharts Need Time Dimension," *The Internal Auditor* (April 1982): 35–37.

Myers, Gibbs. "Forms Management, Part 2: How to Design Business Forms," *Journal of Systems Management* (October 1976).

Pollock, S. L., H. T. Hicks, Jr., and W. J. Harrison. *Decision Tables: Theory and Practice.* New York: John Wiley & Sons, 1971.

Shelly, Gary B., and Thomas Cashman. *Introduction to Computers and Data Processing.* Fullerton, Calif.: Anaheim Publishing Co., 1980.

Squire, Enid. *Introducing . . . Systems Design.* Reading, Mass.: Addison-Wesley Publishing Co., 1980.

Statland, Norman, and Donald T. Winski. "Distributed Information Systems: Their Effect on Your Company," *Price Waterhouse and Company Review* (1978, No. 1): 54–63.

Wetherbe, James C., *Systems Analysis,* St. Paul: West Publishing Co., 1980.

QUESTIONS

1. Explain or define the following:

System flowchart	Block code
Document flowchart	Significant-digit code
Program flowchart	Partial sequence code
Micro document chart	Scheduling charts
Decision table	PERT
Uniform coded chart of accounts	CPM

2. Define the three basic types of flowcharts and give the advantages and uses of each.
3. Draw a flowchart symbol for each of the following:
   a. Manual operation
   b. Magnetic tape
   c. Document
   d. Main processing
   e. On-line storage
4. What are the basic differences between systems and document flowcharts?
5. What is a micro document chart? How is it used? What is its relation to a document flowchart?
6. Explain the use of program flowcharts. Who uses program flowcharting?
7. How does a decision table assist a systems analyst in preparing a system for the computer?
8. Define the four elements of a decision table. Discuss the order of developing the four elements.
9. When documents are being designed, what factors should be considered in order to fit the document to its intended uses?
10. What is a code? What are the different types of codes used in computer applications?
11. What are the design characteristics of a proper coding scheme? Which of these involve accountants?
12. Who should develop the chart of accounts for an organization? Why?
13. What are significant digit codes? When are they used?
14. What is meant by scheduling charts? How can they be used in systems design?
15. Explain the relationship between PERT and CPM.

PROBLEMS

16. Sales Department Flowcharts

The sales department of the Wilson Company prepares a seven-part sales invoice from each customer order and files the order alphabetically by customer. Part 2 is sent to the credit department for credit approval, and the remaining parts are held until credit is approved. Part 2 is returned to sales and filed with the customer's order. Parts 1 (sales invoice) and 3 (posting copy) are sent to the billing department; part 4 is used as a packing slip; part 5 is sent to the warehouse as a stock request; and parts 6 and 7 are sent to the customer.

The warehouse sends part 5 with the goods to shipping. In shipping, the goods are compared with the the stock request and units shipped are noted on the request. Shipping takes the packing slip from the files and sends it with the goods to the customer. The stock request (part 5) is then sent to billing.

Billing enters shipped items (marked on the stock request) on the sales invoice (part 1) and on the posting copy (part 3), makes extensions and checks them, compares prices with the price list, and runs a tape of extended amounts shown on the posting copy. The stock request (part 5) is filed numerically; numerical sequence is accounted for at this time. The sales invoice is sent to the customer. The posting copy is sent to general accounting, where it is placed in the open invoice file. The tape of extended amounts is also sent to general accounting, where it is used to post the total to the sales control account in the general ledger. The open invoice file is balanced monthly to the general ledger sales control.

Required:
   a. Prepare a system flowchart for the sales department.
   b. Prepare a document flowchart of the sales invoice.

17. Procurement and Payables Flowcharts

The purchasing department of Cola Company uses a four-part purchase order prepared from a written purchase request by the superintendents or foremen. Parts 1 and 2 are sent to the vendor; part 3 is filed as a control and follow-up copy for open orders; part 4 is sent to the receiving department for use as a receiving report.

Received goods are indicated on part 4, which is then sent to purchasing where it is compared with part 3. Part 4 is then sent to accounting and held until the invoice is received. When the vendor's invoice is received in accounting, part 4 is taken from the files and checked against the invoice for accuracy of prices, quantities, and computations. The invoice is assigned a number and recorded in the invoice register. The account distribution code is written on the invoice. The invoice and part 4 of the purchase order are sent to the accounts payable clerk, who files these two documents by due date.

In accounts payable, the clerk pulls the invoices and purchase orders and prepares checks and check copies (the copies show account distribution). From the checks, the clerk prepares a tape of the cash amounts and forwards the invoices, purchase orders, checks, check copies, and tape to the general accounting department. In general accounting, a clerk posts the amounts from the check copies in the cash disbursements book and totals the postings made from the batch of check copies. The total of the postings is then compared with the total on the tape forwarded from accounts payable. If the totals are not in agreement, the difference is analyzed and reconciled; if they are in agreement, the general accounting clerk forwards the checks with supporting invoices, purchase orders, and check copies to the controller for signature.

The controller reviews the supporting data, signs the checks, and returns all items to the general accounting clerk. General accounting reviews the checks and mails them to the vendors, files the check copies by number, stamps the invoices "paid," and forwards the invoices and any supporting documents to the purchasing department.

Required:
   a. Prepare a systems flowchart for each function.
   b. Prepare a document flowchart including all activities.

18. Chart of Accounts

Bill Smith has recently been appointed controller of a family-owned manufacturing enterprise. The firm, S. Dilley & Co., was founded by Mr. Dilley about 20 years ago, is 78 percent owned by Mr. Dilley, and has served the major automotive companies as a parts supplier. The firm's major operating divisions are heat treating, extruding, small parts stamping, and specialized machining. Sales last year from the several divisions ranged from $150,000 to more than $3,000,000. The divisions are physically and managerially independent except for Mr. Dilley's constant surveillance. The accounting system for each division has evolved according to the division's own needs and to the abilities of individual accountants or bookkeepers. Mr. Smith is the first controller in the firm's history to have responsibility for overall financial management. Mr. Dilley expects to retire within six years and has hired Mr. Smith to improve the firm's financial system.

Mr. Smith soon decides that he will need to design a new financial reporting system that will:

a. Give managers uniform, timely, and accurate reports on business activity. Monthly divisional reports should be uniform and available by the tenth of the following month. Company-wide financial reports also should be prepared by the tenth.

b. Provide a basis for measuring return on investment by division. Divisional reports should show assets assigned each division and revenue and expense measurement in each division.

c. Generate meaningful budget data for planning and decision-making purposes. The accounting system should provide for the preparation of budgets that recognize managerial responsibility, controllability of costs, and major product groups.

d. Allow for a uniform basis of evaluating performance and quick access to underlying data. Cost center variances should be measured and reported for operating and nonoperating units, including headquarters. Also questions about levels of specific cost factors or product costs should be answerable quickly.

A new chart of accounts, as it appears to Mr. Smith, is essential to starting on other critical financial problems. The present account codes used by divisions are not standard.

Mr. Smith sees a need to divide asset accounts into six major categories; that is, current assets, plant and equipment, and so on. Within each of these categories, he sees a need for no more than ten control accounts. On the basis of his observations to date, 100 subsidiary accounts are more than adequate for each control account.

No division now has more than five major product groups. The maximum number of cost centers Mr. Smith foresees within any product group is six, including operating and nonoperating groups. He views general divisional costs as a nonrevenue-producing product group. Altogether, Mr. Smith estimates that about 44 natural expense accounts plus about 12 specific variance accounts would be adequate.

Mr. Smith is planning to implement the new chart of accounts in an environment that at present includes manual records systems and one division that is using an EDP system. He expects that in the near future most accounting and reporting for all units will be automated. Therefore, the chart of accounts should facilitate the processing of transactions manually or by machine. Efforts should be made, he believes, to restrict the length of the code for economy in processing and convenience in use. *(IMA adapted)*

Required:

a. Design a chart of accounts coding system that will meet Mr. Smith's requirements. Your answer should begin with a digital layout of the coding system. You should explain the coding method you have chosen and the reason for the size of your code elements. Explain your code as it would apply to asset and expense accounts.

b. Use your chart of accounts coding system to illustrate the code needed for the following data:

(1) In the small parts stamping division, $250 was spent by the foreman in the polishing department of the Door Lever Group on cleaning supplies. Code the expense item, using the code you developed earlier.

(2) A new motorized sweeper has been purchased for the maintenance department of the extruding division for $5,112. Code this asset item using the code you developed above.

19. Inventory Flowchart

The Monroe Company maintains a perpetual inventory system where clerks in the accounting department post the data manually from receiving reports, materials requisition forms, copies of purchase orders, and other transactions such as returns and adjustments to the inventory records. The documents are filed by posting date and the inventory records are analyzed after each posting for errors and to determine whether the item should be reordered. If an item needs to be reordered, a purchase requisition is prepared and sent to the purchasing department where clerks select a vendor from a master vendor file, prepare a purchase order (five copies), and update the vendor file to reflect the order. The purchase order is approved and distributed as follows: original and first copy sent to the vendor; copy 2 filed with the corresponding purchase requisition; copy 3 sent to the receiving department; copy 4 sent to inventory control.

Required:

Prepare a systems flowchart for the Monroe Company.

20. Cash Receipts Flowchart

Cash receipts in the Swiss Company are processed in the following manner. The cashier opens all mail containing customer payments and prepares a batch control tape of the total amount received which is sent to the general ledger clerk to support the appropriate journal entry. The cashier prepares two copies of a deposit slip, deposits the cash receipts in the bank, and files the bank-validated copy of the deposit slip by date. She also sends the remittance advices to the accounts receivable clerk, who posts them to customer accounts. Assume that no other operations or personnel are involved in the processing of cash receipts.

Required:
Prepare a document flowchart of the processing previously described.

21. Program Flowchart and Decision Table

In examining the documentation of the Royal Company, the auditor discovered that the program flowchart and the decision table for the following inventory function were missing. Each input record contained the item name, number, quantity on hand, most recent price, and total costs of items in stock. The program prints page headings at the beginning of the output and after each new printout page is started. Each page contains 37 lines. For each input record the program extends the product price times the quantity on hand and compares this with the total cost amount on the input record. If the two figures do not agree, an error is printed at the end of the line on the printout. If the figures agree, the inventory data are printed as output. Besides being used for error messages, the space at the end of each line is used to list high-risk items, those valued above $5,000. When the last record is processed, the items are printed out and the program ends.

Required:
   a.   Prepare a program flowchart of the inventory function.
   b.   Prepare a decision table for the preceding function in accordance with your flowchart.

22. Program Flowchart and Decision Table

Mutual Savings Company is in the process of placing its customer savings accounts on a new computer. The current rate structure for passbook accounts is as follows:
   a.   Interest of 8 percent on accounts with balances over $10
   b.   Interest of 9 percent on accounts with balances over $1,000
   c.   Interest of 9.25 percent on accounts with balances over $1,000 for at least 1 year

Required:
   a.   Prepare a program flowchart for the passbook savings account application.
   b.   Prepare a decision table for the passbook savings account program.

23. Decision Table

Midwest Company crushes grain to sell for animal feed. Because of its large-scale operations, it processes only one product a day. The overall production schedule is determined by the amount of grain in the inventory, which is determined based on market forecasts. Because of its high volume, corn is always crushed first if there is enough corn inventory. For a daily processing run, the following minimum amounts are needed: corn, 50,000 bushels; oats, 38,000 bushels; and soybeans, 30,000 bushels. If the corn inventory is insufficient, oats are processed first. If none of the minimum amounts is available, a mixture of corn and oats is made if there are at least 30,000 bushels of corn and 15,000 bushels of oats. Otherwise, the company shuts down for the day.

Required:

Prepare a decision table for the daily production operations of the Midwest Company.

24. Coded Chart of Accounts

Lorenso and Jacome have recently started a company to import Portuguese fish products. The three categories of fish will be canned, frozen, and dried. There will be 54 varieties of canned fish, 12 varieties of frozen fish, and 14 varieties of dried fish. Initially, the products will be sold along the eastern coast of the United States with Charleston, South Carolina, as the distribution point. The company will employ a sales staff, warehouse workers, shipping clerks, and a business staff. The company owns its building in Charleston and has a fleet of automobiles for its sales staff. Normal operating expenses include: raw materials, packaging, salaries and wages, employee benefits, and depreciation. Selling and administrative expenses include selling commissions, travel, advertising, staff salaries and benefits, and insurance. The company will also have several thousand customers on account and about 14 suppliers. In total, the company will have no more than 137 employees during its first four years of operations.

Required:

Design a coded chart of accounts that will facilitate the preparation of quarterly balance sheets and income statements. Make appropriate allowances for inventory, accounts receivable, accounts payable, and payroll.

25. Coding System for Minicomputer

The Lookout Gift Shop is located next to the entrance of a national park. The lower level is stocked with tourist items related to the park. There are over 5,000 inventory items that can be classified into 39 categories from postcards to engraved dishes. No single inventory item is ever carried in quantities over 200.

On the upper level the shop stocks items frequently needed by travelers. Typical items include toiletries, counter medications, snack food, and outdoor games and equipment. There are 106 categories of items on this level and item quantities range from 12 to 144.

Required:

The shop owner is currently installing a minicomputer and desires to computerize the inventory. Develop a coding system that would permit proper classifications of the inventory items. Allow room for expansion because future plans call for another shop in a nearby tourist village.

26. PERT Network and CPM

Frame Company specializes in large construction projects. The company uses the PERT technique in planning and controlling its projects. The following schedule of separable activities and their expected completion times have been developed for a bank building to be started next month.

Activity	Predecessor Activities	Completion Time (weeks)
a. Excavation	—	2
b. Foundation	a	3
c. Vault foundation	a	7
d. Rough plumbing and heating	b	4
e. Framing	b, c	5
f. Roofing	e	3
g. Electrical	f	3
h. Interior walls	d, g	4
i. Finish plumbing and heating	h	2
j. Exterior finishing	f	6
k. Landscaping	i, j	2

(IMA adapted)

Required:
   a.   Prepare a PERT network.
   b.   Compute the critical path and its completion time.

27. PERT and CPM

Carmine Manufacturing has just made a final decision to install a computerized information system. Before beginning the conversion, the systems analysts developed the following list of activities that must be completed.

Activity	Completion Time (days)	Predecessor Activities
a. Determine requirements	21	—
b. Plan design phase	2	a
c. Assign duties	1	a
d. Design system	30	c
e. Feasibility study of final design	4	d
f. Develop controls	12	b, c
g. Equipment requirements	8	d, f
h. Prepare documentation	6	d, g
i. Install equipment	11	e
j. Test and debug programs	18	i
k. Conduct training	14	h, j
l. Release system to operators	2	g, k

Required:
a. Prepare a network diagram.
b. Determine the critical path and its completion time.
c. Determine which path has the most days of slack. What is the amount of the slack time?

28. Payroll Flowchart

City Papers has a payroll system that is card input oriented. All production employees punch daily time clock cards when entering or leaving the printing facilities. At the end of each week the timekeeping department collects the cards and prepares duplicate batch control slips by department showing the total hours worked and the number of employees. The time cards and original batch control slips are sent to the payroll department. The second copies are filed by date.

The payroll transaction cards are keypunched in the payroll department using the time card information. A total card for each batch is keypunched from the manual control slip. The time cards and control slips are filed by batch for possible reference.

The payroll transaction cards and batch total card are sent to data processing where they are sorted by employee number within each batch. Each batch is edited by a computer program that checks the employee number against a master employee tape file and the total hours and number of employees against the batch total card. A detailed printout by batch and employee number is produced, which indicates batches that do not balance and invalid employee numbers.

The printout is sent to the payroll department which reconciles the differences. Batch total cards and transaction cards are discarded. Upon reconciliation, the computer center processes the payroll producing paychecks, paystubs, a check register, and an updated payroll master file on magnetic tape. *(AICPA adapted)*

Required:

Prepare a systems flowchart of the payroll system.

29. CPM and Network Analysis

Esther Thomas is responsible for finding a suitable building and establishing a new convenience grocery store for Thrift-Mart, Inc. Ms. Thomas enumerated the specific activities that had to be completed and the estimated time to establish each activity. In addition, she prepared a network diagram, which appears here, to aid in the coordination of the activities. The list of activities to locate a building and establish a new store is as follows:

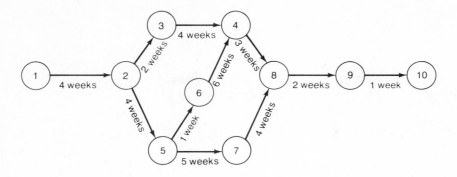

Activity Number	Description of Activity	Estimated Time Required
1-2	Find building	4 weeks
2-3	Negotiate rental terms	2 weeks
3-4	Draft lease	4 weeks
2-5	Prepare store plans	4 weeks
5-6	Select and order fixtures	1 week
6-4	Delivery of fixtures	6 weeks
4-8	Install fixtures	3 weeks
5-7	Hire staff	5 weeks
7-8	Train staff	4 weeks
8-9	Receive inventory	2 weeks
9-10	Stock shelves	1 week

(IMA adapted)

Required:

a. Identify the critical path for finding and establishing the new convenience store.

b. Ms. Thomas would like to finish the store 2 weeks earlier than indicated by the schedule, and as a result, she is considering several alternatives. One such alternative is to convince the fixture manufacturer to deliver the fixtures in 4 weeks rather than in 6 weeks. Should Ms. Thomas arrange for the manufacturer to deliver the fixtures in 4 weeks if the sole advantage of this schedule change is to open the store 2 weeks early? Justify your answer.

c. A program such as the one illustrated by the network diagram for the new convenience store cannot be implemented unless the required resources are available at the required dates. What additional information does Ms. Thomas need to administer the proposed project properly?

CHAPTER THREE

Information Systems and Computer Technology

The more important concepts of computer technology and terminology as related to accounting information systems are presented in this chapter. Assuming that the reader has had a minimum exposure to computer technology, this chapter should provide the basics for a general understanding of the technical tools needed for the study of accounting information systems. References are provided at the end of the chapter to help readers strengthen their knowledge of a particular topic. Other texts and reference books devote relatively more attention to some of the topics found in this chapter so that one may easily reinforce the material, if necessary. An attempt to cover all topics in detail would distract from the accounting emphasis of this text. Although all the areas covered do not relate directly to accounting, they are included because they represent part of the body of knowledge of general information systems. Those readers with a strong computer background could omit this chapter or use it merely as basic reference material.

With an increasing number of developments taking place in computer technology, the accountant needs to keep current in the areas related to various accounting systems. Recent developments have increased the integration of accounting with all aspects of an organization. The computer technology and terminology presented in this chapter reflect the close relationship that has evolved between accounting information systems and computer systems.

In addition to keeping current on primary computer changes, the accountant must also be concerned with the large volume of accounting data that may be affected as the computer changes are implemented. The accountant must constantly be concerned about the accuracy, reliability, control, and timeliness of the data. To assess properly the effectiveness and efficiency of accounting applications, the accountant must be familiar with the organization's computer hardware and software. Items often considered are: (1) amount, type, and preparation of input; (2) recording and storage media; and (3) frequency and formats of outputs, users' needs for printouts, inquiry availability on CRTs, and distribution.

ELEMENTS OF A COMPUTER SYSTEM

The basic computerized system is composed of four major elements: hardware, software, procedures, and personnel. The hardware and software elements are discussed in separate sections, and procedures and personnel matters are integrated throughout the chapter. Manual systems reflect the same elements, although with different characteristics from those of automated systems. Business executives are often awed by the basic computer system even though it parallels, in many instances, the manual system it replaces. *Hardware,* the equipment necessary for a computer system, is discussed first.

Central Processing Unit

The central processing unit (CPU) is the primary performing element and the most complicated feature of an electronic data processing system. The CPU consists of a control section that coordinates all systems activities, an arithmetic/logic unit that performs the calculations, and an internal memory that holds program information during the actual processing of a program, see Figure 3.1.

The CPU is primarily a binary device with electronic impulses used as the instructions during the processing cycle. After being transferred to the CPU, the electronic impulses are manipulated in accordance with the instructions of a program. They are then combined to form digital representations of data. The CPU must follow specific rules in manipulating the impulses. These rules are laws of logic, the four mathematical functions, comparisons, and transfers of data between files. The specific rules must be performed in a predetermined sequence as described in the program being processed. Also, the

MAIN COMPUTER COMPONENT SYSTEMS.

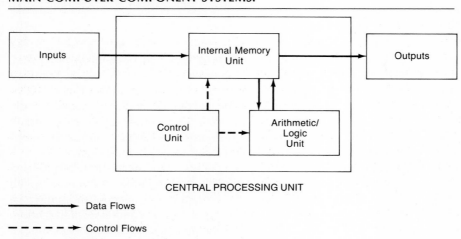

CENTRAL PROCESSING UNIT

———————▶ Data Flows

— — — — ▶ Control Flows

Figure 3.1

CPU can store in internal memory the program being executed and follow the directions of the specific program without further instructions. These characteristics distinguish the computer from other mechanical devices such as bookkeeping machines, desk calculators, and punch card systems.

The CPU is surrounded by other equipment that aids in the total processing function. The main items of equipment are input devices, output devices, and primary and secondary storage elements. These elements, along with the CPU, comprise the basic EDP hardware configuration. The specific hardware used for any given EDP installation is known as a *configuration.* When these elements are coupled directly to a CPU, they are labeled as *on-line* equipment or elements, and elements that are not attached directly to the CPU are labeled *off-line.* An input tape drive, for example, would be on-line; the keying machine that prepared the tape would be off-line.

Input

The input element of a computer performs the basic translation function for the system, converting data to an acceptable form for processing. Data can be converted from the language symbols of society into machine language through magnetic disk drives, paper tape readers, magnetic tape readers, and communication terminals. The sections on the various types of peripheral equipment discuss most of the devices available for use in a system, including those applicable to input.

Output

The output element of a system reverses the processing steps of the input element. This phase of the system converts the symbols of machine language into human interpretable symbols or into other machine language forms, or both, for additional processing by other programs or routines. A variety of output devices are discussed in the communications section.

Storage

Primary storage is generally used only to hold programs and data being processed. Examples of primary storage are core, plated wire, semiconductor, and bubble memory. Secondary storage, which is used for the voluminous data files that most organizations have, is usually much cheaper than primary storage. Secondary storage is usually on disk, magnetic tape, drum, or other mass storage devices. Also, certain types of secondary storage enable sensitive and priority data to be removed and stored in remote locations for security and control. This concept is discussed further in Chapter Four.

The data contained in secondary storage media are made available when needed by the system, and when not in use they are generally stored off-line or have controlled on-line access. The two procedures of storing such data are direct access and sequential access. *Direct access* is provided on devices that store the data in addressed and random order so that each item can be accessed without having to read from the beginning of a file to find specific data. Magnetic disks are examples of such devices. *Sequential access* requires that data be stored in a controlled sequence on the storage device, necessitating the reading of all records until the desired data are found. Magnetic tape is the most common example.

Data Transmission and Storage

Input and output devices are the communicating means between one computer and other computers or human users. Regardless of the communication needs, peripheral equipment today can handle any task, including the transmissions of sound, touch, and temperature to and from the environment and the CPU. Each new generation of computers introduces more sophisticated communication techniques.

Magnetic Tape Units   Magnetic tape is one of the most widely used input/output and storage media. Its popularity stems from four advantages. First, its speed is far superior to that of cards. Most magnetic tape units can read up to 320,000 characters per second; the average card reader reads only 6,000 characters per second. Second, it is unsurpassed as a storage and transfer medium because of its compactness. A 10 × ¾-inch reel of tape can hold as much data as 500,000 punched cards. Third, the tapes can be reused, a major cost savings over cards. Fourth, record lengths can vary without adverse consequences to other records. This advantage provides for flexibility in establishing data fields and minimizing space. Records can be packed together if necessary. These advantages offset many of the disadvantages of magnetic tapes for most users. For example, tapes are only machine readable, internal labels must be used for control so that good tapes are not accidentally erased or written over, and they must be sequentially written and read.

Although magnetic tapes are used primarily as storage, recent changes in technology have increased their input/output role. Organizations refer tapes containing check payments to banks for checking account reconciliation. Plants, and branches of large organizations, send payroll data to the home office through communication lines where it is recorded on tape pending the next payroll processing. Many companies that use service bureaus send all their data on magnetic tape to the service center's processing unit.

Magnetic Disk Units   Magnetic disks and the somewhat less popular magnetic drums are used primarily for mass storage when direct access of data is important. The data need not be stored sequentially since these units have direct access capabilities to all stored data. On-line, real-time systems dominate such applications, which permits the processing of a variety of programs without the need for mounting or changing tape reels, instructing the computer, or otherwise responding to user needs. Inventory, accounts payable, and accounts receivable applications frequently employ such configurations. Entire systems are sometimes organized by using direct access units such as those used by banks and brokerage firms where customers constantly demand information from as well as supply information to the system. Also, magnetic disks permit real-time applications for relatively small EDP systems that have limited needs for such files.

Magnetic Ink Character Recognition Devices (MICR)   These input devices are designed to read magnetic ink characters. Common examples are coded checks and other bank documents and customer statements of utility and credit card companies. These devices minimize input errors and are relatively fast (up to 1600 documents per minute). They are often combined with sorters to process documents that must be separated by some special grouping such as the type of customer or product line.

Optical Readers These input devices have gained wide acceptance in organizations where large volumes of documents must be read. They are generally less expensive than special character readers, and they can be designed to read almost any type of characters, whether handwritten, typed, or computer-generated. By circumventing the manual step of keying input data, these machines greatly reduce the number of input errors, speed the processing, and reduce preprocessing costs. The major handicap of most optical readers is the restrictions on the type and quality of paper used. Blemishes in the paper, dirt, wrinkles, or other foreign particles may cause the scanner to misinterpret the actual characters or reject the document entirely. This extra or exception processing can be costly and inefficient.

Although optical readers do not require characters to be printed in magnetic ink as do MICRs, they can read only a limited number of fonts. A *font* is a set of specific characters that must adhere to strict requirements of size, shape, and style. These readers are most often used in processing turnaround documents, such as credit card statements, and in reading price tags in retail stores.

A less sophisticated device is the *optical mark reader.* Rather than reading a set of characters, these devices read only a few types of marks. Pencil marks on test answer sheets is a common example. Companies often use this concept in manufacturing plants so that the inputs to the system can be kept in the simplest form—a pencil mark in a selected field.

Teleprinter Terminals Teleprinter terminals, the most common of on-line devices, are used primarily for data input and inquiry. Although they can be used for output purposes, they are efficient only for low-volume applications. Remote communications are accomplished via direct telephone lines, eliminating the need for transfer documents.

The major advantage of these terminals is the direct accessibility to other elements of the computer system. Although such terminals are necessary for the on-line feature of a real-time system, several weaknesses must be controlled. Errors in input are difficult to control. The computer must be programmed to detect and denote such errors. Multiprocessing in on-line systems creates problems when concurrent inputs attempt to update identical records. Again, controls must be implemented to monitor updating requests. These controls are discussed in Chapter Five. Other disadvantages are (1) the slow speeds for output, (2) delays in transmission because of line problems, (3) input error detection and correction, and (4) unclear audit trails because permanent hard-copy files are often not maintained.

Cathode-ray Tube (CRT) Terminals Equipped with a video screen and keyboard (some models may also have a printing device similar to the teleprinters), CRTs serve the same general purpose as teleprinters. Many CRTs have graphic capabilities, and some can be adapted to accept light pens as an input stimulus. These are especially convenient when engineers are using the computer to aid in construction design and to effect changes in a particular blueprint directly on the screen. Computer programmers find CRTs useful in modifying and updating computer programs currently on file. After retrieving the file, the programmer can make line-by-line changes in the program, test the changes, and return the program to storage.

The lack of printing capabilities is the main disadvantage of CRT devices. However, the flexibility and convenience provided by CRTs make them the overwhelming choice in many on-line situations. Also, they are cheaper than most other devices and do not require paper.

Voice Terminals   These devices are used mainly for inquiry response, and possess only limited input/output capabilities. The most common voice terminals are push-button telephones, through which the user transmits a combination of voice and push-button messages for communication with the system. Retail store clerks use audio devices to check customers' credit at the time of sale, and manufacturing operations use them to monitor stock status reports between the inventory control system and the various plant locations.

Intelligent Terminals   These devices are usually improved CRTs with a memory that can perform certain data input checks and simple arithmetic operations—microcomputers, or minicomputers. Intelligent terminals are designed primarily for input and inquiry. Their main advantage over other terminals is that they can transmit partially processed data to the CPU, which not only increases the speed of the communication process, but also relieves the main CPU of many routine activities. Terminals of this type are increasing in popularity in situations where the user requires immediate processing of simple programs and, in addition, needs access to the main computer system for input, output, or inquiry. A department that monitors its own budget would be a good application of these terminals.

Organizations making major systems changes find these terminals useful in expanding the capabilities of the computerized system without the need to expand the basic CPU. The costs of adding several intelligent terminals are generally much less than the costs of acquiring a larger CPU. Another subtle advantage is that these terminals provide the users with flexibility unavailable from a system with simply a larger CPU.

Microfilm Recorders   Microfilm recorders are output units that are used if information needs to be stored on permanent files but will be used infrequently. *Microfilm rolls* are used to store such items as newspapers or government records. Another medium, the *microfiche,* is a sheet of film containing a number of images, and is used in search and reference processes. The sheets can be used for locating parts, determining part numbers, names, model applications, and the like at inventory warehouses and for student record inquiries at universities.

Printers   Printers are output devices that vary from simple keyless teleprinters to complex photographic printers. The most common printers are high-speed impact line printers. They print one or two full lines of prearranged data at a time. Impact printers use the electric typewriter concept with either bars, drums, or chains as the lettering media. Nonimpact line printers are even faster than impact printers; examples are electrosensitive, electrostatic, electrophotographic, and ink jet printers. The primary advantages of nonimpact printers over other printers are speed, quiet operation, superior quality, and lower equipment costs. Disadvantages include higher paper costs, although these devices cannot provide multiple copies. The nonimpact printers require a higher-quality paper to withstand the speed.

Plotters   Plotters draw sketches, graphs, and designs on paper. In contrast to normal printing devices, plotters use a mechanical pen that moves freely over the paper. Digital or numerical data accepted by the plotter are transmitted to create the desired drawing. Plotters can be used for drawing maps, building designs, recording vital signs of the human body, and making break-even charts for products.

Card Devices   Basic card devices can read cards as input, or punch cards as output of a computer program. Few systems use cards as a primary input medium today; however, many systems employ cards as output. Cards as output are often necessary for payroll programs, as paychecks, for utility company billing systems, and for monthly statements of credit card companies.

The advantages of cards include human readability, data correction, record replacement, and ease of use. The disadvantages, which often outweigh the advantages, include limited record size, bulkiness of storage, vulnerability to changing temperature and humidity, and the inability to correct and reuse cards. A large card input/output operation can be expensive relative to the other available choices when all factors are considered—that is, card costs, preparation, storage handling, and control. Card output has maintained popularity because of certain user needs, but overall they have become less acceptable as other techniques improve.

Software

Systems software consists of all the programs and routines needed to instruct the hardware in performing its processing functions. Software emanates from two sources, the vendor and the user. *Vendor software* is prepared by computer manufacturers for their own components or by software companies that sell to any computer user. This software may be standardized (canned) or custom-made. *User-prepared software* is custom-made by the organization for uses by its departments.

Software programs can be categorized as *control* or *application.* Control programs are required with all computerized systems to oversee the interaction of the hardware components and to control the processing of the three functions of the CPU: memory and storage, control, and logic and arithmetic. Application programs control computer functions in the performance of specific tasks in the daily operation of the system.

A brief review of the primary elements found in most software systems is necessary because of their use in accounting information systems. In-depth discussions of these elements can be found in the information systems references at the end of the chapter.

Programming Languages   Computer programs begin as flowcharts that are converted into programming commands by using one of the languages adaptable to the hardware of the given system. These language commands are converted into machine sensible language which the computer understands. *Machine language* is a coding system based on a binary system of 0's and 1's. The machine language is interpreted by the computer. Because machine languages are very difficult for humans to use, each computer operation has a software system to communicate between the computer and programmer.

The next level in the hierarchy of languages is known as *assembly* or *symbolic language.* These languages use *mnemonic* (memory) codes. Mnemonic codes use words such as "add," "move," and "store." With this type of language the programmer writes most instructions by using a defined set of mnemonic codes. By using a software package called an assembler, the computer converts the assembly language into its binary equivalents. These types of languages are considered *machine-independent;* that is, they may be translated into any type of machine language.

Higher-level languages represent the next software level in the hierarchy. These languages are oriented toward people users versus machine. They use software complier programs to translate the user-oriented language into binary equivalents.

Most programming languages today are *procedure-oriented,* the most common being FORTRAN, COBOL, BASIC, and PL/1. They specify a set of instructions to be followed by the computer. For example, the word "read" is understood by a person examining a program and by the computer processing the program to mean certain things. In a *non-procedure-oriented* or *symbolic* language "read" may be symbolized as "RD." Although the computer still knows what this means, a human reading or writing a program in symbolic language may be confused by the many relationships that must be remembered. In contrast to other languages, procedure-oriented languages are easy to read, write, correct, and change. Just as some languages are easily understood by different people, others are easily used by different computers.

File Maintenance   File maintenance is the process of updating files stored by the computer. The programs are developed to process recurring activities such as payroll, inventory, and accounts payable. In each case a master file must be accessed and updated as transactions are processed. File maintenance occurs on the file itself when new inventory items are added, current items are dropped, or changes are made in the data fields of each account.

Utility Routines   As the name implies, utility programs have many applications. They are usually attached to larger programs to perform activities such as sorting data, merging files, converting data from one medium to another, and printing. These routines save programmers valuable time because the basic instructions for a given hardware configuration should be similar for all processing. For example, a memory dump for payroll should follow the same basic steps as a memory dump for accounts payable.

Report Generation   A primary element of processing the financial transactions is the function of report generation. Statements, reports, and listings are prepared according to direct or indirect requests from users. These outputs come from previously stored data and from results of processing data. Outputs may be generated in batches (payroll) or upon individual requests (customer credit check). Reporting may be combined with processing functions or programmed as a separate activity.

Edit Processing   This function prepares input for transaction processing by examining data for errors. Edit may be programmed to detect data transmitted from an unauthorized source, to prevent data from being applied to the wrong transaction processing (an inventory transaction in accounts payable, e.g.), and to detect errors in the data itself (an incorrect account number or a missing data field).

Edit checks are usually separate programs that review data entering the system. The edit check results in a listing of data items that cannot be processed. The valid transactions are placed on tape or disk to await processing. The invalid items may be immediately corrected and processed or held for processing until the next regular run. An *error log* is usually kept to detect whether the same errors are made frequently, whether a particular terminal or equipment device is making the errors, or whether a particular input source (department, store, person) is at fault.

Operating Systems   The operating systems perform the activities of storage control; scheduling, program execution, data security, and resource control—assigns time and cost to users. The software is composed of an integrated series of sequential commands that instruct the CPU and the input and output functions, and interface the utility routines, application programs, and other programs with each other. The operating systems developed by hardware manufacturers in recent years are much more effective and efficient in error control and prevention. The newer systems perform activities such as scheduling jobs based on predetermined priorities, multiprogramming, and basic tasks formerly performed by console operators.

Auditing Packages   The basic similarity of most auditing procedures has encouraged auditors to develop generalized software packages to assist in certain audit routines. In some cases there may be several software packages for a single client; in other cases individual software packages may be used for multiple clients. The audit programs may range from a statistical test of inventory items to a test of an entire computer application, such as an inventory system where input, processing, and output are examined and analyzed for effectiveness and internal control.

Word Processing   The most recent addition to this area is specialized software known as *word processing.* Word processing applications require very little computer manipulation and are primarily used to store letters, reports, and other types of text that need to be used repeatedly or modified frequently. The primary advantage is the elimination of repeated typing of the same material.

Word processors also come as stand-alone equipment without computer connections. In such cases the configuration consists of a specialized microcomputer, CRT, keyboard, printer, and an input device, usually a diskette reader. These are very popular in offices that must do lots of similar reports, letters, and proposals. The normal typing time can be cut drastically as compared to regular typewriter usage, and quality improves greatly.

AUTOMATED SYSTEMS

Automation in the accounting sense refers to the degree of sophistication practiced in the processing of financial data. The automation spectrum extends from purely mechanical on the one hand to purely electronic on the other. Automation is, of course, particularly apropos in accounting systems with high document (input) activity volumes, routine (standardized) processing, and uniform results (output). Automation may be introduced in any or all of an organization's information systems and may vary from microcomputer processing techniques to large on-line real-time systems. This section discusses the most common types of systems, hardware configurations, and applications.

Card Systems

Card systems generally use punched card input and output, although output may also include printouts. The process begins with the input punched into cards and verified. A master file is prepared for each major system function (such as payroll, personnel, or fixed assets), and input cards are processed with these masters. Although card preparation is a minor part of most computerized systems, cards play a major role when used as turnaround documents. Today most card processes are part of larger, more complicated systems.

The nature of card processing may dictate several additional preliminary operations. For example, if two decks (a master file and an input file) of cards must be merged before processing, they are passed through a *collator*. The *reproducer* punches data in one card from the data in another card. Complete or partial duplication can be selected for the new cards. Such duplication is used to prevent manual keypunching of recurring data. The *interpreter* reads cards and prints the contents on the face of the same cards.

Electronic Tape Systems

The major storage medium for these systems is magnetic tapes, with either cards or tapes as the primary input media. Output may take a variety of forms with no strict limitations. Figure 3.2 illustrates a typical tape-oriented system. Notice that cards are the input media, tapes are the storage media, and paper printouts are the output media.

For many years tape-oriented systems were the most advanced type of EDP design and, as a result, many complex tape-oriented applications still exist. Although other improved methodologies and devices are on the market, large organizations still maintain elaborate tape-oriented systems. These systems may operate independently of other systems or be a part of the total computer configuration; applications include payroll and fixed assets.

Small Computer Systems

Minicomputers and microcomputers developed as alternatives to time sharing, service bureaus, and large, expensive computer systems. Companies using time sharing or service bureaus wanted a computer for their exclusive use. Today's minicomputers are as large and complex as the mainframe computers of the mid-1960s, giving the users with medium-size systems a choice.

Minicomputers can be equipped with a variety of peripheral devices, and may themselves be peripheral to large, complex macrosystems. The selection of a configuration should depend on organizational needs and the computer applications that can fulfill those needs. Applications should be identified by priority criteria such as cost reductions, improved operating efficiency, and timely reporting.

Microcomputers are often so small and self-contained that they can fit on a desk. Such configurations generally consist of a keyboard, a printing element, internal storage, and CRT. Larger microcomputers can operate and instruct input/output devices, tape

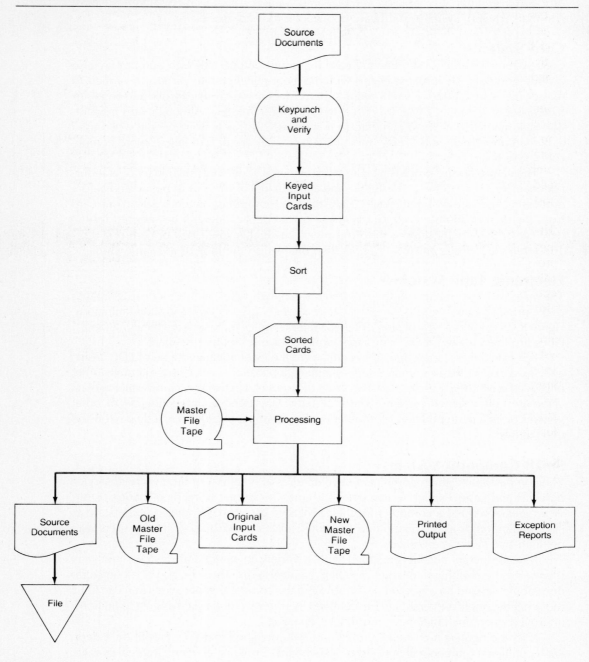

Figure 3.2

devices, and disk packs. Microcomputer configurations may consist of several computers, each specializing in a given function, to provide for decentralization and user accessibility. For example, a large plant may use microcomputers for inventory control. One handles receiving; another, work-in-process transactions; another, finished goods and shipping. And a minicomputer, or perhaps a large mainframe, may coordinate the activities of the microcomputers to provide for consolidated reporting and control. See Chapter Five for additional applications of small computers.

After the hardware is selected, the software must be implemented. Most small computers are easy targets for software salespeople who have multitudes of packages developed especially for "your" computer. Although a large number of these programs can be adapted to almost any computer, the organization must design the computer system to *meet its needs* and not design the organization to meet the demands of the computer system. Management should define its objectives and determine its software needs from these objectives. Either purchased or custom-designed software can meet most of the criteria and can be used separately or jointly.

Direct-access Systems

These types of systems possess the capability of accessing and updating computer files through remote terminals. The user can input data as events occur or in batches to maintain a current status of each stored record. The maintenance of updated master records assures users that responses to their inquiries are based on the most current information.

The configuration of a direct-access system includes a CPU, input/output terminals, and a direct-access storage device such as a disk pack. The complexities of direct-access systems are unlimited, and Figure 3.3 illustrates two different configurations. A *simplex system* or *single processor* is a configuration with only one CPU. It is the cheapest direct-access system and the least complex. The *duplex system* or *multiprocessor* uses two CPUs that work independently and can replace each other during downtime. This particular system utilizes the *shared-file* concept to minimize costs and data storage duplication.

Key-to-Disk Systems

A type of direct-access system, the *key-to-disk system,* has a minicomputer or microcomputer that is used strictly for data input/output. The small computer supports several on-line input/output devices, usually terminals. The computer is connected with one or more disk files onto which all input data are fed. As data enter the system the computer performs several edit control functions to detect errors. After the data have been verified and corrected, control totals are produced for future comparisons with other outputs of the system. When all processing, editing, and correcting steps are completed, the small computer transfers the data to a larger mainframe computer for processing with appropriate master files. Figure 3.4 illustrates a sample key-to-disk configuration.

Because of reduced human involvement, these systems have several advantages over other small computer operations. First, there is the immediate detection of input errors that permits correction before data are permanently entered into the system.

DIRECT-ACCESS COMMUNICATION SYSTEMS.

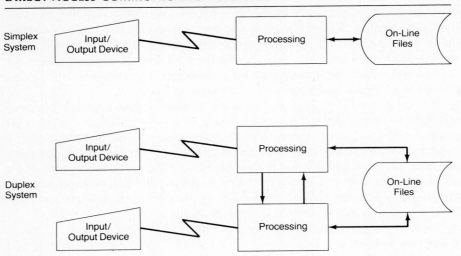

Figure 3.3

KEY-TO-DISK SYSTEMS.

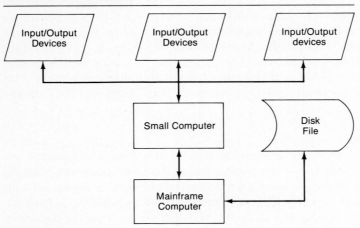

Figure 3.4

·Second, the small computer performs much of the balancing that results in control totals, a great time-saver with a high degree of accuracy. Next, such a system can assist operators in predefining data fields, controlling character acceptance to data fields, and prompting the overall process. Finally, these systems are much faster and more efficient than card input systems. However, as opposed to traditional batch systems, they are more expensive to set up, although other costs may be about the same. Another disadvantage is that the work of the small computer may in fact slow down the process unless the mainframe computer is near capacity. Some configurations allow the key-to-disk system to bypass the small computer if the mainframe computer has unused capacity for a given period with automatic changeover if the workload increases.

PROCESSING PROCEDURES

Several technical characteristics of electronic systems with which accountants should be familiar are now examined, without emphasizing the mechanics of their operation. Awareness of these characteristics should assist users in understanding the capabilities of their system; but, more importantly, it should enable them to take maximum advantage of the capabilities.

Multiprogramming

Multiprogramming is a software technique that allows several programs to be processed concurrently. The computer is so fast that what appears to be simultaneous processing actually involves a rapid switching between programs. Although several operating programs may be stored in primary memory, only one is processed at a time. Multiprogramming generally increases the efficiency of program processing by utilizing every *picosecond* (trillionth of a second) possible. Multiple program tasks are executed in the same time span by interweaving their execution and overlapping their input/output activities. These tasks share the system components and alternate between execution, computation, data transfer, and input/output activities, thereby providing for increased system efficiencies. This procedure maximizes the tremendous speed of electronic processors in systems with many remote terminals constantly demanding processing time. The only overhead time is the switching from one program to another.

This concept is often integrated with a computer system's *overlap* capability, allowing the computer configuration to perform more than one input/output activity and CPU operation simultaneously. Third-generation and later computers generally have this capability. This process enables the system to increase greatly its *throughput*—the amount of work performed by a system in a period of time.

Often in multiprogramming it is necessary for two or more programs to refer to a given data set at the same time. *Multithreading* is a capability that allows simultaneous accessing to take place so that the programs do not have to wait on each other. When many identical transactions enter a system concurrently, *reentrance* allows several of them to be processed by a single application program at the same time. This is usually necessary when multiprogramming is employed to keep the system operating efficiently.

Multiprocessing

When a system has two or more CPUs, more than one program can be processed at the same time. With such an arrangement, the CPUs generally share a central memory and have interfacing capabilities. Unlike multiprogramming, multiprocessing is related to hardware configuration and is actually a simultaneous process. Multiprocessing requires multiprogramming to handle the interfacing capabilities. When a system is capable of multiprocessing, CPU backup is available—a major advantage of such systems.

Multiplexing

Multiplexing is often used in a system with remote terminals. If a CPU is required to handle all the communication activities of a system, its actual processing capabilities are going to be limited. To free the CPU from many of the communicating tasks, multiplexors may be installed between the CPU and the terminals to act as message switching and connecting centers. As shown in Figure 3.5 each multiplexor handles input and output to several terminals.

Program Swapping

The movement of programs between primary and secondary storage is known as *programming swapping*. This capability is necessary when all programs currently being processed cannot be held in primary storage. As a given segment is needed for a program, it is retrieved into primary storage, used, and then returned to secondary storage. This is continued until the program is finished or until primary storage has enough space to hold the entire program. This is an application of the virtual storage access method discussed in Chapter Four.

Fault Tolerance

Many hardware vendors are now manufacturing computers that can continue operating even when a major function fails. This ability is labeled *fault tolerance.* It can be built into each computer chip by use of redundant circuity. Fault tolerance can also be built into a system through intricate software that checks its performance constantly. When one element fails, processing is immediately shifted to an alternative source of achieving the same activity.

The traditional method of fault tolerance, parallel processing on two or more CPUs, is so expensive that it is seldom used. Although the newer approaches are not cheap, the cost/benefit relationship is much more acceptable for most applications. Current demands for such systems include banking, airline and hotel reservation systems, and cable television networks.

Communication Processing

As systems grow, multiplexors become inadequate to handle the large volumes of communication between the CPU and the terminals. To help with the communication function and also to relieve the CPU of many input/output tasks, many systems have either large computers or minicomputers to interface between the multiplexor and the CPU. A communication processor serves as a store-and-forward device that feeds the CPU only when a complete message is sent; that is, the CPU does not have to store fragments of a message until the terminal user completes a transmission. This saves the CPU both time and storage space that can otherwise be devoted to actual processing. Figure 3.4 also includes a communication processor application.

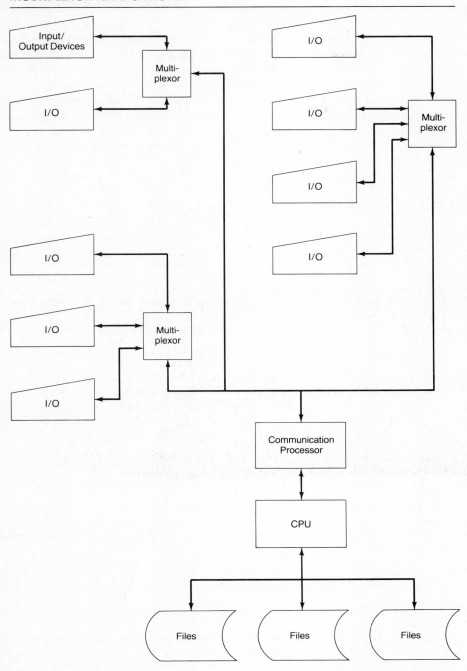

Figure 3.5

SUMMARY

This chapter has covered those components of computers and computer systems that are considered to be important in the study of accounting information systems. With an understanding of the basic concepts presented in this chapter, the reader may proceed to Chapter Four, which is a discussion of various processing applications. These chapters must be understood before proceeding with the study of accounting information systems since they lay the basic groundwork for understanding the computer and information systems as well as their relationships to accounting information systems. Without the tools and techniques of computers and the basic applications available, the user's ability to understand accounting information systems is severely limited. Because many of the information systems and accounting information system concepts are identical, often only the application distinguishes the two systems.

SELECTED REFERENCES

Bergeron, Lionel L. "The Word Processing Survey," *Journal of Systems Management* (March 1975): 20–24.

Berliner, Harold, and Marvin Golland. "Microcomputers for the Uninhibited," *Management Focus* (May/June 1980): 3–7.

Bohl, Marilyn. *Information Processing,* 3rd ed. Chicago: Science Research Associates, 1980.

Bromberg, Howard. "The Consequences of Minicomputers," *Datamation* (November 15, 1978): 98–103.

"Computers That Don't Fail," *Business Week* (May 21, 1984): 52–53.

Datapro Research Corporation. "All About Data Collection Equipment," in *Datapro 70: The EDP Buyer's Bible.* Delran, N.J.: Datapro Research Corp., 1980.

Datapro Research Corporation. "All About Small Business Computers," in *Datapro 70: The EDP Buyer's Bible.* Delran, N.J.: Datapro Research Corp., 1980.

Goldberg, Victor, and Russell Gowland. "How to Select and Install a Minicomputer," *World* (Winter 1980): 7–11.

Heintz, Carl. "Seeking Solutions with Spreadsheets," *Interface Age* (September 1983): 52–54.

Honickman, Howard W. "Minicomputers—A Big Risk?" *CAmagazine* (August 1979): 42–52.

Juliessen, J. Egil. "Where Bubble Memory Will Find a Niche," *Mini–Micro Systems* (July 1979): 48–61.

Kelley, Neil D. "Micrographics: A Role in the Paperless Office," *Infosystems* (February 1980): 52–56.

Konkel, Gilbert J. "Word Processing and the Office of the Future," *The Arthur Young Quarterly* (Winter 1982): 2–9.

Krippaehne, Thomas M. "The Right Way to Select a Microcomputer," *Today's Executive* (Spring/Summer 1982): 12–19.

Lines, M. Vardell, and Boeing Computer Services Company. *Minicomputer Systems.* Cambridge, Mass.: Winthrop, 1980.

Masters, Paul. "Talk Is Getting Cheaper," *Datamation* (August 1981): 71–74.

Pittis, Alan R. "The Future of Large Computer Systems," *CAmagazine* (March 1979): 70–74.

Poppel, Harvey L. "Who Needs the Office of the Future?" *Harvard Business Review* (November/December 1982): 146–155.

Reifer, Donald J., and Stephen Trattner. "A Glossary of Software Tools and Techniques," *Computer* (July 1977): 52–60.

Ross, Edward A., and Lewis I. Solomon. "Technology Trends in Desktop Computers," *Mini-Micro Systems* (December 1978): 46–57.

Schwartz, Donald A. "Microcomputers Take Aim on Small Business Clients," *The Journal of Accountancy* (December 1979): 57–62.

Solomon, Leslie. "A New Approach to Data Storage: Bubble Memories," *Popular Electronics* (February 1979): 74–76.

Worthy, Ford S. "Here Come the Go-Anywhere Computers," *Fortune* (October 17, 1983): 9–11.

Wynne, Robert, and Alan Frotman. "Microcomputers: Helping Make Practice Perfect," *The Journal of Accountancy* (December 1981): 34–39.

QUESTIONS

1. Explain or define the following terms:

   Central processing unit   Primary storage
   Configuration   On-line elements
   Off-line elements   Direct access
   Sequential access   Cathode-ray tube
   Intelligent terminals   Microfiche
   Hardware   Software
   Machine independence   File maintenance
   Utility routines   Duplex system
   Microcomputer   Simplex system
   Multiprocessing   Multiplexing
   Multiprogramming   Picosecond

2. Relate the development of the computer changes to changes in accounting information systems.
3. List the major elements of a computer and define the functions of each. Be sure to separate the functions within the CPU.
4. Discuss the characteristics a system should have if the users need frequent direct access for both input and retrieval.
5. What are the primary differences between a basic card system and a basic tape system? Include both hardware and software differences.
6. Discuss the main advantages of CRTs over teleprinters.
7. How do the applications of magnetic tape systems and magnetic disk systems differ?
8. Explain the differences between software and hardware.
9. What would be some of the general reasons for changing from a
   a. Card system to a magnetic tape system
   b. Magnetic tape system to a direct access system
   c. Magnetic tape system to a combination magnetic tape/disk system
10. What is a microcomputer? In what types of situations is it normally used?
11. Contrast the relationships between a direct-access system and the use of magnetic tapes, magnetic disks, and CRTs. Which components must be used with a direct-access system?
12. Differentiate between file maintenance and report generation.

PROBLEMS

13. Body of Knowledge

To operate an automobile properly the user must know something about driving techniques, maintenance, and operating characteristics of the particular model. As major users of computerized systems, how much and what specifics should accountants know about the computer? Include in your discussion the areas of hardware and software.

14. Computerized Systems Installation

Beta Supply Company is an automotive parts dealer with eight locations throughout the northwestern United States. The company sells to dealers and the general public. Purchasing for all warehouses is handled through the home office. Although one location may be out of stock with certain items, the items are generally available in one of the other locations. Because of favorable quantity discounts, Beta always buys in large quantities. As a result of local out-of-stock situations, the purchasing department often buys enough for all locations when only one actually needs more of an individual item. Management is very concerned with the growing levels of inventory while sales are fairly constant. Beta has a very large computer system at the home office that has available time and flexible capabilities. Discuss how the computer system could be changed to help meet the needs of proper purchasing for the company. Be sure to list any equipment changes required as the result of your recommendations.

15. Systems Analysis

Funderburk Sales Company has sales branches located throughout North America. Each branch has between 10 and 30 employees. All merchandise is shipped from the home office upon confirmation from the sales branches. Because each branch is prohibited from having any bank accounts, all payrolls are processed at the home office and the checks are mailed to the branches for distribution. Recently, the company has experienced delays with check delivery, and you have been assigned to make recommendations as to how the computer system might be utilized to permit each branch to have a remote terminal where the payroll checks could be printed on location. Is this a realistic possibility? What better solution might you suggest to improve timely check delivery?

16. Cost/Benefit Analysis

Your client, IBIGM, Inc., wants to change from a card system to a more computerized operation. Before doing this, however, the company wants you to discuss the pros and cons involved in giving up a very good card system to go with an untested but more flexible magnetic tape-dominated system. The card system is currently operating at 99 percent capacity, and breakdowns are very costly in time delays. The president is concerned with personnel additions, training, equipment costs, and completeness of operations. Discuss how you would satisfy the president's concerns, elaborating on the advantages of a magnetic tape-dominated system. Evaluate on a cost and benefit basis.

17. Microcomputer Analysis

After studying the needs of your company in the area of accounting information systems, you have concluded that a typical microcomputer system is what should be acquired. List the variables and characteristics that might be predominant in a situation that needs a microcomputer system. These may be categorized under headings such as user needs, size, timeliness, and so forth.

18. Information System Capabilities

In a computerized information system that has the latest in technology, tell how each of the following activities would be performed. Answers may be humans, computer processing, or a combination of both.

a. Hiring new employees
b. Processing payroll of employees
c. Determining discounts to be taken on customers' payments
d. Getting variances from a production department cost report
e. Evaluating causes of variances on a cost report
f. Evaluating an accountant's performance
g. Evaluating the performance of a line employee who puts handles on bicycles.

19. Systems Selection

Describe the type of computer system, time-sharing service, or computer service bureau the following companies would find most beneficial. Be sure to include all necessary hardware for the primary operations.

a. Red Company is a wholesale grocer. The company handles 14,000 different items and has 200 retail store customers. It employs 15 drivers, 20 warehouse workers, 4 supervisors, and 6 business office employees. In addition, 4 salespeople handle all of the accounts. Its operation consists of ordering, storing, and delivering grocery items.

b. White Company is a consulting firm. It specializes in geological surveys. The average job lasts 2 years and usually requires about 12 people. The average contract is $450,000. Between 40 and 50 jobs are under contract at all times.

c. Blue Company is a local lending institution. It has offices in three cities and specializes in signature, auto, and home-improvement loans. The average loan is for $5,000 for a 3-year term. Each office has its own collection department which keeps track of loans and their status. The home office does all other accounting functions. A customer's credit is approved at the local office, with larger loan requests sent to the home office. Each of the three offices has about 4,000 contracts.

20. Computer Applications

Brass Candle Company makes brass candleholders in 205 varieties. Most of its customers are retail gift shops although it has several wholesale distributors. Last year sales totaled $3.5 million and resulted in a net income of $400,000. Its income/sales ratio fluctuates widely because of market changes in its raw materials. Purchasing is the most critical aspect of the business. Other than raw materials the operating costs are minor.

Besides keeping up with and improving purchasing, the president would also like to improve the tracking of customer payments. It appears that many of its 3,500 customers are very slow payers and the company often sells to customers who are already delinquent in their accounts.

The company expects to maintain its current level of operation for the next few years if it can keep its cash flow in control. With a sound financial condition, plant expansion is possible in about 4 years.

Required:
    a. Explain the basic information needs of the company.
    b. What specific computer applications can help improve the information system?
    c. What computer hardware does your suggested solution require?

CHAPTER FOUR

Data Processing

There are many activities that data must pass through in a data processing system of an organization. In the processing of accounting data especially, consideration must be given to the recording, classifying, sorting, storing, retrieving, summarizing, analyzing, and communicating activities. Electronic data processing has greatly influenced these activities not only by changing how they are performed, but also by providing alternatives as to how they may be performed.

The basic ways data processing activities may be performed and a detailed discussion about the newest developments in data processing applications are presented in this chapter. Because electronic funds transfers affect every aspect of business and society and because considerable attention is being focused on them by business (especially financial institutions), a portion of this chapter is used to explain the concepts and implications of electronic funds transfer systems.

PROCESSING APPLICATIONS

The methods of processing data have undergone several changes in recent years. Although *batch* processing is most common, it has given way to *on-line* processing. Most organizations select various combinations of these methods if their CPU and peripheral equipment configurations permit. Real-time processing is perhaps the most advanced type of system, requiring a computer with on-line capabilities. Distributed processing, a type of real-time processing, has increased in popularity recently because the cost of multiple computers has been declining. Combination systems (hybrid) are also discussed in relation to the need for flexible computer applications.

Batch Processing

The processing of data that has been grouped, or batched, by some functional characteristic is called *batch processing.* Batch processing is periodic, either selected or sporadic. Payroll is generally selected batch processing at predetermined intervals. On the other hand, inventory updating from the receiving department may be sporadic; that is, data are batched depending on the amount and frequency of goods received. Inventory processing may be performed hourly, daily, weekly, or on demand.

Batched input is usually in the form of punched cards, marked-sensed documents, magnetic diskettes, or magnetic tape. Even though data may be collected on magnetic tape or other media over a period of time, processing is not performed until all the data for the batch are completed. Of the systems noted in this chapter, batch processing can be performed on all of them and is the only practical method available for card and magnetic tape input systems.

Batch processing is either sequential or random. The basic difference during processing is that sequential applications must be sorted, whereas random ones can be processed without preliminary rearrangement. Random batch processing can occur only if the configuration has direct access capabilities, such as with magnetic disks.

A processing concept called *remote batch processing* is used where an organization has several activity locations processing identical types of transactions. The information is electronically transmitted to the central computer. For example, branch sales offices accumulate sales representatives' commission data, batch it, and send it to the home office to be processed once a month. The communication media are usually remote terminals.

Advantages　The batch processing concept with computers is similar to conventional manual accounting systems, in which data are gathered and processed in groups. As such, it offers the following advantages:

1. It is very efficient for large volumes of like transactions where most items in a master file are used during each processing run.
2. Basic accounting audit trail is maintained.
3. Such systems generally cost less than other types of systems.
4. The overall system is not so complicated as on-line systems and is easier to understand.
5. It is generally easier to control than other types of computerized systems; control total concepts are better defined because they have definite cutoffs.
6. The handling of batched data by specialized input processing personnel is more efficient than letting multiple users input data as it is received, a concept usually found in on-line processing.

Disadvantages　Because batching is performed periodically, certain disadvantages must be considered:

1. Processing takes longer for large master files than with most other systems because these files are often in sequential order. This is especially true if the activity is small and every file must still be read.
2. Response time is slow when compared to other systems.
3. Processing is inefficient for files that have lots of additions and deletions. Such activity is very time-consuming during file maintenance.
4. Some data duplication is likely because each batch process often uses its own separate master file.
5. Processing functions between applications are usually not integrated because of timing differences and various master file configurations.
6. Information in files may not be current because of time lags.
7. It normally requires that both transaction and master files be sorted in the same sequential order.

On-line Processing

On-line processing requires no preliminary data preparation, batching, or sorting. An on-line system can accept data directly from the users with various types of terminals: teleprinters, CRTs, or audio terminals. This procedure offers an advantage over batch systems because data can be entered into the system directly from the originator and output is sent directly to the user without passing through other processes or people. Since fewer people handle the data, an on-line system saves time, minimizes human errors, increases security, and eliminates duplication.

Master files and programs are directly accessed by the CPU in on-line systems. Therefore, a data set may be accessible by different application programs, which minimizes file duplication but necessitates strong control features. These controls are discussed in a later chapter. Users who are authorized to access the system strictly for inquiry purposes benefit greatly from the time saved by having the files on-line with the CPU. Again, controls must be implemented to prevent access to unauthorized files.

Before an organization decides it needs an on-line system (as opposed to a batch system), it should carefully consider the additional start-up and equipment costs. Overall, an on-line system requires more hardware to handle the same amount of processing. Another weakness is the increased costs of the additional controls previously mentioned. Partial on-line systems are often found with traditional batch processing systems to meet the complex needs of large organizations.

Real-time Processing

A real-time application provides users with responses quick enough to control the activity being monitored. Some inquiries need immediate responses (e.g., air traffic controllers in large airports); others may require only occasional responses (e.g., raw materials inventory clerks who assign materials for assembly line use). A system can be on-line without being real-time. The reverse is not possible because real-time systems must be designed with hardware configurations that have direct-access capabilities.

On-line real-time systems have several distinguishing characteristics. All files are maintained in an on-line mode and are directly accessible at all times. All input is processed and related files updated immediately upon entry. Files may be accessed at the main console terminal as well as at all the remote terminals. Access to any given file is approved by the control program only when the correct user codes are recognized. Limited access is thereby provided to authorized users only. Finally, these systems frequently provide automatic processing, which occurs when an input entry results in offsetting follow-up actions. For example, when a salesperson places an order through a remote terminal, the system checks inventory files to verify availability. Next, it checks the customer's credit for approval and notifies a waiting salesperson of availability and acceptance. The system then notifies shipping, prepares the shipping and billing documents, updates the accounts receivable records, and records the transactions in the sales journal. These are often referred to as *dispatching systems.*

Advantages   The advantages of real-time processing vary to some degree on the complexity and size of the system and on the applications for a given system. The basic advantages are:

1. The conversion of raw data onto cards or magnetic tape is eliminated at the input stage by entering the data directly into the system through terminals.
2. Edit processing for data errors is done upon entry; inaccurate data are rejected.
3. Timely information is provided for decision making.
4. All files are kept up-to-date.
5. Integration of various subsystems is increased within the organization.
6. Human intervention is minimized.
7. It is ideally suited for master files that are large but have little activity.

Disadvantages Although the advantages are very attractive for many applications, several disadvantages exist. The most noted are:

1. The hardware systems are very expensive.
2. Effective systems integration requires a data base management system, an expensive software package.
3. Extensive controls are needed to guard against unauthorized access because the system is open through the use of terminals and wiretapping.
4. They are more difficult to audit because of technical complexities.

Distributed Processing

The concept of locating the computer system components throughout the organization is known as distributed data processing. This allows inputs to the system to take place where they originate and at the appropriate organizational level. The data can be processed and used locally with key items and summary data forwarded to higher organizational levels. Much of the processing can be assigned to numerous small CPUs, either minicomputers or microcomputers.

The distribution of information processing is accomplished by placing a CPU at various organizational levels. If possible, everyone at a given level should have the same access. Popular locations are at division levels, plants, regional offices, and major responsibility centers (e.g., profit, cost, or investment). Each system element may establish its own configuration, develop its own software, and determine its own data base. The individual systems may contain batch and real-time processing and use various data base formats. The constraining factors are that each distributed system must be able to interface with the corporate system and provide the data that the higher level demands.

Distributed processing systems can have many patterns, of which the three most common are ring, star, and hierarchical. Development of the configuration depends on the primary factors of systems size, complexity, organizational diversity, and demands of top management. Any given configuration might have several types of patterns, with one predominant. Figure 4.1 illustrates a star pattern. A ring pattern has each small system interfacing with other like systems to form a ring or circle. The hierarchical pattern has subordinate/superior relationships and looks like a pictorial of an organization chart.

Another concept of distributed processing known as *local area network* (LAN) is growing in popularity as communication technology expands to meet everyone's needs. LAN is characterized by having work stations (e.g., microcomputers, terminals, word processors, point-of-sale devices, etc.) within everyone's reach. Such systems allow the

DISTRIBUTED DATA PROCESSING SYSTEMS-STAR PATTERN.

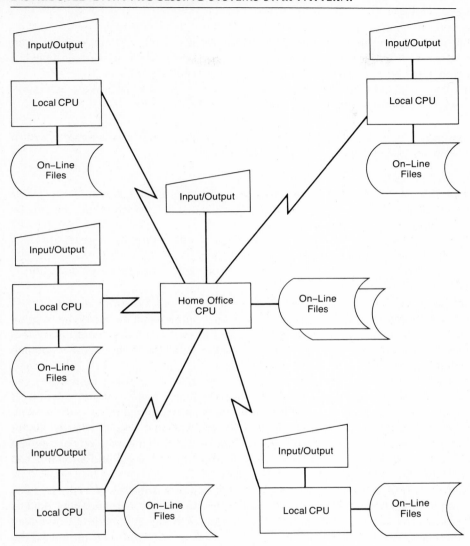

Figure 4.1

individual employee to input, retrieve, and communicate without even leaving the work station. A star pattern might have several LANs surrounding each of its points.

Advantages The rapid growth of distributed processing attests to many advantages. The primary advantages are:

1. It has increased flexibility over other systems because each unit can specialize in its own area of need.
2. It is very responsive to user needs.
3. It has increased reliability over other systems because each unit can operate even if others are down and operating units can help process data from down units.
4. It has better control of costs because units are smaller.
5. It has the ability to share data files through corporate files, thus improving communications between operating units.

Disadvantages Because it is a relatively complex area, several disadvantages exist of which users must be aware. These disadvantages are:

1. It has high initial costs.
2. It has difficulties with auditing because each system is often different.
3. It has reduced specialization with smaller computer staffs, thereby reducing operating and programming efficiencies.
4. It has problems of interfacing local networks with the corporate system.
5. It has the potential for duplication of data.
6. It is often difficult to maintain adequate controls over every phase of operation.

Hybrid Systems

There are several elements in any data processing environment that dictate diversification in techniques and applications. The most important of these are costs, controls, system objectives, and available technology. In some instances these elements work with each other; in others they work against each other.

A totally integrated real-time system is very expensive, and few companies can afford such computerization. As a result, each of the major organizational functions is designed to be as efficient as funds allow while meeting the demands of management. Most organizations tend to develop hardware configurations and systems methodologies that are within their budgets yet flexible enough to meet the changing needs of the next few years. Many systems are left open-ended so that future changes and additions can be made with minimum problems.

Controls also place restrictions on the configuration and design of systems. Even though funds or technology may be available, placing secret or confidential data in on-line modes may not be worth the risk of exposure. Although it would be convenient for the few authorized users to have access to the information on their terminals, the availability to unauthorized users would place a burden on the control system. For example, authorized employees might try to access more information than they are allowed to use and sell the findings to competition. The best way to prevent such access is not to have the information on-line. Whenever management thinks a foolproof system has been developed, it should remember that [*humans developed the system and therefore humans can overcome any controls of the system!*]

Another influence on the system is user needs. Users want the system to meet their every need, regardless of costs, control problems, or available technology. As discussed in a later chapter on system design, designers must be very careful to separate user wants from user needs.

Moreover, available technology influences the configuration. The latest in technology is generally very expensive in comparison to what the same technology will cost in a few years. If possible, organizations generally try to let new technology be tested and proved by someone else before they acquire it.

Although the payroll-personnel system shown in Figure 4.2 is only part of a large system, it illustrates how several hardware design concepts can be integrated into a single organizational function. For payroll processing, punched cards are used as input and magnetic tapes are used to store year-to-date information, both financial and tax. After an edit check of the input data for errors, the files are updated for each payroll run.

PAYROLL-PERSONNEL: A HYBRID SYSTEM.

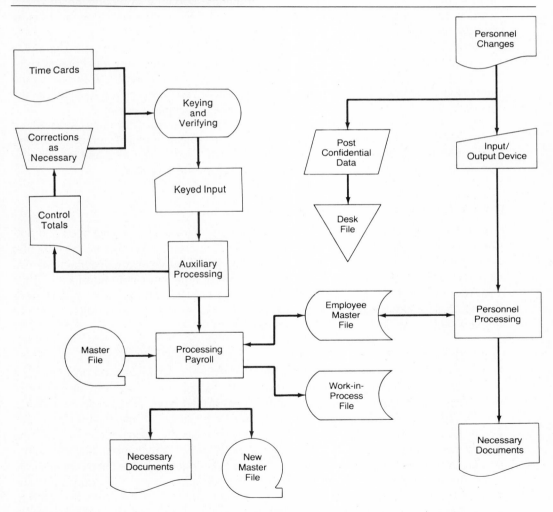

Figure 4.2

During each run the payroll program has direct access to the on-line personnel file to receive information such as changes in the number of taxable dependents for an employee, terminations, and leave-without-pay situations. The payroll process also has access to the work-in-process file, which is on-line. This file is updated for direct labor charges and overhead charges in the case of indirect labor. The necessary documents and files are also furnished. The chapter on payroll provides details for proper input, processing, and output for various types of payroll systems.

The personnel part of the system receives changes from management, employees, and other sources. All except the confidential data are entered through real-time terminals to update the on-line personnel records. The confidential data are manually recorded by employees in file folders. The on-line files are used by payroll, as previously mentioned, and by personnel for making inquiries, updating company employment statistics, meeting governmental requirements, checking credit references, or meeting other demands.

Our example is not a simple payroll-personnel system, nor is it the most complex system available. The example is from an actual organization, so it is also practical for at least one company's needs. It uses cards, magnetic tapes, magnetic disk packs, and manual files. The system employs batch processing concepts (payroll processing), on-line concepts (work-in-process file updating), real-time concepts (personnel inquiry), and manual concepts (confidential data file). Various combinations are normally incorporated into a workable hybrid system. Such systems are very typical, practical, and cost efficient. They meet the needs of the users, provide adequate control features, and employ the technology justified by the informational needs of the organization.

DATA FILES

Every computer system must have a storage mechanism for data that have been computerized. The selection of the storage method is very important in organizing the data files since it influences how the data can be used for updating, retrieval, and file maintenance. After contrasting physical and logical files, we discuss the most common forms of file organization and highlight their characteristics and uses. Currently, most organizations use hybrid data files, combinations of either sequential or direct-addressing, random or indexed-sequential, or virtual storage methods.

Logical Versus Physical Files

A *logical file* refers to the collection of records needed for an application program such as accounts payable. A *physical file* refers to the storage of records on some type of media (e.g., tapes, disks, drums). Physical records do not have to coincide with logical records. Three common situations illustrate this point. First, the physical records may require two disk files (a large inventory system), whereas the logical file is still just one file, the inventory data. Second, the physical file may include much more than is required for a given logical file. The logical file for processing accounts payable checks needs only information such as the vendor's name, address, amount due, and discount rate. The physical file for accounts payable includes the preceding facts plus information such as vendor history, product reliability, and orders on request. Third, a logical file may require information in a different format from that of the physical file. A payroll master may be kept by employee number, but for ease of processing, it may be sorted into groups by departments which closely coincide with data input, pay scales, and output.

Sequential Files

Sequential files are organized in descending or ascending record-key sequence. *Record-key* is the data item in each record that distinguishes one record from another in a file. It is used when retrieval requires that a specific item be accessed. The record-keys for each file are unique, and for efficiency they usually take the form of item identification. Examples are using an employee's social security number as the record-key in the payroll file and a part number as the record-key in a raw materials inventory file.

The most common form of sequential file storage is magnetic tape. Even though designed primarily for other storage methods, magnetic disks and drums are also used for sequential storage of data. Because disks and drums provide flexibility in the type of storage they can handle, they are becoming more popular for sequential storage needs.

Magnetic tape has maintained its appeal in accounting systems because many of the files used in accounting are in sequential order: Customer accounts are in order by account number, inventory files are in order by stock number, and the fixed asset file is often in order by the location number of each item. Another justification for using sequential files for accounting applications is the need to maintain certain activities in chronological order. This applies to keeping sales records by invoice number, purchasing activities by purchase order number, and accounts payable by due date.

Other advantages that apply to sequential files are only indirectly related to accounting. These types of files make efficient use of the storage space since the utilization is continuous, a characteristic not usually found in direct-access files. Sequential files are also efficient when a large number of records are necessary for a single activity such as raw materials inventory. In that type of application the many items that have to be changed during each updating run cause sequential access to be just as efficient as direct access. For files that have frequent printouts of all or most of the records, a sequential method is advantageous because all of the records are stored in the order that they would be printed. This applies to files such as accounts payable, accounts receivable, and payroll check records.

There are several reasons why sequential methods are not normally used with real-time applications. For sequential master files, each updating transaction requires the file to be read one record at a time until the proper record is found. Therefore, an activity with a large master file requires a lot of valuable time. Sequential master files inhibit adding and deleting records within the file.

Direct-access Files

Magnetic disks and magnetic drums are the most common types of direct-access files. The characteristic of these files that is most advantageous is the ability to record each item at an individual address and retrieve it directly from that address. This is ideal for files that require frequent inquiry, updating, and multiple access. Another major advantage is the ability to update the files either in batches or as individual transactions occur.

Although there are several variations, most direct-access systems are organized by using either direct addressing or the hashing approach. The *direct/addressing* approach allows records to be stored by key-controlled locations and the computer creates an index of record-keys and related locations (addresses). This index is maintained in internal storage of the CPU for use at all times.

The *hashing* approach converts the record-key directly to a physical address on the file. This conversion enables the computer to skip the search through the dictionary before accessing a particular record on the file. However, since the system does not use a dictionary, the placement of the data is random and the storage space is usually not filled.

Indexed-Sequential Files

As noted previously, it is important for some files to be kept sequentially. However, because record searches often prove very time-consuming with large sequential files, the indexed-sequential addressing method (ISAM) was developed. By indexing every nth file, one can greatly reduce the search time for a single record. Before searching for a record, the program searches the index for the indexed record closest to the record needed. This method also allows sequential processing.

Assume that the accounts payable master file is in alphabetical order with 20 files per index. For example, if the file for Polk Company is needed, the computer reads the index until it finds a gap where Polk Company would fall. Assume that the computer determines that Polk Company is between addresses 2206 and 2207 as shown in Figure 4.3. Therefore, Polk Company is contained in the sublist headed by 2206. The sublist is then searched sequentially until the desired record is found. In this example the record is shown as being at address 2206, record-key 03. If the sublists are very large, each one of them can also be indexed. In addition to the index area and the prime storage area, an indexed-sequential file also contains an overflow area. This area contains any data of a record that cannot be stored in its prime area.

Virtual Storage Files

Although the virtual storage concept can be used with other systems, in recent years it has developed as a separate method of file access. The *virtual storage access method* (VSAM) stores data in large, addressed, fixed-length blocks. Record access is similar to ISAM except that the blocks in use are moved into and out of primary storage as necessary. The addressing approach is determined by the type of addressing used in the primary storage of the CPU.

VSAM eliminates the need for complex addressing schemas for each record within a file because each record within a block is addressed as if the entire file was in primary storage. This greatly increases the potential for file design because virtual storage expands the file capacity to both primary and secondary storage availability, not just primary storage as with other methods.

DATA BASE SYSTEMS

Traditionally, a data element or set of data belonged to the department or function that created it. Inventory data belonged to inventory control, personnel data belonged to the personnel department, and the same was true of all data files. However, as the utilization

INDEXED-SEQUENTIAL FILE STRUCTURE.

Index Area

Address		Record Keys
. . . .		. . . .
2205		PEA–PIM
2206		PIN–PYZ
2207		QUA–RED
2208		REE–RUM
2209		RUN–SAT
. . . .		. . . .

Prime Storage Area

Address		Accounts Payable File Record				
2205		Record Key 01	Record Key 02	Record Key 03	. . . . . .	Record Key 20
2206		Record Key 01	Record Key 02	Record Key 03*	. . . . . .	Record Key 20
2207		Record Key 01	Record Key 02	Record Key 03	. . . . . .	Record Key 20
2208		Record Key 01	Record Key 02	Record Key 03	. . . . .	Record Key 20
2209		Record Key 01	Record Key 02	Record Key 03	. . . . . .	Record Key 20

*Desired record

Figure 4.3

of the computer became more sophisticated in the 1970s, a new concept emerged that permitted data to be used by more than one department or operating function. The *integrated data base* concept is used today in most large, and in many small, computer operations. The philosophy underlying the integrated concept recognizes data as an organizational resource to be used by the entire organization, not just the creating department or function. In most practical situations the concept assigns applications to data elements and data sets instead of assigning elements and sets to applications.

Under the *total management information systems* concept, the organization should have only one fully integrated data base. In most organizations, this totality concept is not feasible for several reasons. First, it is very expensive to design and build a data base that includes everything that everybody in the organization needs, or thinks is needed. Second, some areas require high levels of security and should be maintained in separate files that can have special controls placed around them. Third, a single data base tends to be very complex and difficult to design—and even more difficult for the users to understand and control.

After the proper combinations of data bases have been established for an organization, management must work with the users to determine accessibility, control, availability, and the amount and kinds of data to be included in the data bases. The specific areas that must be defined are the exact content of each file, file organization, availability, integrity, and security.

Contents

Because the data base is intended to serve various users, the contents of each file must be determined by all areas that will be using the file. Management of the organization must control the content decisions of each file to ensure proper integration and coordination of all potential users and suppliers of the data. With a large diversity of data sources in most organizations, the types and forms of data must be controlled by a centralized management team or group so that no one area or department will dominate the data base.

Specific problem areas related to the contents are method of storage, timing of collection and storage, timing of availability, amount and type of data to be collected, measurement of data (units, dollars, etc.), and order and sequence of storage within each record. Different sources and uses dictate various storage characteristics for the data, and a coordinated effort must be made to meet the basic needs of those who have priority over each given set of data files. The system can help control this by use of a data dictionary. As a minimum the data dictionary should provide the following for each data set: name, source or creation, storage format (numeric, alpha, etc.), character size, file location, and primary and authorized users. In addition to these characteristics, the uses of the data should be described, giving details concerning output format, frequency of output, and accessibility methods.

Data Structure Concepts

Data structure relates to the arrangement of data items in a data base and the type of interface needed between the physical and logical organizations. To accomplish these adjustments, one must incorporate several concepts into the control program of the data base. The inverted file concept is used to allow multiple attribute inquiries. And the file connection concepts of pointers and chains are employed in delineating data relationships.

Inverted Files   Often the data in a file can have many uses other than its main purpose. The *primary keys* in a file are organized to be used with a file's principal aim. However, several *secondary keys* may be implemented so that the file can be used for alternative purposes. Once a secondary purpose is defined, a file attribute related to that purpose is used to invert the file, thereby creating an index of the file for that attribute (secondary key).

This concept can be illustrated by using the accounts payable file for Figure 4.4. The noninverted file is by primary key, vendor numbers, which is also the address of each record in the file. The other attributes listed (not all by any means) in the noninverted file of Figure 4.4 can be used as secondary keys. The inverted file serves as an index of each attribute selected. It provides the address of each record with a given attribute. From Figure 4.5, we notice that New York vendors can be found at addresses 102 and 105, whereas Atlanta vendors can be found at addresses 101 and 103. If we wanted a listing of all raw material vendors, the program would go to the vendor file and addresses 101, 102, 103, 106, and 108. Such systems can also be programmed to select multiple

ILLUSTRATION OF CHAINS AND POINTERS.

Primary Keys	Secondary Keys					
Address Vendor Number	Vendor Name	Location	Type Items	Balance	Pointers A	B
101	TSI Co.	Atlanta	Raw Materials	14,500		
102	Coast	New York	Raw Materials	76,300	103	103
103	Villa	Atlanta	Raw Materials	26,800	104	106
104	Pickens	Dallas	Office Supplies	23,500	106	
105	Sun Co.	New York	Office Furniture	18,800		
106	ABC Co.	Dallas	Raw Materials	56,900	107	**
107	Tom Ltd.	Toronto	Plant Supplies	21,400	*	
108	CCC Co.	Dallas	Raw Materials	12,000		

- - - Single associations
— — Multiple associations
@ Starting point for both associations
* End point for single associations
** End point for multiple associations

Figure 4.4

attributes. If a user wanted to know the raw material vendors in Dallas, the program would match the two secondary attributes and select the common addresses. Dallas vendors of raw materials would be found at addresses 106 and 108.

Information retrieval is considered by many to be the most important area of integrated data base systems. Although the primary advantage of being able to build new files without requiring new input is important, the availability of having the inverted files as backup is also a significant advantage. The requirement of substantial storage space and the need to update the inverted files continually are the primary disadvantages of the application. A later section on relational structures expands this topic further.

ALTERNATIVE FILES.

Single Associations

Attribute Location	Address	Attribute Type Items	Address
Atlanta	101, 103	Plant supplies	101, 107
New York	102, 105	Raw materials	102, 103
Dallas	104, 106, 108		106, 108
Toronto	107	Office suppliers	104
		Office furniture	105

Multiple Associations

Attributes Location & Item	Address	Attributes Item & Balance	Address
New York, raw materials	102	> or < $20,000	
New York, office furniture	105	Plant supplies <	107
Atlanta, raw material	101, 103	Plant supplies >	101
Dallas, raw materials	106, 108	Raw materials >	102, 103
Dallas, office supplies	104		106, 108
Toronto, raw materials	107	Office furniture <	105
		Office supplies <	104

Figure 4.5

Pointers   A *pointer* is any element of a record that allows the accessing mechanism to locate a specific item in another record. They may be placed in an index or within the data fields. If internally placed, they are referred to as embedded pointers. Pointers facilitate the use of stored data to form new list and inverted files. They are also used to store new data in the overflow areas. The pointers link the new data with the intended or normal location. In most structures, each record contains one or more pointers that indicate the address of the next logical record (see Figure 4.4). Including pointers in one record to connect with another record enables the physical and logical files to be completely separated.

Although pointers permit diversification of data utilization, they have several disadvantages. The implementation of such structures requires complicated programming. File maintenance must be performed every time a record is added or deleted and is therefore very time-consuming to the system. Also, some extra storage is necessary to contain the pointers.

Chains   A *chain* represents a logical path through a data base. It allows groups of records to be associated with each other. These logical paths are connected by the pointers just described. Figure 4.4 illustrates how the pointers and chains can be combined to form a logical file. The accounts payable file includes certain information about each vendor. If we desire to evaluate all accounts with balances over $20,000, the software for that part of the data base provides the A pointers to list only those accounts. The chain of desired accounts becomes 102, 103, 104, 106, and 107. This is represented by the solid-line chain in Figure 4.4, a single association.

Often a situation arises where several attributes are needed. If a user is interested in raw material suppliers with balances over $20,000, the chain becomes 102, 103, and 106, controlled by the B pointers. These chains are known as *multiple associations.* Notice from this small example how large the files can become. This is a disadvantage in many situations.

Data Structures

The type of file organization in a data base varies with the uses, complexity, and size of the data base. A *flat structure* is established where all the data records are similar in size and their utilization is very simple or restricted. A batch processed payroll would be an example of a data set with each record containing the same type of data elements, in the same order, and with each element needing the same number of storage spaces. Notice in Figure 4.6(a) the file example with each data element in a flat line. This data structure also permits like data sets to be stored one on top of (or behind) the other. Flat structures are seldom used with integrated data bases because they usually require a sequential-access medium, such as magnetic tape.

A structure often used in accounting data files is the *tree,* or *hierarchical,* data organization, as shown in Figure 4.6(b). A data base subschema is created that defines the relationships between the data that are to be stored in the data base. A *schema* describes the logical overview of the data base file being examined and a *subschema* represents a portion of a schema. A subschema is the part of the data base that generally relates to a specific use. In this type of subschema the data records are organized into echelons. As the relationships are established between echelons, the upper echelons are parents to the next lower echelons, the children. Each parent may have many children, but each child can have only one parent. In a marketing system the top echelon might be each branch officer master record; the second echelon, the various types of customers; and the third echelon, the types of items the customers buy. As the echelons progress, each level must be accessed through some parent in the preceding level. Moving through the levels from parents to children is a one-to-many relationship, whereas moving from child to parent is a one-to-one relationship. These relationships are controlled by pointers and chains.

Figure 4.6(c) shows a *network,* or *complex,* structure. This file may also contain parents and children, but here the relationships are many-to-many. In a network data base, individual files are established for each major element. For a job order production system it is necessary to establish many-to-many relationships among customer, inventory, production, and the like. These relationships, are controlled by establishing a network between all of the interrelated files through pointers and chains.

Although there are other types of file structures, the systems analyst, programmer, and computer manager are more concerned than the accountants are with what can be done with a data set. Accountants should be aware of the possibilities and advantages of the different types of file organizations and design structures.[1]

DATE STRUCTURES, (A) FLAT FILES, (B) HIERARCHICAL FILES, (C) NETWORK FILES.

First Record	Social Security No.	Employee Name	Payrate	Deductions	Etc.
Second Record	Social Security No.	Employee Name	Payrate	Deductions	Etc.
Nth Record	Social Security No.	Employee Name	Payrate	Deductions	Etc.

(a)

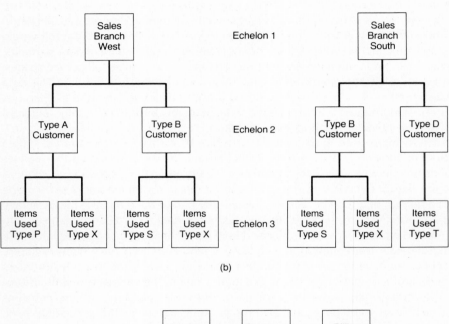

(b)

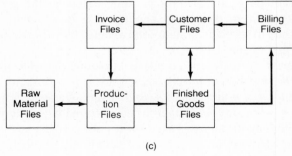

(c)

Figure 4.6

Relational Structures

It is often very difficult to anticipate every future need of data when developing a data schema. All data files discussed previously have required that the data relationships be determined in advance. If a given relationship is ignored, but later needed, the entire file usually has to be reprogrammed and reconstructed.

The logical descriptions of the data can be simplified by *normalization.* This is the process of replacing tree and network structures with two-dimensional flat files or tables called *relations.* This allows the system to access data from the data base in different ways through the use of an index and without complicated pointers and chains.

By using the data in Figure 4.6(b), one can illustrate the relational concept. The basic step is to convert the tree structure to a flat file structure. Converting network files to relational structures takes several more steps, but it is not required here for understanding the concept. The inverted files of Figure 4.5 are also partial relational indexes. A fully relational data structure has an index for every attribute in the master file. However, for most applications it is not necessary to invert a file for every attribute.

The sales reporting system in Figure 4.6(b) must first be simplified by having only one field *(domain)* on which to address. In Figure 4.7 the domain is branch/customer type. Any time that a structure is normalized, some data redundancy will occur. Because our illustration combined two fields into one domain, both sales branch and customer types will be redundant throughout the file. In relational data bases each row *(tuple)* of the file must be uniquely identified. For each combination of branch/customer type and item type there must be a unique address. If compared with the inverted file illustrations, the redundancy may not even be as much because the inverted files must repeat certain data fields every time an inversion takes place.

Relational data structures allow the computer system to develop a variety of files from the same data in a relatively efficient manner. New indexes can also be added as user's needs change. Another advantage of relational structures is the ease with which the data bases can be modified. They are also much more flexible than files that are kept in hierarchical and network forms. These advantages are partially offset by two disadvantages. First, the index part of the file must be maintained along with the records them-

RELATIONAL STRUCTURES.

Address	Domain Branch/Customer Type	Secondary Fields Type of Items
2371	West/A	Type P
2372	West/A	Type X
2373	West/B	Type S
2374	West/B	Type X
2375	South/B	Type S
2376	South/B	Type X
2377	South/D	Type T

Figure 4.7

selves and, second, the index file, which can become quite large, must be searched sequentially.

Availability

The data base must accommodate many types of uses. Each file should include the proper contents to allow all users adequate amounts of data. Availability has different meanings to the various users found in most organizations. To the sales force, availability implies the ability to find out immediately whether a customer has good credit, the limits of the credit line, and the account's status—current or past due. To a managerial accountant, availability implies quick access to anything that may be needed in analyzing the production performance for Department 416 last month. Availability also implies that the computer personnel can revise various files when changes are needed and can maintain a reliable and sound operating system under all conditions.

Integrity

The quantity and quality of the data base must be protected at all times. Integrity is primarily concerned with the quality of the data base, and security is concerned with the physical condition of the data base. To protect the quality of the data base several conditions must be met. Primary to data base quality is the control of incoming data. All inputs should conform to a predetermined standard of elements, size, and content. Control features should be incorporated that measure these standards. For example, it is very easy to install a control feature that checks all inventory item inputs for correct length of stock number. Other checks include verifying alpha and numeric fields for the correct type of character, testing for positive and negative conditions in cash transactions, and verifying completeness of a customer's address. All of these control features are discussed in Chapter Six.

Backup protection is another integrity condition that must be maintained. The user must be assured that the data base can be reconstructed if the data are lost or destroyed. Such losses can occur during power failures, natural disasters, and hardware and software failures, and from user and operator carelessness. When any failure occurs, the system should have some means of backup and restoration.

Another problem with some of the more complex systems occurs when two or more users have accessed the same data file. When multiple users are making changes in a file at the same time, it is possible that some of the data may be lost. This can be controlled through a process called *deadlock* where the first user to access the file locks out any other users until he or she is finished.

Security

Security procedures are implemented primarily to protect the existing data from loss or destruction. Through proper access controls, intrusion can be monitored and unauthorized access attempts detected and prevented. The other objective of security is to prevent the unauthorized dissemination of data. Data are often classified by an organization as confidential, and steps must be taken in the information system to protect the data base from unauthorized receivers of information. Proper management of the data base and the computer operations is one of the best means of providing this security. Detailed security controls are discussed in Chapter Six.

DATA BASE MANAGEMENT SYSTEMS

Data base management systems (DBMS) are large software packages that are used to meet the complexities of today's data structures. DBMS are special computer programs that control the basic data movements within the system by maintaining, manipulating, and retrieving data. Most DBMS can perform functions such as adding, deleting, modifying, sorting, printing, and identifying records, files, and data. DBMS programs can also handle more than one set of data at a time, a restriction in traditional file management systems. Such programs are written to ensure utmost efficiency. Users of a computer system that has DBMS can rely on it to perform most of the tasks involved with data structures, data storage, and data retrieval.

Data base management systems are *application-independent.* They can be used in virtually any environment where data have to be managed within the computer system. DBMS are not structured to any set of files in a system but to the system as a whole (see Figure 4.8). This characteristic enables a user to access, inquire, or update data without being concerned with where or how the data are stored. Unlike traditional data processing programs where the data are specified through format requirements of the given program instructions, DBMS accepts a set of data in various forms and assigns it to a proper file where it may be used by several users. This concept separates the data from the user by making many of the routine decisions that affect the handling of the data.

To assist in defining, developing, and communicating the changes in DBMS, the Conference on Data Systems Languages (CODASYL) Systems Committee has outlined the major features of DBMS. The first feature is *data structures.* This feature permits the DBMS user to handle data without having to be concerned about how the data are stored. The next feature, *data independence,* keeps data separate from the related processing programs. Therefore, either the data or the programs can change independently of each other. This feature is primarily possible through the use of data dictionaries, discussed earlier.

Interrogation, another feature, permits data to be extracted or copied with the results formatted into readable reports or other machine usable forms for further processing. This is accomplished by two programming languages called *data definition languages* (DDL) and *data manipulation languages* (DML). The DDL describes the schema and subschemas to be used and initializes the data bases with data by specifying record formats, record-keys, record sizes and file structures. This is the link between the logical and physical files discussed in an earlier section. The DML enables the manipulation of data stored in the data base. It provides the processing techniques of retrieval, sorting, displaying, deleting, and adding. Once the area of the data base has been defined, interrogation performs whatever instructions it has been given. For example:

    FIND ALL INVENTORY ITEMS IN INVENTORY FILE OF
       DATA BASE ACCOUNTS OVER $4,000
       AND UNUSED IN SIX MONTHS
       AND LOCATED IN WAREHOUSE 106
       AND PRINT IN FORMAT ACCOUNT NUMBER, NAME,
          AMOUNT, DATE OF LAST USAGE

COMPUTER SYSTEM WITH DBMS.

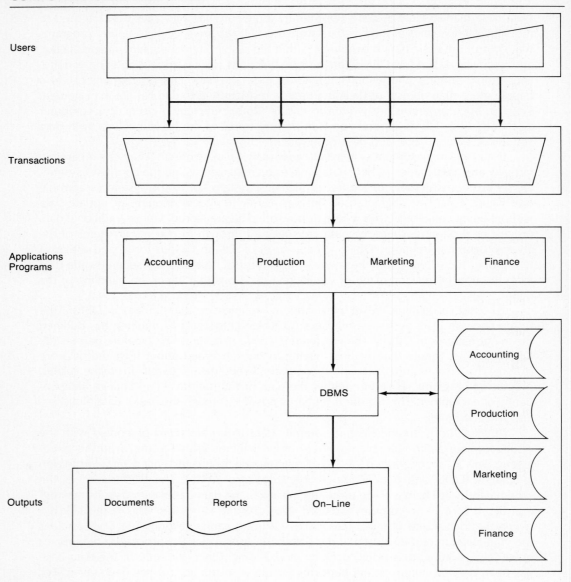

Figure 4.8

The *updating* features of DBMS allows for changing the values of all or part of the data items without changing the logical structure of the data base. Also protected under this feature are the existing security measures and control and validation criteria. Updating allows for adding data to the data base, changing data within the data base, and deleting data from the data base, using DDL and DML.

The *creation* of new sets of data to be placed under the control of an existing DBMS is another feature outlined by the CODASYL Committee. This feature includes activities such as entering a data definition for a file already in existence in machine-processable form but not yet known to the DBMS, or creating a new set of data and telling the DBMS about its existence. When creating new data base files, one must define and communicate the parameters and specifications to the DBMS. Creation also includes the addition of new files to an existing data base of related files. *Re-creation,* a special case of creation, converts an existing file into a structure different from that currently in existence, and redefines the parameters and criteria of the new data file(s).

The last technical feature of DBMS is *storage structure.* This is the concept of physical data storage. The managers of the data base system select the best storage structure for each file according to the uses of the file and its data. Refer to earlier sections of this chapter for detailed discussions of structures.

Most organizations that have DBMS also have a *DBMS administrator.* This person is normally responsible for several activities, including: assigning user access codes, developing retrieval methods, maintaining edit controls over changes, approving all data base changes, and controlling overall DBMS operations. The DBMS administrator is the human interface coordinator, between the users and the data base.

DBMS Advantages

Data base management systems provide a means of solving some of the complicated problems of managing computerized data in a large automated system. The advantages of DBMS over traditional computerized accounting systems are improved data control, utilization, service, and flexibility. Such systems have greatly improved the management information system process, especially the areas related to accounting. The accountant, freed from highly structured data input formats, is able to use the current data forms more effectively without having to modify or change every data element before it is inputted into the system.

Most DBMS offer the following specific advantages:

1. Minimizes data redundancy
2. Has ability to associate data with various uses
3. Has improved interface between users and data
4. Has ability to change programs without changing data base program independence
5. Allows either batch or on-line processing
6. Increases throughput of system

DBMS Disadvantages

Although there are relatively few disadvantages, they have a substantial impact. They are as follows.

1. Very complex systems, difficult to program and implement
2. Very expensive because of extensive programming and large storage requirements
3. Sensitive to incorrect data—under traditional systems, an error in an employee pay record only affects payroll; under a DBMS, possibly affects payroll, personnel, production, and cost accounting because of multiple uses of the same data.

ELECTRONIC FUNDS TRANSFER SYSTEMS

Throughout history each society has adopted or developed some method for handling economic transactions. Some acceptable form of payment must be made in return for goods and services. Economic transactions have been handled through the barter system, which was supplanted by economic systems that utilized money to handle transactions. Money systems are now supplemented by checks, which are being replaced by electronic transfers. This new system, electronic funds transfer (EFT), offers a radical departure from the traditional checking system. Instead of transferring data through paper documents and checks, the EFT system transfers data through electronic records. A product of the computer and telecommunications era, EFT systems today represent a viable, alternative system for handling economic transactions. Although the cash and checking modes have coexisted for many years, EFT systems have now joined these as a third type of transactional medium.

The inefficiency of processing paper documents, along with the delays in receiving information, has encouraged financial and other institutions to develop EFT as an alternative information system. In the technical sense, the AICPA has defined an EFT system as

> a computer-based network that enables payment-system transactions to be initiated, approved, executed, and recorded with electronic impulses and machine-sensible data rather than with paper.[2]

Most common in commercial banks and savings and loan associations, EFT systems represent on-line systems that are used to perform various functions including the maintenance of up-to-date records. EFT systems speed the transfer of funds by communicating information relating to payments via electronic means. Thus, they allow banks to provide faster, more efficient service to customers.

Impact of EFT Systems

As EFT systems become more widely adopted, the impact of EFT will be felt by all segments of the population that engage in economic transactions: businesses, financial institutions, and consumers (i.e., users). Further, EFT will have an important impact on those whose function is to record, summarize, and report on economic transactions—namely, accountants.

EFT systems offer both benefits and costs to users. Benefits may be classified into two major areas: convenience and efficiency. In terms of convenience, an EFT system allows consumers and businesses to pay bills through electronic processing. By making such EFT payments, the consumer or business is relieved of writing and mailing checks.

Such convenience is enhanced when the customer authorizes a financial institution to pay certain bills automatically. In addition, many banks are now installing EFT systems at shopping centers and supermarkets. These systems generally allow customers to withdraw cash as well as provide authorization for cashing checks at the respective merchants.

Another benefit, automatic deposits, eliminates unnecessary delays in fund transfers. The Social Security Administration is the largest user of such transfers. Worries about lost or stolen checks are greatly reduced. Another example of convenience is the capability of fund transfers (e.g., depositing a payroll check) even while an employee may be sick or on vacation.

A potential benefit of EFT systems centers around the capability of such systems for reducing transactional costs. Reducing such costs helps not only financial institutions but also consumers and businesses engaged in economic transactions.

Although initial set-up costs for most EFT systems are quite expensive since they involve sophisticated computer technology and controls, the variable costs are quite low. As a consequence, the marginal cost of processing one additional transaction in an EFT system is extremely small. Little or no additional labor is involved, and only a small amount of computer time is used. In comparison, the marginal cost of processing a check is much higher because of the additional labor costs in handling and transporting checks.

EFT systems may also reduce costs indirectly. For example, when credit data are incorporated into an EFT system, substantial improvements in the control of consumer credit may be effected. These improved credit controls should reduce bad debt write-offs of the companies involved.

With the benefits that EFT systems provide there are certain costs and disadvantages. A primary disadvantage is the large initial set-up cost of an EFT system. Such a heavy fixed investment requires widespread use if per unit costs are to be small.

Other disadvantages of EFT systems center around the potential loss of security and control with respect to personal financial information. Consumers, of course, want to be assured that they do not lose control over their personal financial transactions. Consumers may perceive that they lose control over the payment process in an EFT system in certain areas, such as automated payments and withdrawals. Consumers may also be concerned over the possible access to their accounts from nonauthorized sources. Many consumers also believe certain other controls may be lost in an EFT system. (For example, checks provide written evidence of transactions and may be intercepted during processing by the payor to issue a stop–payment notice). Since most EFT systems instantaneously record transactions, this control is lost. This aspect also eliminates the float of taking several days before a check clears an account.

Consumers and government officials also voice concern over the possible violation of consumer privacy in EFT systems. Computers allow information to be sorted and stored with relative ease. Access to such data presents many possibilities for abuse and misuse such as determining an individual's buying habits, shopping patterns, and debt payments. Americans have traditionally placed a high degree of importance on individual privacy. The possibility of a breach of confidential information represents a serious disadvantage of EFT systems.

EFT can also have an impact on other economic segments of our society. The Securities and Exchange Commission has granted temporary approval of an electronic trading system for the Cincinnati Stock Exchange. This system allows bids to buy and offers to sell to be placed on the exchange electronically on terminals throughout the country. Bids and offers are then matched by the computer and processed.

The impact on accountants should also be noted. Certainly, the CPA who acts as an independent auditor for a client that uses an EFT system will find a significant impact on audit procedures as currently performed within paper-based systems. EFT cannot only capture and record data more quickly but can also have a significant impact on internal accounting controls. Although EFT systems may require changes in the organization and control procedures, the objectives and essential characteristics of internal accounting control are not altered.

Electronic systems may have a pervasive impact on our economic structure, often in ways that few people anticipate. While new industries and services will arise in response to EFT systems, others will disappear. An analogy may be drawn with the advent of the automobile. While the automobile, tire, and petroleum industries emerged, other industries and vocations such as blacksmiths, stables, and railroads declined.

Automated Clearinghouses

The cornerstone of the electronic funds transfer system is the automated clearinghouse. Its function is to transmit debit and credit items through the financial system electronically rather than manually. An automated clearinghouse (ACH) is analogous to a traditional clearinghouse in that it represents a system for the interbank clearing of debits and credits. The main difference between automated and conventional clearinghouses is that the debit and credit items exist on paper in the conventional clearinghouse and as electronic signals recorded on a magnetic medium in the automated clearinghouse. The ACH thus paves the way for the elimination of the often burdensome physical processing of the paper check.

Automated clearinghouses are especially suited for handling recurring payments such as payroll, social security or pension payments, and certain payments by individuals (e.g., mortgage and insurance payments). Payors authorize their banks to pay a specified amount to a payee (e.g., bank or insurance company) on a specified date. Parties participating in these types of payments receive a descriptive statement documenting the payment.

To process preauthorized electronic payments, the company creates a tape listing a routing number and account number for each customer participating, with the amount owed and the date due. The company sends the tape to its bank, which processes and distributes output tapes to receiving institutions through an automated clearinghouse. This process is similar to the forwarding of tapes under the direct deposit plan for payroll. Although this system offers the customer the convenience and time savings of writing checks and mailing, the advantages are often viewed by the banking customer as offset by a perceivable loss of control over payment, error in payment, fear of overdraft, and loss of float. In addition, if the payor reduces float another disadvantage is created. For companies and financial institutions the system has potential for reducing cost of check handling and accelerating availability of funds for the company.

Automated Teller Machines (ATMs)

Machines through which an individual may conduct various routine banking services can be grouped in an area known as teller machines. These services are provided through either remote terminals or Touch-Tone telephones. Much of the recent EFT system development and growth has involved these machines.

Although the capabilities of the system vary from bank to bank, the system generally may be used to make cash deposits, transfer funds between a checking and a savings account, make cash withdrawals from an account, make credit card cash withdrawals, or make payments on an account. Obtaining account balances is another important feature in most on-line systems. Automated teller machines allow customers to make transactions after business hours and at convenient locations. A major concern in using ATMs is unauthorized access to customer accounts. In most systems the customer is required to enter a personal identification number after activating the machine with the plastic card. If the correct number is not entered, no transaction can be completed. In addition, the machine will retain the card on the assumption that the lack of the correct number means unauthorized use of the card.

If the automated teller machine is connected on-line to the bank's computer, the customer's account is updated immediately; otherwise a magnetic disk is maintained in the machine and is periodically delivered to the bank for processing. On-line systems may be categorized into two types: proprietary systems and switch systems. When the terminal communicates with a computer servicing a specific financial institution, the system is called a *proprietary system*. If the terminal communicates with a computer representing a service center that "switches" messages and settles accounts for several financial institutions, the system is known as a *switch system*.

Telephone Transfer Systems

Remote banking does not necessarily require terminals; funds may also be transferred through the use of Touch-Tone telephones. These telephone systems allow customers to transfer funds to a merchant for payments and verify their account balances with the financial institution. In the typical telephone system, the customers use the Touch-Tone telephone to enter their account numbers, their personal identification numbers, the merchant's special account number, and the dollar amount of the transfer. The funds are automatically transferred from the customers' accounts to the merchant's account. The bank involved then sends periodic statements to both customers and merchants verifying the transactions.

Point-of-sale Systems

On-line systems that allow customers to transfer funds to merchants as purchases are made are usually called *point-of-sale* (POS) systems. Of all the EFT systems, the POS system offers the most significant, and potentially the most beneficial, change. A point-of-sale system allows the customer to pay for goods and services at the merchant's location (e.g., a supermarket) by transferring funds from the customer's account to the merchant's account either immediately or at the end of the day. By entering transaction data into the electronic payments network at the time and place of sale, the system promotes the paperless transfer of funds in transactions between customers and businesses.

Point-of-sale systems usually offer three types of services, either individually or in combination: check verification, fund transfer, and data capture. As one of the earlier services of point-of-sale systems, the check verification function allows the merchant to determine the availability of funds in a customer's account before accepting a check or initiating a fund transfer. After the customer's account number is entered in the system, the computer verifies the check and transmits a response back to the terminal (e.g., a green light signals an approved check).

When a funds transfer is involved, the point-of-sale system transfers funds from the customer's account to the merchant's account. This system usually requires the use of a "debit" card to facilitate the transfer. Unlike a credit card that extends credit, debit cards generate a charge (e.g., a debit) against the customer's account at the financial institution. Many point-of-sale systems located at retail stores also have the capability to capture other data for management's use. For example, the system may update inventory data as well as record price and discount information.

As with automated teller machines, unauthorized access to the account is guarded against by the required use of a personal identification number known only to the customer. Data concerning the transaction are entered by the clerk through an electronic cash register or a product code reader. If the customer's bank is different from the store's bank, a switching process center connects the computers of the two banks. Both parties of the transaction receive a printed statement at the time of the transaction, and the customer's regular bank statement contains a descriptive listing similar to the listing used on credit card statements.

Accounting Controls

Although EFT systems offer the advantages of timeliness and reduction of document handling, certain concerns do exist regarding their utilization. Accounting controls are designed to provide reasonable assurance that all relevant transactions are authorized and recorded in accordance with stated policies. To achieve this objective, accounting controls provide methods to identify and locate the relevant documents that support such transactions. Different control methods are necessary for a variety of reasons: to aid the independent auditor in the verification of transactions, to provide additional controls in the form of expected support and documentation, and to satisfy various requirements of governmental and regulatory bodies. These controls are discussed in detail in Chapter Six.

Legal Implications of EFT Systems

The emergence of EFT systems has increased discussion and debate regarding the legal guidelines for such systems. These concerns about legal implications center around three major areas: *privacy, security,* and *banking rules.*

Many people have voiced fears that through EFT systems, companies as well as the government may be able to identify confidential customer information, including customers' financial resources, buying preferences, and shopping patterns. These concerns are aggravated by the lack of present legal safeguards over the privacy of financial transaction information.

The National Commission on Electronic Funds Transfers identifies four areas in which consumer privacy may be violated:

1. New kinds of financial transaction records may be generated.
2. The amount of information currently included in transaction records may increase.
3. Records will be easier to retrieve.
4. The number of institutions with access to an individual's financial records may increase.[3]

EFT systems can capture an individual's financial transactions instantaneously as they occur. In addition, the technological capabilities of EFT systems could allow rapid access to these data. A major concern is the protection of consumer privacy and the protection of these records from unauthorized storage and access by banks, insurance companies, credit bureaus, the government, and others. Many consumers feel that criminals may have easy access to computerized electronic systems with only a slight chance of detection. Computer and security experts agree that the security surrounding EFT systems needs to be reviewed and updated continually, but they believe the systems are as secure as paper-based systems.

The development of EFT has generated significant debate over possible violations of federal and state banking statutes. The basic issue in debate is whether remote terminals are branches. This question is most significant in states that (1) limit bank branches or (2) have different branch regulations for various types of financial institutions (e.g., banks versus savings and loan associations).

For most large systems the processing applications combine a mixture of batch and on-line characteristics. Historically, computer systems began as batch processing and slowly progressed to on-line and later to real-time. However, most organizations today begin with a combination of processing applications thanks to the advances in computer hardware and software. Even organizations with minicomputers have on-line capabilities and the various tools necessary to operate them efficiently.

Accountants generally think of the data base system as belonging to them. However, in the modern and complex information systems of today the accountant is only one of many generators, users, and developers of data and the related systems. Accountants should be aware of the various data base concepts and what a properly designed data base system can provide for them. Data base systems not only ease some of the problems of managing data but allow a multitude of data uses and manipulations that were unavailable just a few years ago. The basic benefits that are provided for accounting users include improved control, reduced costs, and flexibility.

SUMMARY

Data processing can be discussed in terms of processing, files, structures, software, and applications. This chapter has covered the basics of batch and direct processing including real-time and distributed. The advantages and disadvantages of each were explained along with relevant examples. Next, the latest developments in data base concepts were discussed, beginning with the various types of data files. Data structures were presented in great detail, with attention focused on the aspects of file and data integration.

Data base management systems play a very important role in the development of integrated data base systems and should be considered for implementation any time that a system is being redesigned. Although they can be very complex and expensive, DBMS are the leading software application of the future.

Electronic funds transfer systems are part of the continual evolvement of financial transaction systems. Their applications are increasing, and, in some cases, are supplanting the more traditional paper-based transaction systems. The development of EFT systems promises a tremendous impact on accounting, business, and society.

EFT systems are typically divided into three categories: automated clearinghouses, teller machines, and point-of-sale systems. As with other transaction systems, EFT systems require accounting controls to safeguard assets and aid in the generation of reliable information. However, legal guidelines for EFT systems have not been fully developed.

NOTES

[1]See chapter references for a source of technical material on this topic.

[2]AICPA, *Audit Considerations in Electronic Funds Transfer Systems* (New York: American Institute of Certified Public Accountants, 1978), p. 1.

[3]National Commission on Electronic Funds Transfers, *EFT in the United States: Policy Recommendations and the Public Interest* (Washington, D.C.: NCEFT, October 28, 1977). These tables are extracted from work done by Donn Parker for the FDIC in his work with the commission.

SELECTED REFERENCES

Ahituv, Niv, and Michael Hadass. "Identifying the Need for a DBMS," *Journal of Systems Management* (August 1980): 30.

Akresh, Abraham D., and Michael Goldstein. "Point-of-sale Accounting Systems. Some Implications for the Auditor," *Journal of Accountancy* (December 1978): 68–74.

American Institute of Certified Public Accountants. *Audit Considerations in Electronic Funds Transfer Systems,* New York: AICPA, 1978.

Buchanan, Jack R., and Richard G. Linowes, "Understanding Distributed Data Processing," *Harvard Business Review* (July–August 1983): 143–153.

Burch, John C., Felix R. Strater, and Gary Grudnitski, *Information Systems: Practice and Theory.* New York: John Wiley & Sons, 1983.

Canning, Richard G. "What's Happening with CODASYL-Type DBMS?" *EDP Analyzer* (October 1974): 1–14.

Cardenas, A. *Data Base Management Systems.* Boston: Allyn & Bacon, 1979.

Coopers & Lybrand. *Electronic Funds Transfer,* January/February 1979.

Date, C. J. *An Introduction to Database Systems.* Reading, Mass.: Addison-Wesley Publishing Co., 1981.

Donaldson, James R. "Structured Programming," *Datamation* (December 1973): 52–54.

Lyons, Norman. "Segregation of Functions in EFTS," *Journal of Accountancy* (October 1978): 89–92.

Martin, James. *Computer Data-Base Organization.* Englewood Cliffs, N.J.: Prentice-Hall, Inc., 1977.

Martin, James. *Principles of Data Base Management.* Englewood Cliffs, N.J.: Prentice-Hall, Inc., 1976.

Myers, Gibbs. "Forms Management, Part 2: How to Design Business Forms," *Journal of Systems Management* (October 1976): 76–84.

National Commission on Electronic Funds Transfer. *EFT in the United States: Policy Recommendations and the Public Interest.* Washington, D.C.: NCEFT, October 28, 1977.

Nolan, Richard L. "Computer Data Base: The Future Is Now," *Harvard Business Review* (September/October 1973): 98–114.

Nusbaum, Edward E., Andrew D. Bailey, Jr., and Andrew B. Whinston. "Data-Base Management, Accounting, and Accountants," *Management Accounting* (May 1978): 35–38.

Powers, Victor. "Implementing Generalized Data Base Management Systems," *Data Management* (May 1975): 31–37.

Richardson, Dana R. "Auditing EFTS," *Journal of Accountancy* (October 1978): 81–87.

Schaller, Carol A. "The Revolution of EFTS," *Journal of Accountancy* (October 1978): 74–80.

Shelly, Gary B., and Thomas Cashman. *Introduction to Computers and Data Processing.* Fullerton, Calif.: Anaheim Publishing Co., 1980.

Singel, John B., Jr. "Computer Data Base Systems: Who Needs Them?" *Price Waterhouse and Company Review* (1975, No. 2): 18–22.

Squire, Enid. *Introducing . . . Systems Design.* Reading, Mass.: Addison-Wesley Publishing Co., 1980.

Vanecek, M. T., and G. Scott. "Data Bases—The Auditor's Dilemma," *CPA Journal* (January 1980): 26–35.

Walsh, Myles E. "Relational Data Bases," *Journal of Systems Management* (June 1980): 11–15.

Wetherbe, James C. *Systems Analysis.* St. Paul: West Publishing Co., 1980.

QUESTIONS

1. Explain or define the following terms:

Batch processing	Indexed-sequential file
Remote batch processing	Schema
On-line processing	Inverted file
Real-time processing	Pointers
Dispatching systems	Chain
Distributed processing	Normalization
Local area network (LAN)	Data independence
Record-key	Data definition language
Logical file	Data manipulation language
Physical file	Automated clearing house
Direct addressing	Point-of-sale system
Data dictionary	

2. Discuss the differences between batch processing and on-line processing.
3. How do real-time systems relate to batch processing and on-line processing?
4. What is a data dictionary? In what type of system is it used?
5. Define the types of data structures discussed in this chapter.
6. What is a DBMS? Does a data base need or require a DBMS? Why?
7. What are the primary advantages of a formalized data base system?
8. What is the accountant's role in developing a data base system?
9. Contrast single and multiple data associations.
10. Discuss the concept of data integrity.
11. How does a relation structure operate?
12. Distinguish between application-independent and data independence.
13. How does a DBMS work?
14. Briefly describe the role of the data base administrator.
15. What benefits do point-of-sale systems offer? Are there any disadvantages?
16. Identify the areas of vulnerability in an EFT system.
17. Discuss legal implications of EFT on:
    a. Privacy
    b. Security
    c. Banking

PROBLEMS

18. Real-time Systems

Athens National Bank's credit card department issues a special debit card that permits card holders to withdraw funds from the bank's automated teller windows at any time of the day or night. These terminals are connected to the bank's central computer. To use them, a bank customer inserts the magnetically encoded card in the automated teller and enters a unique pass code on the teller keyboard. If the pass code matches the authorized code, the customer indicates (1) whether a withdrawal from a savings account or a withdrawal from a checking account is desired and (2) the amount of the withdrawal (in multiples of $20). The terminal communicates this information to the bank's central computer and then gives the customer the desired cash. In addition, the automated terminal provides a hard copy of the transaction to the customer together with the cash.

The bank has imposed certain restrictions on the use of the debit cards when customers make cash withdrawals at automated teller windows, as follows:

a. The correct pass code must be keyed into the terminal before the cash withdrawal is processed.

b. The debit card must be one issued by Athens National Bank.

Required:
What additional features are needed in this system to ensure proper control?

19. Systems Application

Clayton Wholesale Company is considering the implementation of a marketing information system to assist its sales force. There are approximately 400 salespeople working out of 23 branch offices throughout Canada. The goal of the system is to have at a central headquarters customer sales history files that can be accessed by each branch office. When customer orders and shipments are received from each branch office, the files will be updated as soon as possible.

There are approximately 12,000 customers on the file at any one time. Approximately 10 customers are added, and deleted, daily. History files will be maintained for 18 months by product for each customer. Each customer will have a master record with descriptive data. The average number of product records per customer is expected to be 8. Projections indicate that the volume of order records for updating the history file will increase continually.

Required:
a. What type of system is needed for the new marketing plan of Clayton Wholesale? Define the processing needs.

b. If you did not recommend a real-time system, why not? What problems would likely occur in such an application?

20. Payroll System Applications

Ratchford Company is currently involved in the conversion of its manual data processing system to a computerized data processing system for handling of its accounting functions. One of the major accounting processes that will be handled by the new computer system is the company payroll. The new payroll file will be utilized by several departments within the company. The personnel department will need to access the file in order to prepare the initial employer record and make pay rate changes. The accounting department will need access to the file in order to disburse paychecks. Even the company union association needs to access the file in order to credit employees with contributions.

Required:

    a.   Develop a system for Ratchford's payroll application using a pure or hybrid process. Include facts such as the type of hardware, the number of terminals, and who should have access.

    b.   Does your system have any potential control problems? How could you change your system to minimize these problems?

21. File Structures

For each of the following situations, explain the type of file structure that you think would be best. Justify your answers. Limit your answers to sequential, direct, and indexed-sequential.

    a.   A sales commission file that is updated at the time of sale from a remote terminal

    b.   A fixed asset file in a large manufacturing firm

    c.   A stockholder file in a large corporation that is updated weekly to reflect changes sent in by the brokerage firms that deal in the company's stock

    d.   An inventory file for a large retail organization that is updated daily

    e.   A payroll master file that is updated for each monthly payroll

    f.   A production job file for a large assembly plant that has many jobs in process at the same time

22. Data Base Systems

Oriental Rugs makes carpets to order. Customers may choose from 35 styles and up to 12 combinations of various colors. There are also a variety of sizes for each of the 35 styles. Upon selection of a style, size, and color combination, a sales order is prepared and placed on the computer. The computer then reviews the inventory for mat layouts and color availability. Depending on the inventory level, the computer places orders with suppliers as needed.

After the inventory activities have been completed, the system prepares a work order that is sent to the production manager. The system also keeps up with the status of jobs in process and provides information on demand through access terminals.

Upon completion of all jobs on a particular customer order, the customer is sent a statement. If an order contains more than one item, the billing is made per the instructions on the order, either as each item is completed and shipped or after all items are shipped.

The system also updates the cost accounting system for direct and indirect labor, factory overhead, and direct materials.

Required:

    a.   Describe the data base system you think would be best for Oriental Rugs.

    b.   List the separate master files that would be used in the data base you recommend and the type of storage medium for each.

23. File Structures

Normalize the following tree structure into a flat file.

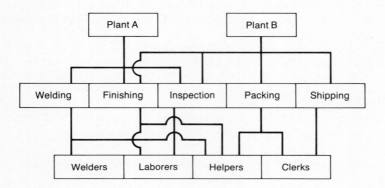

24. Data Base Systems

Stone Mountain Community College is computerizing its student registration procedures and desires to have the following information available for on-line terminal inquiry. Professors should be listed by department and courses taught. Each course should have a listing of students by major. There must be some identification between each student and his or her professors for each course.

Required:

Prepare a network structure representing the stated relationships for the data base.

25. Data Base, File Structure, and Processing

Dublin Manufacturing is converting its accounts payable system from manual to computer operations. It has approximately 425 vendors and both raw material and supplies. Some of the vendors furnish both types of inventory items. Most of the vendors are located within one day's delivery of the plant, although 15 percent of them must have at least a week's lead time. All of the vendors allow some type of payment discount, ranging from 2 percent in 10 days to 1 percent in 30 days.

Required:

    a.   Identify all the data items needed for this file.

    b.   Select a primary key and several secondary keys. Justify why you selected each.

c. Give three examples of using the secondary keys for inverted files and explain why the company might want to have the file inverted in each way.

26. Data Base Implementation

Changes in the design and development of computerized accounting information systems have been very frequent in the last few years. Traditionally, computerized data processing systems were arranged by departments and applications. Computers were applied to single, large-volume applications such as inventory, payroll, and customer billing. Other applications were added once the primary application was operating smoothly.

As more applications were added, problems in data management developed. Businesses looked for ways to integrate the data processing systems to make them more comprehensive and to have shorter response times. As a consequence, a data base system was developed that was composed of the data base itself, the data base management system, and the individual application programs. *(IMA adapted)*

Required:

a. Explain the basic difference between the traditional approach to data processing and the use of the data base systems in terms of (1) file structure and (2) the processing of data.
b. Identify and discuss the favorable and unfavorable issues that a company should consider before implementing a data base system.

27. Files, Pointers, and Chains

Cedartown Electrical Supply has 26 vendors that can be identified by using the letters of the alphabet because each one of them begins with a different letter. The five companies whose names begin with vowels are all raw material suppliers located in Atlanta. Companies B, C, D, and F are located in Denver. Companies G, H, J, K, L, and M are located in St. Paul, whereas Companies N, P, Q, R, X, Y, and Z are in New York. Companies S and T are in Seattle, Company V is in Vineville, and Company W is in Wellington.

In addition to those in Atlanta, the following companies sell raw materials, Companies F, G, J, L, N, P, Q, R, V, and W. Companies A, B, C, F, J, M, N, O, W, and X sell plant supplies to Cedartown Electrical. Office supplies are bought from Companies D, F, K, X, Y, and Z. Companies H, S, T, and W sell equipment to Cedartown Electrical.

All vendors in New York allow discounts of 1 percent in 10 days, Denver vendors allow discounts of 2 percent in 10 days. All other vendors allow a 1 percent discount in 30 days except the one in Wellington that does not allow a discount.

All companies whose names are after the letter M have account balances of over $25,000. Other companies have smaller balances and Companies B, F, and M have zero balances as of today.

Based on experience, Cedartown has rated each vendor based on quality, deliver ability, return allowances, and product technology. The best ranking goes to Companies A, C, F, J, N, R, U, W, Y, and Z. The lowest ranking goes to Companies B, E, K, S, and X. All other companies have a medium ranking.

Required:

    a. Set up a flat file for the accounts payable vendors of Cedartown Electrical Supply.

    b. Show a pointer and chain system for all companies that supply raw materials.

    c. Set up a table for each of the following multiple associations:

        (1) Vendors that carry both raw materials and plant supplies

        (2) Vendors that carry raw materials and have a medium ranking

        (3) Vendors that sell more than one type of item to Cedartown Electrical and have balances over $25,000

28. Systems Analysis and Data Files

Wekender Corporation operates 15 large departmentalized retail hardware stores in major cities of North America. The stores carry a wide variety of merchandise but the major thrust is toward the weekend "do-it-yourself." The company has been successful and has added new stores in each of the last 4 years.

Each store acquires its merchandise from the company's centrally located warehouse. Consequently, the warehouse must maintain an up-to-date inventory that is ready to meet the demands of the individual stores.

The company wishes to keep its competitive position with similar type stores. Therefore, Wekender Corporation must improve its purchasing and inventory procedures. The company's stores must have the proper goods to meet customer demand and the warehouse must have the goods available. The number of stores, their diverse locations, the large number of inventory items, and the volume of business all provide pressures to change from basically manual routines to computerized data processing procedures. Recently, the company has been investigating three different approaches—a magnetic tape input system with batch processing, an on-line system using teleprinters with batch processing and a real-time system with terminals at each store.

Management has determined that the following items should have high priority in the new system.

    a. Rapid ordering to replenish warehouse inventory stocks with a minimum of delay

    b. Quick filling of orders and shipping of merchandise to the stores (this involves determining if sufficient quantities exist)

    c. An indication of inventory activity

    d. Perpetual records to determine quickly inventory level by item

To analyze the system properly the warehouse and purchasing procedures must be reviewed. Most items in the warehouse are stored in bins and controlled by inventory number. The numbers generally are listed sequentially on the bins to facilitate locating items for shipment. Frequently, this system is not followed and, as a result, some items are difficult to locate.

Whenever a retail store needs merchandise a three-part merchandise request form is completed. One copy is kept by the store and two copies are mailed to the warehouse. If the merchandise requested is on hand, the goods are delivered to the store, accompanied by the third copy of the request. The second copy is filed at the warehouse.

If the quantity of goods on hand is not sufficient to fill the order, the warehouse sends the quantity available and notes the quantity shipped on the request form. Then a purchase memorandum for the shortage is prepared by the warehouse. At the end of each day all the memos are sent to the purchasing department.

When ordered goods are received, they are checked at the receiving area, and a receiving report is prepared. One copy of the receiving report is retained at the receiving area, one is forwarded to accounts payable, one is filed at the warehouse with the purchase memorandum, and one is sent to purchasing. All back-orders from the retail stores are reviewed at the end of each day to see if any of the goods arrived. These back-orders are filled the next day.

When purchasing receives the purchase memoranda from the warehouse, purchase orders are prepared. Vendor catalogs are used to select the best source for the requested goods, and the purchase order is prepared and mailed. Copies of the order are sent to accounts payable and the receiving area; one copy is retained in the purchasing department.

When the receiving report arrives in the purchasing department, it is compared with the purchase order on file. The receiving report is also checked against the purchase invoice before the invoice is forwarded to accounts payable for payment.

The purchasing department strives periodically to evaluate the vendors for financial soundness, reliability, and trade relationships. However, because the volume of requests received from the warehouse is so great, this activity currently does not have a high priority.

Each week a report of the open purchase orders is prepared to determine if any action should be taken on overdue deliveries. This report is prepared manually from scanning the file of outstanding purchase orders. *(IMA adapted)*

Required:
  a. Which of three systems under consideration best meets the needs of Wekender Corporation?
  b. Briefly describe the basic equipment components that would be needed for the system you recommended.
  c. Identify the data files that would be necessary for the system.
  d. Indicate the type of information that would be contained in each file.

CHAPTER FIVE

Small Business Systems and Configurations

Although small businesses play an important role in every society, they were the last to receive the benefits of the computer revolution. This chapter discusses the developments of computerized systems for small organizations and presents an application of how a small organization can take advantage of the current technology. Also included is a brief discussion of applications for service and not-for-profit organizations, with special attention to small CPA firms.

Almost everyone can remember when computers were used only by large organizations. In large organizations all of the details about computers, programming, and systems analysis and design are handled by experts. Usually, in these organizations the accountants are not intimately knowledgeable about such matters. However, in small organizations where microcomputers and small business computers are making inroads, accountants and other operating personnel are finding it necessary to learn more about the systems and their applications. Although computer service bureaus and time-sharing arrangements have primarily served small organizations in the past, their popularity has declined in recent years as the cost of owning small business computer systems has also declined.

Both hardware and software companies have made great strides in developing small business systems. Software has become much more user friendly than in the past, and the hardware is much more oriented to users with a minimum of technical training and background.

Low cost, easy installation, and increasing computer literacy have contributed to the fast acceptance of microcomputers in business. In most cities today one can go into a retail store and buy a complete system with a variety of software available. By following instructions, one can have parts of the business applications operating in just a few days or even hours. Many microcomputer systems require no formal training in programming, and the operating instructions are often easier than running a large copy machine.

Because there is often a backlog of computer applications waiting to be installed in large companies, many operating units within such a company have found it more effective to acquire and operate their own micro-information systems. This allows users to control their own applications and have the process operating while the information needs are still relevant.

With all businesses rapidly changing to keep up with competition and inflation, the computer for the small business is more necessary than ever. It is particularly useful for inventories, accounts receivable, and payroll. Also, many small businesses have begun to adapt cash control procedures to the small business computers. Microcomputer popularity has given small businesses a large variety of systems combinations from which to choose because of the abundance of both hardware and software alternatives. Although several manufacturing companies have already dropped out of the competition, software producers seem to be multiplying. This makes it increasingly difficult for the small business to distinguish between good and bad software applications. The selection process can border on confusion for the small business because software vendors claim to have the newest, latest, most up-to-date packages. The best initial criterion for software selection are to keep it simple, flexible, and on a small scale. Small businesses should prefer to have a few applications working than to have many applications not working.

Management and owners should not worry about waiting until the price drops, or a new technology is developed, to consider a computerized system. Most small computers currently available can increase the operating efficiency of manual systems, and they will pay for themselves in a few years through efficiency of record keeping and the amount of time saved. These systems can do wonders for traditional bookkeeping aspects of accounting, improve the reporting of inventory, reduce time and increase accuracy of payroll processing, and keep both accounts payable and receivable subsidiary ledgers in much better condition than manual systems.

SMALL COMPUTER SYSTEMS

Although it is possible to give detailed descriptions of all the major computer systems currently available for small businesses, the information would be out of date before this text ever comes from the printer. Brief descriptions of the categories of computers is therefore presented. Small computer classifications normally include everything from hand-held programmable calculators to minicomputers.

Microcomputers range in price from a few hundred dollars to about $5,000. Although some of them may have very small memories, the typical memory capacity ranges between 32 and 256K. These types of computers are used in the smallest organizations where only a few applications are needed. Larger organizations may use them for specific applications such as sales analyses for district offices where each district keeps track of its own sales history. Most of them are stand-alone systems that do not interface with other systems, although many have that capability. Notice in Figure 5.1 the modem that can link the personal computer to other computers.

Business or *accounting microcomputers* constitute the next category, and they range in price from $5,000 to $40,000 with a minimum memory of 256K. These are the most popular computers for small organizations because they can perform most computerized activities, although on a smaller scale than large mainframes. Most business microcomputers can be programmed using one of the high-level languages, and operate using either floppy disk or hard disk packs. These types of computers are frequently used in networks and are easily adaptable as the organization grows. Typical accounting applications found on these types of computers include: general ledger, accounts receivable, accounts payable, payroll, and inventory. There are also many spreadsheet applica-

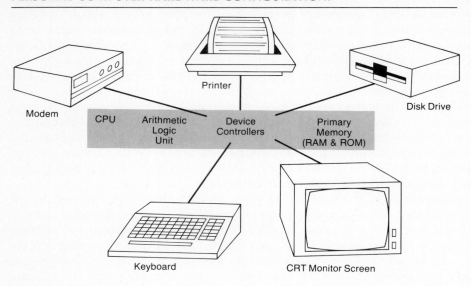

Figure 5.1

tions for this group of computers, with budgeting and cash flow estimates being the most frequently used. Additional packages that are often used are word processing and data file management.

The last category of small computers are the *minicomputers.* They have a memory, before add-ons, of about 512K and range up to 100 megabytes. The price range is $45,000 to $100,000. The best definition of these computers is simply that they are small, mainframe computers. They can operate as fast, handle the same type of peripheral equipment, and form the same type of communication networks. The primary difference is that they lack the capacity of the larger mainframe computers.

SYSTEMS ORIENTATION

Small business systems are either operator-oriented or file-oriented. *Operator-oriented systems* are similar to the old bookkeeping machine method wherein data are entered manually, record-by-record, through the use of a keyboard. The processing of each record is completed before the next record is entered.

Most of the operator-oriented systems are turnkey systems because the user does no programming. Everything is "canned" and ready for processing when acquired. The data are simply used "as is," with the outputs emerging in preprogrammed formats. Accounts payable and payroll are typical applications of turnkey systems.

File-oriented systems receive most of their input in batches. The input data are fed into the computer under machine control rather than human control. Although the operator still enters the data at the console, the records are accumulated and processed as a group. File-oriented systems are capable of supporting multiprogramming capabilities, are larger than operator-oriented systems, usually can handle one higher-level language, and usually include multiple direct storage devices. Most small computer applications are file-oriented.

COMPUTERIZING SMALL BUSINESS SYSTEMS

Computerizing an existing manual system will not necessarily result in a better accounting system. Maximizing the benefits of a small business computer requires that the system being computerized be sound and responsive to the users' needs. It is sometimes advisable to wait until the small business system is acquired before redesigning the existing manual system, although this would never be considered with the acquisition of a large computer. This allows the system and computer to be as compatible as possible. Small organizations usually do not program the applications initially. They buy software packages that best fit their current needs.

Although these software packages have many restrictions, they do allow some flexibility. For example, the following applications are available with most of the basic accounting software packages.

1. A perpetual inventory system can be developed by using an inventory program. This allows better evaluations of turnover and reorder points and reduces the need for frequent periodic inventory taking.
2. A chart of accounts can be created by using a basic general ledger package. All accounts for the balance sheet, income statement, capital valuation reports, and subsidiary ledgers can be controlled and monitored. The chart of accounts can also be used to segregate cost centers and functions and produce product line and departmental reports.
3. Several applications are possible by using the various spreadsheets. The most popular are budgets, pro forma statements, and cash flow estimates. The use of these applications with sensitivity analysis is very helpful to most companies.

Design Considerations

Once the decision has been made to install a small business computer, careful consideration must be given to several of the characteristics of small businesses. Although not all of these apply to every small business, they are certainly representative among all types of businesses.

Lack of Computer Expertise   Very few small businesses have anyone on their staffs who are knowledgeable in computer technology and information systems. However, as more people acquire microcomputers for their homes, the amount of minimum exposure to small computer systems is increasing. The primary vulnerability to the small business is not the lack of computer expertise, but the inability to choose properly the correct software for the applications needed. Consequently, the software may not be compatible with either the hardware or the needed applications.

Limited Applications   Some small businesses may desire a computer simply because all of their business associates have one. They often become status symbols for the organization. Because many businesses do not require external reporting, the applications may be limited to basic internal activities; payroll, accounts payable, and accounts receivable, for example.

Small businesses may have only one function that needs computerizing. If that activity is critical to the efficient operations of the organization, then it alone may justify the new system. Also, it is not uncommon to find small businesses with only a few customers, vendors, inventory items, and employees. These businesses can probably benefit most from budgeting and cash flow application. However, if properly incorporated into the information system, these applications can be of substantial benefit to the organization.

Lack of Financial Resources   Many managers and small business proprietors underestimate the total cost of an operational small business system because they are misled by advertisements for small business computers that cost only "a few dollars a day." Just because a total system is advertised for $3,999 does not mean that additional funds will not be needed. There are installation costs, software costs with related adjustments and requirements, systems redesign (not free by any means), special training for employees, new documentation and forms, and slack time while everyone "feels out" the new system. To be realistic, the $3,999 system may result in immediate resource outlays of $7,500, plus future costs associated with the adjustment and break-in period. Small business computer buyers must be aware of the total costs, not just the advertised price in the newspaper.

Informal Information Systems   Many small businesses simply prepare reports when required to do so by the government and keep no formal records for daily management of the organizations. An organization can become quite large and still evaluate its success by its daily cash balances. Even if the accounting system is very informal, an organization can benefit from computerization if it has a large work force, numerous suppliers or customers, or a large inventory system. One or more of these situations are often found in small organizations. For example, a small CPA firm of 20 professionals may have several hundred clients. Thus a computerized receivables system might provide many benefits to the firm.

These and many other factors peculiar to a given organization might need to be considered before installing a small computer system. Before proceeding with a computer acquisition, make sure that a real need exists and can be cost justified.

Systems Analysis and Design

Although the owners or managers of a small organization might have reasonably good ideas concerning their needs, obtaining someone to examine the system who has a systems design background is usually preferable. Regardless of who does the systems analysis, it should be performed before any major changes are made.

The existing system should be examined in order to understand exactly how it is currently functioning. Operating activities may need to be changed before any attempt is made to computerize the existing system. Computerizing a bad system will only produce bad results more quickly, not better results. During this phase of evaluation a listing of changes should be made, along with any additional controls that will be necessary for the new system.

After the analysis has been made, the changes and controls must be evaluated to determine what improvements are essential before the new system is implemented. Generally, only the most serious weaknesses are corrected during the initial installation phase of the new system. As the system becomes operational the other improvements are made so as not to cause major disruptions to the system in the future.

Next, the software packages best suited for the immediate needs are selected. The more popular packages are available for most hardware configurations, therefore, concentrate on software first and hardware second. After the software needs are determined, the appropriate hardware is then selected.

After the basic package has been assembled, have a meeting of the users to get their ideas about the proposal. During such sessions priorities often change and new ideas are developed that will help improve the system. Because small organizations are close-knit, whether or not they want to be, the support of all key personnel should be obtained. One department, group, or powerful individual can wreak havoc on a small computerized system. Everyone does not have to agree to everything, but everyone does need to support the concept being undertaken. People are the cause of many system failures because people run the system; the computer only follows instructions of the people. Those closest to the system (the major users) must want the system, be willing to learn the system, and, most importantly, be willing to adapt to the new system and the ever changing environment.

Additional items that may be included on the design checklist are:

1. Amount of growth expected and considerations given to growth
2. Evaluation of future needs excluding growth
3. Considerations for leasing rather than purchasing
4. Inclusion of clear audit trails, essential for many purposes other than auditing
5. Backup systems available in immediate geographic area—either the vendors or other businesses with the same type of system will suffice

Installation

A plan of implementation for small computer systems should be developed where the various components and packages are installed over an interval of several weeks or months. The implementation plan must be closely monitored to ensure proper acceptance and operating results. Because extensive training is usually not necessary with such systems, the overall process should be completed in a few months.

There are two popular approaches to the implementation of small business systems. Many people like to install the easiest system first so that by the time they get to the most difficult one, their experience with the preceding packages will make the last system a little easier. This also builds confidence that the system does work. The other approach is to install the most beneficial system first, even if it is the most difficult. This method gives management early assurance that the right decision was made to install the new system, assuming everything works of course.

As might be expected, the software training associated with the new systems is much more difficult than the hardware training. Because of strong vendor competition, the small system configurations have been increasingly easier to operate over the last few years. Although the user friendliness of software has improved, many packages are still very difficult to learn and even more difficult to modify to the needs of particular users. More time and training are needed with software than hardware because there are usually more software users and they are usually less experienced than the people operating the hardware.

Where possible, a new application should be operated parallel with the old system that it was designed to replace. Normally, the parallel process should not take very long. Many analysts recommend only one month, provided one complete cycle can be made. Most cycles, however, take about one quarter to complete so that a variety of activities can take place.

Evaluation and Review

Periodic evaluations and reviews of any operating system must be made. Controls in small systems sometimes get left behind in the rush to implement all of the packages. Things go wrong in small systems just as they do in large systems and controls are no less important. Many of the controls discussed in Chapter Six are applicable to any system, regardless of size.

After the system has been operational for some time, it must be reviewed for relevance to the current needs of the organization. Flexibility is an advantage of most small systems, and change should be undertaken as needed. If the organization is growing, there may be a need to add a larger system or other small systems. Many organizations prefer several small systems that can be integrated, or just connected, rather than a larger, more inflexible system.

ACCOUNTING CONTROLS AS RELATED TO INFORMATION SYSTEMS

There are several specific control areas that must be discussed within the context of microcomputers. Internal controls relating to accounting systems and accounting data are the responsibility of the accounting and internal auditing departments. Since many accountants consider microcomputers to be used strictly on a departmental basis, the controls are often ignored until some unfortunate incident, such as employee theft, occurs. Although controls for both large and small organizations are important, the area surrounding the use of microcomputers in large organizations can be very critical because these systems are often tied to the organization's primary data base and used as input and output devices. Through such access, many careless and fraudulent activities take place. These aspects of controls are discussed in Chapter Seven where the emphasis is placed on the auditing of information systems.

Control of a microcomputer setup should relate to matters such as data integrity, organization plan, safeguarding of assets, and systems interfaces. Protection of the data base is important because of its confidentiality and the need for reliable and accurate data. The scope of the controls surrounding such a system should have a cost benefit relationship to the risks involved in the exposure and accessibility of the data to many organizational units. To the extent that a given risk is very high, there should be related controls to assure management that the system is properly secured and protected. Exposures to risks that must be considered in a microcomputer setting include:

1. Theft of sensitive information
2. Destruction of data/information necessary for operations
3. Data manipulation
4. Unauthorized access by persons within the organization
5. Incompatibility of system with other operating elements.

Evaluation of these five areas should be part of the developmental stage, not an after-the-fact consideration. This matter will be expanded under the general control sections of the next chapter.

An additional risk that is seldom associated with large computers is that of equipment theft. Most small systems can be easily carried by one person, and much of the software can be placed in briefcases and easily smuggled out of the organization. Securing (bolting) the equipment to a work station may help solve part of the problem, but this eliminates the desirable portability of the computer. If portability is important, the best control approach is probably to provide a secure location with limited access during working hours and tight security during nonworking hours. Extensive control may also be required for the various diskettes and software packages used by the system. Most of the controls that relate to microcomputers also relate to the on-line terminals of larger systems.

BUSINESS SOFTWARE AND APPLICATIONS

Applications for small business systems are very diverse and continue to evolve as computer technology advances. Not only can present computers store relatively large amounts of information, they can retrieve it quickly. In addition to the accounting applications discussed in this chapter, other popular applications include financial modeling, forecasting, word processing and telecommunications.

The expanding area of telecommunications is also having a major impact on accounting because it greatly enhances the electronic transfer of data from one place to another. Once fully developed, a microcomputer system with telecommunication capabilities can provide users with access to multiple data bases. These bases can include: (1) industrial financial data, (2) market statistics, and (3) economic statistics and trends.

Transaction Processing Network

The goal of small organizations generally is to have all financial transactions processed in a common network. In most systems this network is centered around the general ledger system with a basic transaction register or journal, a detailed and summary trial balance, an income statement, and a balance sheet. The following brief discussion of the Prater Manufacturing Company highlights many of the characteristics found in a basic general ledger system for a small organization. The basic general ledger system in most organizations comprises: (1) a chart of accounts; (2) a set of master file records; (3) a transaction register or journal; (4) a detailed listing of all transactions; (5) automatic interface with other systems such as accounts receivable, payroll, and inventory; and (6) a set of reports such as trial balance, departmental accounting statements, and comparative financial statements.

Prater Manufacturing Company transactions occur randomly during the day and each category of transactions may be printed out in a transaction register such as that illustrated in Figure 5.2. This register contains all the cash disbursements of March 9, 1986 and provides a general description of each activity, the account involved, the amount, and the total transactions for the period. A transaction register may be provided on a monthly, quarterly, or annual basis to give full details of all activities affecting each account. This register provides a permanent record of activities and an audit trail for control purposes.

Another purpose of the transaction register is to provide a hard copy file of account maintenance, showing all accounts as they were updated, changed, and deleted through the account maintenance program. From the transaction register, a detailed trial balance is provided as shown in Figure 5.3. The detail trial balance program utilized by Prater Manufacturing separates the general ledger by account number and shows all activities that took place during the period for each account number. Although an abbreviated listing is given for Prater Manufacturing, it should be easy to realize the convenience of such a report in balancing and comparing accounts at the end of each reporting period. The system used by this company also allows adjusting entries to be made at the end of the period with sufficient room for explanations as required.

The information system provides a monthly balance sheet with subsidiary schedules as necessary and an income statement with month-to-date and year-to-date figures and with ratios of all activities as a percent of sales. These reports are shown in Figures 5.4 and 5.5.

The Accounts Receivable System

The general ledger system usually relates to several subsystems such as accounts payable, payroll, and inventory. For illustration purposes, however, only the accounts receivable system for Prater Manufacturing will be used. The basic printout for this system is illustrated in Figure 5.6 in which details of the current accounts are shown. This report includes the vital characteristics of credit limit, year-to-date activities, and current balance. The amount of detail and information in such a system can be determined by the organization, although many of the features are preprogrammed. The overall general ledger system ties the activities of the accounts receivable system with the general ledger accounts receivable master file, the inventory and sales accounts, and the operating cash account. This greatly facilitates the reconciliation process at the end of each period between cash receipts and the changes in the general ledger accounts receivable and sales files.

Also integrated with the accounts receivable system is a periodic aged receivables report, see Figure 5.7. This report provides management with an analysis of the collection process and aids in controlling sales to delinquent customers.

For billing purposes Prater Manufacturing has a computerized invoice and monthly

PRATER MANUFACTURING COMPANY
GENERAL LEDGER
TRANSACTIONS CONTROL REPORT

SOURCE CODE: 2   CASH DISBURSEMENTS

ENTRY SESSION 6

LN	REF	DATE	DESCRIPTION	ACCOUNT	AMOUNT
01	001	03/09/86	THE NEWS AND COURIER	36800	$ 550.00
02	002	03/09/86	A T & T	36800	1,500.00
03	002	03/09/86	A T & T	42600	225.00
04	003	03/09/86	STATE FARM INSURANCE	53300	400.00
05	004	03/09/86	AMERICAN FREIGHT	33400	4,200.00
06	005	03/09/86	ACCOUNTS PAYABLE, MISC.	20300	15,000.00
07	006	03/09/86	CENTRAL TELEPHONE	36600	315.00
08	007	03/09/86	DICKENS CONSTRUCTION	68100	875.00
09	008	03/09/86	UPS	50200	25.00
10	009	03/09/86	DREWS FIBERS	38450	50,000.00
11	009	03/09/86	DREWS FIBERS	38500	26,000.00
12	010	03/09/86	AMERICAN LUMBER	35200	111,000.00
13	010	03/09/86	AMERICAN LUMBER	38500	45,000.00
14	019	03/09/86	CASH	10000	255,090.00—

TOTALS:	TRANSACTIONS	14		BALANCE	$0.00
	DEBITS	$255,090.00		CONTROL	$255,090.00
	CREDITS	$255,090.00—		TOTALS	$255,090.00
BATCH:	TRANSACTIONS	14		TOTALS	$0.00
DIFFERENCE:	TRANSACTIONS	0			

END OF TRANSACTIONS CONTROL REPORT

Figure 5.2

PRATER MANUFACTURING COMPANY
GENERAL LEDGER
DETAIL TRIAL BALANCE
PERIOD ENDING 03/31/86

NUMBER	ACCOUNT DESCRIPTION	BEGINNING BALANCE	DESCRIPTION	TRANSACTION DATE	REF	AMOUNT	ENDING BALANCE
1003	CASH, OPERATING	$ 61,500.00	COLLECTIONS	03/01/86	A/R	$ 30,000.00	
			CASH SALES	03/05/86	021	37,863.31	
			DISBURSEMENTS	03/09/86	019	255,090.00—	
			COLLECTIONS	03/14/86	A/R	14,063.69	
			COLLECTIONS	03/21/86	A/R	88,500.00	
			CASH SALES	03/22/86	141	40,000.00	
			COLLECTIONS	03/24/86	A/R	107,128.00	
			COLLECTIONS	03/28/86	A/R	38,200.00	
			DISBURSEMENTS	03/29/86	046	52,505.00—	109,660.00
1010	PETTY CASH	100.00				0.00	100.00
1112	ACCOUNTS RECEIVABLE	105,255.00	A&B FURNITURE	03/14/86	121	14,063.69—	
			BARGAIN TOWN	03/08/86		90,000.00	
			BARGAIN TOWN	03/21/86	138	90,000.00—	
			BOWER'S INC.	03/01/86	026	30,000.00—	
			BOWER'S INC.	03/28/86	279	10,000.00—	
			CONTEMPORARY'S LTD	03/06/86		12,500.00	
			CONTEMPORARY'S LTD	03/12/86		3,000.00	
			CONTEMPORARY'S LTD	03/28/86	280	21,000.00—	
			DALTON INDUSTRIES	03/12/86		74,728.00	
			DALTON INDUSTRIES	03/24/86	201	74,728.00—	
			HABERSHAM'S INTERIORS	03/14/86	206	32,408.69	
			HABERSHAM'S INTERIORS	03/24/86	206	32,400.00—	
			J.P. HAVERLY CO.	03/28/86	286	7,200.00—	$48,500.00
1121	PREPAID EXPENSES	2,325.00	INSURANCE EXPENSE	03/31/86	037	325.00—	2,000.00

NUMBER	ACCOUNT DESCRIPTION	BEGINNING BALANCE	DESCRIPTION	TRANSACTION DATE	REF	AMOUNT	ENDING BALANCE
3000	SALES	270,000.00	CASH	03/05/86		37,863.31	
			CONTEMPORARY'S LTD	03/06/86	021	12,500.00	
			BARGAIN TOWN	03/08/86		90,000.00	
			CONTEMPORARY'S LTD	03/12/86		3,000.00	
			DALTON INDUSTRIES	03/12/86		74,728.00	
			HABERSHAM'S INTERIORS	03/14/86		32,408.69	
			CASH	03/22/86	083	40,000.00	560,500.00 −
3100	SALES RETURNS	5,000.00	BARGAIN TOWN	03/16/86	016	1,500.00	6,500.00
4000	SALARIES	25,000.00	MONTHLY PAYROLL	03/15/86		12,500.00	37,500.00
4100	PAYROLL TAXES	2,750.00	MONTHLY EXPENSE	03/15/86		1,375.00	4,125.00
5000	RENT	1,500.00	PIEDMONT INVESTMENT	03/31/86		750.00	2,250.00
5100	UTILITIES	875.00	POWER COOPERATIVE	03/22/86	132	875.00	1,750.00
5150	TELEPHONE	325.00	CITIZENS TELEPHONE	03/27/86	132	315.00	640.00
5200	ADVERTISING	250.00	GREENMAN AGENCY	03/14/86		2,050.00	2,300.00
5300	INSURANCE	0.00	PREPAID EXPENSES	03/31/86	037	325.00	4,325.00

TOTAL DEBITS	820,067.00		659,382.00	1,479,449.00
TOTAL CREDITS	820,067.00 −		659,382.00 −	1,479,449.00 −
DIFFERENCE	0.00		0.00	0.00

	CONTROL	ACTUAL
CONTROL TOTALS		
TRANSACTION COUNT	43	43
TRANSACTION TOTAL	0.00	0.00

Figure 5.3

RATIO: 290500	THIS MONTH	RATIO	3 MONTHS	RATIO
INCOME				
SALES	290,500.00	100.0	560,500.00	100.0
RETURNS AND ALLOWANCES	1,500.00	0.5	6,500.00	1.2
NET SALES	289,000.00	99.5	554,000.00	98.8
COST OF GOODS SOLD				
BEGINNING INVENTORY	35,000.00	12.0	15,000.00	2.7
COST OF GOODS MFG.	187,000.00	64.4	337,000.00	60.1
FREIGHT-IN	4,200.00	1.4	11,200.00	2.0
COST OF GOODS AVAILABLE	226,200.00	77.9	363,200.00	64.8
LESS: ENDING INVENTORY	45,000.00	15.5	45,000.00	8.0
COST OF GOODS SOLD	181,200.00	62.4	318,200.00	56.8
GROSS PROFIT	107,800.00	37.1	235,800.00	42.0
OPERATING EXPENSES				
SALARIES	12,500.00	4.3	37,500.00	6.7
PAYROLL TAXES	1,375.00	0.5	4,125.00	0.7
RENT	750.00	0.3	2,250.00	0.4
OFFICE EXPENSES	0.00	0.0	900.00	0.2
UTILITIES EXPENSE	875.00	0.3	1,750.00	0.3
TELEPHONE	315.00	0.1	640.00	0.1
ADVERTISING	2,050.00	0.7	2,300.00	0.4
INSURANCE	325.00	0.1	4,325.00	0.8
PROFESSIONAL FEES	300.00	0.1	600.00	0.1
DEPRECIATION	8,667.00	3.0	17,334.00	3.1
MISCELLANEOUS EXPENSES	25.00	0.0	125.00	0.0
TOTAL OPERATING EXPENSES	27,182.00	9.4	71,849.00	12.8
OTHER INCOME/EXPENSES				
INTEREST EXPENSE	1,000.00	0.3	3,300.00	0.6
TOTAL OTHER INCOME/EXP.	1,000.00	0.3	3,300.00	0.6
NET INCOME BEFORE TAXES	79,618.00	27.4	160,651.00	28.6
INCOME TAXES	0.00	0.0	2,500.00	0.4
NET INCOME	79,618.00	27.4	158,151.00	28.2

Figure 5.4

statement program. By simply entering the customer number and sales information, the invoice program creates an invoice with all the necessary details concerning the customer and the sales transactions. At the end of each month the system also generates statements for all customers. These two reporting features are great time-savers in most small organizations where these activities are normally performed manually.

This illustration of the Prater Manufacturing Company shows that even a small company can have a fairly sophisticated reporting system. The overall characteristics of the established formats, input requirements, processing needs, and reports of any subsystem for a small manufacturing company are no different from those presented in Chapters Ten through Nineteen for large companies. The only exceptions are that they are smaller in size and do not have the large volume of transactions. These systems can do the same things except that they operate on a smaller scale, perform the processing steps a little more slowly, and create different types of master files for the system.

APPLICATIONS FOR SERVICE ORGANIZATIONS

Although most of this chapter has been devoted to general applications needed for the typical organization, service and not-for-profit organizations cannot be ignored. The following discussions exemplify firms in that category, using a small CPA firm as an example. Although each type of service industry is different, a small CPA firm provides an example that is typical among attorneys and consulting firms.

Characteristics of Service Organizations

The characteristics distinguishing separate service and not-for-profit organizations from other organizations include: lack of salable inventory, difficulties in measuring output quantities and qualities, much smaller average size, and the large percentage of professional employees. Not-for-profit organizations can have the additional distinguishing characteristics of political emphasis on pleasing constituents, or a higher authority, and the absence of a profit motive.

Of the foregoing characteristics, perhaps the most significant one from an information systems perspective is the lack of salable inventory. This makes a substantial difference in the organization of the information systems because the transformation process (conversion of raw material into finished products) is the center of activity in many other types of organizations. Without this transformation process, the cost accounting system is distinctly different, controls take on a completely different emphasis, and the valuation process is usually much simpler.

With these obstacles removed from the information system, the adaption of microcomputer and small business computer processing is much simpler. The types of inventory these organizations have—supplies, merchandise bought for resale, food supplies in a restaurant, and medicine in a hospital—simply flow into and out of stock without the need to employ some type of product costing process. This does not make inventory control any easier, but it does make the accounting process a lot less complicated.

To offset the absence of inventory processing in these types of organizations, the complication of measuring the outputs (except in the case of retail organizations) challenges the information systems designers. Outputs of hospitals, police departments, even CPA firms, can be difficult to define and measure. When intangible products (services) are provided, problems with quantity and quality standards usually exist.

These problems do not all have to be solved before a small computer is installed, because many of the basic functions discussed in the previous sections (accounts payable, accounts receivable, payrolls, and budgets) can be easily placed in a computerized

RUN DATE 03/31/86

PRATER MANUFACTURING CO.
GENERAL LEDGER
BALANCE SHEET
AS OF 03/31/86

ASSETS

CURRENT ASSETS		
CASH	109,760.00	
ACCOUNTS RECEIVABLE	48,500.00	
PREPAID EXPENSES	2,000.00	
INVENTORY	45,000.00	
TOTAL CURRENT ASSETS		205,260.00
FIXED ASSETS		
OFFICE FURN. & EQUIP.	20,000.00	
PLANT EQUIPMENT	500,000.00	
ACCUMULATED DEPRECIATION	17,334.00—	
TOTAL FIXED ASSETS		502,666.00
TOTAL ASSETS		707,926.00

LIABILITIES AND STOCKHOLDERS' EQUITY

CURRENT LIABILITIES		
ACCOUNTS PAYABLE	45,000.00	
TAXES PAYABLE	4,875.00	
TOTAL CURRENT LIABILITIES		49,875.00
LONG-TERM LIABILITIES		
NOTE PAYABLE—BANK	272,000.00	
TOTAL LONG-TERM LIAB.		272,000.00
STOCKHOLDERS' EQUITY		
COMMON STOCK, $1.00 PAR,		
45,000 SHARES AUTHORIZED		
ISSUED AND OUTSTANDING	45,000.00	
RETAINED EARNINGS	182,900.00	
CURRENT EARNINGS	158,151.00	
TOTAL STOCKHOLDERS' EQTY.		386,051.00
TOTAL LIAB. & EQUITY		707,926.00

SUBSIDIARY SCHEDULE

CASH	
CASH—OPERATING	109,660.00
PETTY CASH	100.00
	109,760.00
ACCOUNTS RECEIVABLE	
A & B FURNITURE	9,009.54
ABE FURNITURE	1,004.00
BOWER'S INC.	77.00
CONTEMPORARY'S LTD.	23,187.81
HABERSHAM'S INTERIORS	8.69
J.P. HAVERLY CO.	14,847.25
LINDSEY COMPANY	365.71
	$ 48,500.00

Figure 5.5

RUN DATE 03/31/86 PRATER MANUFACTURING COMPANY
ACCOUNTS RECEIVABLE
CUSTOMER ACCOUNT LIST

CUST. ACCOUNT	NAME-ADDRESS	TYPE	SHIP CODE	TERMS CODE	TAX CODE
2106	A&B FURNITURE 4718 JONESBORO RD. WEST PARK, GA. 30030 404/366-1567	REGULAR	1	0	1
1481	ABE FURNITURE 118 PEACHTREE ST. SW ATLANTA, GA. 30330 404/524-5267	REGULAR	0	1	1
2119	BARGAIN TOWN 1270 CUSTER AVE. IRMO, SC 29210 803/998-4758	ASSIGNED	3	4	3
2312	BOWER'S INC. 168 MITCHELL ST. CUMMING, WV 20131 804/767-5080	REGULAR	0	0	3
4116	CONTEMPORARY'S LTD 4605 WEST BATTLE AVE. ATLANTA, GA. 30309 404/884-5589	TRIAL	0	3	1
4821	DALTON INDUSTRIES 6500 MAIN ST. AUBURN, AL 39861 205/326-1009	REGULAR	0	0	3
8204	HABERSHAM'S INTERIORS 6102 ORANGE ST. ASHVILLE, NC 27801 206/588-1598	TRIAL	3	2	3
1693	J. P. HAVERLY CO. 206 EDGEWOOD AVE. NW WHIT, TENN. 37301 301/521-6625	REGULAR	0	0	1
7760	LINDSEY COMPANY 6104 ELLIOT ST. TUCKER, SC 29201 803/939-2432	REGULAR	2	1	2
	TOTAL				

END OF CUSTOMER ACCOUNT LIST

Figure 5.6

DISC. %	CREDIT LIMIT	ACTIVITY	DATE	AMOUNT
2.00	50,000.00	BEGINNING BALANCE		23,073.23
		PAYMENT	03/14/86	14,063.69—
		ENDING BALANCE		9,009.54
0.00	50,000.00	BEGINNING BALANCE		1,004.00
		ENDING BALANCE		1,004.00
0.00	150,000.00	BEGINNING BALANCE		0.00
		SALES INVOICE 002019	03/08/86	90,000.00
		RETURNS	03/16/86	1,500.00—
		PAYMENT	03/21/86	88,500.00—
		ENDING BALANCE		0.00
2.00	150,000.00	BEGINNING BALANCE		40,077.00
		PAYMENT	03/01/86	30,000.00—
		PAYMENT	03/28/86	10,000.00—
		ENDING BALANCE		77.00
1.50	50,000.00	BEGINNING BALANCE		28,687.81
		SALES INVOICE 002001	03/06/86	12,500.00
		SALES INVOICE 002020	03/12/86	3,000.00
		PAYMENT	03/28/86	21,000.00—
		ENDING BALANCE		23,187.81
0.00	150,000.00	BEGINNING BALANCE		0.00
		SALES INVOICE 002121	03/12/86	74,728.00
		PAYMENT	03/24/86	74,728.00—
		ENDING BALANCE		0.00
1.00	50,000.00	BEGINNING BALANCE		0.00
		SALES INVOICE 002123	03/14/86	32,408.69
		PAYMENT	03/24/86	32,400.00—
		ENDING BALANCE		8.69
2.00	25,000.00	BEGINNING BALANCE		12,047.25
		PAYMENT	03/28/86	7,200.00—
		ENDING BALANCE		14,847.25
0.00	50,000.00	BEGINNING BALANCE		365.71
		ENDING BALANCE		365.71
				48,500.00

Figure 5.6 (cont'd)

RUN DATE 03/31/86   PRATER MANUFACTURING COMPANY
ACCOUNTS RECEIVABLE
DETAILED AGED RECEIVABLES REPORT

ACCOUNT	CUSTOMER NAME	PHONE	INVOICE	DUE DATE
2106	A&B FURNITURE	404/366-1567	002002	12/31/85
1481	ABE FURNITURE	404/524-5267	001077	04/30/85
2312	BOWER'S INC.	804/767-5080	000841	03/02/84
			001090	04/30/85
4116	CONTEMPORARY'S LTD	404/884-5589	002001	04/06/86
			002020	04/12/86
			001974	02/28/86
8204	HABERSHAM'S INTERIORS	206/588-1598		
1693	J.P. HAVERLY CO.	301/521-6625	001941	01/31/86
7760	LINDSEY COMPANY	803/939-2432	000982	07/03/85
			000896	04/30/84
	TOTALS			

END OF DETAILED AGED RECEIVABLES REPORT

Figure 5.7

mode. These applications are similar in all types of organizations, although budgeting takes on a different role in the not-for-profit organizations.

Applications for a Small CPA Firm

CPA firms have most of the characteristics discussed in the previous section. They have no salable inventories, a high percentage of professional employees, and an output that can be difficult to measure. Although our discussion here is limited to small CPA firms, it should be noted that many large CPA firms have recently begun to install microcomputers in their individual offices to enhance client relationships and to improve overall performance through the advantages that these systems can offer.

Whether any service organization is better off with microcomputers is best determined by the use made of the system. Simply by having a small computer, the CPA firm may be better able to relate to its clients who also have similar systems. The clients can be advised on a first-hand basis. No client ever likes to be the test case.

Another client-related use is the application of spreadsheet analysis while talking with the client about activities such as investments, budgeting, and sales mix analysis. The simulations can be made instantly while the CPA and the client are discussing the future of its operations. Providing instant projections to various alternatives is always impressive for the client that still has a manual system.

With the increasing management advisory services that CPAs are providing, the

CURRENT	1–30	31–60	OVER 60	TOTAL
			9,009.54	9,009.54
			1,004.00	1,004.00
		40.00		
		37.00		77.00
12,500.00				
3,000.00				
	7,687.81			23,187.81
8.69				8.69
		14,847.25		14,847.25
			362.49	
			3.22	365.71
15,508.69	7,687.81	14,847.25	10,456.25	48,500.00

Figure 5.7 (cont'd)

microcomputer also has numerous applications. Feasibility studies (e.g., budgets and pro forma statements) can be greatly enhanced by the use of spreadsheet programs. If a project is not feasible at one level, it takes only a second to see if it is feasible at another level. Other consulting activities that can benefit from microcomputer applications include production schedules and mixes, capital budgeting, time-series analysis, marketing strategies, and inventory modeling.

Administratively, the firm could use the microcomputer for billing, word processing, personnel scheduling, meetings and presentations, and keeping employee time sheets by client. Data management software programs are very popular among CPA firms. They enable the firm to perform a variety of functions such as maintaining mailing lists, providing labels of any sort, writing reports, and keeping all general files in order. Also important for client relations is the use of such programs for *deadline ticklers.* With a variety of clients having multitudes of reporting deadlines, the tickler provides a periodic (usually weekly) report that lists clients that have reports due in the coming weeks or months. The lead time can vary with the complexity of the report due.

Each CPA firm must select the software packages that are best for its needs. Packages other than those mentioned previously that are frequently found in small firms are tax planning packages, tax preparing programs, graphics, general ledger, and various types of financial spreadsheets.

Because of the need to maintain the best client relations possible, every small CPA firm should strive to maintain an operating status on the cutting edge of business technology. Would you engage a CPA firm that was two years behind in its update of federal tax laws? Why then should you go to a firm that was using ten-year-old computer technology and information systems applications?

KEYS TO SUCCESS

Computerized systems have much potential to assist small organizations in the successful operations of their activities. Better cost data, more timely information, improved accuracy, and better management reporting are all potential benefits of a computerized system. For a successful system, it is necessary that several fundamental factors be considered.

1. Software that reflects, or can accommodate, the organization's unique requirements
2. Hardware capacity and performance to handle the level of transaction and processing requirements
3. Appropriate data processing and account controls
4. Proper documentation of user and data processing procedures
5. Adequate training for user and data processing personnel
6. Accurate input and the controls to maintain it
7. Acceptance by users
8. Management involvement and support

SUMMARY

There are many ways an information system can be established for a small organization. Today's small computer technology makes it advantageous to consider using the computer in the smallest organizations. Applications for these computers vary from the simple to the complex and from accounting to production. Also, because of the price ranges, most organizations can afford a computer.

As with information systems in general, the first applications to be placed on these small computers are usually basic accounting functions. The next development phase usually includes the financial spreadsheets for sensitivity analysis in budgeting and other planning areas such as production and marketing.

When designing these small computer systems, one must consider several characteristics of small organizations. These include: lack of computer expertise within the organization, limited applications, lack of financial resources, and lack of an existing information system. Once these limitations have been considered, the phases of implementation begin. For most situations follow-through with each phase is important to ensure a properly functioning system upon completion.

Small computer systems are the trend of the future for small organizations, whether manufacturing, retailing, service, or not-for-profit. Because the computer gives most organizations an operating advantage, organizations should consider the implementation of at least partial computerization.

SELECTED REFERENCES

Anderson, James, and Wendy S. Sternick. "The Computer and You," *The Practical Accountant* (May 1984): 43–46.

Berliner, Harold, and Marvin Galland. "Microcomputers for the Uninitiated," *Management Focus* (May–June 1980): 3–7.

Dascher, Paul E., and W. Ken Harmon. "Assessing Microcomputer Risks and Controls for Clients," *CPA Journal* (May 1984): 37–41.

Goldberg, Victor, and Russell Gowland. "How to Select and Install a Minicomputer," *World* (Winter 1980): 7–11.

Heintz, Carl. "Seeking Solutions with Spreadsheets," *Interface Age* (September 1983): 52–54.

Konkel, Gilbert J. "Word Processing and the Office of the Future," *The Arthur Young Quarterly* (Winter 1982): 2–9.

Krippaehne, Thomas M. "The Right Way to Select a Microcomputer," *Today's Executive* (Spring/Summer 1982): 12–19.

Leitch, Robert A., and K. Roscoe Davis, *Accounting Information Systems.* Englewood Cliffs, N.J.: Prentice-Hall, Inc., 1983.

Muscove, Stephen A., and Mark G. Simkin. *Accounting Information Systems.* New York: John Wiley & Sons, 1984.

Person, Stanley. "A Microcomputer in a Small CPA Firm," *CPA Journal* (March 1984): 20–25.

Shuster, Harvey L., and Paul D. Warner. "Micros for Small Business: The Time is Now," *Management Accounting* (March 1984): 45–48.

Worthy, Ford S. "Here Come the Go-Anywhere Computers," *Fortune* (October 17, 1983): 9–11.

Wynne, Robert, and Alan Frotman. "Microcomputers: Helping Make Practice Perfect," *Journal of Accountancy* (December 1981): 34–39.

QUESTIONS

1. Explain or define the following:

   Microcomputers   Service organization characteristics

   Accounting computers   Not-for-profit organization characteristics

   Minicomputers   Deadline ticklers

   Operator-oriented systems

   File-oriented systems

2. What small business characteristics must be considered when deciding whether or not to install a microcomputer?

3. Explain the major phases in the systems analysis of a small organization considering installing a computerized system.

4. In addition to the basic considerations in the analysis and design of a small computer system, what other items are often considered?

5. Explain the two popular approaches to computer systems implementation. What are the reasons for choosing either method?

6. What type of items are considered in the evaluation and review phase of a new computerized system?

7. Develop a table showing the differences among the microcomputer, business microcomputer, and minicomputer characteristics.

8. In what type of situations are file-oriented and operator-oriented systems justified?

9. What are the keys of success in computerizing a small business's operations?

10. What are the differences among service organizations, not-for-profit organizations, and all other organizations?

11. From an accounting perspective, what is the greatest difference between service and manufacturing organizations?

12. What characteristic of service organizations is more difficult to handle than with other types of organizations?

13. What are some of the major applications for small computer systems in a small service organization?

14. In what ways can a small CPA firm make use of microcomputers?

PROBLEMS

15. Chart of Accounts

Happy Time Company is a wholesale distributor of baby furniture and accessories. All of its sales are on credit, with many of its customers on an installment basis. Its sales categories are classified as: beds, other furniture, and accessories. The company deals with 36 vendors that supply various types of inventory.

From its home office in Augusta, Georgia, Happy Time controls three warehouses; one in Augusta, one in Mobile, Alabama, and one in Baltimore, Maryland. It also has three sales districts with headquarters in each of the three cities. All purchases are handled at the home office, with shipments from most suppliers made directly to the warehouse where the goods are needed. Except in emergencies, each sales territory sells and delivers the goods that it has available in its own warehouse.

The company owns all of its buildings as well as vehicles for its salespeople and top executives. It also has a fleet of delivery trucks that are located at each warehouse. The company has three garages that perform maintenance on all vehicles.

At each sales district there is a sales manager, office manager, and 10 to 15 traveling salespeople. In the warehouse there is a warehouse foreman and several employees who act as loading and shipping clerks and one inventory control clerk. The vehicle maintenance shops have a foreman and several mechanics. The home office is made up of the president and his staff, an accounting department, a purchasing department which also does inventory control for the entire company, and a marketing and sales analysis department.

Required:
    a. Design a chart of accounts that will provide appropriate data for the financial statements of Happy Time.
    b. List the source documents, journals, and ledgers that should be used.

16. Analysis and Chart of Accounts for Microcomputers

Magnetic Music has two stores in a large city and each one is located across the street from a high school. Each store has two major product lines. One is records and tapes and the other is school supplies. Diana and Doreen are the owners of the company and each manages one of the stores. Each store has four sales clerks, two stock clerks, two cashiers, and a janitor. In the original store there is also a purchasing department, an accounting department, and an inventory control department. Each of these departments consists of two people.

The company buys from 143 vendors and each store has approximately 2,000 inventory items, with each record and tape counted as a separate item for control purposes. All sales are for cash or credit card. The company has two bank accounts: one for payroll and the other for operating activities.

All of the furniture, fixtures, and display counters are owned but the buildings are leased. The company also owns a van which is used to transport materials between the two stores.

All purchases of merchandise are on account and payments are made within 30 days unless there is an allowable discount. Also, some of the records and tapes are sold on consignment. The company carries a line of credit with its bank which is used to stock up on inventory at the beginning of each school year. After the initial sales rush is over, all short-term borrowings are repaid. The company is currently keeping its financial statements on a cash basis but desires to convert to an accrual basis at year-end when it installs a microcomputer system.

Required:
  a. Evaluate the microcomputer needs of the company. Be sure to include both hardware and software.
  b. Design an inventory and sales report to show the status of inventory items. Select the type of reporting period you desire (daily, weekly, monthly, etc.)
  c. Design a coded chart of accounts for the system you have recommended.

17. Computer System Configurations

Owl Ceramic Company is a manufacturer of ceramic figurines. It has approximately 60 different varieties of figurines, most of which are owls. It sells only to wholesale distributors and all sales are on credit. The company owns all of its building and equipment and has approximately 50 employees in the manufacturing division. The marketing group is made up of a manager and three traveling salespeople.

Because of the recent popularity of owls, the business has been growing faster than the production department can produce the desired quantities. Although most sales orders are being filled, the delivery dates are sometimes 30 days behind schedule. Because many of their orders are custom designed based on color and size, the overall production process is about half job order and half for inventory stock. The manufacturing status is very difficult to determine because of poor control at the input point of queuing orders for production.

The company has a small office staff with two accountants and several clerks that keep up with payroll, production, production orders, accounts payable, and accounts receivable. The company has only about 14 raw material suppliers and about 10 suppliers of other items such as office equipment and supplies.

Sales in 19X5 totaled $2,000,000 and income was $40,000 after taxes. This represents an increase averaging 14 percent a year for the last 3 years.

Required:
- **a.** Determine an appropriate computer system configuration for Owl Ceramics.
- **b.** Evaluate whether or not the programs for Owl Ceramics should be purchased or tailor-made.
- **c.** Explain what can be done to help improve the control over the production process, especially the status of jobs in process.

18. Cash Control and Systems Analysis

City Bicycles is a chain of stores located in Sun City, Florida. Each location carries a full line of bicycles and supplies. Because the bicycle market is especially competitive during the vacation/tourist season, each shop has a rental fleet of approximately 50 bicycles. During this season the company places its top priority on customer service. For the rental equipment, the customers are sure that if a breakdown occurs, a bike will be brought to them within 30 minutes. For the retail sales, the store carries an extended warranty and assures each customer that they will provide a repair service and a complete inventory of parts with 24-hour service during the tourist season.

All sales are for cash or credit card and all accounts from vendors are paid on a net 30-day basis. The accounting and office staff consist of one accountant, one bookkeeper, and two clerks. Each store location has a manager and two permanent cashiers. Additional cashiers are added during the busy season.

Except during the busy season, the store managers are able to keep track of their inventory parts and the status of their rental bikes. However, during peak seasons they often run out of rental bikes as well as of replacement parts. As a result of stock-outs, lost sales frequently occur and much of their repeat business has begun to diminish. The company has also been having a problem with cash flow because of the need to replenish inventory during the slow season when few funds are available. During the peak season the company generally has excess cash which stays in the checking account. Each store makes the cash deposits into one common account and separate cash receipts by store are not maintained. Also during the peak season there is not enough time to reconcile the cash drawers and the sales receipts on a daily basis. Estimates are made at the end of each week as to the amount of sales made and rental revenue.

Required:
- **a.** Make a recommendation to the company as to how its information system can be improved with computerized applications.
- **b.** Determine the primary software needs of the company.
- **c.** Discuss how the cash control situation may be improved through the use of a computerized system.
- **d.** Evaluate the benefits to be gained from computerizing the inventory system.

19. Financial Modeling

Macon Sales Corporation has encountered difficulties in estimating its cash flows for the last few years. This has caused rather strained relations with its banker. The company would like to develop a means by which improved forecasts can be made to plan the company's monthly operating cash flows. The following data were gathered to facilitate cash forecasting and planning:

a. Sales are expected to increase 0.5 percent each month.
b. Of each month's sales, 30 percent are for cash and 70 percent are on account.
c. Of credit sales, 80 percent are collected during the first month following the sale and 20 percent are collected in the second month. The company incurs no bad debts.
d. Gross profit margin on sales is 25 percent.
e. Inventory purchases are made each month to cover the next month's sales.
f. Inventory purchases are paid for in the month of purchase and include a 2 percent cash discount.
g. Monthly payroll expenses are $15,000; monthly rent, $400; and monthly depreciation, $120. Other cash expenses are variable and are 1 percent of each month's sales. *(IMA adapted)*

Required:
a. Construct a financial planning model that generates the monthly operating cash inflows and outflows for any specified month; ignore income taxes.
b. If sales for a current month are $20,000, compute the cash inflows and outflows for the next 2 months.

20. Microcomputer Applications

Rockmart Builders is a small contractor that specializes in one-story office and marketing buildings in office parks in a large city. Because of its excellent reputation, it is asked to bid on many jobs. During the busy building season each summer, it has difficulty in handling its billings, accounts payable, subcontractor schedules, cost distributions, and inventories. Currently, the company employs one full-time clerk to handle all contract schedulings and a bookkeeper to keep up with cost distributions for each job. Another clerk handles all other accounting matters such as cash and accounts payable.

Despite the hard work of the office staff, the company is always behind schedule in making payments to its subcontractors and in getting bids out on time. Also, many bids are lost simply because of poor cost estimation. Without some relief, the company is very limited in its growth and in the current competitive construction environment, and it will probably lose many profitable bids.

Required:
a. If the company acquires a microcomputer, what applications would be available to assist in improving the operations?
b. What specific hardware needs do you recommend?

SECTION

CONTROLS AND AUDITING

CHAPTER SIX

System Controls

$\mathbf{A}$s is true with most things designed by humans, elements that are incorporated in the design phase tend to work better and more efficiently than those that are added as components in later stages. This philosophy is often useful in designing and installing accounting information systems and has been applied accordingly to systems controls in this chapter. Controls are generally more effective if built into a system rather than added on after a system is implemented. During the development of an information system the proper placement of controls is easier, less costly, and more efficient.

Controls are mechanisms implemented to reduce the risks of adverse effects. They are generally geared to three areas of an organization: safeguarding assets, efficiency of scarce resource utilization, and proper recording and accounting of economic events. In the accounting profession, controls are usually classified as either accounting controls or administrative controls.[1] Accounting controls encompass the procedures and records that safeguard assets and ensure the reliability of financial records. Administrative controls encompass procedures and records that influence the decision processes of management and the adherence to the policies of management. Although controls have been classified in many ways by information system experts, we have chosen classifications generally accepted by most accountants.

Accounting controls in an EDP system are divided into *application controls* and *general controls.* Application controls relate primarily to the accuracy and completeness of data. For example, in an accounts payable system the application controls formalize the computation and preparation of vouchers for payment and the subsequent process of check writing. General controls are the broader standards and guidelines that are followed in a process. In accounts payable, these controls include documentation, data flow, and separation of duties. These control concepts are further expanded in Chapter Seven.

The impact of automation in accounting is often apparent, especially in terminology. Since automated systems now dominate business and require different types of controls than manual systems, this text emphasizes automated control terminology. Fortunately, automated and manual control terms frequently have the same meaning and application. Also, controls tend to be "systems-oriented," rather than "accounting-oriented," as a result of the diversity found in automated information systems and the changes that automation has imposed on controls.

So important is this area that the Foreign Corrupt Practices Act of 1977 included a section related to internal control. The act requires publicly held companies to maintain accurate accounting records and to design and maintain effective internal control systems.

Because accountants work with all kinds of systems in an organization, they should be cognizant of all controls in the information systems environment. This chapter presents six aspects of control important to information systems. First, the two basic types of control systems are discussed with emphasis on accounting applications. The next two sections present preventive and general controls along with relevant accounting illustrations. Because of the complexities of on-line systems, the fourth section deals with basic controls necessary for sound on-line applications. Transaction controls as related to accounting are examined in detail in the fifth section. And last, the impact of automation on controls peculiar to accounting information systems are discussed with relevant examples and applications.

CONTROL SYSTEMS

Control systems are subsystems within information systems. There are controls within accounting, over accounting, and interrelated with accounting. This section discusses the two broad classifications of control systems: feedback systems and feedforward systems. The primary objective of control is to accomplish the directives of management that will satisfy systems requirements and, with the two control systems working together in an organization, provide strong assurances that management's plans and objectives are being properly attained. Since control is a major consideration of information systems design, it is necessary for each of the two control systems to be constantly monitored for inclusion into the overall design scheme of any accounting information system. It is important to realize that a control system is dependent on the information system that it monitors, since that information system provides the data and information input for the control system. Without proper built-in controls most information systems cannot survive. This section perceives control in a cybernetic rather than a coercive sense, and therefore views the information system as a self-regulating system with control a very important subsystem.

Feedback Control Systems

A basic requirement for any control system is an evaluation of current activities, that is, *feedback*. Because many information systems are large and complex, several control subsystems have evolved to provide formal feedback from the system. Most feedback control systems, when isolated, are found to contain four elements: (1) a function or process to evaluate; (2) a set of standards or control totals for comparison; (3) a sensor to detect and measure items for evaluation; and (4) a control device to report and correct variances from standards. A flowchart of a feedback control system is illustrated in Figure 6.1.

Although many items go through a given system function, not every item will be selected for evaluation. Every system function has certain key elements that, when chosen for evaluation, will predict the reliability of the entire function. For example, a payroll system may use *number of checks written* and *total gross pay* as the two primary

A FEEDBACK CONTROL SYSTEM.

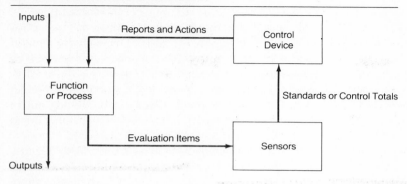

Figure 6.1

control elements. If these two numbers are predetermined for each payroll run, and the output of each run agrees, then the particular run is assumed to be correct and therefore in control. This does not imply that other payroll controls are unnecessary, but these two tests are frequently performed for every run because of their simplicity, reliability, and verifiability. In repetitive operations these three characteristics generally govern the types, quantity, and complexity of items controlled.

Many individual feedback controls exist, such as those for payroll, but there are several broad feedback systems such as standard cost accounting systems, which monitor entire production operations; the internal auditing system, which monitors the entire organization; and inventory control systems, which control all aspects of inventory movement from raw materials to finished products. The complexity of some of these large systems often requires that they contain several control elements. Although basic feedback control systems may contain only a predetermined standard and rely on negative feedback, the more complex ones can recall past experiences, constantly adjusting the goals and collecting and storing new data.

Every function of an organization has certain elements that must be controlled, and management must select the proper control device and set of standards with which to control each function. A major role of the accounting information system is to serve as the regulator or monitor for many aspects of an organization's control system. Accounting information systems exemplify the important interrelationships that the accounting function has with most other functional systems within an organization.

Feedforward Control Systems

Other than concurrent feedback controls, such as for payroll processing, many feedback controls lag the actual system by various periods of time. To overcome the time lag in controlling critical functions, many organizations have developed feedforward control systems. These systems attempt to prevent delays in reporting variances by predicting outcomes based on the inputs used in a particular situation and to predict outcomes if the inputs continue to display their current trends. As predictions from the system are made, inputs can be changed to correct or improve remaining outputs. Therefore, more desired results can be obtained by this concept of continuous control monitoring.

The elements of a feedforward control system are similar to those of a feedback control system (see Figure 6.2). A comparison of Figures 6.1 and 6.2 highlights two major differences: (1) the point of data input to the control system and (2) the place of adjustment from the control system to the function evaluated. The sensors in the feedforward system assess the status of the inputs and the control device attempts to predict the outputs from the selected inputs. Thus, if the inputs appear to be getting out of control, the feedforward system can adjust the inputs or the processing function to improve future outputs or desired results.

Feedforward control systems are particularly applicable in cash budgeting. Because future cash needs must be known in the present, a feedforward control system can continually monitor both inflows and current uses. Therefore, if future cash needs cannot be changed, management will be informed on a timely basis to adjust either the cash inflows or the present cash uses or both, which will result in the desired future outcomes.

Inventory, which may also have a feedback control system, provides another good example of applied feedforward control systems. Although an inventory feedback control system is primarily concerned with price and usage variances, inventory theft, and physical management, the feedforward system emphasizes inventory demand, storage, and ordering. For an inventory system to operate properly, the necessary material items must be on hand when needed. As raw materials are used, the feedforward system compares stock balances to future needs. Models such as economic order quantity (EOQ) and reorder points (ROP) require the system to make the necessary adjustments to the inputs to maintain the desired inventory stock levels—the outputs.

Any system that has critical outputs should be monitored by both feedback and feedforward control systems. Working together, these control systems can assure management that a particular function is either operating within management's objectives or out of control, at which point corrective action may be taken.

A FEEDFORWARD CONTROL SYSTEM.

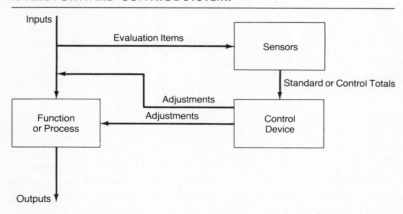

Figure 6.2

PREVENTIVE CONTROLS

Feedback and feedforward control systems are concepts that are tailored to the functional elements of an organization. Preventive controls are more general in nature and are applied on a piecemeal basis whenever needed in the organization. These controls act as guidelines to effect desired results and avert potential problems. It is generally more economical to prevent an undesirable event than to detect and correct it once "inside" the system. That is true for both manual and computerized systems.

Although the accounting information system and all its subsystems contribute to an organization's controls, the individual exercise of sound control procedures cannot be monitored by the accountant in every function of an organization. Thus, it is necessary for the system designer to incorporate preventive controls throughout every systems function in the organization. Many types of preventive controls are needed in accounting, and the following discussions of individual preventive control tools and techniques relate to accounting information systems.

Documentation

Computerized systems are a complex collection of data gathering processes, multiple users, output peculiarities, and technical equipment. Without proper documentation the efficient integration of these diverse elements would be difficult. Documentation assists accountants, computer personnel, and management in evaluating the operational efficiency and effectiveness of the data processing activities. It also provides a tool for training and reduces the impact of key employee turnover.

Documentation serves as a prime communication link between many systems within an organization. If errors and misunderstandings can be minimized through documentation, then its role as a preventive control is fulfilled. Proper documentation provides a means of monitoring changes in the system and should make the process of change easier. This is possible because good documentation provides all users and managers with concise information concerning the status of activities, programs, and processes at any given time, as well as reference material for what has happened in the past. Also, communication of changes in an organization dictates the use of documents if management is to stay ahead of the informal communication processes.

From management's view, documentation provides employees with a clear understanding of system objectives and concepts, and ensures adherence to company policies. Because of its important role in information systems, the three major categories of documentation are examined in detail with references to the preventive characteristics of each.

System Documentation   Since the system must be known to many people in an organization, it is necessary to have sound documentation of the system itself. To prevent the duplication of functions, as well as the omission of functions, the system documentation should include both narratives and flowcharts of the system and related subsystems. The narrative descriptions of the system should correlate with the flowcharts and be supported by procedures manuals for all operations in the system. Specific systems documentation should include:

1. Description of system
2. Systems flowcharts
3. Necessary inputs and source documents
4. Necessary outputs
5. General file and record descriptions
6. Control procedures, defined and explained
7. Backup procedures

Program Documentation   Program documentation relates primarily to computerized systems, although manual systems must also have written details of ledgers, journals, and procedures. Program documentation should contain comprehensive descriptions of the programs on file, their accessibility, and confidentiality. Such descriptions can be used for developing tests of the system, discovering procedural strengths and weaknesses, and assisting management when changes need to be made.

For a proper program documentation file, the following should be included:

1. General narrative descriptions of each system
2. Flowcharts with input, output, data flow, subroutines, and operating sequence
3. Testing procedures
4. Implemented controls
5. Sample printouts of outputs
6. Input formats
7. Operating instructions
8. Authorization list for all changes
9. List of all source programs and documents
10. Interface program (for computer systems)
11. Description of file structures
12. File retention procedures
13. Error detection and correction procedures

Although accountants normally do not get involved with program documentation, someone must verify the soundness of the accounting programs on a periodic basis. Generally, either the internal or external auditors will review the program documentation for authenticity. Documentation may not prevent a person from making unauthorized changes in an accounts receivable program, for example, but when the program printouts are compared to proper program documentation, the discrepancies should be detected. In essence, an accountant cannot be responsible for accounts receivable operations unless there are assurances that the accounts receivable program is operationally sound. Program documentation aids in providing that assurance.

Operating Documentation   Operating documentation relates to the daily conduct of activities within an organization, and should include document flowcharts (see Chapter Two,) input requirements, output distribution, operating procedures and instructions, and information interpretation. Operating documentation applies to the computer center, the accounting department, research and development, and the president's office, to list a few. No system, computerized or manual, large or small, should be exempt from using formal operating documents. Operating documentation can be easily verified by having top management or the auditors observe the operations of a department and compare the results to the written procedures.

The following items are of particular importance when developing operating documentation:

1. Description of system
2. Determination of original source document retention period
3. Procedures controls to prevent source documents from being processed more than once
4. Methods of establishing control totals
5. Error message explanations
6. Handling of error procedures
7. Emergency instructions
8. Equipment requirements

Organizational Independence

The best way to prevent wrongdoings is to have employees check on each other. Although organizational independence (separation of duties) does not demand that employees duplicate activities, it does provide for a checking system by requiring each major function to be performed by more than one individual. As a basic rule, custody of assets should be separated from the recording of transactions, which in turn should be separated from the decision process related to a given function. The concept can also be applied within a function, such as payroll, by assigning the data collection (hours worked) to one employee, file changes (pay raises) to another employee, computations and processing to a third employee (or the computer), and process control (batch totals) to another employee. It does not take many employees in a department to apply sound organizational independence practices. This is a very important control tool of management because a little application can go a long way in preventing hazardous situations from developing.

An important problem faced by many organizations in changing to a computer system is how to separate duties when fewer operational personnel are available with fewer duties to perform. When certain manual operations are computerized, management's ability to separate duties by accounting function is hindered because many traditional activities are combined in the computerized process. To compensate for a lack of functional organizational independence, most organizations have developed operational independence within the data processing department. The Auditing Standards Board of the American Institute of Certified Public Accountants, in Statements on Auditing Standards Nos. 3 and 48 stresses the importance of incompatible functions within the computer operations center.[2] Separations of duties are possible within the average data processing center, however, with four distinct functions generally recommended.

1. Keeping operating personnel limited to machine and hardware functions. These people should not have free access to programs, data files, or libraries. All operating personnel should be closely supervised and monitored for unauthorized activities. Many businesses require job rotation among the operators to prohibit too much familiarity with a given program.

2. Maintaining a separate library for all files and data with a librarian. Predetermined lists should be furnished by management so that access to the files is limited to specific users known to need the files for a particular purpose (e.g., a payroll master file signed out on predetermined pay dates). File usage logs should be kept by the librarian and should include the user's name, data requested, and person authorizing access.

3. Keeping computer programmers and systems analysts from operating equipment and files. Because these groups know more about the operation of the system than anyone else, unrestricted access could be detrimental to the organization. Once a file has been tested, approved, and placed in the library the programmer or analyst should have no need for it unless there are authorized changes to be made. As discussed in the section on documentation, all changes in the system should be well documented and properly authorized. Since file manipulation is one of the largest causes of computer fraud, there is even more reason to have strict control over file access.[3]

4. Providing for separate data processing management. A programmer or analyst should *not* be the part-time department manager. Because of the need to authorize certain transactions, make personnel changes, and establish operating procedures, the manager needs to be responsible only for management functions. The system is weakened if managers can authorize their own access to files and programs.

These separations can be easily illustrated by use of a department flowchart of a medium-size computer installation (see Figure 6.3). By having these types of separated functions in the system, the operations of the data processing function should be in control as much as the other functional areas of the organization. Many times a given functional area may be too small to have adequate separation of duties, and the implementation of its processes on the computer may strengthen the overall control process. Also, auditors regard organizational independence as basic to the achievement of internal control in a system, and, if it can be centered in the data processing function versus "a little here and some there," better control techniques may be applied.

Personnel

An organization may utilize elaborate documentation for business transactions, and the separation of functional assignments may be theoretically sound; yet without the proper placement of well-trained personnel, the overall control system may be ineffective. The screening process for all types of information systems personnel must be carefully conducted. More attention must be given to background information and references than for the average prospective employee. Standards for responsible positions on the information system's staff should include minimum levels of experience, integrity, character, and intelligence. Integrity and character are important for all systems personnel, especially in computerized operations. Since people, not computers, commit fraud, the control emphasis must be placed on people who have direct, and in some situations indirect, access to the information system. This is very evident from the results of Brandt Allen's survey of fraud cases.[4] As shown in Figure 6.4 the positions of people committing fraud varied from clerks to corporate officers.

ORGANIZATIONAL CHART FOR A DATA PROCESSING DEPARTMENT.

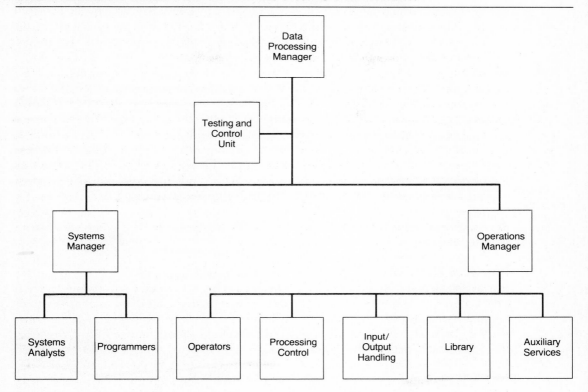

Figure 6.3

PRIMARY PERPETRATORS OF FRAUD.

Job Title	Number of Cases
Data entry/terminal operator	15
Clerk/teller	16
Programmers	15
Officers/managers	21
Computer operators	9
Other employees	5
Outsiders	5
Unknown	3
Total cases	89

Figure 6.4

Once people are hired they should be properly trained for the system function they will perform. Training programs should be geared to familiarize employees with the control requirements of the system and their role in the control scheme. Personnel should know and understand their place in the organization, their responsibilities to the system, and what is expected of employees filling given positions.

Employees holding key positions should be bonded to protect the financial interest of the organization. In some organizations all persons who play a role in information flow and processing are bonded. Another individual control concept requires all key employees to take annual vacations. It is difficult for employees to hide covert activities during extended periods of absence. During such periods their functions are performed by others, and any unauthorized activities hopefully would be noted. Some businesses, such as banks, force all employees to take vacations for the specific purpose of detecting fraud or mismanagement. Another related control concept designed specifically to detect unauthorized activities is the rotation of duties among key employees. Last, the immediate removal of dissatisfied employees from the system is critical because numerous instances of fraud or sabotage have occurred by disgruntled or fired employees before their termination dates.

Physical Controls

Just as the accounting manager of a manual system does not want people to have free access to the journals, ledgers, and accounting machines, the management of computerized systems does not want unauthorized persons tampering with the hardware or data files. Organizations must be concerned about the need for procedures to protect its system components from fire, theft, flood, riot, or other destructive forces. The best protection is to have parallel systems and process everything twice, at different locations. Although this may be done for certain priority processing, most organizations cannot justify the additional costs of such a system vis-à-vis the extra protection gained. Therefore, most systems rely on other means of physical protection.

Physical controls should include such items as (1) fire protection; (2) environmental devices to control temperature, humidity, and static electricity; (3) security devices and personnel to control unauthorized access by both employees and visitors, and (4) screening devices to prohibit persons from taking unauthorized items from the processing center. Both hardware and software can be protected from humans by limiting access to the computer center. For protection from floods, riots, and similar destructive forces, management must place the computer processing, storage, and remote terminals as well as other off-line facilities in minimum risk areas. For example, it would not be wise to place the computer center in the basement of a building near a river floodplain or in a building near an active earthquake center.

More difficult to protect are off-line facilities, remote terminals, and software in the hands of users. These equipment operators and software users should be specially trained in control procedures to protect the items from unauthorized persons and natural disasters. For all types of physical controls there should be backup and emergency procedures available to keep the system operable.

GENERAL SYSTEM CONTROL TOOLS AND TECHNIQUES

The preventive controls discussed in the previous section apply to all types and sizes of systems and are considered management tools because of their general applicability. This section examines the controls related primarily to computer system operations. For purposes of this text, these controls are divided into general system controls (this section), on-line controls, and transaction controls. Although the presence of general system controls is vital to a system, they do not affect daily processing activities as do the transaction controls.

Hardware Controls

Most hardware controls are built into the computer by the manufacturer to improve the controllability of the system. Several hardware controls are basic to most computers. *Parity checking* is one such control with several variations. A parity (or check) bit is used to check the transmission of data in various types of components. The bit is provided in each byte which, when included with the other bits in a byte, makes the total bit count either odd (odd parity) or even (even parity). If the system is based on odd parity, the parity bit will be added if the sum of the other bits is even and will be ignored if the sum of the other bits is odd. After the check bit is entered into the system, every byte should be odd for all following transmissions of that set of data. This can be tested by each data-using component. For remote facilities and terminals that often have noise or static interruptions, a *two-dimensional parity check* is used. This control uses a character check for each record in addition to a block check. Thus each set of records can be verified both vertically and horizontally, in a manner similar to extending and footing a worksheet in a manual accounting system.

Other hardware controls include *duplicate circuitry, echo check, read-write,* and *dual read-write.* Duplicate circuitry provides for the *CPU* to perform computations twice, followed by a comparison of the results. Echo checks authenticate the transmission of data to and from the components of the computerized system. The data are verified by sending back (echoing) the signal received to the sending component for comparison with the source data. Dual reading-writing is another control in which input and output is read or written twice by separate components and compared for accuracy.

Several hardware controls relate to mechanical and power failures. When certain components malfunction, others can be programmed to continue processing, but on a less efficient basis. This is known as *graceful degradation.* To ensure continuous sources of electric power, *uninterruptible power systems* are employed. These include battery and generator systems for temporary backup until normal electricity is restored.

Firmware Controls

Firmware control is a hand-wiring technique that uses solid-state devices such as chips. Read only memory (ROM) is an application, as is the familiar hand calculator that has its logic on a chip. Unlike the traditional hand-wired boards, these chips can neither be altered manually nor modified with conventional software applications. However, they can be physically removed.

Firmware controls essentially eliminate anyone from altering programs internal to the computer, such as the logic function or *the* basic operating system of the CPU. Any manipulations would require technical knowledge about the system and access to the computer equipment. This is a very important control function because it eliminates programmers from altering programs through software changes. Unfortunately, not all computers have the ability to accept many firmware controls.

Software Controls

There are two major categories of software, systems (control) programs and application programs, which must be safeguarded. Most software controls are placed into the computer systems by the manufacturer. They generally control input and output operations of the system. These controls perform such functions as providing appropriate error messages if there is a reading or writing error so that the operator can take the necessary action, screening input for proper record lengths so that all incoming data will be properly accepted, and controlling access when reference is made to an unauthorized file. Such controls ensure users of the systems that the data are correctly entered, properly recorded, and securely stored if necessary. Additionally, access controls must be in existence to prevent programmers from making unauthorized changes in application programs such as the payroll program.

Labels

The two major categories of labels are external and internal. *External labels* are found on magnetic tape reels, disk packs, and other file storage devices. An external label is generally a paper decal and many contain such information as file name, date of last processing, identification number, and related files. The use of external labels should minimize the misplacement, misuse, and untimely replacement of files.

Internal labels are a part of the recorded data and are in machine-readable form, unlike the human-readable form of external labels. This labeling is frequently considered a *programmed* control because it is an integral part of the data in a file. There are generally two types of internal labels—volume and file. *Volume labels* are associated with a particular type of file such as a tape reel or disk pack. All files receive volume labels when they are first prepared for processing. This label is the first record on the file. It contains the volume serial number that should be verified every time the file is read, updated, or printed. Such labels provide control over the proper usage and posting of the data file. In disk systems a volume table of contents follows the volume label. *File labels* for all files stored on the component are placed in the volume table of contents. Each file label contains the name, description, and location of each file on the component. For example, if an inventory program calls for a certain file number during inventory updating, the volume label assures that the proper file is selected.

File labels are found both at the beginning (header labels) and at the end (trailer labels) of a data file. These labels are generally used with tape files or other "sequence files." Both labels contain the file name, date created, last use, and other control information. The trailer label usually contains a block count and sequence number reference. These controls guard against losing records in the file.

Data File Controls

Guarding against the loss or destruction of data, of course, should be a primary concern of management. Good internal control demands that critical data are protected from all possible hazards. Some of the controls discussed previously protect certain aspects of data, but several controls exist specifically for data control and security. The following controls are primary to data security, although the list is not exhaustive.

Basic to most data files are file protection devices and backup files. The most common file protection device is the *tape file protection ring.* This ring is inserted into a groove around the tape reel to permit writing on the magnetic tape. Without the ring, the tape cannot be altered or erased and the data are protected. Tape files should always be stored without the ring, forcing the operator to make a positive decision to write, and preventing careless destruction of data. Such an action would not be taken unless instructed by the operations manual for a given program, thus requiring the operator to read the external label before applying the protection ring and mounting the tape.

Considering the many controls already discussed and those still to be discussed, it would seem that *backup files* would be unnecessary. However, errors do occur in the data files, and data are sometimes destroyed. The problem of reconstruction of erroneous or destroyed files has given birth to duplicate files stored off premises and to the *grandparent, parent, child concept* of file management. This is a convenient concept because most programs produce a new master file with each processing run (see Figure 6.5). As new master files are created, the most recent is labeled *the child,* the previous one is *the parent,* and the oldest is *the grandparent.* If the child is destroyed, the parent can be used as the master file to reprocess the last period's activity, which recreates the lost or damaged child master. Master files not on "removable media" should be reproduced on tapes or removable disks so that the parent or grandparent or both can be stored in separate locations from the child master. Storing all the master files together defeats part of the objective of having backup files. The advantage of this control procedure, when properly conducted, is that data recovery is always feasible. Figure 6.5 also illustrates the proper remote storage of data files.

Forms and Document Design

Although documentation is obviously necessary for overall systems control, forms and documents are equally important for input and output control. Every accounting information system must have several forms and reports for the purpose of recording source data and reporting output. Forms and reports range from invoices and paychecks to balance sheets and sales performance reports. Good forms and documents are critical to the control of a system because they deliver the data and information from one segment to another and from one processing step to the next. Well-designed forms and documents facilitate the compilation of critical business data and enable readers to abstract needed information with ease. Forms that require users to search for data are poorly designed and often lead to communication errors. Ease of recording and efficiency of processing should be the primary characteristics of input forms. Output documents should accentuate and highlight the most important elements of business transactions and provide a logical and systematic flow of information. Output documents should be free of *irrelevant* information as well as an *overabundance* of *relevant* information.

GRANDPARENT-PARENT-CHILD APPLICATION.

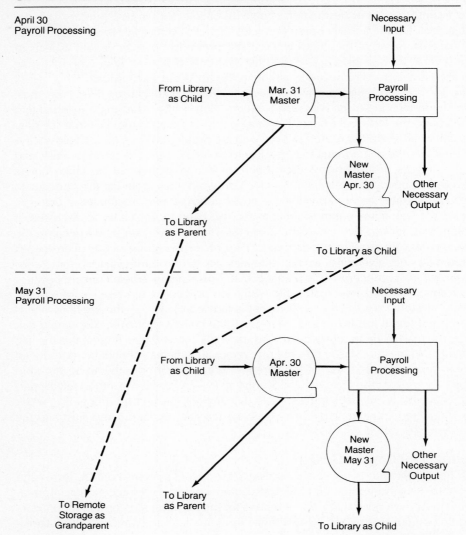

Figure 6.5

Another document control principle is the use of *prenumbered forms,* especially for critical documents such as payable vouchers, invoices, and payroll checks. Sequential numbering of forms with full accountability at every activity point is a traditional control technique used in both manual and computerized systems. Such forms can be traced through the system to assure that all transactions have been properly accounted for and recorded. Several examples of such forms can be found in Chapters Ten to Eighteen.

A different type of document control technique is the *turnaround document,* which contains characteristics of both input and output. The punch cards or magnetic cards that are returned when we pay our utility bills are examples of such documents. Turnaround forms are produced as output from the processing of one subsystem (e.g., billing process of the utility company), and when returned to the system they are input to another subsystem (e.g., the collection process of the utility company). Other examples of such forms are inventory move tickets that follow work-in-process through a manufacturing process and punched time cards of employees used in the payroll process. These documents minimize errors by eliminating many of the human activities necessary in preparing both the input and the output of a process.

ON-LINE SYSTEM CONTROLS

In addition to the foregoing general controls, on-line systems utilize additional safeguards because of the increased vulnerability created by the use of terminals and remote operational centers. These devices are often employed to transmit data over long distances, and this removal from the central processing center requires controls to verify actual transmission, check data security at remote locations, and monitor access to the system. The following discussion of such control features applies generally to both on-line systems and on-line, real-time systems.

Terminal Controls

The terminal controls discussed in this section cover a wide range of error prevention and detection objectives. The major systems functions in need of control are accurate transmission of data, data and data base security, and proper terminal usage. Data transmission parity checks, previously discussed, should be used along with *message indicators.* These indicators appear at the beginning and end of each transmission to let the user know that all data were received and nothing was lost or dropped during transmission. Programs to notify the sender of any errors in transmission and to permit their correction should be built in. Sequence numbers should be contained in the message indicators and verified by the built-in programs to ensure proper receipt of transmissions.

Systems security and terminal accessibility can be controlled by *passwords* and *hierarchy codes.* The programs that control terminal transmissions at the central processing center should be able to determine the authenticity of the sender's code, the terminal location, and the approval to access the files requested. The central processing unit should also keep a *history log* of all terminal transmissions by terminal number, time sent, and user code. This log can be used for message verification, audit trail evidence, and error identification.

Data Access Controls

Although terminal controls screen out many potential problems, other controls are necessary to protect the data base. Sensitive data files must have extra protection through code rotation and multiple codes. Authorized user codes are changed on a random basis.

Multiple codes include terminal access codes, user identification codes, and compatibility codes. Once an authorized user code has been accepted by the system, a compatibility test is performed by the software to verify the user code with the file being requested. Each file is programmed to accept only data and inquiries from certain user codes. For example, an inventory clerk's identification code should not allow the clerk access to the payroll system; likewise, a payroll clerk's user code should not allow access to the inventory files.

Processing Controls

After the user has been properly cleared, the input data should be controlled until processing is completed. The first control is the *completeness test.* This test assures the user that all the data for a particular transaction have been entered. A sales transaction entered by a salesperson from a remote sales office requires the customer's address for billing purposes. If such data have been omitted, the program will alert the salesperson that something is missing, and the omission can be corrected.

After the data are deemed complete, the system can then check for accuracy. The *closed-loop verification check* sends selected data back to the sender for review and confirmation. If the selected data are correct the user must respond, and subsequently the program continues processing. The program sends back to the salesperson the description of the inventory item ordered, which must agree with the inventory number entered by the salesperson. If the correct number has been entered, a response is made and the system accepts the order as correct.

Software controls must also be implemented to guard against the possibility of concurrent processing and updating of the same data base by two or more programs. This occurs in multiprogramming modes where the executing programs are in on-line storage, and one program destroys data of another program by claiming the same storage space. Such processing must be controlled by means of *memory protection,* a concept that allows each processing program to access only its block of storage and thereby prevents one program's errors from adversely affecting other programs or the operating system.

TRANSACTION CONTROLS

Transaction controls are designed to meet the control requirements of specific application events. Transaction controls begin where general system controls end. They ensure the accuracy and completeness of the recording, classifying, summarizing, storing, and retrieving of accounting data and information. These controls also affect the updating of files and permanent records.

There are many types of transaction controls. The predominant ones are discussed here with an emphasis on accounting and related transactions, as opposed to noneconomic transactions. The primary objectives of each control are presented and risks assumed in the absence of such controls are discussed. Because of the uniqueness of these controls, they are defined, with accounting examples, for each control application.

Transaction Validation

Most systems process numerous types of transactions, varying from customer orders to employee retirement fund contributions; from purchase discounts to million-dollar capital expenditures; from petty cash to automated inventory control. Transactions may change files by deletions of records, additions to records, or changes to records. Also, the sources of transactions vary. They may be from customers, employees, governments, sales personnel, and other components of a system's environment. The purpose of transaction validation is to ensure that all processing is correct, complete, authorized, and acceptable to the system. In almost all cases, the prevention of invalid data from entering the system is more efficient than the correction of data already entered into the system.

The primary control techniques used to validate transaction data relate to the editing features of the software components. Most computers have the ability, because of their great speed, to edit or examine all data elements routinely. Such a control feature is impractical with manual systems. The edit features described here can detect most errors not found through the control measures of data preparation and input.

Initial controls related to transaction validation are usually found in the data conversion phase. During this processing phase, non-machine-readable data forms are converted into machine-readable forms such as punched cards or magnetic tape. Because such processing is generally manual, controls must be installed to detect both inadvertent and intentional errors. *Key verification* of input is essential to most input processing. This control consists of verifying the prepared input by sampling primary fields in the data, or the entire record. Verifying devices are available that check the data already entered by sending the prepared cards or tapes through the machine again, this time merely for the purpose of checking the punched holes or magnetic bits for accuracy. The need for key verification can be reduced by the use of turnaround documents and *automated source documents.* Automated source documents are outputs from some phase of processing that are used to capture part or all of the input for the next processing phase. An example would be the recording of a sales transaction on a multiple copy invoice, one copy of which can be optically read by the computer and entered directly into the system without further manual intervention.

The controls previously discussed sometimes fail to provide protection against certain types of errors, such as number transposition. A *check digit* is used for this purpose. It is simply an additional digit added to an original number. The check digit has no value in processing other than indicating that a given numeric field is correct. Check digit schemes are varied and numerous. The mathematical method chosen for a particular set of numbers should maximize error detection and minimize human effort and computer operations. A check digit may be determined by performing some type of mathematical operation on the original digits in a numeric field. Using a five-digit numeric field, for example, the sixth digit (check digit) could be determined by dividing the five digits by a prime number.[5] The check digit becomes the remainder left from the division. If an account number, 61934, is divided by the prime number seven, the new account number becomes 619345, because the quotient of the division is 8847 with a remainder of 5. Comparisons of actual check digits to calculated check digits by the computer can be easily accomplished during processing of incoming data. Although not foolproof, the use of check digits adds another control dimension to data processing which helps ensure correctness.

Another approach to data validation is the use of *sequence checks.* Such checks provide processing control where the order of the data being processed is important, or when it is necessary to verify that all transactions have been processed. Sequence checks can be used in a variety of situations. If a company uses prenumbered sales invoices as a control element, the computer can check all invoices for each reporting period and provide a list of missing numbers that must be accounted for by the users. In the case of systems requiring strict document control, such as payroll checks, the computer can be given the first check number of a processing run and assure the proper sequential use of all check numbers.

Validity tests are edit routines that are used to ensure that transactions contain valid codes and characters, and adhere to predetermined field sizes. Each of these characteristics is defined by the program in use and can be compared to the input as it enters a given process. In a payroll system, for example, a social security number may contain both numbers and dashes for ease of human readability; whereas the payroll program requires only nine numbers. The validity check would detect such errors because the field size is nine, not eleven.

Limit or reasonableness checks test record fields to verify whether predetermined numerical limits have been violated. Many processing activities have normal limits within which certain record fields should fall. The following are examples: (1) The hours-worked field in a weekly payroll processing program should not exceed a reasonable number of hours, such as 70. (2) To control accounts payable expenditures, all checks over $50,000 must be written by hand; therefore, the computer program for accounts payable has an upper limit test of $50,000. (3) The company has a policy of not writing accounts payable checks below $5.00. The payables program has a minimum limit check of $5.00. When a limit check is violated, the program must print out appropriate error messages that should be immediately handled by someone assigned to the task. Such test failures might well be legitimate, (i.e., an employee might actually work 75 hours), in which case the limit test must be overridden. Other violations detected by the limit check could be the result of input errors, such as keypunch mistakes, a clerk placing an amount in the wrong data field, or an employee changing an hours-worked entry without knowing about limit controls.

A control closely related to the limit test is the *logic test.* This is another initial screening control. It is a check of logical relationships between input data and the file or files accessed. For example, a closing entry for an accounting period that debits depreciation expense and credits allowance for doubtful accounts is not a normal transaction. Therefore the logic test would print out an error message for corrective action.

The last two validation routines, the field check and the sign check, are closely related. The *field check* compares the input characters in a data field with characters defined by the program for that field. If an alphabetic character suddenly appeared in an otherwise exclusively numeric field, the field check would initiate an error message. Similarly, if a data field is expected to contain a negative number (such as an inventory withdrawal), the *sign test* would consider any positive number in that field to be erroneous.

Control Totals

Once transactions have been properly validated, processing of the data with the related files begins. After the initial processing steps, consisting primarily of calculations, most programs require the compilation of specified totals so that another control procedure can be implemented. This procedure requires a comparison of totals determined prior to processing with totals determined from the computer processing. Based on this comparison test, action is required to reconcile unmatched totals before processing continues.

The versatility of control total testing has engendered a variety of uses and applications. *Record counts* are one example. Prior to processing, all the transactions comprising a batch are counted. This count is simply compared with the number of transactions actually processed by the computer. An extra record or a missing one requires reconciliation before processing can continue. This assurance is especially critical in such areas as payroll and other check-writing programs. *Batch totals* are the most widely used control totals because they generally apply to dollars (gross pay for a payroll run) or quantities (inventory items on hand). *Hash totals* are generated from data not normally totaled, which would otherwise be considered useless. The numerical sum of all customer numbers in an accounts receivable processing run would be an example of a hash total, to be compared with a predetermined number. Such totals can replace record counts in most processes because the number of records processed is generally incorrect if the manual hash total does not agree with the computer-processed hash total. Hash totals go one step further than record counts in that they can detect a wrong account number or perhaps an improper record substitution.

Another common batch total approach is the *cross-footing test.* This test is particularly applicable when a process requires both vertical and horizontal verification. The totals can then be combined to reconcile all the individual totals. An example is a payroll program, where each individual record must reflect gross pay, less deductions, to compute net pay. Because accounting needs the vertical totals (gross pay, withholding taxes, net pay totals, etc.) for record-keeping purposes, the cross-footing test constitutes both a control and a necessary total.

A typical control total application can best be illustrated by a modified systems flowchart. The payroll application shown in Figure 6.6 illustrates a processing procedure in which a processing delay occurs to permit the payroll department, or control group, to reconcile the control totals and make any necessary corrections. This procedure ensures the correctness of the final output and thereby minimizes the need for manual corrections at a later time.

Error Detection and Correction

As the foregoing discussion suggests, it is important that authorized personnel detect and correct invalid data as early in the process as possible. Once errors have been detected, specific resubmission techniques must be established to ensure that all corrections are made in accordance with predetermined procedures. Several guidelines are basic to error correction.

1. All errors detected after the computerized process begins should be recorded in a *history log* or a special error log. This allows every error to be properly checked when the correction is made and provides an audit trail when files and records are

CONTROL TOTAL APPLICATION.

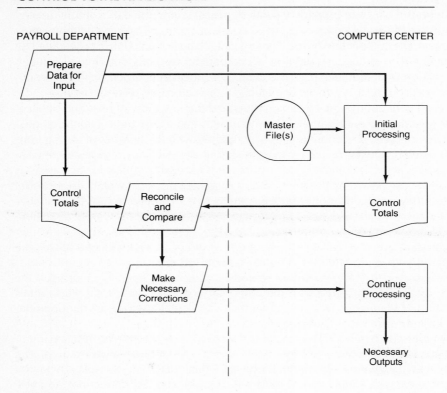

Figure 6.6

being examined by either internal or external auditors. Also, outstanding errors (those not corrected) can be periodically investigated to determine cause-and-effect relationships, as well as reasons for their uncorrected status.

2. Errors should always be resubmitted at the point of original submission if possible. This allows for all necessary files to be properly updated without the necessity of subsequent file adjustments. If not properly handled, error corrections frequently generate more errors and thus complicate the correction process.

3. All errors should be reported to and monitored by a data control group. Such a group provides consistency of corrections and aids in ensuring that all errors are corrected. If a system cannot justify a control group, one individual assigned to monitor all errors can be very effective.

These guidelines, along with the other control features, should give management confidence in the correction process. A compilation of error rates, types of errors, persons responsible, and severity of errors provides comparisons between prior and future periods and helps establish tolerances.

Output Distribution

Even after the source data have been properly prepared, converted into machine-usable form, and processed, the control process must continue during distribution if the system is to be considered in complete control. The function of output controls is to ensure that all processing is authorized, that unauthorized changes have not been made by computer personnel or others, and that the output is correct. Because output may consist of paper printouts, magnetic tapes, checks, or various other instruments, the controls related to distribution must be as varied as those relating to input. In many systems the first step in the distribution process is the reconciliation of the control totals. Next, the output should be reviewed and visually edited if possible for reasonableness, clarity, and format. Last, the processing personnel should know the authorized personnel that are to receive the output.

Although the preceding steps are necessary for most outputs, all vital and sensitive outputs such as payroll checks, product formulas, and so on should receive extra attention. Any output that should not be accessible by computer personnel should be generated under the watchful eye of an authorized user or by output devices at the user's location. All critical documents, such as checks and other "numbered" output, should be accounted for along with the control total reconciliation.

IMPACT OF AUTOMATION ON CONTROLS

As systems become more automated, controls related to the improved systems must change to meet the new characteristics of such systems. Changes in information processing technology also have an impact on controls. In recent years automation has significantly enhanced quantitative approaches to processing, control, and input/output reconciliations. These new techniques have refocused management attention on analysis of output rather than on input controls. Because of the improved reliability of information provided to management, automated systems have, in effect, reduced the amount of human time and effort devoted to control by management.

During the past decade advanced technology has had a noticeable impact on processing and quality control of manufacturing firms. Computers are often devoted exclusively to control problems of organizations ranging from perpetual monitoring of inventory to temperature control in a chemical process and from atomic energy systems regulation to the maintenance of perpetual cash levels in checking accounts. Because management's control problems go beyond economic and financial systems, the accountant must be aware of these shifting priorities within the entire environment. This is necessary since nonfinancial controls are often more important to the organization than financial controls, and the accountant may not always have priority in using the computer to improve the controls of the financial system. No matter where automation improves controls, the accountant gains because accounting, as a system, interacts with myriad other systems in the organization. As other systems improve through control changes, so should accounting.

In many organizations a separate control group is established to monitor, evaluate, and control the computerized system. To separate the operations from control properly, the group must be outside the EDP department. A currently developing trend is for this function to be under a specially trained internal auditing group. For computer operations to maintain their integrity, they must be continuously reviewed by someone outside the operating system, a function that most internal audit departments can provide.

Automation has greatly facilitated the "management by exception" concept. Basically, this concept controls by monitoring and measuring actual performance against established standards, or norms, for any activity. When unsatisfactory performance is indicated, management takes corrective measures. In *open-loop management by exception* the computer monitors, measures, and compares actual performance to established standards, and notifies the appropriate personnel for corrective action. In *closed-loop management by exception* the computer does all the preceding in addition to taking the corrective action itself. An example is an automated inventory system where quantitative replenishment models are used (e.g., economic order quantity, reorder point, and safety stock). In the *open-loop system* the computer notifies purchasing when something needs to be ordered and the purchasing department proceeds from there. In the *closed-loop system* all vendor information is stored in automated files containing updated pricing and ordering information. When inventory replenishment is indicated through exercise of the aforementioned model(s), the automated system places the order and notifies purchasing, receiving, and accounting. Human error is almost completely eliminated, and the need for human judgment is minimized. Other examples of the automation of "exception" controls are delinquent accounts receivable; budget variances by budget line items; and failures to take advantage of all allowable discounts in accounts payable.

The impact of automation on general controls may also be illustrated by comparing manual and automated system flowcharts. Because payroll is relatively simple and easy to comprehend, it will again be used as a sample system. Figure 6.7 shows a very basic hourly payroll system flowchart with separation of duties by personnel within payroll. Although the flowchart does not include every detail, it illustrates all the major elements of a typical system. (See Chapter Fourteen for a detailed discussion of payroll systems.)

The payroll is performed by four people. The supervisor is responsible for updating records for new, terminated, and current employees, and for adding current hours worked to each master file record. Clerk A computes the actual dollars of pay, deductions, and net pay on each record and batches the totals. Clerk B writes the checks from the data prepared by Clerk A. Clerk C prepares batch totals from the checks themselves. The supervisor then reconciles all the control totals and, upon correction and approval, Clerk C releases the checks. This example illustrates two of the dominant control elements discussed in this chapter, *separation of duties* and *control totals.*

When the aforementioned system is computerized, as illustrated in Figure 6.8, a significant change takes place in the separation of duties. This results from the computer performing all the duties of Clerks B and C. The control over input is still performed by the supervisor, who also reconciles the control totals. Because fewer humans handle the data, calculations are much improved. The only data errors likely to occur are during keypunching. Even these are minimized in the new system because Clerk A punches only current employee changes, cards for new employees, and hours worked for all current employees. The preceding payroll processing run has provided the department with a prepunched master deck of cards for all employees containing all pertinent data except

MANUAL PAYROLL SYSTEM.

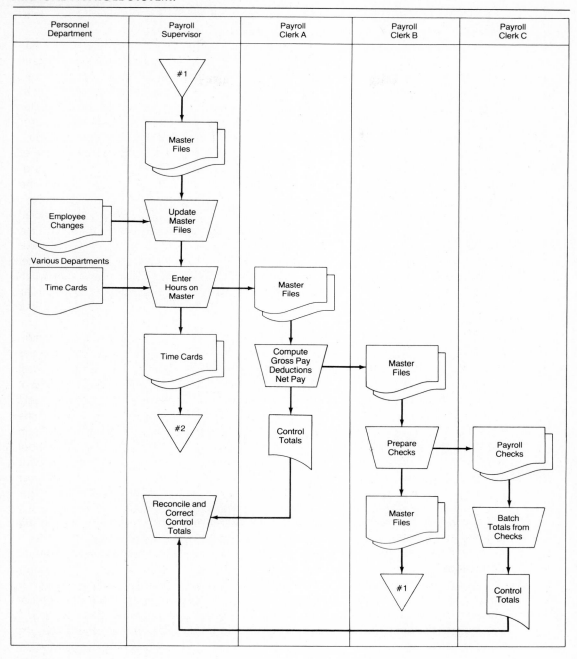

Figure 6.7

COMPUTERIZED PAYROLL SYSTEM.

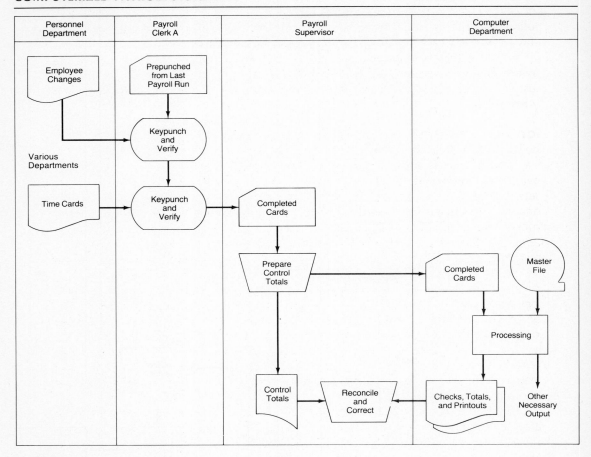

Figure 6.8

hours worked. The control totals under this system include a record count, a hash total of hourly wage rates, and gross pay. The computer printout provides these totals as well as other totals necessary for ledger posting, such as tax withholdings and insurance deductions.

Using inventory and payroll systems as examples, several generalizations can be made about the impact of automation on control. First, there is less need for organizational independence because the computer performs many of the functions that had to be separated when performed manually. It should be recalled, on the other hand, that this consolidation of activities by the computer requires very strict controls regarding the organizational independence of the computer department! Second, the absence of human effort in sorting, calculating, and summarizing data minimizes the need for controls that simply emphasize mathematical correctness. Control totals are still very important as discussed in a previous section of this chapter. Third, the need for manual edit routines of input are reduced because the use of turnaround and computer-prepared source documents minimizes the human inputs into most processes.

With the large amount of processing controls in the hands of so few people the controls that are in use must be the best available. Also, management and internal audit must be very careful in monitoring the use and adherence of the controls implemented by the system.

Control Considerations in a Data Base Environment

The basic control considerations in a data base environment are not different from those in a nondata base environment. However, because of the differences in a data base environment attributable to data independence and the sharing of data among diverse users, the control procedures may differ from those which might be employed in a nondata base environment. Understanding the implications of these different control procedures should aid general management and auditors in evaluating control requirements in a data base environment. There are three areas where control in a data base environment may differ from that encountered in a nondata base environment. These are: access/update, coordination of activity, and concentration of resources.

Access/Update   Access to data is accomplished through data requests by the application programs to the DBMS or through special report-writing facilities of the DBMS. Control considerations normally include: retrieval of data elements, update of data elements, and execution of functions. The necessity for additional or different controls in the data base environment is influenced by the sharing of data by users and by the greater availability of the data elements to the user as a result of on-line access and easy-to-use query languages.

Retrieval of data elements is important to ensure that a user can access only those data elements that are authorized for him or her. These controls include the capability to initiate access to data elements based on direct inquiries (for example, status of an inventory item), and indirect inquiries (for example, status of an inventory item that is being used for job No. 418 in the finishing department).

Control over the update of data elements is similar to that of control over retrieval of data elements. The controls must ensure that each user can update only those data elements that he or she has been authorized to use. Update of data elements includes the capability to change the contents of a data element, add or delete a data element or change the relationships between data elements (for example, inventory item No. 55 is used for job No. 189 instead of job No. 664).

Controls must ensure that if there are two or more authorized programs requesting to update data at the same time, the result should be accurately reflected without loss of data. Further, if one authorized program requests an update, and one or more other programs request retrievals at the same time, the resulting information to end users should be accurate and consistent. Due to the sharing of data between user programs which could be executing at the same time, two programs might request update and retrieval functions of the same data at the same time. If not properly controlled, this could have an adverse effect on the integrity of the data. Therefore, the DBMS procedure for accessing data should essentially "lock" the group of shared data until the update processing is complete before allowing the retrieval function to access the data. There are many DBMS software packages that have built-in safeguards to prevent loss of data when more than one user requests access to a particular data element at the same time.

Coordination of Activity   Because DBMS allows the sharing of data by diverse users, the coordination of their activities must be controlled. The level of control over each data element should be commensurate with the most sensitive and critical user and uses. However, shared use does not imply that every user must have control equality. For example, inventory users who have only retrieval access do not need the same degree of control as do users who are allowed to update and change inventory files. The requirements of the most critical items in a file should be of primary concern in the design of the control features.

Controls over the data must ensure that the descriptions of the data elements are coordinated for consistent interpretation of meaning and appropriate use. They must ensure that cut-off dates are defined and communicated so all users know the status of a file at any given time. This is particularly important for accounting and operating cycle cut-offs.

Concentration of Resources   Controls in this area include physical, data structures, DBMS operations, and key personnel. The physical aspects must be protected from improper alteration and destruction. The sharing of data files means that multiple users rely on the continued availability of that file. Loss of any single file or record can affect many users in a DBMS set-up.

The data structures must be controlled to ensure that the file relationships are maintained as defined. Most DBMS have complex data file relationships (see Chapter Four), and unauthorized changes in these relationships can be confusing to the users. The data base manager must continually evaluate the controls related to this area and have them properly changed and modified as necessary.

The DBMS operations must also have proper controls. Primary areas include installation, daily management, and communications with users as to operating status and system changes. This is usually the responsibility of the DBMS manager in conjunction with the auditors and corporate systems oversight committee.

Controls over key personnel must be in place to ensure that the organization has a sufficient number of trained employees, and such controls extend beyond the computer center to primary users of the systems. Especially important are the controls over the people who input most of the data.

Financial Controls over Computerized Systems

After all the technical and information systems aspects of the organization have been evaluated, consideration must be given to one more important topic related to control —resource evaluation and review. Once a system is operational, its costs must be controlled just as other costs of the organization are controlled. For example, there have been situations where a feasibility study was conducted at the beginning of a system's life cycle (discussed in a later chapter) with no later consideration of the cost associated with operating the system.

Most information systems departments operate under a budget format but many companies do not monitor the costs carefully, since the philosophy is often that all MIS costs are necessary but uncontrollable. A sound responsibility reporting system can greatly improve the efficiency of operating the MIS. Many companies charge users with the time that they use the system and the number and types of reports that they employ. Although much of the costs is indirect and theoretically outside the realm of responsibility reporting, managers should be requested to assess their information needs annually so that a more efficient use of the resources is possible.

For a company implementing a system for the first time, many managers prefer the MIS to be free to the users so that people will use the system. Such a situation should be carefully monitored because there may be some departments and employees who will abuse the privilege and employ the system for meaningless tasks. Once an application gets on the system, regardless of how meaningless, it can be very difficult to remove the application.

SUMMARY

For an organization to survive in the long run, it must have sound system controls. Although an organization will not need every control discussed in this chapter, certain aspects of control are basic to the sound operation of any system. Every organization must have some type of feedback system, although perhaps not as formal or well defined as that discussed in this chapter. Every system must also exercise some preventive controls, although these may vary depending on the type of organization. In reality, several preventive controls are basic in one form or another (i.e., documentation, organizational independence, and asset protection).

Even though control tools and techniques are too numerous to summarize here, every system must select the controls best suited for its operations. The selection will depend on things such as the size of company, amount of automation (if any), and use of real-time or batch processing. Business transactions are the raw materials of information systems, and controls over transactions depend on operational characteristics such as volume of transactions, data sensitivity, data gathering difficulties, and frequency of transactions.

Automation has an impact on manual systems when they are computerized and on computerized systems when they are updated for technology changes or growth. The importance of these changes should be recognized by accountants and auditors. Change is inescapable, and the computer is perhaps the most radical change ever to occur in the business environment. Accountants must know not only how to deal with control changes caused by automation, but also how to implement the controls when advancing technology changes the systems environment.

NOTES

[1] AICPA, Statement on Auditing Standards No. 1 (New York: American Institute of Certified Public Accountants, 1973), p. 20.

[2] AICPA, Statement on Auditing Standards No. 3 (New York: American Institute of Certified Public Accountants, 1974), p. 5, see also SAS No. 48.

[3] Brandt Allen, "The Biggest Computer Frauds: Lessons for CPAs," *Journal of Accountancy,* (May 1977): 54.

[4] Ibid., p. 58.

[5] A prime number is any number that can be divided evenly only by itself and the number 1—for example, 1, 3, 13, 29, and 53.

SELECTED REFERENCES

Allen, Brandt. "Embezzler's Guide to the Computer," *Harvard Business Review* (July/August 1975): 79–89.

Allen, Brandt. "The Biggest Computer Frauds: Lessons for CPAs," *Journal of Accountancy* (May 1977): 55–62.

Cushing, Barry E. *Accounting Information Systems.* Reading, Mass.: Addison-Wesley Publishing Co., 1982, Chap. 14.

Davis, James R. "EDP Control Means Total Control," *Management Accounting* (January 1977): 41–44.

Friedman, Stanley D. "Contingency and Disaster Planning in the EDP Area," *Today's Executive,* (Autumn 1982): 5–10.

Gibson, Cyrus F., and Richard L. Nolan. "Managing the Four Stages of EDP Growth," *Harvard Business Review* (January/February 1974): 76–88.

Hoffberg, Alan M. "Strengthening Controls over Mini- and Micro-Computers, *The CPA Journal* (May 1980): 82–85.

Hoffman, F. William, and Norman Statland. "Security—Will Your EDP System Survive a Disaster?" *Today's Executive* (New York: Price Waterhouse and Co.) (Summer 1979): 14–18.

Laudenan, M. "Document Flowcharts for Internal Control," *Journal of Systems Management* (March 1980): 38–41.

Li, David H. "Control Flowcharting for Internal Control," *The Internal Auditor* (August 1983): 28–33.

Romney, Marshall B., W. Steve Albrecht, and David J. Cherrington. "Red-flagging the White Collar Criminal," *Management Accounting* (March 1980): 51–54.

Sawyer, Lawrence B., Albert A. Murphy, and Michael Crossley. "Management Fraud: The Insidious Specter," *The Internal Auditor* (April 1979): 11–25.

Thorne, Jack F. "Control of Computer Abuses," *Journal of Accountancy* (October 1974): 40–48.

Watkins, Peter, "Computer Crime: Separating the Myth from Reality," *CAmagazine* (January 1981): 44, 47.

Zimmerman, Harry, "Minicomputers: The Challenge for Controls," *Journal of Accountancy* (June 1980): 28–35.

QUESTIONS

1. Define and explain the following:

Accounting controls	Application controls
Systems documentation	Program documentation
Operating documentation	Organizational independence
Parity bit	Duplicate circuitry
Echo check	Graceful degradation
Header labels	Trailer labels
Internal labels	External labels
Tape file protection ring	Check digits

Completeness test	Closed-loop verification
Sequence checks	Validity test
Limit checks	Logic test
Batch total	Record count
Field check	Control totals
Hash total	Cross-footing test
History log	Open-loop management by exception

2. Discuss the concept of feedback control systems and give several examples of proper application.
3. Contrast feedback and feedforward control systems. Give several examples of feedforward control applications.
4. Define preventive control. Discuss several important elements in an organization's preventive control applications.
5. Explain the three types of documentation. Give examples of each.
6. Explain how organizational independence can be a preventive control. What are the distinct applications of independence necessary for a sound data processing department?
7. As related to EDP, what are physical controls? Give several examples.
8. Contrast hardware and software controls. Give several examples of each.
9. Why are so many different types of labels needed in software controls? Explain an application of each type.
10. Discuss the concept of keeping multiple copies of data files. What is the concept called? Give an example of its application.
11. Give several examples of characteristics of good documents. Which characteristics that you listed are required and which are elective?
12. When are terminal controls used? How effective are they?
13. Define transaction validation. When is it applicable? List the most popular transaction validations.
14. Give an accounting application of each of the different types of control totals.
15. What is the importance of error detection? When should error detection be corrected?
16. Discuss the impact of automation on controls. Give a specific example of how automation has changed a traditional accounting control procedure.

PROBLEMS

17. Separation of Duties

The Alpha Company has just terminated all its accounting employees because of a fraud discovered by its CPA. The fraud had continued for 4 years, and the investigation revealed that poor separation of duties caused considerable problems in detecting the wrongdoings. All accounting employees had known about the fraud. To prevent the problem in the future you have been asked to provide a sound basis of separation for the new employees being hired. The five new employees will perform the following duties:

a. Preparing payroll checks
b. Posting accounts payable ledger
c. Posting accounts receivable ledger
d. Posting cash disbursements journal
e. Making cash deposits*
f. Handling petty cash*
g. Preparing accounts payable checks
h. Posting general ledger
i. Posting cash receipts journal
j. Issuing credit memos on returned sales

*These duties require much less time than the others.

Required:

Determine an acceptable set of duties for each employee and list at least three different combinations for a single employee that would be unacceptable from a control perspective.

18. Separation of Duties

The Lee County Savings and Loan Association has the following organizational structure in its data processing department. There are three keypunch operators, two computer operators, one programmer, and a department head who assists with systems analysis and design. The programmer and the department head assist the operators when the work load is heavy, and on occasion the department head has done some programming. The programmer is primarily responsible for maintaining the existing system and for making infrequent changes. When no programming is necessary, she helps user departments interpret output information. How would you evaluate this situation, given the importance of controls in a financial institution? What changes would you recommend?

19. Computer Location

The Southern Petroleum Company is moving its home office and computer center to a more centralized location. It is considering several sites in larger cities, and the president is concerned about having the computer center downtown with the home office. He believes a remote location is better for the computer operations center. Comment on his opinion and list other factors that are important in the location of a large computer operations center.

20. Cash and Receivables Control

Thach Company is engaged in wholesale operations. In evaluating the cash and receivables of the company, you discover that they do not prelist cash receipts before they are recorded and that there are several other minor weaknesses. In discussing the matter with the accounting manager, you find she is mainly concerned with costs savings. Her primary considerations when assigning tasks are the employee's familiarity with the task and his capability and availability. Also, the controller believes he has excellent control over accounts receivable since most of them are pledged as security for a line of credit with the local bank. The bank sends out confirmations periodically with the company's approval. You learn that the bank is satisfied if it gets positive replies of 75 percent; the remaining 25 percent are assumed to be nonresponse. Evaluate this situation of cash control and collection. What are the implications of the bank's nonresponse confirmations? What changes do you suggest?

21. Feedback, Feedforward, and Preventive Controls

For the items listed, state whether they are feedback-, feedforward-, or preventive-oriented. If more than one control applies, give primary and secondary relationships.

a. Evaluation of new employees by the personnel department
b. The cost accounting system of a manufacturing company
c. Separation of duties in the accounting department
d. Trend analysis of sales by territory
e. Annual evaluations of employees by their supervisors
f. Computerized EOQ inventory system
g. Bank reconciliations

22. Control Applications

For the following situations, discuss the various types of controls that would have been appropriate for prevention, detection, or correction. *(AICPA adapted)*

a. A computer malfunction caused the system to be down for 3 days at the end of the month. As a result, payroll was late, end-of-month postings could not be made, and several reports were not on time. During this period the company could not find compatible equipment on which the critical activities could be processed.

b. A computer department employee was given 2 weeks' notice before he was terminated. During this time he removed the external labels from all the files in the library.

c. Late one night an employee was smoking in the data file library and carelessly dropped ashes in a waste paper container. The resulting fire destroyed several reels of tape on which the only master file of inventory and payroll was stored. The files had to be manually reconstructed.

d. During a street riot, several people forced their way into the computer center, which was on the main level of the office building. Several gunshots were fired into the computer and other minor destruction was incurred. The system was inoperable for several days.

e. A night operator knew more about the system than anyone else. During a period of several weeks, he accessed the master payroll program, which was stored on-line, and increased his tax withholding so that he would get a large refund when he filed his tax return.

f. A customer payment was entered by the keypunch operator as $147.22 instead of $14,722.00.

g. An employee using a direct-access terminal entered the wrong account number for a customer. The charges were entered on the account of another customer, who was very irritated when he received the bill for goods not ordered.

h. The accounts payable printout was not verified, and a double payment was made to a vendor. The vendor notified the company.

23. Sales Transaction Controls

A sales transaction card was designed to contain the following information:

Card Column	Information
1–10	Customer account number
11–30	Customer name
31–38	Amount of sale
39–44	Sales date
45–46	Store code number
47–49	Sales clerk number
50–59	Invoice number

Required:

a. If such a card is rejected during computer processing because the sales clerk whose identification number appears on the record does not work at the store indicated by the numbers in card columns 45 and 46, then the error was probably detected by which of the following:

(1) A self-checking number

(2) A combination check

(3) A valid-character check

(4) A limit check

b. If the last letter of a customer's name is erroneously entered in card column 31, which of the following is most likely to detect the error during an input edit run?

(1) A logic check

(2) A combination check

(3) A valid-character check

(4) A self-checking number

24. General Controls

The Martin Utility District is installing an electronic data processing system. The CPA who conducts the annual examination of the Utility District's financial statements has been asked to recommend controls for the new system. *(AICPA adapted)*

Required:

Discuss recommended controls over:

a. Program documentation

b. Program testing

c. EDP hardware

d. Tape files and software

25. Control and Fraud Prevention

Jordan Finance Company opened four personal loan offices in neighboring cities 3 years ago. Small cash loans are made to borrowers who repay the principal with interest in monthly installments over a period not exceeding 2 years. Ralph Jordan, president of the company, uses one of the offices as a central office and visits the other offices periodically for supervision and internal auditing purposes.

Mr. Jordan is concerned about the honesty of his employees. He came to your office in December and stated, "I want to engage you to install a system to prohibit employees from embezzling cash." He also stated, "Until I went into business for myself I worked for a nationwide loan company with 500 offices and I'm familiar with that company's system of accounting and internal control. I want to describe that system so you can install it for me because it will absolutely prevent fraud." *(AICPA adapted)*

Required:

a. How would you advise Mr. Jordan on his request that you install the large company's system of accounting and internal control for his firm? Discuss.

b. How would you respond to the suggestion that the new system would prevent embezzlement? Discuss.

26. Error Detection and Prevention

Oliveria Manufacturing Company produces finished goods on a job order basis. It pays all production employees on an hourly basis with time and a half for overtime hours. The five organizational units actively involved in the payroll and labor cost determination procedures are timekeeping, factory operating departments, payroll audit and control, data preparation, and computer operations. The basic data collection and processing steps, together with their locations, are as follows:

a. *Timekeeping.* Employee time (clock) cards are prepared.

b. *Factory operating departments.* Job time tickets are prepared and forwarded.

c. *Timekeeping.* Employee time cards and job time tickets are compared and forwarded.

d. *Payroll audit and control.* Preceding source documents are reviewed and forwarded.

e. *Data preparation.* Preceding source documents are converted to punched cards and forwarded.

f. *Computer operations.* Data on punched cards are converted to magnetic tape, which is then processed against the employee payroll master file (on magnetic tape) to produce paychecks, hours worked summary by department, a payroll register, and a labor cost distribution sheet. *(AICPA adapted)*

Required:

a. List the possible errors or discrepancies that might occur at each data collection and processing step.

b. For each error or discrepancy list a control feature to prevent or detect its occurrence.

c. What changes in the system would make better use of the control features presented in this chapter?

27. Error Detection and Prevention

What controls could be implemented to prevent, detect, or minimize the occurrences in the following situations?

a. A new computer operator on the night shift accidentally erased the accounts payable master file by using it as an output tape for another job.

b. A vendor payment was keyed onto the input tape as $2,222.00 instead of $222.20.

c. A floppy disk that held the inventory file was removed from the disk drive yesterday and put in the library but cannot be found today.

d. A district sales manager entered a customer order for one thousand toasters instead of for one thousand coasters. The toasters were delivered much to everyone's dismay.

e. A payroll employee accessed the sales ordering system and ordered several hundred items for a fictitious company and had them delivered to a friend's address.

f. Several customer orders go unfilled because the computer printout showed a zero balance for a particular item when in fact the item was in stock.

g. A sales clerk accidentally omits the quantity from a rush order that is supposed to be shipped in the afternoon. The customer cannot be reached until tomorrow.

h. A confidential payroll check register is accidentally sent to the purchasing department.

i. A key operator accidentally entered a set of accounts payable vouchers into the accounts receivable master, both files have identical types of account numbers and sales order forms are similar to payables vouchers.

j. A payroll clerk made a terminal entry to increase the amount of his salary on his next paycheck.

28. Controls and Confidentiality

Toronto Retail is a retailing concern with stores throughout North America. The company is in the process of designing a new integrated computerized information system. In conjunction with the design of the new system, the management is reviewing data processing security to determine what new control features should be incorporated. Two areas of specific concern are: (1) confidentiality of company and customer records and (2) safekeeping of computer equipment, files, and facilities.

The new information system will process all company records, which include sales, purchase, financial, budget, customer, creditor, and personnel information. The stores and warehouses will be linked to the main computer at corporate headquarters by a system of remote terminals. This arrangement will permit data to be communicated directly to corporate headquarters or to any other location from each location throughout the terminal network.

At the present time certain reports have restricted distribution, because either not all levels of management need to receive them or they contain confidential information. The introduction of remote terminals in the new system may provide access to this restricted data by unauthorized personnel. Top management is concerned that confidential information may become accessible and may be used improperly.

The company is also concerned with potential physical threats to the system, such as sabotage, fire damage, water damage, power failure, and magnetic radiation. Should any of these events occur in the present system and cause a computer shutdown, adequate backup records are available to enable the company to reconstruct necessary information at a reasonable cost and on a timely basis. However, with the new system, a computer shutdown would severely limit company activities until the system could become operational again. *(IMA adapted)*

Required:
  a. Identify and explain the problems that could occur related to confidentiality of information and records in the new system.
  b. What measures would ensure the confidentiality of the information and records of the new system?
  c. What can be done to provide physical security for the company's files, equipment, and computer-related facilities in the new system?

29. Control Totals
The following information represents a weekly accounts payable printout of the Sand and Soil Hauling Company.

Vendor Number	Vendor Name	Invoice Amount	Discounts Taken	Net Amount
0123	ABC Co.	$24,500	$400	$24,100
1683	Mr. J. Smith	750	00	750
2644	Fixit Shop	4,312	100	4,212
2777	AAA Repair	2,536	25	2,511
5610	City Trucks	68,750	687	68,063

Required:
  a. Compute a relevant batch total for the weekly run.
  b. Compute a hash total for the weekly run.
  c. How can the totals you computed be used by the company?

30. Internal Control Questionnaires

The following questions came from an internal control questionnaire. If the answer to each question is "no," what are the implied weaknesses in the system?

a. Are your duties related to the computerized payroll system clearly defined?

b. Do you use the results provided by the labor efficiency printout?

c. Do you use all copies of this document?

d. Are all computerized files related to this department kept up to date?

e. Are you familiar with emergency backup procedures if the computer was down on a day when payroll had to be processed?

f. As a computer operator, are you required to take vacations?

g. Do you have batch control totals for the payroll run?

h. Are checks signed by someone outside the accounts payable department?

i. Are changes to the accounting programs approved by someone outside the programming department?

31. Internal Controls and Analysis

The cashier of Alpha Supply received a check from Customer A made payable to the company in the amount of $900. It was deposited in a bank account used only for the petty cash fund, of which he was custodian. He then drew a $900 check on the petty cash fund bank account payable to himself and cashed it. At the end of the month, while processing the monthly statements to customers, he was able to change the statement of Customer A so as to show that A had paid the $900 invoice. Ten days later he made an entry in the cash receipts ledger that purported to record receipt of the remittance of $900 for Customer A, thus restoring the account to the proper balance, but overstating cash. He covered the overstatement by omitting from the list of outstanding checks in the bank reconcilement, two checks, the aggregate amount of which was $900. *(AICPA adapted)*

Required:

a. Describe the deficiencies in the system of internal control.

b. How would you correct each situation?

CHAPTER SEVEN

Auditing, Controls, and EDP

A discussion of controls is not complete unless the interrelationship between controls and auditing are considered. Auditing is the process of examining information with the intent of establishing reliability and is normally performed by someone other than the preparer or user. Since an audit occurs after the transactions and events under examination are completed, it serves as a broad control over the system. In addition, evaluating controls and verifying the existence of controls in the system are often integral components of the audit process. To feel confident in the applications of the controls discussed in Chapter Six, information systems users need to know what controls are in effect, if the controls are being followed, and if they are effective in controlling the system. This chapter examines the types of audits used in computerized systems, the role of the auditor, and the auditor's use of computers. The discussion centers around computers and control and the impact of computers on auditing techniques.

To facilitate the demands of the many users of accounting information, most organizations typically perform two types of audits: internal audits and external, or independent, audits. Internal audits are primarily for internal users, whereas external audits are useful to both internal and external users of information. Internal users, generally the management of an organization, utilize accounting information for decision making, planning, and control. External users, such as creditors and shareholders, also need accounting information for decision-making purposes. Whereas internal users have relatively complete access to information, most external users must depend on accounting reports released by the company. For external users, the assurance that accounting reports are reliable and without bias is generated through the auditing process performed by independent auditors. The independent auditor (generally a certified public accountant) is primarily concerned with external reporting and the related attest function; alternatively, the internal auditor is interested in the management and control processes of the company. Since accounting systems produce information utilized in various types of accounting reports, all auditors must have a solid understanding of the organization's accounting system. As the Commission on Auditors' Responsibilities observed:

> The preparation of financial statements starts with data documented by an accounting system. Accounting systems and the controls over them make possible a comprehensive summary of the myriad, diverse transactions of the typical business. These systems are an important source of information to the auditor, as well as to management.[1]

Our complex business environment requires numerous types of auditors. In addition to the independent auditors and internal auditors, there are General Accounting Office (GAO) auditors, Internal Revenue Service agents, Federal Bank examiners, and auditors of other various federal, state, and local governmental agencies. Although the objectives of these various types of auditors differ, the auditing procedures utilized are often similar. Thus many of the concepts in this chapter apply to most classifications of auditors.

Although all auditors are concerned with compliance and controls, these items are especially significant for the internal auditor. According to the Institute of Internal Auditors,

> Internal auditing is an independent appraisal activity within an organization for the review of operations as a service to management. It is a managerial control which functions by measuring and evaluating the effectiveness of other controls.[2]

Thus internal auditors function as appraisers of accounting systems and as an effective control element of the organization.

INTERNAL CONTROLS

Statement on Auditing Standards (SAS) No. 1 defines internal control as "the plan of organization and all the coordinate methods and measures adopted within a business to safeguard its assets, check the accuracy and reliability of its accounting data, promote operational efficiency, and encourage adherence to the prescribed managerial policies."[3]

SAS No. 1 also divides internal controls into two components: administrative controls and accounting controls. According to SAS No. 1, (paragraphs 26–29):

> *Administrative control* includes, but is not limited to, the plan of organization and the procedures and records that are concerned with the decision processes leading to management's authorization of transactions . . . and is the starting point for establishing accounting control over transactions.
>
> *Accounting control* comprises the plan of organization and procedures and records that are concerned with the safeguarding of assets and the reliability of financial records and consequently are designed to provide reasonable assurance that:
>
> a. Transactions are executed in accordance with management's general or specific authorization.
> b. Transactions are recorded as necessary (1) to permit preparation of financial statements in conformity with generally accepted accounting principles or any other criteria applicable to such statements and (2) to maintain accountability for assets.
> c. Access to assets is permitted only in accordance with management's authorization.
> d. The recorded accountability for assets is compared with the existing assets at reasonable intervals and appropriate action is taken with respect to any difference.[4]

Auditors are generally more interested in internal accounting controls since they represent the means by which a company: (1) processes its accounting transactions so that reliable financial information can be generated and (2) safeguards its assets.

Obviously, a company that processes its accounting information reliably would be preferred by an auditor who is to render an opinion on the financial statements. To provide assurances that the accounting system generates reliable financial information, a company would install internal accounting controls that provide checks and balances so that accounting information is correctly recorded both initially and as it is processed through the accounting system. Clearly, a good internal control system would indicate that the financial accounting numbers are more reliable and thus require fewer audit tests and procedures by the auditor. On the other hand, a poor internal control system would indicate that these financial accounting numbers may not be so reliable and thus would require the auditor to expand auditing procedures.

The internal accounting control systems generally have certain characteristics that give the company reasonable assurance that accounting controls are functioning properly. SAS No. 1 groups such characteristics into the following classifications.

1. Personnel should have competence and integrity.
2. There should be no incompatible functions such that any person is in a position both to perpetrate and conceal irregularities in the normal course of his duties. To accomplish a proper segregation of duties, the system, insofar as possible, should provide for different individuals to perform the functions of (a) authorizing a transaction, (b) recording a transaction, (c) maintaining custody of the assets that result from a transaction, and (d) comparing assets with the related amounts recorded in the accounting records.
3. Authorization for transactions should be issued by persons acting within the scope of their authority and the transactions should conform to the terms of the authorizations.
4. Transactions should be recorded at the amounts and in the accounting periods in which they were executed. The transactions should be recorded in proper accounts.
5. Access to assets should be limited to authorized personnel.
6. There should be independent comparisons of assets with the recorded accountability of these assets.[5]

AUDITING STANDARDS AND CONTROLS

A primary consideration of an auditor is the evaluation of internal controls utilized by the company. Controls have a direct impact on the effectiveness of the accounting system and, as a consequence, the reliability of accounting information. To aid auditors in fulfilling their professional responsibilities, the American Institute of Certified Public Accountants (AICPA) has established a framework of 10 auditing standards.

The second standard of fieldwork, one of the 10 standards, relates specifically to internal controls.

There is to be a proper study and evaluation of the existing internal control as a basis for reliance thereon and for the determination of the resultant extent of the tests to which auditing procedures are to be restricted.[6]

Statement on Auditing Standards (SAS) No. 43 clarifies the auditor's responsibilities regarding the second standard of fieldwork. According to SAS No. 43, the review of controls may be limited to obtaining an understanding of the control environment and the flow of transactions through the accounting system. This is often referred to as the *preliminary phase* of the auditor's review of internal control.

The purpose of this preliminary phase is to provide the auditor with a general knowledge of matters such as the organizational structure; the methods used to communicate responsibility and authority; the methods used to supervise the system; the various classes of transactions; and the methods by which each significant class is authorized, executed, initially recorded and processed. These matters, of course, represent the control environment and the flow of transactions. Ordinarily the auditor obtains this understanding by a combination of previous experience with the client, inquiry, observation, and references to prior-year working papers, client-prepared descriptions of the system, or other appropriate documentation. The auditor is required to obtain an understanding of the control environment and the flow of transactions that allows the auditor to assess auditability and to design substantive tests properly.

The control environment includes the client's organizational structure, the methods used by the client to communicate authority and responsibility, and the methods used by management to supervise the control system. To understand the flow of transactions, the auditor should understand how accounting information flows to the accounts in the client's financial statements.

An understanding of the accounting system, which the auditor must obtain in all audits, should be distinguished from an understanding of the internal accounting control system, which the auditor must obtain only if there is an intent to rely on internal accounting controls. The accounting system is composed of procedures that are established to process transactions as a means of maintaining the records of an entity's operations and financial position. The procedures include those that recognize, assemble, classify, analyze, and record all the entity's transactions. On the other hand, the system of internal accounting control includes procedures to provide reasonable assurance that the financial records produced by the accounting system are reliable and that assets are safeguarded. An accounting system may include procedures that contribute to the achievement of control objectives and, in practice, the two systems may partially overlap. But, theoretically, an accounting system is able to produce reliable financial records without a system of internal accounting control.

Although the auditor is concerned with analyzing and evaluating internal controls, the responsibility for the establishment and maintenance of internal controls rests with management of the company. As noted by the Securities and Exchange Commission,

> a fundamental aspect of management's stewardship responsibility is to provide shareholders with reasonable assurance that the business is adequately controlled. Additionally, management has a responsibility to furnish shareholders and potential investors with reliable information on a timely basis. An adequate system of internal accounting controls is necessary to management's discharge of these obligations.[7]

Thus management must establish internal controls to achieve company objectives. The auditor, on the other hand, reviews and evaluates these controls as a basis for reliance and determination of the extent of subsequent audit procedures.

In 1977 the U.S. Congress passed the Foreign Corrupt Practices Act (FCPA). This act has two major provisions: (1) It is a criminal offense for any American business to offer a bribe to a foreign official or foreign political party or candidate for the purpose of obtaining, retaining, or directing business to any person. (2) It requires every publicly held company to devise, document, and maintain a system of internal accounting controls sufficient to provide reasonable assurances that the four following objectives are met:

1. Transactions are executed in accordance with management's general or specific authorization.
2. Transactions are recorded as necessary (a) to permit preparation of financial statements in conformity with generally accepted accounting principles or any other criteria applicable to such statements and (b) to maintain accountability for assets.
3. Access to assets is permitted only in accordance with management's general or specific authorization.
4. The recorded accountability for assets is compared with the existing assets at reasonable intervals and appropriate action is taken with respect to any differences.

The effect of the accounting provision of the FCPA is to require publicly held companies to maintain reasonably complete and accurate financial records and a reasonable system of internal accounting controls.

RELATIONSHIP OF CONTROLS TO AUDITING

To review and evaluate the company's internal controls, the auditor must identify, test, and evaluate the controls and determine their objectives. To facilitate an understanding of these procedures, Coopers & Lybrand, a national accounting firm, divides this process into seven steps and labels it a *Uniform Audit Approach*. [8]

1. The auditor should obtain an understanding of and record the client's accounting system, including the procedures and controls incorporated in it, and review selected transactions to determine that he has understood and recorded the system properly.
2. Select an appropriate Internal Control Questionnaire [a part of an Internal Control Questionnaire for Cash Receipts for a theater is shown in Figure 7.1].
3. Evaluate the system to identify (a) those internal accounting controls on which he proposes to place some reliance and (b) any apparent weaknesses in the system.
4. Discuss with the client the apparent weaknesses identified in order to ascertain whether they are compensated by some other control; if they are not compensated, the auditor should assess their possible effects on the financial statements and on his audit tests.
5. Design (or modify) and carry out a program of functional tests to determine whether the controls on which he intends to place reliance were operating during the period.
6. Report apparent weaknesses and breakdowns in internal control to the client in a management letter.
7. Based on the results described in (1) to (6), design (or modify) and carry out a program of audit work to substantiate the amounts appearing in the financial statements and related notes.

INTERNAL ACCOUNTING CONTROL QUESTIONNAIRE
CASH RECEIPTS TRANSACTIONS.

CLIENT: Control Procedure	Yes	No
1. Are prenumbered tickets used and subsequently accounted for?	————	————
2. Is there restricted access to rolls of unused tickets?	————	————
3. Is a ticket machine used in issuing tickets?	————	————
4. Are tickets voided upon admission of patrons?	————	————
5. Is there segregation of duties between the issuance of tickets and admission of patrons?	————	————
6. Is there an independent daily cash count and reconciliation with tickets issued?	————	————
7. Are cash receipts deposited in total daily?	————	————

Source: Adapted from Walter G. Kell and Richard E. Ziegler, *Modern Auditing,* 2nd Ed. © 1983, p. 117.

Figure 7.1

As stated in generally accepted auditing standards and reflected in the Coopers & Lybrand approach, internal controls and a review and evaluation of the accounting system should be an integral part of any independent audit designed to express an opinion on the financial statements. Indeed, such a systems approach should permeate the entire audit. Peat, Marwick, Mitchell & Company, another national accounting firm, has flowcharted their systems approach to auditing. This flowchart, as shown in Figure 7.2, clearly shows the importance of internal controls and the accounting system in all phases of the audit.

Figure 7.2 divides the audit process into three phases: (1) planning, (2) interim work, and (3) final work. In the planning phase the auditor gathers initial evidence about the client and its financial statements by obtaining information about general economic activity, the client's industry, financial performance, and internal controls. In the interim work phase the auditor reviews, evaluates, and tests the client's system of internal controls. As a result of these procedures, the auditor determines the extent of other audit work to be performed. In the final work phase the auditor finishes the specific audit procedures that need to be performed and draws conclusions. The audit is then reviewed by appropriate supervisory personnel, and the audit report is subsequently issued.

A CYCLES APPROACH TO AUDITING

The preceding section provided evidence as to the importance of internal controls and the accounting system when external audits are conducted in accordance with professional auditing standards. Auditors, however, in the proper discharge of this responsibility often become frustrated by the seemingly endless maze of controls that are installed for each of the company's various accounts. The economic events generating transactions that impact on the company's accounts are almost limitless. To attempt to understand the accounting system from this perspective of myriad economic events severely limits the auditor's view.

AUDIT OVERVIEW, (1) PLANNING PHASE, (2) INTERIM PHASE, (3) FINAL PHASE.

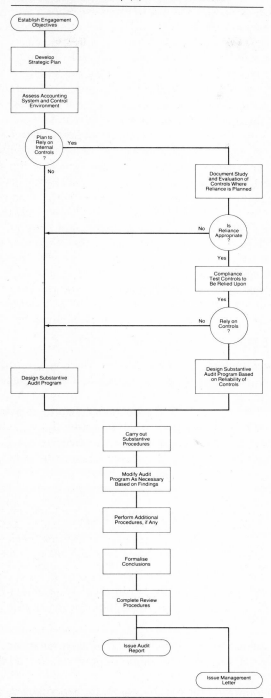

Source: *Systems Evaluation Approach to Auditing,* 1981, Peat Marwick Mitchell & Co., 1981.

Figure 7.2

Instead of reviewing controls from a specific transaction approach, auditors can categorize these economic events into a limited number of cycles that represent the various business activities of the company. Economic events common to a given cycle are related in the sense that their internal control objectives and tasks required for adequate authorization, recording, and reporting are similar.

Cycles are comprised of the various accounting subsystems in operation. In this book the cycles have been broadly categorized into four groups: the spending cycle, the conversion cycle, the revenue cycle, and the administrative cycle. Although accountants may classify cycles in different ways, the important point is that controls can be examined from a cycle viewpoint rather than from a transactional viewpoint.

A cycle approach to auditing has numerous benefits to the auditor. As noted previously, viewing the accounting and control systems in terms of cycles often simplifies the review and evaluation process since commonalties between various controls and transactions are often observed. In addition, when controls are viewed in terms of cycles, the auditor focuses on controls over an entire process (e.g., the sales process from order to payment) rather than the specific transactions that comprise only one phase of the process. In this regard the auditor views controls as a continuous process rather than a hodgepodge of controls broken down by type of transaction and department. As a consequence, a cycle approach to auditing increases both the breadth and depth of the auditor's understanding of internal controls and the accounting system.

IMPACT OF EDP SYSTEMS ON AUDITING

In the professional literature, the concept of accounting controls has been expressed in terms of objectives. Thus the concept is independent of any specific type of data processing that a company may utilize whether that processing is manual, mechanical, or electronic. The auditor's objectives do not change regardless of how accounting data are processed. Although objectives do not differ among the types of data processing, the specific procedures utilized to achieve those objectives may be dependent on the system used. Recognizing these conflicts, the statement on Auditing Standards (SAS) No. 48 states:

> The auditor should consider the methods the entity uses to process accounting information in planning the audit because such methods influence the design of the accounting system and the nature of the internal accounting control procedures. The extent to which computer processing is used in significant accounting applications, as well as the complexity of that processing, may also influence the nature, timing and extent of audit procedures.

SAS No. 48 further observes that in evaluating the effect of an entity's computer processing on an examination of financial statements, the auditor should consider matters such as:

1. The extent to which the computer is used in each significant accounting application
2. The complexity of the entity's computer operations, including the use of an outside service center
3. The organizational structure of the computer processing activities

4. The availability of data. Documents used to enter information into the computer for processing, certain computer files, and other evidential matter that may be required by the auditor may exist only for a short period or only in computer-readable form. In some computer systems, input documents may not exist at all because information is directly entered into the system. An entity's data retention policies may require the auditor to request retention of some information for review or to perform audit procedures at a time when the information is available. In addition, certain information generated by the computer for management's internal purposes may be useful in performing substantive tests (particularly analytical review procedures).

5. The use of computer-assisted audit techniques to increase the efficiency of performing audit procedures. Using computer-assisted audit techniques may also provide the auditor with an opportunity to apply certain procedures to an entire population of accounts or transactions. In addition, in some accounting systems, it may be difficult or impossible for the auditor to analyze certain data or test specific control procedures without computer assistance.

Installation of EDP systems impacts accounting controls in both (1) the types of accounting control features in the EDP system itself and (2) effects of EDP on accounting controls. Thus, for a proper evaluation, an EDP system must be examined in terms of its own control features as well as the impact of the EDP system on the characteristics of control content.

EDP Accounting Control Features

Professional auditing standards (SAS No. 48) categorize EDP accounting control features into two areas: general controls and application controls. General controls relate to all EDP activities and include (1) the plan of organization and operation of the EDP activity, (2) the procedures for documenting, reviewing, testing, and approving systems or programs and changes thereto, (3) controls built into the equipment by the manufacturer (i.e., hardware controls), (4) controls over access to equipment and data files, and (5) other data and procedural controls affecting overall EDP operations.

Alternatively, application controls relate to specific accounting tasks and are broadly divided into three areas: (1) input controls, (2) processing controls, and (3) output controls. Application dependent controls are often dependent on general controls and are designed to achieve specific control objectives.

Input controls are designed to provide reasonable assurance of the EDP process up until the time data are entered into the computer. They are of major importance in an EDP system since the output in such a system depends on the input. These controls include checks for proper authorization, correct data conversion into machine-readable form, and prevention of lost, added, or duplicated data.

Processing controls are designed to provide reasonable assurance throughout the working phase of an EDP application. Processing controls test whether all transactions are processed as authorized and also test for omissions of authorized transactions and for the addition of unauthorized transactions. Processing controls include tests for valid data, cross-footing tests, and reasonableness tests. These were discussed in detail in Chapter Six under Transaction Controls.

Output controls are designed to provide reasonable assurance that EDP outputs are accurate and received only by authorized personnel. Examples of output controls include reviews by authorized personnel of reports and other output for incompleteness, totals that do not reconcile, and missing information.

The process of classifying controls into general and application control categories has no effect on the objective of designing a system of internal accounting control which is to provide reasonable assurance that errors and irregularities are prevented or detected.

Effects of EDP on Other Accounting Controls

Although EDP systems do not change the objectives and essential characteristics of accounting controls, the specific organization and control procedures utilized and the resultant audit trails may differ from those used in non-EDP systems. The introduction of an EDP system impacts on the other elements of accounting control in five areas: (1) segregation of duties, (2) execution of transactions, (3) recording of transactions, (4) access to assets, and (5) comparison of recorded accountability with assets.

Since procedures are often combined in computerized systems, the likelihood of incompatible functions and therefore less segregation of duties increases. *Incompatible functions* relate to such matters as assignment of duties, changes in programs, maintenance of data files, and operating of data management systems. When individuals perform incompatible functions, compensating controls in other areas should be utilized. Independent document and data checks by user departments, rotation of personnel, and internal audit procedures are some examples of compensating controls.

When a program executes the steps in the transaction cycle (e.g., determining inventory items to be ordered and preparation of purchase orders), control procedures should be designed to assure that the steps are executed in accordance with authorizations issued by persons acting within the scope of their responsibilities. In these cases where EDP is utilized to process or initiate and record transactions, the effectiveness of accounting controls depends on (1) the functioning of the EDP procedures that record the transactions and produce the output and (2) the follow-up of other actions by output users.

When EDP activity includes the processing of documents that lead to the use or disposition of assets, then personnel in EDP will also have access to those assets. Accounting controls should be initiated to provide reasonable assurance that computer personnel do not have unauthorized access to assets.

In many companies the computer is utilized to compare recorded accountability with the physical quantity of assets (e.g., during physical inventory counts computer listings of physical counts are compared to book-recorded quantities). If EDP is used in this situation, controls should be designed to prevent errors and irregularities such as misstatement of physical counts, insertion of fictitious physical counts, or errors (intentional or unintentional) in the printout of comparisons between physical counts and recorded quantities.

Evaluation of the EDP System

Even though specific accounting controls may vary, or be modified in an EDP system, the evaluation process should not differ. SAS No. 48 points out that the evaluation of control surrounding the computerized aspects of an accounting information system should not be conceptually different from the evaluation of the other aspects of the system. Also, this evaluation should be integrated with the auditor's overall systems review. All control procedures related to accounting activities, whether manual or computerized, management or staff, decision making or data entry, should be considered as an integrated concept by the auditor. Treated separately, the controls of one area may be strong and those of another weak; without evaluating how the different controls complement and supplement each other the auditor is unable to place proper reliance on the total control aspect of an organization.

In performing an audit of a client with an EDP system, the auditor should consider whether specialized skills are needed to determine the effect of computer processing on the audit, to understand the flow of transactions, to understand the nature of internal accounting control procedures, or to design and perform audit procedures. According to SAS No. 48, if specialized skills are needed, the auditor should seek the assistance of a professional possessing such skills, who may be either on the auditor's staff or with another firm. If the use of another professional is planned, the auditor should have sufficient computer-related knowledge to communicate the objectives of the other professional's work; to evaluate whether the specified procedures will meet the auditor's objectives; and to evaluate the results of the procedures applied as they relate to the nature, timing, and extent of other planned audit procedures.

AUDITING AROUND THE COMPUTER

With this concept of auditing, the primary focus is on input and output rather than on the technical aspects of the computer system. The auditor proves the accuracy of the data inputs, demonstrates that those inputs actually should result in the outputs obtained, and concludes that the processing system is correct and effective. Input controls are examined and sample-tested, and the manually calculated results of the input data are compared with the computer output of the data. If the calculated results and the outputs agree, the system is assumed to be functioning properly.

Auditing around the computer is advantageous because it requires minimum involvement with the computer and the programs of the accounting functions. Its major weakness is its failure to assess and evaluate the actual processing steps of the system; that is, basic system controls against fraud and human error may be missing or data input controls may be absent or inadequate. The processing itself may be inexpensive and efficient, allowing the auditor to give good evaluations when the system is in fact inefficient and ineffective. Because of these weaknesses, auditing around the computer has limited applicability in a computer environment—for example, a small company with computer applications that are independent from each other.

UTILIZATION OF EDP BY AUDITORS

Many companies have used EDP systems for many years in their operations; however, auditors and accounting firms have only recently taken advantage of the many auditing benefits to be derived from using electronic systems. Generally, auditors utilize the computer in one of two ways: (1) processing test data developed by the auditor on the client's system to aid in the review and evaluation of internal controls and (2) testing the client's records that are maintained on the computer as part of the auditor's substantive tests of the client's financial statements.

Auditing Through the Computer

When performing audit procedures through the computer, auditors should be cognizant of the potential risks involved and exercise due professional care. For example, auditors should ascertain that they are auditing actual client files, not bogus files. Auditors should not rely on EDP personnel to process audit applications. Moreover, auditors should guard against the erasure or modification of an EDP file due to an operator or programming error during processing.

Test Data In the test data, or test deck approach, the auditor develops transactions to be processed under the auditor's control using the client's EDP system. The test data approach is shown in Figure 7.3. Generally, the test data include valid and invalid transactions so that the auditor can examine the system to see whether it properly processes both valid and invalid data. The use of test data by the auditor is similar to controlled testing performed by systems analysts where the results of the test data transactions are known before the data are processed.

Test data are basically used to obtain information about the operation of the pro-

TEST DATA APPROACH.

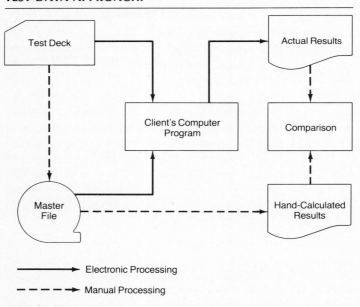

Figure 7.3

grams and the controls surrounding the programs. This is recommended where a significant portion of the organization's internal control system is computerized. It may also be effective where there are gaps in the audit trail and where a particular function has a large volume of transactions. However, this testing process may be difficult to use in a large complex system where the number of data combinations is numerous. Further, the auditor must be careful to ascertain that data created using this approach have not entered the client's data files.

For this approach to be effective, the auditor must be sure that a program being tested is the one the company actually uses to process its data. Although every program cannot be tested on a surprise basis, the auditor can request randomly selected programs for unannounced testing. Another surprise technique is to arrive at the processing center during actual processing of company data and request that the program in use be left on-line after regular processing so that the auditor can utilize the program to process the test data. The second method is preferred over the first because the auditor knows that the program is the one currently being used.

There are several weaknesses of this method that distract from its use. Substitution of programs by computer personnel during testing may be very difficult to monitor and detect. Using test data in real-time systems can be hazardous, because intentionally invalid test data may interfere with the normal updating of files and create erroneous data in actual company files. To avoid this, false files may be used, but they are expensive and time-consuming to create.

Parallel Simulation   In parallel simulation the auditor designs a computer program that can process real data from the client. Whereas a test deck processes simulated data on a client system, parallel simulation processes client data on a simulated system. As shown in Figure 7.4, when utilizing parallel simulation the auditor compares output from the simulated system with output from the client's system.

The primary advantage of parallel simulation is that the auditor is actually examining real data, data that comprise part of the financial records for which an opinion is being rendered. However, parallel simulation requires significant computer expertise. And since the client's computer program is not examined, parallel simulation is often classified as auditing ~~around~~ with the computer.

Auditing ~~through~~ with the Computer

Integrated Test Facility (ITF)   ITF is defined as an approach to computer auditing wherein fictitious test transactions are passed through the client's processing system simultaneously with actual company data without affecting the real data base or files. The auditor establishes a separate data base and master file against which the test data are processed. Once the fictitious data base and files are operational, the auditor can process test data without computer personnel knowing when or what programs are being tested. This approach is especially beneficial for auditing on-line systems or on-line aspects of large complex systems.

Using ITF, the auditor can examine the impact transactions have on the company, how they are processed by the computerized system, and the integration they cause or require in the system. Because the fictitious data are integrated with real data, the ITF has an advantage over the test data approach by letting the auditor know that the correct

PARALLEL SIMULATION.

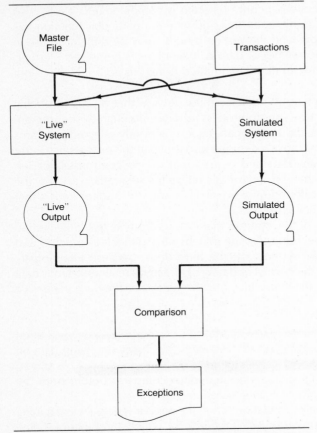

Source: W. C. Mair, "New Techniques in Computer Program Verification,"
Tempo (Winter 1971–1972), p. 14, published by Touche Ross & Co.

Figure 7.4

programs, not substitute programs, are being used for processing. The major advantage is that ITF tests the program as it is operating, not after the fact.

Auditing with the Computer

Software programs allow the auditor to use the computer as an audit tool and is often referred to as auditing with the computer. In this case the auditor is examining the client's financial records rather than the client's computer system. Thus the computer is an audit tool much like an adding machine or calculator. The auditor, for example, may design a program to check extensions, footings, and cross-footings of a client's records or to select appropriate audit samples and print confirmation requests.

Many CPA firms have designed computer programs known as *generalized audit software programs* for their audit personnel. Such programs perform routine audit tests and can be adapted by the auditor to many client situations. These systems usually do not require extensive computer expertise by the auditor (i.e., the auditor does not have to be a computer programmer), and they reduce the time spent for detailed record checking.

Peat, Marwick, Mitchell & Company has designed a generalized computer audit program, referred to as System 2170, to perform a variety of routines and functions for the auditor. A detailed listing and brief description of 13 of the routines and functions that can be performed by System 2170 are listed in the chapter Appendix.

AUDITORS' CHANGING RESPONSIBILITIES

Auditors face ever-increasing societal demands for extensions of their services into areas heretofore not served by the auditing profession. Debate among auditors as evidenced in professional journals and at professional meetings often centers around the auditor's ability to provide services in these nontraditional areas. Audits of interim financial data, future commitments, and involvement with forecasts all represent areas of expansion beyond the auditor's traditional role.

Often overlooked in the debate over extensions of the auditor's responsibilities are the importance of the accounting system, the interrelationship of the system with many of these areas, and the auditor's involvement and familiarity with accounting systems. The Commission on Auditors' Responsibilities has noted that:

> the accounting system establishes an important boundary for the accounting function. This boundary, however, is not static. As the accounting system develops, the audit function can expand accordingly. For example, if the accounting system develops to include more forward-looking information, that information can then be included in the audit function.[9]

The establishment of an accounting system and its resultant internal controls provides the very basis for the accumulation and verification of economic information. The auditor traditionally has developed an extensive knowledge of a client's accounting system. As accounting systems have become more complex and sophisticated, the auditor's responsibilities for understanding, testing, and evaluating the system have remained constant. Thus, expansion of the auditor's knowledge and expertise has become necessary.

Any discussion of the auditor's expanding role should include an evaluation of the auditor's expertise and abilities and an appropriate recognition of the auditor's unique relationship with and insights into a client's accounting system. New demands on the auditing profession will continue. Auditors must respond to societal pressures and expand their services into less traditional areas in which they possess the appropriate expertise.

The Commission on Auditors' Responsibilities emphasized the importance of a systems approach to auditing and urged that auditors become even more involved with accounting systems and internal controls. "The core of the framework that the Commission proposes is the audit of the accounting system and the controls over it."[10] This view is a distinct departure from past views that the audit represents an audit of a specific set of financial statements.

SUMMARY

Despite extensive utilization of controls, any accounting system may generate erroneous financial data. The major control point is at the time of input, and as a consequence auditors must carefully examine that area. However, this is only the beginning of the auditor's examination. The importance of the auditor's understanding and evaluation of a company's accounting system has long been emphasized in professional literature. Auditors are tied to the accounting system and the related internal control system.

Auditors have historically recognized the importance of accounting systems; only in recent years have they devised systems approaches to auditing. This development has been aided by a cyclical approach to systems whereby individual accounting subsystems are viewed in terms of their impact on the basic transactions cycles: spending, conversion, revenue, and financial. As the importance of systems to the auditing process has been increasingly recognized, society has placed new and expanded demands on the auditing profession. Many auditors as well as members of the Commission on Auditors' Responsibilities believe that auditors can respond to such challenges by utilizing a systems approach to auditing.

The emergence of EDP systems has also had an impact on the auditor, who must be cognizant of the complexity of such systems and their effect on accounting controls. Concomitantly, auditors are employing their own EDP systems with increasing frequency to aid in the performance of the audit. Use of test data, parallel simulation, and ITF to check the client's accounting system and utilization of software programs to perform specified audit procedures represent areas in which the auditor now employs the computer. Other areas are continuously being developed by both internal and external auditors to assist in the evaluation of the controls of a system as well as the system itself. It is beyond the scope of this text to develop all the computer auditing techniques in depth. The references at the end of the chapter provide more information on this topic.

APPENDIX: ROUTINES AND FUNCTIONS OF GENERALIZED COMPUTER AUDIT PROGRAMS

1. *Math routines.* The system provides four common mathematical operations—add, subtract, multiply, and divide. There is virtually no limit to the number of mathematical operations that can be performed during a single processing run.
2. *Include/exclude routines.* The use of an include or exclude routine gives the auditor selection ability to include or exclude records over, under, or equal to any given criteria. This allows the auditor to edit files and search for errors and helps select records that meet exception criteria. For example, an auditor who wanted a listing of all accounts over a certain dollar amount would use the include routine.
3. *Summarize routine.* This permits the auditor to summarize two or more input records into one. For example, the client may have multiple records for a given inventory item (same item in various locations). An auditor who wants to summarize the inventory quantity by item to audit for overstocked conditions would use the summarize routine.

4. *Categorize routine.* This permits the auditor to categorize an entire file. For instance, the auditor would use the categorize routine in aging an accounts receivable file by designating each age bracket as a single category.
5. *Match/direct routine.* This allows two files to be matched. For example, the auditor may match inventory test counts to the master inventory file and thus choose various courses of action as a result.
6. *Search routine.* This performs a table lookup function and will normally be used to convert codes to meaningful data. For example, if an accounts receivable file were coded with an alphabetic indication of credit limit (A = $50, B = $100, C = $500, etc.), the search routine could be used to convert the alphabetic code to dollars. These dollar limits could then be individually compared to the receivable balance to determine the extent of excessive credit granted to customers.
7. *Accumulate routine.* This permits the calculation of subtotals and totals by specified control levels. For instance, an auditor may want to determine sales by product line within divisions of a company.
8. *Foot routine.* This enables the auditor to foot all or selected parts of a file, count the records, and print the results.
9. *Sample routine.* This allows the auditor to select certain records for further processing. The selection process is based on every nth record with multiple random starting points.
10. *Output routines.* These direct the computer to print selected details, punch cards in a desired format or prepare a magnetic tape or disk in a desired format.
11. *Confirmation routine.* This permits confirmation of virtually all types of balance-only accounts, as well as statement-type accounts for accounts payable. Both positive and negative confirmations may be prepared and intermixed within a single processing run. For example, the auditor may want to send positive confirmations on all accounts over $5,000 and negative confirmations on selected accounts under $5,000. This could be done in a single processing run. The confirmation may be selected on a systematic sample basis (every nth account), with automatic random selection of the starting point. The routine provides record counts and dollar totals for the entire file and for each confirmation criterion selected. These totals are printed at the end of the confirmation run without additional instructions to the computer. If desired by the auditor, the routine permits preparation of second requests.
12. *Variables test (STAT operation).* The System 2170 variables test is composed of two job streams: sample selection and sample evaluation. During sample selection, the STAT operation will cause System 2170 to scan a population, stratify it, compute the correct sample size, and randomly select and print the sample items for the auditor's use. If desired, the system will generate an output tape containing the sample items, which may be used as input for subsequent System 2170 applications (e.g., the preparation of confirmation requests). After the sample items have been audited, the sample evaluation job stream is performed by using as input the audited values of only those sample items found in error. Along with various statistical results, the auditor receives a statistical recommendation to accept or reject a population. The sample evaluation may also indicate a "no decision" in certain circumstances where examination of additional sample items will be required.

13. *Attribute test (ATT operation).* Whereas the variables test (STAT operation) requires the execution of two job streams, the attribute test requires that only the sample selection job stream be executed. During sample selection, the ATT operation causes Systems 2170 to compute the proper attribute sample size, randomly select and print the sample items, and print an attribute evaluation table for the auditor's use after the sample items have been audited.

SOURCE: Peat, Marwick, Mitchell & Company. System 2170.

NOTES

[1]Commission on Auditors' Responsibilities, *Report, Conclusions, and Recommendations* (New York: American Institute of Certified Public Accountants, 1978), p. 53.

[2]Institute of Internal Auditors, *Statement of Responsibilities of the Internal Auditor* (Orlando, Fla.: Institute of Internal Auditors, 1971).

[3]*AICPA Professional Standards,* Vol. 1 (New York: American Institute of Certified Public Accountants, 1984), p. 32.

[4]Ibid., para 26–29.

[5]Ibid., Section 320.35–48.

[6]Ibid., au 150.02.

[7]Securities and Exchange Commission, Securities Release 34–13185, January 19, 1977.

[8]Coopers & Lybrand, *Uniform Audit Approach,* 1978.

[9]Commission on Auditors' Responsibilities, p. 58.

[10]Ibid., p. 60.

SELECTED REFERENCES

Arens, A. A., and J. K. Loebbecke. *Auditing: An Integrated Approach,* 3rd Ed. Englewood Cliffs, N.J.: Prentice-Hall, Inc., 1984.

Arthur Andersen & Co. *An Analysis of the Foreign Corrupt Practices Act of 1977.* Chicago: Arthur Andersen & Co., 1978.

Arthur Andersen and Co. *A Guide for Studying and Evaluating Internal Accounting Controls.* Chicago: Arthur Andersen & Co., 1978.

Cash, James I., Jr., Andrew D. Bailey, Jr., and Andrew B. Whinston. "A Survey of Techniques of Auditing EDP-Based Accounting Information Systems," *The Accounting Review* (October 1977): 813–832.

Cerullo, Michael J. and John C. Corless, "Auditing Computer Systems," *CPA Journal* (Sept 1984): 18, 20–26.

Commission on Auditor's Responsibilities. *Reports, Conclusions, and Recommendations,* New York: American Institute of Certified Public Accountants, 1978.

Coopers & Lybrand. *Uniform Audit Approach,* New York: 1978.

Davis, Gordon B., Donald L. Adams, and Carol A. Schaller. *Auditing and EDP,* 2nd ed., New York: American Institute of Certified Public Accountants, 1983.

Evaluating Accounting Controls: A Systematic Approach. New York: Arthur Young & Co., 1980.

Institute of Internal Auditors. *Statement of Responsibilities of the Internal Auditor.* Orlando, Fla.: The Institute of Internal Auditors, 1971.

Mair, W. C. "New Techniques in Computer Program Verification," *Tempo* (Touche Ross & Co., Winter 1971–1972).

Mair, William C., Donald R. Wood, and Keagle W. Davis. *Computer Control and Audit,* 2nd ed. Altamonte Springs, Fla.: The Institute of Internal Auditors, Inc., 1976.

Porter, W. Thomas, and William E. Perry. *EDP Controls and Auditing,* 3rd. ed. Belmont, Calif.: Wadsworth Publishing Co., 1980.

Reneau, J. Hal. "Auditing in a Data Base Environment," *Journal of Accountancy* (December 1977): 59–65.

Walker, Michael A., and Thomas Moser. "The Foreign Corrupt Practices Act of 1977: An Auditor's Perspective," *The CPA Journal,* 48 (May 1978): 71–75.

Weber, Ron. *EDP Auditing.* New York: McGraw-Hill Book Co., 1982.

QUESTIONS

1. Explain or define the following:

Administrative controls	Output controls
Accounting controls	Test data approach
Preliminary phase	Parallel simulation
Foreign Corrupt Practices Act	Integrated test facility
Processing controls	Audit software program

2. What is the role of auditors in examining the computerized records and systems of a client for external reporting purposes?
3. How does the auditor differentiate between the evaluations of internal control in manual versus computerized systems?
4. What role does the accountant play in the establishment of controls in the computerized systems of his or her own company?
5. Explain how questionnaires assist in the evaluation of internal controls.
6. In control evaluations, how many separate areas should there be and what are they? Which areas are most important and why?
7. How has computerization changed general accounting controls?
8. How does the computer help the auditor in actual auditing engagements?
9. What is the test deck approach?
10. What is a summarize routine? Where is it used? Who can use it?
11. What is a sample routine? What are the popular uses of such a routine?
12. Contrast auditing around the computer with auditing through the computer.
13. What additional impacts do you visualize the computer having on the auditing process, either internal or external?

PROBLEMS

14. Auditing Techniques for Systems Evaluation

The basic techniques used by auditors in evaluating systems are inspection, confirmation, comparison, observation, inquiry, and sampling. Select a basic technique to perform or detect the following situations, and justify your reason for selecting it.

a. Determining the error rate for keypunching payroll input.
b. There is evidence that the night operators are accessing unauthorized programs and making changes in them.
c. Management makes a special request that the actual payrolls for the year be reconciled to the year-end totals for a computerized payroll.
d. It is reported that some of the audio terminals are giving out erroneous information.

e. A bank needs several surprise checks of tellers during the year.

f. An organization has thousands of accounts receivable in its retail sales division through the use of credit cards. The general ledger accounts receivable is vital for short-term borrowing.

15. Accounts Receivables Controls

Jim Edwards, CPA, has just completed an audit of the Sanders Department Store, a retail chain. He is about to prepare his report when he is notified by management that a terminated employee in the accounting department appears to have left the company with several hundred thousand dollars that he acquired through accounts receivable manipulation. Edwards is somewhat surprised because he did a thorough check of receivables by auditing around the computer. He even sent out confirmations that the employee in question furnished him from the last computer printout of the outstanding receivables. What additional audit work could Edwards have performed that would have improved his chances of detecting the fraud?

16. Implement New Controls

The internal auditor for Toomer Industries has just been informed by management that the external auditors do not give the company's internal controls very high ratings. Although the internal auditor periodically checks the company's internal control features, the external auditors found some serious weaknesses. Management wants to add several controls to the current system. What are the disadvantages of adding controls after a system is operational? What is the best way to make such improvements?

17. Audit Software Programs

Describe how generalized audit software programs could be helpful in auditing the following accounting areas:

a. Accounts payable

b. Payroll

c. Fixed assets

d. Allowance for bad debts

18. Audit Reports and Schedules

The War Eagle Manufacturing Company is being audited by Young, Sells and Peat, CPAs. The auditor in charge of fixed assets is concerned about the lack of a proper audit trail. A computer audit expert is summoned to the job, and he suggests that a generalized audit program be used in the verification of the accounts. The audit package does the following:

a. Foots the file and prints totals by category for all assets. Breakdowns are given for costs, new additions during the period, current depreciation and depreciation balance, and differences between book and tax depreciation.

b. Prepares listings of all additions over $10,000.

c. Recalculates all depreciation for both book and tax purposes.

The year-end master files for fixed assets can be obtained from the company for the last several years. The master file is separated into 11 categories:

Asset number	Useful life
Description	Tax depreciation method
Type	Depreciation this year (books)
Year acquired	Depreciation this year (tax)
Original costs	Accumulated depreciation (tax)
Accumulated depreciation (books)	

Required:
  a. List the reports and schedules that the auditor will need the audit program to generate.
  b. Explain any additional procedures that might be necessary to satisfy the auditor that fixed assets are fairly stated on the books of the company.

19. Procurement and Payables Controls

Roger Peters, CPA, has examined the financial statements of the Solt Manufacturing Company for several years and is making preliminary plans for the audit for the year ended June 30, 1986. During this examination Mr. Peters plans to use a set of generalized computer audit programs. Solt's EDP manager has agreed to prepare special tapes of data from company records for the CPA's use with the generalized programs.

The following information is applicable to Mr. Peters's examination of Solt's accounts payable and related procedures:
a. The formats of pertinent tapes.
b. The following monthly runs are prepared:
  (1) Cash disbursements by check number.
  (2) Outstanding payables.
  (3) Purchase journals arranged by account charged and by vendor.
c. Vouchers and supporting invoices, receiving reports, and purchase order copies are filed by vendor code. Purchase orders and checks are filed numerically.
d. Company records are maintained on magnetic tapes. All tapes are stored in a restricted area within the computer room. A grandparent-parent-child policy is followed for retaining and safeguarding tape files. *(AICPA adapted)*

Required:
  a. Explain the grandparent-parent-child policy. Describe how files could be reconstructed when this policy is used.
  b. Discuss whether company policies for retaining and safeguarding the tape files provide adequate protection against losses of data.
  c. Describe the controls that the CPA should maintain over:
  (1) Preparing the special tape
  (2) Processing the special tape with the generalized computer audit programs
  d. Prepare a schedule for the EDP manager outlining the data that should be included on the special tape for the CPA's examination of accounts payable and related procedures. This schedule should show the:

(1) Client tape from which the item should be extracted

(2) Name of the item of data

20. On-line Testing Controls

As an internal auditor, you have been assigned to evaluate the controls and operation of a computer payroll system. The audit technique you will be using is on-line testing of the computer systems and/or programs by submitting independently created test transactions with regular data in a normal production run. *(AICPA adapted)*

Required:

a. List four advantages of this technique.

b. List two disadvantages of this technique.

21. Separation of Duties

Johnson, CPA, was engaged to examine the financial statements of Horizon Incorporated, which has its own computer installation. During the preliminary review, Johnson found that Horizon lacked proper segregation of the programming and operating functions. As a result, Johnson intensified the study and evaluation of the system of internal control surrounding the computer and concluded that the existing compensating general controls provided reasonable assurance that the objectives of the system of internal control were being met. *(AICPA adapted)*

Required:

In a properly functioning EDP environment, how is the separation of the programming and operating functions achieved?

22. Internal Control Review

An important procedure in the CPA's audit programs is his or her review of the client's system of internal control. *(AICPA adapted)*

Required

a. Distinguish between accounting controls and administrative controls in a properly coordinated system of internal control.

b. What bearing do these controls have on the work of the independent auditor?

c. List the basic principles of a sound system of accounting control.

23. Internal Control Review

Internal control comprises the plan of organization and all the coordinate methods and measures adopted within a business to safeguard its assets, check the accuracy and reliability of its accounting data, promote operational efficiency, and encourage adherence to prescribed managerial policies. *(AICPA adapted)*

Required:

a. What is the purpose of the auditor's study and evaluation of internal control?

b. What are the objectives of a preliminary evaluation of internal control?

c. How is the auditor's understanding of the system of internal control documented?

d. What is the purpose of tests of compliance?

24. Objectives of Internal Control

Jones, CPA, who has been engaged to examine the financial statements of Ajax Inc., is about to commence a study and evaluation of Ajax's system of internal control and is aware of the inherent limitations that should be considered. *(AICPA adapted)*

Required:

a. What are the objectives of a system of internal accounting control?

b. What are the reasonable assurances that are intended to be provided by the system of internal accounting control?

c. When considering the potential effectiveness of any system of internal accounting control, what are the inherent limitations that should be recognized?

25. Internal Control and Auditing Review

Select the best answer to each of the following questions. And explain why it is the best answer. (All *AICPA adapted*)

a. Which of the following is an administrative control?
  (1) Authorizing credit terms
  (2) Execution of transactions
  (3) Recording original data
  (4) Accountability over source data

b. The auditor is **least** concerned with which of the following?
  (1) Administrative controls
  (2) Application controls
  (3) Safeguarding of assets
  (4) Access to assets

c. Which of the following is likely to be **least** important to an auditor who is reviewing the internal controls surrounding the automated data processing function?
  (1) Ancillary program functions
  (2) Disposition of source documents
  (3) Operator competence
  (4) Bit storage capacity

d. Which of the following would **lessen** internal control in an electronic data processing system?
  (1) The computer librarian maintains custody of computer program instructions and detailed program listings.
  (2) Computer operators have access to operator instructions and detailed program listings.
  (3) The control group maintains sole custody of all computer output.
  (4) Computer programmers write and debug programs that perform routines designed by the systems analyst.

e. Which of the following is likely to be of **least** importance to an auditor in reviewing the internal control in a company with automated data processing?
  (1) The segregation of duties within the EDP center.
  (2) The control over source documents.
  (3) The documentation maintained for accounting applications.
  (4) The cost/benefit ratio of data processing operations.

f. Auditing by testing the input and output of an EDP system instead of the computer program itself will
  (1) Not detect program errors that do **not** show up in the output sampled.
  (2) Detect all program errors, regardless of the nature of the output
  (3) Provide the auditor with the same type of evidence
  (4) Not provide the auditor with confidence in the results of the auditing procedures.

g. When testing a computerized accounting system, which of the following is **not** true of the test data approach?
  (1) The test data are processed by the client's computer programs under the auditor's control.
  (2) The test data must consist of all possible valid and invalid conditions.
  (3) The test data need consist of only those valid and invalid conditions in which the auditor is interested.
  (4) Only one transaction of each type need be tested.

INFORMATION SYSTEMS
ANALYSIS AND DESIGN

CHAPTER EIGHT

Systems Analysis and Design

For a system to be properly evaluated, it should be divided into its basic components so that each major segment can be examined and analyzed. The primary objective is to provide a realistic insight into a segment of a system or the entire system. During systems analysis the ideas for a new or improved system are conceptualized and used as the basis for the design stage.

Systems design is the process of formalizing the specifications for the planned changes to be made in the system. This applies not only to computerizing manual systems but also to improving existing manual or computer systems. Systems being designed for the first time also need a formalized design phase. The needs and objectives of the users should provide the basis for developing the characteristics of the system. Systems design covers equipment availability, document needs, output formats, quantity of input and output, frequency of use, and personnel needs and qualifications.

The concepts presented in Chapters Two through Six must be understood before a study of the basic aspects of systems analysis and design can be undertaken. Further, the design of a system cannot be properly completed until the basic control features of information systems are understood. To design a workable, efficient, and effective system, the designer must know the concepts of systems controls and the aspects of controls that auditors consider important in evaluating the reliability of a system.

SYSTEM LIFE CYCLE

Because the environment surrounding an organization is continuously changing, the information system must be able to respond to the new demands placed upon it. The modifications and developments of an information system generally follow a cycle, which is repeated with each major systems change. *Systems analysis* is the first phase of the life cycle. During this initial activity the problems and needs of the users are defined. The scope of the particular study is then outlined and the fact gathering begins. A preliminary analysis of the facts is made and presented for approval to top management. If the general scope and needs of the system are agreed upon, a detailed analysis is undertaken by the systems analysts.

The second phase in the life cycle is the *systems design*. All aspects of the present system are considered in meeting the new needs defined by the systems analysis. The weaknesses of the current system are the focal points of the systems design unless the current system is not going to be maintained. It is generally appropriate to present several design alternatives for consideration in solving the system's needs. Several important aspects of systems design include cost/benefit analysis, impact on employees, and amount of time and training necessary to get the new system operational.

Systems implementation is the third phase in the life cycle. This involves such tasks as hardware changes, software modifications, systems conversion, employee training, and systems testing. To be complete the implementation phase should include a later follow-up to evaluate the effectiveness of the changes.

The last phase of the life cycle is the *operation* of the system. Until the system is changed again, the operating phase should be monitored and modified as necessary. As the environment changes, the system should be flexible enough to permit minor adjustments. Also, when a major or complete systems change is needed, the obsolescence is an indication of the end of the current life cycle and the beginning of a new life cycle.

SYSTEM OBJECTIVES

The first step in the analysis of an accounting information system is to determine the organizational objectives of the system: What are the purposes of the organization? What will be the relation of the information system to the organization? The primary purpose of any accounting information system is to provide information for management planning and control, but this cannot be accomplished unless the objectives of the organization are known. The overall accounting information system should also ensure that the objectives of each of the primary subsystems are carried out in accordance with management's desires. If these purposes are to be accomplished, the accounting information system must provide the information services to support the management decisions.

The objectives of the organization can be adequately defined only by top management. Although many organizations maintain formal written objectives, the systems analyst often has to ask for them before starting the analysis of a system. The importance of accounting information to the organization is generally indicated by the involvement of, and the number of references to, accounting in the stated objectives. The higher the level of references, the greater will be the importance of accounting to the organization. This also relates to the volume of decisions routinely made by accountants and to their role in the overall development of the accounting information system.

If management does not maintain formal written objectives for the system, the analyst can obtain the general objectives simply by studying the system currently in existence. An experienced analyst should know what information a system is furnishing to management by studying the system flowcharts, documentation, and outputs. The outputs, in particular, should provide the analyst with a clear understanding of the goals and objectives of the system.

Once management's goals and objectives are defined, the system analyst should then proceed to establish the general objectives of the system. The most common general objectives are:

1. *Simplicity.* The system should be complex enough to handle all the tasks necessary, but "frills" should not be designed into the system. All systems methodology should be easily understood, and users should not have difficulty in understanding and applying the results of their input.
2. *Flexibility.* The system should be designed to facilitate change and to minimize problems when changes are needed. Contingencies such as organizational growth, product or service changes, and user demands must be considered when designing for flexibility.
3. *Reliability.* The system should be programmed for an acceptable level of accuracy and periodically tested to ensure continued accuracy. Another reliability component of most systems is backup capability. When part of the system fails, another part should be able to assume the work load of the inoperable component, or if the entire system fails, another system should be available through time sharing or other means.
4. *Timeliness.* The system must be able to establish priorities for processing so that critical outputs can be processed on time and other outputs can be processed when time permits. User needs must be coordinated, and users should be aware of their output's priority.
5. *Feasibility.* The relationships of costs and related benefits must be continually monitored during the analysis and design of any system. Users often make demands of the system that are more properly classified as "wants" rather than needs. Such wants should be minimized in the overall plan of the system, although elimination can often be both difficult and political.
6. *Documentation.* The new system must be documented as it is developed. It is much easier to create the documentation as development takes place than to create documentation of the entire system at the completion of the project.
7. *Participation.* Users should be encouraged to participate in systems design. Selection of key personnel who will be using the new system is important to provide user viewpoints and output perspectives. The ideas these employees have should not be underestimated.

When designing a system, designers must consider all the objectives together; they must combine general objectives with the specific objectives of the organization in order to produce a system that meets the needs of users, management, and outsiders, such as governments. As the needs of these groups are designed into the system, objectives may change to accommodate multiple users and meet the needs placed on the system more efficiently.

SYSTEM CONSTRAINTS

After the objectives of the system are determined, the constraints must be evaluated to identify conflicts between the objectives and the constraints. All organizations have limitations, and the success of a system depends on its ability to operate within given constraints while still meeting its objectives. Constraints frequently place limits on user demands, frequency of reporting, auditability, hardware complexity, and capital expenditures. Several common constraints faced by many organizations are examined in the following sections, along with ideas for overcoming them.

Management Policy
Systems design and analysis are foremost constrained by management. The objectives of the system are themselves constraints placed on the organization by management. Although the constraints are necessary to prevent the system from becoming encumbered with unnecessary frills, the limitations placed on the design of the system by management can result in time delays and extra work for the analysts, programmers, and operating personnel. Moreover, if top management does not support necessary system changes, the system may not be accepted by other users. Positive support in the middle-management ranks is especially important, since user involvement at that level focuses on input and output, planning of the systems changes, document design, reporting frequency, and daily control procedures.

Personnel
Another major constraint in modifying an operating system is the possible need to change personnel. Qualifications of current employees are often insufficient to handle the demands of the new system. In designing the new system, the designer must allow time for training existing employees or for hiring and training new employees. Assuming that the need for systems change is obvious, management must evaluate the personnel needs beginning with qualified systems analysts and designers, programmers, and operators. If such personnel are not available, the organization can hire external consultants to perform the analysis and design stages. After the new system is designed, additional personnel must be available to operate and use it. Although users are not involved with the technical aspects of systems design and analysis, implementation, and testing, they still must be trained to work with the new output and input requirements of the system. Without properly trained personnel, the most sophisticated system is rendered inefficient and ineffective.

Resistance to Change
Closely related to the preceding limitation is the human nature characteristic of resisting change. An organization may have qualified and capable personnel, but if they cannot accept change as an effective means of achieving organizational goals, the effectiveness of the new system will be diminished. People become defensive when they feel that their employment security and job status may be adversely affected by a proposed systems change. Since lost jobs and relocation are normally associated with changes involving the computer, the mere mention of changing the system causes many people to assume a negative attitude toward the change. Such employees attack change in principle, disregarding potential benefits to themselves.

Financial Resources
The amount of funds allocated by management to systems analysis and design is another constraint that must be considered in the initial evaluation of what is to be altered. The relationships between costs and benefits will be considered in a later section.

Technology

Often a system must be designed within the limitations of the hardware currently available. When a change is needed in a situation involving such constraints, the possibilities for solving the problems are reduced and the likelihood for obtaining the best solutions are minimal. For example, changes may be easily adapted when operating space is available or difficult when the changes affect areas otherwise not needing change.

When manual systems are changed, the technology constraints are generally and directly related to the organization's financial constraints. Accordingly, system analysis and design must be performed concurrently with the feasibility study to provide compatibility between the hardware and the system being designed. Anytime management considers systems redesign in coordination with the adoption of new equipment, the system and the hardware become each other's constraints.

Environmental Constraints

Designers of systems are always constrained by the users of the system. Although internal users are more influential concerning changes made in a system, the external users of output information have certain needs that require consideration by the organization. Such users indirectly restrict the design of the system merely to satisfy the demands of society and government, not because of organizational restrictions or requirements. The major outside influences on system design are government reporting requirements, unions, customers, and competitors. The influence of competitors is somewhat different from other external influences. Organizations naturally try to prevent proprietary information from reaching competitors, but when it is inevitable, they take care to cast it in the proper perspective.

JUSTIFICATION OF SYSTEMS ANALYSIS

Before systems analysis is attempted, there is usually some demand for change. Although the change may be widely requested, top management must ultimately approve the investigative activities. This approval should include the scope of the analysis, time limits, complexity, and maximum cost. The relationships of these items to each other and the current system vary depending on the functional area being changed. For example, a system study of the accounting information network is more complex and costly than a study of the payroll system.

Although there are many reasons for justifying systems analysis, the following conditions are most often responsible. *Growth* is a reason for change in many situations. Ideally, the current system was designed to last through several growth cycles. Eventually, in a growth situation, systems reach a point at which their ability to accept additional processing becomes marginal. Closely related to growth is the system's *problem-solving* capabilities. Frequently systems analysis is needed to correct malfunctions in a program or process. At other times the problem is new and the current system cannot solve it or self-adjust to correct it. Another reason for analysis arises when *new requirements* are placed on the system. These demands might include such requirements as government reports, new-product evaluation techniques, changes in generally accepted accounting principles, or customer demands. Although less important today than in the recent past, *technological advancements* require systems to be periodically reevaluated. As systems reach their physical capacity or the procedural limits of the available hardware, changes are needed to expand the current configuration or to acquire newer, more advanced capabilities. Lastly, systems analysis may be performed to improve *operating efficiency.* When the organization is criticized by its auditors for inefficient operations, or by top management for poor decision making, systems analysis may be required to improve the process. Improvements are generally in the areas of *internal controls, methodology,* or *timeliness.* Whenever systems analysis relates to accounting, those whose activities are to be affected should ensure that the objectives are properly and clearly stated and that the project has been approved by someone in top management.

APPROACHES TO SYSTEMS ANALYSIS

Several methods of conducting systems analysis are available, and the selection depends on such matters as size of problem, type of organization, complexity of problem, and time available to complete the analysis. Of the approaches discussed in this chapter, several are popular in almost any situation, and some are used only in special situations. Basic approaches are discussed subsequently, each with its own advantages and disadvantages. However, in recent years, combinations of the methods (hybrid methods) have become most popular because they combine the advantages of several methods without increasing the number of disadvantages. The systems analyst must choose the methods that permit analysis and evaluation of the current situation and its status in order to assess the future needs of the system.

Surveys and Questionnaires

Since most accounting systems have been operational for years, analysts have developed special questionnairies dealing with individual functions. The questionnaires (or surveys) are generally standardized for each area to permit easy evaluation of results based on similar experiences in other organizations. Although questionnaires may vary with the function being analyzed, several basic points are found on most surveys. These include function objectives, control elements of the function, role of personnel involved with the function, relationship of function to the computer system, and interfaces of the function with other functions. The assignment of the weighting factor to the various points, indicating the degree of importance, depends on the function being analyzed. Most questionnaires yield a quantitative score the analyst can compare with other results, either laterally (the same function in another organization) or horizontally (another function in the same organization). A partial questionnaire is illustrated in Figure 8.1.

Surveys are easy to conduct, give quantitative scores for evaluation, and require a minimum of preparation time for the analyst. However, there are several disadvantages to the use of questionnaires solely for analysis purposes. Most questionnaires have a limited selection of answers for each question: yes or no, rank from one to five, or a given set of multiple answers. Because the analyst is usually not present when the questionnaire is being completed, vague questions may be answered under false assumptions, or not

ANALYSIS QUESTIONNAIRE
(SAMPLE FORMAT).

1. What is your role in the department that you are currently assigned to?
   _____
   _____

2. How much access do you have to the computer?
   None_____ Unlimited_____ Very restricted_____ Somewhat restricted_____
3. How many user codes and/or passwords are assigned to you?_____
4. The part of the computer system that you use can best be described as?
   Direct access_____ Batch processing_____ Inquiry only_____
   Input only_____ Other (describe)_____
5. Do you have any control functions? Yes_____ No_____
   If yes, explain._____
   _____

6. Do you handle more than one type of accounting transaction? Yes_____ No_____
   If yes, explain._____
   _____
   _____

7. You spend your average day doing the following
Activity	Percent of time
a. _____	_____
b. _____	_____
c. _____	_____
d. _____	_____
	100%

   The following questions should be answered using the scale of 1 to 5 with 1 being
   Strongly Agree and 5 being Strongly Disagree
8. You are well trained for your current job.   1 2 3 4 5
9. You are respected by your superiors.   1 2 3 4 5
10. You are respected by your peers.   1 2 3 4 5
11. You are respected by your subordinates. (If it applies.)   1 2 3 4 5
12. There are enough controls present in the tasks and related areas   1 2 3 4 5
    that you work with.

Figure 8.1

answered at all. Another weakness is the analyst's inability to structure questions without preconceived responses in mind. This limitation biases the results in favor of the analyst's predetermined conclusions.

Personnel Interviews

Many systems analysts believe the interview approach is the most effective means of analyzing and evaluating a system. The person-to-person relationship enables the analyst to immediately improve and correct any communication problems between the interviewer and the interviewee, something not possible with the questionnaire approach. Interviews can be used to evaluate the individuals in the system and the effectiveness of their roles in the system. Also, the analyst is able to minimize rumors by explaining why the systems analysis is being conducted and what impact any changes may have on the employees being interviewed.

Interviews are usually conducted at all operational levels within the function being evaluated, with the most important positions receiving the greatest attention. The interviews may vary from formal to informal. The type of interview depends on the person being interviewed and the place of the interview. Key personnel are generally interviewed in formal surroundings because their inputs into the evaluation process are more incisive, and the analyst needs to concentrate on what is being discussed. Informal discussions may take place in small groups, at lunch, or when the analyst is trying to reinforce information already obtained.

A major disadvantage with the interview technique is the difficulty in distinguishing honest answers from those the interviewee thinks the interviewer wants to hear. Also, the analyst must be able to discern and discount responses motivated solely by the interviewee's concern for his or her own personal welfare.

Input/Output Analysis

In certain situations, the analyst can obtain the best understanding of a system by studying the input and output of the current system. If the organizational and system objectives are known, the analyst can use the actual input and output of the system to evaluate whether the objectives are being met and whether the future objectives can be achieved within the parameters of the current systems environment. Specific areas of evaluation during the input/output analysis include volume capabilities of the current systems and volume demands of the changes to be implemented, cyclical and seasonal fluctuations in volume, audit-type comparisons of current input and output to determine the effectiveness of the current system, and evaluations of the job descriptions and work loads of the employees performing input and output tasks.

An important area of input/output analysis is the extent of utilization of the input. There should be an evaluation of the volume of inputs actually used, frequency of use, and redundancy of input storage. If enough weaknesses are found in this area, the new demands of the functional areas may be adaptable to the current system after it is improved and the inefficiencies corrected.

Input/output analysis is effective in evaluating the current system, but it is limited in its ability to indicate the needs of the future in terms of the present system. Analysts use this method when management is concerned more with making improvements in the current system than with making changes in the way the system operates.

Document Analysis

The four major categories of documents examined by the analyst are source documents, output documents, charts, and procedures and operating manuals. The source documents aid in determining the input needs of the system and indicate whether enough data are being gathered to fulfill the information needs of management. Although the number and kinds of source documents may not need to be changed, the amount, type, and frequency of data collection may need to be adjusted.

The output documents aid in determining the sufficiency of the information provided for the decision-making process. Many complaints of management concerning the adequacy of decision-making information are really directed at incomplete or irrelevant information. This may or may not be caused by weaknesses in input. By studying output documents, the analyst should be able to determine what management currently considers important to the organization.

Charts and procedures and operating manuals tell the analyst how the system should operate. These documents aid in evaluating whether the system is actually functioning as management desires. Charts include organizational charts, all types of flowcharts that the organization may use, and other specialty charts (e.g., Gantt charts, PERT charts and macro document charts). The various types of manuals should indicate the means of processing the input, the controls surrounding the procedures, task responsibility assignment, frequency of performance, level of secrecy, and the formal information requirements of the system under review.

Observation

When people are required to work in groups or interact closely with each other to perform a set of related tasks, the observation technique is sometimes effective. Through observation the analyst may determine what tasks are being performed, how they are being performed, the control and operating procedures being implemented, the length of the process, and where certain tasks are performed. The analyst may then verify the facts gathered during other phases of the analysis, evaluate the effectiveness and efficiency of the working relationships of the employees, and note the adherence to management's objectives in the routine performance of the various activities.

Observation analysis can be time-consuming and expensive because it requires skilled analysts. Moreover, the fact that it must be used in conjunction with other methods adds to the total costs. Observation is more reliable in studies that are easily quantifiable, as opposed to "subjective" research that yields observation bias from both a subjective evaluator and a subjective subject. Technical areas are thus best suited for observation analysis.

FEASIBILITY STUDIES

When a system, either manual or computerized, appears to need change, a preliminary study should be undertaken to determine whether the needed changes can be justified. This type of study is known as a *feasibility study*. A special team is usually formed by management to examine the advantages, disadvantages, and costs of implementing suggested changes in the system. The team may be composed exclusively of internal members, or it may include outsiders such as public accountants, computer consultants, computer vendor representatives, and systems analysts. The role of the outsiders is to bring expertise to the team; the insiders represent management, the concerned operating departments, internal control or internal auditing, and current members of the systems and computer departments (if any exist).

Many aspects of feasibility studies overlap the activities of systems analysis—and when two separate studies are made, they should be coordinated to minimize any duplication of effort. Basically, systems analysis should deal with "what is needed," and feasibility studies should determine the costs and benefits of the alternatives available to meet those needs. To determine the justification of the proposed changes, analysts need to study several specialized aspects of feasibility. Each of these is discussed with the assumption that they can be related to each other upon completion to provide one unified recommendation to management.

Technical Feasibility Study

The selection of the equipment configuration must be made relative to the demands of the proposed changes and the technical capabilities of the currently available equipment and software. If available equipment already has the capacity to handle the changes, the study can be narrowed to an investigation of the current system's ability to control the changes. Similar systems in other organizations may need to be examined when evaluating the ability of a configuration to handle a given system adequately. Also, analysis of similar systems that use hardware of a different vendor may be beneficial in selecting the best configuration available.

To be technically feasible, a configuration must have acceptable training costs, vendor servicing and maintenance, and flexibility for future changes. Proper weight should be given to capacity, speed, ability to handle complex operations, and ability to integrate with existing and future systems of the organization.

Operational Feasibility Study

The changes proposed in the system should be definable under the objectives of management. The changes must not conflict with the basic operational policies of management or with the general philosophies of management. Examples of items to be included in the operational study are replacement of personnel by the computer and its impact on the organization, major changes in the organization that disrupt the normal status of the personnel (job changes), shifting from a centralized to a decentralized form of management or vice versa, and degree and amount of social changes created in the environment. If management opposes any of these types of changes, the proposed system has little chance of being implemented.

Another area of operational feasibility is scheduling. The changes should be made with minimum disruption to the daily operations of the organization. Decision tools such as PERT, CPM, Gantt charts, and linear programming can aid in determining the impact of the proposed changes on the organization. The actual timing of the changes should also be determined so that persons affected by the changes will know what is going to happen to their departments, jobs, and work status.

Legal and Environmental Feasibility Study

With the increased involvement of government in business matters in recent years, the systems designer and analyst must be concerned with legal and environmental aspects of the organization. The interface between business and its environment must be considered when systems changes are proposed. The organization's discharge of its legal obligations should not be hindered by its information system.

Unlike the economic study where the costs were objective and the benefits subjective, this study has benefits that tend to be objective and costs that tend to be subjective.

The benefits derived from a certain systems change may be very clear, but if they conflict with some legal or social responsibility of the organization, the costs of the change may be difficult to determine. Such costs may include legal fees to defend the organization, customer dissatisfaction and reduced business, poor employee morale, and legal penalties. All these items are subjective and may vary widely.

For accounting-related changes, the analysts and designers should consider the time that certain documents must be maintained by the organization, the minimum documents and other source material required by external auditors in conducting mandatory annual audits of certain organizations, and the documents needed by outside agencies such as the Internal Revenue Service, the Federal Trade Commission, and various local governments. Accountants must play a role in this area so that analysts and designers are aware of the type of documents that must be maintained and generated by the system, the length of time the records must be kept, and the audit trail requirements of external auditors, governmental auditors, and various other groups that require some access to the financial records of an organization.

Economic Feasibility Study

Accountants usually get involved with this study even if the changes do not affect them. As costs experts, they find themselves on the feasibility study team for most systems changes. A study of economic feasibility also requires the participation of persons best able to evaluate the benefits of the system; such persons may be accountants, engineers, systems analysts, or management. The objective of this phase of the feasibility study is to match the costs and benefits so that some conclusion may be reached concerning the justification for the change. Benefits may also be related to other factors such as the time consumed to obtain the benefit, the number of people used to generate the benefit as opposed to the number of people aided by the benefit, and its level of use as opposed to benefits of the existing system.

Benefits can generally be classified as direct and indirect. The direct benefits include:

1. Improved processing time for activities
2. Reduced personnel costs
3. Improved control over data processing
4. Better monitoring of critical items such as inventory levels and accounts receivable aging analysis
5. Reduced operation costs

The indirect benefits are more difficult to evaluate and vary with type and size of organization. The more common indirect benefits include:

1. Improved decision making by management
2. Increased audit confidence in internal controls
3. Better budgeting and planning strategies
4. Improved employee morale
5. More accurate processing of inputs
6. Allowed maintenance of current status or improved status within industry or profession

Although the benefits are somewhat difficult to define, the costs can generally be categorized as follows: equipment changes, personnel changes, analysis, design and development changes, and future operating costs versus current operating costs. Accountants are not necessarily experts on the future costs of systems changes, but they are generally responsible for the analysis of current and historical costs of the various operations of the organization. Therefore the team evaluating the costs of the changes is usually comprised of accountants and those familiar with equipment and software costs, including analysis and design costs.

As with the benefits, the costs can be separated into direct and indirect elements. The direct costs are:

1. Operating cost of new system versus current system
2. Personnel needed for new system
3. Maintenance of new system
4. Training of employees
5. Site preparation
6. Analysis, design, and implementation of new system

The indirect costs often include:

1. Resistance to change by employees and customers
2. Loss of control, therefore more time and money must be spent on control
3. Suboptimization by organizational units that avoid or go around the system
4. Backup and recovery becomes more complex, therefore more expensive

Each of the direct costs areas must be carefully evaluated by the feasibility study team, and to the extent that they can be defined, all indirect costs should also be included in the cost analysis.

GENERAL SYSTEM STRUCTURES

The three general approaches to structuring information systems are centralized, decentralized, and distributed. In a *centralized system* all data processing activities are conducted at one processing center; see Figure 8.2(a). A *decentralized system* permits each major organizational unit to have its own data processing center. A *distributed system,* a type of decentralization, uses multiple processing units located throughout the organization, so that computer operations can be delegated to those in closest contact with the system; see Figure 8.2(b). Such systems may have a centralized computer used primarily to gather and summarize period data for organization-wide reporting. With or without the centralized computer, the members of a distributed system are able to interact with each other, share data files, and use each other's hardware configuration for backup. Refer to Chapter Four for additional information about distributed processing.

The philosophy of management regarding centralization or decentralization must be considered in analyzing and designing a system. A centralized philosophy implies that lower organizational levels are heavily constrained and enjoy very few decision-making prerogatives. A decentralized philosophy indicates significant delegation of authority and responsibility to the lower levels of the organization. Management is usually hesitant to

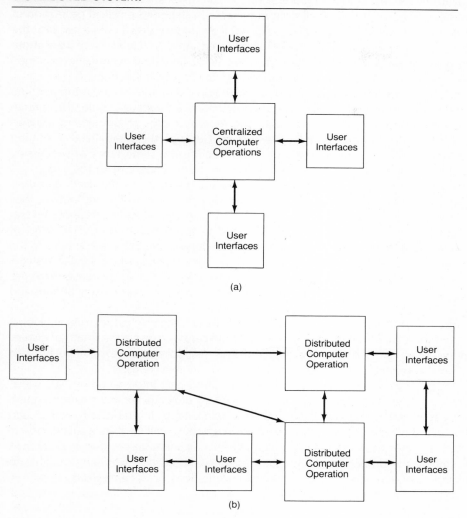

(a)

(b)

Figure 8.2

embrace a processing system that violates its philosophy of organizational structure. Nevertheless, the designer may be able to influence the structural philosophy that best fits the system. In reality, most systems are eventually developed toward the center of a continuum between centralization and decentralization (i.e., centralized systems have some degree of decentralization and vice versa). There are, of course, advantages and disadvantages to each approach in its purest form.

One of the strongest advantages of a centralized processing system is the inherent reduction of redundancy and the minimization of data duplication. Because the processing operations are centrally located, control over the system and physical protection of the facilities are greatly improved. This also tends to control user access, because the controls surrounding access can be closely monitored. A centralized system gives more decision-making power to top management while at the same time minimizing "routine" decision making, which can be accomplished by the processing system.

In the area of systems utilization the centralized operation maximizes computer time used, as opposed to the relatively underutilized distributed systems. Generally, a large system can process larger volumes of data and more complex programs and routines than smaller distributed processing systems can. Because the centralized operation serves a large number of users, many of whom require the same types of processing applications, economies of scale result in lower unit processing cost to the users.

Most of the advantages of decentralized operations relate to the users and their needs. Such systems allow the users to control their input, processing, and output, thus improving processing turnaround time compared to most centralized operations. Several minicomputers can be used in these systems and thereby reduce the overall costs of operating the system. This has occurred primarily in the last few years in response to the substantial reduction in the price of minicomputers. The simplicity of the smaller systems improves processing controls and facilitates error correction. Also, because there are several computers in the system, backup is provided during heavy processing periods and equipment failures.

As new demands are placed on the system through systems changes, organizational growth, and improved technology, necessary modifications cause a minimum of disruption on the other parts of the organization. This responsiveness to change is often considered the greatest benefit of distributed information systems.

The conflict between management's philosophies and information system users' requirements concerning how much to centralize or decentralize information system processing activities can be found in most large organizations. It is difficult to win in such a controversy since the advantages of one approach may well be the disadvantages of another. Once the system has been defined and management agrees that its objectives can be met by the proposed system, the designers should do everything possible to develop the most acceptable system, whether centralized or decentralized.

CONCEPTUAL DESIGN ALTERNATIVES

Once the structural approach has been approved, the specific approach to the actual systems design must be selected. Different approaches may be used for the various systems functions and should be adaptable to either the centralized or distributed concepts. The approach generally depends on the size and complexity of the organization. The long-run conceptual approaches most often used are now discussed.

Top-Down Design

The top-down approach to systems design is appropriate where top management is very involved in the decision-making processes. This method stresses the goals and objectives of the organization and the systems function under consideration. The basis for this type of design is that the information system should be responsive to the organization's needs first and all other needs second. Top management users in the organization have priority in determining the outputs of the system, and the system is designed to respond to their needs first.

The initial phase in developing a top-down design is the analysis of organizational goals and objectives. Next, the systems functions and program applications are defined to meet the goals and objectives previously stated. The designer then considers the objectives and needs of the major operations in the organizations (in some organizations these may be large units such as divisions, and in others they may be departments or plants). Care must be taken not to let the goals and objectives of the subunits conflict with those of the organization. When these types of conflicts occur, *suboptimization* results. If there is another (lower) tier in the organization, it will be treated similarly, maintaining top-down priorities and avoiding suboptimization.

Bottom-Up Design

The bottom-up approach is almost the opposite of the top-down approach. This design method stresses meeting the basic needs of the organization at the operating levels first and the overall goals and objectives of the organization second. The managers who are making the daily decisions and the managers in charge of the basic organizational activities such as payroll and inventory control receive priority in systems design and implementation. This is a very popular approach because the basic needs of the organization are easy to define and implement. After the basic operating levels and functions are designed, the next higher level in the organization is developed and integrated with the previous level.

The system evolves with each higher level in the organization being integrated into the data base. Information flows upward in this type of design, and each higher level receives summarized data from below. The detailed analysis of the summary information is furnished only when needed, thus saving time and effort of each subordinate level.

The top-down and bottom-up methods are often combined, because the overall plans and objectives developed by the top-down approach serve as guidelines in developing the bottom-up procedures. In such combinations, the bottom-up method usually dominates. When these two approaches are combined, top management feels confident that its objectives are being implemented into the system design, and at the same time it is assured that the needs of the operating systems are met.

Integrate-later Design

This method is often used with the bottom-up approach because the organization cannot afford to formalize all its systems functions at one time. Integrate-later design gives priority to the functions that are most critical to the organization or those that are currently overburdened with paperwork or processing activities. The major weakness of this approach is that the separate functions are designed independently of each other—and, as the system grows, the ability to integrate the various functions is severely limited. This weakness can be minimized if the bottom-up approach is coordinated with the overall plan of the system.

Organizational Chart Design

The designer makes the assumption in the organizational chart approach that the information system follows the same flows as the lines of authority and responsibility in the organization's formal structure. This approach saves the designer time because the structure is already defined and the data and information relationships are predetermined. In large organizations this method generally will not be effective because the functional lines and information flows may not be the same. For example, the demands for integrated flows between such functions as marketing, accounting, and production cannot be met with an organizational chart approach. In such situations, the various functions tend to develop their own subsystems with resulting duplication of efforts. This approach might be justified in small organizations because of its simplicity and ease of development.

Data Base Design

The data base approach gives top priority to the collection and storage of critical data in an information system. It assumes that the informational aspects of a system can only be developed after the facts (data) have been collected from the environment. Because it is difficult to predict the needs of management, the data base approach collects everything that *might* be relevant, classifies it according to some information scheme, and stores it accordingly. Although it is convenient to have everything management might need in storage, the cost of such storage, even on the most efficient devices, is usually unjustifiable. Such a system often results in an overabundance of both relevant and irrelevant information. Another disadvantage is the failure to consider the interrelationships of the various functions in categorizing the storage of data. This approach is often used in growing organizations that are not sure what their long-run objectives are going to be and that consequently are uncertain of their future information needs. This method works best in organizations that are very limited in their operations and therefore need only data related to a well-defined environment.

MANAGEMENT SUPPORT SYSTEMS

Before decisions can be finalized about conceptual design, type of computer configuration, and methods of implementation, consideration must be given to the overall needs of the decision makers of the organization. To understand this general topic better, we shall consider the areas of management support systems, decision support systems, and critical success factors.

Management support systems (MSS) are a subclassification of MIS which support the primary responsibilities and functions of managers. These systems provide information for the basic actions of managers—organizing, planning, monitoring, and controlling. Unlike many of the traditional MIS that were very structured, MSS allow the manager to test the consequences of decisions, not merely provide the data for the decision.

Problems that need to be solved using MSS are usually partially structured and do not require every decision element to be quantified. A shortcoming of traditional MIS is its attempt to quantify all possible environmental factors. The developments that have increased the popularity of MSS are the interactive planning models. These models range from personnel scheduling to accounting spreadsheets. Managers who have microcomputers at their disposal generally take advantage of these models to simulate "what if" decisions. For larger, more complicated problems, there are also several modeling packages available for mainframe systems.

Decision Support Systems

Decision Support Systems (DSS) are designed to assist managers in semistructured decisions and are a major element under the MSS umbrella. In addition to assisting managers in semistructured tasks, they also support managerial judgment and improve effectiveness of decision making. To be beneficial in the decision process, the manager must have a proper understanding of the criteria needed to develop the computer-supported systems through the use of interactive planning models such as financial spreadsheets.

DSS allow managers to design and control the implementation of each decision situation to focus on managerial problem solving. The general thrust of the system is then to move from the decision-making activities to the user's needs. This goal of DSS cannot be accomplished until the manager acquires an in-depth understanding of the organization's overall decision process. The managers and others who help design DSS must be sure they comprehend the completeness of the decision situation so that both objective and subjective inputs can be considered. The decision requirements result in telling:

1. Which data are worth collecting
2. When to collect the data
3. How to collect the data
4. How to maintain the data
5. How to store the data

The decision maker should determine how to use the data for the decision situations that arise. The decision maker must define the information needed to support each situation and then turn to the system for that support.

Once this has all been accomplished, each decision situation can then be classified as either structured, semistructured, or unstructured. If the situation is truly structured (sometimes known as artificial intelligence) it does not involve managerial decision making except through preprogrammed decisions; for any given situation the decision is standard. Semistructured situations require managerial action. The solutions are not preset and each situation requires human evaluation and review. The unstructured situations have no basis for predetermined decisions and solutions are not even attempted by the system. For examples of each type of decision see Figure 8.3. This illustration demonstrates that DSS is best at supporting semistructured decision situations.

Critical Success Factors

In addition to developing all the decision models for managers, designers should consider the factors that are important to the decision process itself. The critical success factors (CSF) process was developed several years ago by John Rockart at MIT's Sloan School of Management. It has gone through several evolutionary cycles since its development and currently has many applications in information systems and decision-making processes.

DECISION STRUCTURES.

Management Activity	Structured	Semistructured	Unstructured
Operational control	Inventory reordering	Bond trading	Selecting a cover for a magazine
Management control	Linear programming for production	Setting market budgets for consumer products	Hiring managers
Strategic planning	Plant location	Capital acquisition analysis	R & D portfolio development
Support needed	Clerical or EDP	DSS	Human intuition

Source: Peter G. W. Keen and Michael S. S. Scott, *Decision Support Systems.* Reading, Mass.: Addison-Wesley Publishing Co., 1978, p. 87.

Figure 8.3

As might be suspected, it is a process of determining the factors that are critical to a decision process. These are determined by going through several basic steps.

1. *Identification.* Determine the objectives of each level from the top of the organization to where the decision process will take place. This helps ensure goal congruence and at the same time defines the critical success factors.
2. *Alignment.* Determine which objectives and critical success factors best represent the consensus of the management team. This helps align the CSFs of individual managers with the objectives of the organization.
3. *Information review.* Using the CSF as a guide, managers review the information they receive to determine how it supports the decision process. Irrelevant information can be excluded at this point.
4. *Key measures.* This step determines each person's role in managing the CSFs of the organization, the decisions that are made for each CSF, and the sources of information for each CSF.
5. *Overhaul.* The preceding measures lead to the restructuring of the decision processes in the organization. Reports are redesigned, irrelevant data eliminated, and new data needs added.

Once the system has been converted to CSF decision making, the factors for adherence and change should be monitored as needed. This is but one method of formal decision making; most organizations can improve their overall effectiveness and efficiency with formal rather than informal decision-making processes.

DESIGN AND IMPLEMENTATION PHASES

Once the system has been properly analyzed, but before implementation, several phases are undertaken to ensure that the system meets management's specifications. They are analysis evaluation, output formalization, selection of equipment configuration, controls, testing, personnel, implementation, and operational evaluation.

Analysis Evaluation

The first design phase is the evaluation of the results of the systems analysis. The overall impact on the system must be considered and evaluated in light of the results of the analysis, taking into account management's objectives, resource limitations, available technology, and complexity of proposed changes. Before the designing begins, the relevant decision makers of the system should be consulted with and informed about what is about to take place, the timing of the various design activities, and any possible alternatives that should be considered before design implementation begins.

Output Formalization

The second phase of systems design is the formalization of the outputs to be generated by the proposed system. In this phase, attention is given to the objectives of the system, the quantity and quality of output demanded, and the characteristics of the output. This phase must include communications with the potential users to gather information such as control requirements, security, and the specific contents of the outputs. In contemplating the transition from input to output, the designer must visualize the connections between the available inputs to the system and the desired outputs. Also, the frequency and type of desired reports must be included in the determination of the output design because these items influence the storage medium, output medium, and timing of processing.

Because many decision makers are burdened with an overabundance of information, the system should filter the amount of detail provided to each level of decision making. *Data filtering* is the process of screening unwanted elements as they pass from one point to another. Accounting data are normally filtered through summarizing and classifying. Because demands for detail can vary significantly among individuals at the same decision-making level, this adds to the problem of furnishing everyone with the exact amount of detail needed.

Although data filtering represents a significant improvement over traditional data transfers in reducing useless information, it does have several disadvantages. The difficulty in controlling the various degrees of detail at the same level makes the initial analysis phase very time-consuming. Also, overfiltered information may severely limit retrieving important details after the previous level of data has been summarized and consolidated.

Key variable reporting is also an important aspect of output formalization. This reporting focuses on the items that have significant impacts on the evaluation of the activities of a given decision level. Key variables may be items such as productivity measures, financial ratios, and variance percentages.

The use of the *interrogative method* is another important output consideration. This method requires the decision maker to request the needed information from the system. There are many decision situations that are unknown when an information system is installed and allowances must be made for bringing together information from various data sources. This allows the decision maker to have the best set of information available for the decision at hand. The drawbacks of this method include an expensive data bank and complicated retrieval programs needed to make it operational. However, if there are enough critical decisions that require this kind of on-call information, the advantages can outweigh the disadvantages.

Component Selection

The selection of the components for the systems configuration is the third design phase. The components that comprise the system should be selected early in the design phase so that any new equipment, or equipment modifications, can be installed prior to the time of testing the new system. Configuration selection usually begins with the evaluation of input needs. The availability of a wide variety of input media and devices acceptable for capturing input data generally necessitates a miniature feasibility study to consider the following factors: costs per input element or unit, efficiency of input needed and efficiency of various devices, speed of input, number of input devices and locations, and need for certain types of input controls. Other factors to be considered are related to the source of the input data. The input may be from manually prepared documents such as sales invoices, inventory receiving documents, and periodic adjusting entries. This type of input requires a different means of conversion into machine-readable form than does automated input such as electronic transfers from one bank to another, point of sale devices such as cash registers with pen wands, and automated recording of employees' times when punching in and out.

When selecting the type of input to be used in a given process, designers should consider several characteristics of each method. Manually collected and prepared inputs (1) are easy to use, (2) require a minimum of equipment and accessories, (3) are easy to correct, and (4) provide source documents. But they also (1) are generally slower than other types of input, (2) are prone to human error, and (3) require a conversion or transformation step to machine-readable language. Closely related to manual inputs and processes is machine-assisted input. Although machine-assisted devices vary with the needs of the input process, they all have several similar characteristics. They all (1) reduce human effort, (2) reduce input errors, (3) are easy to correct, (4) are faster than manually prepared input; but they all (5) are more expensive than manually prepared methods, (6) provide some type of source document, and (7) are easy to control. The third general class of input devices and methods is automated processing. Although humans must operate the devices, the devices accomplish most of the actual recording of the input. The major characteristics of automated input devices are that they (1) reduce human contact with the input data, (2) minimize source documents, (3) are expensive to acquire and install, (4) are difficult to correct, (5) are fast and efficient, and (6) are difficult to audit.

The systems designer must next consider the storage and retrieval processes. Like input methods, storage and retrieval methods vary from manual to machine-assisted to automated. Manual methods relate mainly to the storage of paper, punched cards, or punched paper tape. Manual filing systems generally require large amounts of storage space as compared to the other methods, are often unreliable and slow, and are easily destroyed. Accounts receivable files by customer kept in a file cabinet is an example of a manual filing and retrieval process. Machine-assisted storage methods are faster than manual systems, but retain the same negative characteristics; that is, they require a large amount of space, are easily destroyed, and are unreliable. Machine-assisted methods are best used in situations where source documents must be retrieved often and when computer reproductions are not acceptable. These methods have mechanized drawers or trays that can be controlled by the user with a coding storage scheme. Upon entering the correct data, the storage device moves to the location of the user.

Although automated storage and retrieval systems are basically computer-oriented, some microfilm and related systems do not use a computer. Although these systems are much faster than the manual or machine-assisted methods and retrieval is very flexible, they are usually more expensive. Retrieval may be in the form of printouts, punched cards, or video. In most systems the retrieval characteristics are more important than the storage files, and the designer must consider the needs and uses of the output in arranging the total configuration.

The last step in this design phase is the selection of the processing devices and methods. Processing can vary from a completely manual system with no mechanical assistance to a completely automated system with a minimum of human intervention. Because the input system often interfaces with existing computerized systems, the designer may be limited in the processor selection phase or may be required to use the existing facilities. The current systems configuration is known by the designer when the task is undertaken, and any problems that must be solved can be considered during all phases of designing the input, processing, and output.

Vendor Alternatives In beginning this last step in configuration selection the project manager must review the possible alternatives available. The most common alternatives, stated briefly, are:

1. *Mainframe computer manufacturers.* These are the manufacturers of the largest computer systems. Their equipment is mostly used by large corporations, governments, and the military.
2. *Minicomputer manufacturers.* These companies produce machines that have most, if not all, the capabilities of the large mainframes. The primary difference is the size and speed of processing. These systems usually support a small number of peripheral devices and do not use the high-level languages of the mainframes.
3. *Replacement companies.* These companies have organized to make substitute equipment primarily for mainframe computers. These systems are generally faster, smaller, and cheaper than what they replace. They are made to be compatible with the software of the systems they replace.
4. *Microcomputer manufacturers.* These companies make computers for small businesses and specialized functions of larger systems. They are frequently incorporated into large, distributed processing systems.
5. *Service bureaus.* These companies provide data processing for a fee without the user needing to acquire a CPU or do its own programming. The user needs data preparation devices and a medium to communicate the prepared data to the bureau. The bureau normally does all the processing, writes the programs, and owns the CPU. Generally, only batch processing is handled by these systems.
6. *Time sharing.* These are normally service bureaus that provide on-line access to the CPU. The time-sharing service may do the programming, but not necessarily.

If these possibilities do not meet the needs of the organization, there are always leasing companies, used-computer brokers, turnkey systems that include both hardware and software, and peripheral manufacturers that let you buy the CPU from one manufacturer and the other equipment from another manufacturer.

Hardware Selection Criteria   Because organizations are diverse as to size, style, goals, and operating methods, an exact list of what should be used in the selection process is difficult to develop. However, the more common items include:

1. CPU processing capabilities
2. Input/output capabilities
3. Secondary storage capacities
4. Compatibility with other systems and equipment
5. Communication capabilities
6. Guarantees and warranties
7. Maintenance support
8. Backup facilities
9. Error detection and correction capabilities
10. Cost of each particular configuration package
11. Installation and training support
12. Financing arrangements
13. Delivery dates
14. Future operating costs

Each organization should evaluate which of these criteria are most important and then rank each system as to how well it meets the criteria. After the choice of configuration is selected the financing must be arranged.

Software Alternatives   Generally hardware is selected before the software decisions are made. Software usually comes from three basic sources: internally produced, purchased from the equipment manufacturer, or purchased from a software vendor. Occasionally, software is provided by a consulting firm or CPA firm at the request of the client.
   Software developed internally has the following potential:

1. It is made to fit the system currently available.
2. Costs are reduced if the programmers are already employed and are a necessary part of the information system staff.
3. Start-up and training are minimized because development employees already know how to operate it.
4. Confidence of employees is increased because of their participation in the system design and implementation.

   Software developed outside the organization also has certain advantages including:

1. Lower costs because of expertise in programming
2. Quicker development and implementation
3. All programs have standardized formats, thus easier to understand
4. Well-developed and built-in controls, since the software has been tested and used in other systems.

Software Selection Criteria   As is true with hardware, each organization must decide which criteria of software are most important. Possible criteria for software evaluation include:

1. Types of languages used and compliers available
2. Utility packages available
3. Operating system capabilities
4. Data base management capabilities
5. Amount of documentation
6. Ease of user training and acceptance
7. Cost of development, installation, and training.

Most of the criteria can be easily evaluated when comparing outside software vendors to each other. However, when weighing in-house development against outside vendors, comparisons can be more difficult because the internal costs may be harder to determine.

Controls

The fourth design phase is the establishing of controls over the system. Controls are needed to evaluate the effectiveness and efficiency of the system and to ensure that the objectives of management are met. As discussed in Chapter Six, controls can be designed into the system or added to the system at a later date. Because built-in controls are usually more efficient, the designer should include the basic controls necessary for each systems operation in the design of the system. This can be accomplished with the help of the users, management, internal auditors, external auditors, and outside consultants.

Effective controls require knowledge and consideration of the objectives of the individual systems operations, their quantifiable characteristics that can be used for measurements, standards with which to measure the results, the range of acceptable variances, and action to be taken when something is wrong. The nontechnical controls surrounding the systems, such as separation of duties, must also be established by the designer. A consulting team within the organization should assist the designer in development of these types of controls. Environmental controls include the categories of internal controls, managerial controls, and related accounting controls. Such controls are generally effective whether they are built in or added on.

Testing

After the configuration has been installed and the controls selected, the fifth phase, testing, begins. This is probably the most important design and implementation phase. The testing procedures should verify the logical operating activities and the physical interrelationships of the equipment. The computer programs should be tested with correct and incorrect data to ensure that it accepts the former and rejects the latter. *Compliance testing,* in which all controls related to input, processing, and output are tested to verify their proper working condition, should be performed.

The next testing procedures involves testing the data base for security, accessibility, and accuracy. Substantive tests should be used to determine required characteristics. The data base programs should also be tested for file creation, deletion, and retention with the updating procedures for both correct and incorrect data.

The system outputs should be tested for report generating ability, report design, and report distribution. The reports are checked for proper headings, number of copies, data content, extensions and footings, number sequence, dates, and error messages. The users should be involved in this area to evaluate format clarity and readability.

After the initial testing has been completed to the system manager's satisfaction, the organization's auditors, both internal and external if possible, should review the test results, evaluate the controls, and perform independent tests to verify compliance with the designer's test results. These tests results should then become part of the official documentation of the system.

Personnel

The sixth design phase is the selection and training of personnel to operate the new system. This is usually accomplished concurrently with the other early phases of design and implementation. The designer's role in this phase varies with the organization. It may vary from doing all the personnel selection and training to merely indicating the number and qualifications of personnel needed. The personnel department is usually in charge of selection and training. If they do not have the expertise to perform these tasks, they will engage outsiders to train the employees and possibly help with the selection process.

The training and education of personnel is generally separated into user and operating groups. User groups could include managers, sales staffs, production foremen, cost accountants, and customers. Many users are trained throughout the implementation process since they may be involved with the various phases of design and analysis. Other users must be trained in special classes and with hands-on sessions. Without well-trained users, even the best systems can be rendered ineffective.

The operating system employees have generally already been technically trained. Their training at this phase is more concerned with the specifics of the given system. Their training is generally ongoing because most systems continue to change over time, and although every change does not involve every user, it does involve most of the operating system personnel.

Implementation

The implementation phase involves the actual installation of the system or system changes. Generally, the designer or project manager oversees this operation, with the computer and systems technicians doing most of the actual installation. The designer's role is one of management, making sure that the new system is installed as intended, within the time allowed, and tested as appropriate. The amount of time the new system will run *parallel* to the old system depends on the complexity of the changes. During this period, the project manager may make modifications to correct or improve the new system.

The charts and scheduling techniques discussed in Chapter Two are very important in this phase to aid the project manager in keeping things under control. Careful attention must be paid to both timing and costs. The implementation should be kept on schedule because of the many interactions that take place with other parts of the organization. As the overall process nears an end, many activities are being coordinated so that the new system can be started on schedule. Delays by any segment disrupt the entire process and can be very costly.

The last two steps to be completed before the parallel operation begins are *file conversion* and *final system testing.* If the system being changed is already on a computer, the current files must be "cleaned up." This entails validating all existing data, deleting data that are not needed, and possibly converting the data from one file medium to another. For a manual system being converted to a computerized system, all the relevant data must be loaded into the new files and data structures. Both types of conversions can be very difficult and time-consuming.

Once the real data are loaded into the new system, the new programs are tested again. Often the test data used in the initial testing and debugging may not have included every possible characteristic found in the real data. This final testing can save much embarrassment later if a major step or set of data are not being processed correctly. After the project manager is convinced that everything is operating properly, the system begins parallel operations with the old system for a reasonable period of time. This operation time is dictated by the complexity and size of the system and varies from a few weeks to several months.

Evaluation

The next phase is the evaluation of the newly installed system. The designer will be only one of many persons who evaluate the new system. Feedback about the system will come from users, management, internal auditors, external auditors, computer vendors, and others. Initially, the designer should receive the evaluations of the system so that any weaknesses can be corrected immediately. The organization should continually evaluate all its operating systems for efficiency and effectiveness whether or not they have been recently designed.

Specific items to evaluate after the new system is in full operation include:

1. Determination of whether the original objectives of the new system are being accomplished
2. Evaluation of major weak points with immediate corrections
3. Evaluation of the overall project including work of everyone involved
4. Evaluation of the auditability of the system as it relates to accounting
5. Establishment of a monitoring program to review continually the operations for needed improvements and changes.

After these steps have been completed, a final report should be made to the organization detailing every aspect of the system including formal documentation of the system and an itemization of all control features of the system.

SUMMARY

Accountants often serve on organizational teams to analyze and design information systems, especially those involving accounting. Although the tools, techniques, and approaches to analysis and design vary among companies, industries, and nonprofit organizations, a basic understanding of the concepts is important so that employees can better understand their role in the system, especially in accounting.

This chapter completes the introduction to the concepts of accounting information systems, the computer, systems and auditing controls, and information systems in general. The next chapter establishes the basis for the remainder of the text and provides an overall view of the accounting information system.

SELECTED REFERENCES

Ackoff, Russell L. "Management Misinformation Systems," *Management Science* (December 1967): B147–B156.

Burch, J. G., F. R. Strator, and G. Grundnitski, *Information Systems: Theory and Practice.* New York: John Wiley & Sons, 1983.

Crescenzi, Adam D., and Jerry Kocher. "Management Support Systems: Opportunity for Controllers," *Management Accounting* (March 1984): 34–37.

Dearden, John. "MIS Is a Mirage," *Harvard Business Review* (January/February 1972): 90–99.

Drury, D. H. "An Empirical Assessment of the Stages of DP Growth," *MIS Quarterly,* (June 1983): 59–70.

Fried, Louis. "Centralization: 'To Be or Not To Be?'" *Data Processing Management* (Palo Alto, Calif.: Auerbach Publishers, Inc., 1976): 76–88.

Gibson, Cyrus F., and Richard L. Nolan. "Managing the Four Stages of EDP Growth," *Harvard Business Review* (January/February 1974): 76–88.

Hooper, Paul, and John Page. "Organizing Business Data Processing Systems," *CPA Journal* (August 1983): 25–31.

Horwitt, Elisabeth. "Creating Your Own Solutions," *Business Computer Systems* (June 1983): 130–141.

Keen, Peter G. W., and Michael S. S. Scott. *Decision Support Systems.* Reading, Mass.: Addison-Wesley Publishing Co., 1978.

Lowe, Ronald L. "Management Involvement in EDP Planning," *CPA Journal* (June 1980): 28–33.

McFarlan, F. Warren. "Portfolio Approach to Information Systems," *Harvard Business Review* (September/October 1981): 142–150.

Nolan, Richard L. "Managing the Crises in Data Processing," *Harvard Business Review* (March/April 1979): 115–126.

Paretta, Robert L. "Designing Management Information Systems: An Overview," *Journal of Accountancy* (April 1975): 42–47.

Rappaport, Alfred. "Management Misinformation System—Another Perspective," *Management Science* (December 1968): B133–136.

Rockart, John F. "Chief Executives Define Their Own Data Needs," *Harvard Business Review* (March/April 1979): 81–93.

Szatrowski, Ted. "Rent, Lease, or Buy?" *Datamation* (February 1976): 59–68.

Van Rensselar, Cort. "Design the Information System to Match the Organization It Supports," *Datamation* (April 1979): 89–94.

Yourdon, Edward. "A Brief Look at Structured Programming and Top-Down Program Design," *Modern Data* (June 1974): 30–35.

QUESTIONS

1. Explain or define the following terms:

Systems analysis	Integrate-later design
Systems design	Organizational chart design
Systems implementation	Data base design
Feasibility study	Key variable reporting
Centralized system	Data filtering
Decentralized system	Interrogative method
Distributed system	Replacement companies
Top-down design	Service bureaus
Suboptimization	File conversion
Bottom-up design	

2. What is the difference between systems analysis and systems design?
3. What are the general objectives of information systems? Can they be applied to all types of systems—manual, computerized, profit, governmental, and so on?
4. How can a management policy be a constraint to an organization? Give an example.
5. How can resistance to change be overcome in designing a system? Why is it such a problem for the systems designer?
6. What are environmental constraints? Give several examples.
7. List and define the reasons for systems analysis.
8. For each of the approaches to systems analysis, give an illustration of a type of system that best fits each.
9. Why is the questionnaire so popular? Does it have any weaknesses? If so, what are they?
10. Overall, what is the most effective approach to systems analysis? Why?
11. How do feasibility studies and systems analysis differ? How are they alike?
12. Describe each type of feasibility study.
13. Compare centralized and distributed information systems.
14. How is top-down systems design different from bottom-up systems design? Which method is superior in conceptual design?
15. Explain the three types of decision structures.
16. Briefly define each phase of systems design. Explain the possible role of accountants in each phase.
17. What is a scheduling chart? When and how are they used? Can they be used outside the information systems area?

PROBLEMS

18. Systems Analysis Approach

As a systems analyst for RAD Corporation you are assigned the job of improving the sales ordering system. RAD has approximately 149 salespeople working out of 16 regional sales offices. Several regional sales managers have indicated that the salespeople in their region are dissatisfied with the sales order form introduced 6 months ago. A drop in the average number of sales orders filed per salesperson per month, poorly filled-out order forms, and increasing customer complaints about service from salespeople are further indications of trouble.

Required:
  a. Would you suggest interviews or questionnaires to find what is troubling the salespeople? Why?
  b. Develop an interview schedule or a questionnaire in line with your recommendation. If you decide to use a questionnaire, include a cover letter to the salespeople soliciting their cooperation in the study.

19. Accounting Basis for Systems Analysis

Should systems analysis be on a charge basis to the operating department or to company overhead? Explain what factors should be included in making such a decision.

20. Key System Variables

For the following small businesses, suggest several key variables that you would recommend.
   a. Fast food restaurant
   b. Travel bureau
   c. City hospital
   d. Pencil manufacturer, one plant
   e. State bank, one city

21. Filtering Method

Using the filtering method, develop a series of reports for the following decision levels based on the cost system in a company with several plants and divisions.
   a. Plant cost accountant responsible for all direct costs accumulations and variance analysis
   b. Plant cost accounting manager
   c. Plant controller
   d. Division controller
   e. Corporate controller

22. Data Sources

In designing a new system, you have been assigned to determine the data sources for the following areas in your company. Give at least three sources for each area.
   a. Payroll
   b. Accounts payable
   c. Purchasing
   d. Fixed assets

23. Systems Characteristics

In designing an information system, you should follow the practice of keeping the system simple, flexible, reliable, timely, and feasible. However, these objectives often conflict with each other. Give an example of the conflict between each of the following pairs of objectives.
   a. Simplicity versus flexibility
   b. Simplicity versus reliability
   c. Timeliness versus feasibility
   d. Reliability versus feasibility

24. Cash Receipts Analysis and Flowcharting

Ajax Company has just received two proposals for computerizing its cash receipts system. They are:

a. The customer's payment and the remittance advice (a punched card) are received in the treasurer's office. An accounts receivable clerk in the treasurer's office keypunches the cash receipt into the remittance advice and forwards the card to the computer center. The cash receipt is added to a control tape listing and then filed for deposit later in the day. When the deposit slips are received from the computer center in the afternoon, the cash receipts are removed from the file and deposited with the original deposit slip. The second copy of the deposit slip and control tape are compared for accuracy before the deposit is made and then filed together.

In the computer center, the remittance advices received from the treasurer's office are held until 2:00 PM daily. At that time the customer payments are processed to update the records on magnetic tape and to prepare a deposit slip in triplicate. During the update process, data are read from the master accounts receivable tape, processed, and then recorded on a new master tape. The original and second copy of the deposit slip are forwarded to the treasurer's office. The old master tape (former accounts receivable file), the remittance advices (in customer number order), and the third copy of the deposit slip are stored and filed in a secure place. The updated accounts receivable master tape is maintained in the system for processing the next day.

b. The customer's payment and remittance advice are received in the treasurer's office as before. A CRT terminal is located in the treasurer's office to enter cash receipts. An operator keys in the customer's number and payment from the remittance advice and check. The cash receipt is entered into the system once the operator has confirmed that the proper account and amount are displayed on the screen. The payment is then processed on-line against the accounts receivable file maintained on magnetic disk. The cash receipts are filed for deposit later in the day. The remittance advice amount is added to a control tape and the remittance advices are then filed in the order processed.

The computer prints out a deposit slip in duplicate at 2:00 PM for all cash receipts since the last deposit. The deposit slips are forwarded to the treasurer's office. The deposit slips and the control tape are compared for accuracy before the deposit is made. The cash receipts are removed from the file and deposited with the original deposit slip; the duplicate deposit slip is filed for further reference along with the control tape. At the close of business (5:00 PM) each day, the computer center prepares a record of the current day's cash receipts activity on a magnetic tape. This tape is then stored in a secure place in the event of a systems malfunction; after 10 working days the tape is released for further use. *(IMA adapted)*

Required:

    a. For each proposal, draw a system flowchart.

    b. Evaluate and discuss the advantages and disadvantages of each.

25. Property Systems Objectives

Leigh Ann Kyte has recently been promoted to Manager, Property Accounting Section of Milton Corporation. She has had difficulty in responding to some of the requests from individuals in other departments about the company's fixed assets. Some of the requests and problems Miss Kyte has had to cope with are as follows:

    a. The controller has requested schedules of individual fixed assets to support the balances in the general ledger. She has furnished the necessary information, but it has always been late. The manager of the department in which records are organized makes it difficult to obtain information easily.

    b. The maintenance manager wishes to verify the existence of a printing press, which he thinks was repaired twice. He has asked Miss Kyte to confirm the asset number and location of the press.

    c. The Insurance Department wants data on the cost and book values of assets to include in its review of current insurance coverage.

    d. The Tax Department has requested data that can be used to determine when the company should switch depreciation methods for tax purposes.

    e. The company's internal auditors have spent a significant amount of time in the Property Accounting Section recently, attempting to confirm the annual depreciation charge.

    The property account records at Kyte's disposal consist of a set of manual books. These records show the date the asset was acquired, the account number to which the asset applies, the dollar amount capitalized, and the estimated useful life of the asset for depreciation purposes.

    After many frustrations, Kyte has realized that her records are inadequate, and she cannot supply the data easily when they are requested. She has decided that she should have a computerized fixed asset system. *(IMA adapted)*

Required:

    a. Identify and explain four major objectives Kyte's automated property accounting system should possess in order to provide the data that are necessary to respond to requests of information from the various departments.

    b. What data should be included in the file for each asset?

26. Vendor Analysis

Bill Ford Athletic Consultants is in the process of selecting a computer and support software for its company. After talking with several vendors, the study team has eliminated all but three hardware vendors and two software vendors. The software vendor INH is for in-house software. The relevant criteria used, a weighting factor (10 is best), and individual ratings are as follows:

Criteria	Importance Factor	Vendor Rating		
Hardware		**TRT**	**IBN**	**DED**
Processing abilities	8	8	7	9
Input/output abilities	10	7	10	8
Secondary storage	5	7	6	8
Compatibility	4	9	5	7
Maintenance contracts	8	8	9	9
Communication abilities	9	8	6	7
Total costs	10	9	6	8
Training support	8	7	9	10
Deliver date	4	9	5	7
Future operating costs	7	7	6	6
Software		**ABC**	**XYZ**	**INH**
Language compability	9	9	8	10
Utility packages	8	7	9	6
Data base abilities	7	8	7	5
Documentation	8	8	8	7
User friendly	9	8	6	7
Total cost	10	5	7	9

Required:

a. Prepare an analysis of both hardware and software vendors. Include the in-house software preparation.

b. Make a recommendation as to what the company should do and give your reasons.

27. Systems Analysis and Cost Projections

Big Time Company currently processes its sales order system in a batch mode using cards as input. At the end of each day the sales orders are batched and key-punched. The cards are read into the system, edited, and placed on disk storage. The sales invoices are then prepared by the computer.

The company is currently conducting a feasibility study to determine whether it should replace the current sales order system with a new one. This study has rendered the following information about the current system:

a. Each sales order contains 100 characters of data.

b. There are an average of 900 sales orders prepared per day, 20 days a month. Most of the sales are made in person.

c. Because some customers order more than once a day and others call back and cancel their orders, only 800 sales invoices are prepared on an average day.

d. It takes two punched cards per sales order and one half a minute to read each order and punch the cards.

e. The card reader processes the cards at the rate of 400 per minute. It is rented for $500 per month.

f. The cards cost $10 per 1,000, the sales order forms cost $12 per 100, and the invoice forms cost $18 per 100.

g. The current system is rented and $800 per month is allocated to sales order processing. The keypunch machines rent for $200 per month with two machines allocated to sales order processing.

h. The data operators currently earn $1,250 per month and work 8 hours a day.

i. An overhead of $1,000 per month is allocated to sales order processing.

The best proposal the company has received about a new system to replace the current one has the following characteristics:

a. All sales order information will be entered by the sales order clerks and the data operators will not be needed.

b. One additional sales order clerk will be employed and trained to handle corrections and adjustments called in by customers who change their mind about an order. The salary will be $1,800 per month for this person.

c. Terminals at the sales order desks will replace the keypunch machines and card reader. The terminals rent for $450 per month, and four will be needed.

d. A new type of sales order form will be printed by the terminal and will cost $15 per 100. A copy will be given the customer for verification. Telephone orders will be confirmed by mail.

e. The new system will still be stored on disks and the cost of actual computer processing is not expected to change. Overhead will be reduced to $800 per month under this system because the card reader and related operations will not be needed.

Required:

a. Prepare a cost projection for the current and proposed systems.

b. Make a recommendation as to what the company should do about its sales order processing.

28. Inventory and Sales Systems Analysis

Pack Hardware Stores, Inc., maintains nine regional warehouses in widely dispersed locations across North America. Each regional warehouse serves 40 to 50 local stores. A central warehouse in St. Paul, Minnesota, keeps the regional warehouses supplied with goods. Each local store sends a weekly order to its regional warehouse, and a copy goes to the central warehouse. In the event of unexpectedly large sales that result in an inventory shortage, the store can special-order items from the regional warehouse at any time. A copy of each special order also goes to the central warehouse. At the regional warehouse each weekly or special order is filled as it is received, and a confirming copy of the shipping invoice is sent to the central warehouse. Weekly, the central warehouse sorts the copies of the orders from the local stores and the confirmation copies of the shipping invoices from the regional warehouses by warehouse and matches them. For those orders with matching shipping invoices, the appropriate entries are made to adjust the regional warehouse inventory accounts. The regional warehouse inventory for each staple item is replenished whenever the inventory amount drops to the reorder level for that warehouse. A buying department at the central warehouse places orders for seasonal goods and specialty items to be sent to each store, basing order size on past sales records and on "requests" from local store managers. Monthly, each store manager is sent a "catalog" of seasonal and specialty items to use in making store requests. Local store inventory accounts are updated weekly by resorting the filled store orders by store number and updating the store accounts on a tape file.

Required:

Analyze the system description and suggest any improvements (additions or deletions) that you deem appropriate. Drawing a flowchart might be helpful.

29. Data Processing Department Organization

Robertson Industries is a loosely knit conglomerate that offers centralized data processing services to its affiliated companies. To improve the attractiveness of its services, the data processing department this past year introduced on-line service. Several affiliates have become or are becoming users of this service. It has resulted in a reorganization of the data processing department, and Jim Wilson, the senior on the audit, became concerned. Julie Preston, the semisenior on the engagement, reported that the client had not prepared a new organization chart but agreed to see what she could find out. Her report is as follows:

The data processing department now consists of 25 persons reporting to the president through the director of data processing. In addition to these data processing department employees, key committees perform important roles as do the internal and external auditors for the company. The internal auditors now report operationally to the board of directors and functionally to the president.

Selected functions of key committees that are important to the management and control of the data processing department are described briefly as follows:

Data Processing Committee. This committee, composed of three members of the board of directors, meets as required to review and evaluate major changes in the data processing area and to review approval of all pricing of services offered. Their responsibilities also include a review of major agreements with hardware and software vendors.

Audit Committee. In its oversight of the audit function, this committee of the board of directors is directly concerned with the quality of the records and reports processed by the department and the controls employed.

User Groups. These groups consist of representations from on-line users within a specific geographical area. They meet periodically throughout the year to discuss common areas of interest, possible enhancements, and current problems related to the on-line system. The results of these group meetings are reported directly to the data processing department through a user advisory committee.

The data processing department management consists of five managers who report to the director through an assistant director. The department management meets weekly to review the status of projects, customer service levels, and any problems. Weekly status reports are then prepared and distributed to each level of line management. Formal meetings with Robertson's president are held quarterly, or more often if required, to review future plans and past performance.

The following outline describes the sections within the department under the direction of each of the five managers.

I. *On-line Services*
   A. *On-line Technical Staff.* This staff conducts all user training, conversions, and parameter definitions necessary to set up a new user. Training classes are conducted at the data processing center. Conversion assistance is provided to the user prior to the initiation of on-line services. If conversion programs are required, these are defined by the on-line services section to the on-line analyst programmers for program preparation. During the first month after conversion of a new user, calls are directed to on-line services; thereafter, user calls are directed to the user liaison section.
   B. *Applications Coordinator.* This person is responsible for coordinating the approval of user and data processing department project requests, assisting in the requirements definition of a systems maintenance project, monitoring ongoing projects, and approving project test results.
II. *Operations*
   A. *Data Communications Coordinator.* This person monitors all service levels and response time related to the communications network and terminals. The coordinator receives all user calls regarding communications problems. The coordinator logs all calls, identifies the nature of the problem, and reports on the status of the problems until they are corrected.
   B. *Computer Operators.* This section consists of operators, supervisors, and librarians who execute, review, and service the daily computer production runs, special computer runs, and program compilations and tests. The operations are scheduled on a 24-hour basis for 6 days a week. Shift supervisors review all on-line operations and prepare written documentation of each problem encountered.
   C. *Scheduler.* This person is responsible for setting up the computer job runs and adjusting them for on-time special requests.
   D. *User Liaison.* This staff consists of four persons who receive, log, and report all questions or potential problems, other than communications problems, by on-line users. User input is obtained through telephone calls, letters, and on-line messages over the communications network and notes from user committee meetings.
   E. *On-line Reports Control.* This staff is responsible for the distribution of all hard-copy output to all users. Microfiche are sent directly to users from the outside processing vendor. Logs are maintained where appropriate to control distribution and to reconcile items such as check numbers and dividend totals.

III. *Systems and Programming*
   A. *On-line Analyst Programmers.* This staff is responsible for all the applications and system software programming required for the on-line system. Systems analysis and programming consists primarily of maintenance to existing computer programs, correction of problems, and enhancements to the current applications.
   B. *In-house Analyst Programmers.* This staff is responsible for all applications and system software programming not on-line.
IV. *Research and Development.*
   This staff evaluates and conducts preliminary investigations into new applications such as electronic funds transfers.
V. *Marketing.*
   This staff responds to request for information regarding the services provided by the data processing department. Once a user signs an on-line service agreement as a new user, that member is turned over to on-line services for training and conversion. *(Touche Ross & Company)*

Required:

a. Based on Ms. Preston's report, prepare an organization chart of the data processing department and of its relationships to the rest of the organization affecting it.

b. Make recommendations as to how the system could be improved.

CHAPTER NINE

Accounting Information Systems—
A Macro View

The accountant's products are largely based on static concepts. The dynamic business process must be halted for an instant in order to measure, summarize, and analyze the activities of a given period. From this analysis the necessary "adjustments" to asset and equity accounts are made, placing them in *current* status. At this selected point in time the corporate pose is assumed and the accountant strikes the big picture of entity values. Therefore, the accountant's approach to system operations tends to be pragmatic and reasoning retrospective.

Figure 9.1 may be viewed with entirely different attitudes, depending on the angle of perspective. For example, the corporate (internal) accountant is likely to become quite familiar with specific functions and their immediate surroundings. The public accountant, on the other hand, will probably emphasize the broader representation. Both perspectives are important.

Although this "point-of-view" analogy is intended merely to dramatize the divergent philosophical extremes from which information systems analysis may be approached, it does demonstrate the need for an overall plan to aid in the development of detailed subsystems.

A SYSTEMS PERSPECTIVE

Consideration has already been given to the common characteristics of information systems and to the manner in which they may relate to each other. Caution is advised in the development of any functional subsystem without careful consideration of all possible demands that may be placed on it by other information systems. Certainly an intelligent systems analyst would begin a system design by putting the system in its proper perspective within the corporate entity.

Values associated with tangible properties are constantly entering and leaving the business entity, causing a whirlpool of physical and financial value flows as corporate objectives are pursued: (1) manufactured products are constantly absorbing payroll, material, and overhead costs; (2) debts are incurred and liquidated; (3) assets are ac-

PUBLIC ACCOUNTANT'S AND MANAGEMENT ACCOUNTANT'S APPROACHES TO SYSTEM OPERATIONS.

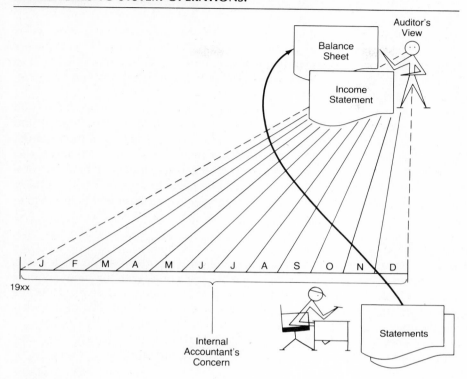

Figure 9.1

quired and diminished through use, (4) sales are made and inventory is converted to cash; and (5) equity is increased or diminished through incomes, losses, stock transactions, and dividends. As the overall cycle is made and endlessly repeated, profit will (must) emerge in order to assure prolonged corporate life. All business information systems exist and function in such an environment. This book follows the philosophy that individual subsystems can best be observed and evaluated in their natural habitat within the whole framework of systems.

Organizations tend to be categorized into three major groups according to their economic purposes: (1) those that provide a service, (2) those that buy and distribute a product, and (3) those that manufacture and distribute a product. Each of these operational forms will be examined from the point of view of the internal activities performed in accomplishing their individual objectives. The service firm (law, dentistry, accounting, television repair, architecture, etc.) receives revenues generated largely from the performance of specialized services and is only minimally affected by the transfer of inventory costs (materials and parts) to the customer. The entire process of (1) performing the service, (2) billing the customer, and (3) collecting the receivable can be viewed as a "cycle" of events.

Similarly, the merchandising company appears to be involved in *two* unique cycles of activity: (1) the process of acquiring and holding merchandise for resale to customers and (2) the separate process of converting the inventory back into cash by selling it to customers. The first group of activities will be called the *expenditure (or spending) cycle,* and the second the *revenue cycle.*

Manufacturing operations introduce a third cycle of internal activities interposed between the expenditure and revenue cycles. It will be referred to as the *conversion cycle* because it involves the transformation of raw materials acquired in the expenditure cycle into finished products for resale in the revenue cycle. Other operating systems such as cash control, property, and general ledger are discussed as a part of a separate cycle labeled *administrative cycle.* It will be helpful to the reader to visualize each of these types of operations from a macro perspective as illustrated in the following pages.

The Service Enterprise

The mode of operation referred to as the service enterprise is portrayed by a single cycle. Figure 9.2 illustrates events within the cycle that are sequential, with the momentum of the cycle directly dependent on the volume of customer contacts and demands for the service. Customer contacts are usually spontaneous, followed by analysis of the work (service) to be done (A).

Identifiable information systems (i.e., operations with unique characteristics and significant activity volumes) are: (1), (2), and (3), the performance and costing of the customer service, including all parts and materials used in its performance; (4), customer billing and collection, if credit transactions are common; (5), supplies and parts inventory maintenance; (6), the liquidation of routine indebtedness, and (7), a few "administrative" systems such as payroll, cash control, property, and the general ledger.

Many service companies have found it economically advantageous to subcontract some of their more voluminous and routine systems to other service enterprises specializing in data processing, although the availability of minicomputers has slowed the trend. Typical of these "delegated" functions are the payroll and the billing (or customer statement) operations.

The Merchandising Concern

Perhaps the most common of all business organizations is the merchandising concern. Its mode of operations is best described as "buying and selling," suggesting two operating cycles umbilically connected at the inventory point as illustrated in Figure 9.3.

Although each cycle is designed to play an important role in the achievement of overall corporate objectives, they move independently in relation to each other. Their common point of contact is the merchandise inventory, and even in this relationship their *individual* interests are somewhat divergent. For example, management within the expenditure cycle is concerned with cash outflows and materials inflows. Policy in these areas is likely to focus on costs, prices, discounts, quality, and delivery schedules, and

BASIC INFORMATION FLOW IN A SERVICE COMPANY.

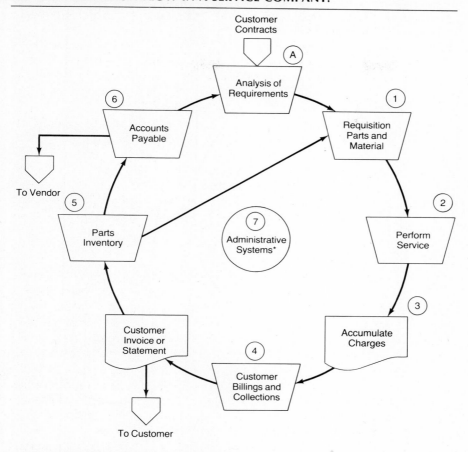

*That is, payroll, general ledger, and cash control.

Figure 9.2

on optimizing ordering and "carrying" costs of inventory. Marketing management, on the other hand, is involved in transactions that move materials out and create cash inflows. These activities are quite naturally motivated by consumer demand and customer service.

The most noticeable difference between the service company and the merchandising concern is the increased number of functional systems that originate, distribute, handle, process, and control critical business documents. In a merchandising business of significant size, uniquely distinctive objectives, responsibilities, and organizational motives can be discerned. These characteristics are reflected in the functions of (1) purchasing, (2) receiving and inspection, (3) accounts payable, (4) and (6) inventory

BASIC INFORMATION FLOW IN A MERCHANDISING COMPANY.

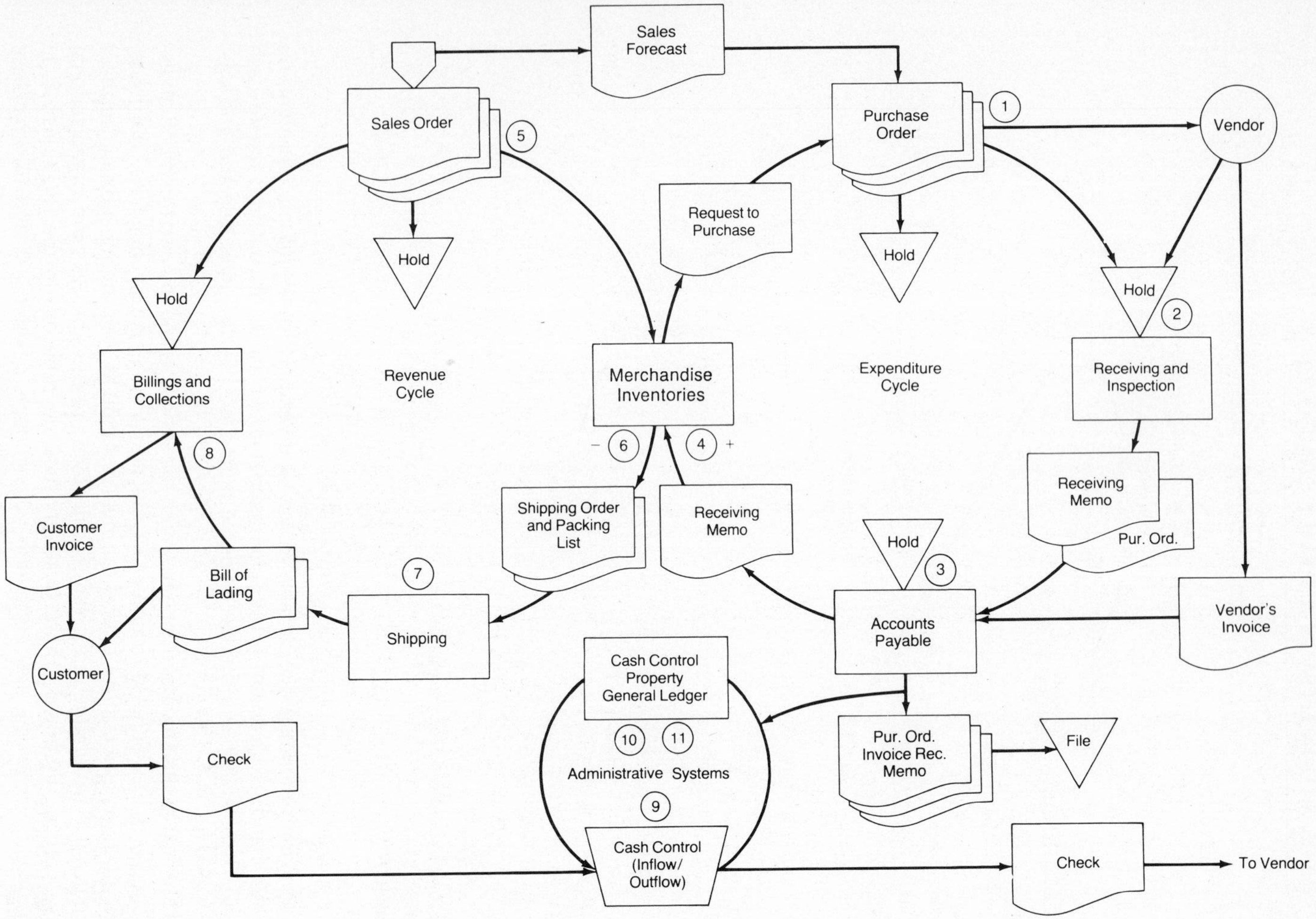

Figure 9.3

control, (5) sales and order writing, (7) shipping, and (8) billing and collection, which includes customer accounts, credit, and history. Also, administrative systems like payroll, cash control, and property are inherent to some extent in both types of enterprises.

Care has been taken not to cast this discussion in the framework of a giant corporation—for example, Sears Roebuck & Company. The complications introduced by multidivisional and multinational operations would tend to obscure *basic* principles, the portrayal of which is the main objective of this book.

The Manufacturing Company

The manufacturing company contains all the information systems operative in the foregoing illustration of the merchandising establishment, plus a vast and complicated operation concerned with converting raw materials into the company's finished product that its marketing group distributes. Without engaging in a moot discussion of the sequence in which these operations occur, it satisfies our purpose to examine the overall functional flows in the manner portrayed in Figure 9.4.

The reader will observe no fewer than nine distinct functional centers of activity within these cycles (numbered 1 through 9 in Figure 9.5), each one geared to a different set of organizational objectives, some of which lead them into contact (if not conflict) with each other. In addition to these systems, the usual administrative systems such as (10) cash control, (11) property control, and (12) general ledger are inherent in the overall pattern of operations. It should also be noted that payroll was listed as an administrative system in both the service and the merchandise illustrations. Because of its unique relationship to the production process through the distribution of direct and indirect labor costs to the manufactured product, we have chosen to show the payroll as an integral part of the production cycle. It must be remembered, however, that the payroll system serves the entire corporate organization, and costs emanating from that system are charged to appropriate cost collection centers throughout the company.

The major purpose of this book is to examine each one of these centers of business activity from the accountant's perspective and to identify the objectives, the business documents created and handled, the flow of information, system interdependencies, management information needs served, the risks of failure in the system, and the effectiveness of financial controls. Although there are possibly many more than 12 major subsystems (see Figure 9.5) functioning in a given manufacturing company of significant size, the ones selected for consideration in the following chapters are those with the highest volumes of activity, in terms of both dollars and transactions.

IDENTIFICATION OF FUNCTIONAL SYSTEMS OF THE OPERATING CYCLES

As a prelude to a more detailed examination of these systems in the following chapters, let us first look at the broad objectives of each, and visualize the document creation and flow associated with the accomplishment of the major objectives of the systems. This includes the major functions of the operating cycles—expenditure, conversion, and revenue.

BASIC INFORMATION FLOW IN A MANUFACTURING ENVIRONMENT.

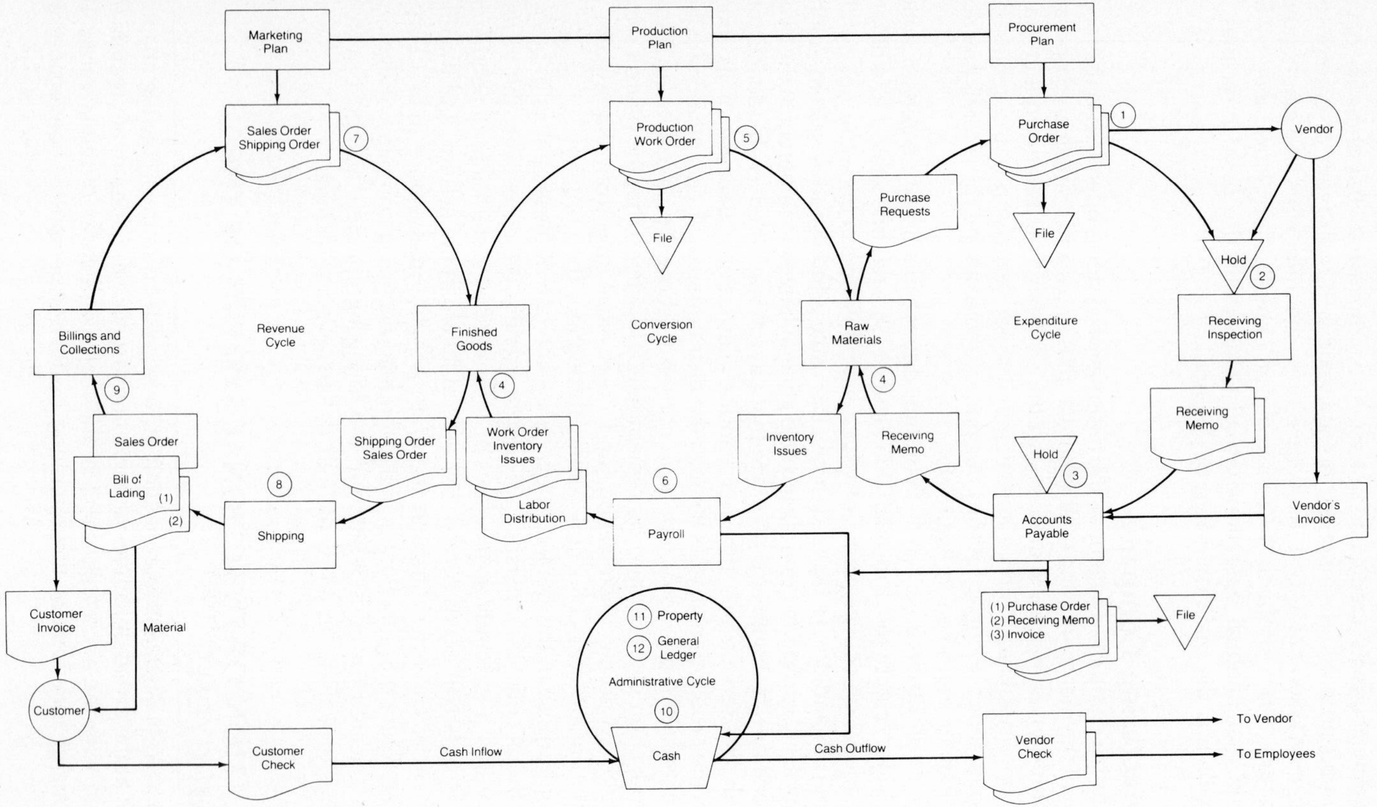

Figure 9.4

FUNCTIONAL SUBSYSTEMS.

The Spending (Expenditure) Cycle
- ① The Procurement and Vendor Control System
- ② The Receiving and Inspection System
- ③ The Accounts Payable System

The Conversion Cycle
- ④ The Inventory Control System
- ⑤ The Production Control System
- ⑥ The Payroll System

The Revenue Cycle
- ⑦ The Marketing System
- ⑧ The Shipping and Transportation System
- ⑨ The Billing and Collection System

The Administrative Cycle:
- ⑩ Cash Receipts and Disbursements
- ⑪ The Property Control System
- ⑫ The General Ledger System

Figure 9.5

The Procurement and Vendor Control System

The task of establishing reliable sources of supply of quality raw materials at competitive prices requires a great deal of expertise in a number of specialized areas. Good buyers will have an intimate knowledge of the company's production and inventory systems because their function is to serve the needs of both. They will be knowledgeable about the many common carriers that make up the nation's transportation system—their routes, schedules, and rate structures. Through various internal sources, the buyer will be familiar with the contract performance history as well as the credit ratings of the suppliers. That knowledge is essential to the successful discharge of the buyer's primary responsibility to (1) meet the raw material requirements of the production process, while (2) preventing excessive accumulations in inventory and (3) assuring efficiency in the procurement function by obtaining quality materials at the proper time and the lowest possible cost. Chapter Ten elaborates on the specific elements of the procurement process, with emphasis on computer operations.

The Receiving and Inspection System

One of the more sensitive points of contact with outsiders is at the unloading and receiving docks, where valuable merchandise and materials exchange hands, and title to such goods is often established. These exchanges involve not only the buyer and seller, but the common carrier as well. Numerous possibilities exist for discrepancies between the time of formalization of the purchase contract and the final delivery of the material. Theft, damage in transit, over- or undershipment, material substitutions, unauthorized shipment, incorrect FOB point (literally "free on board," or point at which title changes hands) and unauthorized carrier (excessive freight charges) are just a few. Testing to determine conformance with engineering specifications is often a precondition of acceptance of a shipment.

The receiving and inspection function thus formally establishes that a procurement contract has been fulfilled, or partially fulfilled, and originates evidence to that effect by the issuance of an official receiving document for use by other authorized internal operations. The *receiving memorandum* reflects all aspects and conditions of the exchange, including the carrier's name and freight bill number. No company of any size can afford to ignore the potential dangers of a poorly controlled receiving operation. A complete analysis of this function is presented in Chapter Ten.

The Accounts Payable (Liability Liquidation) System

Of all the events that follow the establishment of a legal purchase contract, perhaps the payment process is the most visible. It is usually at this point that final settlement of discrepancies between buyer and supplier is reached, facilitating payment of the financial obligation. Payment therefore depends on (1) official purchase, (2) validated performance (receipt), and (3) formal billing.

The vendor can be expected to provide an invoice concurrently with, or immediately following, the shipment. Such invoices will normally be directed to an accounting organization (i.e., the accounts payable department), which should be completely independent of the purchasing and receiving operations. The organization will assume full responsibility for discharging the company's legal obligations to its trade creditors, but not without satisfying itself that the material *was* officially ordered, *was* actually received in good condition, and *is* properly billed in accordance with the terms and conditions specified in the purchase contract. This group is further charged with the responsibility of paying these legal obligations in a timely manner so that the company may be justified in claiming any financial incentive (cash discount) frequently awarded by its trade creditors. Chapter Eleven presents a more detailed analysis of this function.

The Inventory Control System

Materials accepted from carriers and validated in the receiving and inspection department pass directly into the inventory storerooms, accompanied by the official receiving memorandum. At this point, the physical handling of the material and the financial recording are separated. Inventory accounts are "charged" (debited) by the accounts payable operation as it distributes the costs reflected on the approved vendor's invoices. Inventory accounts are "relieved" (credited) through the processing of stores requisitions originating mainly in the production organizations. Inventory prices are maintained according to company policy (FIFO, LIFO, average cost, etc.), and production work orders are charged on the basis of such requisitions.

The inventory system, although seemingly simple in concept, is usually quite complicated in actual practice since it involves much more than the mere inflow and outflow of physical materials and associated costs. A good inventory control system will automatically accomplish most of the middle-management decisions involving stock levels and economic ordering policies. It may also be programmed to anticipate future production requirements possibly resulting in "stockouts" and production line stoppages. A possible by-product of such analysis is the automatically created procurement request. The general process is examined in greater detail in Chapter Twelve.

The Production Control System

Events in the conversion environment introduce a different operating philosophy from those in the expenditure cycle. Unencumbered with the exigencies of relating to and reconciling with "outside" forces, the production operation tends to focus on practical matters such as output, quality, schedule, standards, budgets, and performance. The intricate process of accumulating and allocating the elements of production costs; the application of cost standards and the measurement of deviations from those standards; the loading of production shops for maximum efficiency; the treatment of wastes, by-products, and joint products; combine to make the production operation one of the most complicated and massive systems in the whole superstructure of the management information network. Its direct relationship to marketing, engineering, inventory, payroll, cost accounting, and personnel systems give it a breadth of scope probably unmatched by any of the other subsystems. The accountant's interest focuses on the critical cost flows, accuracy and completeness of the cost distribution process, and the study of budget conformity through the analysis of cost variances. Chapter Thirteen provides an in-depth analysis of this system.

The Payroll and Labor Distribution System

The payroll system is perhaps most appropriately categorized as an administrative information system, since it does not fit exclusively into any one of the three *operating* cycles described in Figure 9.4. The reason for its inclusion in the production cycle is its special involvement in the production costing process. The system in fact relates directly to all functional subentities of the company. No other single system places the company in interface with more "outside" publics than the payroll and its peripheral operations (e.g., the community; banks and other lending agencies; labor unions; federal, state, and local taxing authorities; credit unions; and even the courts in states where wage garnishments are legal). In many of these interfaces, the system serves in a trust capacity, withholding, accumulating, reporting, and remitting on behalf of the respective agencies. Although the payroll system is dependent on the personnel organization for "status" information concerning all employees, it looks to individual organizations and cost centers for input relating to employee performance. In this manner, master records and activity records are brought together, periodic performance is converted into gross pay, and authorized deductions are automatically made and held in trust for appropriate agencies. This system is examined in more detail in Chapter Fourteen.

The Marketing System

Marketing people regard their function as the beating heart of the organization. Although this idea may be an exaggeration, marketing is the intermediary between production and consumption; it provides the fuel that fires other activities in the conversion and spending cycles. The object of sales is to produce a flow of revenue sufficient to cover the cost of *all* other operations within the company, plus a profit for investors.

Obviously, to relegate the marketing function to simple "sales and order-writing" activities would be a gross and dangerous underestimation. In addition to planning, coordinating, and controlling the whole marketing strategy, marketing management has important influences on the routine activities of production, procurement, inventory, finance, and personnel. Sales forecasts, for example, are directly related to establishing production capacity and controlling production scheduling, determining inventory levels, stimulating procurement activity, and the management of cash. Other activities within the payment cycle are indirectly affected.

The accounting information system in turn provides marketing management with data generated from sales, including sales orders, sales analyses and cost reports, invoicing, shipping, customer credit, analysis of doubtful accounts, inventory stock status, and the like. A complete discussion of the marketing system is found in Chapter Fifteen.

The Shipping and Transportation System

Shipping constitutes *performance* of the sales contract and provides evidence to that effect. Its relationships with common carriers and the volume and significance of the documents originating at the shipping point require its treatment as a full-fledged information system. Accounting controls and proper interface with other related and dependent subsystems are vitally important.

Generally, the primary function of shipping is to ensure that all "sold" merchandise is properly packaged and dispatched in accordance with the sales agreement and all "shipped" merchandise is properly billed or invoiced. Once the shipment is officially released to the carrier, the company relinquishes physical control. Misshipments, incorrect routing, improper weights or counts, poor packaging or identification, and other types of shipping mismanagement typically result in rejection of the shipment by the customer. Customer rejection of a shipment entails an excessive number of returned shipments, demurrage charges, further damage in transit, and possible legal expenses.

Shipping is necessarily a cost-oriented function. It must provide a reliable and efficient service because (1) billing and collection depends on its documents as the basis for invoicing the customer, (2) shipping documents provide the legal contractual relationships with carriers, and (3) consummation of the shipping function "starts the clock" for determining due dates for cash discount entitlement. Chapter Fifteen provides a more detailed discussion of shipping systems and related activities.

The Billing and Collection System

The importance of the billing and collection operation is manifested by the fact that it provides the channel through which the vast majority of funds routinely flow into the company. The company relates to its outside customers through its billing and collection operation in much the same manner as it does in the vendor/accounts payable relationships. Because of its important role in the cash flow channel, the system is the object of careful surveillance and control. Its operations are strongly influenced by its interfaces with the credit department, the cashier department, the inventory department, and, of course, shipping.

The system is perhaps best known for the management of customer accounts receivable from the acquisition of an asset to its disposition by conversion into cash, demand deposits, or the like. During this time period, without proper accounting and management controls, the system may be vulnerable to common irregularities such as "lapping" (misappropriation of cash covered by successive misapplications of cash receipts from customers), improper write-offs of doubtful accounts, and billing omissions.

In macro terms, the purpose of the billing and collecting system is to render a customer invoice for each fulfilled, or partially fulfilled, sales contract as evidenced by a validated shipping document, and to follow up the transaction until consummation is evidenced by receipt of the customer's remittance. Chapter Sixteen examines the complete flow of documents and information in this important system.

FUNCTIONS OF THE ADMINISTRATIVE CYCLE

The foregoing discussions of specific information systems have illustrated activities inherent in the *spending* cycle, the *conversion* cycle, and the *revenue* cycle. There are, of course, several other important information systems relating to, but functioning outside, the scope of these three areas.

Three information systems have been selected for discussion under the heading "administrative cycle" because they handle, process, store, control, and report on transactions involving corporate values and value transformations. Other important information systems such as personnel, quality control, budget and forecasting, and engineering are not treated in this book merely because they do not meet that qualification. This does not imply that their role in corporate affairs is any less significant.

The Cash Control System

No other asset receives more constant and intense scrutiny than does cash. The physical characteristics of cash and cash representations tend to stimulate creativity in the minds of employees bent on fraud—all the way from the mail room to the highest executive office. Accounting controls must therefore follow cash flows from the entry point to the bank. Similarly, fraud can be perpetrated in the spending cycle (cash outflows) through improper payment schemes. Obviously, no discussion of cash would be complete without consideration of both receipts and disbursements.

Typical of accounting controls in the handling of cash is the principle of separation of duties in recording and custodial functions. The practice of bonding employees who work in proximity to cash operations is also common.

On the receipts side, cashiers and/or mail personnel identify cash transactions and initiate the separation of recording and handling responsibilities by routing checks and cash to the cashier office and transaction identification and other remittance advice to accounts receivable. Accounts receivable personnel update customer records. In the cashier office the cash sales are usually recorded by journal voucher that is prepared from cash register tapes that are supported by sales slips.

On the payments side, the accounts payable operation usually prepares the checks and distributes cash disbursements to the proper asset and expense accounts. The cashier operation then takes control of the unsigned checks and journalizes the cash disbursement.

As indicated, custody of cash involves some intricate relationships among payables, receivables, the customer, the vendor, the mail room, internal auditing, the bank, and the cashier department. Chapter Seventeen delineates more clearly the controlled movements of these values, along with the carefully performed audits and reconciliations.

The Property Control System

Fixed assets represent an investment of major proportions in most businesses. The gradual diminution in value and service of such assets owing to wear and obsolescence contributes significantly to the cost of producing goods and delivering services. It is essential that a complete and efficient property accounting system be maintained to help keep the business financially strong and productive.

To be effective, the property control system must be based on complete and accurate master records that can be modified to show acquisitions, transfers and relocations, improvements and modifications, replacements, and retirements. The first and continuing responsibility of the system is to monitor and maintain physical control over all tangible fixed properties and provide for adequate insurance. This function envisages the use of a property tagging system to aid in assigning responsibility for use of an asset, its physical location, regular surveillance of its operation, and (in some cases) the automatic cuing of preventive maintenance.

Depreciation computation and accounting, a vital function of the system, directly affects two kinds of taxes: *ad valorem* and income taxes. Both the expense of depreciation itself and the resulting book value of the related asset directly impact the financial operations of the company.

Since fixed assets can be acquired through either purchase or construction, the system must be tied to several subsystems in the spending and conversion cycles. Accounts payable cost distributions as well as material, labor, and overhead cost absorptions against in-house construction work orders are essential to initial asset valuation. The various aspects of property accounting and the general ledger system are discussed in Chapter Eighteen.

The General Ledger System

Each system previously described directly or indirectly provides input into the company's financial records. Through careful systems design and efficient computer programming, essential data are extracted from the routine processing of each system, coded, and formatted for consolidation in the general ledger system. Through this process, corporate general ledger accounts are kept constantly current, and formal statements are readily available without much of the trauma associated with normal closings.

Data not generated by one or more of the operating subsystems must be provided by special journal vouchers. These data would include adjustments and reversals, stock transactions, dividends, and other relatively infrequent events and activities handled outside the standard accounting information systems.

The reader can visualize how a general ledger master file, including the entire corporate chart of accounts, could be updated by this input. Subsequent to such updating, the entire standard closing procedure could be consummated by the computer, resulting in the automatic preparation of the full range of period-end financial statements.

AUDITING CONSIDERATIONS

Until relatively recently, public accountants followed the "transaction approach" in determining the completeness and accuracy of recorded business history on which to base their opinions. For the most part, this procedure required the examination of a rather large sample of randomly selected transactions of specific types. Modern auditing philosophy focuses on the chain of sequential events constituting a *completed* transaction. We have referred to these related events as cycles.

For example, an auditor sought to confirm the accuracy and completeness of a client's accounts by testing a certain percentage of payment and receipt transactions, inventory balances, cash operations, payroll data, and other critical high-volume operations. Satisfactory results from such tests established the basis for confidence in both the recording and reporting of financial information.

Using the "cycle approach," however, the auditor may select a much smaller sample of transactions and trace them through all phases, or events, leading to consumation. For example, a selected purchase contract may be traced through receiving, vouchering and payment, and finally, into inventory where both quantity and pricing can be verified. A given sales contract may be traced through inventory, shipping, billing and collection, and into the cash operation. This procedure accomplishes much more than the simple verification of account accuracy. It confirms the correct (or incorrect) interaction among dependent subsystems, and has the effect of testing the efficacy of internal controls.

SUMMARY

The major objective in the foregoing discussion was to establish a framework of corporate operations within which to view more specifically each operating subsystem. The remaining chapters of this book attempt to scrutinize these individual systems in some detail.

Readers should *not* look for standard, or universally applicable, solutions to systems problems in these chapters. Rather, they should seek an understanding of the vital elements and functions of each system and attempt to visualize alternative solutions for individual situations. After all, systems design is an art. Therefore, the systems analyst must be able to "paint what he or she sees," being careful only to follow the basic rules imposed by the state of the art. Above all, the reader is encouraged to view the subsystem in its place as a part of the whole.

SELECTED REFERENCES

The Auditors Study and Evaluation of Internal Controls in EDP Systems; Computer Services Executive Committee, AICPA, 1977.
Controlling Assets and Transactions; Touche Ross & Co. 1979.
Evaluating Internal Control; Ernst & Whinney, 1979.
A Guide for Studying and Evaluating Internal Accounting Controls, Chicago: Arthur Anderson & Co., 1978.

QUESTIONS

1. From the standpoint of perspective, what single characteristic might differentiate the traditional corporate accountant from the public accountant?
2. What forces are causing the accountant to devote an increasing amount of attention to internal controls as opposed to detailed audits?
3. Although a particular merchandising company may be three times the size of a given manufacturing company, the latter may have several more information subsystems than the former. Why?
4. Discuss and compare the series of events that transpire in the expenditure cycle, the conversion cycle, and the revenue cycle.
5. Identify the major subsystems likely to be found in most large-scale manufacturing companies.
6. In general terms, describe the major responsibilities of a procurement operation.
7. Give reasons for maintaining a separate (from purchasing and accounts payable) materials receiving and inspection operation.
8. Explain why it would be inadvisable to include accounts payable in the same organization with purchasing and receiving.
9. Explain why an accounting processing system should be tailored to the characteristics of the entity.
10. Compare the number of accounting information subsystems found in a manufacturing company with those in a merchandising company. What accounts for the difference?
11. What are the overall objectives of a purchasing system?
12. What factors strongly suggest that the accounts payable operation be completely independent of procurement activities?
13. What role does the production information system play in the determination of the entity's inventory valuation?
14. In what way does the payroll information system act in a "trust" capacity on behalf of agencies outside the entity?
15. What indispensable service does the marketing organization provide that other systems rely on in estimating their level of activity?
16. Without the proper systems controls, what kinds of fraud might be encountered in the billings and collections systems? The cash receipts system? The cash disbursements system?
17. Describe how all the systems discussed might provide selected input into a general ledger system.

PROBLEMS

18. Centralizing Accounting Systems

You are a member of the management services staff of Begg, Borra and Steele, an accounting firm. One of your clients is a large retail establishment with branch stores in several cities surrounding the home store in Memphis. Discuss how you would approach the problem of centralizing the major accounting systems in such a way as to maintain a current general ledger master file at the computer center in the home store.

19. Systems Analysis and Flowcharts

Charting, Inc., a new audit client of yours, processes its sales and cash receipts documents in the following manner:

Cash receipts. The mail is opened each morning by a mail clerk in the sales department. The mail clerk prepares a remittance advice (showing customer and amount paid) if one is not received. The checks and remittance advices are then forwarded to the sales department supervisor, who reviews each check and forwards the checks and remittance advices to the accounting department supervisor. The accounting department supervisor, who also functions as the credit manager, reviews all checks for payments of past due accounts and then forwards the checks and remittance advices to the accounts receivable clerk, who arranges the advices in alphabetical order. The remittance advices are posted directly to the accounts receivable ledger cards. The checks are endorsed by stamp and totaled. The total is posted to the cash receipts journal. The remittance advices are filed chronologically. After receiving the cash from the preceding day's cash sales, the accounts receivable clerk prepares the daily deposit slip in triplicate. The third copy of the deposit slip is filed by date, and the second copy and the original accompany the bank deposit.

Sales. Salesclerks prepare the sales invoices in triplicate. The original and the second copy are presented to the cashier. The third copy is retained by the salesclerk in the sales book. When the sale is for cash, the customer pays the salesclerk, who presents the money to the cashier with the invoice copies. A credit sale is approved by the cashier from an approved credit list after the salesclerk prepares the three-part invoice. After receiving the cash or approved invoice, the cashier validates the original copy of the sales invoice and gives it to the customer. At the end of each day the cashier recaps the sales and cash received and forwards the cash and the second copy of all sales invoices to the accounts receivable clerk. The accounts receivable clerk balances the cash received with cash sales invoices and prepares a daily sales summary. The credit sales invoices are posted to the accounts receivable ledger, and then all invoices are sent to the inventory control clerk in the sales department for posting to the inventory control catalog. After posting, the inventory control clerk files all invoices numerically. The accounts receivable clerk posts the daily sales summary to the cash receipts journal and sales journal and files the sales summaries by date. The cash from cash sales is combined with the cash received on account, and this constitutes the daily bank deposit.

Bank deposits. The bank validates the deposit slip and returns the second copy to the accounting department, where it is filed by date by the accounts receivable clerk. Monthly bank statements are reconciled promptly by the accounting department supervisor and filed by date. *(AICPA adapted)*

Required:

a. Prepare separate flowcharts of the sales and cash receipts applications of Charting, Inc.

b. Identify potential internal control weaknesses in Charting, Inc., procedures.

20. Systems Analysis

Delmo Inc. is a wholesale distributor of automotive parts that serves customers in the states east of the Mississippi River. The company has grown during the last 25 years from a small regional distributorship to its present size.

The states are divided into eight separate territories in order to service Delmo customers adequately. Delmo salespersons regularly call upon current and prospective customers in each of the territories. Delmo customers are of four general types:

a. Automotive parts stores

b. Hardware stores with an automotive parts section

c. Independent garage owners

d. Buying groups for garages and service stations

Because Delmo Inc. must stock such a large variety and quantity of automotive parts to accommodate its customers, the company acquired its own computer system very early and implemented an inventory control system first. Other applications such as cash receipts and disbursements, sales analysis, accounts receivable, payroll, and accounts payable have since been added.

Delmo's inventory control system is comprised of an integrated purchase ordering and perpetual inventory system. Each item of inventory is identified by an inventory code number; the code number identifies both the product line and the item itself. When the quantity on hand for an item falls below the specified stock level, a purchase order is automatically generated by the computer. The purchase order is sent to the vendor after approval by the purchasing manager. All receipts, issues, and returns are entered into the computer daily. A printout for all inventory items within product lines showing receipts, issues, and current balance is prepared weekly. However, current status for a particular item carried in the inventory can be obtained daily if it is desired.

Sales orders are filled within 48 hours of receipt. Sales invoices are prepared by the computer the same day that the merchandise is shipped. At the end of each month, several reports are produced that summarize the monthly sales. The current month's and year-to-date sales by product line, territory, and customer class are compared with the same figures from the previous year. In addition, reports showing only the monthly figures for product line within territory and customer class within territory are prepared. In all cases the reports provide summarized data; that is, detailed data such as sales by individual customers or product are not listed. Terms of 2/10, net 30 are standard for all of Delmo's customers.

Customers' accounts receivable are updated daily for sales, sales returns and allowances, and payments on account. Monthly statements are computer prepared and mailed following completion of entries for the last day of the month. Each Friday a schedule is prepared showing the total amount of accounts receivable outstanding by age—current accounts (0 to 30 days), slightly past-due accounts (31 to 90 days), and long overdue accounts (over 90 days).

Delmo Inc. recently acquired Wenrock Company, a wholesale distributor of tools and light equipment. In addition to servicing the same type of customers as Delmo, Wenrock also sells to equipment rental shops. Wenrock's sales region is not so extensive as Delmo's but the Delmo management has encouraged Wenrock to expand the distribution of its product to all of Delmo's sales territories.

Wenrock Company uses a computer service bureau to aid in its accounting functions. For example, certain inventory activities are recorded by the service bureau. Each item carried by Wenrock is assigned a product code number that identifies the product and the product line. Data regarding shipments received from manufacturers, shipments to customers (sales), and any other physical inventory changes are delivered to the service bureau daily, and the service bureau updates Wenrock's inventory records. A weekly inventory listing showing beginning balance, receipts, issues, and ending balance for each item in the inventory is provided to Wenrock on Monday morning.

Wenrock furnishes the service bureau with information about each sale of merchandise to a customer. The service bureau prepares a five-part invoice and records the sales in its records. This processing is done at night, and all copies of each invoice are delivered to Wenrock the next morning. At the end of the month the service bureau provides Wenrock with a sales report classified by product line showing the sales in units and dollars for each item sold. Wenrock's sales terms are 2/10, net 30.

The accounts receivable function still is handled by Wenrock's bookkeeper. Two copies of the invoice are mailed to the customer. Two of the remaining copies are filed—one numerically and the other alphabetically by customer. The alphabetic file represents the accounts receivable file. When a customer's payment is received, the invoice is marked "paid" and placed in a paid invoice file in alphabetic order. The bookkeeper mails monthly statements according to the following schedule:

Tenth of the month	A–G
Twentieth of the month	H–O
Thirtieth of the month	P–Z

The final copy of the invoice is included with the merchandise when it is shipped.

Wenrock has continued to use its present accounting system and supplies Delmo management with monthly financial information developed from this system. However, Delmo management is anxious to have Wenrock use its computer and its information system because it will reduce accounting and computer costs, make the financial reports of Wenrock more useful to Delmo management, and provide Wenrock personnel with better information to manage the company.

At the time Delmo acquired Wenrock, it also hired a new marketing manager with experience in both product areas. The new manager wants Wenrock to organize its sales force using the same territorial distribution as Delmo to facilitate the management of the two sales forces.

The new manager also believes that more useful sales information should be provided to individual salespersons and to the department. Although the monthly sales reports currently prepared provide adequate summary data, the manager would like additional details to aid the sales personnel.

The acquisition of Wenrock Company and expansion of its sales to a larger geographic area has created a cash strain on Delmo Inc., particularly in the short run. Consequently, cash management has become much more important than in prior years. A weekly report that presents a reliable estimate of daily cash receipts is needed. The treasurer heard that a local company had improved its cash forecasting system by studying the timing of customers' payments on account to see if a discernible payment pattern existed. The payment pattern became the model that was applied to outstanding invoices to estimate the daily cash receipts for the next week. The treasurer thinks that this is a good approach and wonders if it can be done at Delmo. *(IMA adapted)*

Required:

a. Identify and briefly describe the additional data Wenrock Company must collect and furnish in order to use the Delmo data processing system. Also identify the data, if any, currently accumulated by Wenrock that no longer will be needed due to the conversion to the Delmo system.

b. Using only the data currently available from the Delmo data processing system, what additional reports could be prepared that would be useful to the marketing manager and the individual salespeople? Briefly explain how each report would be useful to the sales personnel.

c. If Delmo Inc. were to use a cash forecasting system similar to the one suggested by the treasurer, describe:

   (1) The data currently available in the system that would be used in preparing such a forecast

   (2) The additional data that must be generated

   (3) The modifications, if any, that would be required in the Delmo data processing system

SECTION

THE SPENDING CYCLE

CHAPTER TEN

The Procurement and
Receiving Systems

In Chapter Nine we portrayed the purchasing and receiving functions as separate accounting information subsystems in the expenditure cycle, which they indeed are. However, because of their direct relationship to each other and because we wish to avoid certain duplications necessitated by separate chapter treatment, they are discussed in separate sections in this chapter. This decision should not cause the reader to infer that the two vital functions are not operationally independent, or that they are less important than any of the other functions in the whole accounting information network of subsystems.

Large manufacturing concerns often place both of these functions under a director of material (logistics), along with the inventory control function as shown in Figure 10.1. In order to avoid confusion in our discussions of functions, responsibilities, and controls, we have attempted to maintain the appearance of separation by dividing the presentation into Sections A (purchasing) and B (receiving).

SECTION A

The study of specific accounting information subsystems begins with a function of vital interest to accountants: the procurement, or purchasing system. This interest is generated by the system's pervasive impact on other systems and its tremendous volume of activity. The cost of materials and services purchased annually by industrial companies averages 50 percent or more of the total dollar value of sales. The significant amounts involved and the delicate nature of internal and external relationships require the accountant to consider carefully the overall procurement function not only from the standpoint of (1) efficiency and (2) orderly information flow but also with due attention to (3) controls.

This discussion is limited, for the sake of simplicity, to the acquisition of materials and supplies for production and operation. Other procurement functions relating, for example, to the in-house construction of capital assets, the acquisition of real estate and securities, and contracting for advertising and other professional services are readily adaptable to the techniques outlined herein. Accordingly, these discussions may be adapted to apply to retail stores, transportation companies, and the like.

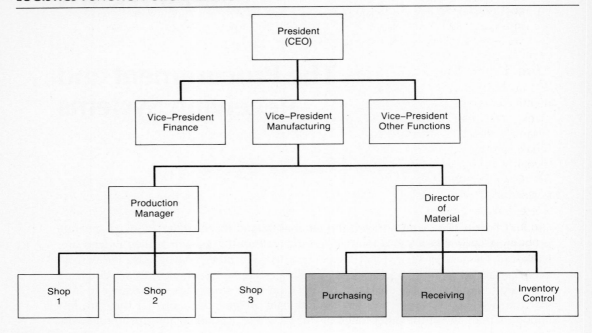

Figure 10.1

The assumption has also been made that our system is sufficiently large and complex to warrant the employment of modern data processing technology in its operation. Although computers stand ready to serve corporate data processing and information needs, they exact a certain price. They demand standardization of data elements, codes, and formats. They likewise demand discipline from management and precision from operating personnel. The following discussion attempts to blend sufficient detail with broad concepts to yield a maximum understanding of salient issues involved in purchasing operations.

FUNCTIONS OF THE PROCUREMENT SYSTEM

Among their corporate regulations most companies of reasonably large size will maintain written statements of policy and procedure governing the procurement functions, as well as all systems areas. Such procedures may be supported by organization charts, specific responsibility delegations, and even individual job descriptions in an effort to control this massive activity. Such procedural documents commonly include a statement of objectives, which might be worded as follows:

The purchasing function involves the procurement of materials, supplies, equipment, and services at the lowest possible cost consistent with required quality standards to support the production of merchandise and products that meet (the company's) image and reputation for excellence in its field. The main goal must always be the promotion of (the company's) best interests through intelligent action and fair dealing that results in the acquisition of maximum value for each dollar of expenditures.

Minimizing Material Cost

The purchasing department, through the exercise of its considerable flexibility in implementing purchasing policy, exerts a tremendous impact on perhaps the largest category of expenditures in the company operations. Its decisions to "make or buy," to issue "blanket orders" with a single vendor, and to buy in quantity and earn favorable price breaks, along with other decision alternatives directly affect (1) cash requirements, (2) inventory levels, and (3) production costs.

One of the ways material acquisition costs can be minimized is through the prudent business practice of eliciting competitive bids for significant purchases. To protect the interests of the shareholders, the board of directors and top management should formulate and approve the policy on this matter. The degree of formality of the bid process probably should vary depending on the size of the purchase. A typical policy might reflect the following variations:

1. Purchases of $500 or less: No formal bids required. Savings that may result on such orders would not justify the cost of obtaining bids.
2. $501 to $2,500. Verbal or telephone quotations from price catalogs should suffice. Such information should be made part of the permanent record.
3. $2,501 to $10,000: Written quotations should be obtained from several approved suppliers and opened in the presence of at least two other persons in the department office. The person opening the bids should sign all documents and make them part of the permanent file.
4. Purchases over $10,000: Written bids should be obtained and opened in the presence of a representative of the treasurer's office at an announced time and date, with vendors invited to attend. Signed bids are then made official, permanent records, and the supplier is selected. This process is referred to as the *sealed bid* procedure.

It is common practice to require quotations from at least three vendors, that being the minimum number considered necessary to assure competition. Most companies will establish more than three approved sources for each product. This raises the question of how the potential bidders are selected. A vendor rating plan often provides the answer, or a rotation system that gives the last successful bidder a repeat opportunity may be preferred. If quotation files indicate consistent overbidding by certain vendors, management should be alerted to the possibility that the bidding system is being "manipulated" through vendor-insider contacts or even through agreement among vendors.

"Rigged" bidding arrangements are occasionally reported by the press. When skillfully executed, such arrangements are practically impossible to detect through observation of contract award patterns. The company should, therefore, constantly search for new suppliers who may qualify for the "approved vendor list."

Another awkward situation occurs when a favorable bid is received *after* the announced bid closing date. Such bids are generally not considered eligible for consideration. In order to hold late bids to a minimum, buyers should be careful to allow vendors sufficient time to prepare their quotations. Vendors whose quotations have not been received by the deadline should be contacted by telephone as a precaution against the possibility that an insider favoring a particular vendor may have obtained a potentially lower bid from a competitor and "misplaced" it.

From the foregoing discussion, the reader should readily perceive the favorable impact on material cost accruing from a sound bidding procedure. One final element of internal control is a strict system of authorizations for purchase contracts. Levels of approval are usually set by the president and the board of directors, and might reflect the pattern shown in Figure 10.2.

Establishing and Maintaining Reliable Sources of Material

For most purchases, individual buyers decide which vendors shall receive the invitation to bid, although such decisions are controlled to some extent through periodic review by higher authority. To protect the company against the possibility of acquiring inferior materials that might adversely affect production scheduling and product quality, potential vendors should be thoroughly investigated and approved or disapproved. Sources of information are abundantly available: printed registers and catalogs, trade magazines, trade shows, financial statements and credit agency reports, and personal contact with the vendor's own sales, production, research, and engineering personnel.

Evidence supporting such investigations should be maintained as a part of the purchasing department's record of vendors, which we have called the *approved vendor list*. Entry and exit from this list should be based on vendors' consistent performance and should be reviewed periodically by upper management.

Some companies utilize a vendor rating system, which may range from a simple grading of "good, satisfactory, or unsatisfactory" to a complex cost-ratio plan involving analysis of all cost factors including material price, telephone calls, delays, and visits. A company should carefully weigh the advantages to be gained from such plans. Often, the results obtained do little more than mirror the opinion of a good buyer who maintains close daily contact with the vendor.

AUTHORIZED APPROVALS FOR PURCHASE CONTRACTS.

Purchase Amounts	Level of Approval Required					
	Buyer	Asst. Pur. Agent	Pur. Agent	Dir. of Material	Pres. or Exec. VP	Board of Directors
$500 or less	x					
$501 to $2,500	x	x				
$2,501 to $10,000	x	x	x			
$10,001 to $25,000	x	x	x	x		
$25,001 to $100,000	x	x	x	x	x	
Over $100,000	x	x	x	x	x	x

Figure 10.2

Assuring Ethical Standards in Procurement

The Sherman Act, the Federal Trade Act, the Clayton Antitrust Act, and the Robinson-Patman Act are laws basically intended to eliminate unfair competition and price discrimination in selling. Certain sections apply to the buying function as well. A buyer, for example, is prohibited from knowingly inducing or receiving price advantages deemed to be discriminatory under the law or from receiving any form of "compensation" from the seller.

Conflicts of interest related to the procurement process normally take one of two forms: a buyer's financial interest in the vendor's company or outright commercial bribery. Fraud possibilities are naturally inherent in relationships with outside parties when personal interests come in conflict with job responsibilities, particularly when so many buying decisions are made on a personal basis.

A desirable feature of a strong conflict of interest policy should require that any officer, member of management, or employee, report outside equity interests in vendor companies. Whether a company specifically prohibits persons with financial interests in vendor companies from engaging in procurement activities or disregards *minor* investments in large enterprises whose shares are traded on the major exchanges, a determination of all such interests should be established and maintained in current status.

One of the most effective ways to uncover and deter conflict-of-interest situations in a purchasing operation is an annual review of the volume of business conducted with each supplier by a responsible official not connected with the procurement function. Such a report should be prepared by someone outside the purchasing organization and may be reviewed by the internal auditing department in consultation with the designated official as needed.

The possibility of commercial bribery can also be minimized by a strong and widely publicized company policy on the matter. Bribery in procurement activities may be construed to include gifts, entertainment, and luncheons as well as "kickbacks." The effectiveness of company policy may be increased by distributing copies of the stated policy to both buyers and vendors periodically, and especially just prior to Christmas and other holiday seasons when abuses tend to be more prevalent.

Vendor-buyer relationships are more likely to be formal and independent when purchasing organizations practice a policy of buyer rotation. In spite of the training problem involved, the optimum result can be the development of a staff of versatile buyers equipped to move into positions of greater responsibility as the company grows.

Financial and Operations Planning

The purchasing department should play a vital consultative role when production budgets, schedules, and material cost standards are being established for the ensuing year. Purchasing knowledge of impending price fluctuations and new product developments can prevent costly mistakes in price and cost estimating.

When a company is considering the advantages of making components of their products in their own production shops, as opposed to buying them from outsiders, purchasing experts can be of great assistance. The maintenance of current "price files" should be a standard requirement of each purchasing agent in each material category of responsibility.

Supportive Role

Finally, as the originator of the critical source document (purchase order) that sets the procurement cycle in motion, the purchasing operation provides the very cornerstone of contract authority in support of the accounts payable, receiving, and inventory control functions. A close working relationship between these functions is essential.

PROCUREMENT SOURCE DOCUMENTS

The procurement process is energized by a formal request to purchase, generally called a *purchase requisition,* which is prepared and approved by an authorized person in the company who has recognized an existing or impending need for a vital material or service. Purchasing activity is not self-motivating except in small companies where the overall material control function might include purchasing, matching and paying, inventory, traffic, shipping, and receiving. The dangers inherent in such a combination of activities should be readily apparent to the accountant.

Subsequent to receipt of the purchase requisition comes the *request for quotation,* which is used by the buyer in the solicitation of bids. This request, like the purchase requisition, can take a variety of forms but should include the standard information needed to support the purchasing decision.

Finally, the contract is awarded to one of the competitive bidders, and a *purchase order* is prepared and distributed. Typical examples of these forms commonly found in manufacturing companies are given in the following discussion.

Document Content

The *purchase requisition,* Figure 10.3, is a multiple-copy form that bears a serially controlled number in the upper right corner that provides specific identification for each ordering action, guarantees such action by forcing purchasing to "clear" the request, and guards against duplicate action. The requesting authority may even suggest one or more existing suppliers. However, specificity will be focused on the quantity and description of the material needed. The original and first copy is sent to the purchasing department; a second copy is retained by the requisitioner for follow-up.

After the contract has been established, the purchasing department returns the confirmation copy to the requisitioner. That copy shows such details as purchase order number, name of buyer, terms, FOB, shipping instructions, delivery schedule, price, and the necessary procurement approval.

The *request for quotation* form, illustrated in Figure 10.4, elicits the preceding details from suppliers participating in the competition, and when returned reflects the conditions quoted by the bid winner. This form is distributed in duplicate to each potential bidder: One copy is returned to the purchasing department to communicate the conditions and details of the bid. The vendor's quote number (upper right corner) provides the key reference of this phase of the transaction.

The resulting *purchase order,* illustrated in Figure 10.5, reflects the quotation details contained in the winning bid. Special attention is directed to the purchase order number, which now becomes the controlling number for all activities relating to the contract. That number *must* appear on all vendor invoices, packages and cases, bills of lading, receiving

RUSSELL CORPORATION

17216

PURCHASE REQUISITION

SUPPLIER: _____   SHIP TO: _____

_____   _____

_____   _____

DATE REQUIRED _____   ROUTE _____   DATE _____

DEPARTMENT _____   CHARGE TO _____   TAX _____

QUANTITY	UNIT OF MEASURE	DESCRIPTION	COST

SPECIAL INSTRUCTIONS: _____

RECEIVING COPIES _____   WEIGHT _____

PERSON ORDERING _____   APPROVED _____

Figure 10.3

REQUEST FOR QUOTATION _____

QUOTATION NO. _____

Ship Via & Route _____

VENDOR NAME _____   Date Delivery Required _____

VENDOR ADDRESS _____   Terms _____

    " _____   F.O.B. _____

    " _____

PART NUMBER	QUANTITY	DESCRIPTION	ANNUAL NEEDS	UNIT COST	DISCOUNT	NET AMOUNT

PLEASE SUBMIT BY RETURN MAIL YOUR BEST QUOTE BASED ON THE DESCRIPTION ABOVE. IF YOU WISH TO SUBSTITUTE FOR SPECIFICATIONS LISTED, PROVIDE FULL DETAILS. WHERE TOOLING IS NECESSARY, QUOTE SEPARATELY - DO NOT INCLUDE IN UNITE PRICES. QUANTITY DISCOUNTS ARE EXPECTED.

NOTE*   THIS IS NOT AN ORDER   _____

                                          Director of Purchasing

Figure 10.4

memoranda, inspection reports, and correspondence that pertains to this transaction. Copies of this purchase agreement are often distributed as follows:

Copy 1 is sent to the vendor. Standard legal terms and conditions are preprinted either at the bottom or on the reverse side of the original copy. These terms need appear only on the vendor's original copy.

PURCHASE ORDER

RUSSELL CORPORATION
ALEXANDER CITY, ALABAMA 35010 • (205) 234-4251

IMPORTANT

ADDRESS ALL SHIPPING TAGS, INVOICES,
AND CORRESPONDENCE TO:

S
H   **RUSSELL CORPORATION**
I T
P O

ALEXANDER CITY, ALABAMA 35010

TO ▶ .

DELIVERY REQUIRED	SHIP VIA		PURCHASE ORDER DATE
REQUISITIONING DEPARTMENT	DEPARTMENT CHARGED - ACCOUNT NUMBER		

✓ REC'D.	QUANTITY	UNIT OF MEASURE	DESCRIPTION	PRICE

RUSSELL CORPORATION

1. SUBMIT INVOICE IN DUPLICATE WITH ORIGINAL BILL OF LADING WITH ROUTING
   SHOWN.
2. RENDER A SEPARATE INVOICE FOR EACH SHIPMENT AGAINST THIS ORDER IF
   PARTIAL SHIPMENTS ARE MADE.
3. OMIT SALES OR USE TAX FROM INVOICES TO US. WE PAY DIRECT TO THE STATE
   OF ALABAMA. OUR AUTHORIZED BLANKET CERTIFICATE IS NO. 26.

J.L. WILLIS, DIRECTOR OF PURCHASING

Figure 10.5

Copy 2 is sent to the vendor with the original. The vendor is required to sign this copy and return it immediately to the buyer. The official signature constitutes formal acknowledgment and acceptance of the order, which at this point becomes a legal contract. In the case of rush orders where bids are not solicited, the vendor must provide information regarding price, terms, and delivery. This acknowledgment is usually forwarded to accounts payable.

Copy 3 is sent to accounts payable as notification of commitment and support for payment. Often, the purchase requisition is attached.

Copy 4 is sent to the receiving department as notification of impending shipment. Frequently the quantity column on this copy will be "blacked out" or omitted to ensure an independent count by the receiving clerk. The impact of this omission on the company's receiving operation is discussed in Section B, "Functions of the Receiving System."

Copy 5 is sent to the requisitioning authority as notification of procurement action.

Copy 6 is sent to material control as notification that materials are on order.

Other copies may be retained by the purchasing department for follow-up and commodity files and vendor history files.

Record Retention

Since "open commitment" reporting and "volume of business by vendor" are more appropriately extracted as by-products of other automated information systems such as accounts payable, purchasing operations produce little in the way of management reports. As a consequence, there is scant need for massive filing operations involving hard copy other than the currently active documents kept for interim follow-up purposes. After a brief retention period, therefore, completed transaction documents (requisitions, vendor quotations, purchase order acknowledgments, and closure notices) may be routed to central files to be stored in accordance with corporate records policy.

The only permanent hard-copy files needed are current vendor information files and material price history files. These files should be purged and updated routinely to provide pertinent information to support buying activities without undue clerical effort.

DOCUMENT FLOW AND TIMING

When approaching an examination of a procurement system, an accountant is apt to be particularly interested in the assignment of functions and responsibilities—an important characteristic of any satisfactory system of internal control. The flow of the foundation documents in the procurement and receiving systems is illustrated in Figure 10.6 Following the logical steps and observing the timing of the activities involved make it easy to see why strict controls are necessary. An explanation of the numbered events follows:

1. A using department will determine the need for a particular product or service and prepare a requisition, obtain the necessary approvals as specified in company policy, and forward it to the purchasing organization. "Using department" will typically be synonymous with "stores," or inventory control, since the majority of purchasing activity relates to that function. Fully automated and computerized

PROCUREMENT AND RECEIVING SYSTEMS CRITICAL DOCUMENT FLOW.

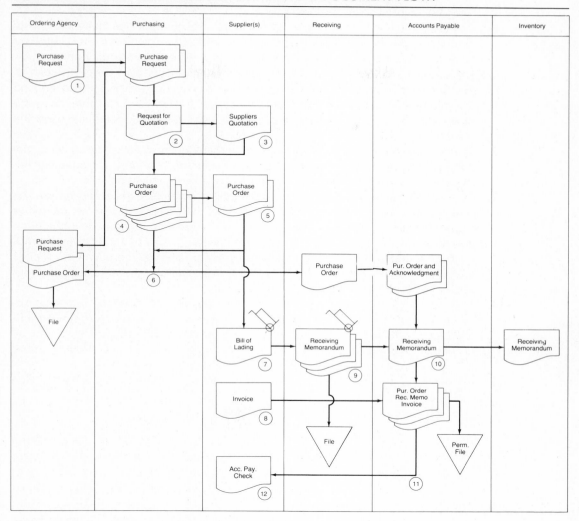

Figure 10.6

inventory systems are often programmed to automatically create requisitioning paperwork when stock levels fall below predetermined minimums.

2. As previously indicated, the buyer will act on the requisition by soliciting bids from selected vendors.
3. The several competing suppliers will submit bids to the buyer in response to the request for quotations.
4. A purchase order will be prepared on the basis of the most favorable quotation and forwarded in duplicate to the winning bidder as well as to using departments.

5. The selected vendor will approve the contract by signing and returning the acknowledgment copy to the buyer.
6. Complete distribution of copies of the purchase contract has been previously described. The key copies for accounts payable, to support payment, and for receiving, to support receipt of the shipment, are shown in the diagram.
7. The supplier processes the company's purchase order (its *sales* order) through its own inventory, shipping, and billing operations. A bill of lading is prepared, and the shipment is consigned to a common carrier for delivery. In some cases the supplier may use its own delivery system, but this does not materially affect the process.
8. Immediately following the shipment, or perhaps even concurrently with it, the supplier's billing and collection operation dispatches a request for payment (invoice) directly to the company's accounts payable organization.
9. When the shipment arrives, it is examined for possible damage en route. The shipment is validated by verification of the purchase order number on the bill of lading. The delivery is not consummated if this connection is not made. Otherwise, normal receiving functions ensue as discussed later. A copy of the receiving memorandum is routed directly to accounts payable to facilitate the payment process. Necessary document copies travel with the material through inspections and ultimately to stores or other designated recipients.
10. Inspection "certifies" the document upon completion of its testing function. Another copy is "receipted" and returned to receiving by the recipient (inventory), whereas the final copy stays with the merchandise. Other copies may also be distributed as company policy dictates, but sound systems design limits the number of copies circulated to avoid redundant filing operations.
11. Accounts payable assembles the document set for payment on the invoice due date.
12. Final payment consummates the transaction.

From point 4 in the foregoing cycle, the transaction is in complete control by the serial number shown on the purchase contract. The reader can recognize the abundant opportunities for fraud in a situation where authority for all these functions and steps in the cycle rests with one individual or even in a small group within a single departmental unit. Obviously, if that person is dishonest, activities and accompanying paperwork can be arranged to bring about self-payment or payment to fictitious vendors. If the authority for making disbursements rests elsewhere, only a fraudulent invoice is needed to complete the cycle. Similarly, if disbursing authority requires other *independent* support for payment of the invoice, then other documents must be falsified.

Purchasing executives feel that the cause of efficiency is best served by combining these steps (including the matching function) in the purchasing heirarchy. Finance executives, on the other hand, insist that control over expenditures is the primary responsibility of the controller's division. Since accounting is not directly involved in purchasing transactions, performance of the matching and payment function by that department serves as a check on the purchasing department. Independent requisitioning and receiving operations and a separate inventory control system further remove the possibility of collusion and fraud by separate reporting on quantity and quality of receipts.

ACCOUNTING CONTROLS AND RISKS OF FAILURE

The reader has perhaps concluded that purchasing activities tend to be "freewheeling" in nature when conducted in an unstructured environment. That fact is partially attributable to the pressures and influences placed on buying agents by salespeople. In any event, there are some serious risks involved in loosely controlled procurement operations.

Some of the risks are that purchases may be made from unauthorized suppliers, from vendors whose interests are in conflict with the entity, or from vendors whose salespeople solicit gifts and kickbacks from customers or request that payment be made in an illegal manner. These irregularities could result in intentional or unintentional disbursements of cash to an unauthorized party, undetected sensitive payments, and payments at higher than satisfactory prices. Such consequences could adversely affect operating results and cash flows.

Another risk is that unneeded goods and services or substandard quality materials may be purchased, or purchases may be made too far in advance (or arrears) resulting in failure to meet short-term entity objectives. Such failures may result in (1) write-downs and write-offs of unusable or unsalable inventory, (2) production of unmarketable finished products because of failure to meet customer quality specifications, (3) costly production line delays or shutdowns, (4) use of higher quality (and cost) materials than is necessary, and (5) strains on working capital and increased warehousing costs.

We have already mentioned some of the control features inherent in a large purchasing operation. Most of them have focused on the buyer and concern vendor selection, bidding procedures, and a system of transaction approvals based on total value. Some of the other control techniques might include (1) periodic internal audit of procurement files and procedures, (2) formal documentation of overall procurement plans (e.g., material requirements schedule, economic order quantities, safety stocks, reorder points, capital expenditure budgets, etc.), (3) centralized purchasing operations to assure control of procurement of all goods and services, and (4) executive authorizations of all orders for materials not reflected on "bills of materials" (production material requirements).

MANAGEMENT INFORMATION REQUIREMENTS

We have seen how the requirement for control has forced the separation of the buying functions from related follow-on activities and the status of open commitment. Purchasing management should not assume from this arrangement that they have been relieved of responsibility for the consequences of their actions or the processing of purchasing transactions delegated to the computer. Only the clerical effort is relinquished. Responsibility remains exactly where it was. Purchasing management should have sufficient knowledge of the operating capability of the computer to satisfy themselves that adequate controls are built in. They must assume full responsibility for the accuracy and completeness of the input to the system and for the reliability of the output. Some of the needed management control information might take the following forms.

Analysis of Large Purchases

An analysis of this kind may be useful when issued in several different sequences such as: (1) the basis of awarding the contract—if by lowest bid, quality, schedule, freight/routing, or other considerations; (2) by purchasing agent; (3) by type of material; (4) by vendor. The net difference between the actual price accepted and the "lowest" or "best" vendor quotation would give the purchasing manager a good review of the work of individual buyers and vendors. The format for such a report is suggested in Figure 10.7.

Vendor Performance Analysis

Essential input from the accounts payable and receiving departments should be provided to permit a periodic comparison of each vendor's overall performance vis-à-vis the contract agreement. Such information as invoice pricing, over- and undershipments, quality record, schedule performance, and discount terms can be stored in each purchase order and/or vendor record. Periodic printouts of vendors who have built up large cumulative overcharges within tolerance limits can be easily obtained. A review of the supporting documents can then be made to determine whether such charges are legitimate or whether the vendor is deliberately overcharging because of inside knowledge of the company's tolerance range. Such a report should be issued at least annually and might reflect the data shown in Figure 10.8.

Analysis of Cost of Purchases

Although not a part of the visible information flow, and thus not routinely available as an output of the operating system, the various cost elements of the purchasing function must be constantly observed and critically reviewed by purchasing management. We refer, of course, to such semihidden costs as (1) preprinted forms, (2) clerical costs, (3) telephone costs and buyers' time utilized in telephone contacts, (4) purchase order changes, and a host of other items that go relatively unnoticed but can impose a signifi-

Report No. _____		PROCUREMENT PERFORMANCE ANALYSIS					Date _____	
Purchase Order	Vendor Code	Part No. and Description	Award Code	Qty.	Unit Price	Best Price	Gross Difference
A1-12345	00250	26-36-567A Flange	20	100	1.50	1.50	.00
A1-13268	00250	1796-583L Valve	21	275	15.25	13.98	349.25
B1-36879	00250	No. 3 Type Blivitt	21	1000	.20	.19	10.00
A2-17171	00250	XL-100 Reversible	20	700	2.10	2.10	.00
		Vendor Total					x,xxx.xx

NOTE: Award Code 20 signifies lowest bid/comparable quality; " " 21 signifies user preference of product features.

Figure 10.7

Report No. _____		VENDOR PERFORMANCE ANALYSIS					Date _____	
Vendor Code	Purchase Order	Gross Overcharge	Price Var.	Over-Shipment	Shipment/ Invoice Var.	Frt. & Disc. Terms	Days Behind Schedule	Qual. Rejects
00251	A1-12356	10.15	10.15				0	0
00251	A2-34567	36.50	6.50	20.00		10.00	0	0
00251	A2-35601	5.18	5.18				0	0
		51.83T	21.83T	20.00T		10.00T		
00935	A6-98765	600.00		600.00			0	0
00935	A6-98766	10.00		10.00			0	0
00935	B1-12346	30.00		30.00			0	0
00935	B1-23460	25.00		25.00			0	0
		665.00T		665.00T				

Figure 10.8

cant financial burden on the company. Sound purchasing management requires that these costs be identified, measured, and expressed in relation to some other more visible measure of accomplishment, such as the number of purchase contracts awarded per period or dollar value of purchases per period.

No attempt will be made to speculate on the form and content of such a report because it can take whatever shape, form, and content that prudent management deems appropriate. The aggressive procurement executive will welcome the challenge of conducting a continuous profit improvement or cost reduction program because the favorable results of such efforts will certainly be recognized.

Activity Lists
Finally, the department must receive as a minimum requirement, a computer listing of the items introduced into the system at each processing date. This list should include input introduced from other related systems and be sorted by activity code to facilitate its use as an audit medium. For convenience, one report could reflect the activity from all input sources (see Figure 10.9).

Exception Notices
The system should be designed and the program written in such a way as to highlight for management/vendor action all abnormal and conflicting conditions. For example, typical exceptions are: (1) behind schedule, (2) price and terms discrepancy, (3) cancellation for cause, (4) notification of closure, and (5) incorrect address.

Stored messages should be made available or be on call by the program and printed on continuous form mailing pieces for easy handling by buying personnel. An example is shown in Figure 10.10.

Management information requirements in receiving tend to focus on status information as opposed to the financial information normally processed in such areas as cash,

The Procurement and Receiving Systems   **283**

ACTIVITY LIST

Vendor Code	Purchase Order	Part Number & Description	Amount	Activity Code								
				P/O Amend	P/O Canc.	P/O Close	New Vendor	Vendor Change	Vendor Delete	Credit Rating	New P/O	P/O Ackno.
24135	B1-8102	A-X2 Flange	3,280.00	01								
28360	A2-2695	25-1A Valve	750.00	01								
36830	A9-1621	5/8" Extruded R	1,295.15	01								
		Total	T5,325.15									
38950	B2-7501	ABC L Brace	79.50		02							
45678	B3-3310	Casting XX-3	895.50		02							
		Total	T 974.00									
		ETC				03	04	05	06	07	08	09
		ETC										
		ETC										

Figure 10.9

EXCEPTION NOTICES AND ACTION MESSAGES

```
                         THE COMPANY NAME

        Vendor Name
        Street Address
        City, State  Zip

        Dear Sir:              RE:  P.O. No. _____

            Your attention is directed to our referenced purchase order which
        is now _____ days behind the contract delivery schedule.  We ask that
        you investigate this transaction in your plant and advise us concerning
        the status of this order.  If shipment has been made, please provide the
        necessary freight bill number to permit us to trace the shipment with
        the carrier.

            Thank you.            Signed: _____
```

Figure 10.10

payroll, or accounts receivable. What materials and services have been received? What shipments have been rejected and why? What shipments are past due? What procurement contracts have been completed and/or canceled by receiving action? These information needs must be satisfied by the documents and reports generated by the receiving department.

The major users of this information are the inventory, procurement, and accounts payable operations. Inventory personnel prefer reports to be in part number sequence for obvious reasons. Accounts payable personnel operate in the "transaction mode" and are vendor-oriented. Assume, for example, a shipment containing quantities of several parts purchased on the same order. If listed in part number order, the splintered elements of a single receiving memorandum could be scattered throughout the report, making the total transaction clumsy to discern. For this reason, their report will usually be printed in sequence by purchase order number within vendor code number.

A SYSTEM FOR PURCHASING

Procedures prescribing the flow of procurement documents must naturally be tailored to the degree of centralization considered appropriate by the top management of the company. We have chosen not to dwell on multidivisional companies in this discussion because the document handling will be essentially identical from a functional point of view regardless of the form of organization. Thus, it should suffice to visualize a procurement operation purely from an operations standpoint by looking primarily at the basic elements in the cycle.

The small size of some purchasing operations may require a few "generalist" buyers rather than specialists in certain product lines. If the number of products a company purchases is limited, the advantages of buyer specialization are minimized if not completely negated.

As with all well-controlled and well-organized information systems, all incoming (and perhaps outgoing) documents should be funneled through a document control station. Based on a thorough knowledge of the company's material codes and categories, the document control clerk is able to route the documents to the proper action group typically headed by a purchasing agent. The purchasing agent then distributes the work load as appropriate to the buyers. In strict accordance with company policy and procedure, the buyer then performs all the preliminary procurement functions previously discussed that lead up to the formalization of the purchase contract.

The finalized document set is then forwarded to the procurement clerical section where the purchase order is prepared and distributed. Here an input operator prepares a "trial" copy of the purchase order on one of several types of document-creating machines that produce a by-product magnetic tape or disk. Next the trial copy is audited against the supporting documents. If errors exist that require correction, they are clearly marked and reentered on the input medium. Upon passing the audit, the supporting documents are routed to a record maintenance and statistical operation while the input data move to an order distribution and data transmission station. The purchase order is automatically transcribed to a multipart purchase order form. While this process is being performed, extracted data are being captured for the computer, either through the preparation of punched cards or by direct transmission to the computer center via other sophisticated communication media. Copies of the official purchase order may then be returned to the document control station for logging and distribution.

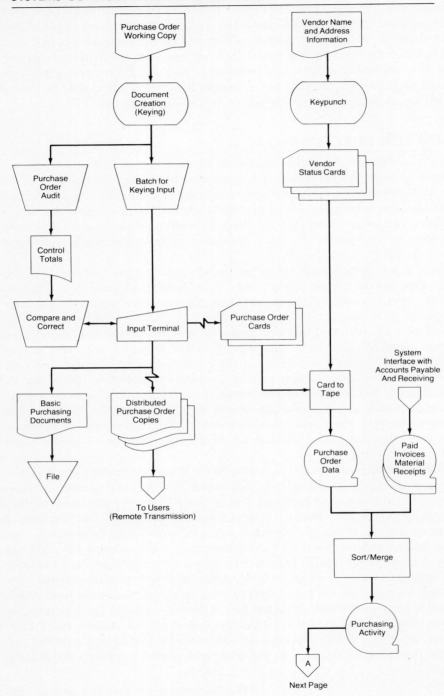

Figure 10.11

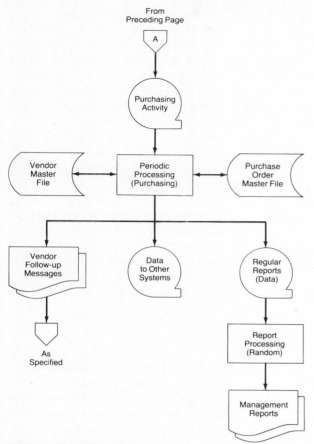

Figure 10.11 (cont'd)

Data Processing

It is apparent from the foregoing discussions that two major master files are required in the data processing center for adequately discharging the information function of a normal procurement system: the purchase order master and the name-and-address master. We have just described a clerical operation that could facilitate the problem of data capture and transmission at the point of creation of the formal purchasing contract, leaving only the matter of communicating vendor identification data to data processing. The purchasing organization should be held responsible for establishing and maintaining current vendor information, including the designation of a "pay-to" address when different from the "buy-from" address. Let us now review in chart form a theoretical processing arrangement (including a hardware configuration) extending from the clerical operation to the accomplishment of the computer processing, as shown in Figure 10.11

The activity file, the purchase order master file, and the vendor name and address file are maintained in vendor code number sequence. This arrayal, in effect, amounts to an alphabetical arrangement of all purchasing information. In the purchase order master file, individual purchase orders are in sequence by purchase order number *within* the *major* vendor code sequence. This type of file arrangement facilitates processing and produces output that requires a minimum of additional sorting and arranging for printing. The process is simple and straightforward. Activity is introduced, matching master records are located (if in existence), and appropriate action is taken.

Record Content and Sequence

After examining the purchasing system and the accounts payable system in Chapter Eleven, the reader may question the maintenance of *two* purchase order files and wonder why procurement and accounts payable could not share a common master file in the interest of efficiency. That is, of course, technically feasible. Accountants are inclined to view such a sharing of files as a weakening of internal control, however, particularly where each system acts as a check on the other.

Both master files maintained in the procurement system should contain *variable-length* records. This is necessary to provide for both single- and multiple-item orders and to reflect a measure of flexibility in vendor identifications (buy-from and pay-to addresses, for example).

SECTION B

As indicated previously, the elements of a purchase contract must be provided to an independent receiving operation to serve as the *authority* to accept incoming shipments. This may be done by a copy of the purchase order, as previously mentioned, or by some other expedient medium such as punched cards. We now examine the receiving systems more closely before considering the various document flows and interrelationships.

One of the most serious errors a systems analyst can make is to underestimate the efficacy of an independent receiving operation. Even some accountants regard the function as a simple unloading and unpacking operation situated somewhere in the vicinity of purchasing—or perhaps stores. They ascribe little more functional responsibility to it than to count, weigh, or measure the contents of delivered shipments and to issue verifying reports.

This attitude is dangerously naive. In modern, large-scale companies, millions of dollars worth of materials flow annually through the hands of a few individuals who make decisions affecting literally every phase of company operations. They encounter endless combinations of order-ship-bill-receive variations that stagger the imagination. They hopefully maintain an unbiased interface with the often conflicting interests of suppliers, purchasing agents, accounts payable, production, common carriers, and stores.

Perhaps most important, the receiving dock is the point at which title to valuable merchandise generally changes hands. Three legal interests are involved—the company, the carrier, and the supplier. In almost every other phase of information systems we have recognized a separation of document processing and physical handling for control purposes. Here the two converge to provide both the opportunity and the temptation to practice larceny and blame other parties.

The receiving operation must accept responsibility for preventing such activities. It must, therefore, be considered an independent function with exclusive authority to open, inspect, verify quantity, test quality, and issue irrefutable documentary evidence of receipt, or *rejection,* of a shipment on behalf of the company.

FUNCTIONS OF THE RECEIVING SYSTEM

On the surface, receiving operations may appear quite simple. However, *eight* vital control functions are actually being performed. This discussion envisages a physically remote, voluminous operation of a fairly large company.

First, authorized receiving personnel *do* unload the shipment and perform a cursory inspection of its condition in the presence of the carrier's representative. Was the shipment damaged while in transit? Is the apparent damage severe enough to refuse acceptance of delivery from the carrier? The importance of such a judgment cannot be overstated. Once the company's agent accepts delivery by signing the shipping document, the carrier's legal liability is greatly reduced. Damage must therefore be accurately assessed in advance. Goods arriving FOB shipping point leave the company with recourse only against the common carrier when damage is sustained en route. Shipments establishing the FOB point at the company's receiving dock require the vendor and the carrier to settle damage disputes between themselves. In cases where shipment was made FOB shipping point in violation of the terms and conditions of the purchase contract, the latter solution would apply *if* the damage was detected prior to acceptance.

Second, the authenticity of delivered shipments is established. Under no circumstances should a shipment be accepted from a carrier until it has been determined that the goods or services were officially ordered, that the contract is still open (unfilled), and that the delivery is not a duplication of a former shipment. The receiving operation is forced to maintain supporting documentary evidence to make such a positive identification. Moreover, it requires the supplier to reference the purchase order identification number.

Third, verification is made that the contents of the shipment match precisely the items specified on the purchase order. No material substitutions can be accepted. Authority to permit a deviation from the original purchase contract can come only through a formal purchase order amendment. Receiving personnel, although independent, cannot be permitted to make judgments concerning the acceptability of vendor-substituted parts or materials that may later adversely impact the production process. In cases where differences of opinion exist concerning identification of materials, the buyer should be contacted to resolve the matter.

Fourth, differences between ordering and shipping practices are reconciled. For example, materials ordered in bulk or lot quantities often specify *approximate* weights or counts. In such cases, the shipping documents will seldom reflect the exact quantity measurements as those specified on the purchase order. A company may order 10,000 ⅝-inch hex-head screws at 3¢ each (total price = $300), whereas the vendor customarily ships this item in a 150-pound barrel containing approximately 10,275 screws, priced at $308 per barrel. Most companies have policies establishing under- or overshipment tolerance limits within which such transactions may be consummated without further negotiation. The extent of such tolerances is often limited to the cost of processing the paperwork required to solve the problem. In other cases, the receiving department is often forced to make unpopular decisions (e.g., when a vendor deviates from purchase agreements on quantities, when there are differences between shipping manifests and actual counts, when shipments arrived ahead of schedule). Companies whose procurement procedures prohibit the referencing of *quantity* information on the receiving copy of the purchase order may experience serious repercussions in receiving as a consequence. Receiving personnel generally must accept in good faith whatever quantity is shipped. Such "blind" receiving may result in unacceptable over- or undershipments, significant freight discrepancies, and follow-on inventory and accounts payable problems. Such practices appear to be enjoying less popularity as "control features" improve in today's more sophisticated receiving systems.

Fifth, a determination is made concerning compliance with special engineering and/or other specifications. This responsibility may involve functional testing, X-ray testing, or even destructive sample testing as a means of assuring quality. The inspection role should not be taken lightly by receiving personnel and is important to the maintenance of product quality in the conversion cycle.

Sixth, within the parameters established by company policy the receiving department usually has the authority to "close" (or consider complete) a purchase contract when, in its best judgment, no further deliveries are likely to occur. Such situations arise, for example, when the unfilled portion of an order is considered too small to ship economically or when the last expected delivery date is long past due. This closing action is important to all users of purchasing and receiving information, particularly accounts payable and the computer center whose suspense files should be regularly purged of inactive documents and records.

Seventh, the receiving department is the *only* organization in the company authorized to originate official documentary evidence of receipt of a supplier's shipment. In the case of special purchases of small, high-value items, company procedures sometimes provide for special pickup and delivery to a designated individual within the company. Nevertheless, a serially numbered and controlled receiving memorandum is always issued and distributed according to procedure.

Eighth, the receiving department is responsible for delivering the merchandise and a copy of the official receiving memorandum to the designated recipient—usually raw material stores and parts inventories. A receipted copy of the receiving memorandum absolves the department of any further responsibility for the transaction.

These eight functions are inherent in *all* receiving operations, regardless of the operation's position in the "size spectrum." This presentation has attempted to describe a medium- to large-scale operation utilizing some degree of sophistication in method.

RECEIVING SOURCE DOCUMENTS

The receiving process cannot, or should not, begin without visible proof that the delivery is in response to an official purchase contract. Neither the supplier nor the carrier can be relied upon to provide such proof. Advance notice of impending shipments must therefore be provided within the company and kept on file until delivery is made. Almost universally, such notice is in the form of a *purchase order,* or excerpted data therefrom (i.e., hard copy, punched card, on-line display, etc.).

The shipment, when delivered by a common carrier, is always accompanied by an identifying document known as the *bill of lading;* see Figure 10.12. Sometimes a vendor will attach a copy of the invoice, or some other shipping document known variously as a shipping list, packing slip, or shipping manifest. The purpose of such documents is

BILL OF LADING.

REFERENCE THIS NUMBER ON ALL CORRESPONDENCE CONCERNING THIS ORDER

*FREIGHT CHARGE CODES: 1 - Collect 2 - Prepaid 3 - Prepaid & Add 4 - Pick-up 5 - Deluxe Delivery 6 - Our Truck 7 - Freight Only

SHIPPING ORDER NUMBER	CUSTOMER CODE					CUSTOMER ORDER NUMBER	DATE ACCEPTED			SHIP DATE REQUESTED			SHIP FROM	SLS. NO.	BACK ORDER FROM	*FRT. CODE	DISC. CODE
	NUMBER	LOCATION	DEPT	CL	TYPE		MO.	DAY	YR	MO	DAY	YR					

SHIP TO

PLEASE PRINT FULL NAME

RECEIVED BY: DATE

RECEIVER: Indicate below all discrepancies you found upon receipt of this merchandise. (Reference the catalog No's when describing.)

FREIGHT CLASSIFICATION

Note A - Dumbbells or Barbells (Item 16190 NMFC) note item 16192.
Note B - Gymnasium apparatus (Item 16600 NMFC, sub 2) Note item 16602.
Note C - Horseshoes, pitching pegs or stakes (Item 16660 sub 2 NMFC).
Note D - Table tennis, KD (Item 17480) note 17482 NMFC.
Note E - Store display racks or stands (Item 57410, sub 6) NMFC.
Note F - Goals, basketball, steel, with or without nets or mounting hardware, R, S, or L (Item 16430 NMFC).
Note G - Balls N O I (not otherwise indicated) inflated (Item 15560 NMFC).
Note J - Nets, other than wire in packages (Item 16960 NMFC).
Note K - Table tennis balls, in boxes (Item 15550 NMFC).
Note L - Shuttle cocks (Item 17260 sub 2 NMFC).
Note M - Dart sets (Item 84060 NMFC).
Note N - Wheel weights (Item 132220) NMFC).
Note O - Weights lawn or umbrella (Item 196960 NMFC).
Note P - Weights counter balance N O I (Item 107420 NMFC).

the property described below, in apparent good order, except as noted (contents and condition of contents of packages unknown), marked, consigned, and destined as indicated below, which said carrier (the word carrier being understood throughout this contract as meaning any person or corporation in possession of the property under the contract) agrees to carry to its usual place of delivery at said destination, if on its route, otherwise to deliver to another carrier on the route to said destination. It is mutually agreed, as to each carrier of all or any of said property over all or any portion of said route to destination and as to each party at any time interested in all or any of said property, that every service to be performed hereunder shall be subject to all the terms and conditions of the Uniform Domestic Straight Bill of Lading set forth (1) in Uniform Freight Classification in effect on the date hereof, if this is a rail or a rail-water shipment, or (2) in the applicable motor carrier classification or tariff if this is a motor carrier shipment.

Shipper hereby certifies that he is familiar with all the terms and conditions of the said bill of lading, including those on the back thereof, set forth in the classification or tariff which governs the transportation of this shipment, and the said terms and conditions are hereby agreed to by the shipper and accepted for himself and his assigns.

Subject to Section 7 of Conditions of Applicable bill of lading, if this shipment is to be delivered to the consignee without recourse on the consignor, the consignor shall sign the following statement:

The carrier shall not make delivery of this shipment without payment of freight and all other lawful charges.

Per X

"Shipper's imprint in lieu of stamp, not a part of Bill of Lading approved by the Interstate Commerce Commission."

*If the shipment moves between two ports by a carrier by water, the law requires that the bill of lading shall state whether it is "carrier's or shipper's weight."

NOTE Where the rate is dependent on value, shippers are required to state specifically in writing the agreed or declared value of the property.

The agreed or declared value of the property is hereby specifically stated by the shipper to be not exceeding

per

DELIVERING CARRIER CAR NO CAR OR VEHC INITIALS

SHIP VIA	TRIP NUMBER	DATE SHIPPED	PARCEL POST	FREIGHT AMOUNT
			$	$

ITEMS ORDERED	ITEMS SHIPPED	CATALOG NUMBER	UNIT	CARTONS ORDERED	CARTONS SHIPPED	DESCRIPTION	NOTE	ITEMS BACK ORDER	ITEMS CANCELLED	WEIGHT

RECEIVED $______ TO APPLY IN PREPAYMENT OF THE CHARGES ON THE PROPERTY DESCRIBED HEREON

AGENT OR CASHIER

PER

(THE SIGNATURE HERE ACKNOWLEDGES ONLY THE AMOUNT PREPAID) CHARGES ADVANCED

TOTAL CARTONS SHIPPED

CARRIER

TOTAL WEIGHT SHIPPED

FREIGHT CHARGE CODE

If Charges are C.O.D. Collect $

REMIT TO:

PERMANENT P.O. BOX OF SHIPPER ABOVE

THE CUBAGE OF THE INDIVIDUAL PACKAGES OR PIECES IN THIS SHIPMENT SUBJECT TO CLASSES APPLICABLE TO A SPECIFIC DENSITY GROUP ARE:

Note Q ____ cu. ft./ctn. decl. den.____ resu. wt./ctn.____
Note R ____ cu. ft./ctn. decl. den.____ resu. wt./ctn.____
Note S ____ cu. ft./ctn. decl. den.____ resu. wt./ctn.____
Note T ____ cu. ft./ctn. decl. den.____ resu. wt./ctn.____
Note V ____ cu. ft./ctn. decl. den.____ resu. wt./ctn.____
Note W ____ cu. ft./ctn. decl. den.____ resu. wt./ctn.____
Note X ____ cu. ft./ctn. decl. den.____ resu. wt./ctn.____
Note Z ____ cu. ft./ctn. decl. den.____ resu. wt./ctn.____

SHIPPER PER AGENT PER

Figure 10.12

twofold. First, they inform receiving authorities exactly what the vendor purports to have packaged and shipped. Second, they provide information to assist in associating the shipment with other documents supporting the transaction. Buyers usually ensure that this important connection is made by insisting that suppliers reference the purchase agreement number on all shipping and billing documents. By whatever name it is called, it is an important source document and should be permanently associated with other receiving documents.

The format of the Uniform Straight Bill of Lading is fairly standard, with the controlling document numbers of the three principals appearing prominently for easy transaction identification. Information pertinent to the method of payment of freight charges appears on the forms, with provision for the shipper to declare the value of the property. Otherwise, the document merely specifies the contents of the shipment and includes basic facts relative to the carrier and the route to be followed to final destination.

The bill of lading is usually prepared in four copies; the original is retained by the shipper to facilitate invoicing. (See Chapter Fifteen for a complete discussion.) The second copy accompanies the shipment to its destination and energizes the receiving process. The third copy is sent to the shipper's traffic and transportation department, and the fourth is kept on file in the shipping department as part of its control procedure.

Next to appear in the receiving process is the receiving document itself. Authorized receiving personnel authenticate the shipment and assure compliance with all terms and conditions of the purchase agreement; then they create the official *receiving memorandum;* see Figure 10.13. This can be accomplished in a variety of ways, as discussed later in the section on system configuration. The receiving memorandum must be a serially prenumbered and controlled document which must be accounted for. Maintenance of a "receiving log" facilitates the numbering procedure.

The receiving memorandum may take many forms and reflect varying amounts of information from the purchase contract. The internal functions served by the document largely determine its form and content. The form may be used by inventory personnel as the vehicle to price, extend, classify by catalog part number, and enter the items on stock records. Accounts payable uses the form to audit the shipment against the vendor's invoice and distribute the charges to the appropriate accounts. Contents common to most forms are the (1) purchase order number, (2) serial receiving number, (3) vendor identification, (4) carrier identification, (5) purchase order item number and material description, (6) date received, (7) quantity received, (8) freight charges, and (9) resulting status (balance) of the order. These are the basic facts essential to follow-on processing.

As a control measure, many companies block out the quantity field on the purchase order document provided to receiving. The receiving agent is forced to verify counts, weights, and measures physically. Thus, the temptation for receiving dock personnel to *assume* vendor compliance is avoided and an independent quantity count is established. The receiving memorandum does not reflect the current status of the order when the quantity field on the purchase order is blocked out. In systems where the computer is used to generate the receiving document based on skeletal information provided by receiving operations, this problem is resolved. Otherwise, "balance on order" must be obtained by some other means.

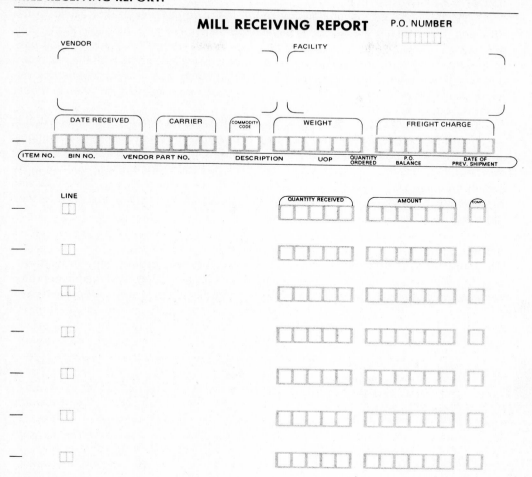

Figure 10.13

Although not a common practice, *freight bills* are sometimes left at the receiving docks to be handled by receiving personnel. When such shipment is made FOB shipping point, one of two methods of payment is acceptable: (1) the vendor may prepay the freight and include the charges on the invoice or (2) the company may pay the freight charges directly to the carrier. In the first case, the freight bill should be attached to the accounts payable copy of the receiving memorandum so that confirmation of the charges may be obtained from traffic and transportation and the vendor properly reimbursed. In the second case, the bill should be routed directly to the traffic and transportation department, where it will usually be grouped with other bills from the same carrier and summarized monthly on a *freight statement* for payment.

Record Retention

Ironically, the receiving documents are more vital to using organizations than to the receiving department itself. Accounts payable permanently files a "document set" containing purchasing, invoicing, shipping, and receiving documents to support each payment. The data files maintained in central data processing also contain all the necessary details of transactions with suppliers. Consequently, the maintenance of separate receiving document files in the receiving, purchasing, and stores organizations would appear to be duplications of effort.

Users of receiving documents need to know the total of all receiving activity during each reporting period to assure the completeness and accuracy of their own operations. Such an activity report is attainable from the input supplied to data processing from the receiving log. The receiving log, Figure 10.14, which accounts for the disposition of every serially numbered receiving document, is a part of the permanent records of the receiving department. It provides the necessary audit trails to trace receiving activities to their ultimate conclusion.

Files

Active purchase orders held in suspense pending supplier performance constitute the only file maintenance operation in receiving. Such files are usually arranged in purchase order number sequence for easy accessibility and refiling. Since several thousand open

RECEIVING DOCUMENT LOG											
Vendor	Purchase Order	Receiving Memo	Date	Carrier	Freight Bill No.	Description	Qty.	Accept	Reject	Rej. Code (Below)
Allied Chem. Co.	B1-9810	382574	293	A-2801	39386-B	Perma-Dye	10 bbl.	✓		
Rock Mills Inc.	B6-1235	382575	293	A-1733	12813	Sheeting	5000 yd.	✓		
Avondale Mill	A1-1875	382576	293	R-0050	6163-6	Canvas	1000 yd.	✓		
N-Line Knits	C2-3210	382577	293	T-0163	1773	Tube Knit	8000 yd.	✓		
ABC Greige Gds.	C3-4321	382578	294	T-0163	1779	Percale	5000 yd.		✓	3

Rejection Reason Codes: 1—No purchase order, 2—Excessive quantities shipped, 3—Unacceptable material substitution, 4—material of unacceptable quality, 5—Duplicate shipment, 6—Damage in transit, 7—Purchase order closure, 8—Shipment ahead of schedule, 9—Shipment too long past due, 10—Freight terms unacceptable.

Figure 10.14

purchase contracts may be on file at any time, constant purging of closed, inactive, canceled, or "consider complete" orders is necessary.

ACCOUNTING CONTROLS AND RISKS OF FAILURE

The whole concept of receiving is service-oriented in that it produces a document on which other systems depend. It is therefore essential that these documents be reliable. Accountants must assure that the entire receiving function operates in a controlled environment if company objectives are to be achieved. Several techniques may be used to maintain control.

Techniques for Maintaining Control

1. Maintenance of closely supervised central receiving locations that are separate from shipping, purchasing, and storing functions—tight security is essential.
2. Use of purchase order forms that (a) instruct vendors to deliver to a specific location, (b) require vendors to reference the authorizing purchase order number, and (c) include preprinted terms and conditions reflecting legal practices.
3. Performance of a count and appearance check for damage at the receiving dock, and comparison of the contents of the shipment with the bill of lading.
4. Detailed comparison of merchandise received versus a copy of the purchase order. Shipments for which no order exists are returned to the vendor or held in suspense pending receipt of an order.
5. Preparation of a receiving document at the dock for each shipment.
6. Use of prenumbered and controlled receiving documents that are subsequently accounted for as they are used by inventory and accounts payable functions.
7. Concurrent distribution of receiving documents to inventory and accounts payable.
8. Preparation, maintenance, and accessibility of documented procedures for (a) receiving and reporting *services* received, (b) receiving, handling, and reporting sold merchandise returned by *customers,* (c) returns to vendors, (d) treatment of over-shipments, partial shipments, and shipments ahead of schedule, and (e) the establishment of receiving operations cutoffs (daily and period end).
9. Maintenance of a system that assures accurate and complete processing of receiving activity and provides input to other dependent systems.
10. Careful training, close supervision, and bonding of key receiving personnel.

Controls are expensive to maintain and are considered optimal when their cost equals their potential benefits. Excessive controls are as undesirable as the absence of controls. Therefore, management must decide what is best for its own operation. A company takes serious risks when management fails to place the proper emphasis on the receiving function.

Risks Resulting from Insufficient Controls

1. Goods and services may be received and never reported, or reported inaccurately, either of which could result in a misstatement of inventory and cost of sales or an unrecorded liability.

2. Incorrect perpetual inventory records would cause operating problems.
3. Company relations with suppliers could be severely damaged.
4. Partial shipments, customer returns, and other unusual transactions may be improperly treated, resulting in unprocessed or inaccurate sales adjustments and accounts payable adjustments.
5. Liabilities may be recorded for goods and services billed but not received; conversely, liabilities may not be recorded for goods and services actually received.
6. Cash may be incorrectly or even fraudulently disbursed.
7. Duplicate payments may be made, and cash disbursements may occur in advance of receipt of goods and services.

Success Factors

Independence, timeliness, accuracy, and control are critical to the success of any receiving operation. Independence implies the absence of bias and influence from other organizations (inside or outside the company) and the finality of authority in judging supplier performance. Timeliness is especially important to the accounts payable system, which relies on the receiving document to support payment of the vendor's invoice—ideally within the cash discount period. Accuracy and reliability in counts, weights, and measures, as well as in inspection testing results, are characteristics that give the whole operation integrity. Control, not only of the receiving process but of the physical materials as well, is essential. Most receiving operations utilize such physical security measures as fenced-in limited-access receiving areas and enforce a strict policy of admission only to authorized personnel.

MANAGEMENT INFORMATION REQUIREMENTS

Receiving Rejections

Of particular importance to purchasing is information pertaining to shipments that have been found unacceptable by receiving. The explanation need not be lengthy, but sufficient information must be shown to permit the purchasing agent to negotiate a solution with the vendor. A possible format for this report is illustrated in Figure 10.15. Codes are sometimes used to denote standard reasons for rejection, such as:

Codes	Rejection Reason
1.	No purchase order
2.	Excessive quantities shipped
3.	Unacceptable material substitution
4.	Material of unacceptable quality
5.	Duplicate shipment
6.	Damage in transit
7.	Purchase order canceled or closed
8.	Shipment ahead of schedule
9.	Shipment too long past due
10.	COD terms not acceptable

REJECTION REPORT.

REJECTION REPORT

				Receiving Rejections	Week Ending _____
Vendor	Pur. Ord.	Carrier	Date*	Part No.	Rejection Reason
24135	B1-8102	A3906	298	A-X2 Flange	Substitute Unacceptable
28360	A2-2695	A1624	265	25-1A Valve	Cracked Casing
36830	A9-1621	T0035	277	5/8" Extruded R	Overshipment
38950	B2-7501	R1003	280	ABC L Brace	Early Shipment
45678	B3-3310	R0309	278	Casting XX-3	Bubbles in Housing
48909	C1-7218	R1820	278	Forging 132-X	See P.O. Specification No. 1
END					
*Date of Purchase Order					

Figure 10.15

Inspection Report

If the shipment is determined to be legitimate and acceptable at the receiving dock, a receiving memorandum will be issued and distributed. If inspection later reveals that part, or all, of the merchandise is of unacceptable quality, the receiving procedure is "reversed" by the issuance of a correcting document. Since the accounting copy of the receiving memorandum was dispatched immediately upon its creation, one of two actions is required. If payment has *not* been made, the invoice can be canceled and returned for reissuance. If payment has already been made, an accounts payable debit memorandum will be issued and either processed against future payments or sent to the vendor for reimbursement.

Management in the inventory and production operations are vitally concerned that only quality materials and parts are accepted. In cases of repeated below-standard performance, these executives have the prerogative of removing a vendor's name from the approved suppliers list. Coded comments are often used to indicate the inspector's reason for rejecting materials. Figure 10.16 illustrates the format and content of such a report.

Open Orders and Past-due Shipment Report

Behind-schedule shipment notifications are important to those departments in the expenditure and conversion cycles. As will become apparent in inventory and production systems (Chapters Twelve and Thirteen), production operations are often delicately balanced and scheduled to meet customer delivery expectations and to provide efficient

INSPECTION REPORT.

INSPECTION REPORT

Inspection Report						Date 9/27/8X
Part No.	Description	Vendor	R.M. No.	Acpt.	Rej.	Remarks
163A-1	Strut Support	03692	382567	X		
31-318-3XXX	Flabus Forpus	10468	382568	X		
32-419-30A1	Holy Kow	12895	382569	X		
39-162-1X2Y	Akin Bakus	23358	832570	X		
AX2 Flange	Corner Angle	24135	382571		X	Substitute Mat'l
219-831-XX3	Super Floppa	25554	382572	X		
25-1A Valve	Hydraulic Flutter A	28361	382573		X	Cracked Casing

Figure 10.16

utilization of the company's physical resources. Logistics play an important role in this process. Procurement lead times are precisely calculated to keep the production shops supplied with raw materials and to prevent overstocking of expensive inventory. Timely performance by the supplier is essential.

Receiving personnel are in a better position than those in other organizations, including purchasing, to determine the vendor's intentions with respect to minor unshipped balances on open purchase orders. In fact, shipping documents commonly indicate the vendor's intention to "back order" or "consider complete." Even in the absence of such notification, experience should help clerical personnel decide when it is not economically reasonable to expect further deliveries from a supplier. Listing of purged open orders should prove helpful to management in keeping files in current condition.

A SYSTEM FOR RECEIVING

The simplicity of the flow of *information* through receiving, as contrasted to the complexity of associated physical operations, suggests a rather straightforward data processing application. Essentially, the system has three major objectives: to bring receiving activity together with matching purchase order masters, to accomplish the routine updating automatically, and to print predetermined reports and documents required by other systems and organizations.

Four basic procedures have been suggested for handling the clerical functions in receiving. There are no doubt other variations. Using a copy of the purchase order as the authorizing master is a reliable procedure in receiving. Current receiving information is added in the appropriate space on the purchase order, and the document is reproduced and circulated to users. This procedure requires a minimum of expensive equipment and gets the receiving document in circulation almost instantly. Reports present a problem, however. Typically, receiving documents must be keypunched for processing against a purchase order master file where report data are extracted.

The use of punched cards, a by-product of the procurement system, is another common technique for providing authorizing receiving documents. The filing is simpler and less expensive, and the preparation of the receiving memorandum is largely automatic. The updated cards can be transmitted to the data processing center where report data are readily available from the match of purchasing and receiving documents.

Another technique involves the use of a punched and printed paper tape captured as a by-product of the purchase order typing process. The tape is transmitted over ordinary telephone lines via a transceiver and is easy to file, requires very little storage space, and is simple to handle and update. The updated tape automatically creates the receiving document and at the same time, also via remote communications equipment, transmits input data to the computer center.

The computer offers another alternative, of course. Skeletal information on incoming shipments (i.e., purchase order number, quantity received, carrier code, freight bill number, etc.) can be introduced into the computer to match the master purchase order and create a complete receiving memorandum. This method is illustrated in Figure 10.17.

Regardless of the solution to the clerical problem, receiving data must eventually enter the information stream of the expenditure cycle. Receiving activity processed in the system should be passed on to other dependent information systems to avoid needless duplication of keypunching in those areas.

Record Content and Sequence

Processing techniques and file management are within the purview of the central data processing department, but usually the last word on information retention and disposition rests with the user organization. The schematic diagram presented in Figure 10.17 contemplates the use of a master file of active purchase orders formatted in a manner similar to the example presented in Figure 10.11. Actually, with minor adaptations the same master could be shared by the two systems if an agreement were reached delegating responsibility to maintain the file. The same sensitive control problems inherent in relationships between accounts payable and purchasing are not present in this relationship. Receiving data would merely be used to update the master and produce the necessary management reports.

In any event, the purchase order master should contain all the information necessary for the computer to make positive detail comparisons and decisions with respect to supplier and carrier performance and to determine the current status of the order. Receiving activity for purposes of this discussion, is introduced through on-line terminals with formats designed to meet the needs of the particular user department.

SUMMARY

The purchasing process described in this chapter relates to a large single operation. Although a multiplant, multidivisional, or multistore operation would complicate the system somewhat, organization and size have very little, if any, effect on the *nature* of the functions performed. Generally, when the organizational unit and its operations are

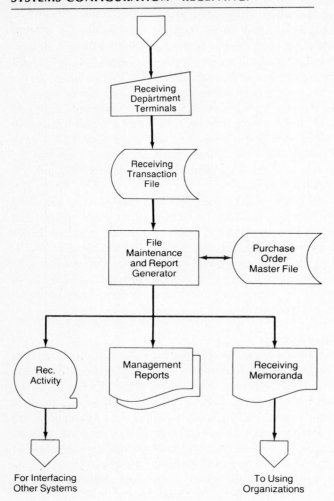

Figure 10.17

small and simple, the functions of purchasing, accounts payable, and perhaps even inventory are more likely to be consolidated into a single system. Conversely, the larger and more complex the operation is, the more likely these functions will be semiautonomous. This tendency is attributable not only to the need for specialization and efficiency but also to the need for controls in the form of functional checks and balances. Each independent system relies on the functional integrity of its information supplier; thus, collusion to commit fraud becomes a complicated and risky business.

A good procurement system must provide reliable sources of quality products. Beyond that initial responsibility, the purchasing function plays a vital role in the ultimate success of the business through its bidding and contracting activities and the influence on the cost of products and services it produces. Inventory management, production schedules, cash flows, and in large measure *company image* are all inextricably related to, and dependent on, sound, timely, and efficient purchasing operations.

Although the system as we have described it provides no direct information for accounting treatment (e.g., journalization), source data originating in the system is vitally important in a supportive way to the liquidation of accounts payable liability and to the determination of legal commitments to purchase. In order to understand the procurement system in its broadest perspective, accountants especially will want to consider it in relation to inventory, production, accounts payable, traffic and transportation, inspection, and, to an increasing extent, the legal department.

As the second major subsystem operating in the expenditure cycle, the receiving function plays a sensitive role between purchasing and accounts payable. It must be strictly independent of the ordering function; it must serve the needs of accounts payable and inventory. The broad objectives of the receiving function may therefore be succinctly restated: receiving must provide assurance that (1) all goods and services ordered are received, (2) all goods and services received are ordered, and (3) all reports are prompt and accurate.

SELECTED REFERENCES

Arthur Andersen & Co. *A Guide for Studying and Evaluating Internal Accounting Controls* (an in-house publication), January 1978.

Coopers & Lybrand. *Internal Control Reference Manual: Payments Cycle* (an in-house publication), 1978.

Ernst & Whinney. *Evaluating Internal Control: A Guide for Management and Directors* (an in-house publication), 1979.

Fielding, J. "Gearing Adjustment—What Is the Best Method?" *Accountancy* (May 1979).

Maudler, P.S. "Asset/Liability Management Today," *Bankers Monthly* (November 1979).

Murdick, Robert G., and Joel E. Ross. *MIS in Action.* St. Paul: West Publishing Co., 1975.

Prince, Thomas R. *Information Systems for Management Planning and Control,* 3rd ed. Homewood, Ill.: Richard D. Irwin, Inc., 1975.

QUESTIONS

1. In what ways does the procurement function impact an entity's inventory decisions?

2. Why is it essential to follow a competitive bidding procedure in purchases exceeding an established dollar amount?

3. Do you see anything "unethical" in a buyer accepting an expensive Christmas gift from an established supplier of standard materials regularly purchased by the buyer? What legal implications, if any, are involved?

4. Of what value is an "approved vendor list," and what should be the basis of supplier entry and exit from it?

5. Should the entity maintain control over the issuance of requests to purchase? Why? What kind?

6. What elements contained in a purchase order, formally acknowledged by the vendor, make it a legal contract? Is the vendor required to perform as agreed? Is the buying company required to accept standard performance?

7. What inherent weaknesses may be found in companies whose purchasing, receiving, and vendor payment functions are organized under one executive?

8. On what bases can a vendor's performance under a purchase agreement be evaluated?

9. What control purpose is served by the use of serially prenumbered purchase order forms? Should all forms be accounted for? Why?

10. What organizations normally receive copies of approved purchase orders? For what functional purpose?

11. What circumstances might constitute a conflict of interest situation in the procurement organization? How can these situations be discovered and controlled?

12. What kinds of management reports are needed by purchasing executives?

13. What are the primary functions of a receiving operation?

14. What financial considerations make the receiving function of special interest to accountants?

15. What authority and responsibility are delegated to the receiving operation relative to (a) the physical condition of incoming shipments, (b) shipments violating FOB terms and routing instructions, (c) overshipment, (d) over- or underbillings (price and quantity)?

16. What special characteristics are critical to the success of a receiving operation?

17. List and discuss some of the inequities that might reflect in corporate records as a result of poorly controlled receiving functions.

18. Vendor shipments are often accompanied by several related documents such as the bill of lading, the packing slip, a carrier freight bill, the vendors sales order, and sometimes even an invoice. What disposition should be accorded these documents by receiving personnel?

19. Should receiving memoranda be controlled by serial number? Why?

20. Under what conditions may an "open" purchase order be considered *closed* by authorized receiving personnel?

21. Should the receiving department have the authority to reject vendor shipments significantly ahead of scheduled delivery? Shipments long past due? Why?

22. List and discuss some of the control techniques used to achieve receiving department objectives.

23. Who (what organization) should authorize deviations from the purchase order (e.g., substitute materials, reduced price, excess freight)?

24. What responsibility does the receiving operation have in the invoice payment process?

PROBLEMS

25. Procurement Controls

The Blue Chip Company frequently experienced the need to acquire small, high-value items for both its production operations and certain "ceremonial" occasions. Such purchases were often made on a short lead-time basis. The company produced a highly technical product under government contract and followed the public relations practice of giving expensive miniature replicas of its product to visiting senators and high-ranking military personnel.

Mr. Allgood, an experienced buyer, usually handled such purchases for the company. Allgood knew company procurement policy and procedures like the palm of his hand. The particular procedure that he used to make such "special purchases" specified that delivery should be made to a designated company representative whose signature constitutes official acceptance, which was then used to support the issuance of a receiving document.

A request to purchase 30 such items valued at $10,000 came to Mr. Allgood's desk marked "Rush."

Allgood followed the standard procedure of obtaining several competitive bids for the order, adding a new twist that he had been planning for some time. He had decided to become a bidder himself! He had set up a fictitious company with a legitimate-sounding name using a post office box address in a nearby large city. Being in a position to review all bids, Allgood had no difficulty assuring that his bid was the lowest. Since company procedure required no formal review of bids of $10,000 or less, he naturally awarded the contract to himself (his "company"). An official purchase order was issued and subsequently acknowledged.

In due time, Allgood shipped a box containing filler materials of approximately the same weight and size as the real merchandise, specifying on the packing list that the shipment was to be picked up at the dock, unopened, by Mr. Allgood. Delivery was accomplished without incident, and an official receiving report was issued and distributed. Shortly thereafter, Allgood dispatched his invoice—an impressive document especially printed for his purpose by a friend in the printing business, bearing attractive discount terms of 2/10, net/30.

In the meantime, the accounts payable department was routinely assembling all the documents supporting the "transaction." Desiring to earn the $200 cash discount, the department paid the obligation promptly on the due date. Account distribution was made to the expense account specified on the purchase order, and the completed transaction was put to rest in permanent record storage.

Ironically, the accounting firm that audited the company's affairs miraculously discovered the fraud through its sample testing techniques. Much of the money was recovered from Allgood and his accomplice, who had falsified the purchase request resulting in the rush order.

Required:
   a. Point out as many control weaknesses as you can that might have allowed this fraud to happen.
   b. What procedural changes would you recommend to preclude a recurrence of this kind of activity?

26. Purchasing and Receiving Controls

The company had acquired a large punch press from Germany. The giant machine had been cocooned in a petroleum jelly compound for 25 years and required complete cleaning prior to use. Part of the cleaning process called for sandblasting and refinishing much of the exterior of the machine.

The maintenance supervisor placed a *Request to Purchase* calling for the rental of a sandblasting machine and the purchase of one bag of silica sand. The request was marked "Emergency—Rush." The buyer, Mr. Phillup Space, executed the order for rental of the sandblaster and decided to place the sand order by phone, which he would follow up later with a formal purchase order. He called a salesman he knew at Portland Cement Company in Chattanooga, Tennessee, about 50 miles away. His instructions to the salesman were "to put a bag of silica sand costing approximately $4.50 on the next Trailways bus to be picked up at the bus depot by a company driver." Phillup gave the salesman a purchase order number that he had obtained from the serially controlled purchase order log and asked him to reference the number, as usual, on his packing list and invoice. Freight charges were to be prepared and billed on the invoice.

The Portland salesman promptly complied with the request, and within 3 hours the sand arrived at the local bus station. A courier picked it up and delivered it to the receiving dock as instructed. Receiving personnel could find no supporting purchase order, however, and refused to accept delivery, asking the driver to return the bag to the bus station and send it back COD to Chattanooga.

The next day, upon receiving the rejected bag, the puzzled salesman called Phillup Space for an explanation. Embarrassed, Space explained that under the press of a very busy schedule, he had failed to follow up with the issuance of the official purchase order. He asked that the bag be once again placed on a bus, and assured the salesman that there would be no slipup this time. He suggested that Portland Cement rebill the shipment to include the triple transportation charges that had accumulated by this time.

Space quickly referred back to the control log to verify the order number he had given the salesman the day before. In his haste to cover the error, he inadvertently selected a number one "units digit" removed from the correct one. A formal purchase order was expeditiously typed and rushed to the receiving dock to await the immediately impending shipment.

Soon the bag of sand arrived the second time, somewhat lighter and leaving an abrasive trail flowing from the several small holes caused by so much rough handling. Again the receiving agent could *not* accept the bag (1) because the purchase order number on the packing list did not exist, and (2) the merchandise was obviously damaged in transit. The severely depleted bag was once again returned to Chattanooga.

The irate salesman had Mr. Space on the telephone at 8:00 A.M. the next morning, beating the frantic maintenance supervisor to the punch by only a split second. His opening remark was: "Hey, Space, I'm standing here at the Chattanooga bus station literally holding an *empty* bag. What would you like me to do with it *and* the accumulated freight charges of $12.00?"

Required:

    a. What standard purchasing procedure did Space violate in verbally arranging a contract with the Portland Cement Company salesman?

    b. Could the purchasing company be held liable for the excessive freight charges?

    c. Did the receiving department act responsibly in rejecting the shipment repeatedly? Should they have taken the initiative in seeking an internal solution after the first rejection?

d. How might this kind of misunderstanding be procedurally avoided in the future?

27. Risk and Preventive Controls

You have completed an audit of activities within the purchasing department of your company. The department employs 30 buyers, 7 supervisors, a manager, and clerical personnel. Purchases total about $500 million a year. Your audit disclosed the following conditions:

a. The company has no formal rules on conflicts of interest. Your analysis produced evidence that one of the 30 buyers in the department owns a substantial interest in a major supplier and that he procures supplies averaging $50,000 a year from that supplier. The prices charged by the supplier are competitive.

b. Buyers select proposed sources without submitting the lists of bidders for review. Your tests disclosed no evidence that higher costs were incurred as a result of that practice.

c. Buyers who originate written requests for quotations from suppliers receive the suppliers' bids directly from the mail room. In your test of 100 purchases based on competitive bids, you found that, in 75 of the 100 cases, the low bidders were awarded the purchase orders.

d. Requests to purchase (requisitions) received in the purchasing department from other departments in the company must be signed by persons authorized to do so. Your examination of 200 such requests disclosed that three, all for small amounts, were not properly signed. The buyer who had issued all three orders honored the requests because he misunderstood the applicable procedure. The clerical personnel charged witn reviewing such requests had given them to the buyer in error. *(AICPA adapted)*

Required:

For each of the four conditions, state:

a. The risk, if any, that is incurred if each condition described previously is permitted to continue

b. The control, if any, you would recommend to prevent continuation of the condition described

28. Purchase Requisition Procedures

Long, CPA, has been engaged to examine and report on the financial statements of Maylou Corporation. During the review phase of the study of Maylou's system of internal accounting control over purchases, Long was given a document flowchart for purchases as shown in Figure 10.18. *(AICPA adapted)*

Required:

a. Identify the procedures, relating to purchase requisitions and purchase orders, that Long would expect to find if Maylou's system of internal accounting control over purchases is effective. For example, purchase orders are prepared only after giving proper consideration to the time to order, and quantity to

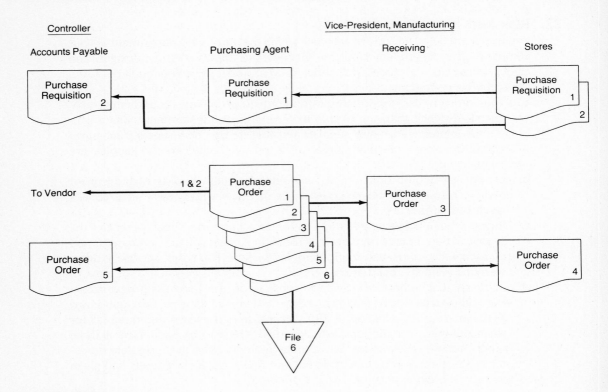

Figure 10.18

order. Do not comment on the effectiveness of the flow of documents as presented in the flowchart or on separation of duties.

b. What are the factors to consider in determining
  1. The time to order
  2. The quantity to order

29. Receiving Controls

A dispute developed between the E. Z. Rigg Company and one of its suppliers whose invoice was being held without payment pending receipt of the shipment. The terms of the purchase agreement established the FOB point at the shipper's plant, with the freight to be prepaid and included on the invoice. Rigg Company's experience with this particular supplier had not been good. The supplier consistently billed weeks ahead of shipment, and the company often had to prod the supplier's sales representative to effect delivery. Attractive discount terms of 2% 15 days from date of invoice were rarely available under the circumstances.

In response to the supplier's demand for payment, Rigg Company's chief accountant explained the company's position and concluded that payment could not be made until receipt of the merchandise ordered. As proof that shipment had been made, the supplier mailed a photostatic copy of the carrier's freight bill. The chief accountant contended that the freight bill *alone* proved nothing except that the goods had been released to a common carrier. For all he knew, the shipment could be resting in a switching yard somewhere miles away.

After several exchanges of this sort, the accountant decided to take the initiative in resolving the matter. He asked the traffic department manager to check out the photostatic document for him. Investigation confirmed the legitimacy of the freight bill, and the carrier even produced a copy of the bill of lading, which had been "receipted" by a check (✓) in the signature space. There were no other identifying marks. The accountant carried this evidence to the receiving department, where a thorough search of the entire receiving dock area failed to yield any clues concerning the whereabouts of the missing shipment. The purchase order was still "open," no receiving report had been issued, and it was established that the material had not reached the stores.

A solution was reached in a meeting with the management representatives from accounts payable, receiving, traffic, and stores. It was agreed that arrangements should be made to permit payment of this aging account and that purchasing should be required to strike the supplier's name from the approved vendor list. In order to consummate the transaction, it was also agreed that a "dummy" receiving report would be issued to support payment and that inventory would record the receipt. Subsequently, the imbalance in the perpetual inventory account would be written off to an expense account.

Required:
Criticize:
a. The decision to pay the obligation
b. The legitimacy of the "receipted" bill of lading
c. The inventory "washout"

30. The Legal Environment of Shipping and Receiving

A large order for steel I-beams valued at approximately $75,000 was placed with Jerusalem Steel by the Majestic Company. The shipment was to be made via Coastal Rail, FOB vendor, freight to be paid direct to Coastal by Majestic.

The purchase order and the Jerusalem Steel invoice were routinely received by the Majestic accounts payable department and filed pending arrival of the confirming receiving report. Terms of payment were 10 days EOM.

Considerable time elapsed after receipt of the invoice with no evidence of receipt of the shipment. The manager of accounts receivable at Jerusalem Steel finally called the accounts payable manager at Majestic and expressed concern over the status of the rather large invoice. He was advised that payment could not be made until the shipment arrived, whereupon the Jerusalem manager quoted the carrier's freight bill number as proof of shipment. The Majestic manager reminded his counterpart that a freight bill number could hardly be considered evidence of *delivery* of $75,000 worth of bulky steel, but that he would check into the matter.

No evidence of the shipment could be found, and ensuing contacts between the two companies' representatives resulted in threats of legal action. In the meantime, the carrier could not account for the shipment and could not prove that the shipment had been delivered. Eventually, Jerusalem Steel was fully compensated for the value of the shipment by the carrier's insurance company and the matter was laid to rest.

About six months after the conclusion of the unfortunate transaction, a Majestic Company maintenance crew discovered the missing I-beams scattered along the banks of the rail spur serving the company's receiving docks. The side supports had broken as the train rounded a curve, and the entire shipment tumbled into the high weeds no more than 200 yards from the security gate. The beams, although slightly rusty, were in acceptable condition and still in demand. In the meantime, the purchase order with Jerusalem had been canceled and the unpaid invoice returned.

Required:
   a. Who owned the shipment at the time of its disappearance?
   b. Was the transaction properly settled?
   c. If Majestic decides to keep the I-beams, from whom must it purchase them?
   d. What really constitutes "proof" of delivery?
   e. Differentiate between proof of shipment and proof of delivery.

31. Flowchart Analysis

Anthony, CPA, prepared the flowchart in Figure 10.19, which portrays the raw materials purchasing function of one of Anthony's clients, a medium-size manufacturing company, from the preparation of initial documents through the vouching of invoices for payment in accounts payable. The flowchart was a portion of the work performed on the audit engagement to evaluate internal control. *(AICPA adapted)*

Required:

Identify and explain the systems and control weaknesses evident from Figure 10.19. Include the internal control weaknesses resulting from activities performed or not performed. All documents are prenumbered.

32. Purchasing and Receiving Systems Design

Lecimore Company has a centralized purchasing department which is managed by Joan Jones. Jones has established policies and procedures to guide the clerical staff and purchasing agents in the day-to-day operation of the department. She is satisfied that these policies and procedures are in conformity with company objectives and believes there are no major problems in the regular operations of the purchasing department.

Lecimore's internal audit department was assigned to perform an operational audit of the purchasing function. Their first task was to review the specific poli-

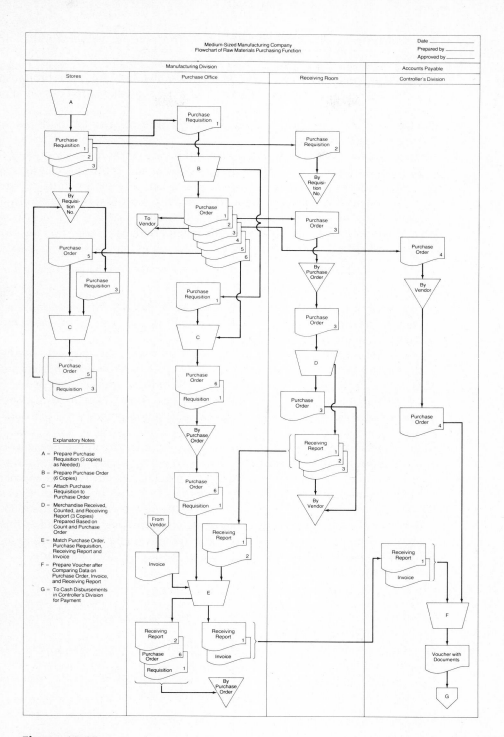

Figure 10.19

cies and procedures established by Jones. The policies and procedures are as follows:

All significant purchases are made on a competitive bid basis. The probability of timely delivery, reliability of vendor, and so on are taken into consideration on a subjective basis.

Detailed specifications of the minimum acceptable quality for all goods purchased are provided to vendors.

Vendor's adherence to the quality specifications is the responsibility of the materials manager of the inventory control department and not the purchasing department. The materials manager inspects the goods as they arrive to be sure the quality meets the minimum standards and then sees that the goods are transferred from the receiving dock to the storeroom.

All purchase requests are prepared by the materials manager based on the production schedule for a 4-month period.

The internal audit staff then observed the operations of the purchasing function and gathered the following findings:

One vendor provides 90 percent of a critical raw material. This vendor has a good delivery record and is very reliable. Furthermore, this vendor has been the low bidder over the past few years.

As production plans change, rush and expedite orders are made by production directly to the purchasing department. Materials ordered for canceled production runs are stored for future use. The costs of these special requests are borne by the purchasing department. Jones considers the additional costs associated with these special requests as "costs of being a good member of the corporate team."

Materials to accomplish engineering changes are ordered by the purchasing department as soon as the changes are made by the engineering department. Jones is very proud of the quick response by the purchasing staff to product changes. Materials on hand are not reviewed before any orders are placed.

Partial shipments and advance shipments (i.e., those received before the requested date of delivery) are accepted by the materials manager who notifies the purchasing department of the receipt. The purchasing department is responsible for follow-up on partial shipments. No action is taken to discourage advance shipments. *(IMA adapted)*

Required:
Based on the purchasing department's policies and procedures and the findings of Lecimore's internal audit staff.
a. Identify weaknesses and/or inefficiencies in Lecimore Company's purchasing function.
b. Make recommendations for those weaknesses/inefficiencies that you identify.
Use the following format in preparing your response.

Weaknesses/Inefficiencies   **Recommendations**

33. Purchase Order Controls

Properly designed and utilized forms facilitate adherence to prescribed internal accounting control policies and procedures. One such form might be a multicopy purchase order, with one copy intended to be mailed to the vendor. The remaining copies would ordinarily be distributed to the stores, purchasing, receiving, and accounting departments.

The following purchase order (Figure 10.20) is currently being used by National Industrial Corporation *(IMA adapted):*

Required:

    a. In addition to the name of the company, what other necessary information would an auditor recommend be included in the illustrative purchase order?

    b. What primary internal control functions are served by the purchase order copies that are distributed to the stores, purchasing, receiving, and accounting departments?

34. Control Points

Good Lumber Company is a large regional dealer of building materials that requires an elaborate system of internal controls. The flow chart of the purchasing activities is presented in Figure 10.21.

The activities in the purchasing department start with the receipt of an approved copy of the purchase requisition (PR) from the budget department. After reviewing the purchase requisition, a prenumbered purchase order (PO) is issued in multiple copies. Two copies are sent to a vendor, one retained in the purchasing department, and the remainder distributed to other departments of Good Lumber. The second copy of the purchase order is to be returned by the vendor to confirm the receipt of the order; this copy is filed according to PO number in the PO file.

A receiving report (RR) is completed in the receiving department when shipments of materials arrive from vendors. A copy of the receiving report is sent to the purchasing department and attached to the purchase order and purchase requisition in the vendor's file.

The accounts payable department normally receives two copies of a vendor's invoice. These two copies are forwarded to the purchasing department for review with various documents related to the order. Purchasing will either institute authorization procedures for the payment of the invoice or recommend exception procedures. *(IMA adapted)*

Required:

    a. A primary purpose for preparing a flowchart is to identify system control points. Explain what a control point is.

    b. Control points are not specifically identified in the flowchart presented for the purchasing department of Good Lumber Company. Review the flowchart and identify where control points exist. For each control point:

PURCHASE ORDER

SEND INVOICE ONLY TO:

297 HARDINGTEN DR., BX., NY 10461

TO _____

SHIP TO _____

DATE TO BE SHIPPED	SHIP VIA	DISC. TERMS	FREIGHT TERMS	ADV. ALLOWANCE	SPECIAL ALLOWANCE

QUANTITY	DESCRIPTION

PURCHASE CONDITIONS

1. Supplier will be responsible for extra freight cost on partial shipment, unless prior permission is obtained.

2. Please acknowledge this order.

3. Please notify us immediately if you are unable to complete order.

4. All items must be individually packed.

Figure 10.20

(1) Identify where the control point exists in the flowchart. Use the reference number that appears to the left of each symbol.

(2) Describe the nature of the control activity required for each control point.

(3) Explain the purpose of or justification for each control activity.

Using the following format in preparing your answer.

Reference Number   **Control Activity**   **Purpose or Justification**

PURCHASING DEPARTMENT.

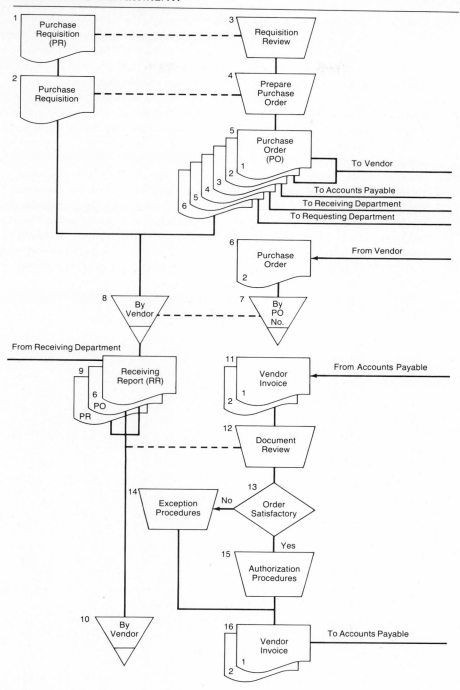

Figure 10.21

CASES

35. The Apogee Company Case presented in Appendix C represents a real-life example of a potentially disasterous procurement operation. Not only are vital contractual agreements *not* documented, the company violates or completely ignores most of the standard control features one would expect to find in a system responsible for spending (projected) $2,000,000 annually for raw material purchases.

Study the case in the light of the concepts and principles you learned in Chapter Ten, and design reliable information systems for purchasing and receiving. Treat them separately. In this, and all the remaining systems relating to the Apogee Company, assume the acquisition and use of a computer of appropriate size and configuration.

36. Bubbling Stone Beverage Co. (Appendix D) is apparently a well-managed, successful enterprise. Often, operating success is a reflection of the personalities and capabilities of a *few* key persons. Review the procurement and receiving practices of this company and speculate on who, or what, is responsible for its efficiency (success). Is it the people who do the job, or is it the "system" within which they operate? Can the systems' integrity endure a series of key personnel turnovers? Indicate how *you* might modify and improve purchasing procedures and receiving functions in Bubbling Stone Beverage Co.

CHAPTER ELEVEN

The Accounts Payable System

Responsible handling and processing of a company's current trade obligations are vital for many reasons, not the least of which are its direct effects on the *current ratio* (ratio of current assets to current debts) and the possible loss of sizable sums through failure to earn cash discounts. The process of liquidating the current trade liabilities of an organization requires the assembly of *support* documents for payment that involve the operations of at least two directly related internal functions (purchasing and receiving) and an external entity (the supplier). No payment should ever be made without an authorizing document, typically an approved purchase contract. In most cases, payment will also be withheld until receipt of the material or satisfactory performance of the service specified in the purchase agreement.

The "document set" supporting payment to outsiders typically consists of (1) a vendor invoice, (2) a matching purchase order or other contractual obligation, and (3) a matching receiving report bearing inspection certification. Furthermore, these documents must be in agreement with respect to the basic terms of the contract, such as part number and description, quantity, unit price, shipping terms, carrier mode or routing, discount terms, taxes, and delivery schedule.

FUNCTIONS OF THE SYSTEM

Depending on the size of the company, the accounts payable system may vary in organizational form and characteristics from a simple manual system of payment authorizations to a complex computer operation in which transaction audits and payments are automatically and remotely accomplished on due date. Regardless of the degree of technical sophistication, however, there are several basic functions that all good accounts payable systems *must* perform.

Prompt Payment of Liabilities

The most obvious and essential function accomplished by a payables system is the timely liquidation of trade debts. Prompt action within the specified discount periods (2/10 n/30, or 1% EOM, e.g.) can yield significant savings on gross trade accounts payable and cannot be lightly regarded. Although accountants appear unable to agree on whether such discounts are a reduction of material price or a reward for early payment, failure to *earn* them is an almost unforgivable financial practice.

With three independent agencies originating the foundation documents to support payment, we might expect certain variations between the documents to occur periodically. One of the most difficult problems of any reasonably complex accounts payable system is the mediation of these differences in the best interests of the company whenever possible. Examples of situations that require corrective measures are:

1. Over- and underbilling due to vendor price discrepancies
2. Overshipments, undershipments, and early shipments relative to the contract terms
3. Variations in quantity among shipping documents, invoice, and receiving report
4. Materials damaged or lost in transit
5. Vendor substitutions for materials ordered
6. A situation in which the vendor's document creation system causes invoices to be dated and mailed ahead of actual shipment, thus making it virtually impossible to earn cash discounts
7. Incorrect routing, causing freight charge discrepancies
8. Invoice discrepancies in FOB terms, taxes, discount terms, extensions, totals, and so on.

There seems to be an endless combination of "order-ship-bill-receive" variances that make an extremely complicated process out of an otherwise straightforward event sequence. Typically, companies will establish "tolerance limits" within which minor variations can be handled without exception. Such tolerances should be established at the point where the cost of processing corrective documentation approximates the amount of the discrepancy. One of the hazards of a policy of this sort is the fact that vendors often are able to discern the extremes within which they can operate. They may tend consistently to press this advantage to the limit.

Accounting Distribution

The accounts payable operation is usually given the responsibility for distributing invoice charges to the appropriate accounts. In a very real sense, the automated accounts payable system corresponds to the voucher register system taught in most introductory accounting courses. Using periodic distribution summary listings, the by-product of a fully automated process, the accountant makes a periodic journal entry. Even that manual function is eliminated when the general ledger is maintained on the computer (see Chapter Eighteen).

Businesses often require that all general fund payments and transfers be processed through accounts payable. In such cases, the *net* payroll amount flows through the accounts payable system via special input from the payroll system. The function of the accounts payable system is simply to transfer funds from the general fund to a special bank account balance against which payroll checks would be charged. This procedure provides a cash control and will be discussed in more detail in the payroll system chapter.

Accrual of Open Liability

The master file of unpaid vendor invoices serves the same purpose as the conventional voucher register for determining the gross balance and the subsidiary detail of trade accounts payable. Logically the system should be expected to provide the basis for accruing open liability on cue (i.e., monthly, quarterly, and/or annually). This vital function is accomplished by extracting a detailed printout of each vendor's unpaid claims substantiated by proof of delivery (receiving memo). From this information, the accountant may prepare an accrual journal entry. Alternatively, the computer could prepare the journal voucher automatically.

Purchase Commitments

Purchase orders duly accepted and acknowledged by suppliers constitute legal and binding contracts. The company shares a contingent obligation with the supplier during the interim period prior to actual performance and consummation of the transaction. This does not imply that such contracts may not be legally terminated without penalty to either party.

The logical source of such information is the master purchase order file maintained in the accounts payable system and used as the "authorizing" document in determining the validity of vendor invoices. This file will reflect not only the original gross amount of the purchase agreement, but, as partial fulfillment is accomplished, will also yield the uncompleted balance of open purchase commitments. A periodic listing of such commitments in vendor sequence provides an important clue concerning the purchasing habits of individual buyers.

Vendor Identification and Control

The manner in which a company discharges its responsibilities to outsiders, particularly with respect to payment of its legitimate debts, may have a greater impact on its image than any other single business activity. Accounts payable authorities are more consistently in direct contract with outsiders in the settlement of accounts than either purchasing or marketing operations. Therefore, the maintenance of an up-to-date vendor name and address file is absolutely essential to a good payables operation. The bare necessities of any vendor file would include the vendor identification number (for internal control), the complete name and address, credit information relating to the payables operation, and provisions for accumulating the volume of business conducted with each vendor during a given year.

Large multidivisional suppliers often have organizational and operational complexities that must be handled by an automated payables system. For example, there is often a "buy-from-pay-to" complication wherein a vendor may contract, ship, and invoice from a divisional facility but require that payment be made to a central corporate finance office. Conversely, order taking and shipping may be a normal divisional function with centralized billing requiring payment to either the central *or* divisional operation. Aside from the obvious difficulties of physically *matching* related documents bearing different organizational designations, there is the possibility of legal involvement should payment be directed to the wrong recipient.

Many companies are also finding a well-organized and up-to-date vendor file advantageous in meeting the increasing governmental reporting demands relating to small businesses, minority businesses, area operations analyses, and other selected organizational characteristics.

SOURCE DOCUMENTS

As previously indicated, the accounts payable system depends principally on three independently prepared documents: the transaction authorization (the purchase order discussed in Chapter Ten), the supplier's request for payment after performance, that is, the invoice (Figure 11.1), and the proof or acknowledgment of satisfactory performance (receiving report); see Chapter Ten. When the terms of the contract specify that the buyer will absorb the freight charges, another source document, the freight bill, may be required to support the latter two documents. The combination of these documents (if in agreement) constitutes a liability, often referred to collectively as "vouchers payable."

Assuming freight terms "FOB shipping point," the vendor may elect to prepay the freight and include the charges on his or her invoice. Otherwise, the freight charges would be billed directly to the buyer by the carrier. In the first case the vendor would be obligated to support the invoice with a paid freight receipt as a condition of payment. In the latter case, carrier freight bills would be treated similar to regular invoices supported by evidence of receipt of material (or internal traffic department approval) as a condition of payment.

Other significant documents playing a role in the accounts payable system are the adjusting documents: debit and credit memoranda. A credit memorandum is shown in Figure 11.2. These documents relate to specific transactions and are typically used to reconcile and adjust differences between the documents supporting payment.

Document Control and Validation

A matter of particular importance in the accounts payable system is the official registration of each vendor document submitted for payment. It is common practice for vendors to provide duplicate copies of their invoices, particularly in cases where payment may be delayed pending the settlement of one or more of the discrepancies previously discussed. Such superfluous documentation should be identified and prevented from entering the normal system processing.

Many companies accomplish this by maintaining a "document control register," in which each original billing document is entered. The document is assigned a unique identifying code number. Such a number may consist of 10 digits (86-12-30-1234), the first six representing the calendar identification and the last four being an exclusive serial number ranging daily from 0001 to 9999. Once assigned, the document bearing such a number *must* be officially disposed of either through normal payment or voiding due to lack of performance or irreconcilable difference.

Document Reference Numbers

In addition to the material identification, price, and quantity information normally expected on business transaction paper, documents entering the accounts payable system from outsiders must reflect sufficient information to permit matching with other related

RUSSELL CORPORATION KNIT DIVISION
ALEXANDER CITY, ALABAMA 35010 ▪ (205) 234-4251 ▪ D·U·N·S 339-5902

REMIT TO:
RUSSELL CORPORATION
BOX 272
ALEXANDER CITY, AL. 35010

SHIPPER   VIA   PAGE

AGENT	OUR ORDER NO.	CUSTOMER ORDER NO.	CUSTOMER DEPT. NO.	STORE NO.	ACCOUNT NO.	TERMS	DATE	INVOICE NO.

(SAME AS SOLD TO UNLESS SHOWN)

SOLD
TO

SHIP
TO

1 STRING 2 PAPER BUNDLES 3 POLY BUNDLES 4 BOXED

CASE NUMBER	STYLE	PACKAGE CODE	COLOR	SPECIAL STYLE										UOS	PRICE	AMOUNT
					A	2	4	6	8	10	12	14	16	18			
					B	6 MO.	1	2	3	4	5	6	6X	8			
					C	S	M	L	XL				XS				
					D	30	32	34	36	38	40	42	44	46			
					E	38	40	42	44	46	48	50	52	54			

WE DISCLAIM LIABILITY FOR FURNISHING "PROOF OF DELIVERY" UNLESS REQUESTED IN WRITING BY YOU WITHIN NINETY DAYS AFTER SHIPMENT.
NO CLAIMS ALLOWED UNLESS MADE WITHIN FIVE DAYS AFTER RECEIPT OF GOODS.
WE HEREBY CERTIFY THAT ALL GOODS AND SERVICES COVERED BY THIS INVOICE WERE PRODUCED AND FURNISHED IN COMPLIANCE WITH THE REQUIREMENTS OF THE FAIR LABOR STANDARDS ACT OF 1938, AS AMENDED, AND ANY REGULATIONS AND ORDERS ISSUED THEREUNDER.
WE GUARANTEE THAT THE TEXTILE FIBER PRODUCTS SPECIFIED HEREIN ARE NOT MISBRANDED NOR FALSELY NOR DECEPTIVELY ADVERTISED OR INVOICED UNDER THE PROVISIONS OF THE TEXTILE FIBER PRODUCTS IDENTIFICATION ACT AND RULES AND REGULATIONS THEREUNDER.
INTEREST AND SERVICE CHARGE WILL BE MADE ON ALL PAST DUE INVOICES.   **ORIGINAL INVOICE**

Figure 11.1

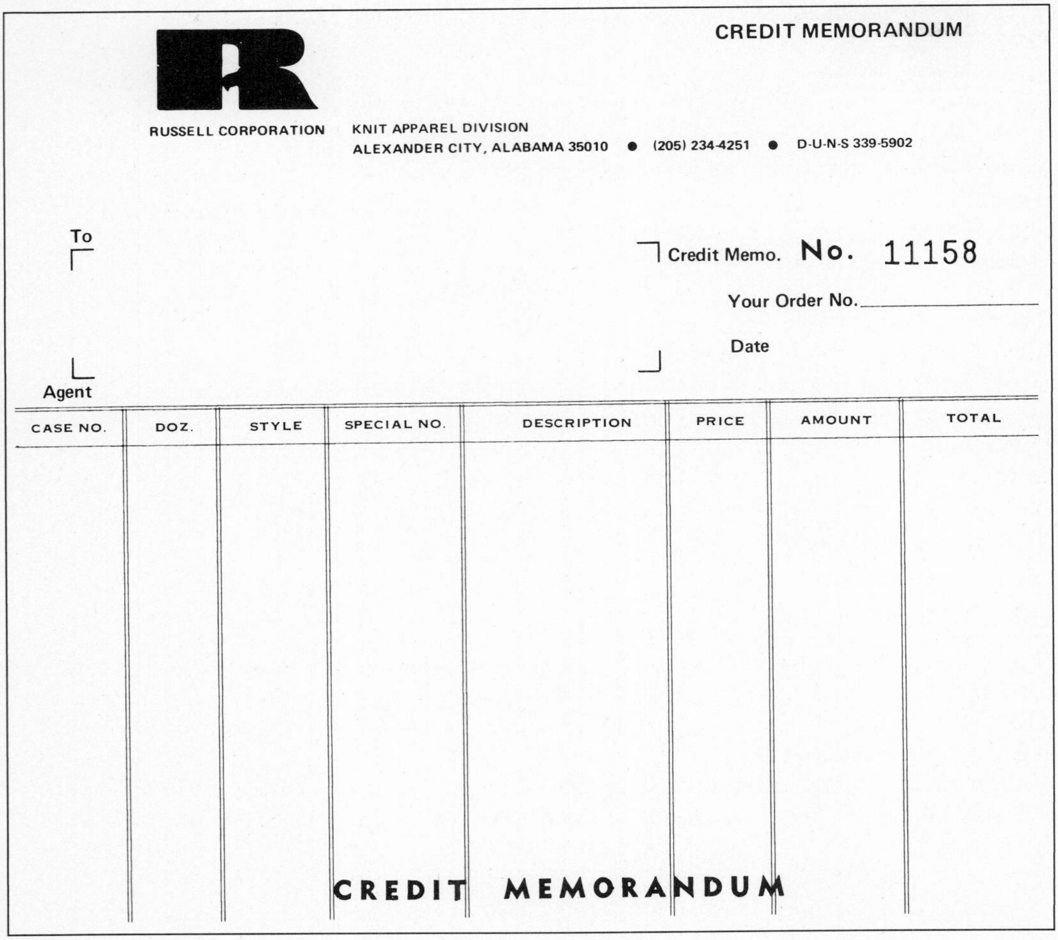

CREDIT MEMORANDUM

RUSSELL CORPORATION   KNIT APPAREL DIVISION
ALEXANDER CITY, ALABAMA 35010   ● (205) 234-4251   ● D-U-N-S 339-5902

To

⌐ Credit Memo. **No. 11158**

Your Order No._____

Date

Agent

CASE NO.	DOZ.	STYLE	SPECIAL NO.	DESCRIPTION	PRICE	AMOUNT	TOTAL

CREDIT MEMORANDUM

Figure 11.2

internal documents. The most important numbers in this interrelationship process are the purchase order serial number and the carrier's freight bill number.

Upon receipt, a document control clerk will note the purchase order number on the vendor's invoice and make a cursory check to determine whether a previous billing has been recorded and paid or is still pending payment. If it is still pending, the clerk destroys the duplicate invoice. If not, the invoice is formally registered and entered into the system. By following this simple procedure, possible duplicate payment and distribution are avoided, along with the attendant reversal and corrective measures necessitated by erroneous data entering other systems such as inventory control, cash, and general ledger.

Appropriate inclusion of the carrier's document number on the vendor's invoice provides a key link in the transaction cycle, particularly when there are multiple shipments and billings against a single authorizing purchase contract. Receiving operations routinely show the carrier's number on all receiving reports, thus providing irrefutable evidence of performance and assuring the assembly of proper document sets to support payments.

It can be seen that an invoice presented for payment, assigned a unique registration number, related to a specific purchase contract, and matched to a receiving report bearing the carrier's proof of delivery can be paid with confidence (and paid *only once*)—assuming, of course, there are no irreconcilable differences between the terms of agreement and actual performance.

Record Retention

Subsequent to payment, which terminates the transaction cycle, the completed document sets are physically removed from the active files and stored in vendor name sequence in central files. After a period of time, usually corresponding to the applicable statute of limitations, such documents may either be stored in dead files or destroyed. Computer printouts of payment and distribution details may be kept for an indefinite period for reference since their lesser bulk makes them more economical to retain than the original documents.

DOCUMENT FLOW AND TIMING

The sequence of events in the accounts payable cycle follows a uniform pattern: order, accept, receive, invoice, and pay and distribute. The reader should examine the document flow diagram in Figure 11.3 and relate the numbered events to the following explanation of functions.

Someone in the organization holding the delegated authority will perceive a need and originate a request to purchase (1). Such a request may automatically emanate in the inventory control system if it is programmed to detect and take action on strategic inventory conditions. This function is detailed in the inventory system chapter.

The appropriate buyer will act on the request to purchase (2) by possibly "letting out bids" to *approved* suppliers. The bid winner becomes the official supplier when he signs the acknowledgment copy of the purchase order and returns it to the buyer. At this point a legal contract exists. The signed acknowledgment copy of the purchase order is received by the buyer, who makes the proper notation on his or her file copy and routes the acknowledgment to accounts payable (3).

In the meantime, the supplier's focused attention is on assembling the material for shipment and arranging for carrier pickup in time to meet the specified schedule delivery terms of the purchase agreement (4). The completion of the bill of lading and the actual shipment gives rise to the preparation of an invoice requesting payment (5). The invoice is mailed directly to accounts payable.

Upon receipt of the shipment (6), the receiving organization originates a receiving report. The issuance of this document is contingent upon the existence of an authorizing purchase order (7). Each receiving report is assigned a unique identification number that distinguishes it from all other receipts. Prior to release of the receiving report, the shipment is inspected for conformance with the purchase agreement and possible dam-

DOCUMENT FLOW AND TIMING—ACCOUNTS PAYABLE.

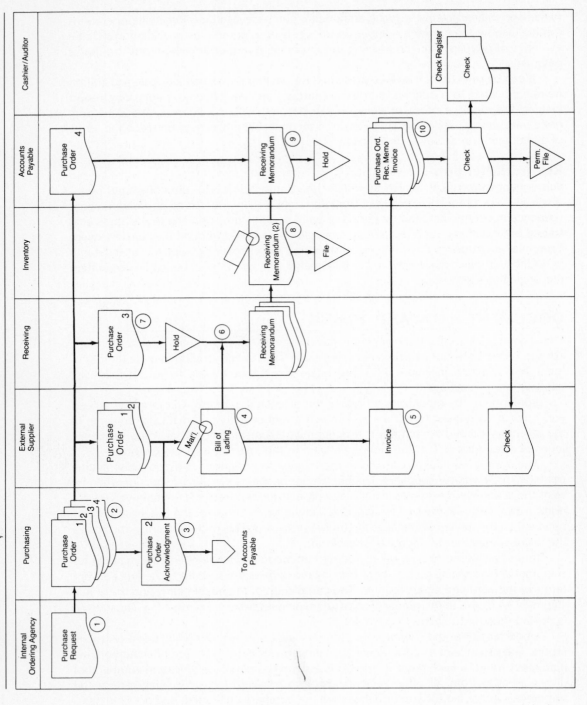

Figure 11.3

age in transit. Depending on the FOB terms, the carrier may send a freight bill to either the buyer or the supplier (not shown in the flow diagram).

Receiving reports are released, one being sent to accounts payable (9) to support payment and another routed with the material to stores (8).

Physical inventory is updated on the basis of the receiving report, and inventory prices are updated by accounts payable distribution. The process provides a control feature that separates physical handling and record keeping. Status reports are also prepared, and the cycle begins again.

The arrival of all support documents in accounts payable makes it possible for the transaction to be consummated by payment (10), hopefully within the discount period. Some companies will pay reliable vendors *before* receipt of the shipment to take advantage of discount terms. This procedure can also be programmed, but care must be taken that duplicate payments are prevented when the receiving report is entered. Further, when a receiving report is not processed within, say, 30 days, an exception report needs to be prepared. All unpaid bills, together with related documents, are held in active vendor files in sequence by purchase order number within vendor code.

Document integrity, accuracy, and timing are critical factors in the successful operation of an accounts payable system. Deviations from contract terms outside the payment tolerance limits usually cause delay of payment, loss of discount (unless the supplier accepts responsibility for the delay), and expensive corrective action.

ACCOUNTING CONTROLS AND RISKS OF FAILURE

To assure achievement of the entity's objectives in the accounts payable area, the system needs (1) a method of vendor selection and approval, (2) a management policy governing quantities, prices, and terms of goods and services purchased, (3) regular performance audits of purchasing activities, and (4) detailed procedures for documenting and approving liquidation of trade obligations. Some of the risks that the accounts payable system must guard against are:

1. Liabilities may be recorded for goods or services billed but not received.
2. Liabilities may be recorded at incorrect amounts due to clerical errors, incorrect prices, incorrect terms, and so forth.
3. Liabilities for goods and services received may not be recorded.
4. Accounting distributions (debits) may be incorrect (e.g., charging items to administrative expenses rather than to manufacturing expenses). This results in an incorrect calculation of the burden rate used in inventory valuations (work-in-process), improper classifications in the income statement, and inaccurate reports.
5. An incorrect amount of cash may be disbursed.
6. Cash may be fraudulently disbursed.
7. Duplicate payments may be made.
8. Checks may be fraudulently altered.
9. Cash may be disbursed in advance of receipt or for goods and services never received.
10. General ledger inputs may be inaccurate as a result of clerical errors.

11. Timing problems may develop, resulting in a failure to record all liabilities or disbursements in the proper period and the loss of purchases discounts.
12. Imbalances between the control account and the subsidiary ledger could result from inaccurate posting.
13. Financial statements may reflect incorrect and misleading data.

The foregoing list of potential dangers is not meant to be exhaustive, but merely to demonstrate the breadth and depth of the impact of accounts payable functions. Some of the techniques designed to assure control in these areas of concern are enumerated here. Such control techniques may also extend into related organizations.

1. Use of prenumbered and controlled critical forms (e.g., vouchers, check requests, adjustment forms, and checks)
2. Perforating, voiding, safeguarding, or otherwise canceling source documents to prevent reuse (e.g., vouchers, invoices, checks, and adjustments forms)
3. Restricted access to check-signing equipment and signature plates
4. Established procedures for recording, voiding, explaining, and disposing of voided and/or mutilated check forms
5. Requiring manual and/or dual signatures on checks, especially large ones
6. Separation of check preparation and signing functions
7. Prohibition against signing blank checks, or drawing checks payable to cash or bearer
8. Requiring computer-prepared or mechanically prepared checks to agree in total with the check register, voucher register, account distribution list, and check-signing machine counter
9. Segregation of duties in manual systems
   a. Voucher posting from invoice/order checking
   b. Check preparation from voucher posting
   c. Mailing of checks from check preparation
10. Automatic check preparation by computer, where possible, based on scheduled payment (due) date entered when voucher is processed
11. Documented processing, cutoff, and period-end closing procedures
12. Documented chart of accounts
13. Maintenance of logs at receiving locations, which may be used to
    a. Accrue liabilities as of activity dates rather than of processing dates
    b. Check completeness of voucher registers
14. Written cutoff and closing schedules, with procedures stating, by functions, the sources to be used to prepare journal entries for accruals
15. Automatic journal entry generation by computer-based system where possible
16. Limited access to on-line files and other data base master files to authorized personnel, effected by the use of passwords

MANAGEMENT INFORMATION REQUIREMENTS

Standard procedure in any good information system requires a printout of daily activity introduced for processing. Such a list is essential for audit and internal control purposes. Beyond this minimum requirement, the basic management information needs focus on payment, accounting distribution, open liability, and unfilled purchase commitments. As previously mentioned, the accounts payable system must be designed to provide this essential information either on automatic time (date) cue or through a special "report generator"—which is itself a system. A daily activity list might take the form and content illustrated in Figure 11.4.

Daily Payments List

Such a report itemizes the invoices processed for payment on the current date. The report is controlled on vendor number and reflects all the pertinent document numbers needed to trace any element of a particular payment. With totals reflected for each vendor, the auditor can easily ascertain that each item listed also appears on the remittance advice attached to the check. A facsimile list is demonstrated in Figure 11.5.

Check Register

The listing of accounts payable checks, or check register, is the permanent record of payments. Three copies are usually prepared: one to accompany the checks to the cashier's office, one to the internal auditors, and a copy retained for a time in the accounts payable organization. An illustration of the check register is found in Figure 11.6.

Accrued Liability Report

A summary of all unpaid liabilities at the time of closing, arranged in account number sequence, provides the basis for recognizing legitimate obligations to outsiders and for distributing the related charges to the inventory accounts involved. The entry will be reversed at the beginning of the subsequent period after its effects are reflected in the financial statements. Often companies maintain their unpaid liability file by due date rather than by vendor.

		ACCOUNTS PAYABLE			
Report #: AP-001		Daily Activity List		Date: 12/24/8X	
Act*	Vendor	Name	Purchase Order	Document Code	Amount
01	12345	ABC Company	AB12345	J25750001	10.50
01	23456	Badminton, Inc.	AB34567	A13750310	5,280.00
01	67890	Goodminton, Inc.	CA25791	A20754025	999.00
		TOTAL			6,289.50
02	25689	Brown, Jones, & Smith	BX12567	--	372.00
02	88888	XYZ Company	AB35791	--	154.00
		Etc.			
		Etc.			

*ACTIVITY IDENTIFICATION CODE NUMBER.

Figure 11.4

ACCOUNTS PAYABLE
Daily Payments List

Report #: <u>AP-002</u>   Date: <u>12/24/8X</u>

Vendor	Name	Document Code	Purchase Order	Invoice No.	Amount	Subtotals
12345	ABC Company	M16756540	AC83210	12567	1,750.62	
12345	ABC Company	M16756539	AC83210	12568	1.98	
12345	ABC Company	A21752159	B513579	23285	67.00	1,819.60
25689	Brown, Jones, & Smith	M05756051	B356271	XA510	139.13	139.13
34567	Dan River, Inc.	A09753939	A175651	1919A	25.25	
34567	Dan River, Inc.	A09754201	A175651	1919B	750.16	775.41
45678	Goodbody Parts	F10751314	C632133	A5105	10.10	10.10
Etc.						
Etc.						
	TOTAL				XX,XXX.XX	

Figure 11.5

ACCOUNTS PAYABLE
Daily Check Register

Report #: <u>AP-003</u>   Date: <u>12/24/8X</u>

Vendor	Name	Check No.	Gross	Disc.	Net
12345	ABC Company	A1235679	1,819.60	.00	1,819.60
25689	Brown, Jones, & Smith	A1235680	139.13	1.39	137.74
34567	Dan River, Inc.	A1235681	775.41	15.51	759.90
45678	Goodbody Parts	A1235682	10.10	.00	10.10
Etc.					
Etc.					
	TOTAL				X,XXX,XXX.XX

Figure 11.6

Cash Forecasting

The accounts payable system should be expected to provide information to support the preparation of a short-range cash payments forecast, which can be obtained as a by-product of the system. This task can be accomplished by accumulating the gross amounts of unpaid invoices in a "due date" pattern. Such a summarization of maturing obligations may also be adjusted slightly by some experience factor to give effect to anticipated cash discounts. The resulting information would yield an important input in the intelligent management of cash. An illustration of such a report is found in Figure 11.7.

A perceptive systems designer may also be expected to provide summaries on a moving 12-month basis of gross liabilities that have been liquidated and discounts taken

Report #: AP-051	ACCOUNTS PAYABLE Projected Cash Requirements — Short Range					Date: 12/24/8X
Vendor Code	First Day	Second Day	Third Day	Fourth Day	Fifth Day	Beyond 5 Days
00359	.00	.00	250.00	7,527.15	.00	75.00
00526	15.00	397.00	.00	.00	3,369.82	.00
01684	750.00	.00	.00	.00	.00	.00
09807	.00	1,625.00	.00	.00	.00	193.00
18673	.00	.00	67.00	.00	.00	.00
ETC.						
ETC.						
Totals	1,019,301.25	852,316.14	931,062.27	1,403,677.12	540,461.83	1,185,501.69

Figure 11.7

as perceived in Figure 11.8. The application of regression analysis to these data will yield vital information for intermediate-range cash planning, performance analysis, and forecasting.

Discrepancy Reporting

Finally, as the computer performs the programmed audits of the documents supporting payment, discrepancies requiring vendor action may be brought to attention through the automatic preparation of "vendor advisory messages" ready for mailing. Such messages relating to price variances, quantity variances, freight discrepancies, overshipments, and the like may be stored in memory for instant recall when the occasion demands. Depending on the volume of such discrepancies, significant clerical savings might be effected by employing this technique. An example is shown in Figure 11.9.

ACCOUNTS PAYABLE SYSTEM

The primary functions of an accounts payable system, the source documents feeding it, the flow and timing of such documents, and the essential outputs expected of the system have been discussed. The arrangements for handling these data, both manually and in a large sophisticated operation requiring the utilization of a computer, are now considered.

Manual Operations

A very high degree of order and organization should be maintained in accounts payable, regardless of the volume of documents handled. Separation of manual functions should promote efficiency in document handling, transaction auditing, registration, filing, matching, and final disposition after payment.

Original documents are usually received, sorted, and classified at a single checkpoint, and their validity and originality are determined through a cursory check with the

ACCOUNTS PAYABLE CASH REQUIREMENTS FORECASTS.

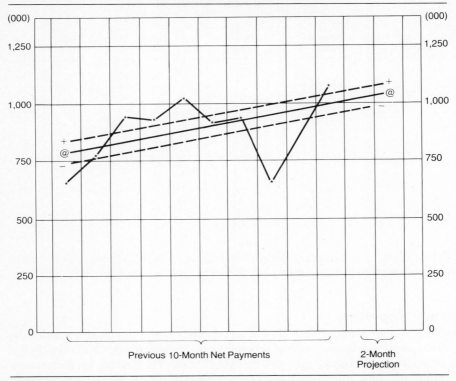

(Computer plots points: * = raw accumulated data, @ = calculated regression points, and + and − indicating standard deviations above and below the trend line)

Figure 11.8

invoice processing personnel. Receiving memoranda and purchase orders are filed without further action. If valid, the vendor's invoice is referred to a "document control" station, where the vendor's identification number (code) and an official document registration number are assigned to each invoice. Invoices are then routed to the next operation, where pertinent data are captured by either keypunching or automatic transmission to the data processing center. The documents come to rest in the invoice processor's files where they are ultimately matched to corresponding purchasing and receiving documents. At this point, discrepancies are resolved so that the document set is "payable." An auxiliary operation is generally necessary to maintain current vendor name, address, and credit information, and to control the assignment of vendor code numbers essential to automatic data processing. This operation may be performed through a separate program on a microcomputer and transferred to the main computer or entered directly to the main computer through a terminal.

ACCOUNTS PAYABLE VENDOR ADVISORY MESSAGE.*

```
        Towson Products, Inc.                    Date  8/15/8X
        Box 80 Midtown Station
        Lochapoka, NY

        Dear Sir:

            Your invoice No._____ dated _____ incorrectly includes
        freight charges of $_____.  Our Purchase Order_____ which
        you acknowledged (date)_____ specifies freight terms "FOB
        our plant."  Please submit a corrected invoice for immediate
        payment.

                            Sincerely,


                            Company Name
```

*Notice of discrepancies of all kinds; preprogrammed and selectively printed in appropriate situations.

Figure 11.9

When the system generates checks to pay the invoices, the resulting accounting distribution list is audited against the paid document sets, which are then placed in "paid" files for limited storage and quick reference. The accountant responsible for the distribution audit also prepares all necessary accounts payable journal vouchers. Daily payment is audited by an accountant who is responsible for control of accounts payable checks (used, unused, and voided). Interrelationship with the cashier's operation is also a responsibility of this accountant. For control effectiveness, it is important that these two activities be assigned to different individuals.

Data Processing

Master file maintenance and transaction processing in a central data processing facility are the responsibility of an independent EDP staff. Bringing the related master files into precise interface with a variety of input activity requires the programmer to solve all the matching, updating, voiding, and other file decisions previously performed by human processors. Computers then assume the complicated transaction audit functions and make the necessary payment and distribution decisions. As emphasized in Chapter 6, this type of consolidation of activities through computer processing requires that separation of duties be strictly defined and continually enforced.

Figure 11.10(a) demonstrates the preliminary manual handling. Figure 11.10(b) shows a series of computer runs for accomplishing the accounts payable objectives. By analyzing the processing steps in the computer portion of the flowchart, the student can visualize how computers have absorbed much of the manual burden of accounts payable processing.

In step (1), documents that affect the entity's liability to outsiders (i.e., invoices, freight bills, debit and credit memoranda) are summarized into some convenient machine-sensible form. Punched cards are used in this illustration for the sake of simplicity.

The other two groups of related documents (purchase orders and receiving reports) must enter the system to match and support invoices for payment. These forms would

TRADE ACCOUNTS PAYABLE PREPROCESSING OF DOCUMENTS.

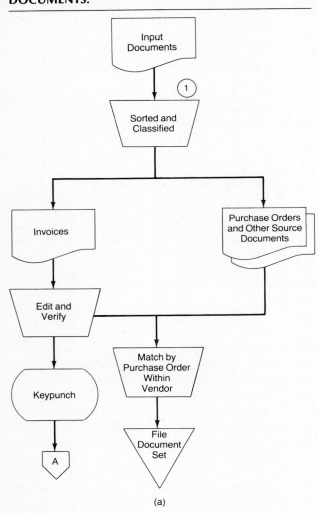

(a)

Figure 11.10(a)

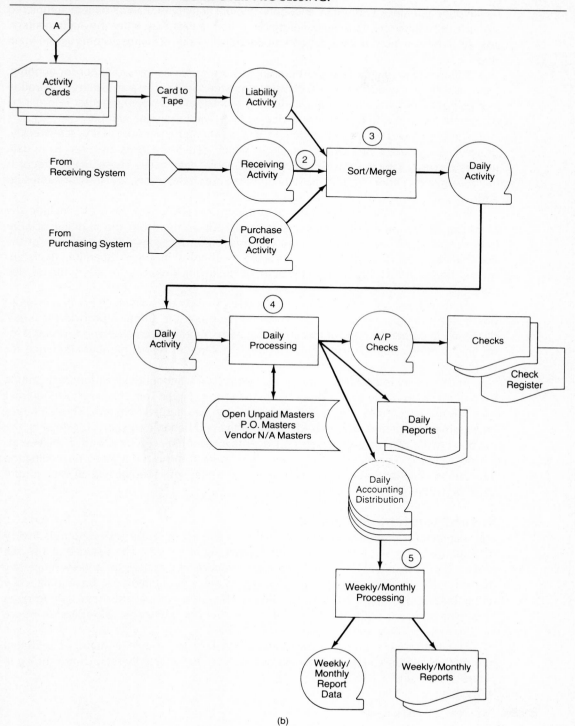

(b)

Figure 11.10(b)

be keypunched along with other accounts payable activity in manual or semiautomated systems. Alternatively, data representing these documents may enter the accounts payable system from interfacing independent purchasing and receiving systems as shown in step (2) of Figure 11.10.

If these basic payment-support documents are to be brought together for auditing, they must be arranged in some common sequence. Step (3) is a sort-merge operation that places all the documents (magnetic tape records at this point) together in order by document "type" within purchase order number within vendor number.

The sequenced records emerging from step (3) enter a periodic (daily, semiweekly, or weekly) computer processing run (4) in which activity records are used to update master records, which form the accounts payable data base. These master records include unpaid vendor invoices (liability), unfilled purchase orders, and vendor name and address data.

Some of the functions performed in this processing phase, step (4), include the matching of the principal documents (records) for comparison, the auditing of contract details (price, description, quantity, terms, etc.), decisions concerning any of the possible discrepancies previously discussed (variations in price, quantity, overshipments, freight terms, etc.), and selection of qualifying invoices for payment on due date.

An assortment of output emerges from step (4). Accounts payable checks constitute one of the principal products, along with a check register. Other report details (lines) discussed in earlier sections of this chapter may be randomly created and formatted for off-line printing. Step (5) sorts these report line items in report number sequence for printing.

Another very important output of the system is the accounting distribution resulting from accounts payable processing. As discussed in Chapter Ten, the purchase contract specifies the account to which each purchase is to be charged (debited). These charges are summarized periodically (weekly or monthly) and become the basis for debiting the various inventory, expense, asset, and overhead accounts resulting from liabilities incurred and paid. The weekly processing run (5) performs this function by producing the "accounting distribution reports" that serve as the basis for journalizing all expenditure cycle activities.

Record Content and Sequence

The matching of the master and activity files of the accounts payable system is a very delicate operation and requires the strict sequencing of records. The absence of any one of the records essential to normal processing requires the system to ignore completely the possibility of effecting a payment. Prolonged delay of payment can be automatically recognized and brought to the attention of the accounts payable manager through computer prepared notifications similar to the "vendor advisories" illustrated in Figure 11.9, which give apparent reason(s) for the delay.

The individual records on the various master files should contain all pertinent information relating to a purchase contract. Illustrations of activity records are shown in Figures 11.11 and 11.12.

ACTIVITY RECORDS (80-COLUMN CARDS).

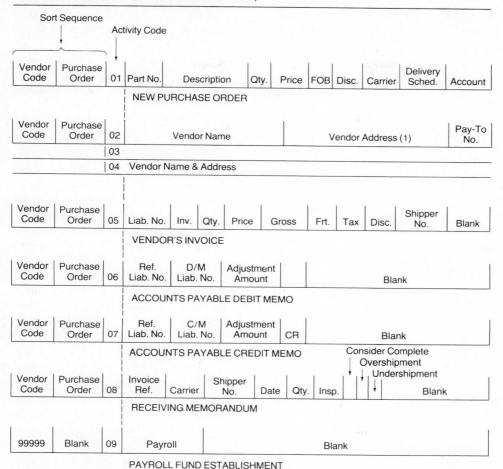

Figure 11.11

Systems Logic

Through interpretation of the system designer's diagrams, the computer programmer must convert to precise machine commands the step-by-step procedure normally followed by an invoice processing clerk in consummating a transaction. The degree of complexity, and perhaps even the methodology, will vary in each individual system depending on a variety of factors such as the size and nature of the business or industry. Each system tends to be tailored to the management needs of that company. The basic functions are universal, however, and are readily apparent.

MASTER RECORDS (MAGNETIC DISK).

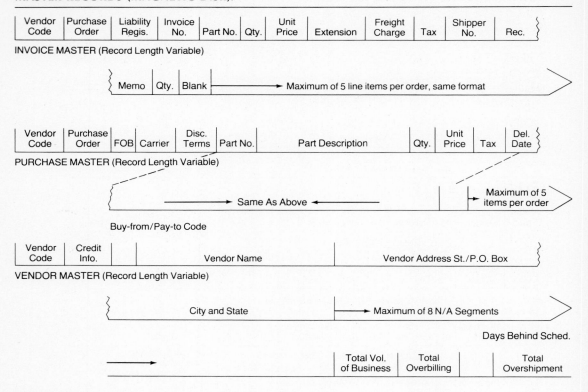

| Vendor Code | Purchase Order | Liability Regis. | Invoice No. | Part No. | Qty. | Unit Price | Extension | Freight Charge | Tax | Shipper No. | Rec. |

INVOICE MASTER (Record Length Variable)

| Memo | Qty. | Blank | Maximum of 5 line items per order, same format |

| Vendor Code | Purchase Order | FOB | Carrier | Disc. Terms | Part No. | Part Description | Qty. | Unit Price | Tax | Del. Date |

PURCHASE MASTER (Record Length Variable)

Same As Above

Maximum of 5 items per order

Buy-from/Pay-to Code

| Vendor Code | Credit Info. | | | Vendor Name | Vendor Address St./P.O. Box |

VENDOR MASTER (Record Length Variable)

City and State — Maximum of 8 N/A Segments

Days Behind Sched.

| Total Vol. of Business | Total Overbilling | Total Overshipment |

Figure 11.12

File Protection

The possibility of accident, deliberate sabotage, and natural disaster makes it necessary to provide a means of recovery in the event vital records are destroyed or damaged. A common practice is to maintain duplicate sets of such records in fireproof storage vaults inaccessible to unauthorized persons. The procedure of holding the master files and activity tapes for a completed cycle until current processing is accomplished and then replacing the older files with the freshly updated ones provides an effective way to recover from disaster. Should a destructive event occur during the current cycle (month, e.g.), accumulated activity could be processed against the previous month-end master files to bring the current cycle back up to the present, from which point normal processing could resume. See the grandparent-parent-child system discussed in an earlier chapter.

SUMMARY

This chapter narrates a reasonably sophisticated accounts payable system in general terms, presenting the important characteristics without too much detail. The reader should first attempt to visualize the "traffic pattern" of documents and events, along with the contact points and dependencies on other related subsystems. Next, he or she should focus on the action points, an understanding of the flow and the timing, and then the problems inherent in any accounts payable operation should easily follow. An understanding of the macro aspects of the system should permit accountants to adapt their thinking to any accounts payable situation, regardless of the degree of complexity.

Critical functions in the accounts payable system include: proper recording of all liabilities, prompt payments, and supporting documentation for each payment. The activities all require good documentation and a controlled flow of documents from one department to another. The effectiveness of this system also affects several other systems within the organization. Especially important is the interface with the cash and property control functions. These are considered in detail in later chapters.

SELECTED REFERENCES

Arthur Andersen & Company, *A Guide for Studying and Evaluating Internal Accounting Controls: Expenditure Cycle* (an in-house publication), January 1978.

Coopers & Lybrand, *Internal Control Reference Manual: Payments Cycle* (an in-house publication), 1978.

Ernst & Whinney, *Evaluating Internal Control, A Guide for Management and Directors* (an in-house publication), 1978.

Fielding, J. "Gearing Adjustment—What Is the Best Method?" *Accountancy* (May 1979): 63–69.

Madler, P. S. "Asset/Liability Management Today," *Bankers Monthly* (November 1979): 29–34.

Murdick, Robert G., and Joel E. Ross. *MIS in Action.* St. Paul: West Publishing Co., 1975.

Prince, Thomas R. *Information Systems for Management Planning and Control,* 3rd ed. Homewood, Ill.: Richard D. Irwin, Inc., 1975.

QUESTIONS

1. What internal and external documents support the payment process?
2. Whether accomplished manually or by the use of computers, what minimum audit steps should be accomplished prior to approval of a vendor's invoice for payment?
3. What kind of variations might one expect to find between the various documents supporting the payment transaction?
4. Under what circumstances might a vendor overshipment or overbilling be acceptable to the purchasing entity?
5. Why would the positioning of accounts payable under the aegis of the director of material be considered a control weakness? Under the procurement department manager?
6. Do open (unfilled) purchase orders constitute a liability for the purchasing entity? If so, what kind, and why?
7. Why is it necessary to maintain control over the vendor name and address file?
8. By what means might an accounts payable department reconcile price and quantity differences between an invoice and the purchasing document to make the invoice payable?
9. What procedures can be established to preclude the registration and payment of duplicate vendor invoices?
10. What kinds of information should management expect to receive from a well-organized and highly automated accounts payable system? From a simple manual system?

11. Summarize the role of accounts payable in the expenditure cycle and discuss its interfaces with other systems in the cycle.

12. What accounting entries normally result from the execution of the accounts payable function?

13. What control features should be established for handling accounts payable checks, used and unused?

14. How might accounts payable information contribute to short- and medium-range cash forecasts?

15. On what basis is accrued liability for transactions with trade creditors established? Should invoices not supported by receiving memoranda be considered legal debts?

16. A CPA learns that his client has paid a vendor twice for the same shipment, once based on the original invoice and once based on the monthly statement. Suggest control procedures that could have prevented this duplicate payment.

PROBLEMS

17. Systems Analysis and Recommendations

A very large West Coast manufacturing company opened an autonomous eastern division. Although the products and services it would produce under government contract were different from those of the West Coast operation, it moved all its paperwork systems intact from the California plant.

One of those systems was accounts payable. The California operation was designed in the mid-1940s by a management accountant who had *made* the system work, in spite of its obvious shortcomings, by simply overwhelming it with "invoice processing clerks." He was rewarded with a promotion to chief financial accountant at the new eastern division largely because of his familiarity with this key system, plus, of course, his natural ability as a manager.

Under the pressures of the new operation, it did not take long for the system to become hopelessly bogged down under the flood of new and different purchase contracts. At one point prior to remedial action, the average age of unpaid vendor invoices rose to 180 days, and an estimate of cash discounts lost the first year reached $400,000.

The "California system" was designed to physically bring the three payment support documents together in an invoice processing department. Physical matching was then followed by the transaction audit, accounting distribution, and finally by payment. The three documents entered the department in random sequence and were promptly filed as follows:

a. Purchase orders were filed separately in sequence by purchase order number within vendor code number.

b. Receiving reports were also separately filed in strict purchase order number sequence.

c. Vendor invoices were maintained in a third file, kept in alphabetical order by vendor name.

A crew of 20 invoice processors were assigned groups of vendor accounts. These processors arranged unpaid invoices in approximate order by due date so as to meet as many of the invoice payment terms as possible.

The process of bringing the document sets together was clumsy at best. A processor would take a stack of due invoices to the purchase order files and pull matching orders. Successful matches were then taken to the receiving report files in search of supporting receiving memoranda. Failing to find the latter, all other documents were returned to their respective files. Full three-document sets emerging from this search then became candidates for payment.

Aside from the wear and tear on official documents, many of which became badly frayed from repeated handling, the master files became the center of a mass of disorganized human traffic. Clerical time was unproductively spent waiting, pulling, and refiling. Standard production per processor (payable document sets) averaged about three to four per hour, totaling less than 600 successful payments per day for the unit. Current purchase order volume was averaging 1,200 per day and increasing. It became clear that the system could not handle the current volume of activity, even with twice the number of invoice processors presently employed. In fact, the marginal productivity of new personnel would surely decrease under such limited access to files.

The chief accountant finally appealed to all personnel in the payables department for fresh new ideas on how to speed up the operation. A $500 savings bond was offered for the best proposal, regardless of whether it was fully implemented.

Required:

Submit a proposal for solving the backlog problem, speeding up the matching process, and earning the allowable cash discounts.

18. Receiving Systems Analysis

Pucker Chemicals, Inc., followed a written policy of routinely accepting vendor shipments in excess of order quantity on high-volume-usage raw materials, provided the overshipment did not exceed 5 percent of the order quantity. On manufactured parts, assemblies, and other materials the tolerance limit was set at $50, since the company estimated that the cost of creating and processing the paperwork to reject and correct such violations would cost at least that much.

Certain suppliers became aware of the overshipment tolerance limits and consistently shipped and billed quantities in excess of the purchase agreements—many exceeding even the tolerance limits.

Company procedure required that the quantity field be blocked out on the copy of the purchase order provided to receiving. Management felt that this practice would assure accuracy in weights, counts, and measurements established at the receiving docks. As a result, however, overshipments were not usually detected until after the official receiving reports were issued. Detection and remedial action usually became the responsibility of accounts payable.

Although intimately aware of the company's policy, accounts payable personnel felt strongly that it was not procedurally correct to impose enforcement at the point of payment. At that late point, remedial action was limited to the issuance of accounts payable debit memoranda, thus precluding payment for the overshipped portion of transactions. This recourse was most unpopular, since buyers almost always conceded to vendor pressure and issued amendments to original purchase orders making the overshipments "legal." Accounts payable would then be forced to issue credit memoranda that were accorded the same routine handling for payment that a regular invoice received.

Receiving and accounts payable management agreed that Pucker's overshipment policy was, in effect, being completely ignored. In a joint memorandum to top management, they recommended the establishment of operating procedures that would ensure strict and uniform enforcement of the policy in the future. They concluded that a vendor's performance should properly be evaluated at the receiving dock, and that unacceptable overshipments should be rejected at that point and returned to the vendor at his expense.

Since inventory pricing procedures were adversely affected by the flood of "adjustment" documents (accounts payable debit and credit memos) distributed by accounts payable, the inventory manager gave his unqualified endorsement to what became known as the "clean transaction" movement.

Required:
    a. Comment on the company's policy requiring that order quantity *not* be made known to receiving personnel.
    b. In light of your answer to (a), how would you recommend handling vendor overshipments?
    c. What role should accounts payable, purchasing, and inventory operations play?

19. Audit Objectives of Accounts Payable Systems

Mincin, CPA, is the auditor of the Raleigh Corporation. Mincin is considering the audit work to be performed in the accounts payable area for the current year's engagement.

The prior year's working papers show that confirmation requests were mailed to 100 of Raleigh's 1,000 suppliers. The selected suppliers were based on Mincin's sample that was designed to select accounts with large dollar balances. A substantial number of hours were spent by Raleigh and Mincin resolving relatively minor differences between the confirmation replies and Raleigh's accounting records. Alternate audit procedures were used for those suppliers who did not respond to the confirmation requests. *(AICPA adapted)*

Required:
    a. Identify the accounts payable audit objectives that Mincin must consider in determining the audit procedures to be followed.
    b. Identify situations when Mincin should use accounts payable confirmations and discuss whether Mincin is required to use them.
    c. Discuss why the use of large dollar balances as the basis for selecting accounts payable for confirmation might not be the most efficient approach and indicate what more efficient procedures could be followed when selecting accounts payable for confirmation.

20. Internal Auditors Role in Payables Control

You are the director of internal auditing at a university. Recently you met with the manager of administrative data processing and expressed the desire to establish a more effective interface between the two departments.

Subsequently, the manager of data processing requested *your views and help on a new computerized accounts payable system being developed.* The manager recommended that internal auditing assume line responsibility for auditing suppliers' invoices prior to payment. The manager also requested that internal auditing make suggestions during development of the system, assist in its installation, and approve the completed system after making a final review.

Required:

State how you would respond to the administrative data processing manager, giving the reason that you would accept or reject each of the following:

a. The recommendation that your department be responsible for the preaudit of suppliers's invoices.

b. The request that you make suggestions during development of the system.

c. The request that you assist in the installation of the system and approve the system after making a final review.

21. Systems Analysis and Recommendations

ConSport Corporation is a regional wholesaler of sporting goods. The systems flowchart (Figure 11.13) and the following description present ConSport's cash distribution system.

a. The accounts payable department approves for payment all invoices (I) for the purchase of inventory. Invoices are matched with the purchase requisitions (PR), purchase orders (PO), and receiving reports (RR). The accounts payable clerks focus on vendor name and skim the documents when they are combined.

b. When all the documents for an invoice are assembled, a two-copy disbursement voucher (DV) is prepared and the transaction is recorded in the voucher register (VR). The disbursement voucher and supporting documents are then filed alphabetically by vendor.

c. A two-copy journal voucher (JV) that summarizes each day's entries in the voucher register is prepared daily. The first copy is sent to the general ledger department, and the second copy is filed in the accounts payable department by date.

d. The vendor file is searched daily for the disbursement vouchers of invoices that are due to be paid. Both copies of disbursement vouchers that are due to be paid are sent to the treasury department along with the supporting documents. The cashier prepares a check for each vendor, signs the check, and records it in the check register (CR). Copy 1 of the disbursement voucher is attached to the check copy and filed in check number order in the treasury department. Copy 2 and the supporting documents are returned to the accounts payable department and filed alphabetically by vendor.

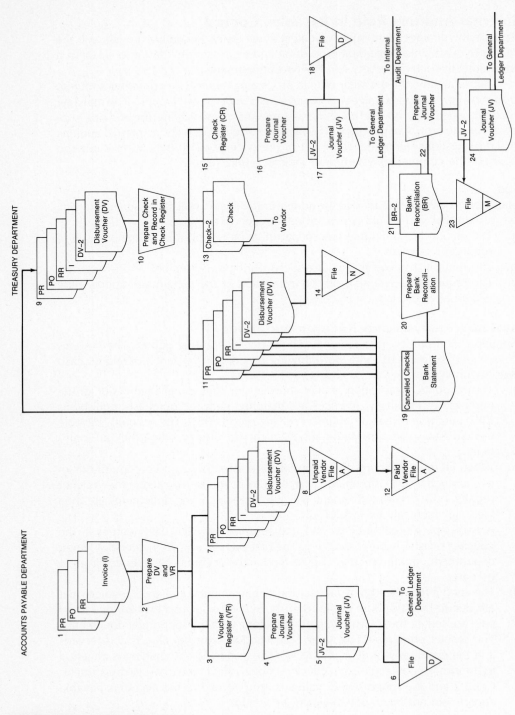

Figure 11.13

e. A two-copy journal voucher that summarizes each day's checks is prepared. Copy 1 is sent to the general ledger department and copy 2 is filed in the treasury department by date.

f. The cashier receives the monthly bank statement with canceled checks and prepares the bank reconciliation (BR). If an adjustment is required as a consequence of the bank reconciliation, a two-copy journal voucher is prepared. Copy 1 is sent to the general ledger department. Copy 2 is attached to copy 1 of the bank reconciliation and filed by month in the treasury department. Copy 2 of the bank reconciliation is sent to the internal audit department. *(IMA adapted)*

Required:

ConSport Corporation's cash disbursement system has some weaknesses. Review the cash disbursement system and for each weakness in the system:

a. Identify where the weakness exists by using the reference number that appears to the left of each symbol.

b. Describe the nature of the weakness.

c. Make a recommendation on how to correct the weakness.

Use the following format in preparing your answer:

Reference Number	Nature of Weakness	Recommendation to Correct Weakness

22. Accounts Payable Systems Design

Tralor Corporation manufactures and sells several different lines of small electric components. Its Internal Audit Department completed an audit of the expenditure cycle for the company. Part of the audit involved a review of the internal accounting controls for payables including the controls over the authorization of transactions, the accounting for transactions, and the protection of assets. The following comments appear in the internal audit staff's working papers.

a. Routine purchases are initiated by user activities on authorized purchase requests. Such purchases are actually made by the purchasing department using prenumbered purchase orders approved by authorized purchasing agents. The original of the five-part purchase order goes to the vendor, a copy is retained in purchasing, a copy is sent to the user department, a copy is sent to the receiving department to be used as a receiving report, and a copy is sent to the accounts payable section of the accounting department.

b. Because of complex technical and performance criteria, purchases of specialized goods and services are negotiated directly between the user department and the vendor. Established procedures require that the specialist-user and the purchasing department approve invoices for such purchases prior to recording and payment. Strict budgetary control of such purchases is maintained at the specialist-user level.

c. The accounts payable section maintains a list of persons in purchasing authorized to approve purchase orders and of persons in operating departments authorized to approve invoices for specialized purchases. The list was last updated 2 years ago and is seldom used by accounts payable clerks.

d. All vendor invoices are numbered upon receipt and recorded in a prevoucher register. The register is annotated to indicate the dates invoices involving special purchases are forwarded to operating departments for approval and the dates they are returned. Review of the register indicated that there were seven open invoices for special purchases that had been forwarded to operating departments for approval over 30 days ago and had not yet been returned.

e. Prior to making entries in accounting records, a transaction audit is performed by an accounts payable clerk. This involves matching the accounts payable copy of the purchase order with a copy of a properly authorized receiving report and the vendor's invoice, or obtaining departmental approval of invoices for special purchases. Other aspects of the transaction audit involve checking the mathematical accuracy of all documents and determining the appropriate accounting distribution.

f. After invoices are recorded in the approved voucher register, they are filed in alphabetical order. Unpaid invoices are processed for payment on the fifth and twentieth of each month, and all cash discounts are taken whether or not earned.

g. Supporting documents are canceled upon payment by an authorized person in the treasurer function who signs the checks. Payments are made based on original documents only.

h. Prenumbered blank checks are kept in a locked safe and access is limited to authorized persons. Other documents and records maintained by the accounts payable section are readily accessible to all persons assigned to the section and to others in the accounting function. *(IMA adapted)*

Required:

Review the eight comments that appear in the internal audit staff's working papers. Determine whether the internal audit staff's findings indicate that a strength or weakness exists in the controls of the expenditure cycle.

a. For each internal control *strength* identified, explain how the described procedure contributes toward achieving good authorization, accounting, or asset protection controls.

b. For each internal control *weakness* identified, explain why it is a weakness and present a recommendation to correct the weakness.

Use the following format to present your answer.

Comment Number	Strength(s) or Weakness(es)	Explanation as to Why Finding Is a Strength or Weakness	Recommendation to Correct Weakness

23. Flowchart Concepts

The following illustrates a manual system for executing purchases and cash disbursements transactions. *(IMA adapted).*

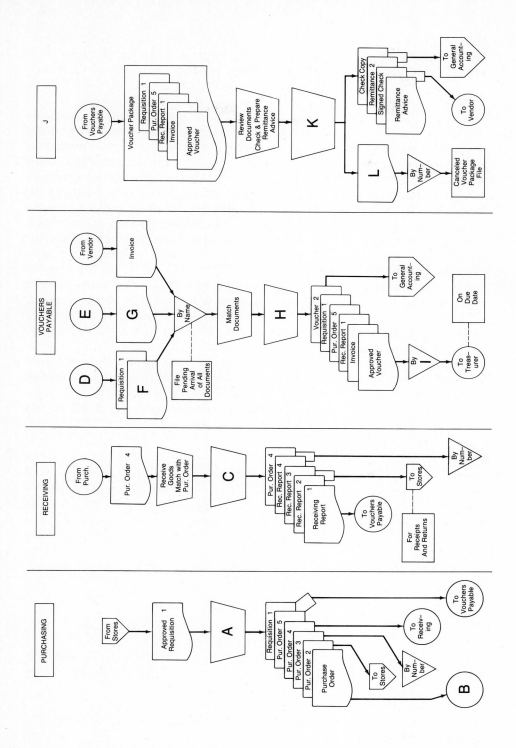

Required:

Indicate what each of the letters (A) through (L) represents. Do not discuss adequacies or inadequacies in the system of internal control.

CASES

24. The manner in which normal trade accounts payable are liquidated by the Apogee Company (Appendix C) leaves it dangerously vulnerable to fraud. Among other serious weaknesses, the company maintains no formal and accurate filing system for assembling documents to support the payment process; for making the necessary accounting distributions resulting from payment; and for determining (accruing) open liability at period-end. Cash discounts are largely ignored, and there is a general disregard for basic internal controls to prevent financial improprieties.

    Applying the principles presented in this chapter (and other sources), design a full-scale accounts payable system tailored to the needs of Apogee Company.

25. Figure D.3, Exhibit D, outlines the purchasing, receiving, and accounts payable procedures of the Bubbling Stone Beverage Co. Judging from the sequence of events described in the case narrative, would you conclude that all traditional accounts payable functions are properly controlled and effectively accomplished? Justify your conclusion.

    Speculate on why the company vested its chief financial officer (treasurer) with the responsibility for making the "go ahead" decision on all payments of legitimate (documented) vendor claims.

    Characterize the role of the accounts payable function in the routine liquidation of trade debts.

SECTION

CHAPTER TWELVE

Inventory Control Systems

Webster defines logistics as the "science dealing with the procurement, maintenance, and transportation (movement) of . . . materials, facilities, and personnel."[1] Flanked by the procurement and marketing functions, the inventory system, as it relates to materials, resides at the heart of logistics management.

Effective management of materials, from production to customer, exerts an important influence on product costs and profits. Just as important, materials management often requires the commitment of substantial amounts of corporate resources. Material costs may constitute 50 percent or more of total product costs in manufacturing concerns. In wholesale and retail establishments, "merchandising costs" may include an even higher proportion of material costs. With the exclusion of service-oriented businesses, we may generalize that inventory management is an area of primary concern to all business firms involved in supplying goods to the market.

Casting the whole approach to information systems analysis within an industrial framework requires that we consider two phases of inventory management: raw materials and finished goods. Figure 12.1 may assist in visualizing the physical flow of materials through an organization.

Several different types of inventories may be maintained separately in large industrial organizations. The more common ones include:

1. Raw materials, the basic ingredient for the company's finished product
2. Purchased parts and assemblies from outside suppliers, the component parts of the finished product
3. Work-in-process, representing the finished product, with accumulated costs at various stages of completion
4. Finished goods, complete and available for sale
5. Operating (factory) supplies used in support of production operations
6. Small tools and equipment used in the production process, which are ultimately expensed to the end product as overhead
7. Office supplies and equipment

Inventory elements that represent the most significant financial investment consist of physical products that are (1) held for sale in the normal course of business, (2)

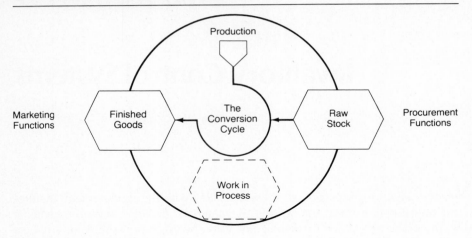

Figure 12.1

consumed in the production of marketable end products, and (3) expensed or capitalized in the manufacturing process. Although this chapter focuses mainly on those elements, the physical controls and flow of financial information may follow the same general pattern in each of the preceding situations.

OBJECTIVES OF THE INVENTORY SYSTEM

The overriding objective of any inventory system is to provide logistic support to the production and marketing functions with the lowest practicable investment in inventories while at the same time generating timely and reliable financial information. In regard to inventory the accounting information system should be designed to provide reasonable assurance that:

1. Inventory transactions are recorded and processed in accordance with management's general or specific authorization.
2. Inventory transactions are recorded in a manner (a) to permit preparation of financial statements in conformity with generally accepted accounting principles or any other criteria applicable to such statements and (b) to maintain accountability for inventory assets.
3. Access to inventory assets is permitted only in conformity with management's authorization.
4. The recorded accountability for inventory assets is compared with the existing inventory assets at reasonable intervals, and appropriate action is taken with respect to any differences.
5. Data required to make appropriate business decisions are available on a timely basis.[2]

TYPES OF TRANSACTIONS

To facilitate an understanding of the inventory system, we can categorize inventory transactions into three different types:[3]

1. Transactions affecting inventory quantities
2. Transactions affecting inventory costs
3. Transactions affecting other inventory master file information

Of course, by definition, inventory represents a quantity of physical items on hand. In a manufacturing concern, such items are often classified as raw materials, goods in process, and finished goods. Both purchases and sales represent transactions that affect inventory quantity.

Transactions that affect inventory cost are somewhat more complex since they depend on the company's cost system and pricing method. For example, costing will be affected by whether a company uses an actual or a standard cost system. In addition, factors such as obsolescence and damaged goods affect inventory costs.

Transactions that affect other inventory master file information would include the addition of a new finished good and its related bill of raw materials, changes in inventory codes, and replacement of raw materials with substitutes.

SOURCE DOCUMENTS

As previously mentioned, at least three major inventories must be considered and separately accounted for in any manufacturing environment. Although the forms and records employed to execute the material control procedures are industry designed, they tend to conform to a standard functional pattern. These patterns are graphically illustrated in Figure 12.2.

Based on the illustrated analysis, we can observe at least seven basic kinds of information (numbered 1 through 7 in Figure 12.2) emanating from other related organizations that impact the inventory system, plus three types that are indigenous to the inventory system (numbered 8 through 10 in Figure 12.2) which impact other systems.

Raw Materials

The procurement function becomes involved in inventory operations at both ends of the ordering spectrum. It is cued by requests to purchase that routinely emanate in the raw material inventory cycle as a by-product of automatic stock status analysis. As the purchase contract is consummated, the resulting purchase order is introduced into the inventory system to provide "on-order" and "expected delivery date" for inventory management. Purchased raw materials enter the entity at the receiving docks, where a memorandum of receipt is issued. The material is routed to raw stock stores accompanied by this receiving memorandum. On the basis of this document, physical quantities are updated. A facsimile copy of this document is shown in Figure 12.3.

The warehouse, or raw stock stores area, may be physically separated from the inventory control organization. In such cases, the warehouse manager may be required to provide a daily materials-received report from which input data are extracted for

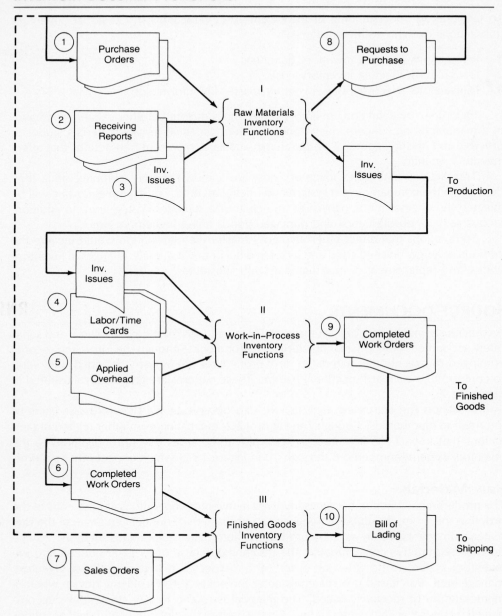

Figure 12.2

RECEIVING MEMORANDUM.

	REC BY	RECEIVED FROM	DESCRIPTION	CARRIER	PRO NUMBER	WEIGHT	PPD / COLL	KEY-REC NO.	DATE REC
1						$		SHORT □ DAMAGE □	

	PART NUMBER	DESCRIPTION	QUANTITY	UOM	P.O. NUMBER	L.C. NUMBER	SCHEDULED DELIVERY DATE

REMARKS: **CALIFORNIA**

(left margin vertical text: INVENTORY CONTROL)

Figure 12.3

computer updating of the inventory master records. Alternatively, validated copies of the receiving memoranda may be keypunched, or otherwise converted to machine-sensible input media, for the updating process.

Work-in-Process

Moving from the raw material area to the production shops, the withdrawal of raw materials for consumption in the production process may be accomplished in a variety of ways, but never without the support of an authorizing document. Such a document may vary from a simple "issue ticket," as illustrated in Figure 12.4, to an elaborate multipart stores requisition designed to serve a number of subsidiary and related functions. The importance of this document is apparent: It authorizes reductions in raw materials inventory and serves as the basis for posting raw material usage and cost data to work orders in the production process. It also serves as a transmittal receipt to control the movement of materials between stores and the various requisitioning departments.

The introduction of direct labor and overhead into the production process is fully discussed in Chapter Thirteen and will not be repeated here. It may be appropriate to point out that work-in-process accounts are normally charged with "standard" material quantities and prices, standard labor hours and rates, and standard overhead applied on

ISSUE TICKET.

SUPPLIES REQUISITION

RUSSELL

DATE OF ISSUE: _____

LOCATION: _____ (Mill)

DEPARTMENT: _____

COST CENTER NO.: ☐☐☐☐☐

STORE NO.: _____

☐ Budget No. _____
☐ Work Order No. _____
☐ Garment Merchandise
☐ Packing Supplies
☐ Machine Supplies
☐ Mill Supplies
☐ Office Supplies

QUANTITY WANTED	SPECIFICATION AND DESCRIPTION	QUANTITY ISSUED	STANDARD PRICE UNIT	COST	TOTAL
				$	$
GRAND TOTAL					$

Departmental Supervisor Approval: _____

Material Received By: _____

Material Issued By: _____

ROUTE: White-Cost Dept.; Yellow-Stores; Pink-Dept. Supervisor

COST DEPARTMENT USE ONLY:

Costing: _____ Date _____

Extended: _____ Date _____

Verified: _____ Date _____

Account Distribution: _____

Figure 12.4

a predetermined usage basis. Variances from such standards are extracted for management consideration at the beginning, leaving work-in-process to be valued on the basis of standard costs. The balance of work-in-process inventory at any time, therefore, is the sum of all standard costs accumulated against unfinished work orders in the production shops.

Finished Goods

Completed products arrive at the finished goods storage area accompanied by completed and fully "costed" work orders. Such documents provide the basis for updating the finished goods inventory accounts. An example of a completed work order is shown in Figure 12.5.

Sales orders are often accompanied by *packing slips,* which authorize the release of finished products for packaging and subsequent shipment to customers. This document may have many names (e.g., order packing list, shipping assembly list), and it may appear in a variety of forms. Its basic purposes, however, are (1) to authorize the assembly and release of specified inventory items to shipping, (2) to effect a reduction in quantity and total value of appropriate items reflected in the inventory master records, (3) to serve as a transmittal receipt between the finished goods storage area and the shipping dock, and (4) to support the billing function in the preparation of customer invoices.

COMPLETED WORK ORDER.

JOB COST SHEET

RUSSELL CORPORATION   KNIT APPAREL DIVISION

Job Order No. _12345_ Date Order Received _9-2-86_
Item _AMPHIB BLIVIT_ Date Delivery Promised _9-27-86_
For _ABC COMPANY_ Date Job Completed _9-23-86_

Direct Material			Direct Labor			Factory Overhead		
Date	Reference	Amount	Date	Reference	Amount	Date	Rate	Amount
9/2		350 00	9/3		80 00	9/23	30% DL	153 00
9/11	(Materials Requisition Number)	25 00	9/4	(Payroll and Labor Distribution Cross-refer.)	80 00		(Predetermined Aug. Rate)	
9/2		8 00	9/7		160 00			
			9/8		20 00			
			9/10		70 00			
			9/23		100 00			
TOTAL		383 00	TOTAL		510 00	TOTAL		

Summary

Direct Material... 383 00
Direct Labor 510 00
Factory Overhead.. 153 00
   Total... $1,046 00
Number of Units.. 1
Unit Cost $1,046 00

Figure 12.5

In more sophisticated information systems, the standard *bill of lading* form may emerge as an automatic by-product of the inventory updating process. This document is required by law when common carriers are used to transport goods between buyer and seller. Since the form is essentially a shipping contract, we shall defer its discussion to the chapter on shipping systems.

SYSTEM CONFIGURATION

We turn our attention now to the problem of organizing the various operations that constitute the inventory system. The arrangements contained in the following illustrations are intended to represent normal data flows inherent in any large industrial firm so that we may observe how they are handled, controlled, and processed. By the term *system configuration* we allude not only to the complex of computer, peripheral, and auxiliary equipment that are essential in modern inventory processing systems, but also to the human organization for handling material control input and its preparation and transmission for computer processing.

Although many of the descriptions and examples that follow are assumed to exist in a modern computer environment, the reader should try to visualize how the same operations might be accomplished manually, or with microcomputer systems, in a smaller situation. In this section the approach taken envisions a large-scale material control organization, separate and apart from warehouses and plants, whose responsibilities include (1) managing the overall material logistics function, (2) planning, controlling, handling, and processing inventory-related documents and activities, and (3) reporting vital inventory information to corporate management.

Efficiency in a large inventory system demands a high degree of order and organization. The combination of a broad variety of inventory items and the tremendous volume and randomness of inventory activity invites chaos in the absence of such order.

Manual Handling

Most reliable information systems preface the data processing function with a careful analysis and preconditioning of the input data. In Figure 12.6 the reader can visualize a random inflow of inventory activity into a control station where it is classified, sorted, registered, coded, and routed to personnel specialized in handling each particular category of transactions. The variety of inventory transactions arriving at inventory document control includes requests to purchase, purchase orders, receiving memoranda, raw material requisitions, inventory adjustments, costs and standards, completed production work orders, sales orders, packing assembly lists, bills of lading, and returned sales notices. In accordance with detailed procedures, these activity records are redistributed to the appropriate inventory responsibility groups.

At designated work stations specialized inventory clerical personnel administer the procedurally prescribed processing, obtain necessary authorizations, apply appropriate material codes, indicate correct accounting distribution, and ''condition'' the activity for input into the inventory-updating computer runs. On the finished goods side of the operation, specialists are performing similar tasks for the inventory activities.

Last, all inventory-related transactions are converted to machine-sensible input media for transmission to the computer center, where inventory master records are maintained. Prior to the advent of computers in commercial data processing, all processing subsequent to this point was accomplished manually through the use of specially designed accounting machines, or electromechanically through the use of punched card equipment that preceded the computer. Although processing techniques have changed dramatically, the fundamentals of the inventory system have remained fairly constant.

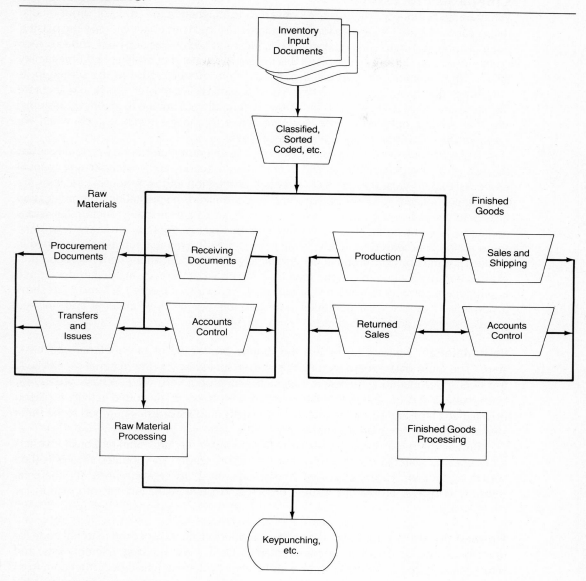

Figure 12.6

Computer Processing

When inventory master records are converted to magnetic tape, disk, or drum media, the visual card-form files are no longer required. Still the need to actually *see* the master, not as it appeared on the last "status" report but as it is *today,* has persisted. Video screen computer access devices have solved this problem. This kind of on-line, real-time facility enables the inventory clerk to call a particular item master record to the screen in its current condition, and to read it as one would a printed card master. Quick and accurate decisions are thus facilitated. This technique is certainly not unique to inventory systems. We shall see it employed in an even more active role in the revenue cycle when we consider the marketing system in Chapter Fifteen.

Today, the effective operation of a large-scale inventory information system requires the use of a computer. The sheer volume of transactions would render any manual approach expensive and inefficient. Although production and warehousing facilities are often decentralized, record keeping must be centralized, necessitating communication links between individual facilities and the centralized data processing function. Divisions and branches are connected to central control organizations by ordinary telephone transmission lines leased from telephone companies. The manual functions described in Figure 12.6 may be performed at geographically dispersed locations with microcomputers that automatically transmit the data to the central data processing department. Such equipment is commonly used throughout many industries. Figures 12.7 and 12.8 show a condensed overview of computer configurations for the raw material and finished goods inventory control systems.

Raw Material   Figure 12.9 breaks the routine processing of raw material into basic steps. The input data stream feeding this system includes: (1) raw material receipts, (2) transfers to production, (3) issues (openings) to production, (4) purchase orders, (5) accounting cost distribution, and (6) inventory adjustments. The coded activity is placed on magnetic tape and sorted by material code (part number or stock number) in the same sequence as the raw material master file.

Processing run 1 updates the raw material master file, and simultaneously extracts a current raw material inventory position, or status, report. The updated master is then sorted by location (warehouse site) and rerun (run 2) to create reports summarizing receipts, transfers, production issues, orders, and other management information for each location.

Finished Goods   At this point, the finished product code replaces the material code (or raw stock code) as the major focus of interest. Daily sales, packing assembly lists, and returned sales are accumulated weekly and converted to magnetic tape. Other data from production are similarly processed. These weekly transactions are sorted by style (finished product number) and processed against the inventory master file to produce an updated inventory master file in the first processing run (see Figure 12.10). In run 2, a style master file containing all pertinent qualitative and descriptive information and a style cost master are matched with the updated (quantity) inventory master file to produce an "extended, costed style master." This tape now includes all quantitative, qualitative, and

INVENTORY CONTROL CONFIGURATION—RAW MATERIAL.

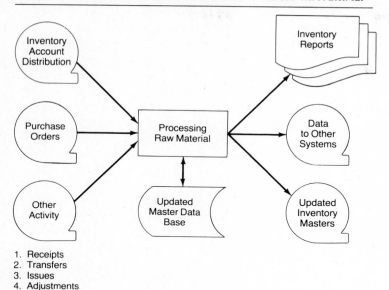

1. Receipts
2. Transfers
3. Issues
4. Adjustments
5. Returns

Figure 12.7

cost data pertaining to each style or finished product. Finally, the costed style master is sorted by division location and used to process the finished goods inventory reports previously discussed.

As can be seen in the configuration diagram for finished goods (Figure 12.10), accumulated inventory activity is passed through several more computer runs to produce special information required by company management (i.e., transaction audit listing, aged inventory, production for customer order, and free-for-sale inventory).

The processing logic is similar for that of the raw material system and will not be simulated here. In fact, all computer processing logic consists essentially of (1) accessing and matching various input files, (2) updating data base files, (3) performing routine decisions concerning disposition, recalculation, procedural adjustments, and so on, (4) extracting information for reports, (5) sorting and resequencing interim data, and (6) preparing updated files for reintroduction in subsequent processings.

ACCOUNTING CONTROLS

We have observed the many organizational interfaces that impact on the inventory information system: the replenishment (inflow) relationships through purchasing, receiving, accounts payable, and production and the depleting (outflow) relationships through

INVENTORY CONTROL CONFIGURATION—FINISHED GOODS.

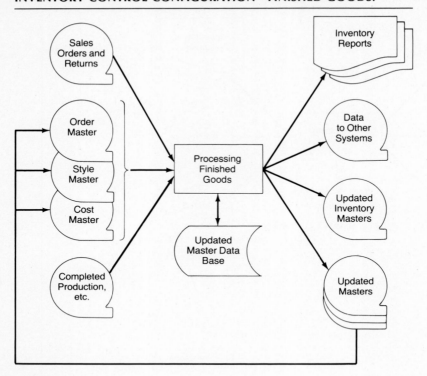

Figure 12.8

production, marketing, and shipping. Inherent in all these relationships is the standard control principle of "separation of handling and recording."

Throughout these relationships several salient principles generally prevail. First, inventory is created in the expenditure cycle through the acquisition of raw materials, parts, and supplies. Although the inventory system accepts and executes the custodial function, control in terms of costs and total financial investment is exercised by other organizations.

Second, in the conversion cycle where raw materials are transformed into finished products through the application of direct labor and overhead, both physical and cost controls are relinquished to production, payroll, and cost accounting. We may consider the application of raw materials in the production process as an intermediary transfer of value from raw stock to finished goods inventory. Although minor inventory reductions may result from inventory management decisions to scrap, write off, sell at a loss, or otherwise dispose of obsolete raw materials, the major flow is what must be observed and controlled.

Third, finished goods inventory is reduced in final analysis through the efforts of the

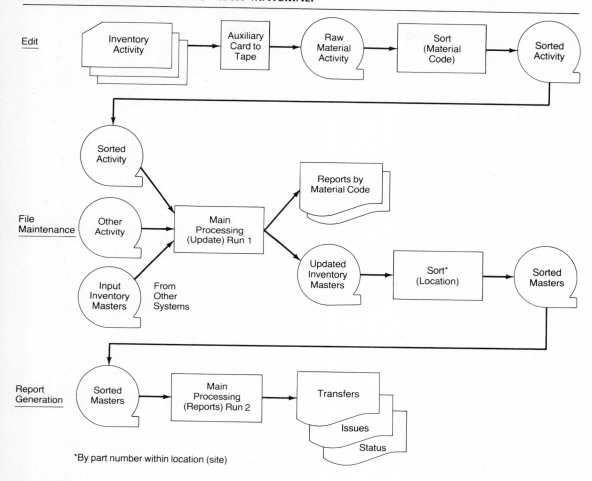

Edit

Inventory Activity → Auxiliary Card to Tape → Raw Material Activity → Sort (Material Code) → Sorted Activity

File Maintenance

Sorted Activity, Other Activity, Input Inventory Masters, From Other Systems → Main Processing (Update) Run 1 → Reports by Material Code / Updated Inventory Masters → Sort* (Location) → Sorted Masters

Report Generation

Sorted Masters → Main Processing (Reports) Run 2 → Transfers / Issues / Status

*By part number within location (site)

Figure 12.9

sales function. Although cost/price information may be provided by the inventory system, the actual charge to cost of goods sold is generally executed by the billing and collection function.

Fourth, overall management policy governs total investment in inventory. Although materials management plays a vital role in the critical balancing of inventory size and cost, it by no means exercises final control.

Finally, effective inventory control is comparative and relative, not absolute. The maintenance of accurate inventory records alone does not achieve inventory control. It is achieved through the activities of human beings exercising varying degrees of judgment and experience in the performance of their assigned tasks. Rules and procedures, al-

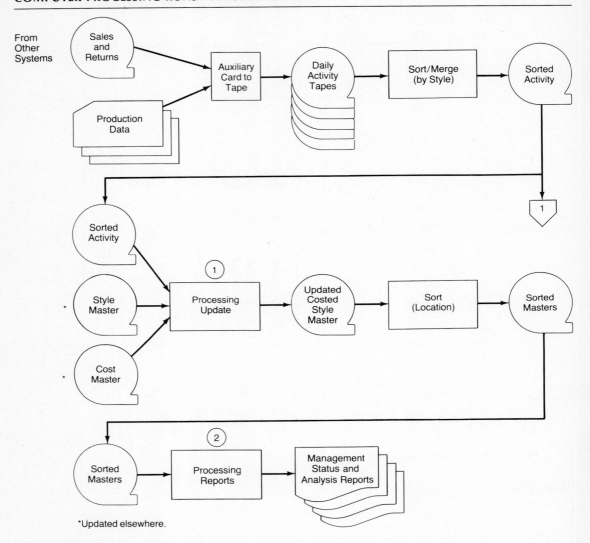

Figure 12.10

though essential, merely guide these individuals in making sound evaluations and decisions.

To examine controls in more detail, we shall discuss a computerized inventory system next. Each type of control—input, processing, or output—will be considered separately.

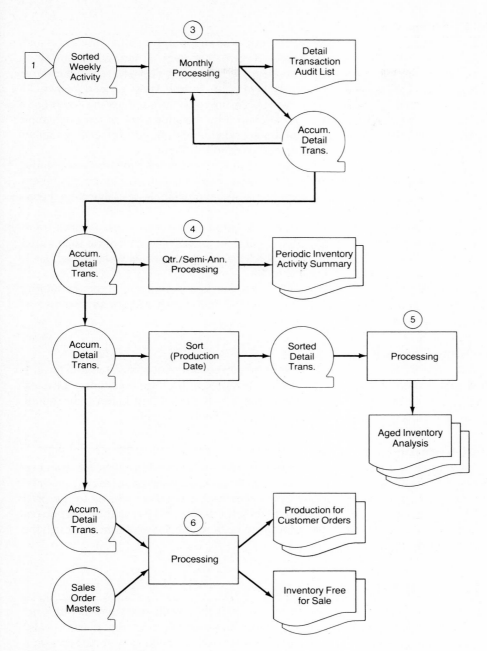

Figure 12.10 (cont'd)

Input Controls

Input controls include controls over (1) authorization of input, (2) input conversion and code verification, (3) data movement, and (4) error handling.[4] There are a variety of methods to control the authorization of input. The use of approval procedures by supervisory personnel represents a primary inventory control. These procedures would include requiring that batches of transactions be approved before processing and requiring that file maintenance transactions be approved by the supervisor of the originating department. Preprinted sequentially numbered documents provide for accountability and thus represent another control over authorization of input.

Input conversion and code verification represent a second classification of input controls. These would include such controls as scanning of documents for completeness and errors, key verification when data are converted into machine-readable form, batch controls, and batch balancing.

Data movement, the third classification of input controls, represents controls over the transporting of data between departments and processing steps. Controls in this area include the logging of batches, the use of batch transmittal forms with sequential batch numbers, and the calculation of control totals.

The fourth area of input controls, error handling, is concerned with the monitoring and handling of errors. These controls include error monitoring and the generation and logging of error control totals.

Processing Controls

Processing controls in an inventory system generally consist of control totals and reasonableness tests. Control totals are used in the processing of inventory quantities, physical inventory, and file maintenance. Reasonableness tests may be instituted over routine inventory processing as well as periodic physical inventory counts.

Output Controls

Output controls in inventory may be categorized into two broad areas: review of processing results and distribution of output. The accounting department should review processing reports to ascertain that balances appear reasonable, that balances tie to the prior period closing balances, and that totals tie to the general ledger. Only authorized personnel should receive distribution of the output. Such control can be established through the use of a report distribution manual.

INVENTORY INTERFACE

As noted earlier, the inventory system interfaces with a wide spectrum of other accounting information subsystems. Many transactions that impact on inventory also have a direct impact on some other area of the overall accounting system. For example, purchases are inextricably tied to the accounts payable system. Figure 12.11 illustrates the interface of the inventory system with the other accounting information subsystems.

INVENTORY INTERFACE.

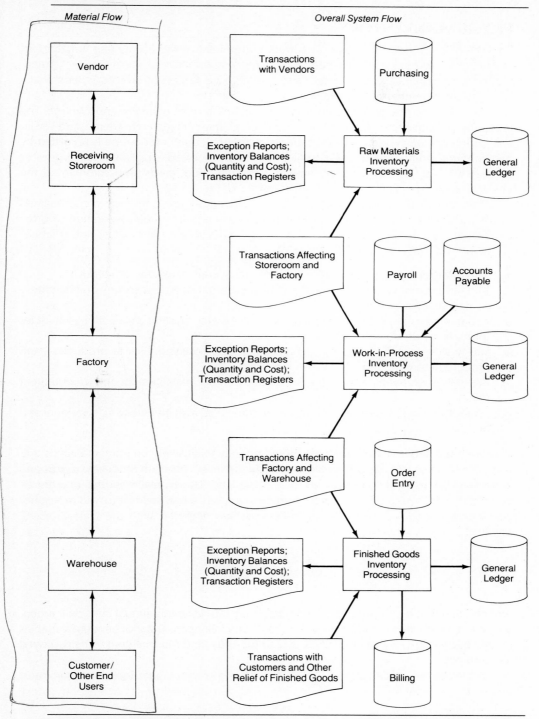

Source: AICPA, *Audit Approaches for a Computerized Inventory System* (New York: American Institute of Certified Public Accountants, 1980) Copyright © 1980 by the American Institute of Certified Public Accountants, Inc. Adapted by permission.

Figure 12.11

PHYSICAL INVENTORY

Physical inventory counts are an important component of the accounting function. Of course, all companies utilizing a periodic inventory system take physical counts. Companies on a perpetual inventory system also take physical counts of inventory periodically to verify their perpetual records.

An accurate physical inventory count requires proper planning and control. The company must institute physical count procedures that will generate the desired result. In a computerized system, when a count is made, the count information is recorded by personnel on prenumbered cards, which are then processed. The computer processes the batch totals, checks for duplicates and missing count cards, and summarizes the physical inventory. This process is illustrated in Figure 12.12.

The responsibility for maintaining optimum inventory levels imposes a complicated set of variables on inventory management. The task requires the amelioration of often conflicting organizational goals, needs, timing, and safety requirements, and financial concerns such as:

1. Minimization of investment in inventory (an overall company concern)
2. Minimization of warehousing and handling costs (an overall company and inventory management concern)
3. Maintenance of proper inventory levels to service normal production schedules (primarily a production concern)
4. Safety stock requirements to cushion unforeseen catastrophies (a production and procurement concern)
5. Prevention of inventory obsolescence (an inventory management and procurement concern)
6. Establishment of economic ordering quantities (EOQ) (an inventory management and procurement concern)

Sophisticated inventory systems should not rely exclusively on human analysis and response to these variables. They should utilize "built-in" decision models to detect and automatically respond to critical inventory balances. The typical response may be an automatic request to purchase a predetermined quantity when an inventory item reaches an unacceptably low level. This quantity may be computed with the classical EOQ formula:

$$EOQ = \sqrt{\frac{2(C \times D)}{R}}$$

where C equals the cost per purchase order processed, D equals annual units demanded, and R equals the inventory carrying cost rate. The values for the independent variables in the equation are established only after careful study, and must be constantly reviewed for currency.

Although this procedure may help resolve the how-much question, the system must first make the when-to-order decision. This decision is based on (1) average inventory

INVENTORY COUNT PROCESSING.

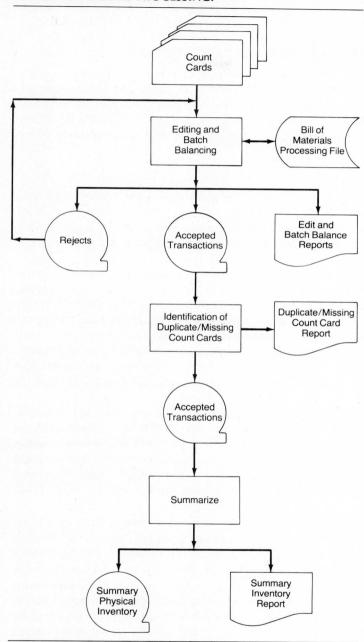

Source: AICPA, *Audit Approaches for a Computerized Inventory System* (New York: American Institute of Certified Public Accountants, 1980) Copyright © 1980 by the American Institute of Certified Public Accountants, Inc. Adapted by permission

Figure 12.12

level, (2) expected demand during an intervening period, and (3) procurement lead time required for reorder.

MANAGEMENT INFORMATION REQUIREMENTS

Inventory management reports are typically designed to serve at least three essential functions or areas of concern: (1) analysis, (2) position or status, and (3) planning and coordination. These basic management information requirements can be visualized even though we must consider raw materials and finished goods reporting separately. The following discussion represents a typical company's inventory reporting procedures.

Raw Materials

The logistics system for raw materials is fed by input from procurement, receiving, production control, and accounting. On order, receipt, issue, and moving balance information on both quantity and cost are routinely maintained in the master inventory records. Such information is readily available for periodic analysis and reporting.

Analysis Reports   In accordance with preprogrammed self-analysis routines, the inventory system performs computer audits of each inventory item against a set of control parameters. As inventory balances are diminished and approach established reorder points, purchase request forms are printed for validation by management and transmitted to purchasing. We have already examined the sequence of events engendered by these documents. Other activity includes receiving memoranda and production requisitions. It is customary in most information systems to list activity items to serve as an audit trail. In this case, classification of activity by type of material would greatly enhance the usefulness of the report.

Another useful analysis report, especially with respect to raw materials inventory, is a listing of inventory items at reorder point. Items appearing in this report (see Figure 12.13) would be expected to match the items for which reorder documents (requests to purchase) were created. The listing would reflect sufficient information from the updated master records to permit management to execute intelligent reorder decisions rather than blindly validate automatic procurement requests.

Usage Reports   Since the computer can maintain current, month-to-date, quarter-to-date, and year-to-date statistics on individual inventory items requisitioned for production use, the extraction of all kinds of usage information is relatively simple. Even minor problems imposed by time and distance factors should not seriously complicate the processing.

If the raw stores warehouse is located in a remote area, special control problems result. To control materials in transit from the warehouse to production control, a *transfer notice* (issue slip) is executed (see Figure 12.14). These transfers result in an interim report, the *raw material transfer register* (see Figure 12.15).

Later, as the raw material is entered into production, the lower half (detachable) of

ITEMS AT REORDER POINT
DATE: 10-31-86

Item Number	Bin Number	Prefrd. Vendor Item Number	Description	On Hand	On Order	Months of Stock	Item Type	Vendor Item Number	Last Order Date	Vendor Name
000631	025961	263221	Shuttles	32	250	.1	Prod.	X 0396	6/27/86	Shutco
061270	003164	000754	Coolant	1	3	.3	Maint.	Y 0479	8/13/86	Coolco
000973	000917	001964	Paper tape	—	10	.9	Ofc.	A 0420	9/26/86	Sanders

Figure 12.13

RAW MATERIAL TRANSFER NOTICE.

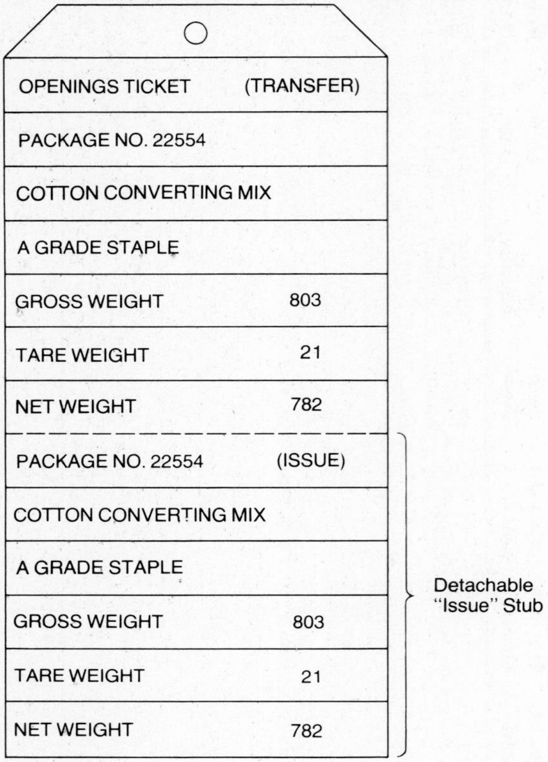

OPENINGS TICKET	(TRANSFER)
PACKAGE NO. 22554	
COTTON CONVERTING MIX	
A GRADE STAPLE	
GROSS WEIGHT	803
TARE WEIGHT	21
NET WEIGHT	782
PACKAGE NO. 22554	(ISSUE)
COTTON CONVERTING MIX	
A GRADE STAPLE	
GROSS WEIGHT	803
TARE WEIGHT	21
NET WEIGHT	782

Detachable "Issue" Stub

Figure 12.14

RAW MATERIAL TRANSFER REGISTER.

Type Grade	Bales Shipped	Pounds	Weighted-Average Cost per Pound	Total Cost
Denim mix cotton				
B	40	20,040	48.54¢	$ 9,727.42
C	51	25,653	44.61	11,443.80
E	63	31,752	42.19	13,396.17
Total shipped	154	77,445	44.63¢	$34,567.39

Figure 12.15

the transfer ticket is returned to inventory control to effect the actual "book transfer" of materials to production. The transfer is summarized in a periodic *monthly raw materials consumption report* (see Figure 12.16).

Position/Status Reports   We have already observed that there are several different kinds of inventories in most large business operations: factory supplies, office supplies, maintenance supplies, and spare parts, as well as raw material and finished goods inventories. We have chosen to demonstrate only two kinds of material: bulk direct materials (bales) and supply items. Such position listings help fulfill the management need for status information; see Figures 12.17 and 12.18.

Copies of these reports are used extensively by stores and production control as the basis for long-range replenishment decisions and coordination of production and inventory. Accounting departments use the weighted-average costs from these reports to determine inventory valuation in "lower of cost or market" decisions. When inventory is geographically dispersed, these reports, sorted in sequence by location code, yield valuable control information.

Finished Goods

The finished goods inventory control system is fed by production data, sales tapes (from billings and collections), customer orders (from marketing), and reports of merchandise returned for credit (from accounts receivable). Inventory master records are maintained in sufficient detail so that all production costs (i.e., direct materials, direct labor, and applied overhead) are clearly distinguishable. Further, the ultimate disposition of the finished product is indicated by production control on the completed production transfer documents: (1) items produced to customer order and (2) items free for sale. The marketing department uses this information to focus its sales efforts and advise customers of the current status of their orders.

MONTHLY RAW MATERIAL CONSUMPTION REPORT.

Type Grade	Number of Bales	Total Pounds	Weighted Average Cost per Pound	Total Cost
Duck mix cotton				
A	41	16,523	56.13¢	$ 9,274.36
B	436	173,528	53.29	92,473.07
C	19	7,581	50.74	3,846.60
D	11	4,367	49.10	2,144.20
E	5	2,050	46.26	948.33
F	7	2,786	43.10	1,200.77
G	1	399	40.21	160.44
Total	520	207,234	53.10¢	$110,047.77

Figure 12.16

INVENTORY POSITION REPORT—SUPPLY ITEMS.
DATE: 10-31-86

| Category #004 Item # | Category Description Item Count | | Inactive | Inventory Objective |
	Total	New		
4811	60	50	10	100
4812	43	39	4	40
4813	1,160	1,103	57	1,000
4814	1,290	1,153	137	1,300
Category Total	2,553	2,345	208	2,440

Figure 12.17

Several special summary reports are produced by the typical company studied, but they are not illustrated here because of the duplication in format.

In most manufacturing concerns, especially those engaged in an operation such as textiles, not all of the finished product is of uniform quality. This is especially true at the start and conclusion of a "production run." The resulting "off-quality" merchandise, or "seconds," is identified by production control and becomes inventoried and marketed separately. Reports similar to those discussed earlier would also be appropriate for off-quality stock.

Notification of merchandise returned for credit (or refund) reaches inventory control through the billings and collections (accounts receivable) department, or it may arrive as a specially coded item on the sales tape provided by accounts receivable, to which inventory control has *read-only* access. As a service to accounts receivable, sales transactions (including returns) are costed at standard by the inventory control system and returned to provide the basis for the "cost of goods sold" journal entries.

SUMMARY

The purpose of this chapter has been to highlight inventory flows, documentation representing those flows, problems and assumptions inherent in systematic inventory operations, controls and risks in the absence thereof, relationships between the inventory system and the production system, and organizing corporate resources to meet management expectations in the inventory operation. Systems analysts must understand these forces if they are to view the inventory function in its proper perspective relative to other related and dependent subsystems and design an effective systems solution to the supply

(Over) Under Objective	Issues		Receipts		Percentage Turnover	
	QTD*	YTD**	QTD	YTD	QTD	YTD
40	16	59	18	61	.27	.93
(3)	40	126	53	129	.93	3.06
(160)	534	1,211	605	1,300	.46	1.04
10	2,064	6,123	3,000	7,000	1.49	4.79
(113)	2,654	7,519	3,676	8,490	1.04	9.82

*Quarter to Date
**Year to Date

Figure 12.17 (cont'd)

RAW MATERIAL INVENTORY POSITION.
DATE: 7-25-86

Type Grade	Number of Bales	Total Pounds	Weighted Average Cost per Pound	Total Cost
Nylon				
A	575	286,924	56.25¢	$161,395.31
B	274	136,452	52.99	72,305.91
C	126	62,622	47.54	29,770.50
D	54	26,784	42.01	11,251.96
E	2	990	36.24	358.78
	1,031	513,772	53.54¢	$275,082.46

Figure 12.18

needs of the entity. It is hoped that this discussion has yielded a *broader* understanding of logistics management.

NOTES

[1]*Webster's New Collegiate Dictionary* (Springfield, Mass.: G. & C. Merriam Company, 1975.)

[2]AICPA, *Audit Approaches for a Computerized Inventory System* (New York: American Institute of Certified Public Accountants, 1980).

[3]Ibid, p. 46.

[4]Ibid, p. 51.

SELECTED REFERENCES

AICPA, *Audit Approaches for a Computerized Inventory System*. New York: American Institute of Certified Public Accountants, 1980.

Arthur Andersen & Co. *A Guide for Studying and Evaluating Internal Accounting Controls* (an in-house publication), January 1978.

Ballou, Ronald H. *Business Logistics Management*. Englewood Cliffs, N.J.: Prentice-Hall, Inc. 1973.

Bonczek, Robert H., Clyde W. Holsapple, and Andrew B. Whinston. "Aiding Decision Makers with a Generalized Data Base Management System: An Application to Inventory Management," *Decision Sciences* (April 1978): 228–245.

Coopers & Lybrand. *Internal Control Reference Manual: Production Cycle* (an in-house publication), 1978.

Ernst & Whinney. *Evaluating Internal Control: A Guide for Management and Directors* (an in-house publication), 1979.

Kanter, Jerome. *Management-oriented Management Information Systems*. Englewood Cliffs, N.J.: Prentice-Hall, Inc., 1972.

Karchner, Quinton L., Jr. "How Our Plant Automated Its Collection of Data," *Management Accounting* (September, 1980): p. 45–48.

Keegon, David P. "Some Second Reflections on MRP," Price Waterhouse and Co. *Review* (1977) (No. 3): 38–43.

Mautz, R. K., and Winjum, James. *Criteria for Management Control Systems*. A Research Study Prepared for the Financial Executives Research Foundation, 1981.

Whelan, W. James, and Jan R. Williams. "Lost Inventories—Where Did My $8,000,000 Go?" *Todays Executive*. New York: Price Waterhouse and Co. (Summer 1979): 21–24.

QUESTIONS

1. Name as many different kinds of inventories as you can for a large shoe manufacturer, a large auto manufacturer, a food processor.
2. In a highly automated inventory system, who is best qualified, under existing criteria, to decide when and how much to order?
3. What overall plan governs the level of inventory activity?
4. What kinds of indicators assist management in assessing the efficiency and effectiveness of inventory control procedures?
5. Discuss the relationship between inventory control and purchasing, receiving, accounts payable, and production control.
6. What chain of events and accounting entries are set in motion when merchandise is returned by the customer for credit?
7. What control weakness, if any, do you see in assigning material control the responsibility for journalizing cost of goods sold?
8. In a company whose materials and supplies include a great number of items, would you object to combining the storekeeping function with production and inventory record keeping? On what grounds?
9. Why is it more appropriate for charges to inventory accounts to be made by accounts payable in computerized systems than by material control?
10. What role does the inventory system play in accepting (or rejecting) merchandise returned by the customer for credit?
11. What are the three major types of inventory transactions?
12. Explain how it is possible for an inventory control system to automatically replenish itself?

13. How has the principle of "separation of handling and recording" been implemented in the inventory systems to assure the necessary accounting controls.
14. What are the major objectives of an inventory control system?
15. What responsibility, if any, does inventory control have in the assessment and valuation of work-in-process inventory.

PROBLEMS

16. Computer Equipment Functions and Applications

Executive management of Wolfe Incorporated, a rapidly expanding manufacturing company, has been reviewing a proposal prepared by the manager of the data processing department to update the computer equipment now in use. The present equipment includes a central processing unit, tape drives, card punch, card reader, card sorter, and a line impact printer.

The data processing manager suggests that new equipment be acquired to provide an on-line, real-time capability for inventory stock control and more efficient operation.

Required:
  a. Briefly describe the function of each item of equipment now in use.
  b. Identify two types of equipment not previously mentioned that would be required for the proposed on-line, real-time application.

17. Stores and Warehousing Analysis and Control

As auditor in charge of a stores and warehousing audit of a large distributor, your findings include the following:
  a. Preliminary analysis of inventory levels indicates that, on the average, there is a 2-year supply on hand.
  b. Scanning the inventory reveals that some individual items haven't moved in 5 years.
  c. Many items held in long supply are catalog items readily obtainable from suppliers.
  d. There appear to be no special controls over sensitive inventory items such as electronic supplies, precious metals, and the like.
  e. Out-of-stock conditions were noted for some critical items.
  f. An excessive number of inventory adjustments have been made. *(IIA adapted)*

Required:
Assuming that the audit has established the absence of adequate control procedures:
  a. Give a recommendation that you would make to provide the means of correcting each of the six conditions noted and to prevent their recurrence. Explain the purpose from a control standpoint of each of the six recommendations.
  b. Describe three benefits to operating management that would result from correcting all these conditions.

18. Raw Material Controls

You have been engaged by the management of Alden, Inc., to review its internal control over the purchase, receipt, storage, and issue of raw materials. You have prepared the following comments which describe Alden's procedures.

a. Raw materials, which consist mainly of high-cost electronic components, are kept in a locked storeroom. Storeroom personnel include a supervisor and four clerks. All are well trained, competent, and adequately bonded. Raw materials are removed from the storeroom only upon written or oral authorization of one of the production foremen.

b. There are no perpetual inventory records; hence, the storeroom clerks do not keep records of goods received or issued. To compensate for the lack of perpetual records, a physical inventory count is taken monthly by the storeroom clerks who are well supervised. Appropriate procedures are followed in making the inventory count.

c. After the physical count, the storeroom supervisor matches quantities counted against a predetermined reorder level. If the count for a given part is below the reorder level, the supervisor enters the part number on a materials requisition list and sends this list to the accounts payable clerk. The accounts payable clerk prepares a purchase order for a predetermined reorder quantity for each part and mails the purchase order to the vendor from whom the part was last purchased.

d. When ordered materials arrive at Alden, they are received by the storeroom clerks. The clerks count the merchandise and check the counts against the shipper's bill of lading. All vendor's bills of lading are initialed, dated, and filed in the storeroom to serve as receiving reports. *(AICPA adapted)*

Required:

Describe the weaknesses in internal control and recommend improvements of Alden's procedures for the purchase, receipt, storage, and issue of raw materials. Organize your answer sheet into two columns, headed "Weaknesses" and "Recommended Improvements," respectively.

19. Systems Flowchart Analysis and Control Evaluations

A company maintains its detailed inventory records and its general ledger inventory account on a perpetual basis. Thus, the cost of materials entering into production and the cost of inventory on hand for financial statement purposes can be readily determined. Nevertheless, the company takes periodic physical inventories. State four reasons why the company should make periodic physical inventory counts.

20. Document Flowcharts and Internal Controls

R. Brown Company manufactures and distributes small electronic control devices to producers of other, more sophisticated, consumer products. Brown is a fairly large and complex company containing all the automated information systems found in other large companies. Due to the high quality of its products and the somewhat limited number of its customers, the company has experienced very few sales returns.

On December 29, 19X1, a sizable shipment of its products was returned, unopened, by a customer because the shipment was inadvertently made several months ahead of contract need date. The carton was routinely accepted upon its arrival at the receiving dock by an authorized receiving clerk. Company procedure required the processing of a special form (customer returns credit form), copies of which were immediately distributed to accounts receivable, inventory control, and other interested organizations. Following acceptance, the shipment was carefully inspected and found to have suffered severe damage as a result of being dropped from a forklift while being loaded onto the carrier's vehicle. Damage was not apparent from outward appearances. Inspection personnel refused to allow the material to be returned to inventory, pending a negotiated settlement with the customer.

In the meantime, accounts receivable processed the normal adjustment as follows:

DR. Returned Merchandise Clearing Account	15,000	
CR. Cost of Sales		15,000
DR. Sales Returns and Allowances	20,000	
CR. Accounts Receivable		20,000

Standard operating procedure required inventory control to offset the returned merchandise clearing account and debit inventory when the material was officially returned to inventory. This event had not occurred at December 31, 19X1.

On January 18, 19X2, the decision was made by management to junk the shipment on the basis of a negotiated settlement, whereupon the following entry was made.

DR. Inventory Loss and Damage	15,000	
CR. Returned Merchandise Clearing Account		15,000

Required:

a. Assuming that the timing error was not clear at the time of closing on December 31, what was the total impact of the preceding events on the financial statements?

b. Based on your knowledge of marketing and inventory operations at this point, what conditions could have precipitated the early shipment in the first place?

c. Design procedures to preclude a recurrence of this situation.

21. Systems Applications, Equipment Requirements, and Data Files

Peabock Company is a wholesaler of soft goods. The inventory is composed of approximately 3,500 different items. The company employs a computerized batch processing system to maintain its perpetual inventory records. The system is run each weekend so that the inventory reports are available on Monday morning for management use. The system has been functioning satisfactorily for the past 15 months, providing the company with accurate records and timely reports.

The preparation of purchase orders has been automatic as a part of the inventory system to ensure that the company will maintain enough inventory to meet customer demand. When an item of inventory falls below a predetermined level, a record of the inventory item is written. This record is used in conjunction with the vendor file to prepare the purchase orders.

Exception reports are prepared during the update of the inventory and the preparation of the purchase orders. These reports identify any errors or exceptions identified during the processing. In addition, the system provides for management approval of all purchase orders exceeding a specified amount. Any exceptions or items requiring management approval are handled by supplemental runs on Monday morning and are combined with the weekend results.

A system flowchart of Peabock Company's inventory and purchase order procedure is shown in Figure 12.19. *(IMA adapted)*

Required:

   a. The illustrated system flowchart of Peabock Company's inventory and purchase order system was prepared before the system was fully operational. Several steps that are important to the successful operations of the system were inadvertently omitted from the chart. Now that the system is operating effectively, management wants the system documentation complete and would like the flowchart corrected. Describe the steps that have been omitted and indicate where the omissions have occurred. The flowchart does not need to be redrawn.

   b. In order for Peabock's inventory/purchase order system to function properly, control procedures would be included in the system. Describe the type of control procedures Peabock Company would use in their system to assure proper functioning, and indicate where these procedures would be placed in the system.

22. Inventory Systems Design

Beccan Company is a discount tire dealer that operates 25 retail stores in the metropolitan area. Both private brand and name brand tires are sold by Beccan. The company operates a centralized purchasing and warehousing facility and employs a perpetual inventory system. All purchases of tires and related supplies are placed through the company's central purchasing department to take advantage of quantity discounts. The tires and supplies are received at the central warehouse and distributed to the retail stores as needed. The perpetual inventory system at the central facility maintains current inventory records, designated reorder points, optimum order quantities, and continuous stocktakings for each type of tire by size and other related supplies.

The documents employed by Beccan in their inventory control system and their use are as follows:

PEABOCK COMPANY'S INVENTORY AND PURCHASE ORDER PROCEDURE.

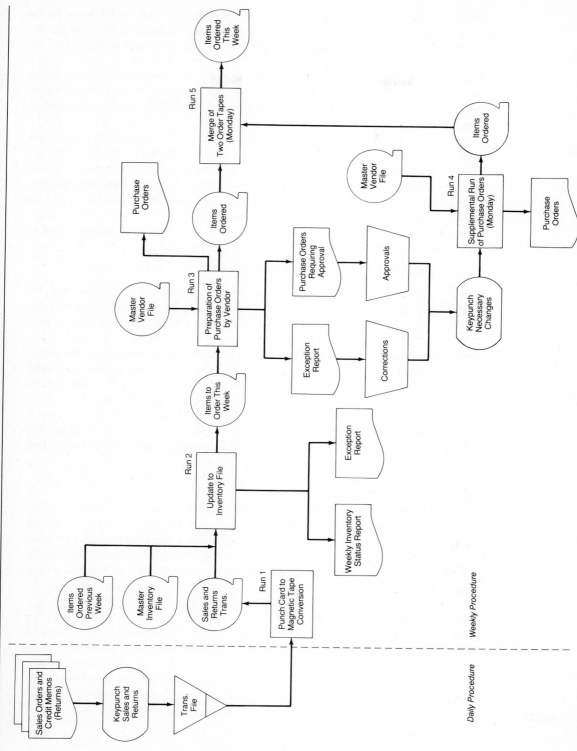

Figure 12.19

Retail stores requisition. This document is submitted by the retail stores to the central warehouse whenever tires or supplies are needed at the stores. The shipping clerks in the warehouse department fill the orders from inventory and have them delivered to the stores.

Purchase requisition. The inventory control clerk in the inventory control department prepares this document when the quantity on hand for an item falls below the designated reorder point. The document is forwarded to the purchasing department.

Purchase order. The purchasing department prepares this document when items need to be ordered. The document is submitted to an authorized vendor.

Receiving report. The warehouse department prepares this document when ordered items are received from vendors. The receiving clerk completes the document by indicating the vendor's name, the date the shipment is received, and the quantity of each item received.

Invoice. An invoice is received from vendors specifying the amounts owed by Beccan.

The departments involved in Beccan's inventory control system are:

Inventory control department. This department is responsible for the maintenance of all perpetual inventory records for all items carried in inventory. This includes current quantity on hand, reorder point, optimum order quantity, and quantity on order for each item carried.

Warehouse department. This department maintains the physical inventory of all items carried in inventory. All orders from vendors are received (receiving clerk) and all distributions to retail stores are filled (shipping clerks) in this department.

Purchasing department. The purchasing department places all orders for items needed by the company.

Accounts payable department. Accounts payable maintains all open accounts with vendors and other creditors. All payments are processed in this department. *(IMA adapted)*

Required:

Prepare a flow diagram to show how these documents should be coordinated and used among the departments at the central facility of Beccan Company to provide adequate internal control over the receipt, issuance, replenishment, and payment of tires and supplies. You may assume that the documents have a sufficient number of copies to assure that the perpetual inventory system has the necessary basic internal controls.

23. Logistics Activities Flowchart

Wekender Corporation owns and operates 15 large departmentalized retail hardware stores in major metropolitan areas of the southwest United States. The stores carry a wide variety of merchandise but the major thrust is toward the weekend "do-it-yourselfer." The company has been successful in this field, and the number of stores in the chain has almost doubled since 1970.

Each retail store acquires its merchandise from the company's centrally located warehouse. Consequently, the warehouse must maintain an up-to-date and well-stocked inventory that is ready to meet the demands of the individual stores.

The company wishes to hold its competitive position with similar type stores of other companies in its marketing area. Therefore, Wekender Corporation must improve its purchasing and inventory procedures. The company's stores must have the proper goods to meet customer demand, and the warehouse in turn must have the goods available. The number of company stores, the number of inventory items carried, and the volume of business all are providing pressures to change from basically manual data processing routines to mechanized data processing procedures. Recently, the company has been investigating three different approaches to mechanization—unit-record equipment, computer with batch processing, computer with real-time processing. No decision has been reached on the approach to be followed.

Top management has determined that the following items should have high priority in the new system procedures:

a. Rapid ordering to replenish warehouse inventory stocks with as little delay as possible.

b. Quick filling and shipping of merchandise to the stores (this involves determining if sufficient stock exists).

c. Some indication of inventory activity.

d. Perpetual records in order to determine inventory level by item number quickly.

A description of the current warehousing and purchasing procedures follows.

Warehouse Procedures

Stock is stored in bins and is located by an inventory number. The numbers generally are listed sequentially on the bins to facilitate locating items for shipment; frequently this system is not followed, and as a result, some items are difficult to locate.

Whenever a retail store needs merchandise, a three-part merchandise request form is completed—one copy is kept by the store and two copies are mailed to the warehouse the next day. If the merchandise requested is on hand, the goods are delivered to the store accompanied by the third copy of the request. The second copy is filed at the warehouse.

If the quantity of goods on hand is not sufficient to fill the order, the warehouse sends the quantity available and notes the quantity shipped on the request form. Then a purchase memorandum for the shortage is prepared by the warehouse. At the end of each day all the memos are sent to the purchasing department.

When ordered goods are received, they are checked at the receiving area, and a receiving report is prepared. One copy of the receiving report is retained at the receiving area, one is forwarded to accounts payable, and one is filed at the warehouse with the purchase memorandum.

Purchasing Department Procedures

When the purchase memoranda are received from the warehouse, purchase orders are prepared. Vendor catalogs are used to select the best source for the requested goods, and the purchase order is prepared and mailed. Copies of the order are sent to accounts payable and the receiving area; one copy is retained in the purchasing department.

When the receiving report arrives in the purchasing department, it is compared with the purchase order on file. The receiving report is also checked with the invoice before forwarding the invoice to accounts payable for payment.

The purchasing department strives periodically to evaluate the vendors for financial soundness, reliability, and trade relationships. However, because the volume of requests received from the warehouse is so great, this activity currently does not have a high priority.

Each week a report of the open purchase orders is prepared to determine if any action should be taken on overdue deliveries. This report is prepared manually from scanning the file of outstanding purchase orders. *(IMA adapted)*

Required:

    a. Wekender Corporation is considering three possible automated data processing systems; unit-record system, batch-processing system, real-time computer system. Prepare a systems flowchart for each of the three proposals.

    b. Regardless of the type of system selected by Wekender Corporation, data files will have to be established. Design a record (schema) to illustrate these data.

CASES

24. As you observed from your analysis of Apogee Company operations (Appendix C), the production and inventory functions appear to operate homogeneously. Although they *are* closely related, financial integrity demands that they operate independently. Among many other apparent weaknesses, there are no vital documents to record and trace the critical value flows from inventory, through the production shops, to finished goods.

    Selectively apply the concepts and practices presented in Chapter Twelve and design separate accounting information systems for Apogee's inventory operations.

25. Criticize Bubbling Stone Company's philosophy of holding raw materials inventory (particularly flavor syrups, aluminum cans, and bottles) to an absolute minimum. Does this philosophy place the company's overall operation in jeopardy in the short run in case of strikes and other temporary disruptions of supplier operations?

    Flowchart your perception of the company's logistical procedures, beginning with purchasing and including receiving, raw materials inventory, production, and finished goods. Enumerate and explain any weaknesses you observe.

CHAPTER THIRTEEN

Production Control Systems

The process of converting raw materials into marketable finished products directly involves three massive accounting information subsystems: production control, inventory control (raw materials, work-in-process, and finished goods), and payroll/labor distribution. These systems are, or should be, completely independent of each other, yet each makes a unique and vital contribution to the conversion process. We examined the inventory systems first because they provide the connecting links between the expenditure cycle (raw material) and the revenue cycle (finished goods). Actually, the production function initiates the flow of costs (values) that culminates in the creation of finished goods.

Unlike many other operating subsystems in a company, conversion cycle systems have few direct financial relationships with outside organizations. Their role is generally confined to the task of tracking and controlling manufacturing cost flows as raw materials are transformed by the application of direct labor and factory overhead. This transformation requires unique documentation, systems configurations, controls, and reports.

THE PRODUCTION CONTROL SYSTEM

With respect to *financial* information, the production process is generally regarded as the arena of the cost accountant. It is an environment in which normal cost flows are often metered and measured against predetermined production cost standards, and where deviations (variances) from such standards are carefully scrutinized by efficiency-conscious management for possible corrective action. By isolating the production environment from the purely "financial" cost/value flows that immediately precede and follow it, as shown in Figure 13.1, we can visualize how the production cost stream may be analyzed. Moving from left to right, the normal cost/value flow is interrupted as it enters the conversion cycle functions. Management will have attempted to regulate and control these flows by establishing "acceptable" standards (quantity and price) for each of the elements of production in the planning and budgeting process. Only the established standards will be allowed to flow through the work-in-process account(s) as

MANUFACTURING COST FLOWS—AN OVERVIEW.

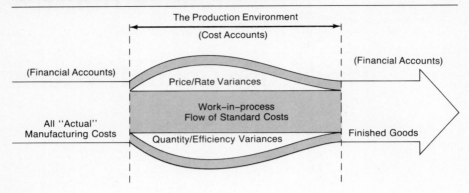

Figure 13.1

production work is accomplished. As business transactions occur, related variations from established standards are channeled into separate accounts by "cause."

Management accountants, unfettered by generally accepted accounting principles, are free to redirect certain elements of the cost stream in almost any manner deemed useful for control purposes. Typically, this means diverting several types of "cost variances" from the "standard cost flow" for special analysis, such as (1) the material *price* and *usage* variances, (2) the direct labor *rate* and *efficiency* variances, (3) the variable overhead *spending* and *efficiency* variances, and (4) the fixed overhead *budget* and *volume* variances. At the end of any given accounting period, however, all such variances must be rechanneled back into the "full" cost stream as it reenters the financial accounts through finished goods and cost of goods sold. This procedure is referred to as the redistribution of production cost variances. In the interest of accurate product costing and the correct determination of net income, such redistribution should follow the tempo of the cost stream. That is, when inventory turnover is rapid, most of the *standard* production costs will reside in the costs of goods sold at period-end. Commensurately, a relatively larger portion of standard cost variances should be reallocated to that account.

The cost flow is more precisely delineated in Figure 13.2, showing the sources of manufacturing costs and their paths through the manufacturing environment to their ultimate destination, finished goods.

THE PRODUCTION PLAN

It is generally acknowledged that the entire business tempo is governed by the sales forecast. Following the cycle approach discussed in Chapter Nine, Figure 13.3 demonstrates how the whole budgeting and planning process emanates from that critical source of information. The sales forecast (1) is extrapolated into a production schedule (2), which

PRODUCTION CONTROL THROUGH STANDARD COSTS.

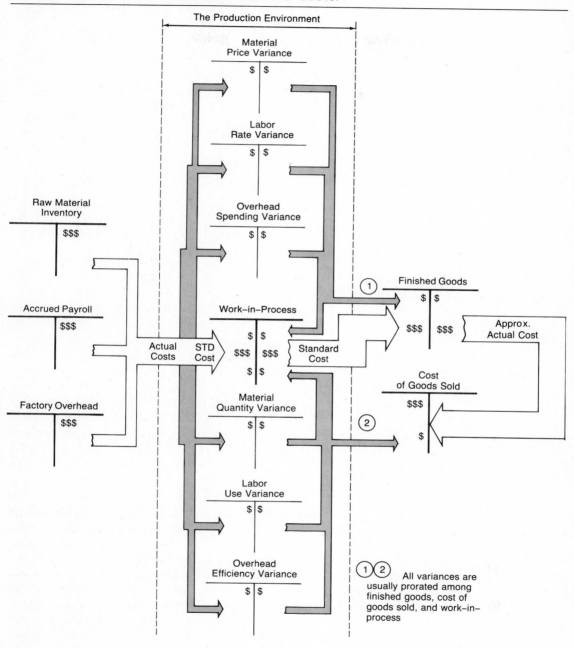

Figure 13.2

THE PRODUCTION PLANNING PROCESS.

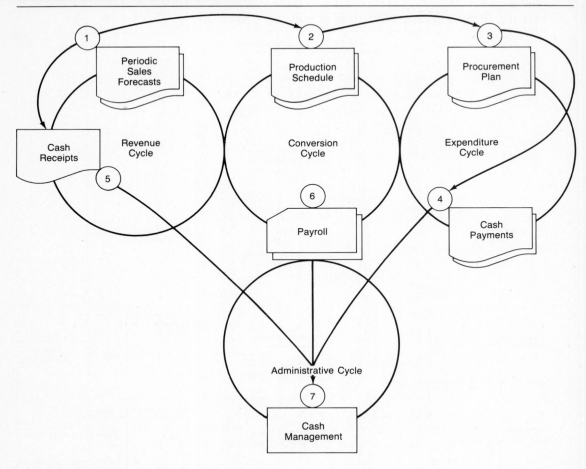

Figure 13.3

of course takes into consideration both the existing inventory of finished goods and the level of inventory desired at the end of the period. The production schedule then provides the basis for the development of a procurement plan (3) in the form of a carefully controlled series of purchase contracts with outside suppliers of raw materials. Again, the existing inventory of raw materials and the inventory level desired at period-end must play a deciding role in the determination of the volume of purchases. Shipments by suppliers eventually result in cash outflows through accounts payable (4), while sales transactions stimulate cash inflows through the accounts receivable function (5). The other significant cash outflow occurs in the payroll system (6). All these cash flows converge in the administrative cycle (7) where the company's cash control system is managed.

Objectives of the Production Control System

The overriding objective of the production operation is to transform the systems' inputs into desired outputs (finished products) in the most effective and efficient manner possible. Some kind of production planning group can be found in almost any manufacturing organization, regardless of size. The formal production control organization is quite visible in large-scale manufacturing organizations. Execution of its responsibility involves forecasting and planning, routing, scheduling, dispatching and expediting, and coordinating. These activities ensure the orderly supply and movement of materials, the performance and application of labor, and the utilization of machinery and equipment, and they effect a smooth interface of internal organizations.

Actual production must be preceded by carefully conceived plans governing quantity to be produced, raw materials needed, labor and machine requirements, and prescribed manufacturing methods. Understandably, marketing and engineering departments play important roles in this preliminary planning process.

Through its analysis of the overall market for the company's product, and a projection of the market share accruing to the company, the sales organization prepares a sales forecast. Meanwhile, engineering will have broken the product down into its components. Matching these two inputs permits the explosion of material and part requirements into an overall bill of materials, or parts list.

Consulting inventory stock status reports aids in the determination of current procurement requirements. Planners may then study purchasing history records to establish lead-time requirements for procurement action on items to be stocked. Control continues through the now familiar stages of requisitioning, ordering, receiving, storing, issuing, and handling along the production line.

Source Documents

A variety of source documents are utilized in the production system. Beginning in order of impact in the physical process, the following forms, reports, and documents are considered: sales forecasts, stock status reports, material assembly parts lists, bill of materials, routing sheets, production work orders, stores requisitions, and job cards (time tickets).

Sales Forecast In the overall scheme of company affairs, the single most important informational instrument is the forecast of sales. It provides the basis for allocation of resources throughout the entire firm and establishes the projected level of activity to which production and expense budgets must be geared.

Sales forecasts are the products of market research representing a conglomerate of sales history, economic indicators, trends, demographic and environmental data, and other information gathered from in-depth studies, trade publications, governmental pamphlets, promotional literature of competitors and direct communications with customers. They serve not only as planning aids but as a means of establishing sales quotas and exercising management control over the sales force.

Our discussion is concerned exclusively with the reports' use as input to the production planning process, where critical decisions are made that govern the types and quantities of products to be manufactured. The reader may wish to glance ahead to the chapter on marketing systems for a preview of the form and content of this vital report.

Stock Status Report   The production schedule, based on a forecast of sales, determines the quantities of the various raw stock, parts, and subassemblies needed for manufacturing activities. Procurement activities initiated in response to this planning are tempered by several important conditions: (1) inventory account balances at regular intervals, (2) established minimum stock levels, (3) production demands on inventory during the ensuing period(s), and (4) the most economical quantities of raw materials to purchase. For these and other reasons, many efficiency experts feel that the most effective material control system exists when production control is given full responsibility for all stores requisitioning and ordering.

In any event, the role played by frequent reports on the current status of all items in stock is important. Such a report was illustrated earlier in our discussion of inventory systems. That system described the procedure for acquiring, storing, issuing, and reporting inventory quantities and values.

Material Assembly Parts List   The engineering organization develops specifications that list in detail all the raw materials, component parts, and subassemblies with which production personnel will be working to fabricate the finished product. The complete specification plan is often referred to as the MAPL (material assembly parts list). Its importance varies directly with the size, complexity, and number of stages necessary to complete the manufacturing process. In large manufacturing companies, the MAPL is one of the key data base files utilized by production control. It may contain thousands, even hundreds of thousands, of records itemizing the makeup of each assembly, subassembly, and part. Each item is controlled by a unique manufacturing part number.

For purposes of this discussion, the MAPL is considered a manufacturing "catalog" against which individual work orders are processed to produce bills of materials required to complete a more advanced part or assembly. This process is known as exploding the work order, somewhat as illustrated in Figure 13.4.

Bill of Materials   Having demonstrated a possible origin, or source of preparation, of the bill of materials, we can examine its contents and purpose. As previously indicated, a "part" is an item that, when assembled together with other parts, forms a subassembly, which is also identified by a unique part number. The assembling of subassemblies ultimately produces a finished product. The bill of materials lists the kinds and quantities of materials, parts, and subassemblies required to produce a more advanced part, or the finished product itself.

Bills of material give dispatchers the information they need to requisition the necessary materials from stores prior to starting the manufacturing process. As Figure 13.5 suggests, the list may take almost any form as long as it reflects three basic facts: (1) the identification (part) number of each element, (2) a reasonable description, and (3) the quantity of each element required to make the item(s) for which the work order was issued.

Routing Sheet   Labor operations in sequential order, together with machine requirements and standard completion times (labor and machine), are itemized on routing sheets. These documents become a road map for shop activities, guiding workers through the order of operations in a manner prescribed to promote efficiency, minimize

BILL OF MATERIALS.

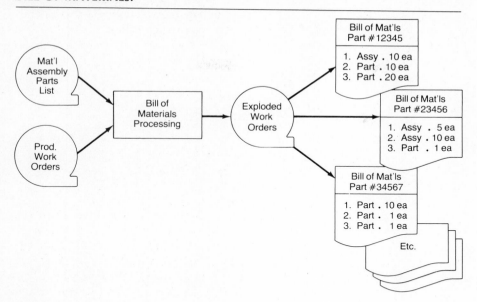

Figure 13.4

cost, and ensure uniformity in product quality. "Operations lists," such as the one suggested in Figure 13.6 may remain constant over a period of time and change only when the configuration of the product or the product process changes.

Production Work Order   Having developed an overall production plan, interpreted it into a schedule of manufacturing activities, arranged for the procurement of the necessary materials, and described the sequence of operations required to accomplish a specific task, we can then set the process in motion with an authorization to begin. That authority is provided by a work order issued by production control.

The work order illustrated in Figure 13.7 serves a number of needs. One copy is dispatched to the cost accounting section for purposes of establishing a work-in-process record for the job. In manual systems, the reverse side of the form may be used for this purpose. One copy remains in production control as a record of open orders for follow-up. Another copy, usually the original, is placed in a protective packet and sent to the department where work begins. From there it travels with the work through the factory. Figure 13.8 illustrates these cost, physical, and document flows in a production environment.

Stores Requisition Form and Job Card   Two internal forms play an important part in determining the cost of production: the stores requisition form, which authorizes the withdrawal of materials and parts from inventory, and the job card (or time ticket), which records the labor time consumed in each production operation.

BILLS OF MATERIALS LIST   TUBING
RUN DATE 01/09/81
PAGE **11

B.O.M.   099200   167CM 5 1/2"BAR 86CM34"SL

REF NO.	STRUCTURED PART NO.	DRAWING NO.	GROUP CODE	DESCRIPTION	UNIT OF MEASURE	QUANTITY/ ASSEMBLY	EXT. CODE
001	31015015		30	BAR, BARBELL, SOLID, CUT, PAINTED BLACK 1" X 66"	EA	1.0000	3
002	30092767		30	SLEEVE,1 1/8" X .028 X 31,STEEL,ZN PLT	EA	1.0000	3
003	50078600		30	CARTON,TUBULAR,KRAFT,.050 X 68	EA	1.0000	3
004	09008600		30	PLUG, END, PLAS., TUBE CARTON, B/B BARS (ALLIANCE #49)	EA	2.0000	3
005	24005100		30	STAPLE, 3/8", DUO-FAST #9512 (T.T.T. ACC.)	EA	6.0000	3
006	62064000		30	LABEL,66" SOLID BAR,PURPLE	EA	1.0000	3
007	16001000		30	GLUE, CARDBOARD, CLEAR, 83534 (H. B. FULLER OR EVANS # 8109)	GL	.0001	3

Figure 13.5

Oprn. No.	Function Description	Classif.	Oprn. Time	Set-up Time	Specific Instruc.
001	Cut Pattern	Cutter	.47	.10	
002	Join Edges	Operator	.24		
003	Fold and Stamp	Operator	.15		
004	Insert Liner	Operator	.81		
005	Trim	Operator	.52		to .25 inch
006	Finish Edges	Operator	.46		
007	Mount Decal	Operator	.05		
008	Pull Tickets	Helper	.05		to packing

OPERATIONS LIST (Routing Sheet)

Date Prepared: _____

Approved: _____

Part No. _____

Figure 13.6

MANUFACTURING COST ACCOUNTING SYSTEMS

Regardless of the nature of the manufacturing operation, production management (as well as inventory and marketing management) is vitally interested in product cost *per unit.* Unit-cost information serves two basic management needs: (1) It aids in the establishment of selling prices that permit not only the recovery of related costs, but also the earning of a fair return on sales. (2) It provides experience data essential to cost control.

Cost accumulation systems are designed to receive input from other related subsystems in the form of (1) raw materials consumed in the production process, (2) direct labor expended to convert such materials into finished products, and (3) factory-related overhead to be absorbed by the products. The two common cost accumulation systems are job order costing and process costing. The election to use one or the other of these systems depends primarily on the nature of the product and the manufacturing process by which it is created.

Job Order Costing Systems

Job order costing accounts for product costs by customer, job, or batch. It is characterized by the "specialized" nature of the product: for example, building construction, weapons systems (aircraft, satellites, submarines), athletic uniforms, movies, textbooks, and so on. As the product moves through the manufacturing sequence the work order moves with it, accumulating increments of direct material, direct labor, and applied overhead costs. The manufacturing sequence is "discontinuous" in the sense that the job can be halted or delayed without noticeable impact on other jobs that may also be in progress. The product itself is identifiable at various stages of completion. The value of work-in-process inventory can be precisely determined at any point in time by simply summarizing costs accumulated on all *incomplete* work orders.

DETAIL
PRODUCTION ORDER

| DIVISION-CALIFORNIA | DATE ISSUED 01/09/81 | PRODUCTION NO. 118-00346 |

CATL/PART NO. 29060618 HARDWARE SET, 11-0173

ORDER QUANTITY- 1,000 START DATE 1- 8-81 DUE DATE 1- 8-81
OPERATING DESCRIPTION - PACK HARDWARE SET FOR 11-0173

CST RPT OPM I CTR STA NO T	PART NO. JOB CODE	DESCRIPTION	CREW SIZE UOM SIZE	QTY EA PCS/HR	TOT STD QTY REQ	TOT SPEC QTY REQ	STD COST PER UOM	DISBURSEMENT	QTY ACTUAL RET USAGE
118	R 54000100	BAG, POLY, 6" X 8" X 4 EA	1.0000	1,000	1,000	.0100		
118	R 20010600	SCREW, SHEET METAL, TY EA	6.0000	6,000	6,000	.0102		
118	R 02010000	CAP, LEG, PLASTIC, BLA EA	2.0000	2,000	2,000	.0104		
118	R 02018000	PLUG, BALL, TUBE INSER EA	2.0000	2,000	2,000	.0270		
118	R 21009200	SCREW, MACH, RHS, 5/16 EA	4.0000	4,000	4,000	.0426		
118	R 23000300	BOLT, CARRIAGE, 5/16" EA	6.0000	6,000	6,000	.0288		
118	R 25000400	NUT, HEX, DB'L CHAMF. EA	10.0000	10,000	10,000	.0079		
118	R 26000667	WASHER, RADIUS,.075,FG EA	14.0000	14,000	14,000	.0087		
118 60 010 183		PACK HARDWARE	HRS 3.0	66.6666					
		TOTALS			690	690			

Figure 13.7

PRODUCTION LOGIC FLOW.

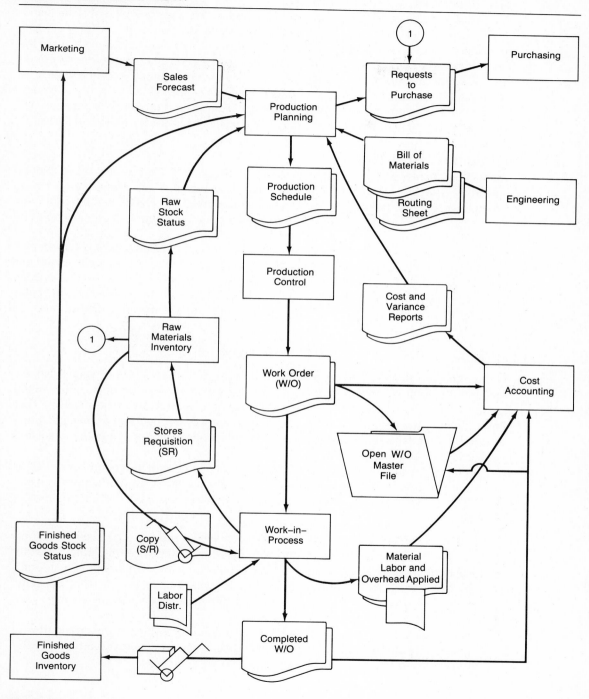

Figure 13.8

The Process Costing System

Perhaps the most distinctive characteristic of a process costing environment is the manufacturing procedure itself. Because of the homogeneous nature of the product, the production process is "continuous." A unit of product is not clearly identifiable until the entire process is completed. This inherent condition requires that management periodically *estimate* the degree of completion of unfinished work-in-process at each stage (cost center) in the production cycle. "Equivalent whole units" produced must then be computed for use in determining unit cost to produce.[1] Examples of products manufactured in a process costing environment are cement, paint, beverages, wire, oil, food, and the like.

Production Cost Flows

Production cost factors should flow in synchronization with the physical movement of inventory. The process is set in motion when raw materials are requisitioned by an expediter at strategic points in the production sequence. The costed materials requisition form is used to update the work order issued by production control. Facsimile copies of these documents are found in Chapter Eleven.

Shop supervisors in each production cost center keep detailed records of direct and indirect labor expended in the production process. This labor application is audited vis-à-vis employee time cards and, after discrepancies are resolved, are used to update the work order. Factory burden is applied to individual work orders, usually on the basis of direct labor hours or machine usage hours, using predetermined overhead rates.

ACCOUNTING CONTROLS AND RISKS

Despite the fact that production operations involve exclusively *internal* value transformations requiring no exposure to cash, no negotiations with outsiders, only limited authority over the resource costs it absorbs, and no responsibility for journalizing cost flows, there *is* the definite need for accounting controls throughout the manufacturing process. Accountants must be concerned about the consequences of a poorly regulated and controlled production system.

Some of the undesirable effects of loose production control procedures are obvious to accountants, although perhaps they are not quite so visible to production management. The reader will have little difficulty in conceptualizing the following undesirable potential risks:

1. Production of unauthorized products or quantities of products in excess of authorized levels. This could result in obsolete, excess, or otherwise unsalable inventory or abnormal sales returns because of unacceptable quality. Other detrimental results could be excessive inventory carrying costs, unprofitable use of plant capacity, strained financial resources, dissatisfied customers, uncollectible receivables, and loss of sales.
2. Untimely processing of conversion cycle transactions resulting in the erratic flow of management information, lost or misapplied data, and inaccurate reporting of work-in-process and finished good inventories.

3. Implementation of operating procedures that circumvent existing internal control techniques and reduce safeguards over sensitive assets.
4. Unauthorized release of production orders to mask shortages, thefts, or excessive spoilage.
5. Incorrect accounting distributions (e.g., labor, material, and overhead costs may be charged to expense when they should be inventoried, and vice versa). Overhead rates may be incorrect because of inaccurate assumptions with respect to allocations of fixed costs, depreciation, and amortization. Sales prices might therefore be established on the basis of incorrect cost information, thus adversely affecting operating results.

MANAGEMENT INFORMATION REQUIREMENTS

In the expenditure cycle, management reporting tends to concentrate primarily on cash handling and related activities and on the generation of documents resulting in cash outflows. In the revenue cycle we shall see similar concerns from a reverse point of view. Up to this point, even in the production system, we have alluded mainly to controls for costs and value flows.

However, production management has an equally pressing need for reports measuring time and quantity performances to complement cost information. Clearly, fraud and other employee deceit in the production system must be motivated by some objective other than cash. To practice "cash fraud" through payroll padding in modern computerized systems would be extremely difficult. Even if briefly successful, the rewards would hardly justify the risks. Misrepresentations in the production system are therefore generally intended to cover mistakes, camouflage poor performance, or conceal shortages and waste.

Production management reports can be summarized into three groups: cost control, performance, and quality control.

Cost Control

To determine the kinds of cost reports needed, we need to distinguish between job order and process manufacturing systems. When production fits the job order pattern, production orders are written for the *job* and manufacturing costs are assigned to the job as it passes through the factory. Costs are accumulated by cost class (labor, material, and overhead) on the work order itself. Incomplete work orders constitute the inventory of work-in-process and serve as a subsidiary ledger to the controlling work-in-process account in the general ledger.

When units of a product are identical, they may be most effectively manufactured on a continuous process basis, with finished production moving routinely into finished goods inventory in a continuous flow. Costs are assigned to a time interval rather than to a specific job. It is necessary then to calculate completed production in order to allocate total production costs equitably between the finished production and the work remaining in progress.

Performance Reports

Information on volume and schedule performance is essential to effective production management. The primary objective of performance reports is to help determine whether plant capacity is being utilized effectively to produce the quantities desired on schedule in accordance with the production plan. Examples of such reports are:

1. Finished goods/assemblies/parts actually produced measured against the established production level
2. A comparison of scheduled completion dates of work orders versus actual completion dates
3. A list of behind-schedule work orders, with reasons
4. Utilization of labor and machines compared to available plant capacity
5. Analysis of factory burden applications versus actual expenditure data

Quality Control

Production management is interested not only in cost, schedule, and volume performances, but also in the quality of finished products flowing through its shops. An independent quality control organization normally inspects production at each stage of completion. Items not passing this quality test are either returned for reprocessing under separate work orders, rated as "seconds" to be disposed of at a reduced price, or declared scrap. Production control management must have regular information pertaining to (1) total quality control rejections—with reasons, (2) rework orders and accumulated cost, and (3) spoilage, scrap, and waste—with reasons.

The nature of the product, the diversity of styles, the process of manufacture (which may even be patented), and the complexity of the company itself combine to create an almost infinite variety of form and content for performance and quality control reports. Simple production quantity and cost reports are exhibited in Figures 13.9 and 13.10.

Date _____ **LABOR EFFICIENCY REPORT** Dept. _____

Job No.	Operator	Operation	Labor Std. Rate	Labor Std. Hours	Actual Rate	Actual Hours	Total Cost Std.	Total Cost Actual
101	Smith	Cut	3.75	2.5	4.00	2.4	9.38	9.60
102	Roe	Route	3.75	.5	3.80	.4	1.88	1.52
103	Jones	Form	3.50	1.0	3.45	1.1	3.50	3.80
104	Doe	Trim	3.80	.5	3.75	.7	1.90	2.63
105	Bean	Assemble	3.75	2.0	3.80	2.2	7.50	8.36
		Etc.						
		Etc.						
		Etc.						
		Total Dept A					1,350.80	1,375.20

Figure 13.9

			Quantity		Price		Cost		Variances (Unfavorable)	
Job	Operator	Material	Std.	Act.	Std.	Act.	Std.	Act.	Qty.	Price
101	Smith	14-271	2	2	.80	.82	1.60	1.64	.00	(.04)
102	Roe	14-301	10	11	1.01	1.00	10.10	11.00	(1.01)	.11
105	Bean	16-799	3	2	.10	.12	.30	.24	.10	(.04)

Date _____   MATERIAL EFFICIENCY REPORT   Dept. _____

Figure 13.10

A PRODUCTION SYSTEM CONFIGURATION

Considering the almost infinite variety of products created in response to consumer demand, coupled with wide variations in organizational size and data processing sophistication among those firms that manufacture them, it is difficult to speculate on a "standard" configuration. Let us assume, however, that the production control *function* is performed somehow, by someone, in all manufacturing companies. We cannot imagine a successful manufacturer who disdains the need to coordinate the intricate processes of production and the attendant problems of product costing. This assumption permits us to speculate on what a system configuration might look like in a large company that depends on computer-processed production data for management decisions.

Figure 13.11 exemplifies such a configuration in a hypothetical situation. In run I, engineering design standards and manufacturing engineering procedures are brought together with inventory records to produce operations lists (routing sheets) for each manufactured part and assembly. A manufacturing assembly parts list (MAPL) may also emanate from this processing, to be used later in run II to produce the basic documents that are essential to accounting for production cost flows, that is, bills of material, inventory requisitions, and shop work orders.

The newly created work orders are then used in the daily work-in-process update, run III, where they enter the production data base and are matched with (1) costed material issues, (2) preaudited job time tickets, (3) production "move" tickets transferring production to the next process in the sequence, and (4) material, labor, and overhead standard costs. The output from this processing run provides three important kinds of management information: (1) production performance reports that contain the quantity and quality information needed to measure productivity; (2) control data in the form of labor, material, and overhead cost variances from standard; and (3) a report of work orders that are completed. Completed work order information is then used by the inventory system to update finished goods inventory records.

Next, reports may be sorted by cost center and/or work order number prior to listing for management analysis.

A PRODUCTION SYSTEM CONFIGURATION.

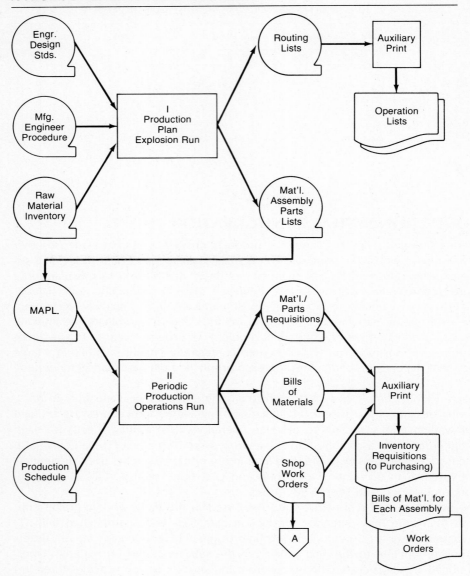

Figure 13.11

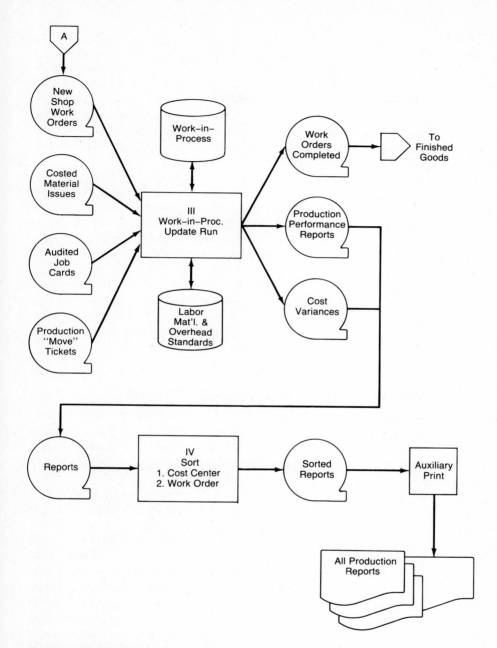

Figure 13.11 (cont'd)

SUMMARY

Production control systems reside at the heart of the largest value flow in a manufacturing company. Management of these flows and value transformations presents unique problems for accounting information systems. The three basic cost elements (direct labor, direct material, and factory burden) must first be distributed to and summarized by cost centers so that organizational performances may be measured against predetermined budgets. Organizational costs are then assigned to the flow of physical products in order to determine *unit costs.* Accurate unit cost determination is the very essence of effective production management and control.

Cost control is often facilitated through the application of *standard* costs (in lieu of actual costs) as the elements of costs are utilized in the production process. Any differences (variances) between actual costs and standard costs are isolated by cause and used by management to effect corrective action. As both the physical product and the accompanying cost flows exit the manufacturing environment upon completion of the production process, standard costs and variances are reunited so that financial accounts once again reflect actual costs.

The accounting information systems designed to track and account for these flows are generally operated by cost accountants. Like most other systems, attention tends to focus on the accuracy and reliability of input data, precise distribution of production costs, maintenance of complete and accurate data bases, and the accurate apportionment of production costs to equivalent whole units of the product.

APPENDIX: COMPUTATION OF EQUIVALENT UNITS

Students who have already completed the basic cost accounting course may wish to refresh their memories by referring back to any standard cost accounting or managerial accounting text. Others who have not experienced the procedure for computing equivalent whole units may find the following brief presentation helpful in understanding its nature and purpose.

First, it must be emphasized that the procedure will differ depending on a company's "cost flow assumption" (FIFO, or weighted average). It is sufficient for the purposes of this book to illustrate only the FIFO method.

Figure 13.12 gives an overview of the FIFO procedure, using small numbers for the sake of simplicity. Keep in mind that the management of each cost center is held accountable for (1) the total physical units passing through that particular production process and (2) all costs charged to the process. The units are usually accounted for by determining (1) units completed and released to the next operation in sequence and (2) units remaining in the cost center in various stages of completion. Of course, when units are spoiled in production they are accounted for by eliminating them from the physical flow. Spoiled units are not considered in order to keep the procedure simple.

The accounting period is the time span within which both physical product and associated cost flows are measured. That is, production costs within a given accounting period must move in harmony with *completed* production. It follows, therefore, that the cost to produce a *single* completed unit must be established so as to determine how

DETERMINATION OF EQUIVALENT UNITS.

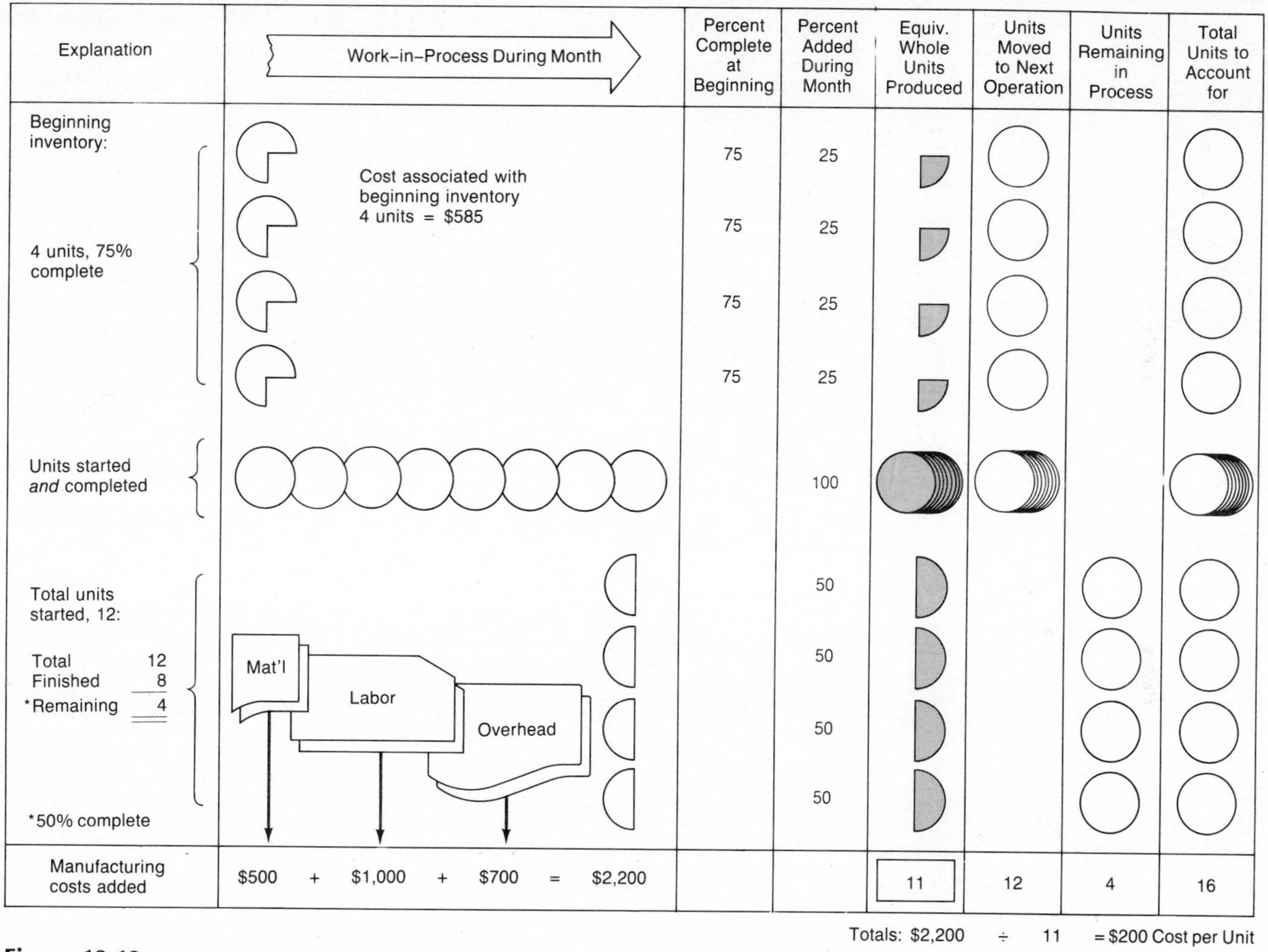

Explanation	Work-in-Process During Month	Percent Complete at Beginning	Percent Added During Month	Equiv. Whole Units Produced	Units Moved to Next Operation	Units Remaining in Process	Total Units to Account for
Beginning inventory:							
	Cost associated with beginning inventory 4 units = $585	75	25				
4 units, 75% complete		75	25				
		75	25				
		75	25				
Units started *and* completed		100	100				
Total units started, 12:			50				
Total 12 Finished 8 *Remaining 4			50				
			50				
*50% complete			50				
Manufacturing costs added	$500 + $1,000 + $700 = $2,200			11	12	4	16

Totals: $2,200   ÷   11   = $200 Cost per Unit

Figure 13.12

much of total production costs assigned to a cost center should accompany the product to the next operation, and how much should remain in the cost center associated with unfinished production.

The illustration shows that 4 units, each 75 percent complete, were in process at the beginning of the accounting period. This condition indicates that 25 percent *more* materials, labor, and overhead costs are required to complete the units during the period. In the meantime, 12 additional units were placed into production. Of these, 8 were completed during the period, leaving 4 *half-completed* units still in process at the cutoff time.

The question is simply this: How many *equivalent* whole units were completed during the period? Of course, it is only logical to consider that one fourth of the resources required to finish the 4 beginning units, together, are the equivalent of one whole unit. Similarly, the 4 half-finished units left in work-in-process have consumed the equivalent of *2* whole units of resources. Considered together with the 8 units that were started *and* completed during the period, it is clear that the equivalent of *11* whole units were manufactured (1 + 8 + 2). The column entitled "equivalent whole units produced" in Figure 13.12 graphically demonstrates how this total is derived.

Total costs of $2,200 were allocated to the cost center during the period, representing direct materials ($500), direct labor ($1,000), and factory overhead ($700). These resources were required to (1) complete the four units in process at the beginning, (2) start and finish 8 additional units, and (3) accomplish half the work required to complete 4 units left in inventory. We can determine the cost to complete *one whole unit* by spreading the production costs of $2,200 over the equivalent whole units of production ($2,200 ÷ 11 = $200 per unit).

Management may now respond intelligently to the following requirements:

1. Account for the 16 units worked on during the period.
   Response:
   a. Transferred to next operation   12
      (4 from beginning inventory and 8
      started and completed)
   b. Still in process, 50% complete   <u>4</u>
      Total accounted for   <u>16</u>
2. Account for the flow of costs charged to the cost center ($585 in beginning inventory and $2,200 of current period cost.)
   Response:
   a. Cost transferred:
      Beginning Inventory $585
      Add: Cost to Complete
         (4 × ¼ × $200)   <u>200</u> $ 785
      Units started and completed
         (8 × $200)   <u>1,600</u>
         Total cost transferred $2,385
   b. Cost in Unfinished Inventory
         (4 × ½ × $200)   <u>400</u>
         Total cost accounted for   <u>$2,785</u>

NOTE

[1]See Wayne J. Morse, James R. Davis, and Al L. Hartgraves, *Management Accounting,* Addison-Wesley Publishing Co., for a discussion of equivalent units computation. Also refer to Appendix A.

SELECTED REFERENCES

Anthony, Robert N., and Glenn A. Welch. *Fundamentals of Management Accounting,* 3rd ed. Homewood, Ill.: Richard D. Irwin, Inc., 1981.

Arthur Andersen & Co. *A Guide for Studying and Evaluating Internal Accounting Controls,* January 1978.

Cashin, James A., and Ralph S. Polimeni. *Cost Accounting.* New York: McGraw-Hill Book Co., 1981.

Coopers & Lybrand. *Internal Control Reference Manual: Production Cycle,* 1978.

Dearden, John. *Cost Accounting and Financial Control Systems.* Reading, Mass.: Addison-Wesley Publishing Co., 1976.

DeCoster, Don T., and Eldon L. Schafer. *Management Accounting: A Decision Emphasis,* 3rd ed. New York: John Wiley & Sons, Inc., 1982.

Ernst & Whinney. *Evaluating Internal Control: A Guide for Management and Directors,* 1979.

Garrison, Ray H. *Managerial Accounting,* 3rd ed. Plano, Tex.: Business Publications, Inc., 1982.

Gray, Jack, and Don Ricketts. *Cost and Managerial Accounting.* New York: McGraw-Hill Book Co., 1982.

Horngren, Charles T. *Introduction to Management Accounting,* 6th ed. Englewood Cliffs, N.J.: Prentice-Hall, Inc., 1984.

Morse, Wayne, James R. Davis, and Al L. Hartgraves. *Managerial Accounting.* Reading, Mass.; Addison-Wesley Publishing Co., 1984.

"Process Computers Head for Wide Role in Plant Automation," *Business Week* (June 29, 1968): 60, 64.

Schrier, Elliot. "Production Planning in a Multiplant System," *California Management Review,* 11(4) (Summer 1969): 69–78.

QUESTIONS

1. Discuss the functions of the production work order and the operations list (routing sheet) in controlling the production process.
2. Enumerate some major risks inherent in a poorly controlled production system.
3. What are some of the physical and financial controls used in the production process to help minimize the risks elucidated in question 2?
4. Identify the source documents that support and feed the production control system, and discuss their origins and controls.
5. Differentiate the two recognized cost accumulation systems, job order and process.
6. What is "equivalent units of production," and what role does it play in production costing?
7. Explain the functions of a bill of materials.
8. How does the use of standard costs aid management in the control of production costs?
9. Why is it necessary to reunite cost variances with standard costs at the end of an accounting period?
10. Explain the impact on inventories caused by isolating the material price variance at the time of purchase of raw materials, as opposed to the time of issuance to production.
11. Discuss the role of the cost accountant in production operations.
12. Given the organization chart shown here, enumerate any concerns you might have concerning controls.

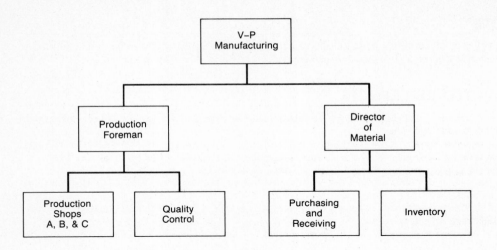

13. Why is it necessary, or desirable, to reconcile employees time cards with the supervisors record of the time employees spend working on various jobs?

14. Why would it be necessary to restrict access to production control data bases, since manufacturing has few (if any) relationships with outside organizations?

15. Describe the similarities and differences between manual and computer techniques in processing production information (consider documents, information flows, controls, and management reports).

16. What purposes might be served by using on-line real-time processing techniques in the production systems.

17. Comment on the organization and record content of work-in-process master files in a job order costing system as opposed to a process costing system.

PROBLEMS

18. Production Systems Controls

Random C. Quence Company manufacturers a fairly expensive consumer product on which a decorative ornament is installed during the final stages of production. The ornament is very popular among teenagers in the community and has become a sort of status symbol when mounted on bicycles, motor bikes, jalopies, and other vehicles.

During one of the company's rather infrequent studies of its production operations efficiency, it was discovered that each unit of finished product consumed about 1.3 of these attractive little ornaments. As a single component of the total direct material cost, the gadget is not a significant item. Its average inventory value is about $3.75. Nevertheless, based on the company's annual production volume of 60,000 units of finished product, it is apparent that $67,500 worth of direct materials is being misappropriated each year.

Following discovery of the discrepancy, the production manager assigned a "troubleshooter" to observe direct material requisitioning procedures very carefully. The investigation revealed that the correct quantities of raw materials were being withdrawn from inventory by the production dispatcher as each order entered the final stage of production. Subsequently, the floor supervisor would issue "supplemental requisitions" to cover shortages, charging a material spoilage account for the excess usage.

Further observation at the factory lunchroom revealed several assembly workers surreptitiously dropping ornaments into empty lunch boxes to take home at the end of their shift.

Required:

    a. Do you consider this petty theft a control weakness?

    b. Should the consistently high balance in the material use variance (spoilage) account have suggested corrective action to management before now?

    c. What procedures would you recommend to stop the pilferage of ornaments?

19. Inventory and Production Control

Production control procedures for the Rand Company require hand delivery of completed work orders to cost accounting at the close of each workday. Cost accounting processes these documents by adding standard costs for labor and materials and applying overhead on the basis of actual labor hours used. A journal voucher is prepared debiting finished goods inventory and crediting work-in-process at standard costs.

Inventory master records are independently updated when the inventory control copy of the completed work order is received directly from production control. Procedurally, inventory clerks match their own "information copy" of the work order with the "costed" copy from cost accounting. The inventory "receipt" is then keypunched and introduced into the computer system, where quantity is updated and costs are reaveraged on the basis of the new data.

A particularly large work order was completed on Friday, December 29, 198X, just prior to year-end closing. The production expediter delivered the documents to cost accounting just as the office was closing at 5:00 PM for the long holiday weekend. On the following Tuesday morning, January 2, the routine processing was accomplished by cost accounting according to procedure. In the meantime, the inventory copy of the work order was delayed because of spoilage inspection problems imposed by customer specifications. This problem was cleared on Friday, January 12, and the remainder of the production documentation was released. Neither cost accounting nor inventory control was aware of the inspection delay until after all data were compiled for preparation of financial statements. The formal statements were published on January 15.

Required:

    a. What affect does this timing error have on inventories? Net income? Balance sheet?

    b. Should the errors be corrected retroactively so that the year-end statements are correct?

20. Evaluation and Analysis of Cost Centers for Control Purposes

Denny Daniels is production manager of the Alumalloy Division of WRT Inc. Alumalloy has limited contact with outside customers and has no sales staff. Most of its customers are other divisions of WRT. All sales and purchases with outside customers are handled by other corporate divisions. Therefore, Alumalloy is treated as a cost center for reporting and evaluation purposes rather than as a revenue or profit center.

Daniels perceives the accounting department as a historical number-generating process that provides little useful information for conducting his job. Consequently, the entire accounting process is perceived as a negative motivational device that does not reflect how hard or how effectively he works as a production manager. Daniels tried to discuss these perceptions and concerns with John Scott, the controller for the Alumalloy Division. Daniels told Scott, "I think the cost report is misleading. I know I've had better production over a number of operating periods, but the cost report still says I have excessive costs. Look, I'm not an accountant, I'm a production manager. I know how to get a good quality product out. Over a number of years, I've even cut the raw materials used to do it. But the cost report doesn't show any of this. Basically, it's always negative, no matter what I do. There's no way you can win with accounting or the people at corporate who use those reports."

Scott gave Daniels little consolation. Scott stated that the accounting system and the cost reports generated by headquarters are just part of the corporate game and almost impossible for an individual to change. "Although these accounting reports are pretty much the basis for evaluating the efficiency of your division and the means corporate uses to determine whether you have done the job they want, you shouldn't worry too much. You haven't been fired yet! Besides, these cost reports have been used by WRT for the last 25 years."

Daniels perceived from talking to the production manager of the Zinc Division that most of what Scott said was probably true. However, some minor cost reporting changes for Zinc had been agreed to by corporate headquarters. He also knew from the trade grapevine that the turnover of production managers was considered high at WRT, even though relatively few were fired. Most seemed to end up quitting, usually in disgust, because of beliefs that they were not being evaluated fairly. Typical comments of production managers who have left WRT are:

> Corporate headquarters doesn't really listen to us. All they consider are those misleading cost reports. They don't want them changed and they don't want any supplemental information.
>
> The accountants may be quick with numbers but they don't know anything about production. As it was, I either had to ignore the cost reports entirely or pretend they are important even though they didn't tell how good a job I had done. No matter what they say about not firing people, negative reports mean negative evaluations. I'm better off working for another company.

A recent copy of the cost report prepared by Corporate headquarters for the Alumalloy Division is shown here. Daniels does not like this report because he believes it fails to reflect the division's operations properly, thereby resulting in an unfair evaluation of performance. *(IMA Adapted)*

ALLUMALLOY DIVISION COST REPORT
FOR THE MONTH OF APRIL
($000 OMITTED)

	Master Budget	Actual Cost	Excess Cost
Aluminum	$ 400	$ 437	$ 37
Labor	560	540	(20)
Overhead	100	134	34
Total	$ 1,060	$ 1,111	$ 51

Required:
    a. Comment on Denny Daniel's perception of:
        (1) John Scott, the controller
        (2) Corporate headquarters
        (3) The cost report
        (4) Himself as a production manager and discuss how his perception affects his behavior and probable performance as a production manager and employee of WRT.
    b. Identify and explain three changes that could be made in the cost information presented to the production managers that would make the information more meaningful and less threatening to them.

21. Production Schedules, Requirements, and Controls

Calen Company manufactures and sells three products. The three products are manufactured in a factory consisting of four departments. Both labor and machine time are applied to the products as they pass through each applicable department. The nature of the machine processing and labor skills required in each department is such that neither machines nor labor can be switched from one department to another.

Calen's management is attempting to plan its production schedule for the next several months. The planning is complicated by the fact that there are labor shortages in the community and some machines will be down several months for repairs.

The following information regarding available machine and labor time by department and the machine hours and direct labor hours required per unit of product has been accumulated to aid in the decision. These data should be valid for at least the next 6 months.

	Department			
Monthly Capacity Availability	**1**	**2**	**3**	**4**
Available machine capacity in machine hours	3,000	3,100	2,700	3,300
Available labor in direct labor hours	3,700	4,500	2,750	2,600

Labor and Machine Specifications per Unit of Product

		Department			
Product	Labor and Machine Time	1	2	3	4
401	Direct labor hours	2	3	3	1
	Machine hours	1	1	2	2
403	Direct labor hours	1	2	—	2
	Machine hours	1	1	—	2
405	Direct labor hours	2	2	2	1
	Machine hours	2	2	1	1

The sales department believes that the monthly demand for the next 6 months will be as follows:

Product	Monthly Sales Volume in Units
401	500
403	400
405	1,000

Inventory levels are at satisfactory levels and need not be increased or decreased during the next 6 months. The unit price and cost data that will be valid for the next 6 months are presented here. *(IMA Adapted)*

	Product		
	401	403	405
Unit Costs:			
Direct material	$ 7	$ 13	$ 17
Direct labor			
Department 1	12	6	12
Department 2	21	14	14
Department 3	24	—	16
Department 4	9	18	9
Variable overhead	27	20	25
Fixed overhead	15	10	32
Variable selling	3	2	4
Unit selling price	$196	$123	$167

Required:

a. Calculate the monthly requirement for machine hours and direct labor hours for the production of products 401, 403, and 405 to determine whether the monthly sales demand for the three products can be met by the factory.

b. What monthly production schedule should Calen Co. select in order to maximize its dollar profits? Explain how you selected this production schedule.

c. Identify the alternatives Calen Co. might consider so it can supply its customers with all the product they demand.

22. Production Centers, Responsibility Accounting, and Output Reporting

Kelly Petroleum Company has a large oil and natural gas project in Oklahoma. The project has been organized into two production centers (petroleum production and natural gas production) and one service center (maintenance).

Maintenance Center Activities and Scheduling

Don Pepper, Maintenance Center Manager, has organized his maintenance workers into work crews that serve the two production centers. The maintenance crews perform preventive maintenance and repair equipment in both the field and the central maintenance shop.

Pepper is responsible for scheduling all maintenance work in the field and at the central shop. Preventive maintenance is performed according to a set schedule established by Pepper and approved by the production center managers. Breakdowns are given immediate priority in scheduling so that downtime is minimized. Thus, preventive maintenance occasionally must be postponed, but every attempt is made to reschedule it within 3 weeks.

Preventive maintenance work is the responsibility of Pepper. However, if a significant problem is discovered during preventive maintenance, the appropriate production center supervisor authorizes and supervises the repair after checking with Pepper.

When a breakdown in the field occurs, the production centers contact Pepper to initiate the repairs. The repair work is supervised by the production center supervisor. Machinery and equipment sometimes need to be replaced while the original equipment is repaired in the central shop. This procedure is followed only when the time to make the repair in the field would result in an extended interruption of operations. Replacement of equipment is recommended by the maintenance work crew supervisor and approved by a production center supervisor.

Routine preventive maintenance and breakdowns of automotive and mobile equipment used in the field are completed in the central shop. All repairs and maintenance activities taking place in the central shop are under the direction of Pepper.

Maintenance Center Accounting Activities

Pepper has records identifying the work crews assigned to each job in the field, the number of hours spent on the job, and parts and supplies used on the job. In addition, records for the central shop (jobs, labor hours, parts, and supplies) have been maintained. However, this detailed maintenance information is not incorporated into Kelly's accounting system.

Pepper develops the annual budget for the maintenance center by planning the preventive maintenance that will be needed during the year, estimating the number and seriousness of breakdowns, and estimating the shop activities. He then bases the labor, parts, and supply costs on his plans and estimates and develops the budget amounts by line item. Because the timing of the breakdowns is impossible to plan, Pepper divides the annual budget by 12 to derive the monthly budget.

All costs incurred by the work crews in the field and in the central shop are accumulated monthly and then allocated to the two production cost centers based on the field hours worked in each production center. This method of cost allocation has been used on Pepper's recommendation because he believed that it was easy to implement and understand. Furthermore, he believed that a better allocation system was impossible to incorporate into the monthly report due to the wide range of salaries paid to the maintenance workers and the fast turnover of materials and parts.

The November cost report for the maintenance center that is provided by the accounting department is shown in the next column.

Production Center Manager's Concerns

Both production center managers have been upset with the method of cost allocation. Furthermore, they believe the report is virtually useless as a cost control device. Actual costs always seem to deviate from the monthly budget and the proportion charged to each production center varies significantly from month-to-

OKLAHOMA PROJECT MAINTENANCE CENTER COST REPORT
FOR THE MONTH OF NOVEMBER
(IN THOUSANDS OF DOLLARS)

	Budget	Actual	Petroleum Production	Natural Gas Production
Shop hours	2,000	1,800	—	—
Field hours	8,000	10,000	6,000	4,000
Labor-electrical	$ 25.0	$ 24.0	$ 14.4	$ 9.6
Labor-mechanical	30.0	35.0	21.0	14.0
Labor-instrumentation	18.0	22.5	13.5	9.0
Labor-automotive	3.5	2.8	1.7	1.1
Labor-heavy equipment	9.6	12.3	7.4	4.9
Labor-equipment operation	28.8	35.4	21.2	14.2
Labor-general	15.4	15.9	9.6	6.3
Parts	60.0	86.2	51.7	34.5
Supplies	15.3	12.2	7.3	4.9
Lubricants and fuels	3.4	3.0	1.8	1.2
Tools	2.5	3.2	1.9	1.3
Accounting and data processing	1.5	1.5	.9	.6
Total	$ 213.0	$ 254.0	$ 152.4	$ 101.6

month. Maintenance costs have increased substantially since 1980, and the production managers believe that they have no way to judge whether such an increase is reasonable.

The two production managers, Pepper, and representatives of corporate accounting have met to discuss these concerns. They concluded that a responsibility accounting system could be developed to replace the current system. In their opinion, a responsibility accounting system would alleviate the production managers' concerns and accurately reflect the activity of the Maintenance Center. (IMA adapted)

Required:

a. Explain the purposes of a responsibility accounting system, and discuss how such a system could resolve the concerns of the production center managers of Kelly Petroleum Company.

b. Describe the behavioral advantages generally attributed to responsibility accounting systems that the management of Kelly Petroleum Company should expect if the system were effectively introduced for the maintenance center.

c. Describe a report format for the maintenance center that would be based on an effective responsibility accounting system, and explain which, if any, of the maintenance center's costs should be charged to the two production centers.

CASES

23. At first glance, the production shops in Apogee Company may appear to be the only functions that have definite purpose and organization. Closer scrutiny, however, reveals an almost total absence of control over the use of scarce resources, the physical movement of production, and the accumulation and assignment of manufacturing costs. Much of the difficulty may be attributable to the fact that the use of resources is totally undocumented and that there is no planning in the form of budgets and/or standards by which to measure production efficiency.

Considering a probable 200 percent increase in production requirements, suggest remedies and procedures to control adequately and manage effectively the production operation.

24. Based on the concepts you studied in this chapter, and perhaps in your cost accounting course, evaluate the production function in Bubbling Stone Beverage Company. Some of the points you should address are:

a. Is there a formal production planning and control process?

b. Are production activities effectively managed?

c. What kind of cost accumulation system, job order or process, would you say is followed?

d. Are cost standards effectively utilized?

e. Are production activities properly documented?

f. Are inputs into the system satisfactorily controlled?

g. Suggest any changes you feel might improve the system.

CHAPTER FOURTEEN

The Payroll System

From the standpoint of volume of activity and records processed, payroll probably constitutes the largest operating system for most companies. In labor-intensive businesses the system may also rank among the most important in terms of dollars expended. Certainly the payroll system is among the most sensitive of all accounting information systems since it represents the company's financial interface with its employees and the community. A missed production schedule, a late vendor payment resulting in loss of discount, a minor stockout condition in inventory are all situations likely to engender immediate management attention. But nothing reverberates with the resounding impact of a late payroll or an incorrect paycheck.

Irrespective of size, the payroll system must be designed to accomplish the company's specific goals as they relate to employees, external interests, and internal needs and to provide for a variety of contingencies imposed both by law and company policy. The requirements for accuracy and timeliness impose stringent deadlines on all payroll activities, and the system is further complicated by governmental reporting requirements associated with such agency funds as income and social security taxes.

Because payroll represents an expenditure of funds for all employees, the payroll system impacts on most components of any organization. In this book, the payroll system has been categorized as part of the conversion cycle since, in most manufacturing concerns, payroll primarily represents the company's expenditure for labor involved in converting raw materials into finished products. Strong arguments could also be made for classifying the payroll system as a component of the expenditure cycle, especially in service organizations.

FUNCTIONS AND OBJECTIVES

Many factors impact on the payroll system. For example, the size of the company might be a deciding factor in whether the system is manual or computerized. The nature of the company's business certainly would affect the timekeeping and labor cost accumulation procedures. A broad divisionalization of company operations, by geography or by product line, may play an important role in the decision to centralize or decentralize the payroll processing. Nevertheless, since so many *basic* characteristics are inherent in all payroll operations, emphasis is focused on these fundamentals used in a payroll system.

Organization

Payroll operations are usually performed under the aegis of the controller, even though the treasurer exercises ultimate control over payroll disbursements through validation and check-signing responsibilities. Frequently, personnel in the treasurer's or controller's office (i.e., the paymaster) are also responsible for the physical distribution of checks or pay envelopes to employees. Typically, however, pay instruments are batched by operational unit or cost centers and distributed to responsible first line supervision for final dissemination to the proper recipients.

A typical organization chart, greatly simplified, is presented in Figure 14.1. It will

ORGANIZATION OF A MANUFACTURING COMPANY.

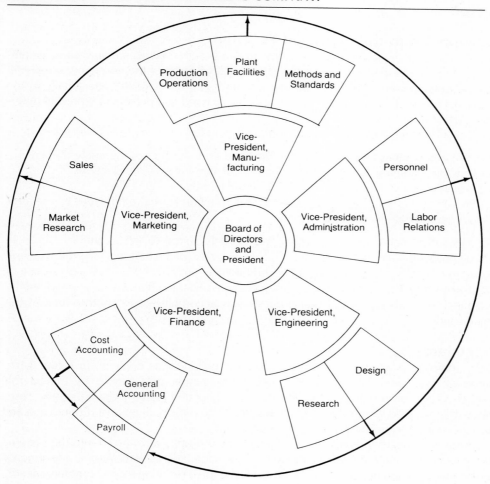

Figure 14.1

become apparent in the discussion that only the payroll system requires the participation and cooperation of *all* organizational units. In a very real sense, every department is a regular contributor to the payroll system and a major subscriber to its products. For purposes of control, however, payroll-related activity is usually channeled through a limited number of direct participants. Thus, in a narrow sense, payroll is directly related to three main operational channels: the personnel function, the production or manufacturing system, and several functional units of the financial operation—primarily accounts payable, the cashier, and cost accounting. Broadly speaking, the personnel operation feeds the system authorized data that determine the pay status of all bona fide company employees. The production control system provides information concerning the precise assignment of factory labor sources. Finally, the accounting subsystems record the results of the payroll and perform the necessary banking transfers to meet the cash needs of the system.

Relationship to the Personnel Function

The payroll cycle logically begins with the acquisition (hiring) of human resources (employees) that takes place in one of the administrative areas of the company, usually an administrative vice-president. Of course, the payroll process relates specifically to the personnel function. However, in most companies payroll and personnel represent different functions.

The objectives of the personnel function include:

1. Hiring personnel who are properly qualified and can be appropriately trained
2. Providing training programs as necessary for employees' job functions
3. Providing for a viable and useful review and evaluation process
4. Providing the necessary data to the payroll function so that employees can receive payment for their services.

The personnel operation is therefore uniquely suited to act as official liaison in payroll matters concerning status of employee, rate of pay, hours of work, payroll deductions, and subsequent changes in conditions of employment. Thus, authenticity of the payroll and the distribution of labor costs associated therewith are provided by personnel, even though the actual processing is accomplished in another area of the organization.

Procedures

Each employee is assigned to an organizational unit such as depicted in Figure 14.1. Labor costs are initially accumulated under cost center designations by the payroll system. As demonstrated in the inventory and production systems chapters these costs are further assigned to shop operations, and finally to individual units of product that are carried forward to finished goods inventory.

Routine changes in employee status must be promptly introduced into the system. Such changes may result from promotion or demotion, cost center transfer, adjustments in pay rate, or union negotiations. Employee severance resulting from retirement, death, resignation, dismissal, and leaves of absence are other common forms of status change. Although most of these decisions originate at the cost center level, responsibility for transmitting them to the payroll system rests exclusively with the personnel office. Individual cost centers are therefore in constant communication with the personnel office concerning employee status.

Record Maintenance

Every employer who is subject to the provisions of the Fair Labor Standard Act of 1938, as amended, is required to maintain records containing information and data described by the specific sections of the act. Although the law does not attempt to specify the form these records should take, it leaves no doubt as to the content or the period of retention of such records.

As a consequence, the very foundation of any good payroll system is the master employee earnings history record, which includes the following basic information:

1. Employee full name and address
2. Employee number
3. Account number—department code
4. Social security number
5. Birth date
6. Job or occupation title and code
7. Shift or work schedule
8. Rate of pay
9. Regular and overtime earnings (current and accumulated for three years)
10. Withholding data

The source documents supporting this information are preserved and must be available for inspection for a minimum period of 3 years. Payroll and personnel departments must work closely to establish detailed company policies and procedures governing (1) employment, (2) retirement, (3) promotion/demotion and transfer, (4) leaves of absence and vacation eligibility, (5) pay rate, bonus, and incentive pay, (6) fringe benefits, (7) group insurance, (8) performance reviews, and (9) disciplinary action, and other conditions pertinent to employment.

Timekeeping and Attendance Reporting

Having identified the personnel function as the authorized channel for transmitting employee status information, we now turn to the matter of documenting the employees' pay entitlement. Such evidence is provided through the use of time cards and attendance reports, a process that places individual cost centers in direct communication with the payroll department. Clearly, one channel establishes authority for payment while the other provides performance information by which pay is calculated, as illustrated in Figure 14.2.

The broad payroll function typically consists of three, often departmentalized, operations: timekeeping, payroll, and labor distribution. The Fair Labor Standards Act requires that formal time and attendance records serve as the basis for all payroll computations. These documents originate in various ways.

Attendance reporting is normally associated with "salaried" occupations that are

TIMEKEEPING AND ATTENDANCE REPORTING.

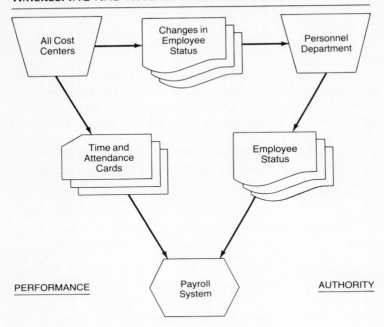

Figure 14.2

not readily adaptable to precise measurement. Such records may take the form of prepunched cards that require both the validating signature of the employees' supervisor or manager and the appropriate noting and coding of absences to effect the proper payroll processing. An alternate form may involve the use of an approved attendance roster that is keypunched to yield the same end product.

"Hourly" occupations require more precise measurement, not only for computing gross pay but for product costing as well. Although time cards may be manually marked and subsequently keypunched, common procedure in most companies requires the use of electromechanical equipment such as the time clock. The operating payroll system should yield a time card prepunched with appropriate employee data for each employee in advance of the payroll period. The timekeeper collects the signed time and attendance cards at the end of the payroll period and prepares them for processing.

A common control feature in most manufacturing companies requires that labor time distribution be accomplished independently of the routine payroll and timekeeping operations. For purposes of this discussion, assume that production job cards are channeled to the cost accounting department following a cursory test for accuracy by the timekeeping department. Matching these two independent data sets ensures accuracy and prevents fraudulent payroll entries. Factory supervision assumes primary responsibility for the execution of company policies covering labor time allocations and coordinates directly with the cost accounting department, as shown in Figure 14.3.

TIMEKEEPING, ATTENDANCE, AND LABOR DISTRIBUTION.

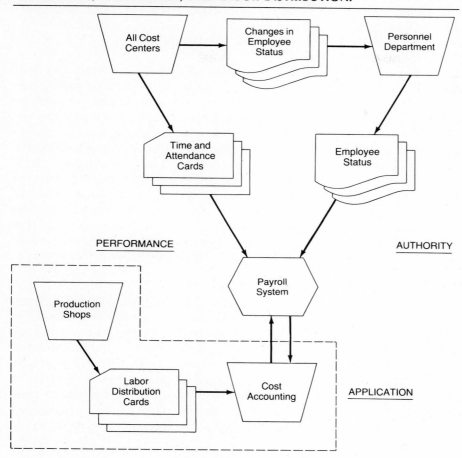

Figure 14.3

SOURCE DOCUMENTS

Each company is likely to design its own payroll-related forms, use its own systems jargon, and operate uniquely in a variety of ways. Nevertheless, certain input records are essential to any good payroll system. In the preceding illustrations, document origination and handling restrictions have been emphasized as a means of controlling payroll improprieties. The form and content of the most important of these documents will now be examined.

Personnel Action Forms

The personnel operation may utilize many types of forms for special purposes such as job applications, change of status, work performance review, employee injury reports, employee counseling, and severance notices. Selected forms and documents that directly affect an employee's status and pay are shown in Figure 14.4 (status change) and Figure 14.5 (personnel action). Through the use of such forms, employee master records are maintained in current condition to support payment of wages, salaries, and commissions.

Time and Attendance Forms

The distinction between time cards and job cards is often confusing. Figure 14.6 may prove helpful in conceptualizing their respective purposes. Time cards, containing only clock-in and clock-out recordings, remain near the clock station at all times. Job cards, on the other hand, may take several forms, depending on the design of the system. Often the card travels with the employee from assignment to assignment, requiring a manual entry of time spent in separate operations by the responsible supervisor. In other situations, the employee may clock in and out of each assignment, creating a separate job card for each operation, the total of which must approximate total hours worked as shown by the time card. Regardless of the form of the job card, it represents a crucial document in the production control system. The job card is the source document for job costs collection relating to direct labor, one of the three components of total production cost. Thus, the data on the job card and its accuracy have a direct impact on job cost, labor distribution, and cost variances. Examples of daily time cards and job cards are shown in Figure 14.7.

Payroll Deduction Forms

Another category of payroll input documents is the authorized payroll deduction. These forms, which must be validated by the employee's signature, provide the authority to withhold specified amounts for designated purposes from the employee's pay. Some are mandatory (Federal Form W-4, "Employees Withholding Allowance Certificate"), and others optional, but all are handled in essentially the same manner. Depending on state laws and the company's contract with its union, the employee may be required to authorize deductions for union dues and legal levies such as court orders and garnishments. Other deductions for items such as credit unions, savings bonds, participatory retirement and group insurance, are accomplished at the request of the employee.

Payroll Adjustment Forms

No matter how well planned and carefully executed the payroll system is, operational inconsistencies, problems, and mistakes invariably occur. Such instances will normally be minimal. If they persist in significant volume, payroll procedures should be carefully reviewed for possible weaknesses in data flow and controls. A good payroll system must include a procedure for making adjustments and corrections and at the same time provide for adequate controls. A general format for such documents does not exist, for their variety in form and content is infinite.

DOCUMENT FLOW AND TIMING

Despite the fact that payroll-related events are more attuned to the expediency of the production process than to any planned sequence, they do tend to flow in an organized pattern. Attention is directed to the document flowchart, as shown in Figure 14.8. Tracking the numbered events in the chart will help bring the whole process into focus.

PERSONNEL CHANGE OF STATUS
PLEASE TYPE OR PRINT

A. ACTION TO BE TAKEN:

[ ] EMPLOYMENT   [ ] RECLASSIFICATION   [ ] LEAVE OF ABSENCE   [ ] TERMINATION

01. New Hire	12. Merit Increase	21. Personal	31. Discharge
02. Re-Hire	13. Plant Transfer	22. Medical	32. Retirement
03. Return From L.O.A.	14. Dept./Shift/Job Chg.	23. Military	33. Lay Off
05. Part Time	15. General Increase	24. Maternity	34. Quit
06. Military Re-Instatement	16. Name Change		36. Other
	17. Change Tax Code		
	18. Change Marital Status		
	19. Other		

KEY	LEVEL 1	LEVEL 2

B. PERSONAL DATA:

EMPL. NO. _ _ _/_ _/_ _ _ _   NAME _____   _____

ADDRESS _____ CITY/STATE _____ ZIP CODE _ _ _ _

DATE OF BIRTH _____ EEO CODE _____ MARITAL STATUS _____ NO. OF DEPENDENTS _____

PHONE NO. _____ FEDERAL TAX CODE _ _ _ STATE TAX CODE _ _ _ PAY CODE _____

ADDITIONAL FEDERAL WITHHOLDING _____ ADDITIONAL STATE WITHHOLDING _____

PAY BASIS: □ PERMANENT   □ PART-TIME   □ WEEKLY   □ BI-WEEKLY

C. JOB DATA:

PLANT NO. _____ PLANT NAME _____ DEPT. NAME _____ DATE BEGAN WORK _____

	HRS. PER SHIFT	JOB NUMBER	SHIFT	OVERSEER CODE	PAY RATE
FROM:	1-4-6-8				
TO:	1-4-6-8				

JOB TITLE _____

D. LEAVE OF ABSENCE: FROM _____ TO _____   LAST DATE WORKED _____

E. EXPLANATION:

EFFECTIVE DATE: _____

PEFORMANCE RATING (Circle one):   Above Average,   Good,   Average,   Fair,   Poor

ATTITUDE _____ ATTENDANCE _____ QUALITY _____

WOULD YOU REHIRE?   YES ( )   NO ( )

F. APPROVALS:

PLANT _____ PERSONNEL _____ PAYROLL _____

PERSONNEL WHITE, PAYROLL YELLOW, PLANT PINK

Figure 14.4

PERSONNEL ACTION.

AUBURN UNIVERSITY   **AUBURN, ALABAMA**

Name _____   Title _____
        (Last)   (First)   (Middle)

Address _____   _____

Effective Date This Action _____   Date Prepared _____

Annual Rate $ _____ Full-Time ( ) Part-Time ( )   If Part-Time, Indicate
Budget Position Number _____ 12 Months ( ) 9 Months ( )   Percent of Full Time _____
CLASSIFICATION:
        Continuing ( )   Indefinite ( )   Temporary ( )   Probationary ( )

        Estimated Length of temporary appointment _____

Citizen of _____ Annual Value of Perquisites $ _____
            (Specify Country)

FUND	DEPARTMENT	ACCOUNT CODE NO.	Annual Amount This Department
1			$
2			$
3			$
4			$
5			$

☐ **APPOINTMENT:** New Position ( )   Replacement ( )   Extension of Appointment ( )
   If replacement, give name of employee replaced: _____
   Previously employed by Auburn University?   Yes ( )   No ( )
   If yes, give name under which employed _____

☐ **CHANGE:** ( ) In Classification/Title from _____

☐ **CHANGE:** In rate from $ _____ per _____ to $ _____ per _____
☐ **CHANGE IN or REDISTRIBUTION OF FUNDS:**
☐ **SEPARATION:** Retirement ( ) Resignation ( ) Termination ( ) (If termination, give specific reason under "Other")
   Last official day of work _____ plus Accrued vacation leave _____ days; Accrued sick leave _____ days.
☐ **TRANSFER:** To _____ From _____ Department of Division
   Accrued vacation leave _____ days; Accrued sick leave _____ days.
☐ **LEAVE OF ABSENCE:** ( ) With pay through _____ , ( ) Without pay through _____ ,
   ( ) With half pay under Salary Continuation Plan as set out under "Other". Continuation of Insurance requested? Yes ( ) No ( )
☐ **REINSTATEMENT FROM LEAVE.**
☐ **OTHER:** _____
   Reason for above action: _____

_____ Designated Supervisor _____

Department Head _____ Dean or Director _____

        Date _____   Date _____

_____ Vice President(s)   APPROVED:

_____ Personnel Office   PRESIDENT _____

_____ Budget Verification   DATE _____
                       Business Office

To be completed by Personnel Office

   Unemployment Compensation Code _____ F.L.S.A. Code _____ Title Code _____

UPO-3 (REV. 1978)   **PERSONNEL OFFICE**   Submit form to University Personnel Office.

Figure 14.5

TIME CARDS AND JOB CARDS.

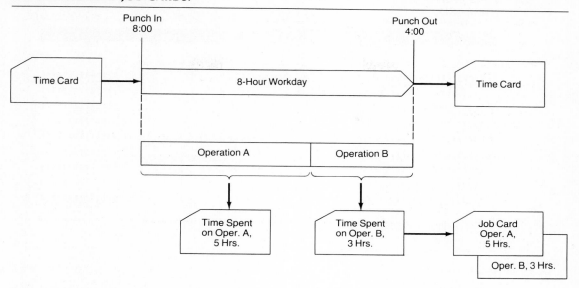

Figure 14.6

We shall begin with the acquisition of a new employee to demonstrate how the process is initiated.

1. Someone in authority initiates a personnel request form in response to a budgeted work load demand. The employment office recruits and hires a person with the specified credentials. The essential employment information is routed to the payroll department where the new employee is "placed on the payroll" by the establishment of an employee master record. A time card is prepared and placed near the new employee's clock-in station.

2. When reporting for work, the new employee clocks in with fellow employees and reports to an assigned work station (cost center). As assigned tasks are performed, the employee's time is charged to a coded operation number, or job, as previously described. For purposes of illustration, time sheets are used in lieu of cards.

3. At the end of the payroll period the timekeeper collects the time cards from the clock stations and the job time sheets from production control. Attendance reports are also received from other departments in the company. A comparison is made between clock time and job time, and discrepancies are resolved. The time cards are then routed to the payroll department and thence to data processing. Job sheets are routed to cost accounting where the labor cost distribution is accomplished and journalized.

4. The payroll is processed, producing among other things (a) employee paychecks, (b) a payroll register, (c) new time cards for the following pay period, and (d) required management reports. The timekeeper distributes the new time cards to the appropriate clock stations.

TIME CARD.
JOB CARD.

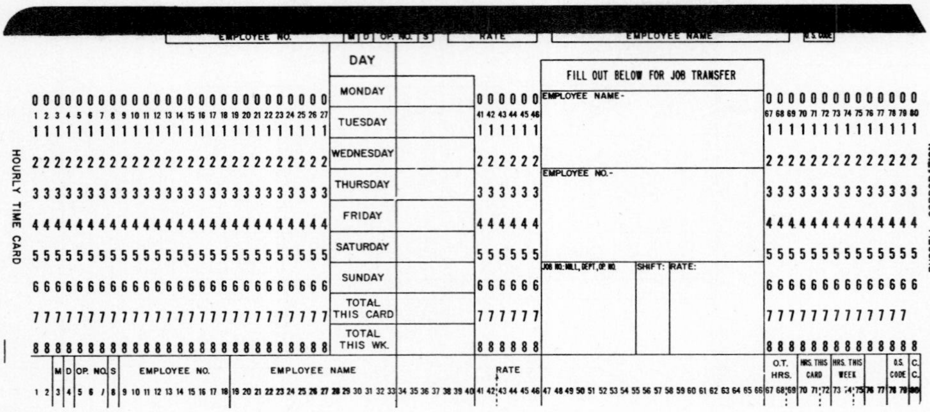

COST CENTER	REPORT STAT'N	START TIME	DIRECT LABOR						*LOST TIME CODE	*INDIRECT LABOR		AUTH'N
			PRODUCTION									
			JOB ORDER NO	PART NUMBER	OPER'N	CREW	QUANTITY	SCRAP COUNT		EXPENSE ACCT. NO.	REWORK/ C.E.R. NO.	
STOP TIME →												

*SEE REVERSE SIDE FOR CODES, EXPENSE ACCOUNT NO'S. AND REWORK/C.E.R. NO'S.

SIGNATURE DATE

— LABOR/PRODUCTION CARD —

DIRECT LABOR LOST TIME CODES

2 NON-STANDARD PROCESS OR ROUTING
3 IDLE TIME: POWER FAILURE
4 . . . . . . EQUIPMENT BREAKDOWN
5 . . . . . . WAITING FOR MATERIAL
6 . . . . . . WAITING FOR ASSIGNMENT
7 . . . . . . QUALITY CONTROL STOPPAGE
8 . . . . . . SPECIAL CLEAN-UP
9 . . . . . . SPECIAL EVENTS
0 . . . . . . OTHER

INDIRECT LABOR EXPENSE ACCT. NO'S.

1220 PROFESSIONAL TECHNICAL - HRLY
1320 CLERICAL - HOURLY
1400 INSPECTION & QUALITY CONTROL
1511 MATERIAL HANDLERS
1520 STOCKROOM ATTENDANTS
1530 TRUCK DRIVERS (OFF CO. PREMISES)
1610 JANITORS & SWEEPERS
1650 PRODUCTION EQUIPMENT CLEANING
1700 MAINTENANCE & REPAIR LABOR
1850 INVENTORY LABOR

REWORK/AFE NO.

NUMBERS FOR REWORK PROJECTS AND AFE CAPITAL EXPENDITURE PROJECTS ARE TO BE OBTAINED FROM THE PLANT MANAGER'S OFFICE AND USED ONLY WHEN AUTHORIZED BY THAT OFFICE.

MAKE NO NUMBER ENTRY ON THE EXPENSE ACCT. NO. COLUMN LINE WHEN A NUMBER ENTRY HAS BEEN MADE ON THE SAME LINE IN THE REWORK/AFE COLUMN.

LUNCHTIME CODE 99

Figure 14.7

PAYROLL DOCUMENT FLOW.

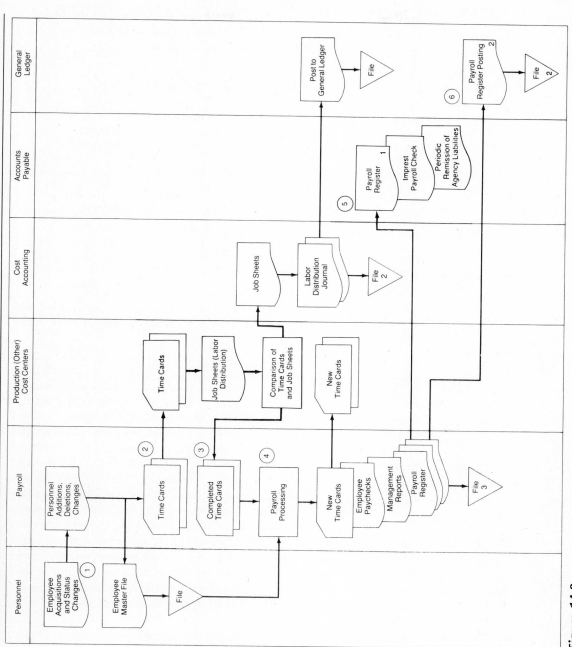

Figure 14.8

The Payroll System **421**

5. A copy of the payroll register goes to accounts payable where an imprest payroll check is prepared, transferring the exact amount of the net payroll to a special bank account. The payment of the payroll is journalized.
6. The distribution of the payroll expenses from the payroll register and the payment from the accounts payable journal are entered in the general ledger.

Entries resulting from operation 3 would appear as follows:

Factory Labor	500,000	
General and Administrative Expense	75,000	
Factory Overhead Accounts	225,000	
Other Charges	200,000	
Accrued Payroll (net)		750,000
Liabilities (Payroll Deductions)		250,000

Entries resulting from operation 5 would appear as follows:

Accrued Payroll (net)	750,000	
Cash		750,000

Employer payroll tax must also be recorded as follows:

Factory Overhead Accounts	27,000	
Administration and Other Expenses	8,000	
Liability (FICA, FUTA, etc.)		35,000

Many of the processes shown in Figure 14.8 can easily be performed by a microcomputer. For example, payroll computations and the resulting payroll register can be generated in a microcomputer.

ACCOUNTING CONTROLS

The sheer preponderance of payroll data and the diversity of its sources suggest the possibility of large-scale fraud. The more obvious examples involve listing fictitious names on the payrolls, or failure to remove terminated employees from active payroll status. Collusion among employees in reporting attendance or punching time cards for each other to cover absences, especially in areas where precise labor measurement and cost assignment are not required, is another common example of payroll impropriety. When abuses occur with the knowledge and perhaps even the participation of first-line supervision, detection becomes more difficult. Consequently, to ensure payroll systems integrity, most companies rely on administrative controls in addition to those imposed by routine accounting procedures. These are exemplified by a system of authorizations and approvals coupled with distinct separation of physical handling from related record keeping. In addition, the internal auditing department constantly observes the payroll operation, alert not only for contrived breaches of procedure but for system weaknesses that could be used to perpetrate fraud. They also verify that the control totals are being utilized and that proper audit trails are being maintained.

For most accounting systems, primary controls for payroll center on the proper separation of duties, processing controls, and maintenance of independently verifiable records. Controls in these areas provide reasonable assurance that large-scale fraud is not being committed and that financial data generated from the system are properly recorded.

Typical accounting controls for a payroll system generally include these provisions:

1. Separation of duties among persons controlling time cards, preparing payroll, and distributing payroll checks
2. Maintenance of personnel files and salary authorizations and updates of employee status performed through the personnel department, not the payroll department
3. All employee status information channeled through the personnel department
4. Time and attendance records and labor utilization records developed by line organizations independently of the payroll operation
5. Payroll employees to have no relationship with or responsibility for the hiring and firing process
6. Payroll obligations paid exclusively by check
7. Unclaimed payroll checks returned to a department not involved in payroll preparation or paycheck distribution
8. Maintenance of payroll activity for control and audit purposes, including hash and batch totals of specified data fields, and record counts of checks used and employees paid
9. Periodic rotation of payroll personnel
10. A bonded person in custody of inventory, issuance, use, and reordering of check forms
11. Periodic surprise pay distributions by personnel other than those normally assigned the task

RISKS OF FAILURE

Clearly, the risks of failure in such an important system are large. Thus, the proper functioning of the payroll system and its related controls should be a vital concern of management. When a proper control in payroll is not functioning, the organization encounters several risks. These risks broadly relate to employees, the government, safeguarding the company's assets, and financial reporting.

Employees

When payroll controls are not functioning, employees may not be paid for hours worked or remittances for payroll withholding may be incorrect. Such errors impact directly on employees and their families and indirectly on employee morale and community relations. Further, employees may be improperly evaluated due to inadequate information.

Government

Clearly, when a payroll system is not properly designed, any business risks the possibility of violating laws and governmental regulations. Laws and regulations relating to minimum wages, income taxes, fair labor practices, and payroll taxes represent some of the areas in which the company may incur fines and other penalties for violations due to failures in the payroll system.

Safeguarding the Company's Assets

If a control function in payroll fails, then a company runs the risk of losing or improperly managing the company's assets. Examples include duplicate payments, fraudulent cash disbursements, inefficient use of labor, use of company labor on noncompany projects, and hiring unqualified employees.

Financial Reporting

A fault in the payroll system could have a serious impact on the financial reporting of the company. Incorrect reporting of payroll accruals, payroll expense, payroll tax accruals, withholding liabilities as well as the possibility of unrecorded liabilities represent areas of potential adverse impact on the company's financial statements. In addition to incorrect liabilities and expenses, payroll errors could very easily impact upon the labor distribution of a manufacturing company. Errors in the labor distribution, of course, could cause misrepresentations in areas other than those previously mentioned, such as cost of goods sold and inventories.

The risks of failure discussed are but some examples of risks involved when the payroll system is not functioning properly. As should be expected with any system that impacts on a large number of people, improper functioning of the controls of the payroll system subjects the company to a large and diverse range of risks.

MANAGEMENT INFORMATION REQUIREMENTS

Since the payroll operation is essentially a "service" function whose primary concern is prepayroll control, many of the reports generated by the system are actually intended for use by other organizations inside and outside the company. Nevertheless, the sensitive nature of both input and output forces the payroll department to act as a repository of extremely confidential data available only to a limited number of authorized users. The department thus serves as the company's interface with federal and state agencies and a host of other special interest organizations such as the labor union, credit union, group insurance company, and pension and retirement funds.

This brief discourse can hardly be expected to anticipate all possible reporting demands that might be placed on payroll systems. Instead, some of the more obvious and most commonly used outputs are illustrated here; many of the possibilities for by-product management information are omitted.

Payroll Checks

The most visible of the system's products are the employee paychecks. These instruments emerge from matching audited time and attendance cards with the employee master records. Relying on the status information stored therein, payroll computations of gross pay, deductions, and net pay are routinely and simply accomplished. Limiting decisions such as the maximum FICA withholding are made according to programmed computer instructions. Paycheck output is programmed to fit a preprinted, continuous-form document such as is shown in Figure 14.9, a punched card with attached earnings and deductions summary, or a watermarked paper form with a "remittance advice" reflecting earnings and deduction data attached.

SAMPLE OF PAYROLL CHECK.

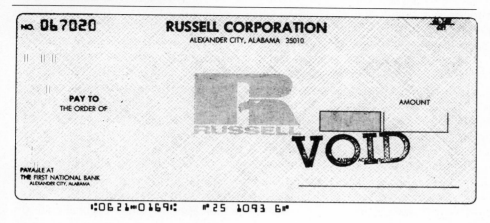

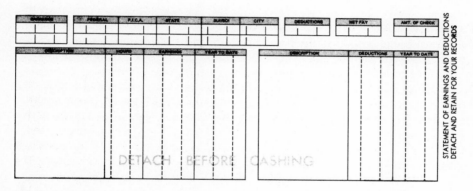

Figure 14.9

The check-creation process in a computerized operation consists of an off-line printing operation following the main payroll processing. A magnetic tape reader or disk file attached to a high-speed printer can transcribe payroll data to continuous-form checks in a matter of minutes. This approach suggests the maintenance of a fairly large stock of such blank forms, which in turn poses a serious control problem for payroll management.

Such control can be effected by adhering to a few strict but simple procedures. First, all check forms should be placed in the custody of an individual and kept under tight security. Second, all check forms should be serially prenumbered and the custodian made accountable for each number. Third, check forms supplied to the computer center for printing, and subsequently returned in finished form for distribution, should be transmitted under serial number control. Fourth, check forms mutilated or improperly printed must be returned to the custodian along with the good ones for accountability. Checks destroyed in the process must be promptly reported and the circumstances carefully documented. Finally, check reordering should be the sole responsibility of the designated custodian. The reader will observe that similar control procedures should regulate the handling of accounts payable checks, as discussed in Chapter Eleven.

The paychecks and earnings statements are sent next to the cashier's department for validation, signature, and physical distribution. A special procedure should be established in this operation for the handling and control of unclaimed payroll checks.

As an alternative to processing individual employee paychecks, many companies offer a direct deposit service to employees in which the employee's payroll check is automatically deposited to the bank checking account designated in writing by the employee. In this situation, the company will send remittance information along with authorization to charge the company account for the total amount of the employee's payroll. Such a direct deposit system, a type of electronic funds transfer (EFT) system, reduces paperwork and, as a consequence, has been increasingly used by business. Nevertheless, controls over payroll, regardless of the payment system, should still be maintained. Characteristics of EFT systems and their special control problems are discussed in detail in Chapter Four.

The Payroll Register and Master File
One of the most useful outputs of the payroll system, and a major supporting document for journalizing payroll activity, is the payroll register. This report provides the impulse and the data for accounts payable to generate the cash transfer establishing the imprest payroll fund. This can be seen in more detail in the system logic charts that follow. The payroll department also uses the register to journalize the gross and net payroll together with the authorized deductions. A payroll register format is shown in Figure 14.10.

PAYROLL REGISTER.

Employee					Earnings			
Dept.	Number	Name of Employee	Hours Worked	Base Rate	Regular	Over Time	Other	Total
014	13271	Barry C. Barfield	40.0	5.00	200.00			200
011	62914	Robert E. Bowers	44.5	8.00	356.00	18.00		374.00
102	37984	Norma W. Deitrick	40.0	7.20	288.00			288.00
008	24677	Robert L. Harris	48.0	7.00	336.00	28.00	14.00	378.00
011	12471	Charles Joseph	40.5	5.00	202.50	1.25		203.75
009	10508	James A. Maloy	40.0	4.70	188.00			188.00

Figure 14.10

Generally printed in alphabetical order by department, it also includes year-to-date information allowing it to double as a master file.

The Payroll Deductions Report

Total voluntary deductions for each employee shown in the payroll register are further itemized by specific agency funds on the weekly payroll deductions report. This report serves as a subsidiary listing to support the total deductions column appearing in the payroll register.

Periodic Payroll and Deductions Summaries

By using formats identical to the payroll register and payroll deductions report (except of course for report title and date), the system provides on cue a summary of payroll activity for the month, quarter, and year-to-date. These periodic summaries are used to support the federal, state, and local tax filings, including income tax and FICA withheld, as well as remittances to other agencies for which funds have been held in trust.

The Check Register

A simple listing of the checks issued to employees to cover the payroll liability serves several useful purposes. The principal user is the cashier's department, which performs the check audit, affixes the validating signature, journalizes the payment, and controls and distributes the checks. Minimally, the report need contain only check number, date, employee name and number, cost center, and net amount of the check. In addition to functions described previously, the check register aids in controlling unclaimed payroll checks at pay date. It is usually listed in check number order.

Period Ending September 27, 1985

| | Deductions | | | | | | Year-to-Date | | |
| | | | | Other | | | | | |
FICA	Federal Inc. Tax	State Inc. Tax	Union Dues	Amount	Description	Net Pay	Earnings	Federal Inc. Tax	State Inc. Tax
12.00	34.14	4.22	5.00			144.64	6,110.03	1,081.38	109.72
22.61	52.72	13.01		18.75	Bond	266.91	8,137.78	1,642.17	184.62
17.28	79.04	10.19	5.00			176.49	16,422.16	3,871.24	569.90
23.08	39.48	4.84				310.60	19,800.74	3,992.09	861.63
	54.62	6.67		40.00	Credit Union	102.46	18,014.20	4,711.91	670.18
11.28	38.73	4.50				133.49	11,074.19	2,719.46	312.26

Figure 14.10 (cont'd)

Agency Fund Reports and Filings

In its role as liaison with noncompany organizations in matters involving payroll activity, the payroll department relies on the system to provide the raw material to facilitate these relationships. Employee master records are programmed to receive and accumulate balances of all earnings withheld from each employee's pay, both legal and voluntary, for periodic remission to the various revenue services (federal, state and local), the credit union, the labor union, and other authorized recipients.

Labor Distribution Reports

For purposes of this discussion, we assume that the cost accounting department plays the key role in processing, verifying, and journalizing the distribution of all labor costs. Referring back to Figure 14.8, the reader can observe the flow of labor time data contained on job sheets (in lieu of job cards) through timekeeping to the cost accounting department. This information is converted into job time cards and processed along with the daily time cards and other payroll activity against the employee payroll master file. Along with a number of other "proof" reports, a preliminary labor distribution list is produced showing the number of hours applied to production and the cost to be charged to each account and cost center.

Cost accountants carefully audit these data vis-à-vis gross amounts (control totals) reflected in the weekly payroll register and resolve all discrepancies. Authenticated labor data are then processed into weekly labor distribution reports for accounting use and for the management of individual production departments. Weekly tapes containing these data are merged on a monthly basis to yield monthly, quarterly, and year-to-date summaries. The report contains regular and overtime hours, and regular earnings, with premium pay distributed as to cause. This information is useful to administration, particularly production management, in achieving the most effective and efficient use of labor resources.

SYSTEM CONFIGURATION

As in the case of some of the other, equally pervasive, information systems involving the centralized clerical functions of decentralized physical operations, the payroll must be tailored to the individual needs of the company. This discussion has focused on the fundamentals of a payroll system in order that the reader may view the whole spectrum of related activities without struggling with complications imposed by geographic dispersion and product diversification. Consideration of the source documents that feed the payroll system necessarily included some attention to organization. The major channels that regulate the flow of payroll data have been observed as having a number of control features that assure an orderly movement. At this point, consideration will be shifted to the data processing system, where all the input information converges for processing.

A very generalized payroll system with its major inputs, outputs, and master files can be reviewed in Chapter Nine. To facilitate understanding, the system has been subdivided into logic segments to consider separately matters such as file updating, time and job card input, resolution of discrepancies, payroll deductions, paycheck preparation, labor expense distribution, payroll accounting, employer payroll tax, and preparation of W-2 forms to demonstrate the handling of agency funds and associated reporting.

The first operation must be the updating of the payroll master file, which governs the whole procedure. The process is straightforward, with the output (updated master file) returning at the beginning of the next processing cycle for further updating. Occurring concurrently with, but apart from, the master file maintenance routine is the input and processing of time cards and job cards. Both sets of independent data are converted to machine-sensible form and reconciled, and discrepancies are resolved. The major product of this operation is a reel, or reels, of magnetic tape containing the details of the periodic payroll activity, the most crucial of which is the total number of hours each employee worked, or, in the case of salaried employees, total dollars, earned. These hours are classified by regular time and premium time, with premium time further broken down as to type—overtime premium, shift premium, holiday premium, and possible hazard pay (see Figure 14.11).

The next step is the main payroll processing, using updated information from the preceding steps and payroll deduction authorizations provided by the personnel department through status change forms. The output from this sequence of operations provides the data for preparation of the paychecks and earnings summaries, the payroll register, the check register, deduction registers, and other management information as may be required. The payroll master file is also updated and stored until the next payroll is processed.

During main processing, the work-in-process file is accessed to allow the updating of the production records for direct and indirect labor. Labor cost distribution, although a very simple and straightforward process, often requires consumption of a significant amount of computer time because of the high volume of activity. Labor distribution reports, by-products of the processing step, aid in the ongoing review of production labor standards and provide the basis for analysis of production efficiency.

The final flowchart, Figure 14.12, illustrates the preparation of year-end tax reports and W-2 forms. Subsequent to the final payroll of the year, the master payroll file produces summary statements for employee tax withholdings. Assuming all interim payrolls have been reconciled and corrected, W-2 processing should require minimum effort.

SUMMARY

The payroll system considered in the preceding pages is accomplished by electronic data processing (EDP) methods. Payroll is usually one of the first applications to be converted to EDP for several reasons. The high volume of input and the multiplicity of calculations required place a great strain on manual and electromechanical processing techniques. Also, the payroll department has found it expedient and beneficial to delegate many of its routine, repetitive clerical operations to EDP.

Although techniques of handling and processing data have changed dramatically in recent years, the basic functions of the payroll operation have not changed appreciably. Essentially, the payroll department conditions the input for and audits the output of the computer processed payroll. As they relate to input, the department's duties are to maintain an updated employee payroll master, preaudit time attendance cards and other

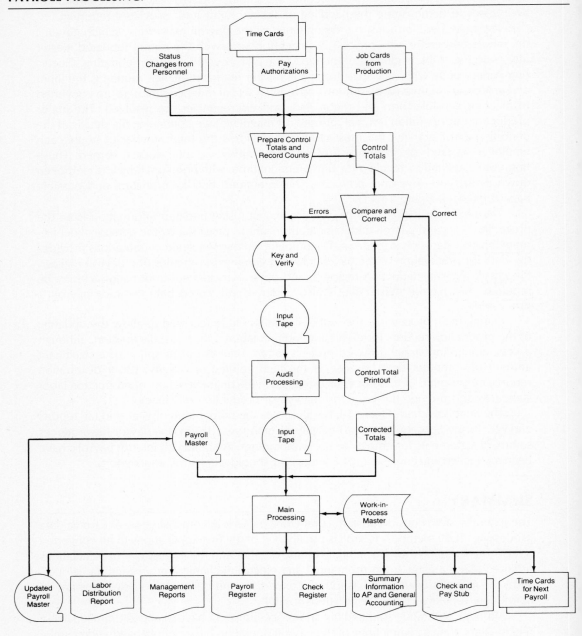

Figure 14.11

PREPARATION OF W-2 FORMS.

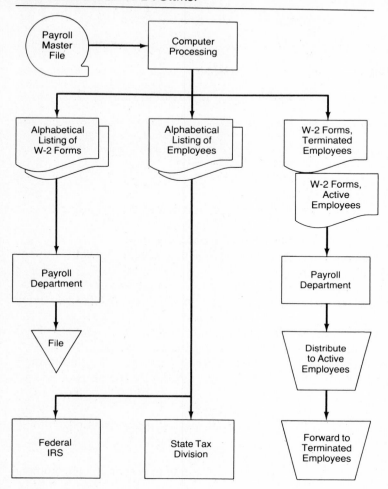

Figure 14.12

payroll activity, channel *all* payroll inputs to the data processing center under strict batch control, and act as custodian of all paychecks (issued and unissued). Output duties consist primarily of auditing all computer-prepared pay instruments, documents, and reports, distributing printouts to the appropriate recipients, detaching and signing payroll checks, and responding to the needs of the outside agencies who have legitimate claims against the payroll.

Maintaining good accounting controls over both input and output files is essential for the proper functioning of the payroll department. All areas of the payroll system should be designated to reflect well-functioning accounting controls.

SELECTED REFERENCES

Arens, Alvin A., and James K. Loebbecke. *Auditing: An Integrated Approach,* 4th ed. Englewood Cliffs, N.J.: Prentice-Hall, Inc., 1984.

Arthur Andersen & Company. *A Guide for Studying and Evaluating Internal Accounting Controls.* Chicago: Arthur Andersen & Company, 1978.

Cushing, Barry E. *Accounting Information Systems and Business Organizations,* 3rd ed. Reading, Mass.: Addison-Wesley Publishing Co., 1982.

Florida Software Service, Inc. PAYCER General Purpose Payroll System: Detailed System Description. Orlando, Fla.: Florida Software Service, nd.

General Computer Services, Inc. Payroll 111: Systems Summary Guide. Huntsville, Ala.: General Computer Services, nd.

Management Science America, Online Data Communications, Payroll/Personnel, Atlanta, 1980.

Management Science America, Payroll Accounting System, Atlanta, 1981.

QUESTIONS

1. Why are there time constraints on the payroll system?
2. Discuss the administrative organization of the payroll system.
3. Discuss the interrelationship of the personnel function with production, with cost accounting, and with the cashier.
4. Why does the personnel function act as a control over labor costs?
5. Discuss the necessary content of payroll records. Justify the items that you would include.
6. What is the purpose of a personnel action form?
7. Discuss the relationship between time cards and job cards.
8. List at least three examples of deductions requiring a payroll deduction form.
9. Cite four common internal accounting controls and discuss the purpose of each control.
10. Describe a payroll register. Why is it important?
11. What uses would a company have for a periodic payroll and deductions summary?
12. What is a payroll master file?
13. Describe the audit of time and job cards.
14. What are the risks of failure in a payroll system to employees? To the government?

PROBLEMS

15. Internal Control Procedures

Kowal Manufacturing Company employs about 50 production workers and has the following payroll procedures. The factory foreman interviews applicants and on the basis of the interview either hires or rejects the applicants. The hired applicant prepares a W-4 form (Employee's Withholding Exemption Certificate) and gives it to the foreman. The foreman writes the hourly rate of pay for the new employee in the corner of the W-4 form and then gives the form to a payroll clerk as notice that the worker has been employed. The foreman verbally advises the payroll department of rate adjustments.

A supply of blank time cards is kept in a box near the entrance to the factory.

Each worker takes a time card on Monday morning, fills in his or her name, and notes in pencil on the time card his or her daily arrival and departure times. At the end of the week the workers drop the time cards in a box near the door of the factory.

The completed time cards are taken from the box on Monday morning by a payroll clerk. Two payroll clerks divide the cards alphabetically between them, one taking the A to L section of the payroll and the other taking the M to Z section. Each clerk is fully responsible for her section of the payroll. She computes the gross pay, deductions and net pay, posts the details to the employee's earnings records, and prepares and numbers the payroll checks. Employees are automatically removed from the payroll when they fail to turn in a time card.

The payroll checks are manually signed by the chief accountant and given to the foreman. The foreman distributes the checks to the workers in the factory and arranges for the delivery of the checks to the workers who are absent. The payroll bank account is reconciled by the chief accountant who also prepares the various quarterly and annual payroll tax reports. (AICPA Adapted)

Required:

List your suggestions for improving the Kowal Manufacturing Company's system of internal control for the factory hiring practices and payroll procedures.

16. Payroll Analysis and Evaluation

Ted Mason, a junior auditor for a regional CPA firm, was assigned the job of reviewing the computerized payroll system of a medium-size client, Tool-All Manufacturing. Ted was to review the systems and procedures of Tool-All's data processing department to establish the reliability of computer-generated payroll data.

Tool-All Manufacturing produces metric tools for both commercial and industrial use. The firm consists of a factory in Waterloo, Iowa, where the tools are made, and a warehouse, where they are stored for sale to wholesalers. The company's information processing facility has an IBM 360/148 with both disk and tape drives.

Ted defined the scope of his payroll application review at the basic information gathering stage to include the following:

Identify the various types of input transactions related to payroll and review the controls thereon.
Review the controls over the processing of payroll information.
Review the various payroll reports to determine whether they are effectively used and properly controlled.

Results of the Review

Through the use of a questionnaire, supplemented by other inquiries and observations, Ted gathered information about the input, processing, and output of the payroll application, together with the applicable controls. He summarized his findings in the following memo written for the work papers.

Memo Re: EDP Payroll Processing

Company procedures: The payroll department accumulates the hours reported by factory and warehouse, applies appropriate pay rates, and forwards the results to the EDP department where pay is calculated and payroll checks are prepared simultaneously with a payroll register and other reports listed below. Checks are protectograph-signed in the EDP department and distributed to the departments by the general manager's secretary.

Factory personnel are hired and terminated by the factory manager in coordination with the personnel department. The payroll department adds and removes personnel from the payroll master file based on notices received from the personnel department. Changes in pay rates are similarly processed. Factory personnel submit their clock-punched time cards to their department heads at the end of each week, for review and initialing and forwarding to the payroll department. Factory personnel are paid a week later.

Warehouse personnel are hired by the warehouse manager in coordination with the personnel department. The warehouse personnel report their hours daily to their department head, who prepares a time summary report by individual and forwards it to the payroll department at the end of each week. The employees are paid every other week, on an hourly basis, for two standard 40-hour weeks plus or minus any adjustment from the previous 2-week period for overtime, time off, and so forth. The payments are staggered so that half the employees are paid at the end of any one week.

The payroll department receives the following reports from the EDP department for each payroll:

The payroll checks/vouchers (approximately 2,000 to 2,500 per week) for distribution to employees.

A weekly payroll distribution report for making the accounting expense entry and determining the amount to deposit in a payroll imprest bank account.

An account distribution report for supplementing the weekly payroll distribution report.

A payroll register of each individual's pay, for reference.

A weekly year-to-date earnings trial balance for verifying that year-to-date earnings and accumulations are in balance each week.

A weekly year-to-date deductions trial balance for verifying that year-to-date deduction accumulations are in balance each week.

An employee payroll master listing (microfiche), providing all records on the employee payroll master file, for reference.

(A simplified flowchart of the payroll system is included in Figure 14.13.)

Findings

The programs and procedures used to process various payroll applications lack adequate documentation. The programs were written by persons no longer with the company. These systems lack current flowcharts and user and operator manuals. This complicates the maintenance process.

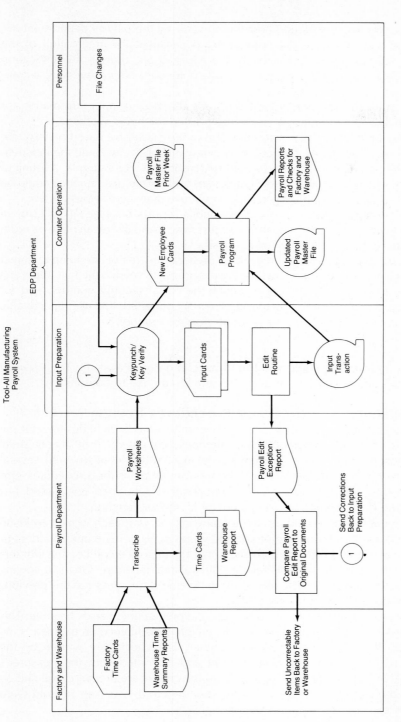

Figure 14.13

Tool-All Manufacturing Payroll System

EDP Department

| Personnel | Computer Operation | Input Preparation | Payroll Department | Factory and Warehouse |

- File Changes
- Payroll Master File Prior Week
- New Employee Cards
- Payroll Program
- Payroll Reports and Checks for Factory and Warehouse
- Updated Payroll Master File
- Keypunch/Key Verify
- Input Cards
- Edit Routine
- Input Transaction
- Payroll Worksheets
- Payroll Edit Exception Report
- Transcribe
- Time Cards
- Warehouse Report
- Compare Payroll Edit Report to Original Documents
- Send Corrections Back to Input Preparation
- Factory Time Cards
- Warehouse Time Summary Reports
- Send Uncorrectable Items Back to Factory or Warehouse

The Payroll System **435**

Unused payroll checks/vouchers held in the vault by the payroll department are forwarded weekly to the data processing department for preparation of the payrolls. Although the checks/vouchers are logged out, there is no verification that all checks/vouchers are returned or accounted for after processing is completed.

No batch control or transmittal documents are attached to input information for new employees, file maintenance, checks issued, or hours worked.

Since the payroll department initiates changes to the master file based on information from various sources, a direct, postreview function—by someone independent of the payroll department—would be reasonable. For example, a listing of changes to the master file for new employees and for file maintenance could be provided to the factory manager and warehouse manager for postreview.

The payroll system generates several erroneous reports because of an error in program logic. The payroll department must now manually recalculate or redetermine this information on a regular basis.

In some cases, the edits performed by input preparation are not adequate to detect material errors. For example, no limit checks are performed in the field reporting overtime hours worked. Failure to check the social security number field for blanks results in an error in processing, when encountered, that uses up valuable processing time. (*Adapted from Touche Ross Foundation*)

Required:

What other information would you like to have in order to evaluate Ted's review of the payroll processing system and why would you like to have it?

17. Payroll Systems, Controls, and Procedures Review

The Vane Corporation is a manufacturing concern that has been in business for the past 18 years. During this period, the company has grown from a very small family-owned operation to a medium-size manufacturing concern with several departments. Despite this growth, a substantial number of the procedures employed by Vane Corporation have been in effect since the business was started. Just recently Vane Corporation has computerized its payroll function.

The payroll function operates in the following manner. Each worker picks up a weekly time card on Monday morning and writes in his or her name and identification number. These blank cards are kept near the factory entrance. The workers write on the time card the time of their daily arrival and departure. On the following Monday the factory foremen collect the completed time cards for the previous week and send them to data processing.

In data processing the time cards are used to prepare the weekly time file. This file is processed with the master payroll file, which is maintained on magnetic tape according to the worker identification number. The checks are written by the computer on the regular checking account and imprinted with the treasurer's signature. After the payroll file is updated and the checks are prepared, the checks are sent to the factory foremen who distribute them to the workers or hold them for the workers to pick up later if they are absent.

The foremen notify data processing of new employees and terminations. Any changes in hourly pay rate or any other changes affecting payroll are usually communicated to data processing by the foremen.

The workers also complete a job time ticket for each individual job they work on each day. The job time tickets are collected daily and sent to cost accounting where they are used to prepare a cost distribution analysis.

Further analysis of the payroll function reveals the following:

a. A worker's gross wages never exceed $300 per week.
b. Raises never exceed $0.55 per hour for the factory workers.
c. No more than 20 hours of overtime is allowed each week.
d. The factory employs 150 workers in 10 departments.

The payroll function has not been operating smoothly for some time, but even more problems have surfaced since the payroll was computerized. The foremen have indicated that they would like a weekly report indicating worker tardiness, absenteeism, and idle time, so they can determine the amount of productive time lost and the reason for the lost time. The following errors and inconsistencies have been encountered the past few pay periods:

a. A worker's paycheck was not processed properly, because he had transposed two numbers in his identification number when he filled out his time card.
b. A worker was issued a check for $1,531.80 when it should have been $153.18.
c. One worker's paycheck was not written, and this error was not detected until the paychecks for that department were distributed by the foreman.
d. Part of the master payroll file was destroyed when the tape reel was inadvertently mounted on the wrong tape drive and used as a scratch tape. Data processing attempted to reestablish the destroyed portion from original source documents and other records.
e. One worker received a paycheck for an amount considerably larger than he should have. Further investigation revealed that 84 had been punched instead of 48 for hours worked.
f. Several records on the master payroll file were skipped and not included on the updated master payroll file. This was not detected for several pay periods.
g. In processing nonroutine changes, a computer operator included a pay rate increase for one of his friends in the factory. This was discovered by chance by another employee. (*IMA adapted*)

Required:

Identify the control weaknesses in the payroll procedure and in the computer processing as it is now conducted by the Vane Corp. Recommend the changes necessary to correct the system. Arrange your answer in two columns, headed "Control Weaknesses" and "Recommendations," respectively.

18. Systems Flowchart Analysis

A CPA's audit working papers contain a narrative description of a segment of the Croyden Factory, Inc., payroll system and an accompanying flowchart (Figure 14.14) as follows:

CROYDEN INC., FACTORY PAYROLL SYSTEM

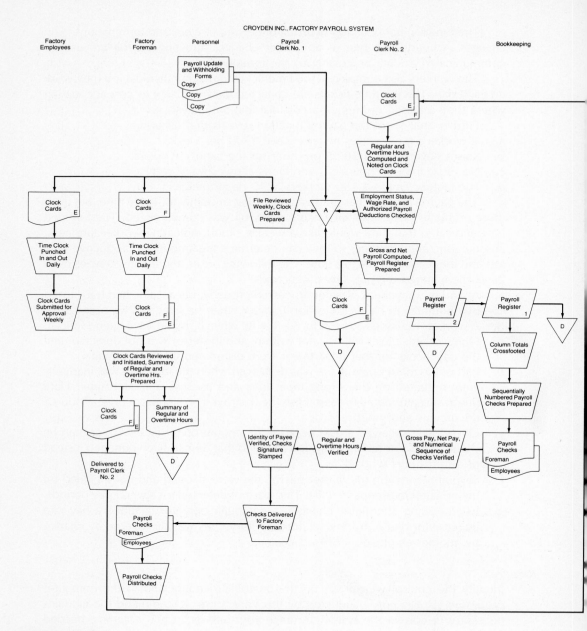

Figure 14.14

Narrative: The internal control system with respect to the personnel department is functioning well and is not included in the accompanying flowchart.

At the beginning of each work week payroll clerk no. 1 reviews the payroll department files to determine the employment status of factory employees and then prepares time cards and distributes them as each individual arrives at work. This payroll clerk, who is also responsible for custody of the signature stamp machine, verifies the identity of each payee before delivering signed checks to the foreman.

At the end of each work week the foreman distributes payroll checks for the preceding work week. Concurrent with this activity, the foreman reviews the current week's employee time cards, notes the regular and overtime hours worked on a summary form, and initials the aforementioned time cards. The foreman then delivers all time cards and unclaimed payroll checks to payroll clerk no. 2. *(AICPA adapted)*

Required:

a. Based on the narrative and accompanying flowchart, what are the weaknesses in the system of internal control?

b. Based on the narrative and accompanying flowchart, what inquiries should be made with respect to clarifying the existence of possible additional weaknesses in the system of internal control?

Note: Do not discuss the internal control system of the personnel department.

19. Internal Control Questionnaire

You are the audit manager of a company with 600 salaried employees and 1,400 hourly rate employees, all of whom are paid by check. You already have an audit program for auditing the payroll department. You plan to supplement your program with a questionnaire on internal control particularly designed for the payroll audit. *(IIA adapted)*

Required:

List 18 questions for an internal control questionnaire covering a payroll audit. The questionnaire should include 18 separate questions, each of which invites a "yes" answer where adequate control is indicated. The questions you provide may apply to any or all of the various facets of the payroll system, including timekeeping, disbursement arrangements, salary and wage rates, computations, and/or segregation of duties and authorities.

20. Payroll Systems Design

You have accepted an assignment as systems consultant to Toomers Paper Manufacturing, a manufacturer of tissue paper. Due to a winning season for the local college's football and basketball teams, there has been rapid growth in the market for tissue paper to roll the trees around the campus. To meet the increased demand, Toomers has grown and much overtime has been required. Management has indicated concern for the company's payroll system.

Toomer's payroll function is manually operated. In addition to required overtime, management has expressed concern about the lack of management reports and potential weaknesses in internal control. Management is considering three options: (1) hiring additional employees in the payroll department, (2) purchasing an electronic accounting machine, or (3) installing a small computer.

Management has assured you that its staff is available to assist and support your study. You have engaged assistants to complete a preliminary evaluation of alternatives that will provide the basis for your decision and recommendations.

Required:

Prepare for your assistants a schedule of procedures to guide their assignment. Include the type of information they might find in a payroll system, the methods for obtaining this information, and the method for analyzing the information. Describe how you would proceed through the initial phases of the systems investigations.

21. Systems Design Procedures

You have been engaged to audit the 19X2 financial statements of Bob Porter, an independent contractor. Bob believes that his employees prefer to be paid with cash, and since it will reduce clerical expenses, he has agreed to do so.

While performing the audit of cash you note that the petty cash fund has a balance of $300. Porter explained that $200 consists of unclaimed wages. Porter's bookkeeper explains that Porter has instructed unpaid wages to be put in the petty cash fund, his reason being that cash can be used for disbursements. Claimants are paid from the petty cash fund. Porter says that this reduces the number of checks drawn to replenish the petty cash fund. It also, he contends, establishes responsibility for cash with one person since the petty cash custodian distributes the pay.

Required:

a. Does this system establish good internal control over unclaimed wages? Explain.

b. What procedures provide good internal control over unclaimed wages when salaries are paid in cash?

22. Payroll Internal Control

Select the best answer to each of the following questions *(all AICPA adapted):*

a. To minimize the opportunity for fraud, unclaimed salary checks should be:
   (1) Deposited in a special bank account
   (2) Kept in the payroll department
   (3) Left with the employee's supervisor
   (4) Held for the employee in the personnel department

b. The sales department bookkeeper has been crediting house account sales to her brother-in-law, an outside salesman. Commissions are paid on outside sales but not on house account sales. This might have been prevented by requiring that:

- **(1)** Sales order forms be prenumbered and accounted for by the sales department bookkeeper
- **(2)** Sales commission statements be supported by sales order forms and approved by the sales manager
- **(3)** Aggregate sales entries be prepared by the general accounting department
- **(4)** Disbursement vouchers for sales commissions be reviewed by the internal audit department and checked to sales commission statements

c. In the audit of which of the following types of profit-oriented enterprises would the auditor be most likely to place special emphasis on testing internal controls over proper classification of payroll transactions:
- **(1)** A retailing organization
- **(2)** A wholesaling organization
- **(3)** A manufacturing organization
- **(4)** A service organization

d. From the standpoint of good procedural control, distributing payroll checks to employees is best handled by the:
- **(1)** Treasury department
- **(2)** Personnel department
- **(3)** Payroll accounting section.
- **(4)** Departmental supervisors.

e. A CPA reviews a client's payroll procedures. The CPA would consider internal control to be less than effective if a payroll department supervisor was assigned the responsibility for:
- **(1)** Distributing payroll checks to employees
- **(2)** Reviewing and approving time reports for subordinate employees
- **(3)** Hiring subordinate employees
- **(4)** Initiating requests for salary adjustments for subordinate employees

f. Effective internal accounting control over the payroll function should include procedures that segregate the duties of making salary payments to employees and:
- **(1)** Controlling unemployment insurance claims
- **(2)** Maintaining employee personnel records
- **(3)** Approving employee fringe benefits
- **(4)** Hiring new employees

g. Which of the following is the best reason an auditor should consider observing a client's distribution of regular payroll checks:
- **(1)** Separation of payroll duties is less than adequate for effective internal control.
- **(2)** Total payroll costs are a significant part of total operating costs.
- **(3)** The auditor did not observe the distribution of the entire regular payroll during the audit in the prior year.
- **(4)** Employee turnover is excessive.

h. Which of the following is an effective internal accounting control used to prove that production department employees are properly validating payroll time cards at a time-recording station:

- (1) Time cards should be carefully inspected by those persons who distribute pay envelopes to the employees.
- (2) One person should be responsible for maintaining records of employee time for which salary payment is not to be made.
- (3) Daily reports showing time charged to jobs should be approved by the foreman and compared to the total hours worked on the employee time cards.
- (4) Internal auditors should make observations of distribution of paychecks on a surprise basis.

i. Effective internal control over the payroll function would include which of the following:
- (1) Total time recorded on time clock punch cards should be reconciled to job reports by employees responsible for those specific jobs.
- (2) Payroll department employees should be supervised by the management of the personnel department.
- (3) Payroll department employees should be responsible for maintaining employee personnel records.
- (4) Total time spent on jobs should be compared with total time indicated on time clock punch cards.

j. Effective internal accounting control over unclaimed payroll checks that are kept by the treasury department would include accounting department procedures that require:
- (1) Effective cancellation and stop payment orders for checks representing unclaimed wages
- (2) Preparation of a list of unclaimed wages on a periodic basis
- (3) Accounting for all unclaimed wages in a current liability account
- (4) Periodic accounting for the actual checks representing unclaimed wages

k. An example of an internal control weakness is to assign to a department supervisor the responsibility for:
- (1) Reviewing and approving time reports for subordinate employees
- (2) Initiating requests for salary adjustments for subordinate employees
- (3) Authorizing payroll checks for terminated employees
- (4) Distributing payroll checks to subordinate employees

l. It would be appropriate for the payroll accounting department to be responsible for which of the following functions:
- (1) Approval of employee time records
- (2) Maintenance of records of employment, discharges, and pay increases
- (3) Preparation of periodic governmental reports as to employees' earnings and withholding taxes
- (4) Distribution of paychecks to employees

m. A factory foreman at Steblecki Corporation discharged an hourly worker but did not notify the payroll department. The foreman then forged the worker's signature on time cards and work tickets and, when giving out the checks, diverted the payroll checks drawn for the discharged worker to his own use. The most effective procedure for preventing this activity is to?

(1) Require written authorization for all employees added to or removed from the payroll

(2) Have a paymaster who has no other payroll responsibility distribute the payroll checks

(3) Have someone other than persons who prepare or distribute the payroll obtain custody of unclaimed payroll checks

(4) Rotate persons distributing the payroll from time to time

n. Which of the following best describes proper internal control over payroll:

(1) The preparation of the payroll must be under the control of the personnel department.

(2) The confidentiality of employee payroll data should be carefully protected to prevent fraud.

(3) The duties of hiring, payroll computation, and payment to employees should be segregated.

(4) The payment of cash to employees should be replaced with payment by checks.

CASES

23. Payroll Systems Design with Internal Control Considerations

After carefully studying the payroll practices of the Apogee Company (Appendix C), list as many processing and control weaknesses as you can, drawing on the discussions in Chapter Fourteen as a guide. A general analysis of the company's income statement and supplementary statement of cost of goods sold suggests that the gross annual payroll could be several hundred thousand dollars. This volume of cash outflow is entirely too significant to be managed haphazardly.

Design a practical and well-controlled payroll system for Apogee, giving due consideration to the problem of labor distribution in production (and elsewhere), and assuming the establishment of an independent personnel/employment department.

24. Payroll System Evaluation

Although payroll is not a significant factor in the conversion cycle of Bubbling Stone case, due primarily to the highly automated production processes, its several hundred employees make it a rather large system. The system is under the treasurer's function. Carefully analyze the payroll procedures, including related functions implied in the case, and comment upon its reliability and integrity. Construct a payroll systems flowchart as currently described in the case.

SECTION

THE REVENUE CYCLE

CHAPTER FIFTEEN

The Marketing and Shipping Systems

The marketing and shipping systems are shown as separate functions in the treatment of revenue cycle systems in Chapter Nine. This portrayal is quite appropriate, since they are considered independent operations serving vital, though different, purposes in overall entity operations. They are of course directly related. However, for essentially the same reasons that we combined the procurement and receiving systems in Chapter Ten, we have chosen to discuss marketing and shipping together, although in separate sections. Again, we do not wish to discount the importance of each in the overall framework of accounting information systems.

SECTION A

MARKETING INFORMATION SYSTEMS

Marketing has been described as a system of interrelated activities designed to develop, price, promote, and distribute goods and services to groups of customers.[1] Marketing is literally the "fueling function" of business as it engages in the perpetual search for survival, growth, and profits. Marketing activities must generate a flow of revenue sufficient to (1) absorb all out-of-pocket costs and expenses, (2) replace diminishing capital assets, and (3) provide a return on investment to capital suppliers.

The basic philosophy of the marketing concept is that the customers' wants and needs should be the focus of the firm's activities. Under this concept research, engineering, finance, personnel, production, and all other business functions must concentrate on satisfying customer needs.[2] With this myopic concentration on service, it is not surprising to find the literature dealing with marketing information systems fragmented along the lines of (1) marketing concepts and philosophy, (2) marketing mix, (3) marketing strategies, (4) marketing planning, (5) marketing organization, (6) product pricing, (7) consumer behavior, and (8) market research. It is often difficult for accountants to perceive such a general pattern of information flow.

Dalrymple and Parsons have developed a model (see Figure 15.1) targeting areas of contact with *internal* organizations where vital support and control information flows.[3] Even from this perspective, however, *marketing information systems* cannot be

MARKETING PLANNING MODEL.

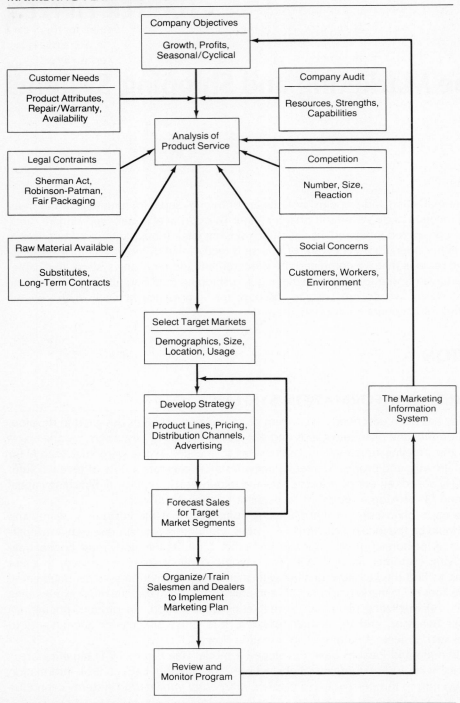

Source: Adapted from Douglas J. Dalrymple and Leonard J. Parsons, *Marketing Management* (New York: John Wiley & Sons, 1980), p. 9. By permission.

Figure 15.1

distinguished from *marketing research.* Until recent years the traditional role of marketing research was that of primary information supplier to management for marketing decisions. The provision of acceptable information bases for marketing decisions is also the goal of modern marketing information systems. How do these terms differ?

Marketing research ordinarily follows an eclectic path—at one time examining the prices of a product line; at another, reviewing competitors' packaging innovations or concentrating on spot projects. But the mission of a marketing information system goes beyond intermittent examinations and provides a *continuous* study of marketing factors important to a firm. It utilizes more data sources, both internal and external, and accepts the responsibility for receiving, analyzing, and distilling a far greater volume of information inputs than the traditional research role.[4] Perhaps it would be appropriate to expand the information service function of the Dalrymple model to portray this larger role, as shown in Figure 15.2.

Increasingly, effective marketing management depends on the development of an operating system with the capacity to obtain and make effective use of marketing information. Marketing performance feedback information serves as the foundation on which

MARKETING INFORMATION SYSTEMS RELATIONSHIPS.

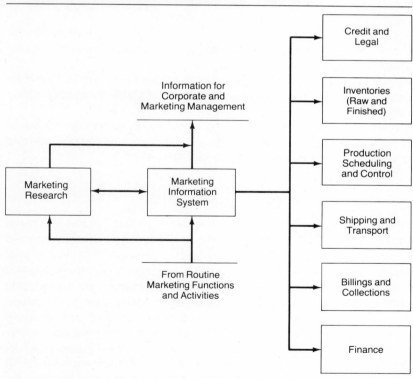

Figure 15.2

the cycle of marketing management, through adaptive control, can ensure continued effectiveness in the marketplace. Strategies and plans are made, activities are implemented, and controls are designed and imposed. As a result of feedback control information, deficiencies in the plan or its implementation, and/or opportunities for innovative strategies are discovered, and these in turn lead to a new cycle of marketing planning.[5]

The importance of developing a sound factual basis for marketing planning is hardly controversial. Long-term trends in marketing, and in business generally, are having an important impact on current information systems activity.[6] These trends include:

1. The increased complexity of business calls for more data and better performance. The organization that previously had firm control of its business in a limited market area now finds itself on uncertain grounds in competition with similar enterprises on a national or international basis.
2. Product life cycles are shorter, and skillful management is required to extract a profit during the limited time available.
3. A marketing concept in which the various marketing functions are organized under one executive (the marketing manager) has taken root in American industry. Effective integration of a far-ranging variety of marketing activities requires a great deal more "refined" information.
4. Many companies have grown so large that, in the absence of a formal marketing information system, retrieval of information is ineffective.
5. The speed with which business decisions have to be made has dramatically increased, and thus a burden is placed on marketing information systems to provide current information to support such decisions.
6. The development of quantitative techniques to refine marketing decision information requires more input data than could previously be made available by normal market research approaches.
7. Although the marketing information system is not entirely dependent on the use of computers, their common use in other business systems makes the organization and retrieval of marketing-related information far more effective.

FUNCTIONS AND OBJECTIVES

Historically, marketing has emphasized sales goals, whereas production has attempted to minimize costs and maintain high standards of quality. Today the marketing concept envisages close coordination between these related functions toward the common goal of profit maximization. As mentioned in the production and inventory discussions, and as will be reemphasized in the discussion of the billings and collections system, marketing decisions and activities simply cannot be isolated from other areas of the firm's operations. In their role as corporate planners, marketing executives must do their homework before corporate resources are committed to products, inasmuch as they must accurately forecast sales *before* production is scheduled, inventory levels are established, procurement activities are initiated, personnel assignments are made, and financing is arranged.

From the viewpoint of the organization, the marketing executive is responsible for six major categories of specialized activity. See Figure 15.3 for a hypothetical arrangement. The functions of advertising and promotion, new product development, marketing

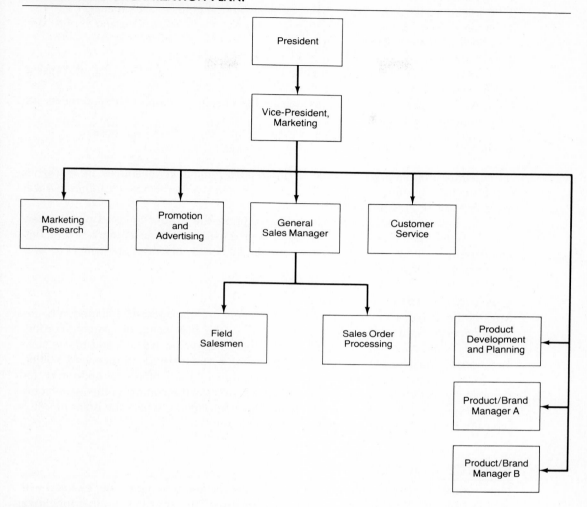

Figure 15.3

research, and customer service are self-explanatory and beyond the scope of this discussion. However, we cannot ignore the primary activities of sales order processing and the product managers (or their equivalents).[7]

The Product/Brand Manager

Product/brand manager is a common designation in the marketing literature and is used to facilitate the delineation of several key functions that must be performed by someone in the marketing organization. Consider, for example, the following primary activities indigenous to the marketing operation, whatever form of market segmentation is used:[8]

1. Recommend product prices, discounts, and allowances.
2. Forecast sales, and establish sales quotas with the general sales manager.
3. Analyze sales results, market share, competitive activity, and brand profits, and adjust marketing plans where necessary.
4. Initiate market research when prudent judgment dictates.
5. Prepare marketing plans for the ensuing year, including merchandising, advertising, and selling activities, to reach sales and profit goals.
6. Initiate product improvements as indicated by changes in customer requirements and competitive action.
7. Continually appraise product performance, quality, and package design.
8. Recommend the elimination of certain products.

Clearly, product price information and related remittance incentives are marketing inputs of vital importance to the billings and collections system where customer invoices are prepared (or at least validated).

The function of sales forecasting is to support the production and procurement organizations and to regulate the tempo of their activities. Of course, marketing recommendations for new products and for the elimination of old ones are critical to both production and inventory operations.

Customer Order Processing

Most of the activities in the marketing environment are management-oriented in nature and concern accountants only in general terms. The processing of customer orders, however, is the main-line connection with other information systems and merits close attention. Companies tend to develop their own unique methods of receiving, editing, controlling, entering, and processing customer orders. In the interest of uniformity and completeness, this book examines information systems in the context of the manufacturing environment rather than the merchandising environment, where the point of sale is typically the cash register (whether cash or charge).

SOURCE DOCUMENTS

Unlike most of the other information systems, the marketing system is not charged with responsibility for matching, reconciling, or "buffering" the activities of other functional systems. As a consequence, the sales function does not handle or process a wide variety of external and internal documents. Beyond its own input responsibility, the hard-copy files maintained by marketing are discretionary and center mainly around customer accounts.

The only three documents to be considered here are (1) the sales order, (2) the sales order acknowledgment, and (3) the customer name and address record. Other related documents already mentioned have been, or will be, treated in other chapters of this book.

The *sales order* is illustrated in Figure 15.4. It includes the company's serial number and the customer's purchase order number. These are the cross-referenced control numbers that unite the buyer and seller documents and establish the contract. A normal lapse of time between the date on the customer's purchase order and the date of receipt

SALES ORDER.

CUSTOMER CODE	ORDERED BY			SHIP TO	

CUSTOMER ORDER NUMBER		DEPT.	AGENT	TERMS: NET 30 DAYS F.O.B. MILL	ROUTING

BOX COLOR	BOX LABEL	GARMENT HANGER	GARMENT PACK	GARMENT PREP	DMD	R/O	LT	TYP	O/T	
									P	S

SHIP DATE   REQ DATE   DSB DATE   DSA DATE

1. STRING ☐   2. PAPER BUNDLES ☐   3. POLY BUNDLES ☐   4. BOXED ☐

SPECIAL STYLE	MILL STYLE	COLOR	NO. CASES	TOTAL DOZ.	A	2	4	6	8	10	12	14	16	PRICE	DELIVERY WEEK
					B	6MO.	1	2	3	4	5	6	8		
					C	S	M	L	XL	XXL	XXXL		XS		

Figure 15.4

by the selling company is to be expected. These times are important because performance under the contract is usually based on the date of receipt.

The sales order from one division of a large, complex organization will often specify shipment to another division at a different address, and may direct that the invoice be mailed to a third address. It is incumbent on the seller to adhere strictly to such instructions. The remainder of the order reflects the product identification, quantity, price, terms, and other specificity relevant to packaging, routing, and delivery.

The buyer organization usually includes its own purchase order acknowledgment form along with its order. Obviously, the buyer would like the seller to simply sign and return this form, since it facilitates the processing in the buyer's expenditure cycle system. Also, legal terms and conditions are usually preprinted on the back of the form. Alternatively, the selling entity may prefer to use its own order acknowledgment form for precisely the same reasons. Aside from the ease of identification and the familiarity of handling one's own documents, it matters very little which form is used as long as both parties are in agreement concerning all aspects of the transaction. Order acknowledgments play no functional role in the information system, but become permanently attached to the related order document.

Customer name and address master records constitute an important data base for the marketing system. In addition to the normal ordering, shipping, and billing addresses that the customer uses to accommodate his own systems, the master file should reflect other pertinent information such as (1) credit rating, (2) payment history, (3) order quantity limit, (4) legal qualifications and/or restrictions, and other special information required by the entity.

DOCUMENT FLOW AND TIMING

Chapter Ten discussed the buyer/seller interface from the viewpoint of the purchasing function. We shall now examine this interface from the seller's perspective. It is necessary to consider receipt of sales requests from a variety of sources, including buyer purchase orders, internal sales orders, personnel sales slips, telephone inquiries, wires, and letters. Through whatever channel orders are received, good business practice suggests that they all be eventually confirmed by the buyer in writing. Transcription, either manually or electronically, to an internal sales order form results in more timely and efficient handling and tends to diminish errors. Figure 15.5 delineates the sequence of events in the revenue cycle that begins with the confirmed order and ends with billing. The following explanations relate to the numbered events appearing in Figure 15.5.

1. The typical initiating instrument is the purchase order reflecting the customer's own document control number and specifying the terms and conditions of the sale/purchase.
2. A preaudit of the proposed transaction, including legal aspects pertaining to performance and shipment, and a routine credit check precede the decision to accept or decline an order—or perhaps to accept it under modified terms. Approval and return of either the purchase order acknowledgment or the sales order confirmation legalizes the contract.

DOCUMENT FLOW OF CUSTOMER ORDERS.

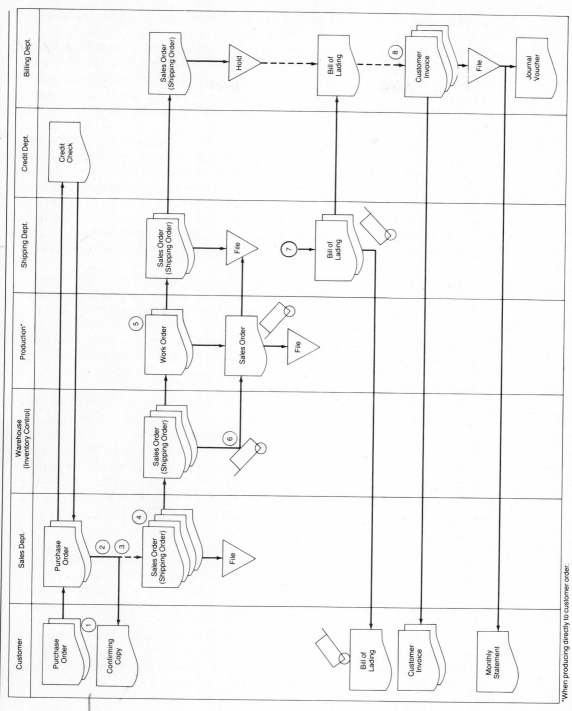

*When producing directly to customer order.

Figure 15.5

3. The confirmation is also preceded by an analysis of the company's ability to perform. Increasingly this analyzing is accomplished via on-line real-time connections with computer data bases. The investigator quickly ascertains product availability, delivery capability, customer credit standing, and order quantity restrictions and reviews legal constraints pertaining to conflicts of interest and related party conditions as well as other stored information governing transactions with individual customers. Additionally, the confirmation document may be produced as a by-product of this initial inquiry.

4. If the sale is confirmed, the customer order processing clerk transmits a coded signal that generates a series of preprogrammed computer functions: Inventory balances are encumbered, and internal documentation is produced (i.e., sales orders, packing assembly lists, bills of lading, production authorization, etc.). These documents are usually printed "off-line" for distribution the following day.

5. When production to customer specification is routine procedure, the normal production process must precede order assembly and packaging. In the meantime, sales and shipping documents are prepared and held until receipt of the finished product from production.

6. Inventory personnel assemble the customer's order, authenticate the necessary documents supporting this stage of performance, extract the necessary information to update the material control system, and route the assembled order with all documentation to the shipping dock.

7. Shipping personnel arrange carrier pickup, assemble shipments for convenient loading and subsequent off-loading, supervise the actual loading, execute the bill of lading with the carrier's representative, and release appropriate copies of all shipping documents to billings and collections.

8. Customer invoices are promptly prepared and mailed, giving due consideration to ship-to and bill-to address variations. In sophisticated systems customer invoices may be partially or completely prepared by the computer. Consummation of the marketing transaction (the full cycle) takes place with the billings and collections function. Although the foregoing discussion has presumed extensive use of electronic data processing and communications equipment, the reader should have no difficulty visualizing the same general functions in a less mechanized, if not a totally manual, environment.

ACCOUNTING CONTROLS

Although the primary marketing function is to generate sales and ultimately revenues from sales, it plays no direct role in the handling of cash or the application of cash to customer accounts receivable. As in the expenditure cycle where the functional systems operate independently in the interest of controlling cash outflow and liability valuation, revenue cycle functions interface with each other in such a way as to control cash inflow and asset valuations.

Control of revenue cycle processing focuses on written operations policies and procedures, customer selection, document control, pricing and terms, financial relationships with customers, and the operation of the system itself.

Written Policy and Procedure

Corporate policy as it pertains to marketing activities should serve as the basis for development of a detailed marketing procedures manual. These procedures should cover every facet of marketing operations including, but not limited to, job duties and responsibilities, training routines, supervisory functions, a system of executive approvals, forms control and handling, and a complete documentation of the information system including periodic review and verification and audit of computer programs. This manual should be required reading for all marketing personnel.

Customer Selection and Approval

The continuous evaluation and rating of customers is certainly no less important than the establishment of an approved vendor list in the procurement operation. Management should establish basic criteria for such evaluation, and sales to potential customers not authorized and approved in accordance therewith should be prohibited. Such criteria might include an evaluation of (1) financial condition and stability, (2) general reputation in the business community, (3) past credit history, and (4) legal restrictions such as export limitations, fair credit, related parties, conflicts of interest, and sensitive payments. These criteria, since they are somewhat confidential, should be coded and maintained as a part of the customer master file.

Control Documentation

An approved *written* request (order) should be required before goods or services are provided. The process is greatly facilitated by the use of standard entity forms, preferably prenumbered and serially controlled. All *authorized* orders should be processed, assembled, shipped, and invoiced on a timely basis.

Price and Payment Terms

Management criteria for establishing prices and cash discount incentives should be included in the policy and procedures manual. Such criteria should be in common use in the marketing environment and appropriately reflected in published catalogs, price tags, bids based on written specifications, trade discounts, and shipping and credit terms. Any deviation from these standards should be authorized by responsible management.

Adjustments to Revenue-Related Accounts

Management criteria governing postsale adjustments should be clearly established and tightly controlled. A system of executive authorizations and approvals should cover *all* adjustments to revenue (sales returns), cost of sales, customer accounts receivable, and accounting distribution. These procedures should include the following: (1) corrected billings, (2) charge-backs, (3) write-offs of uncollectible accounts, (4) service and finance charges, (5) compromise agreements and concessions, (6) volume rebates, (7) returned merchandise for cash or credit, (8) correction of processing errors, (9) cash discounts, and (10) sales commission corrections.

Information System Control

Only authorized personnel should have access to any aspect of the marketing information system. This restriction should encompass document preparation; data collection, coding, and handling; input to the computer; programming; processing; access to data bases; file control; and feedback. Persons authorized to input data into the system and to access data bases should operate on the basis of unique access codes.

RISKS OF FAILURE

There is no standard, or universally applicable, set of controls for marketing and shipping operations. However, the general controls discussed previously can and should be tailored to minimize, and to prevent if possible, the consequences of certain system failures.

Unauthorized Acceptance of Orders

If the procedures do not prevent indiscriminate acceptance of customer orders, the entity opens the way for embarrassing, if not legally disastrous, circumstances resulting from: (1) contractual obligations in excess of established credit limits, (2) contracts for products not in inventory or scheduled for production, and (3) contracts for quality standards the entity is not capable of meeting. The consequences of any of these actions could reflect in warranty liabilities, penalties and/or contingent liabilities, uncollectible accounts, and dissatisfied or lost customers.

Shipments to Unauthorized Customers

When shipments are made in violation of export regulations and fair trade laws, or when orders are shipped illegally to related parties or other conflict-of-interest purchasers, penalties and contingent liabilities are to be expected. Even shipments executed too early or too late in violation of the purchase/sale agreement can have unfavorable consequences such as (1) abnormal rejections and returns for credit, (2) accounts receivable and inventory adjustments, (3) damage to merchandise in transit, (4) excessive freight charges, (5) increased handling costs, and (6) lost customers.

Violation of Pricing Policies

Sales contracts that violate authorized and published prices and terms reverberate widely through the system, and often result in (1) dissatisfied customers, (2) abnormal returns, (3) adjustments to revenue and related accounts, (4) uncollectible accounts, (5) over- or underpayment of sales commissions, (6) incorrect statement of customer accounts, (7) and variations in sales quotas and budget realization, not to mention (8) possible fines, penalties, and contingent liabilities for violation of governmental regulations and laws.

Negligent Handling of Returned Sales

Several organizations may be involved in the recording of sales returns in large and complex companies. Poor timing and incorrect adherence to procedure could result in serious misstatements of receivables, inventories, net sales, costs of sales, profits, and taxes.

Improper Write-offs of Customer Accounts

The decision to declare a customer account uncollectible is usually made in conjunction with the accounts receivable operation and the credit department, and only after executive authorization. Wherever controls are lax, collusion may occur and a misapplication of cash may result.

MANAGEMENT INFORMATION REQUIREMENTS

Marketing executives often feel deluged with ''data'' but rarely feel they are receiving enough ''information.'' They must often intuitively evaluate the risks of a poor decision in the absence of perfect information about the probable consequences of their actions.[9] Marketing management relies more heavily on external intelligence than on refined historical information based on internally accumulated sales data. Appeals for marketing information usually produce the same results—summaries of what has happened or is happening—not what is likely to happen if. . . . not how the firm can exploit an opportunity or cope with a threat; and not what the cost-profit benefit will be of possible future action.[10] Corporate information systems simply have not been designed to produce, and may never be capable of producing, that sort of intelligence.

Existing data processing systems do provide, within their limitations, accounting summary reports from which corporate efficiency may be measured and from which financial and market intelligence may be extrapolated. For the other kinds of intelligence (i.e., economic, political, competitor strategy, threats, opportunities, etc.) the marketing executive must continue to rely heavily on research and a very fertile imagination.

Marketing management usually requires three basic kinds of information from standard internal reports; (1) product availability, (2) operating efficiency, and (3) customer reports.

Product Availability

Product availability is most often served by the primary output of the inventory control system: the stock status and inventory analysis reports. These reports are sequenced by product code number and reflect, among other things, quantities of each item available for sale. Standard unit costs are also included, permitting comparison with base unit selling prices and computation of profit by item. Usually these inventory reports, while emphasizing balance on hand, will contain all the activity relating to issues, receipts, and adjustments. These reports are illustrated in the chapter on inventory.

Operating Efficiency

Although sales analysis is based on historical data, its goal should transcend the mere evaluation of sales personnel and product performance, and serve as the basis for predicting future sales and profitability. The information system can do little more than classify historical sales data in such a manner that prudent management may exercise its judgment in anticipating the future, spotting potential difficulties, and evaluating the reward system designed to achieve entity objectives. Sales analyses can be categorized by personnel, by product, and by territory.

Analysis by Sales Personnel   This information supports the budget process, which, as we have seen, starts with the sales forecast. Basically it measures and evaluates the performance of sales personnel and highlights areas of concern and possible corrective action. The inclusion of product cost data in the report permits the computation of gross profit contributed by each salesperson, in terms of both dollars and percentages, and allows management to structure an evaluation and reward system that will contribute most effectively to the achievement of company goals.

Analysis by Product   Although it is not predictive in nature, this information assists management in discerning shifting trends in product demand and aids in the formulation of future sales policies. Decisions concerning product promotion and advertising are also influenced by this type of sales analysis, as are decisions relative to future inventory levels.

Analysis by Territory   If a salesperson can operate only in one territory at a time, a resequencing of the sales personnel analysis by a salesperson within the territory code would serve this purpose. However, the sales personnel report is essentially an "activity" listing, and the territory report demands summary information. Territory information not only provides a good barometer of the effectiveness of marketing management in a given area, but it also indicates the comparative effectiveness of sales promotion and advertising in the various geographic, demographic, and cultural (urban vs. rural) segments of the whole market.

Customer Reports

Reports of sales and profits by customer draw attention to the relative contribution of a customer's purchases to the entity's objectives. Significant variations in gross profit between customers suggest unusual circumstances requiring special management attention. Small and unprofitable accounts may be accorded less sales emphasis, or even discontinued: Profitable accounts may be accorded extra attention in matters such as terms, discounts, special ordering, and volume rebates.

It is certainly not suggested that management be limited to the reports we have discussed. As stated in an earlier chapter, the value of refined information relates directly to the price management is willing to pay for it. There is tremendous flexibility in the manner in which sales activity can be fragmented, summarized, sequenced, compared, analyzed, refined, and subjected to all types of quantitative analysis.

SYSTEM CONFIGURATION

The basic components of a modern marketing information system are the sales and customer data banks, access to the inventory data bank, a set of analytical tools and models, and a communications network. The system must be able to interpret and process routine sales input and to accommodate the more sophisticated needs of management by reducing masses of random data to forms easily read and interpreted.

Successful information systems for marketing often start very simply and evolve into mature and powerful systems as management is able to visualize the larger potential. As is often the case in other systems, it may be easier to build and integrate several subsystems than to construct a total information system all at once.

Marketing Data Bases

The structure and content of data bases and master files depend entirely on the needs and expectations of individual companies. A key consideration in building such data files is the amount of detail, or "level of disaggregation," desired. In the illustrations that follow, the reader will observe that sales order activity is detailed by individual part numbers at one extreme and aggregated by territory, salespeople, and customer at the other. This procedure is necessary in order to obtain (1) specific cost information for recording cost of sales, (2) customer summary information for invoicing and updating accounts receivable and computing volume rebates, and (3) other summaries for computing salespeople's commissions and statistical analyses of sales.

Processing

Figure 15.6 demonstrates in a general way how sales activity might be processed through a series of computer passes to produce hard-copy documents, activity listings, updated data bases and master files, status reports, and analytical information for marketing management. Alternative approaches to inputting sales activity have been mentioned. The reader should envisage a variety of such approaches and an almost unlimited capability of expanding, contracting, fragmenting, rearranging, and sequencing these data to produce the desired results.

In Processing Run 1, sales order data are used to update a customer master file from which a wealth of analytical data can be periodically extracted. The various hard-copy documents already discussed are produced in this run, including the invoice to be finally completed by the billing clerks. Records to facilitate the updating of customer accounts receivable are prepared here for input into the billings and collections systems where the journal voucher debiting accounts receivable and crediting sales will be made.

Sales orders covering multiple parts or products are split into detailed records that are controlled by inventory part number. These records are computer-generated and reflect reference numbers and other data common to the original sales order so that they may be reassembled or sequenced in some other fashion for detailed analysis. The most important objective of this separation, however, is to permit matching with inventory records where product cost data are extracted, and extensions are made to support the cost of the sales journal entry (see Processing Run 2).

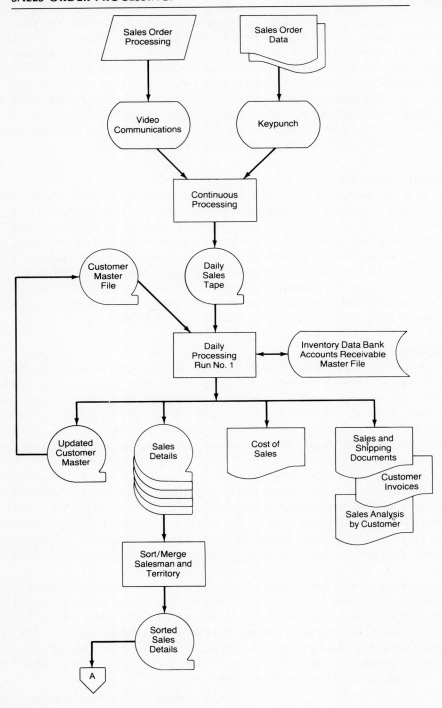

Figure 15.6

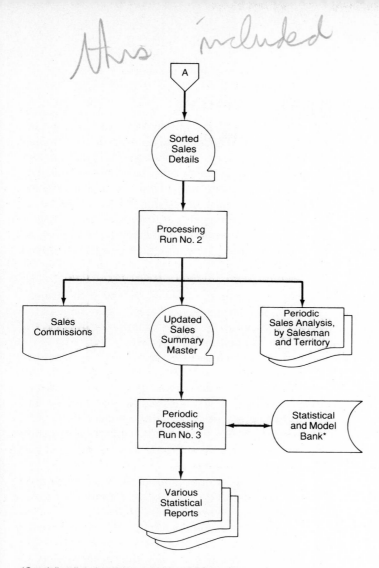

*Specially tailored analyses—similar to EOQ in inventory.

Figure 15.6 (cont'd)

Sales order data are then resequenced by sales personnel within the territory and run "against" the sales summary master where sales information is accumulated on an annual basis. During Processing Run 2, sales commissions are computed, sales analyses are made in accordance with the market segmentation plan chosen by the company, and the historical data in the sales summary master are analyzed by time factor (week, month, quarter, season, and annually).

SECTION B

SHIPPING AND TRANSPORTATION SYSTEMS

In the same manner that the receiving function provides the physical links among purchasing, raw material inventory, and the payment of accounts to trade creditors, shipping operations physically execute transactions involving sales, finished goods inventory, and the creation and collection of accounts receivable. Shipping is the independent originator of vital corporate information. Sales activities at one end of the revenue-generating spectrum and collection activities at the other must be connected by *evidence* of physical performance. Thus, a highly visible and adequately controlled system for assembling, shipping, and delivering sold merchandise is essential to the entire revenue cycle. The paperwork systems of all three functions should move in sequence and with speed and precision.

The shipping function may not involve as many independent judgments and decisions as its counterpart in receiving because shipping deals essentially with insiders. Familiarity with company products, operations, and paperwork ameliorates many of the problems that are inherent in dealings with outsiders. This circumstance permits the presentation of a shipping system in simple, straightforward terms.

To observe and discuss the full range of shipping-related activities, it is necessary to impinge slightly on the operations of inventory and traffic. In doing so, we do not assume that these operations are organizationally related, although they very well may be in many cases. Physical functions often appear to overshadow the shipping and delivering processes, relegating the information system to the status of clerical red tape. Nevertheless, the accountant must be aware of the tremendous value transformation taking place—from inventory, to receivables, to cash—and provide well-designed and controlled information systems to facilitate this conversion.

Critical to the shipping system is the type of transportation used. It is necessary to distinguish between the concepts of *delivery* and *shipment.* Delivery connotes a local, geographically limited, service utilizing company-owned delivery equipment, or leased facilities over which complete control is exercised. Shipment implies the involvement of an independent common carrier, into whose custody goods are consigned for safe transport and ultimate delivery. In return for the carrier's services, the carrier renders an invoice (freight bill) to the party (buyer or seller) responsible for paying transportation costs. The entry of a third party into transactions between buyer and seller introduces some interesting questions concerning title to such merchandise and legal liability in case of in-transit theft or damage. These matters, however, are more appropriately addressed in the area of traffic management.

FUNCTIONS AND OBJECTIVES

The overall objectives of a shipping and transportation organization can be summarized as follows: to assure that (1) all merchandise sold is properly packaged and shipped in accordance with customer specifications (if contractually expressed) and (2) all shipped merchandise is promptly and accurately billed to the customer. This responsibility places the operation squarely between the starting and ending functions of the revenue cycle. As mentioned earlier, the documents in shipping perform at least three very important functions. First, they provide proof of shipment, which authorizes the billing and collections operation to establish the receivable asset and relieve the inventory asset. Second, shipping documents establish the date of seller performance under the contract, and provide a starting time for measurement of the cash discount period or the determination of payment due date. Third, receipted transfer of goods to the common carrier implies the legal responsibility for the safe passage of such goods to the customer.

Traffic Functions

Economic value is added to the product by the transportation function. In the same sense that freight-in increases the cost of inventory to the customer, freight-out affects the selling expenses of the seller. Transportation charges associated with getting goods to a place at the time they are needed must be borne by one of the principals in the transaction. This is true whether delivery is made by company-owned or by contracted facilities, or through the medium of the independent carrier.

Internal traffic affairs are typically conducted by a separate department staffed by experienced transportation experts that are knowledgeable about the optional modes of transportation, and the individual carriers within each mode—their reputations, rates and schedules, and routes covered. Traffic management often includes the following responsibilities:

1. The movement of merchandise from the warehouse to the shipping docks, and packaging and labeling of shipments (often shared by the warehouse functions)
2. The arrangements for transporting and delivering shipments to customers, which include:
   a. Selecting and scheduling of carriers
   b. Negotiating rates with carriers
   c. Routing of shipments, including diversion and reconsignment
   d. Auditing and approval of freight charges for payment, or inclusion on the invoice
   e. Expediting the movement of shipments en route
3. The negotiations and processing of claims arising out of transportation contracts and agreements
4. The handling of all shipments returned by customers
5. The maintenance and control of transportation-related documents

We can only consider internal traffic functions randomly, since they span the entire time period from acceptance of an order to final loading for shipment. With the preceding responsibilities in mind, traffic assistance will be assumed wherever appropriate. Other shipping-related functions are simultaneously occurring in the finished goods stockroom.

The completely assembled order is checked for accuracy against the shipping order before it is approved by authorized personnel. The authenticated packing list labels are then physically associated with the shipment. The merchandise and all associated documents are then transported to the shipping dock, receipted, and left in the custody of shipping personnel.

Stockroom (Warehouse) Functions

Except in cases where circumstances require the "drop shipping" of an order from *another vendor* directly to the customer, most sales are made on the basis of stock carried in inventory. This introduces the need for a physical operation to assemble the customer's order and prepare it for pickup and delivery to the shipping dock. Those industries whose "shipments" are transported and metered over wire, cable, or pipeline are excluded (e.g., electricity, cable TV, oil, gas, etc.).

Once stockroom personnel receive the shipping order and its associated packing list, they select and assemble the designated items. Care must be taken to record *only* what is selected (available) for shipment. When the quantity of an item ordered exceeds the quantity available, a partial shipment is made and a back order is issued for the unfilled portion of the order. Highly automated sales order processing systems can detect inventory shortages in advance by remote inventory inquiry. Back-order decisions can be made at that time and the necessary reorder documents prepared so as to minimize the chances of error in "fractionated" transactions.

Shipping Functions

Under ideal circumstances, the shipment will arrive at the dock at precisely the time the carrier shows up for loading. Unfortunately, actual schedules are not perfect; there is usually a time lag between dock arrival of the shipment and carrier pickup. One of the continuing functions of the shipping department is to plan the physical storage and placement of goods to ensure easy movement and efficient loading of carrier vehicles.

Preparation of the shipping document is one of the most crucial activities performed at the shipping dock. The shipper prepares the bill of lading or other documents only when all items listed are released into the custody of the carrier (i.e., the carrier's agent or representative). The bill of lading, shipping order and other related documents are dated as of that time. The in-house functions related to the physical movement of the merchandise are completed at this point.

SOURCE DOCUMENTS

Independent carriers, whether "common" or "contract," transport shipments under contract. This contractual relationship requires documentary evidence. Shippers who prefer to deal exclusively with a single carrier may do so under the negotiated terms and conditions of *special* contracts. Contractual agreements with common carriers usually take the form of uniform *bills of lading.*

In any transaction between carrier and seller, evidence of a contractual relationship is required by law. Such evidence serves several basic purposes. First, these documents constitute the "contract of carriage," the terms and conditions of which are printed on the form. Second, they convey the shipper's instructions concerning route, delivery date, special handling, and other matters to the carrier. Third, they describe the shipment in terms applicable to rate structures and fee computation. Fourth, they provide a "receipt" for goods described on the bills that are transferred in good condition to the carrier. Fifth, they contain the reference numbers needed to associate the control documents of all parties involved—shipper, carrier, and customer. Finally, the documents serve as evidence of title when negotiable, and may under certain conditions give the consignee the right to claim the goods.

The field of transportation is highly specialized and may involve the use of other document forms in unique situations. Special forms do not, however, affect the design of the seller's shipping information system. Our discussion will focus on four basic shipping documents: (1) the shipping order, (2) the packing list, (3) the bill of lading, and (4) the freight bill. These documents support critical financial data flows, and are of particular interest to accountants.

The Shipping Order

Various methods may be used to create the shipping order, depending on the nature of the business, the size of the organization, and the degree of sophistication of the data processing and peripheral equipment used. In some companies, the sales order processing clerk manually prepares a multicopy shipping document upon receipt of a valid sales order. A copy of the document may serve as a packing list. Other companies may create the shipping order, packing list, and bill of lading with a multipart sales order form. Obviously, the information flow pattern may be different in these two methods, although the basic functions of the system remain essentially unchanged.

Companies employ a variety of techniques for creating shipping documents as automatic by-products of inventory status inquiries. For example, when a customer order arrives by mail, the sales order clerk keys selected data into a remote inquiry device that causes the entire inventory master record to appear on a video screen. An instant decision is made concerning the availability of materials ordered, and the order is "confirmed" with the customer. Keying in certain additional codes "encumbers" (in effect, diminishes) the inventory balance by the amount of the order. The entire revenue cycle is set in motion by the clerk's action, and all related documents are automatically prepared—sales order, shipping order, packing list, and uniform bill of lading.

A variety of document origins and techniques for preparing the shipping order have been presented without prescribing a best method. Wherever possible, and to the extent that data processing capabilities permit, the systems designer should make every effort to minimize manual document preparation and eliminate repetitive entry of data on a variety of single-purpose forms.

By whatever techniques shipping orders are prepared, they serve a number of important purposes. For the traffic function, shipping orders specify (1) the destination and point of delivery of the shipment, (2) the date the goods are needed, (3) the mode of transportation, (4) the route to be followed, (5) the shipping terms, and (6) designate who shall pay the freight charges. For warehouse operations, shipping orders authorize the physical assembly of merchandise sold and give directions on how it should be packaged. For the shipping dock, they first alert shipping supervision of an impending shipment, then specify the date and time of pickup, initiate the preparation of a bill of lading (if not done by other means), and authorize the release of the merchandise into the custody of the carrier. Most importantly, perhaps, the control copy of the shipping order is proof that shipment was made and authorizes the preparation and release of the customer invoice.

Figure 15.7 shows a reasonable representation of a standard shipping order form. The upper half of the form reflects control information such as the preprinted serial

33228

SHIPPING ORDER

RUSSELL CORPORATION   KNIT DIVISION
ALEXANDER CITY, ALABAMA 35010 ■ (205) 234-4251 ■ D-U-N-S 339-5902

REMIT TO:
RUSSELL CORPORATION
BOX 272
ALEXANDER CITY, AL. 35010

SHIPPER   VIA   PAGE

AGENT	OUR ORDER NO.	CUSTOMER ORDER NO.	CUSTOMER DEPT. NO.	STORE NO.	ACCOUNT NO.	TERMS	DATE	INVOICE NO.

(SAME AS SOLD TO UNLESS SHOWN)

SOLD
TO

SHIP
TO

1 - STRING   2 - PAPER BUNDLES   3 - POLY BUNDLES   4 - BOXED

CASE NUMBER	STYLE	PACKAGE	COLOR	SPECIAL STYLE	A										UOS	PRICE	AMOUNT
					A 2	4	6	8	10	12	14	16	18				
					B 6 MO.	1	2	3	4	5	6	6X	8				
					C S	M	L	XL				XS					
					D 30	32	34	36	38	40	42	44	46				
					E 38	40	42	44	46	48	50	52	54				

WE DISCLAIM LIABILITY FOR FURNISHING "PROOF OF DELIVERY" UNLESS REQUESTED IN WRITING BY YOU WITHIN NINETY DAYS AFTER SHIPMENT.
NO CLAIMS ALLOWED UNLESS MADE WITHIN FIVE DAYS AFTER RECEIPT OF GOODS.
WE HEREBY CERTIFY THAT ALL GOODS AND SERVICES COVERED BY THIS INVOICE WERE PRODUCED AND FURNISHED IN COMPLIANCE WITH THE REQUIREMENTS OF THE FAIR LABOR
STANDARDS ACT OF 1938, AS AMENDED, AND ANY REGULATIONS AND ORDERS ISSUED THEREUNDER.
WE GUARANTEE THAT THE TEXTILE FIBER PRODUCTS SPECIFIED HEREIN ARE NOT MISBRANDED NOR FALSELY NOR DECEPTIVELY ADVERTISED OR INVOICED UNDER THE PROVISIONS
OF THE TEXTILE FIBER PRODUCTS IDENTIFICATION ACT AND RULES AND REGULATIONS THEREUNDER.   OFFICE COPY
INTEREST AND SERVICE CHARGE WILL BE MADE ON ALL PAST DUE INVOICES.

Figure 15.7

number of the document, the customer's order number and date, the customer's name and address (or the entity to be billed for the shipment), date of the shipping order, shipping schedule information, the destination if different from the "sold-to" address, and the origin of the shipment. The main body of the form contains details pertinent to the type and quantity of merchandise ordered.

The Packing List

If the packing list is a copy of the shipping order, it will naturally be in the same format and show identical preinserted information as that illustrated in Figure 15.7. One noticeable difference will be the inclusion of a separate column for quantity shipped to be entered by the order filler.

The Bill of Lading

The uniform straight bill of lading is fairly standard in format. Figure 10.5 in the chapter on receiving illustrates a common six-part short form. This particular document set may be distributed as follows after it is receipted by the carrier:

Copy 1: Receipt copy, to billing and collection for invoicing
Copy 2: Carrier's copy
Copy 3: Serves as a freight bill (distributed to the traffic department of either the buyer or the seller, as appropriate)
Copy 4: Memo copy for receiver (customer)
Copy 5: Traffic department file copy
Copy 6: Shipping department file copy

The accountant will be alert to two important, though seemingly minor, items on the bill of lading. The first is the *date shipped*. As pointed out in previous chapters, procurement activity is usually geared to an established production schedule. Customers will usually specify a firm delivery (need) date on their purchase orders. Acceptance obligates the seller to comply with this timing. Some contracts contain a clause giving the buyer the legal right to cancel an order, or any part of it, when shipment is unreasonably behind schedule. Similarly, early shipments may be rejected and returned. Moreover, the seller may be liable for any loss resulting from his failure to perform. It is clear that the shipping and transportation function is under pressure to perform expeditiously, and the system must provide a means of alerting supervision to such strict contract terms.

The second item of importance, particularly to traffic, is the manner in which the shipment is made. Customers may state on their orders, "Ship cheapest way except when specified otherwise." This places the burden of discretion on the shipper. The customer often reserves the right to "charge back" transportation costs that exceed the cheapest rates obtainable. Inattention to these two matters can complicate an otherwise simple transaction.

The Freight Bill

It is easy to confuse the freight bill (Figure 15.8) and the bill of lading, particularly in situations where so many different functional documents seem to originate from the same source—and often from the same multipart document set. The following analogy may

FREIGHT BILL.

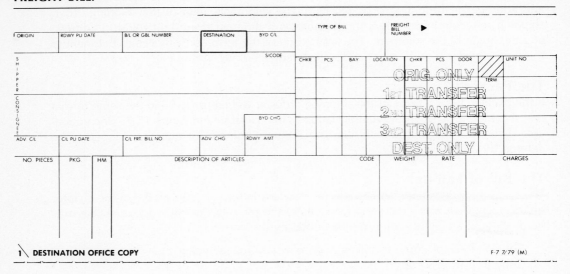

| 1 \ **DESTINATION OFFICE COPY** | | | | | | F-7 7/79 (M) |

Figure 15.8

help make a clear distinction. The bill of lading serves the same purpose for merchandise that a ticket serves for human passengers. It provides evidence to the carrier's agents that the merchandise is legally on board, that the fare has been paid or billed to someone, and that the consignee is authorized to accept the merchandise at destination. The freight bill on the other hand, is the carrier's invoice to the party responsible for paying the transportation charges. When the shipment is prepaid, the freight bill is rendered to the shipper (seller). When shipping charges are to be borne by the customer (buyer), the bill is presented to the receiver at the time of delivery.

The FOB Point

The term FOB (free on board) in effect indicates the point where title to merchandise shifts from seller to buyer. The importance of the point comes into focus mainly when there is evidence of damage or theft in transit, but it is of relatively less concern to the carrier, whose main interest is "who pays the freight." The carrier realizes that it is legally responsible for the safe passage of the shipment, regardless of who holds title. Figure 15.9 illustrates several ways in which the buyer and seller may handle the problems of title and freight cost absorption.

In the first and second situations shown in Figure 15.9 the terms of the sale specify "FOB buyer," signifying that title to the goods does not pass until the buyer accepts delivery. The seller may agree to absorb the transportation cost in each case. In the first case he elects to prepay the freight, but in the second the freight is paid by the buyer and *deducted* from the seller's invoice.

METHOD OF HANDLING FREIGHT BILLS AND FREIGHT CHARGES.

Contract Negotiations Between Buyer and Seller	Seller / Buyer	Title in Transit	Freight Paid by	Sellers Invoice Adjustment	Freight Charges Absorbed by
1. FOB Buyer, Freight Prepaid	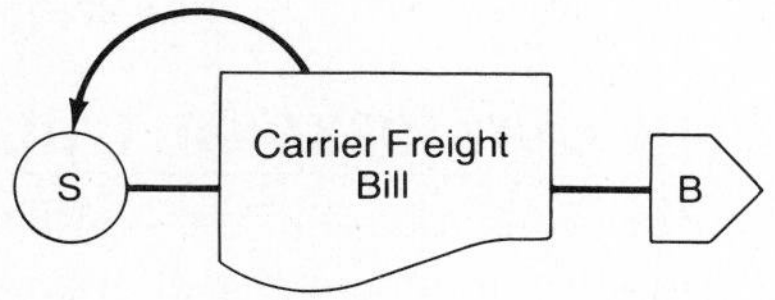 Carrier Freight Bill	S	S		S
2. FOB Buyer, Freight Collect, "Allowed" on Invoice	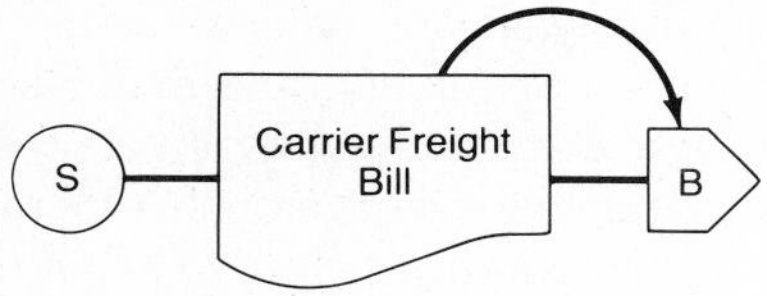 Carrier Freight Bill	S	B	–	S
3. FOB Seller, Freight Collect, "Allowed" on Invoice	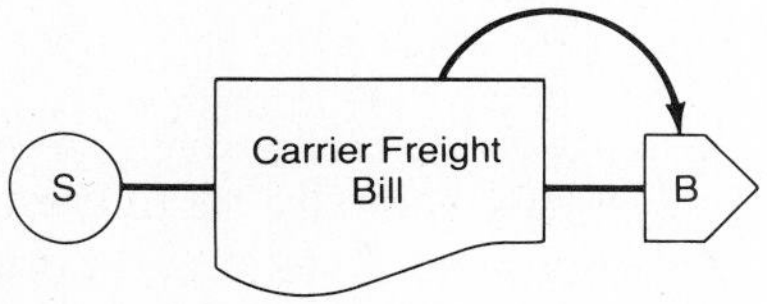 Carrier Freight Bill	B	B	–	S
4. FOB Seller, Freight Prepaid, Billed on Invoice	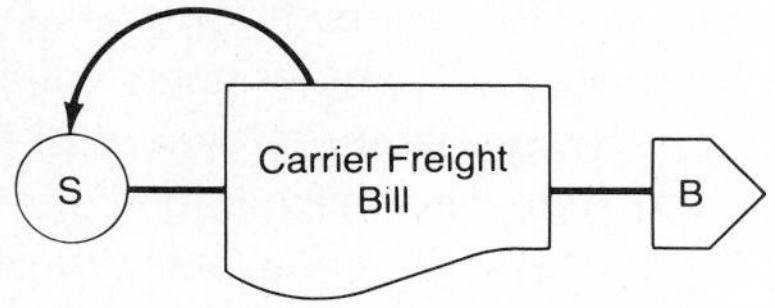 Carrier Freight Bill	B	S	+	B
5. FOB Seller, Freight Collect	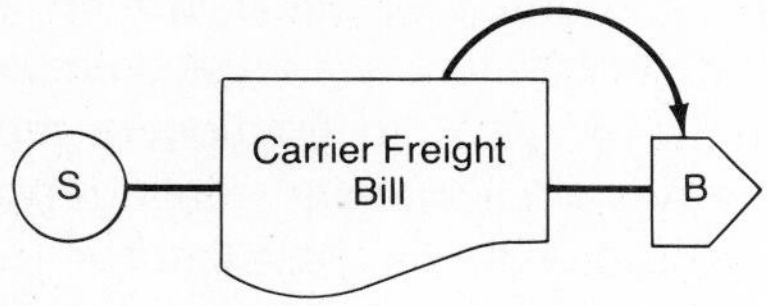 Carrier Freight Bill	B	B		B

Figure 15.9

In the other three situations the sales contract specified "FOB seller," indicating that title passes at the point of release of the goods to the common carrier. Nevertheless, the seller may agree to absorb the transportation charges even though title to the merchandise belongs to the buyer while it is in transit. This may be done by "allowing," or deducting freight charges from the invoice.

The buyer absorbs the freight in situations four and five, although in one instance the seller prepays the freight and includes it along with the merchandise charges on the invoice to the buyer.

ACCOUNTING CONTROLS AND RISKS OF FAILURE

Since shipping activities are not directly involved in the handling of cash or near-cash items, it is tempting to conclude that the maintenance of accounting controls is not an important consideration. Far from it! In fact, a loosely controlled shipping dock can quickly become a major channel for significant material losses. The chances for larceny are directly related to the size, value, popularity, and marketability of the product.

The shipping function can best be controlled by the existence and observance of good operating procedures and effective management. Operating procedures should focus on critical points such as document origination, material movements, information flow, transaction completion, area security, and specific delegation of authority and responsibility.

Document Control

The accountant and systems analyst will naturally be interested in the precomputer mechanics of the shipping and transportation system, particularly with regard to three points: (1) the manual functions related to the creation of key documents, (2) the conformity to the terms and conditions of the sales contract, and (3) the early detection and handling of back-ordered quantities. Most system designers will find many opportunities to streamline document forms and their preparation; they must take advantage of every chance to reduce human error and minimize the number of separate forms used. To avoid costly repercussions from customers, document control procedures must prevent deviations from the established sales contract (e.g., substitutions of materials, violation of carrier and route instructions, and timing of the shipment). Finally, when inventory inquiries and stock checks indicate insufficient quantities on hand to complete an order, arrangements should immediately be made to fractionate the original order and to reschedule the back-ordered portion. If customer concurrence cannot be obtained, arrangements should be made to drop-ship the balance from another source.

Movement of Materials

Tight control of the in-house movement of goods and the flow of documents are matters of special concern. The careful accountant will look for receipted transfers of valuable goods between inventory and traffic operations, between traffic and shipping operations, and between shipping operations and the carrier. To avoid unnecessary accumulations of files, the accountant can destroy such receipts upon completion of the transaction.

It is critical to manual systems that the physical flow of goods be accompanied by the flow of associated documents. Timing is important at the point when shipping functions are completed and invoicing functions begin. Procedures must reduce elapsed time between these functions to an absolute minimum.

Transaction Completion

Whenever inventory shortages make it necessary to "short-ship" an order and back order the balance, procedures must ensure regular followup until the original order is completely filled and the entire order billed. Partial shipments are perhaps best handled as separate transactions, each separately billed. In any case, the system should be designed to "red flag" partially completed sales orders for routine investigation in accordance with the feedback principle discussed in a previous chapter.

Area Security

The problem of physical control is essentially the same at the shipping dock as at the receiving dock. Typical measures of control are limited numbers of entrances and exits, fenced-in areas for storage of packaged merchandise awaiting carrier pickup, and admission only to authorized personnel. Some may consider such matters beyond the scope of an accountant's concern. However, custodial responsibility requires that the accountant be concerned with any aspect of corporate affairs that is vulnerable to fraud. Security measures are especially critical in situations where small, high-value items are handled (i.e., jewelry, drugs, electronics, optics, and the like). Bonding of key shipping personnel is a common control measure in such cases.

Responsibility and Authority

The organization structure should designate a specific shipping function, and operating procedures should make specific assignments of responsibility and authority for the accomplishment of critical tasks. These assignments should go beyond general management responsibilities and extend to the detailed paperwork and physical handling functions as well. Shipping management should be empowered to make independent judgments and initiate action to correct discrepancies in quantities, packaging, loading instructions, and scheduling.

MANAGEMENT INFORMATION REQUIREMENTS

Unlike some of the more pervasive systems previously discussed, the shipping organization does not become involved in period-end accounting entries, adjustments, accruals, deferrals, and the like. In fact, the system really does not *require* special electronic data processing operations, although it would make a good microcomputer application. Accordingly, this chapter gives no consideration to a possible configuration of computer and peripheral devices to accomplish such processing, or to the maintenance of shipping record master files. Instead, we assume the existence of sophisticated sales order writing and billing and collection systems from which an abundance of shipping information is readily obtainable.

Shipping line management must be prepared to respond intelligently to queries from administrative superiors concerning the efficiency and effectiveness of shipping operations. Its information needs will naturally be of the performance, planning, and status (backlog) variety.

Performance Information

Any good manager will collect statistics to help in reading the vital signs of his or her area of responsibility. Most prefer to express performance in terms of some standard resource or facility. As a result, the manager is apt to use indicators like "shipments per day," "orders processed per employee," "average weight per shipment," and "average time shipments held for carrier pickup"—all ideal microcomputer applications.

The best source of performance data is a summary of daily shipping activity. The listing should contain the essential facts from each shipping order processed to completion. Simple computations will yield the indicators needed to evaluate employee and carrier performances, and effectively to plan, organize, schedule, and execute shipping activities. Figure 15.10 suggests a possible format for a status listing. The information should be easily obtainable from the daily billing and collection processing system.

For planning and controlling routine operating loads, it is helpful to know in advance what shipping orders have been issued. "Daily shipping orders issued," also shown in Figure 15.10 contains information that is useful for this purpose. Such information may be obtained easily from the daily sales order processing system.

DAILY SHIPPING ACTIVITY REPORTS.

Date 9/20/86   Daily Shipping Orders Issued   Report SH-002

Shipping Order	Date	Consignee	Customer Order No.	Sales Order No.	Ship Date	Need Date
98765	09/20/86	Langs Sporting Goods	17 to 16	A-2341	09/30/86	10/02/86
98766	09/20/86	Olin L. Hill, Inc.	6310-5	A-2342	09/29/86	10/01/86
98767	09/20/86	Froshins Dept. Store	36830	A-2298	09/29/86	10/02/86
98768	09/20/86	Montgomery Fair	EZ-3030	A-2318	09/29/86	10/02/86
98769	09/20/86	Sears, Roebuck & Co.	SX-159A	A-2336	09/30/86	10/03/86
98770	09/20/86	Pizitz Dept. Stores	821-6163	A-2343	09/29/86	10/01/86
98						
98						
98						
98						
-						
-						
-						

Date 9/20/86   Daily Shipping Activity   Report SH-001

Sales Order No.	Consignee	S/O Date	Shipping Order No.	Carrier	Date Shipped	WT (000#)	Frt. Charges	PP/ Col.
A-2295	Higgins Sportswear	09/05/86	98620	Sou. Rwy.	09/20/86	12	$60	PP
A-2298	Universal Uniforms	09/05/86	98621	McLean Trk	09/20/86	105	$525	COL
A-2300	Sports Distrib., Inc.	09/05/86	98622	UPS	09/20/86	26	$130	COL
A-2302	Fun 'N Games	09/06/86	98702	McLean Trk	09/20/86	87	$435	COL
A-2303	J. C. Penney's	09/06/86	98681	Red Ball Exp	09/20/86	26	$130	COL
A-2304	Loudell's Sport Duds	09/06/86	98690	Orange & Blue	09/20/86	18	$90	PP
A-2305	Loveman's	09/07/86	98691	ABC Motor Fr	09/20/86	15	$75	COL
A-2339	Casual-Wear, Inc.	09/07/86	98692	Dpx Frt Line	09/20/86	75	$375	COL

Figure 15.10

Status Information

The term *backlog* immediately strikes a discordant note in the minds of most people. Actually, the absence of any backlog of uncompleted work should be equally disquieting to management. Such a condition may indicate overstaffing or, more alarmingly, declining business activity. There is a certain reasonable level of uncompleted work at the end of any period. Shipping management must know the status of its backlog, not only to control department costs and schedule employee overtime, but to assist in judging the performance of carriers. A report listing open shipping orders, Figure 15.11, highlights behind-schedule conditions needing special expediting and, in the long run, assists management in decisions to change carriers or even transportation modes where alternatives exist.

The backlog report can be easily prepared by simply matching the information contained in the two activity reports just discussed. Shipping orders issued, reduced by shipments completed daily, plus those carried forward from previous periods, yields shipments awaiting carrier pickup. However prepared, aging items appearing on the report should be followed through to completion.

Unbilled Shipments

Although the completion of the revenue cycle is beyond the purview of shipping responsibility, shipping department management (and the accountant) has a natural interest in matters that retard the completion of that cycle. Normally, the sensitivity of billing

SHIPPING STATUS REPORTS.

Date 9/20/86 Open Shipping Order Report SH-003

Shipping Order	Rec'd	S/O Date	Pkg	Customer	Carrier Pick-up	Scheduled Delivery	Destination
85673	08/10/86	08/09/86	10	After Dinner Sports	9/18	09/18/86	Lochapoka, AL
96302	09/05/86	09/02/86	10	Metro Athletic Wear	9/18	09/19/86	Notasulga, LA
98775	09/20/86	09/18/86	25	His'n & Her'n Shop	9/20	09/21/86	St. Petersburg, Fla.
98776	09/20/86	09/18/86	30	Wearall Sporting Good	9/22	09/24/86	Memphis, Tenn.
98777	09/20/86	09/18/86	12	Cowboy Sport Wear	9/20	09/25/86	Pisgah, Mont.
98778	09/20/86	09/18/86	18	Athletic Distrib.	9/20	09/25/86	Lynchburg, Tenn.

Date 9/20/86 Unbilled Shipments Report SH-004

Customer	Sales Ord.	Date	Ship Ord.	Date	B/L	Carrier
Habbit Sports Wear	35465	08/05/86	85609	08/15/86	123456	Master Fleet
Lang's Sporting Goods	46576	08/05/86	85613	08/15/86	234567	Ryder
Court, Track & Pool	57687	08/19/86	86575	08/20/86	345678	Fleetrite Line
The Sportsperson, Inc.	68798	09/05/86	96344	09/08/86	456789	Shady Van Lines
Fred Sington, Inc.	79809	09/05/86	96345	09/08/86	567890	Baggett Mtr Frt
The Athlete's Foot	80981	09/05/86	96346	09/08/86	678901	L & N Ry.

Figure 15.11

activities should keep the volume of unbilled shipments down to a routine backlog of items. Nevertheless, occasional short shipments and other discrepancies will complicate both the shipping and billing procedures. Resulting unbilled shipments may appear on a report such as the one shown in Figure 15.11 and stimulate constant follow-up until the transaction is complete.

Other reports may be in common use by shipping management, of course. The purpose here is merely to demonstrate some of the types of control information available from shipping operations and to relate such information to the decisions and problems management continually faces.

SUMMARY

The marketing information system is similar in objective to any other data processing system in that it collects and processes the basic knowledge needed to plan and control operations. Unlike other entity functions, only the sales contracts and other related sales activity are introduced into the system, stimulating certain internal actions that culminate in the exchange of marketable products/services for cash.

Although this customer input constitutes the essence of marketing's contribution to the marketing system, management must receive the necessary sales and marketing information to measure achievement of the company's objectives. Marketing management therefore requires something more than presales research. The system must provide a readout of vital signs to permit control of the system and a comparison of planned performance with results. These vital signs necessarily focus on the product, salespeople, the customers, and the preperformance promotion.

The main objective of marketing management is to put together a set of marketing strategies that will achieve the goals of the firm. This is not an easy undertaking because of the nonlinear relationship between the many variables, the interaction among the variables, the unknown character of competitive responses, and the sometimes fickle nature of the customers. Management must therefore act intuitively in designing its marketing strategy, and then rely on a variety of classified, refined, and summarized historical sales information to assess the results of past performance.

There are as many different types of shipping arrangements as there are different companies, different products, and different modes of available transportation. Anyone studying a shipping system will wish to look behind the surface features and concentrate on the control of goods in motion between inventory and the shipping area, including release to the carrier. Documentary evidence should mark each exchange, especially that between the seller (shipping agent) and the carrier's agent. This evidence, particularly the executed bill of lading, is critical to the invoicing process.

NOTES

[1]William J. Stanton, *Fundamentals of Marketing.* (New York: McGraw-Hill Book Co., 1984), p. 5.

[2]Douglas J. Dalrymple and Leonard J. Parsons, *Marketing Management.* (New York: John Wiley & Sons, 1980), p. 4.

[3]Ibid., p. 9.

[4]Conrad Berensen, "Marketing Information Systems," *Journal of Marketing,* 33 (October 1969): 16–23.

[5]Martin L. Bell, *Marketing: Concepts and Strategy,* 3rd ed. (Boston: Houghton Mifflin Co., 1979).

[6]Raymond J. Coleman and M. J. Riley, *MIS: Management Dimensions.* (San Francisco, Holden-Day, Inc., 1973), p. 372.

[7]One must be able to visualize several possible organizational structures or configurations based on other criteria such as geographical region, brand name, separate profit center or divisions of the company, and so forth.

[8]Dalrymple and Parsons, p. 7.

[9]Raymond J. Coleman and M. J. Riley, *MIS: Management Decisions.* (San Francisco: Holden-Day, Inc., 1973), p. 335. Reprinted from Robert L. Johnson and Irwin H. Derman, "How Intelligent Is Your MIS," *Business Horizons* (February 1970).

[10]Ibid., p. 336.

SELECTED REFERENCES

Adler, Lee. "Systems Approach to Marketing," *Harvard Business Review* (May/June 1967): 105–118.

Bell, Martin L., *Marketing: Concepts and Strategy,* 3rd ed. Boston: Houghton Mifflin Company, 1979.

Berensen, Conrad. "Marketing Information Systems," *Journal of Marketing,* 33 (October 1969): 16–23.

Bodnar, George H. *Accounting Information Systems.* Boston: Allyn & Bacon, 1980.

Coleman, Raymond J., and M. J. Riley. *MIS: Management Decisions.* San Francisco: Holden-Day, Inc., 1973, p. 335. Reprinted from Robert L. Johnson and Irwin H. Derman, "How Intelligent Is Your MIS," *Business Horizons* (February 1970): 148–163.

Dalrymple, Douglas J., and Leonard J. Parsons. *Marketing Management.* New York: John Wiley & Sons, 1980.

Doppelt, Neil. "Down-to-Earth Marketing Information Systems," *Management Advisor* (September/October 1971): 19–26.

Hughes, G. David. "Computerized Sales Management," *Harvard Business Review* (March–April 1983): 102–112.

Montgomery, David B., and Glen L. Urban. "Marketing Decision-Information Systems: An Emerging View," *Journal of Marketing Research;* 7 (May 1970): 226–234.

Page, John R., and H. Paul Hooper. *Accounting and Information Systems.* Reston, Va.: Reston Publishing Co., 1979.

Stanton, William J. *Fundamentals of Marketing.* New York: McGraw-Hill Book Co., 1984.

QUESTIONS

1. What essential function is performed by the marketing operation on which all other systems are based?
2. Differentiate between marketing research and the marketing information system.
3. What single subfunction in the marketing organization interfaces most closely with other operating information systems? How?
4. Why is it necessary to maintain an "approved customer file," and what organizations play a role in the establishment and maintenance of such a file?
5. What internal actions are generated by the introduction of a customer sales order into the system?
6. What advantages do you see in using on-line real-time devices in the marketing information system to access the related data bases over, say, a manual system or a semiautomated batch processing system?

7. Describe the accounting impact of postsale adjustments such as:
   a. Compromise agreements and concessions
   b. Volume rebates
   c. Write-offs of uncollectible accounts
   d. Sales returns
   e. Invoice error corrections
   f. Charge-backs
   g. Cash discounts
8. Discuss the risks associated with accepting and honoring sales orders from unauthorized customers.
9. What are the accounting consequences of improper handling of returned sales?
10. What are the basic kinds of information needed by marketing management?
11. What essential data bases are required by a fully automated marketing system?
12. What are some of the trends in the field of marketing, as well as business in general, which are seriously impacting the marketing information system?
13. Compare the role of the shipping system in the revenue cycle to that of the receiving system in the expenditure cycle.
14. List and discuss the major objectives of the shipping operation.
15. What purposes are served by the use of a uniform straight bill of lading? A packing list?
16. How does a carrier freight bill differ from a bill of lading?
17. What does the term *FOB* mean and what is its significance to accountants? To common carriers?
18. Describe five ways in which the buyer and seller may agree to handle the related problems of title passage and freight charges.
19. Considering its role in revenue cycle events, what impact (if any) does shipping operations have on cash flow?
20. What kinds of information does shipping management need to run an effective and efficient shipping operation? Explain.
21. What are some of the common risks of a poorly controlled shipping operation?
22. Why would it *not* be good business practice to combine the shipping and receiving functions of a large company?
23. What is a "drop shipment," and how might such a transaction be handled within revenue cycle procedures?

PROBLEMS

24. Systems Flowchart and Analysis

Plainsman Industries is a small, privately owned, and rapidly growing company located in a midwestern city of about 400,000 people. The company manufactures quality wiring assemblies and switches for the large automobile companies and several hundred other smaller customers. It ships approximately $80,000 to $90,000 worth of its products each week, and has been growing at an annual rate of 20 percent over the past several years.

The company's shipping department consists of four workmen, two typists, and a supervisor who work a variable 8-hour workday depending on the work load and specified shipping modes. Considering its present size, Plainsman has elected to "keep its functions and information systems simple." There is to be a minimum of paperwork, and the shipping and receiving functions share a common dock area situated at one end of the factory building. Responsible executives visualize no special security problems in this arrangement, since the area is locked except when loading or off-loading is in progress.

Plainsman's production operations are initiated by a customer's purchase order which, upon acceptance (routinely in most cases), is sent directly to the shipping department where a multipart invoice is typed for distribution as follows:

1 customer copy held for pricing and mailing
1 production copy attached to customer order
2 shipping copies (one a packing slip) retained in shipping

All typing except insertion of product prices is done by the two typists in the shipping department. A list of these invoices is prepared daily and given to the shipping foreman as a schedule log.

The production copy of the invoice is assigned a unique job number by shipping and routed to the assembly shops. Later, upon completion, the order is given its first quality check, weighed, and stamped with a large black "X" signifying release by production. If the delivery date is more than 2 weeks away, the completed production is temporarily stored in inventory awaiting shipment. Of increasing concern to management is the fact that this "transient" inventory sometimes reaches unmanageable proportions.

The shipping foreman calls for release of the customer's order a few days in advance of the required shipping date. Upon arrival at the shipping dock, the order is deleted from the foreman's log, and the customer's copy of the invoice is sent to the "war room" (a conference room where key managers meet for special purposes) for costing and pricing. The customer's copy of the priced invoice is then mailed independently of the shipment. In the meantime, the shipping department performs a final quality check and verifies the quality reflected on the production copy of the invoice. Errors are corrected at this point.

Plainsman maintains no delivery facilities of its own. The customer usually specifies a common carrier of its choice, and shipping terms generally are "FOB destination." The packing slip and a copy of the short-form bill of lading prepared by the carrier are placed in an envelope and stapled to the carton at the time of loading. Carrier pickups are scheduled from 3:00 PM to 6:00 PM each weekday, and the dock area is secured following the last shipment.

The war room keeps a set of records similar to that maintained in shipping (i.e., *in* orders are added to a log, and *outgoing* shipments are marked off when the invoice is mailed). A cursory audit of these two logs is performed each day.

Required:

    a. Flowchart the system as previously described.

    b. Criticize the document flow, the sequence and timing of events, and the controls.

    c. In view of Plainsman's continued growth, recommend a more efficient system for future operations.

25. Documents and Internal Control

When a shipment is made, the shipping department of BAP Company prepares a shipping order form. This form is in three copies. The first copy is sent out with the goods to the customer as a packing slip. The second copy is forwarded to the billing department. The third copy is sent to the accountant. When the billing department receives the second copy of the shipping order, it uses the information thereon to prepare a two-part sales invoice. The second copy of the shipping order is then filed in the billing department. The first copy of the sales invoice is sent to the customer. The second copy of the sales invoice is forwarded to the accountant. Periodically, the accountant matches his copy of the shipping order with his copy of the sales invoice and files them alphabetically by customer name. Before doing so, however, he uses his copy of the sales invoice to post the sales entry in the subsidiary accounts receivable ledger. *(IIA adapted)*

Required:

    a. For use in appraising internal control over shipping, prepare a flowchart covering the flow of documents reflected in the preceding situation.

    b. List those deficiencies and/or omissions revealed by the flowchart that would lead you to question the internal control.

26. Flowchart Evaluation

A partially completed charge sales systems flowchart is shown in Figure 15.12. The flowchart depicts the charge sales activities of the Bottom Manufacturing Corporation.

A customer's purchase order is received and a six-part sales order is prepared from it. The six copies are initially distributed as follows:

Copy No. 1: Billing copy—to billing department
Copy No. 2: Shipping copy—to shipping department
Copy No. 3: Credit copy—to credit department
Copy No. 4: Stock request copy—to credit department
Copy No. 5: Customer copy—to customer
Copy No. 6: Sales order copy—file in sales order department

When each copy of the sales order reaches the applicable department or destination, it calls for specific internal control procedures and related documents. Some of the procedures and related documents are indicated on the Figure 15.12

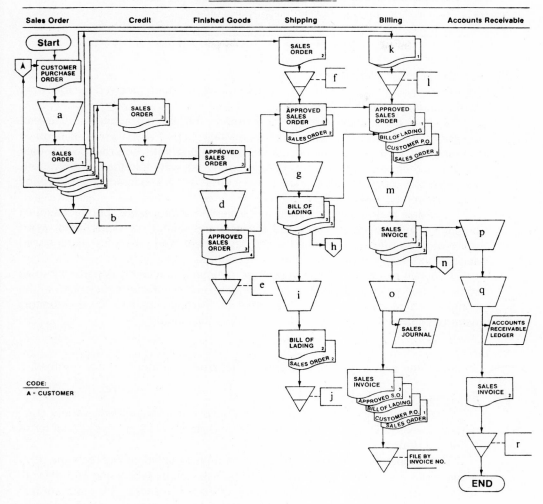

BOTTOM MANUFACTURING CORPORATION
Flowchart of Credit Sales Activities

| Sales Order | Credit | Finished Goods | Shipping | Billing | Accounts Receivable |

Figure 15.12

flowchart. Other procedures and documents are labeled letters a to r. *(AICPA adapted)*

Required:

List the procedures of the internal documents that are labeled letters c to r in Figure 15.12. Organize your answer as follows (note that an explanation of the letters a and b that appear in the flowchart are entered as examples):

Flowchart Symbol Letter	Procedures or Internal Document
a	Prepare six-part sales order
b	File by order number

27. Analysis of Authority

The director of internal auditing for a marketing organization received the following memorandum from the controller:

"During the last audit of my department, the internal auditors on several occasions told the accountants and accounting clerks what they should do in carrying out their respective accounting tasks along with how and when they should do them. Some of my accounting supervisors were told that certain adjusting entries should be made to correct prior period errors and to adjust the carrying values of certain assets.

"I realize that the internal audit staff is very knowledgeable about accounting principles, accounting systems, and the activities within my department, since some of them previously worked in the department, and others are experienced accountants with various professional credentials.

"There is no question that the auditors' directions helped my department solve some of its problems and did, in fact, correct some significant deficiencies in the company's financial statements. Nevertheless, I strongly believe that the auditors went beyond their authority while performing this audit."

Required:

Identify three problems that may arise if the issue of authority is not resolved.

28. Systems Flowchart

Trivia Manufacturing Company produces Trinkets for a nationwide variety store market. It sells to large regional wholesalers and grants 1/10, n/30 discount terms to all its customers.

The company's marketing department recently installed on-line real-time communications equipment in order to speed up sales order processing and delivery service, and thereby improve deteriorating customer relations. An important feature of the new system is its instant accessibility to inventory records that permits immediate responses to an increasingly large volume of the telephone orders. Telephone commitments to customers cue the automatic preparation of (1) a sales order acknowledgment for the customer, (2) the inventory requisition (packing slip), (3) the four-part shipping order set, (4) a standard multipart short-form bill of lading, and (5) a three-part invoice document set, complete except for date and shipping information. The system controls include a cursory credit check by reference to an internally published *list* of credit codes assigned by the credit department. These codes are also reflected in a customer master file maintained manually by the marketing clerical pool. Since the credit list is more widely distributed, sales order processing clerks find it more expedient and convenient to use.

Risky Sales, Inc., a large privately owned wholesale business, is one of the many customers registering complaints about delivery service from Trivia in recent years. On September 30, Risky Sales "called in" an exceedingly large Christmas order for 10,000 dozen Trinkets, requesting immediate delivery. All elements in the routine sales processing procedure indicated "go," so the order was confirmed (accepted) and delivery was expedited.

Although Risky Sales was not considered a particularly poor credit risk by Trivia credit management, it was regarded as a "slow payer." Its annual reports, including changes in financial position, and other credit-related information had been carefully analyzed in June. At that time certain key financial ratios (e.g., current ratio, debt-to-equity ratio, inventory turnover, times interest earned, and return on investment) were only marginally acceptable and appeared to be rapidly deteriorating. Accordingly, credit management decided that a sales volume of 2,500 dozen trinkets during any 30-day period would be immediately imposed on Risky Sales. This restriction was reflected in the customer master file.

Shortly after the new year began, Risky Sales was forced into bankruptcy.

Required:
a. Flowchart the current (new) system as you perceive it from the foregoing narrative. Include the distribution, use, and handling of all documents.
b. Prescribe controls to make the system more reliable and pervasive. Go beyond the immediate situation described previously.
c. Flowchart the improved sales order processing system you have created.

29. Design of Marketing and Shipping Systems

Pinta Company is a regional discount chain in the Southeast selling general merchandise. The company is considering acquiring a point-of-sale (POS) system for use in its stores.

There basically are three types of firms that currently use POS systems—large retailers, grocery stores, and fast food chains. Pinta would probably employ cash registers that use light pens to read the universal product code (UPC) printed on packages.

Charles Brenski, President of Pinta, knows that the equipment is very expensive. He has asked his systems' staff to prepare a report on POS systems including a survey as to what companies are employing POS systems and why they have adopted them. *(IMA adapted)*

Required:
a. Explain briefly how a POS system operates.
b. Identify the potential (1) advantages and (2) disadvantages of a POS system for a company's operations and record-keeping system.
c. Identify and explain the special control problems that a POS system could present to Pinta Company's system personnel.

CASES

30. Although the nature of Apogee Company's product and its marketing strategy greatly simplify both the selling and shipping operations, the company's anticipated growth (in terms of markets, customers, and volume of business) makes it necessary to streamline and "systematize" each of these functions.

After carefully studying Appendix C, present a proposal for marketing and shipping systems, keeping the two independent of each other but functionally related. Describe the documents required, the flow and timing of the documents and related events, the controls needed to assure dependability and integrity, and the kinds of reports needed by management. Be sure to include the customer invoicing and inventory connections.

31. The nature of Bubbling Stone Beverage Company's operation forces it to adopt the unique marketing and shipping/delivery style explained in the case. Actually, its operation is identical in many respects to the system followed by a world famous cola bottler and distributor in the same city. Yet the controller frankly admits that the system could stand some refinements.

Describe the present system in flowchart form (document and systems flowcharts), and isolate those functions and procedures that can be improved. Recommend specific improvements.

CHAPTER SIXTEEN

The Billing and Collection System

In the United States a definite trend away from cash transactions toward an exchange system based on credit has emerged. Since World War II there has been a steady and rapid increase in the use of credit cards. Most business people consider this method of consummating business to be a stimulus to business growth and development. Actual payment follows conveniently and routinely through various forms of funds transfers.

The exchange of goods and services must ultimately be reciprocated with cash, however, if the revenue cycle is to produce the desired results. For each sales transaction, the revenue cycle ends with billing and collection. Customer obligations are satisfied in either a timely manner (transferring the appropriate funds) or an untimely manner (being referred to a collection agency or written off as bad debts).

Transaction forms in society have evolved from simple barter, through various forms of cash, to credit and the checkless society of the electronic funds transfer age. Regardless of the transaction system, the accountant must not lose sight of the real issue—the exchange of values for claims to values.

The billing and collection system represents the logical conclusion to the revenue cycle. The revenue cycle is initiated in the marketing system when a sale is made to a customer. The company agrees to provide certain goods and services in return for payment by the customer. Once the company performs its task, the customer is obligated to pay for the goods or services. The billing and collection system is established to monitor these payments and maintain appropriate customer records.

The vital connection between the revenue cycle and the administrative cycle is provided by the billing and collection system. The end result is the receipt of cash. Controls over cash receipts and procedures for processing them are covered in Chapter Seventeen.

FUNCTIONS AND OBJECTIVES

Broadly speaking, a billing and collection system has three major functions. First, it must assure that all goods and services provided to customers are promptly and properly billed to the recipients. Second, the cost of goods and services provided must be established and recorded. Finally, customer accounts must be managed with accuracy and integrity.

In fact, if any one single characteristic could be used to exemplify the whole billing and collection operation, it would be *integrity.* From the initial billing to the final settlement of the account, good customer relations must be promoted and maintained. Account mismanagement creates customer suspicion and antagonism and may ultimately cause the customer to change to a competitor.

Nevertheless, the system must be designed to provide collection activities that ensure rapid cash inflow while minimizing bad debt losses. Internal controls must effectively preclude the manipulation of accounts and the misapplication, misdirection, and misuse of remittances.

The execution of these broad functions must be accomplished under the aegis of strict operating procedures. Normal business activities may produce several kinds of accounts receivable—namely, trade accounts, employee accounts, and other receivables resulting from claims, legal proceedings, and the like. The general procedures for handling these obligations are not dissimilar, however, and can be discussed together. In this text no distinction has been made between businesses whose customers are predominantly business-oriented and those who sell to retail customers. Beyond the finite details of systems operations, the broad functions and objectives are identical in each case. To describe the general flow of documents, data, and information, we shall use a large-scale manufacturer selling to other manufacturing and retail establishments.

The operating procedures that describe in detail the routine execution of the three broad functions mentioned earlier must provide for numerous subsidiary functions. Billings must be promptly and accurately rendered on the basis of support documents that include the sales order, shipping order, packing list, and bill of lading. Such billings must also be promptly and accurately applied to the proper customer accounts and immediately dispatched to the customer.

Adjustments to customer accounts affecting revenues and cost and account distributions must be promptly and accurately classified, summarized, and recorded. These adjustments are then applied to the proper customer subsidiary accounts. Most adjustments are in the form of accounts receivable debit and credit memoranda, and include the following activities:

1. Corrected billings, especially when mechanical errors reflect in item extensions and invoice totals
2. Charge-backs (e.g., for discounts taken in error)
3. Service, finance, and interest charges for overdue account balances
4. Write-off of uncollectible accounts
5. Concessions and compromise agreements with the customer
6. Volume rebates
7. Merchandise returned by the customer for credit
8. Cash discounts allowed

Cash items received representing collections on account must be promptly and accurately classified, summarized, and reported and applied to the proper customer subsidiary accounts. Accountability for cash should be firmly established in accordance with management's directions in the aforementioned operating procedures. Bonding of key employees who operate in close proximity to cash is a common practice in business. The procedure, of course, covers the handling of cash sales.

Tax information derived from revenue-producing operations must be accurately and promptly reported—both the amounts billed and the amounts collected. Although the billing and collection operation is not generally held responsible for filing and paying such taxes, input from this system provides the basis for such activities in the accounts payable system.

Revenue journal entries and entries to journalize cost of goods and services sold, sales-related expenses, and accounts receivable adjustments must be prepared in accordance with management's plan at the end of each accounting period. Individual accounts receivable balances must be periodically substantiated, aged, and evaluated for management review and determination of action to be taken.

Physical control of processing areas must be maintained. This is usually accomplished by the enforcement of limited access to critical forms and records, data base files, and areas where cash collections and billing operations are performed.

Reliable management reports must be promptly rendered in accordance with management's plan. Although the nature and content of such reports will vary from company to company, some of the more common management information needs are discussed later in this chapter.

SOURCE DOCUMENTS

A variety of source documents are necessary for a properly functioning billing and collection system. As a result of the interface of the system with other relevant systems, several source documents for billing and collection are generated by outside entities.

An example of an outside document is the sales order, which is produced by the marketing system (Chapter Fifteen). This document is forwarded by the marketing system to the credit department for an indication of credit approval and is subsequently received by billing and collection for processing.

The primary source documents generated by the billing and collection system include the sales invoice, the customer statement, the remittance advice, and the bad debt write-off listing. Other source documents may be included in a billing and collection system, but these represent the typical source documents.

The sales invoice, as shown in Figure 16.1, includes the customer name and address, a description of items ordered, the quantity, prices, and shipping terms, and total invoice price. The invoice is prepared by the billing person upon receipt of the sales order and requires the checking of footings, extensions, and prices against the price list. A copy of the invoice is mailed to the customer indicating the purchase and the liability of the customer to the vendor.

At periodic intervals, usually monthly, the company should send customers a statement of their accounts. The statement, as shown in Figure 16.2, should show the balance owed to the company as well as the details making up that balance—that is, the balance brought forward from the preceding statements plus purchases referenced to sales invoice numbers less payments by the customer. Mailing of such statements is an important function of the billings and collections system. The procedure aids in both control and conversion of receivables into cash. Often attached to the customer statement is a remittance advice that is mailed back to the company along with payment by the customer. This document facilitates the recording of cash receipts and credits to accounts receivable. Remittance advices are discussed in greater detail in Chapter Seventeen.

SALES INVOICE.

RUSSELL CORPORATION KNIT DIVISION
ALEXANDER CITY, ALABAMA 35010 ■ (205) 234-4251 ■ D-U-N-S 339-5902

REMIT TO:
RUSSELL CORPORATION
BOX 272
ALEXANDER CITY, AL. 35010

SHIPPER   VIA   PAGE

AGENT	OUR ORDER NO.	CUSTOMER ORDER NO.	CUSTOMER DEPT. NO.	STORE NO.	ACCOUNT NO.	TERMS	DATE	INVOICE NO.

(SAME AS SOLD TO UNLESS SHOWN) .

SOLD TO

SHIP TO

1 - STRING   2 - PAPER BUNDLES   3 - POLY BUNDLES   4 - BOXED

CASE NUMBER	STYLE	PACKAGE CODE	COLOR	SPECIAL STYLE	A									UOS	PRICE	AMOUNT
					A	2	4	6	8	10	12	14	16	18		
					B	6 MO.	1	2	3	4	5	6	6X	8		
					C	S	M	L	XL				XS			
					D	30	32	34	36	38	40	42	44	46		
					E	38	40	42	44	46	48	50	52	54		

Figure 16.1

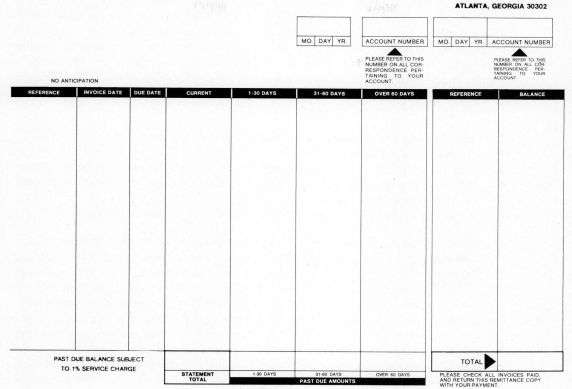

Figure 16.2

Typically, the maintenance of accounts receivable includes the periodic write-off of some of these accounts to bad debts. That determination should be performed by the credit manager with subsequent approval by the treasurer. To facilitate this process, control procedures often require that a listing of such bad debts be prepared to initiate the write-off of these accounts. The listing should include the accounts and amounts written off and a properly authorized signature.

DOCUMENT FLOW AND TIMING

The constantly changing and evolving business environment introduces an ever-increasing volume and variety of sales-related problems with which management in all revenue cycle operations must contend. The design of efficient information systems in this area requires an understanding of all the functions involved in accounting for sales from the time the customer's order is received until final payment is made. Concomitantly, an in-depth perception of management's information needs for planning, operating, and controlling these functions is essential.

For this reason, a discussion of the flow of documents and the sequence of events in the billing and collection system impinges on sales order writing and warehouse-traffic-shipping operations, as well as the involvement of the customer. These events are inherent, to some extent and in some fashion, in all basic systems for sales accounting whether it be a simple retail store or a multidimensional organization. Obviously, a simpler model would describe the former, but major adaptions of the paperwork and information flow systems would be necessary when the following circumstances and business practices (among others) are involved:

1. Central billing and decentralized warehousing and shipping
2. International operations
3. Shipment and delivery by company-owned or -leased carriers, or contract carriers
4. Certain government contract sales calling for "progress payments" based on percentage of contract completion
5. The practice of using "drop shipments" in cases of inventory shortages

Nevertheless, Figure 16.3 describes the essence of billing and collection transactions.

The revenue cycle is initiated by the customer's order. When that order is placed, the marketing department sends a copy to the credit department. Upon approval, marketing is notified, and the customer is sent an acknowledgment. Marketing then prepares a multicopy sales invoice. One copy is sent to billings and collection as notice of an impending shipment, two copies of the sales invoice are forwarded to inventory and one copy to shipping. At this point, shipping prepares a bill of lading and forwards one copy to billings and collection as notification of shipment. The goods are then sent to the customer. Billings and collection records the transaction in the sales journal and accounts receivable ledger and forwards one copy of the sales invoice to the customer as notification of billing. These activities may be either manual or computerized or a combination of both. This is also an area where many companies make extensive use of microcomputer networks to handle each of the activities mentioned.

If there are no complications requiring negotiated adjustments, the final step in the cycle is accomplished when the customer's payment is received and processed. This step provides the important interface with the cash control system.

MANAGEMENT INFORMATION REQUIREMENTS

The format and content of management information requirements is likely to depend on the data processing capabilities employed by the company. Sales analyses, for example, are important planning and forecasting tools, but are usually clumsy and expensive to compile by manual methods. There are, however, certain information requirements that must be served. These needs can be ascertained by asking a few simple, but vital, questions.

DOCUMENT FLOW AND TIMING—BILLINGS AND COLLECTIONS.

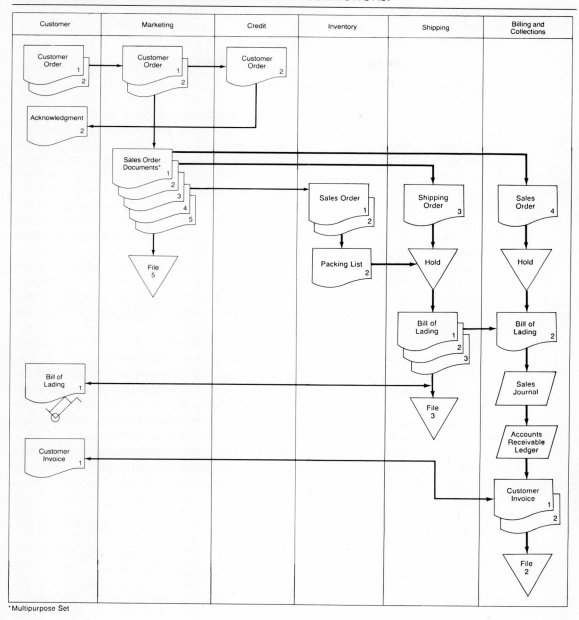

*Multipurpose Set

Figure 16.3

1. How quickly are sales being converted to cash?
2. What percentage of sales are returned for credit? Why?
3. Are there any unbilled shipments on hand?
4. Are cash discount policies speeding up the billings and collection cycle?

Sound management practices and decisions require answers to all these questions and others. The reader can easily visualize how the data available in the billing and collection operation can serve many of the needs of both financial and marketing operations. What information is required for management to determine how quickly sales are converted to cash (question 1)? With a fully automated and computerized operation, instant statistics on accounts receivable turnover and average length of the collection period would be easily available. Additionally, an *aged analysis of open customer accounts* could be extracted from a master customer file during any single processing cycle. A possible format for such a report is illustrated in Figure 16.4. This type of information could be summarized and merged with historical data to produce a short and medium range cash receipts forecast similar (in reverse) to the cash payments forecast demonstrated in Chapter Eleven (accounts payable). Such a forecast could be helpful in the management of cash.

A report listing classified and summarized *adjustments to customer accounts* would indicate the percentage of sales returned for credit (question 2). Arranged in sequence by customer name, and classified horizontally by type of adjustment, this report could serve a variety of management needs in cash, credit, and marketing organizations (see Figure 16.5).

The question of unbilled shipments (question 3) presents a problem, since it alludes to activities that are not yet "in the system." We are assuming here, of course, a sequential process in which billing naturally follows shipping. At any time, it must be presumed that there could be a backlog of shipments to be billed. A report on the status of such items would naturally require manual preparation. If the shipment-billing sequence is automated to the extent that invoicing occurs simultaneously with shipping, then the need for unbilled shipments information would be obviated.

The evaluation of the effectiveness of cash discount policy in speeding up the cash flow (question 4) will usually be a judgment decision by management. The billing and collection system will yield information concerning discounts allowed, as well as those

AGED ANALYSIS OF OPEN CUSTOMER ACCOUNTS									
Customer Name	Code	Invoice Number	Date	Terms	Customer Order Number	Aged Analysis in Days			
						Current	30–60	60–90	Over 90
Smith, E.B.	04	17216	1/18	2/10, n/30	14327				1,001.27
Toomer Corp.	01	33228	12/15	n/30	S-7412	1,327.88			
Volunteer, Inc.	01	21200	9/27	n/30	16001				714.71
Tiger Company	07	49226	11/27	2/10, n/30	R-7111		10,148.33		

Figure 16.4

ADJUSTMENTS TO CUSTOMER ACCOUNTS										
Customer	Code	Invoice	Amount	Negotiated Change	Merchandise Return	Volume Rebate	Service Charge	Corrected Billing	Charge Back	Write Off
Alcoa Alum.	00198	025	751.39		(751.39)					
Allen Co.	00360	A7921	5,280.00			(528.00)				
Baldwin Inc.	07582	297BA	1,279.50					(4.50)		
Lee Corp.	39076	L123L	120.00	2.00			2.00			
Zaco Lowel	93825	3Z777	79.81							(79.81)
TOTAL			7,510.70	2.00	(751.39)	(528.00)	2.00	(4.50)	---	(79.81)

Figure 16.5

not taken or disallowed. The reasons for failure to pay within a discount period, however, may have very little to do with the size of the discount percentage or the time span within which it is allowable. Often a customer's remittance is delayed because of a delay in delivery of the shipment by the carrier. In such cases, the customer has very little choice. The customer's own cash position may be another reason for failure to act within the allowed time period.

Finally, collection follow-up in the form of routine statements of unpaid balances, or "customer reminders," automatically produced by the computer should be a standard product of any good billing and collection system. No attempt is made here to illustrate such forms, since their variety in form and content is unlimited.

SYSTEM CONFIGURATION

The reader will recall that this presentation assumes a sophisticated environment, utilizing not only a large-scale computer, but highly automated paperwork systems as well. This approach does not suggest that the discussion has minimum application in a less "mechanized" operation. Stripped of all the peripheral activities in EDP applications, the foundation elements of any billing and collection system should still be visible. After all, the mystery of the computer is diminished considerably when we remember that it must be programmed to perform these voluminous and repetitious functions that humans would otherwise be forced to do. The input, the processing decisions, the output, and the follow-up required in this system are common to all such systems—mechanized or manual.

It is not necessary to dwell on precomputer processing, which took place earlier in the marketing system (sales order processing). Figure 16.6 briefly reiterates the process merely to show the full spectrum of events. This discussion begins with the receipt of a computer-prepared invoice in response to a firm sales contract. Obviously, without EDP facilities, the invoice would be manually prepared.

Some form of suspense filing will normally be necessary pending receipt of "proof of shipment," at which time the invoice will be promptly updated and released to the customer. The documents supporting the completed sales transaction will then be trans-

SALES ORDER PROCESSING.

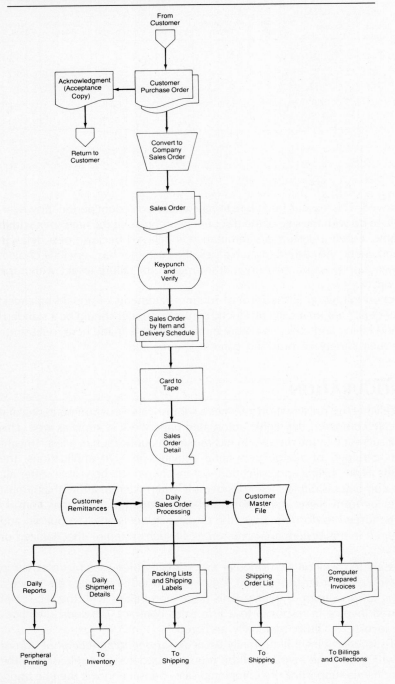

Figure 16.6

ferred to an accounts receivable subsystem, where they then will await the customer's remittance.

Daily Processing

Sales order details, customer remittances, account adjustments, shipments completed, new customer name and address data, and other routine activity will be appropriately coded and sorted together on an "activity" input tape in customer number sequence. These records are then processed against the major data base files. The system envisages the maintenance of two major master files; the current customer master file and the sales summary master file by period (usually a year).

Daily processing yields several critical outputs. Foremost among these are the vital documents, including the shipping order (or shipping list), the packing list if not a part of the shipping order set, package labels for shipment, and the multipart invoice set. The updated customer master disks also emerge for use as feedback in subsequent processings.

Daily reports (see previous illustrations) that are extracted as master files are adjusted by normal activities. These reports are coded for subsequent sorting to the desired sequence, to be followed by off-line listing.

Finally, the daily processing "run" will produce a reel of tape containing records of products shipped. These records will provide input into the inventory control system to accomplish two important purposes: (1) the records officially reduce inventory balances and (2) they are "priced" and returned to the billing and collection system for periodic reporting of sales cost.

Weekly Processing

The weekly summary of priced shipments are resorted for processing against a product price list and a sales summary master file. At this time, data are prepared for the periodic journalization of cost of goods sold, and for the computation of sales commissions when applicable. From this processing, all weekly sales reports are prepared for subsequent sorting and off-line printing.

Monthly Processing

All that remains at this point is the extraction of information needed for operations management. By running the sales summary master file together with the customer master file, both of which will be in customer number sequence, valuable status information is available. Typical of the management reports required are the aged analysis of receivables, customer statements or past-due notices, and adjustments. At this time only minor programming is required for an optional, short-run daily cash inflow forecast.

RISKS OF FAILURE

Failure of the billing and collection system can have a significant and widespread impact on the company. Receivables often represent a major portion of the company's current assets. Further, the interrelationship of receivables to sales and cash receipts adds to the significance of the billing and collection system.

The most obvious risk that a company incurs when the billing and collection system fails to function properly is the misstatement of accounts receivable. Whether or not intentional, such a misstatement could cause a material misrepresentation of the financial statements.

The important interface that the billing and collection system has with customers represents another area in which the company is exposed to possible significant risks if the system fails. Sending the sales invoices, mailing customer statements, and giving the customer appropriate credit for cash payments are all areas of interaction between customers and the billing and collection system. When these functions are not working properly, customer ill will with its often pervasive impact is created.

Improper functioning of the billing and collection system also exposes the company to several types of employee fraud:

1. Issuance of fictitious credits for returns and allowances
2. Creation of fictitious deductions for freight and other charges
3. Write-offs of active and paying accounts receivable
4. Lapping (i.e., posting Customer B's payment to Customer A's account to hide the theft of Customer A's payment) when posting to accounts receivable subsidiary records
5. Falsification of customer's statements

Risks of failure in the billing and collection system may also occur in the critical areas of sales and cash receipts. Risks in these areas, however, are covered in Chapter Fifteen (The Marketing System) and Chapter Seventeen (The Cash Control System).

ACCOUNTING CONTROLS

As with accounting controls in other functional areas, accounting controls in billings and collections are designed to meet two broad objectives: that transactions are properly executed and recorded and that custody of assets is maintained.

To meet the objective that all billings are properly executed and recorded, the company should design internal accounting control procedures to provide reasonable assurance that all shipments are billed at authorized prices and terms. Controls over billings and collections would thus include matching shipping documents with sales orders, preparing and mailing sales invoices, preparing batch or daily sales summaries of billings, and accounting for prenumbered sales orders.

Processing controls are an important component of internal accounting control for billings and collections. Posting to customers' accounts should be made directly from the sales invoices or sales orders. After posting to the customers' accounts, the sales invoice and supporting documentation should be filed. Completeness of the sales journal should be verified by an independent clerk who should determine that the numerical sequence of sales is accounted for and that the daily sales summary agrees with the sales journal totals.

In addition, the customers' account files (accounts receivable subsidiary ledger) should be kept in locked and fireproof files and access restricted to authorized personnel. Mailing of monthly statements to customers and investigation of differences reported by customers should be performed by someone in the accounting department who is independent of billings and collections. Likewise, agreement of the control total of accounts receivable to the total of the subsidiary ledger should be performed by someone who is independent of billings and collections.

SUMMARY

The billing and collection system provides the bridge between sales and cash receipts. As a consequence, the system is closely intertwined with the marketing system and the cash control system. In addition, the billing and collection system represents a very important interface between the company and the customer.

A properly designed billing and collection system should function efficiently and effectively. To function in this manner, the system should include certain source documents that can flow smoothly within the billings and collection system and other related systems. In addition, accounting controls over the system should be implemented to assure that all valid accounts receivable transactions are correctly recorded and that these assets are properly safeguarded. Finally, the billing and collection system should generate management information reports that can be readily and effectively utilized by management.

SELECTED REFERENCES

Akresh, Abraham D., and Michael Goldstein. "Point-of-Sale Accounting Systems: Some Implications for the Auditor," *Journal of Accountancy* (December 1978): 68–74.

Carpenter, N. D., and J. E. Miller. "Reliable Framework for Monitoring Accounts Receivable," *Financial Management* (Winter 1979): 181–186

Landsberg, J. "Managing the Accounts Receivable Portfolio," *Credit and Finance Management* (April 1980): 14–18.

Milling, B. E. "How to Find Hidden Profits in Your Accounts Receivable," *Canadian Business Magazine* (March 1980): 36–48.

Management Science America, Inc. Accounts Receivable II: Commercial Systems, Atlanta, 1980.

Management Science America, Inc. Realtime Online Accounts Receivable, Atlanta, 1980.

NCR Corporation. *NCR Interactive Accounts Receivable System.* Sayton, Ohio: NCR Corporation, 1977.

Parker, D. "Receivables and Bottom-line Credit Management," *Industrial Distribution* (May 1979): 49–52

Wade, P. "False Billing Schemes Tap Your Conscience," *Security Management* (June 1979): 19–24.

QUESTIONS

1. Explain why billings and collections represents the conclusion of the revenue cycle and the connector to the administrative cycle.
2. Describe the major objectives of the billings and collections function.
3. List at least four items that could be used to adjust a customer's account.
4. Identify the four major source documents in billings and collections.
5. Distinguish between a sales order and a sales invoice.
6. Explain the relationship between sales invoices and customer statements.
7. Why should the bad debts listing have an authorized signature?
8. Identify three questions that management may have that could be answered by information generated by the billings and collection system.
9. Why would management want to examine an aged analysis of open accounts?

10. Identify outputs that could be generated by daily computer processing.
11. Discuss the risks of failure when the billings and collection system fails.
12. Identify areas of potential employee fraud in a billings and collection system.

PROBLEMS

13. Preventive Controls and Recommendations

A prolonged strike at the Lettum Havitt Company resulted in a 10 percent across-the-board layoff of company employees. One such casualty was a computer programmer assigned to the billings and collections system. Upon learning of the impending dismissal, the programmer became very bitter and secretly resolved to somehow punish the company for this injustice.

Several days before departing, the programmer came to work one evening ostensibly to make necessary corrections to the accounts receivable update program. Within a few hours a program modification had been installed that was to be "run" on Friday evening after the programmer's termination became effective that afternoon.

The billings and collections runs were executed on schedule, but the operator became concerned when no customer statements and no customer account additions and deletions came out of the process. On attempting to rerun the job, the operator discovered that the entire customer accounts receivable data file had been completely erased by the program modification.

Lettum Havitt advertised their dilemma widely, and wrote letters to all their known regular customers appealing to their integrity for accurate information to reestablish the accounts. As might be expected, the responses were negligible. The company subsequently filed for bankruptcy.

Required:

a. What routine preventive measures could Lettum Havitt have taken to preclude, or at least minimize, this kind of risk?

b. Suggest a "disaster control and recovery" procedure to cover future instances of this sort.

14. Revenue, Sales, and Marketing Systems Review

The customer billing and collection functions of the Robinson Company, a small paint manufacturer, are attended to by a receptionist, an accounts receivable clerk and a cashier who also serves as a secretary. The company's paint products are sold to wholesalers and retail stores.

The following describes all of the procedures performed by the employees of the Robinson Company pertaining to customer billings and collections:

a. The mail is opened by the receptionist who gives the customers' purchase orders to the accounts receivable clerk. About 15 to 20 orders are received each day. Under instructions to expedite the shipment of orders, the accounts receivable clerk at once prepares a five-copy sales invoice form which is distributed as follows:

    (1) Copy 1 is the customer billing copy and is held by the accounts receivable clerk until notice of shipment is received.

    (2) Copy 2 is the accounts receivable department copy and is held for ultimate posting of the accounts receivable records.

    (3) Copies 3 and 4 are sent to the shipping department.

    (4) Copy 5 is sent to the storeroom as authority for release of the goods to the shipping department.

b. After the paint ordered has been moved from the storeroom to the shipping department, the shipping department prepares the bills of lading and labels the cartons. Sales invoice copy 4 is inserted in a carton as a packing slip. After the trucker has picked up the shipment the customer's copy of the bill of lading and copy 3, on which are noted any undershipments, are returned to the accounts receivable clerk. The company does not "back-order" in the event of undershipments. Instead, customers are required to reorder the merchandise. The Robinson Company's copy of the bill of lading is filed by the shipping department.

c. When copy 3 and the customer's copy of the bill of lading are received by the accounts receivable clerk, copies 1 and 2 are completed by numbering them and inserting quantities shipped, unit prices, extensions, discounts, and totals. The accounts receivable clerk then mails copy 1 and the copy of the bill of lading to the customer. Copies 2 and 3 are stapled together.

d. The individual accounts receivable ledger cards are posted by the accounts receivable clerk by a bookkeeping machine procedure whereby the sales register is prepared as a carbon copy of the postings. Postings are made from copy 2, which is then filed, along with staple-attached copy 3, in numerical order. Monthly the general ledger clerk summarizes the sales register for posting to the general ledger accounts.

e. Since the Robinson Company is short of cash, the deposit of receipts is also expedited. The receptionist turns over all mail receipts and related correspondence to the accounts receivable clerk, who examines the checks and determines that the accompanying vouchers or correspondence contains enough detail to permit posting the accounts. The accounts receivable clerk then endorses the checks and gives them to the cashier, who prepares the daily deposit. No currency is received in the mail and no paint is sold over the counter at the factory.

f. The accounts receivable clerk uses the vouchers or correspondence that accompanied the checks to post the accounts receivable ledger cards. The bookkeeping machine prepares a cash receipts register as a carbon copy of the postings. Monthly the general ledger clerk summarizes the cash receipts register for posting to the general ledger accounts. The accounts receivable clerk also corresponds with customers about unauthorized deductions for discounts, freight or advertising allowances, returns, and so forth, and prepares the appropriate credit memos. Disputed items of large amounts are turned over to the sales manager for settlement. Each month the accounts receivable clerk prepares a trial balance of the open accounts receivable and compares the resultant total with the general ledger control account for accounts receivable. *(AICPA adapted)*

Required:

Discuss the internal control weaknesses in the Robinson Company's procedures related to customer billings and remittances and the accounting for these transactions. In your discussion, in addition to identifying the weaknesses, explain what could happen as a result of each weakness.

15. Internal Control Evaluation and Recommendations

Steve Rutledge, CPA, is examining the financial statements of the Opelika Sales Corporation, which recently installed an on-line electronic computer. The following comments have been extracted from Mr. Rutledge's notes on computer operations and the processing and control of shipping notices and customer invoices:

Opelika, to minimize inconvenience, converted without change its existing data processing system, which utilized tabulating equipment. The computer company supervised the conversion and has provided training to all computer department employees (except keypunch operators) in systems design, operations, and programming.

Each computer run is assigned to a specific employee, who is responsible for making program changes, running the program, and answering questions. This procedure has the advantage of eliminating the need for records of computer operations because each employee is responsible for his or her own computer runs.

At least one computer department employee remains in the computer room during office hours, and only computer department employees have keys to the computer room.

System documentation consists of those materials furnished by the computer company—a set of record formats and program listings. These and the tape library are kept in a corner of the computer department.

The company considered the desirability of programmed controls but decided to retain the manual controls from its existing system.

Company products are shipped directly from public warehouses, from which shipping notices are forwarded to general accounting. A billing clerk enters the price of the item and accounts for the numerical sequence of shipping notices from each warehouse. The billing clerk also prepares daily adding machine tapes ("control tapes") of the units shipped and the unit prices.

Shipping notices and control tapes are forwarded to the computer department for keypunching and processing. Extensions are made on the computer. Output consists of invoices (in six copies) and a daily sales register. The daily sales register shows the aggregate totals of units shipped and unit prices, which the computer operator compares to the control tapes.

All copies of the invoice are returned to the billing clerk. The clerk mails three copies to the customer, forwards one copy to the warehouse, maintains one copy in a numerical file and retains one copy in an open-invoice file that serves as a detail accounts receivable record. *(AICPA adapted)*

Required:

Describe weaknesses in internal control over information and data flows and the procedures for processing shipping notices and customer invoices and recommend improvements in these controls and processing procedures. Organize your answer sheets in two columns, headed "Weakness" and "Recommended Improvement," respectively.

16. Information and Data Flow Analysis

Dragano, Inc., a regional distributor of building products with headquarters in New York, had been operating on the East Coast for a number of years. By the end of 1981 there were 15 local sales branches, and annual sales totaled $15 million.

In an effort to expand its area of sales coverage, Dragano acquired Gruendo, Inc., in 1982 and operated the company as a wholly owned subsidiary. Gruendo, also a distributor of building products, with 10 branches and annual sales of $10 million, is located in the Midwest with headquarters in Chicago.

Both companies sell to individuals as well as to contractors. Terms of sale to individuals are cash; sales to contractors are made on 30-day open account provided the contractor's credit is cleared by the headquarters office. The bulk of the dollar volume of sales is to contractors on account.

Dragano customers are billed from the New York office and Gruendo customers are billed from the Chicago office, on a cycle basis. The billings are completed on the basis of daily sales listings along with prenumbered charge slips, rendered by the branches to headquarters. The listings identify cash and charge sales separately. All cash receipts are deposited daily and intact by the branches in local depositories. Charge accounts are paid directly to the office from which the account was billed.

Early in 1984, Dragano management became concerned about the apparent excess of accounts receivable on the books of Gruendo relative to Dragano. Both companies utilized the same credit policy and had approximately the same mix of cash account sales. Gruendo's accounts, however, represented 50 days' sales, whereas Dragano's represented 30 days' sales.

This concern prompted the management of Dragano to call on the corporate accounting staff to investigate the situation. In confirming the accounts of Gruendo and clearing exceptions, the accountants conducting the audit discovered that (1) 10 percent of account balances represented invoices already paid by customers and (2) an additional 20 percent of the account balances represented underpayments by customers on specific invoices.

The audit disclosed that the cashier opened the mail and deposited some checks to a company-named account for which his signature was the only authorized one. He was responsible for preparation of monthly statements and thus was able to remove from the statements invoices already paid by customers.

The underpayment of accounts was the result of arrangements made by the branch salesmen with the knowledge of the credit manager, a long-time employee of Gruendo, whereby favored customers were quoted lower prices than list prices. This granting of discounts in this fashion had been a practice of long standing. The Chicago office billed at list prices, but the customers paid at the quoted rates.

The amount of the overstatements totaled $600,000. *(IMA adapted)*

Required:

Assume that you are the Dragano accountant in charge of this job.

a. Comment critically on the accounting and other procedures described previously.

b. Recommend any changes that you think should be made in the company's procedures. Explain your answer.

17. Systems Analysis and Design

Steve Ostensen, a systems analyst, has just been given a new assignment. He is to analyze and make recommendations to CWA Enterprises, a Corporation that has 20 product lines, with 10 to 15 items in each product line. The company has recently opened two West Coast warehouses to mitigate shipping costs. This was viewed as necessary due to recent growth in the West Coast market.

With the establishment of the warehouses, CWA has also decided to install a real-time sales order processing system. Sales orders are entered into the system by members of the sales force via portable terminals. When an order is received at headquarters, instructions are sent to the warehouse nearest the customer location. Billing is to be done from the warehouse where merchandise is shipped.

The salesperson merely enters his or her user identification number, customer account number, the item number, quantity, and price. In addition, the salesperson enters the credit terms on which the agreement is based.

Required:

Instruct Ostensen as to the means by which the system should be programmed to check the accuracy and validity of the data entered by the sales force.

18. Controls Through Proper Programming

Audio-Video Concepts (AVC), Inc., has just established a Video Rental Club that will allow members to rent videos at reasonable rates. Members are required to rent a minimum of 24 videos per year and also to pay a monthly membership fee. AVC buys the videos in large quantities at 30 percent off the regular list price.

In order to attract new customers, AVC offers two free rentals for each five rented in 1 month. This advertisement is run in the local newspaper weekly.

As a systems analyst, you have been asked to design a computerized billing system. The managers are also interested in knowing which videos are rented most often along with those seldom rented. The credit manager would like for the system to provide an aged accounts receivable report so that delinquent memberships may be evaluated.

Required:
  a. List the input transactions that the system will have to process.
  b. Identify reports that the system will need to produce.
  c. Assuming that master files will be stored in a magnetic disk, others will be stored on magnetic tape, and transaction inputs will be on punched cards, flowchart the new system.

19. Transaction Controls

You are performing the year-end audit of Alsop Company, a designer of design clothing and jewelry. The founder, Michelle Alsop, employs her cousin, Peter Doyle, as the accountant. Peter had studied accounting in a "degree by mail" course but had never graduated.

While you are testing accounts payable, an unusually large number of confirmations had been returned and differences were noted. The accounts payable listing had been given to you by Doyle. When questioned, he explained that he kept no subsidiary ledger for either receivables or payables. You also learn that Doyle has made no provision for bad debts due to a lack of readily accessible information.

Required:
  a. Explain to Doyle the need for subsidiary ledger and accounts receivable aging.
  b. Assuming Alsop is installing a computerized system, identify information needed to input for both purchase and sales transactions.

20. Billing and Collections

Select the best answer to each of the following questions. *(AICPA adapted)*
  a. Smith Manufacturing Company's accounts receivable clerk has a friend who is also Smith's customer. The accounts receivable clerk, on occasion, has issued fictitious credit memoranda to his friend for goods supposedly returned. The most effective procedure for preventing this activity is to:
    (1) Prenumber and account for all credit memoranda
    (2) Require receiving reports to support all credit memoranda before they are approved
    (3) Have the sales department independent of the accounts receivable department
    (4) Mail monthly statements
  b. Salespersons' commissions are based on gross sales. Sales continue to increase, but uncollectible accounts receivable are also increasing at an alarming rate. The most effective procedure for preventing the increase in uncollectible accounts receivable is to
    (1) Have the sales manager review activity of individual salespeople
    (2) Age accounts receivable regularly
    (3) Have the write-off of accounts properly approved

       (4)   Have the credit department approve credit extended to customers before shipment

c. A salesclerk at Schackne Company correctly prepared a sales invoice for $5,200, but the invoice was entered as $2,500 in the sales journal and similarly posted to the general ledger and accounts receivable ledger. The customer remitted only $2,500, the amount on his monthly statement. The most effective procedure for preventing this type of error is to:
   (1) Use predetermined totals to control posting routines
   (2) Have an independent check of sales invoice serial numbers, prices, discounts, extensions, and footings
   (3) Have the bookkeeper prepare monthly statements that are verified and mailed by a responsible person other than the bookkeeper
   (4) Have a responsible person who is independent of the accounts receivable department promptly investigate unauthorized remittance deductions made by customers or other matters in dispute

d. A CPA auditing an electric utility wishes to determine whether all customers are being billed. The CPA's best direction of test is from the:
   (1) Meter department records to the billing (sales) register
   (2) Billing (sales) register to the meter department records
   (3) Accounts receivable ledger to the billing (sales) register
   (4) Billing (sales) register to the accounts receivable ledger

e. For good internal control, the credit manager should be responsible to the:
   (1) Sales manager
   (2) Customer service manager
   (3) Controller
   (4) Treasurer

f. The authorization for write-off of accounts receivable should be the responsibility of the:
   (1) Credit manager
   (2) Controller
   (3) Accounts receivable clerk
   (4) Treasurer

g. For good internal control, the billing department should be under the direction of the:
   (1) Controller
   (2) Credit manager
   (3) Sales manager
   (4) Treasurer

h. Which of the following internal control procedures will most likely prevent the concealment of a cash shortage resulting from the improper write-off of a trade account receivable?
   (1) Write-offs must be approved by a responsible officer after review of credit department recommendations and supporting evidence.
   (2) Write-offs must be supported by an aging schedule showing that only receivables overdue several months have been written off.

> **(3)** Write-offs must be approved by the cashier who is in a position to know if the receivables have, in fact, been collected.
>
> **(4)** Write-offs must be authorized by company field sales employees who are in a position to determine the financial standing of the customers.

i. Which of the following is an effective internal accounting control over accounts receivable?

> **(1)** Only persons who handle cash receipts should be responsible for the preparation of documents that reduce accounts receivable balances.
>
> **(2)** Responsibility for approval of the write-off of uncollectible accounts receivable should be assigned to the cashier.
>
> **(3)** Balances in the subsidiary accounts receivable ledger should be reconciled to the general ledger control account once a year, preferably at year-end.
>
> **(4)** The billing function should be assigned to persons other than those responsible for maintaining accounts receivable subsidiary records.

CASES

21. Billing and Collection Systems Design

Apogee Company's billing and collection system (Appendix C) is not very large in terms of the number of customers at the present time. Tremendous growth is expected during the coming year(s), however, and a more structured and systematic method of invoicing customers and managing customer accounts receivable is required.

Using concepts and practices that you consider appropriate, design a dependable, timely, and well-controlled system for billing customers and collecting customer payments on account. Be sure to incorporate the important relationships with cash control, inventory, and shipping.

22. Billing and Collection Evaluation

Comment on the separate billings and collection systems for route and outside customers of Bubbling Stone Beverage Company.

THE ADMINISTRATIVE CYCLE

CHAPTER SEVENTEEN

The Cash Control System

Cash is a company's most liquid asset, representing the medium of exchange and the unit of accounting measurement. This attribute of liquidity generates unique characteristics for the cash control system. Primary areas of emphasis in the cash control system include the design of accounting controls over cash and the need for reliable cash forecasts and budgets.

The cash control system not only should be designed to maintain control over cash and generate the appropriate information and reports for management, but should also interlock effectively and efficiently with the other systems of the company. The cash system interfaces closely with the accounts payable system (cash disbursements), the payroll system (cash disbursements), and the billing and collection system (cash receipts).

Although the cash system should be effectively integrated with components of the spending, conversion, and revenue cycles, the system itself is properly classified as a component of the administrative cycle. Maintaining cash balances and controls over cash truly represents a financial function of the company. Broad in scope, these functions impact on all the other cycles of the company. This extensive impact throughout the company's operations indicates the importance of cash and the need for a properly designed and maintained cash control system in the administrative cycle.

FUNCTIONS AND OBJECTIVES

Typically, the treasurer's office maintains the cash control system. This results primarily from the broad impact of the cash control system and the need for adequate controls over this valuable resource.

The financial manager is concerned not only with the cash balance, but also with activities that have an effect on this balance. These activities may be classified as either inputs (cash receipts) or outputs (cash disbursements). To control and manage cash properly, the financial manager must monitor the cash balance, cash receipts, and cash disbursements. To achieve this broad goal, the design of the cash control systems should include three objectives: (1) maintenance of proper cash balances, (2) records maintenance, and (3) internal controls over cash receipts and disbursements.

Maintenance of Proper Cash Balances

A major objective of any viable cash control system is to maintain adequate cash sums to meet the transactional needs of the organization. Failure to meet this objective exposes the company to two types of risk, depending on whether the cash balance is too high or too low. The more immediate and obvious danger is the maintenance of a cash balance that is too low. An inadequate balance may prevent the company from functioning properly, with resultant losses of credit and production.

Having large, unnecessary cash balances also exposes the company to certain risks. Excess cash balances represent an opportunity cost (e.g., interest revenue lost) to the company and indicate that the company is not properly investing its funds. Although this risk is somewhat subtle and not so important in the short run, continual excess cash balances indicate poor management and may reduce the company's ability to compete over the long run.

Records Maintenance

Certain records regarding cash receipts and cash disbursements of the company should be maintained. These records serve a variety of purposes: providing audit trails for external and internal auditors, documentation and proof for cash disbursements, and backup records and support for cash receipts. Canceled checks, bank credit and debit memos, duplicate deposit slips, bank statements, and company-prepared bank reconciliations all represent records that are normally kept on file by the company.

Internal Controls

Effective functioning internal controls over cash is a primary objective of a well-designed cash control system. Controls center around monitoring of cash receipts that flow into the organization and exercising proper authority for cash disbursements. Cash receipts are obtained from four major sources:

1. Collections on accounts receivable and cash sales
2. Conversion of other assets into cash
3. Bank loans, bond issues, and sales of stock
4. Refunds from suppliers

Alternatively, cash disbursements are applied in four major ways:

1. Payments on trade accounts payable and payrolls
2. Investments in other assets
3. Repayments of bank loans and bond issues
4. Payments for operating expenses

Internal control objectives for cash receipts and disbursements should recognize the need to establish proper safeguards over the physical handling of such receipts and disbursements and at the same time assure that these activities are recorded and posted properly. For internal control over cash receipts to be effective, the following objectives should be met:

1. Recorded cash receipts represent funds actually received.
2. Such recorded cash receipts are deposited intact.
3. All cash receipts are recorded in the cash receipts journal in a timely manner as well as properly classified, summarized, and posted in the accounts receivable subsidiary ledger.
4. All cash discounts are authorized.

For internal control over cash disbursements to be effective, the following objectives should be met:

1. All cash disbursements are recorded.
2. Recorded cash disbursements represent only disbursements for actual goods and services.
3. Recorded cash disbursements are authorized.
4. Cash disbursements are recorded in the cash disbursements journal in a timely manner.

Achievement of these internal control objectives over cash receipts and disbursements aids in the safeguarding and proper recording of this vital asset.

SOURCE DOCUMENTS

The design and format of many of the source documents in a cash control system do not vary significantly among companies. The interface of the cash control system with the banking community necessitates that certain source documents be standardized. Although other source documents may differ in minor ways from company to company, the basic purpose and function of such records do not vary significantly. A brief examination of many of these documents, categorized as either cash receipts or cash disbursements, will now be presented.

Cash Receipts Documents

Most cash receipts of a company are generated through sales. Sales, of course, may be made either for cash or on account. Although sales on account are handled through the company's billings and collection system, the end product of sales on account and subsequent billings is the receipt of cash.

A cash sale results in the preparation of a sales slip by the salesclerk. Typically the sales slip is made in duplicate, with one copy given to the customer and one copy kept by the company for subsequent posting of cash sales. When the company uses cash registers or an on-line terminal a record of the cash sale is automatically made and a receipt for the customer is generally provided.

Cash payments on accounts receivable are generally received in the mail room, where a daily remittance listing of all such payments is prepared. This listing provides a control total of cash receipts that may be verified against the bank deposit. Enclosed with the customer's payment should be a remittance advice that was sent to the customer by the company during the billing process. The remittance advice, as shown in Figure

17.1, generally includes the customer name and number and the billed amount. After batching the remittance advices, the mail room forwards them to accounts receivable for posting (see Chapter Sixteen).

All cash receipts, whether from cash sales, payments on account, or other sources, should be deposited daily. Once the cashier receives the cash, a deposit slip should be prepared. Deposit slips, as shown in Figure 17.2, are generally provided by the bank,

REMITTANCE ADVICE.

INVOICE NUMBER	INVOICE DATE			INVOICE AMOUNT	CREDIT MEMO	DISCOUNT OR ANTICIPATION	NET AMOUNT	CHECK NUMBER
	MO.	DAY	YR.					

RUSSELL CORPORATION   ALEXANDER CITY, ALABAMA

Figure 17.1

DEPOSIT SLIP.

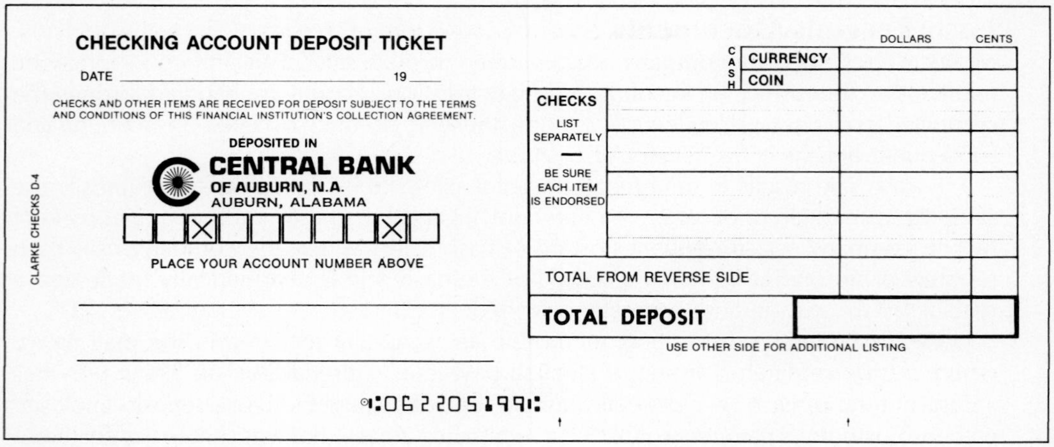

Figure 17.2

512   The Administrative Cycle

and show the company's name, address, and account number; the bank's name and code number; and a space for providing a detailed listing of the deposit. One copy of the deposit slip is sent to the bank; the other is kept for control purposes.

Cash Disbursements Documents

Cash disbursements result primarily from payments to vendors (accounts payable) and employees (payroll). To initiate a cash disbursement, accounts payable prepares a check request, or voucher, and forwards it to the cashier. This chapter covers the process from receipt of the voucher or check request through to the final disposition of the payment. In fully automated systems, the check is usually prepared by the computer in the accounts payable system. This procedure was covered in detail in Chapter Eleven.

The appropriate procedure, of course, upon receipt of a properly verified check request is to write a check for payment. An example of an unused check is shown in Figure 17.3. Checks should be written in numerical sequence. Checks are generally preprinted and include the company's name, address, and account number; the bank name and code number; and a check number. When the check clears the bank, the bank appropriately marks the check to indicate that it has been canceled. Files of unused, canceled, and voided checks should be maintained under tight security.

Banks periodically provide customers with checking account statements. These statements show cash receipts (e.g., deposits) and cash disbursements (e.g., checks that have cleared) recorded at the bank, as shown in Figure 17.4. These canceled checks and deposit slips along with any credit memos (e.g., collections) and debit memos (e.g., charges to the account) are forwarded to the company with the bank statement. Bank statements are necessary for the proper preparation of a bank reconciliation, a very useful management information and control procedure.

DOCUMENT FLOW AND TIMING

The cash control system is typically triggered by sources external to the system. In the case of cash receipts, such impetus usually comes from customers. Cash disbursements, on the other hand, are generated from within the company but from another system, accounts payable. Differences in sources, source documents, and other characteristics suggest that a review of document flow and handling in the cash control system should be dichotomized into cash receipts and cash disbursements.

Cash Receipts

The critical document flow for cash receipts from customers with payments on account is illustrated in Figure 17.5. The document flow begins when the customer initiates the cash receipts cycle by sending payment to the company. When such payments are received by the mail room, a remittance listing is prepared. Payments and the remittance listing are forwarded to the cashier, whereas the remittance advices are forwarded to accounts receivable to post to the subsidiary ledger accounts. Discounts are then approved by the treasurer and duplicate deposit slips are prepared. One copy of the deposit slip is filed and the other deposit slip accompanies the cash receipts to the bank. The validated deposit slip is forwarded to internal auditing. The cashier sends the remittance

SAMPLE OF UNUSED CHECK.

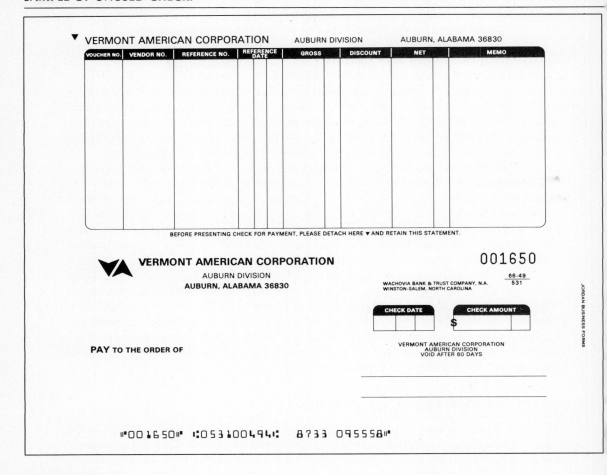

Figure 17.3

listing to accounting, where cash receipts are booked in the cash receipts journal. Accounting prepares two copies of a cash journal voucher, which indicates the journal entry to post to the general ledger. One copy of the journal voucher is forwarded to internal auditing and verified against the validated deposit slip and the other journal voucher is used to make the appropriate entry into the general ledger.

The preceding discussion, of course, assumed that cash receipts represented customer payments on account. The procedure would differ for cash receipts from cash sales. Although cash sales often represent a minor component of cash receipts for manufacturing concerns, they generally represent a substantial portion of cash receipts for retail establishments.

BANK STATEMENT.

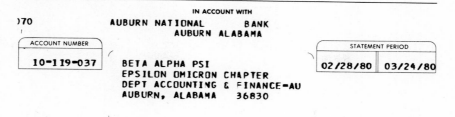

IN ACCOUNT WITH

AUBURN NATIONAL BANK
AUBURN ALABAMA

ACCOUNT NUMBER		STATEMENT PERIOD	
10-119-037	BETA ALPHA PSI EPSILON OMICRON CHAPTER DEPT ACCOUNTING & FINANCE-AU AUBURN, ALABAMA 36830	02/28/80	03/24/80

BALANCE LAST STATEMENT	WE HAVE ADDED		WE HAVE SUBTRACTED		SERVICE CHARGE	RESULTING IN A BALANCE OF	ITEMS ENCLOSED
	NUMBER	DEPOSITS TOTALING	NUMBER	CHECKS TOTALING			
812 29	3	1721 13	13	1 258 73	00	1 274 69	16

CHECKS PAID AND OTHER DEBITS

DATE		DATE		DATE		DATE	DEPOSITS AND OTHER CREDITS	BALANCE
28	6 23							806 06
29							70 00	876 06
04	100 00							776 06
05	29 00							747 06
06	10 00		29 00					708 06
07	29 00						918 00	1 597 06
10	15 00		29 00					1 553 06
11	7 20		29 00					1 516 86
13	29 00		694 30					793 56
20	252 00						733 13	1 274 69

PLEASE REPORT PROMPTLY ANY CHANGE IN ADDRESS

If no exceptions are reported within ten days the account and checks will be considered correct. All items credited subject to final payment.

PRE-AUTHORIZED PAYMENT CODES		·OTHER CODES·	
CC · CHRISTMAS CLUB	BA · BANKAMERICARD PAYMENT	SC · SERVICE CHARGE	OD · ACCOUNT OVERDRAWN
SV · AUTOMATIC SAVINGS	MP · MORTGAGE PAYMENT	IC · INSUFFICIENT CHARGE	P · PAYROLL DEPOSIT
IL · INSTALLMENT LOAN PAYMENT	UP · UTILITY PAYMENT	OC · OVERDRAFT CHARGE	C · CREDIT ADJUSTMENT
IN · INSURANCE PAYMENT		EX · EXCHANGE CHARGE	DA · DEBIT ADJUSTMENT
		LS · LIST POSTED	E · ERROR CORRECTION

Figure 17.4

DOCUMENT FLOW AND TIMING—CASH RECEIPTS.

Document Flow and Timing—Cash Receipts

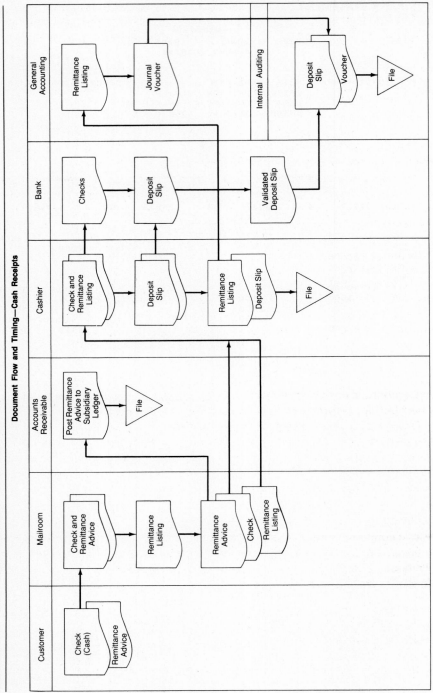

Figure 17.5

In the case of cash sales, the customer once again initiates the process through a cash sale. A duplicate sales slip is prepared: one copy goes to the customer; the other is forwarded to accounting, where the sale is entered in the sales journal and a journal voucher for cash sales is prepared. When cash registers are used, the company copy of the sales slip is maintained on the register. A total is obtained at the end of the day and used for the entry into the sales journal. Cash from cash sales is forwarded to the cashier and the same deposit procedures are applied as in the case of cash receipts from collections on account.

Cash Disbursements

The critical document flow for cash disbursements is shown in Figure 17.6. A substantial portion of cash disbursements is generated by accounts payable. Accounts payable receives all supporting documents (invoices, purchase orders, receiving reports, etc.) and prepares a duplicate payment listing. One copy is forwarded to internal auditing, the other to accounting. The check signer(s) in the treasurer's office reviews the payments and the source documents, signs the checks, and mails them directly to the vendors. This person then stamps all documents as "paid." All documents are returned to accounts payable to be filed. A clerk then prepares a journal voucher distributing the payments to the various inventory, asset, and expense accounts. The treasurer (cashier's office) journalizes the cash credit. The journal vouchers are utilized to post to the general ledger and copies are forwarded to internal auditing. Finally, internal auditing receives a copy of the journal vouchers and verifies them against the payments list.

ACCOUNTING CONTROLS

Accounting controls over cash are designed to safeguard this crucial asset and to aid in the proper, prompt recording of cash transactions. Once again, a dichotomization into cash receipts and cash disbursements should facilitate the discussion. As cash receipts and cash disbursements differ in initial source, source documents, and interaction and relationship with other systems, differences in accounting controls should also be expected. Accounting controls for cash receipts and cash disbursements will be presented along with a discussion of general cash controls.

Cash Receipts

The basic accounting control objectives for cash receipts are to establish control over all cash (including checks) received and to ensure that such cash is deposited promptly in the company's bank accounts. To achieve these objectives, the following specific controls should be established:

1. Do not permit any one employee to handle a transaction from beginning to end.
2. Separate physical handling of cash from record keeping of cash.
3. Record cash receipts promptly.
4. If possible, deposit cash receipts daily intact.
5. Do not permit payments out of undeposited cash receipts.

DOCUMENT FLOW AND TIMING—CASH DISBURSEMENTS.

Document Flow and Timing—Cash Disbursements

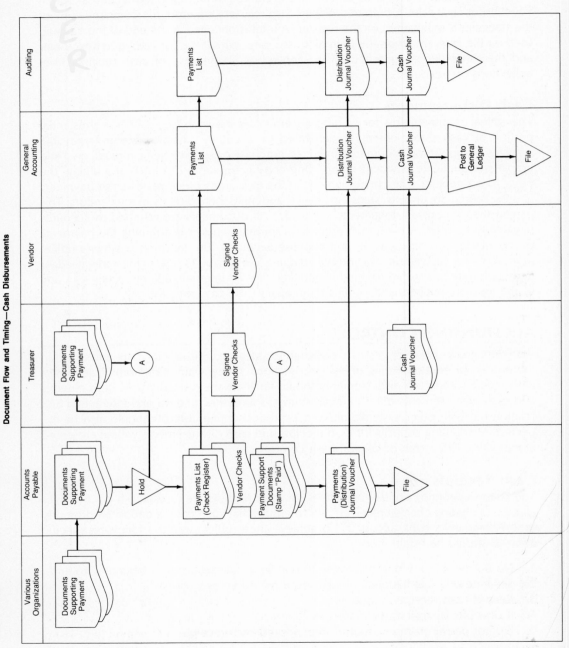

Figure 17.6

6. Prepare detailed listings of cash and checks received in the mail room by persons other than those who deal with accounts receivable, accounts payable, and the general ledger.
7. Mark or endorse checks (i.e., "For Deposit Only") at the point of receipt to ensure deposit in company accounts.
8. Provide for an internal auditing staff to perform audits of cash receipts and monitor the cash control system.
9. Provide procedures to monitor and control cash receipts from cash sales.

A frequently used aid in the control of cash receipts that provides for earlier availability of cash is the "lockbox." Customers are instructed to send their payments to the lockbox, where the cooperating bank opens the box at frequent intervals, often several times each day, to remove the contents. The bank deposits the cash received to the company's checking account and prepares a listing of the checks received. This listing, along with remittance advices, is forwarded to the company. Although the bank may charge for this service, the company strengthens its controls over cash receipts, avoids the cost of handling these items at the company's office, and ensures the availability of cash through earlier deposits of cash receipts.

Cash Disbursements

The primary objective of accounting controls over cash disbursements is to ensure that disbursements from bank accounts are made only in the case of valid transactions. To achieve this objective, the following specific controls should be established:

1. The function of authorizing payment and recording accounts payable should be separated from the function of writing checks.
2. All cash disbursements should be made by check.
3. Checks should be prenumbered, and voided checks should be mutilated and filed.
4. Checks should be signed only when all appropriate documents are attached.
5. All documents should be stamped "Paid" when checks are signed in order to prevent duplicate payment.
6. Supplies of unused checks should be properly safeguarded.
7. Checks that have been written should be accounted for by persons other than those who have custody of unissued checks.
8. The signature plate for the check-writing machine should be secured when not in use.
9. A petty cash fund should be established so that small cash disbursements can be made promptly and efficiently.
10. An internal auditing staff should properly monitor cash disbursements and related controls.

General Cash Controls

In addition to cash controls that are specific to either cash receipts or cash disbursements, there are certain control procedures over cash. A primary objective of these general controls is to ensure that adequate steps are taken to confirm the accuracy of bank balances. To achieve this objective, the following specific controls should be established:

1. Reconciliation of the balance per bank statement with the balance per the general ledger should be made on a regular basis (generally, monthly).
2. Such reconciliations should be prepared by persons not involved with cash receipts or cash disbursements.
3. Personnel performing the reconciliations should obtain the bank statement directly and retain control over the statement until the reconciliation is completed.
4. Reconciliations should include a comparison of each entry in the bank statement with the cash books and records.
5. Reconciliations should be reviewed and approved by a responsible official.

MANAGEMENT INFORMATION REQUIREMENTS

Cash information requirements often vary among companies as a result of differences in asset size, characteristics of cash flows, type of operation, needs for funds, and a host of other attributes. Nonetheless, there are certain information requirements that are common to most companies—including the cash receipts journal, the cash disbursements journal, and cash forecasts.

The cash receipts journal should be designed to facilitate the recording of cash receipts and recognize any special factors that are specific to the company. A typically designed cash receipts journal (Figure 17.7) shows columnar headings for the date, the account credited, any explanation, reference, and amounts to be posted to specific accounts.

The cash disbursements journal or check register as shown in Figure 17.8 maintains a record of all cash disbursements, including accounts and amounts. A column should be provided indicating the check number and voucher or check request number. Both the cash receipts and cash disbursements journal may be prepared manually, by an EDP system, or by a microprocessor that handles only cash receipts.

Although the cash receipts journal and cash disbursements journal serve a record-keeping function in addition to providing accounting controls, they do not, by themselves, give information to management regarding cash needs and flows. Maintaining proper cash balances is a vital aspect of the management function. Clearly, this important objective is best achieved through a properly designed cash control system.

Determination of "appropriate" cash balance is not an easy task. Although the company exercises control over cash disbursements, there is no such control over most cash receipts, since these must come from outside sources (e.g., customers). Nonetheless, certain tools do exist to project both cash receipts and cash disbursements. Projections based on historical experience and utilizing regression analysis or simulation represent primary ways to project cash receipts and disbursements.

Cash forecasts show two types of information: information on current cash status and information on future cash requirements. The cash forecast reflects recent transactions in the cash account with related historical information for management use. Such historical information might include reports of cash activity for the prior week, the prior month, or the same week in the prior year. The cash forecast also includes information on future cash requirements based on projections utilizing appropriate techniques. This information enables management to manage cash properly and maintain a reasonable cash balance.

COMMERCIAL SYSTEMS

RUN DATE: 2/02/81

C A S H   R E C E I P T   J O U R N A L

CUST NO	NAME CHK-NO	CHK-DATE	CHK-AMOUNT	APPLY TO	AMOUNT PAID	DISCOUNT	ALLOWANCE	ALLOWNC ACCT-NO	TOTAL-CR TO A/R	REFERENCE
1	SOUTHERN FLORAL GROUP, INC			1	136.80				136.80	DISCOUNT LOSS
	115	2/02/81	25,365.00	15	296.00				296.00	
				18	3,157.41				3,157.41	
				21	19,405.37	52.00			19,457.37	DISCOUNT ALLOWED
				41	500.00				500.00	
				42	310.00				310.00	
				180	1,559.42				1,559.42	
			CHECK TOTALS:		25,365.00	52.00			25,417.00	
2	DOTHAN GREENHOUSE, INC			16	300.00				300.00	
	265	1/15/81	300.00							
2	DOTHAN GREENHOUSE, INC			1	102.00				102.00	
	3658	2/02/81	2,589.00	9	505.00		23.00	0710-000	528.00	ALLOWANCE FOR FREIGHT CHARGES
				16	845.00				845.00	
				260	1,137.00				1,137.00	
			CHECK TOTALS:		2,589.00		23.00		2,612.00	
4	AUBURN LAWN AND GARDEN			BAL-FWD	2,000.00				2,000.00	
	3369	2/02/81	2,000.00							
5	ATLANTA METRO HOSPTALS			NON-A/R	250.00	CR TO G/L ACCT-NO 0710-000				
	9684	2/02/81	250.00	CASH						
5 ENTRIES			TOTALS:		30,504.00	52.00	23.00		30,329.00	

Figure 17.7

***** COMPANY NAME ******
REF: AP-08-06

RUN DATE: 2/02/81

ACCOUNTS PAYABLE CHECK REGISTER

CHECK #	CHECK DATE	VENDOR #	NAME	VOUCH #	P.O.-#	INVOICE #	INVOICE DATE	INVOICE AMOUNT	DISCOUNT AMOUNT	CHECK AMOUNT
150	1/31/81	1	SMITH & COMPANY	8	122	223	8/19/80	125.50	0.00	125.50
			SMITH & COMPANY	10	12334	123	8/21/80	500.00	0.00	500.00
			SMITH & COMPANY	11		254	8/25/80	250.00	0.00	250.00
			SMITH & COMPANY	12	55		5/28/80	256.00	0.00	256.00
			SMITH & COMPANY	13	125	888	8/20/80	900.00	0.00	900.00
			SMITH & COMPANY	14		521	8/20/80	500.00	0.00	500.00
			SMITH & COMPANY	15	123	1234	8/25/80	500.00	0.00	500.00
			SMITH & COMPANY	16	SDF	ADF	8/25/80	500.00	0.00	500.00
			SMITH & COMPANY	17			8/25/80	100.00	0.00	100.00
			SMITH & COMPANY	19			8/25/80	500.00	0.00	500.00
			SMITH & COMPANY	20			8/29/80	150.00	0.00	150.00
			SMITH & COMPANY	31	211	117	9/10/80	550.00	0.00	550.00
			SMITH & COMPANY	32			9/15/80	1,000.00	0.00	1,000.00
			SMITH & COMPANY	35			9/26/80	1,000.00	0.00	1,000.00
			SMITH & COMPANY	38	347	112	9/22/80	1,369.00	0.00	1,369.00
			SMITH & COMPANY	40		4456	9/22/80	14,589.63	0.00	14,589.63
							CHECK TOTALS:	22,790.13	0.00	22,790.13
151	1/31/81	2	JACKSON SECURITY SYSTEMS	18			8/25/80	200.00	0.00	200.00
			JACKSON SECURITY SYSTEMS	37		456	9/15/80	200.00	6.00	194.00
			JACKSON SECURITY SYSTEMS	39		544	9/15/80	897.52	0.00	897.52
							CHECK TOTALS:	1,297.52	6.00	1,291.52
152	1/31/81	6	FULLER BRUSH	30	900	091480	9/14/80	450.00	0.00	450.00
							CHECK TOTALS:	450.00	0.00	450.00
							CASH ACCOUNT TOTALS:	24,537.65	6.00	24,531.65

3 REGULAR CHECKS THIS CASH ACCOUNT
0 PREPAID CHECKS THIS CASH ACCOUNT
0 MANUAL PAID CHECKS THIS CASH ACCOUNT
0 VOID CHECKS THIS CASH ACCOUNT
3 CHECKS TOTAL THIS CASH ACCOUNT

Figure 17.8

SYSTEM CONFIGURATION

Activation of the cash receipts sector of the cash control system occurs when a customer initiates a cash payment. As shown in the systems configuration for cash receipts, Figure 17.9, customer payments are received and opened in the mailroom. The mailroom prepares a remittance listing and assembles remittance advices in batches. Remittance advices are forwarded to EDP while the remittance listing is sent to the cashier along with the checks. EDP keypunches and verifies the remittance advices and runs an accounts receivable update to the accounts receivable master file. A summary report is also prepared and sent to internal auditing.

Upon receipt of the remittance listing and checks, the cashier has all discounts approved by the treasurer and deposits all receipts intact. The remittance listing is sent to accounting where a journal voucher for posting to the general ledger is prepared. The general ledger is updated, a cash receipts journal is produced, and a copy of the journal voucher is sent to internal auditing. There, the journal voucher is compared to the receivables summary report and any difference is reconciled.

Internal auditing plays a vital role in the maintenance of proper controls over cash receipts. Reconcilement of the journal voucher and the duplicate deposit slip represent important control functions. As shown in Figure 17.10, the internal auditor must compare these documents, determine if any differences exist, and investigate said differences with an emphasis on improprieties and necessary corrective actions.

Cash disbursements, on the other hand, are initiated by either the accounts payable or the payroll system. The systems flow chart for cash disbursements to vendors is shown in Figure 17.11. Accounts payable prepares check requests (i.e., vouchers) or the checks themselves, if computer processed, and also payment listings. Check requests and supporting documentation are forwarded to cash disbursements, where the documents are reviewed and canceled, checks are written and mailed, and a check register is maintained.

Copies of the payment listing are forwarded to accounting and internal auditing. Accounting uses the listing to prepare a journal voucher to enter the transactions in the general ledger. A copy of the journal voucher is forwarded to internal auditing, where the voucher is compared against the payment listing and any differences are investigated and reconciled.

RISKS OF FAILURE

Risks of failure in the cash control system are broadly related to the primary objectives of the system. Recall that these objectives are (1) maintenance of proper cash balances, (2) records maintenance, and (3) internal controls over cash receipts and disbursements.

If the system fails to maintain proper cash balances, numerous failures may occur. When the cash balance is inadequate, the company risks bad checks, cash overdrafts, and ill will with vendors, employees, and the community. These factors can lead to delays or cancellations by vendors regarding shipping and, as a consequence, could cause problems in production, inventory, and marketing. Other potential problems include the loss of purchase discounts, payments of fines and penalties by the company for late payments, and loss of credit ratings.

CASH RECEIPTS SYSTEMS FLOWCHART.

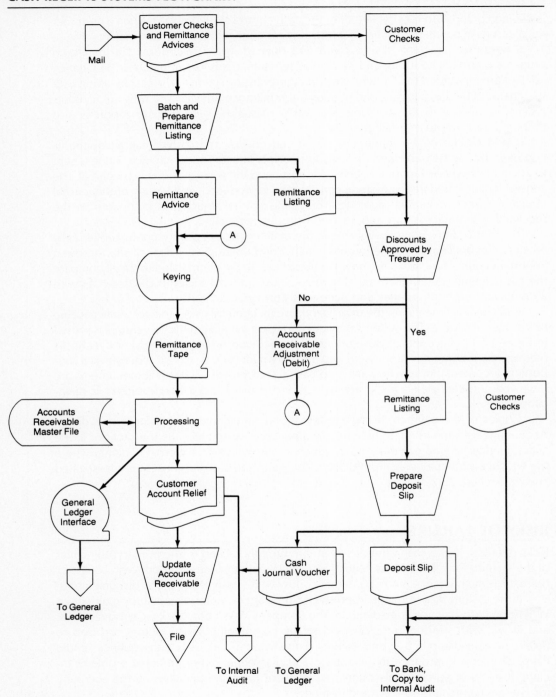

Figure 17.9

FUNCTIONAL FLOWCHART—INTERNAL AUDITING RECONCILEMENT OF CASH RECEIPTS.

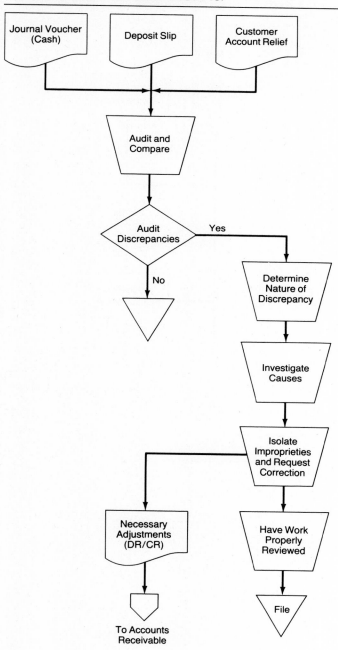

Figure 17.10

CASH DISBURSEMENTS FLOWCHART.

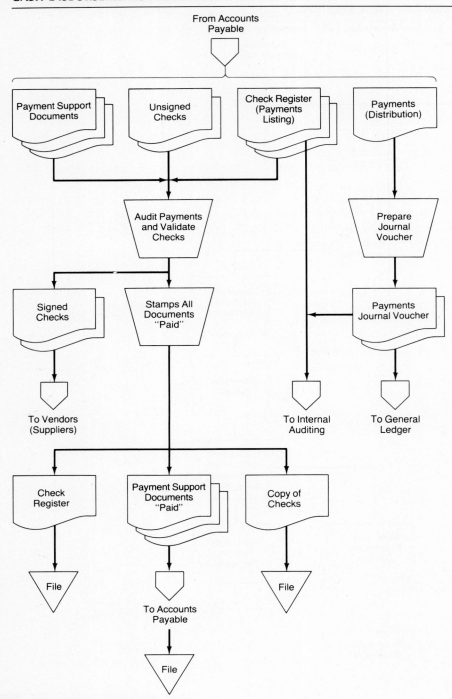

Figure 17.11

At the other extreme, maintenance of excessively large cash balances indicates poor management of company resources. Forgone revenues from the investment of these funds and possible inadequate FDIC insurance coverage for these funds represent two areas of impact when such excess cash funds are kept.

When records maintenance is inadequate, controls over cash receipts and disbursements may not function properly. Audit trails are often lost, along with data needed for proof of previous payment (e.g., canceled checks). Weakening of internal controls in the cash system can, of course, often be disastrous. With its inherent liquidity, cash represents one asset where adequate safeguards and controls must be maintained. A weakening of controls over cash exposes the company to numerous risks—embezzlement of cash by employees (whether in the mail room, in accounts receivable, or by the cashier), kiting, fictitious payments, duplicate payments, incorrect cash balances, or erroneous postings to customers' accounts.

Cash represents one of the company's most important and necessary assets. As a consequence, the company's cash control system must achieve the objectives outlined earlier in the chapter. If the system fails to achieve these objectives, then the company exposes itself to numerous, and quite possibly critical, risks.

SUMMARY

Representing the company's most liquid asset, cash must be properly managed and controlled by the company. To achieve this objective, the company needs a well-designed, properly functioning cash control system. Most systems are separated into cash receipts and cash disbursements subsystems.

The cash control system should provide good internal controls and satisfactory record maintenance and aid management in the maintenance of adequate cash balances. Institution of proper accounting controls over both cash receipts and cash disbursements along with the generation of necessary management reports enables the cash control system to achieve these important functions.

SELECTED REFERENCES

Cerrone, R. A. "Cash Flow Checklist," *Hospital Financial Management* (April 1979): 28–32.
Ijiri, Y. "Recovery Rate and Cash Flow Accounting," *Financial Executive* (March 1980): 110–113.
Murdick, Robert G., and Joel E. Ross. *MIS in Action.* St. Paul: West Publishing Co., 1975.
Page, John R., and H. Paul Hooper. *Accounting and Information Systems,* 2d ed. Reston, Va.: Reston Publishing Co., 1983.
Westerfield, W. U. "Guide to Accounting Controls," *Chain Store Age Executive* (October 1979): 32–37.

QUESTIONS

1. What are the characteristics of cash that differ from those of other assets? How do these characteristics impact on the design of a cash control system?
2. How does cash interface with the other accounting subsystems?
3. Why is it important for a company to maintain a cash balance that is neither too large nor too small?

4. Discuss the differences in document flow between cash receipts from cash sales and cash receipts from collections on credit sales.
5. What are the objectives of internal control over cash receipts and cash disbursements?
6. What is the purpose of the daily remittance listing?
7. Why are cash receipts opened in the mail room rather than by the cashier? By the accounts receivable clerk?
8. What is a remittance advice? What control purpose does it serve?
9. Why should cash receipts be deposited intact daily?
10. What is the purpose of forwarding a duplicate deposit slip to the internal auditing department?
11. Who are the major payees from a company's cash disbursements?
12. Why should tight controls be maintained over unused checks?
13. Should voided checks be filed or discarded? Why?
14. What supporting documents should be in place before a check in payment of an invoice is written?
15. Why are invoices marked "Paid" once checks are written to payees?
16. Why do companies separate the physical custody of cash from cash record keeping?
17. What is a lockbox? What advantages does it offer?
18. Why is a bank reconcilement prepared on a regular basis? Who prepares it?
19. What is the purpose of a cash forecast?
20. What is the role of internal auditing in a cash control system?

PROBLEMS

21. Cash Receipts Control

For each of the following situations describe a cash receipts internal control feature that, if implemented, would prevent or detect the situation. Consider each situation independently.

a. Theft of checks in the mail room
b. Granting an unjustified cash discount
c. Theft of checks by the cashier
d. Theft of cash from cash sales by retail clerks
e. Lack of posting cash receipts to the accounts receivable subsidiary ledger
f. A cash receipts shortage concealed by the cashier who also prepares the monthly bank reconcilement

22. Cash Disbursements Controls

For each of the following situations describe a cash disbursements internal control feature that, if implemented, would prevent or detect the situation. Consider each situation independently.

a. Payment of an invoice twice
b. Payment for goods not received

c. Payment of an invoice with prices higher than the purchase order and sales acknowledgment

d. Payment of an invoice with errors in the extensions on the invoice

e. Payment to an employee who has set up a fictitious company

f. Writing of checks by an employee who does not record the cash disbursement

23. Cash Receipts Control

The United Charities organization in your town has engaged you to examine its statement of receipts and disbursements. United Charities solicits contributions from local donors and then apportions the contributions among local charitable organizations.

The officers and directors are local bankers, business professionals, and other leaders of the community. A cashier and a clerk are the only full-time salaried employees. The only records maintained by the organization are a cashbook and a checkbook. The directors prefer not to have a system of pledges.

Contributions are solicited by a number of volunteer workers. The workers are not restricted as to the area of their solicitation and may work among their friends, neighbors, co-workers, and so forth, as convenient for them. To assure blanket coverage of the town, new volunteer workers are welcomed.

Contributions are in the form of cash or checks. The donations are received by United Charities from the solicitors, who personally deliver the contributions they have collected, or directly from the donors by mail or personal delivery.

The solicitors complete official receipts that they give to the donors when they receive contributions. These official receipts have attached stubs that the solicitors fill in with the names of the donors and the amounts of the contributions. The solicitors turn in the stubs with the contributions to the cashier. No control is maintained over the number of blank receipts given to the solicitors or the number of receipt stubs turned in with the contributions. (*AICPA adapted*)

Required:

Discuss the control procedures you would recommend for greater assurance that all contributions received by the solicitors are turned over to the organization. (Do not discuss the control of the funds in the organization's office.)

24. Cash Collections and Remittances Control

You are auditing the Alaska Branch of Weeks Distributing Co. This branch has substantial annual sales, which are billed and collected locally. As a part of your audit you find that the procedures for handling cash receipts are as follows:

Cash collections on over-the-counter sales and COD sales are received from the customer or delivery service by the cashier. Upon receipt of cash the cashier stamps the sales ticket "paid" and files a copy for future reference. The only record of COD sales is a copy of the sales ticket, which is given to the cashier to hold until the cash is received from the delivery service.

Mail is opened by the secretary to the credit manager, and remittances are given to the credit manager for his review. The credit manager then places the remittances in a tray on the cashier's desk. At the daily deposit cutoff time, the cashier delivers the checks and cash on hand to the assistant credit manager, who prepares remittance lists and makes up the bank deposit which he also takes to the bank. The assistant credit manager posts remittances to the accounts receivable ledger cards and verifies the cash discount allowable.

You ascertain that the credit manager obtains approval from the executive office of Weeks Distributing Company, located in Birmingham, to write off uncollectible accounts, and that she has retained in her custody at the end of the fiscal year some remittances that were received on various days during the last month. *(AICPA adapted)*

Required:
- **a.** Describe the irregularities that might occur under the procedures now in effect for handling cash collections and remittances.
- **b.** Give procedures that you would recommend to strengthen internal control over cash collections and remittances.

25. Cash Systems Evaluation

The town of Oaks Park operates a private parking lot near the railroad station for the benefit of town residents. The guard on duty issues annual prenumbered parking stickers to residents who submit an application form and show evidence of residency. The sticker is affixed to the auto and allows the resident to park anywhere in the lot for 12 hours if four quarters are placed in the parking meter. Applications are maintained in the guard office at the lot. The guard checks to see that only residents are using the lot and that no resident has parked without paying the required meter fee.

Once a week the guard on duty, who has a master key for all meters, takes the coins from the meters and places them in a locked steel box. The guard delivers the box to the town storage building where it is opened, and the coins are manually counted by a storage department clerk who records the total cash counted on a "weekly cash report." This report is sent to the town accounting department. The storage department clerk puts the cash in a safe, and on the following day the cash is picked up by the town's treasurer, who manually recounts the cash, prepares the bank deposit slip, and delivers the deposit to the bank. The deposit slip, authenticated by the bank teller, is sent to the accounting department where it is filed with the "weekly cash report." *(AICPA adapted)*

Required:
Describe weaknesses in the existing system and recommend one or more improvements for each of the weaknesses to strengthen the internal control over the parking lot cash receipts.

Organize your answer sheet in two columns, headed "Weakness" and "Recommended Improvement(s)," respectively.

26. Cash Control Evaluations and Recommendations

You have been asked by the board of trustees of a local church to review its accounting procedures. As a part of this review you have prepared the following comments relating to the collections made at weekly services and record keeping for members' pledges and contributions:

The church's board of trustees has delegated responsibility for financial management and audit of the financial records to the finance committee. This group prepares the annual budget and approves major disbursements but is not involved in collections or record keeping. No audit has been considered necessary in recent years because the same trusted employee has kept church records and has served as financial secretary for 15 years.

The collection at the weekly service is taken by a team of ushers. The head usher counts the collection in the church office following each service. He then places the collection and a notation of the amount counted in the church safe. Next morning the financial secretary opens the safe and recounts the collection. She withholds about $100 to meet cash expenditures during the coming week and deposits the remainder of the collection intact. In order to facilitate the deposit, members who contribute by check are asked to draw their checks to "cash."

At their request a few members are furnished prenumbered predated envelopes in which to insert their weekly contributions. The head usher removes the cash from the envelopes to be counted with the loose cash included in the collection and discards the envelopes. No record is maintained of issuance or return of the envelopes, and the envelope system is not encouraged.

Each member is asked to prepare a contribution pledge card annually. The pledge is regarded as a moral commitment by the member to contribute a stated weekly amount. Based on the amounts shown on the pledge cards, the financial secretary furnishes a letter to members that supports the tax deductibility of their contributions. *(AICPA adapted)*

Required:

Describe the weaknesses and recommended improvements in procedures for:
a. Collections made at weekly services
b. Record keeping for members' pledges and contributions. Organize your answer sheets in two columns, headed "Weaknesses" and "Recommended Improvements," respectively.

27. Cash Disbursement Systems Analysis, Design, and Recommendations

The King Company manufactures and distributes duplicating machines and related supplies. The company has grown rapidly since its formation by the merger of two smaller manufacturing companies in 1963. Sales last year reached $80 million. This growth has been particularly attributable to a management policy emphasizing high product quality and fast, responsive customer service.

Initially, the duplicating machines were manufactured entirely in King Company factories. The rapid growth in machine sales, however, has forced the company to buy an increasing number of subassemblies rather than produce and assemble all the parts itself. All duplicating supplies, however, are purchased from outside vendors.

King's four manufacturing plants and 13 warehouses located in the midwestern and western states are managed from corporate headquarters in Des Moines, Iowa. Sales are made through local sales agents who place orders with the nearest warehouse.

To provide greater flexibility in meeting local needs, purchases of parts, subassemblies, materials, and supplies are made by the individual plants and warehouses. Each manufacturing plant purchases the raw materials and subassemblies for its own production requirements. Warehouses order machines from the factories and purchase duplicating supplies from the best local vendors. Corporate headquarters does not interfere with this decentralized purchasing function unless a plant or warehouse is not providing an adequate return on investment or shows other signs of difficulty. All cash disbursements for purchases, however, are centralized in the headquarters at Des Moines.

Processing at purchase location

Purchases by manufacturing plants and warehouses are made with prenumbered purchase orders issued by a separate purchasing section. One copy of each purchase order goes to accounting, which also gets and date-stamps a copy of each receiving report and all copies of the vendor's invoices. The accounting department accounts for purchase order numbers and matches their detail to the receiving reports and vendors' invoices. The latter are also checked for clerical accuracy.

When all the detail is in agreement, a prenumbered disbursement voucher is prepared by accounting summarizing the detailed information of each purchase. These disbursement vouchers, together with supporting documents, are reviewed and approved for payment by plant controllers or warehouse office managers. The vouchers, together with the supporting documents, are then turned over to the approver's secretary who holds the former, cancels the latter, and returns them to accounting for filing. Periodically, the secretary batches the approved disbursement vouchers, attaches a transmittal slip indicating the number of vouchers in the batch and forwards them to Des Moines for payment.

The corporate office at Des Moines distributes to each plant and warehouse a report listing the checks prepared that week, cross-referenced to the disbursement vouchers submitted. At the four manufacturing plants the controller's office compares the checks listed to a retained copy of each disbursement voucher. The warehouse accounting offices are severely understaffed and do not perform this reconciliation. Vendor statements and inquires about unpaid bills are replied to by the purchase location if invoices have not yet been forwarded for payment. Otherwise, they are sent to Des Moines for a response.

Cash disbursement processing

Corporate headquarters in Des Moines processes each disbursement voucher using the combination of manual and computer data processing activities flow charted in Figure 17.12.

Group	Activity Performed
Input	Open the mail containing approved disbursement vouchers and transmittal slips from the manufacturing plants and warehouses. Make test counts of disbursement vouchers against transmittal slips and forward both for further processing.
Vendor code	File transmittal slips. Sort disbursement vouchers alphabetically by vendor. Scan vouchers for completeness and check vendor code, name, address, and terms to vendor master file. Initiate changes or additions to vendor master file if warranted. Forward acceptable vouchers for further processing.
Batching	Scan vouchers for missing data and check calculations. Group acceptable vouchers by type, in batches of approximately 50. Forward batches to comptometer operators.
Comptometers	Create batch control totals on dollars and hash totals on quantities. Forward batches and control totals for processing.
Control desk	Scan batches for missing data and recalculate control totals. Assign control numbers to batches. Log them in with their control totals. Forward batches with control numbers and totals for further processing.
Data entry	Key punch and key verify data. Send batched documents to control desk for cancellation and return to accounting for filing. Create tape transfer status report. Convert cards to tape. Forward tape with control and summary cards for processing.
Data center	Perform program edits for completeness and reasonableness as well as appropriate limit and validity checks. Process acceptable data against vendor master file and transaction history file. Mechanically sign resulting prenumbered checks. Forward signed checks, reports, and unresolved rejects to control desk.
Control desk	Log and reconcile data center totals. Distribute data center output as appropriate. Foot, balance, and mail checks. Correct errors and otherwise resolve rejects.

Required:

a. What additional information would you like to obtain before making your evaluation of the cash disbursement system?

MANUAL AND COMPUTER PROCESSING ACTIVITIES—CASH DISBURSEMENTS.

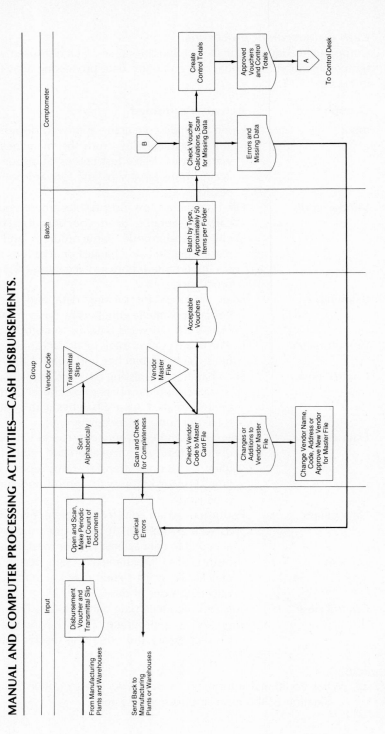

Figure 17.12

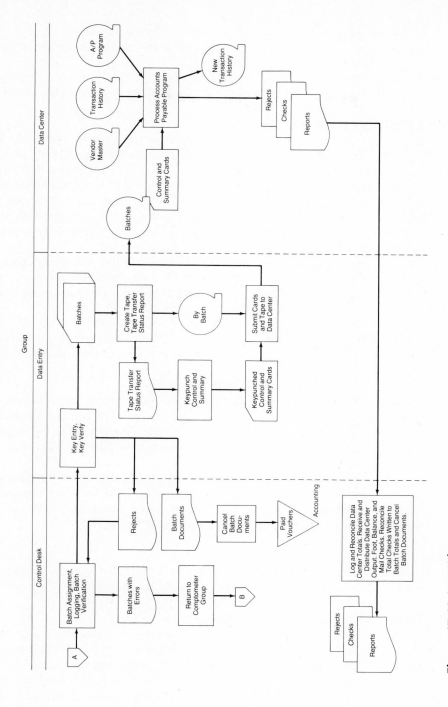

Figure 17.12 (cont'd)

b. What are the objectives of the cash disbursement system?

c. How are these objectives accomplished in this system and what controls are available to assist?

d. What recommendations would you make to King Company management about the internal control over their centralized disbursements system?

28. Retail Cash System Controls

You are auditing Schusters, a local restaurant that was recently opened by Odette Schuster. Although Schuster is a marvelous cook, she knows very little about business and trusts her employees too much. The waiters are given a note pad each day on which to take orders. The sheets are turned over to the kitchen to prepare the orders as instructed. The waiters then deliver the prepared meal to the restaurant patrons. When the customers are ready to leave, the waiters merely sum the bills and take the cash. Since there's no cashier, they give the customers their change. The restaurant accepts no checks or credit cards.

Recently, the owner remarked that even though she was always busy in the kitchen, daily sales just have not been as high as she imagined. The restaurant has been experiencing cash flow problems and Schuster is considering closing.

Required:

Explain to Schuster what internal controls need to be implemented over cash sales. Also, explain what has likely happened due to a lack of these internal controls.

29. Vending Machine Cash Controls

Trapan Retailing, Inc., has decided to diversify operations by selling through vending machines. Trapan's plans call for the purchase of 312 vending machines that will be situated at 78 different locations within one city, and the rental of a warehouse to store merchandise. Trapan intends to sell only canned beverages at a standard price.

Management has hired an inventory control clerk to oversee the warehousing functions and two truck drivers who will periodically fill the machines with merchandise and deposit the cash collected at a designated bank. Drivers will be required to report to the warehouse daily. *(AICPA adapted)*

Required:

What internal controls should the auditor expect to find in order to assume the integrity of the cash receipts and warehousing functions?

30. Ticket Sales and Cash Control

At University basketball games, the cashier, located in a box office near the gate, receives money from spectators and gives them a ticket. The tickets are serially numbered. The spectator hands his ticket to the gatekeeper who is stationed at the entrance of the coliseum. The gatekeeper tears the ticket in half and returns the stub to the spectator. At this point the spectator is allowed to pass through the turnstile. The other half of the ticket is dropped into a locked box.

Required:

a. List the internal controls that are present in the handling of cash receipts.

b. List steps that management can take to strengthen the effectiveness of these controls.

31. Cash Review Questions

Select the best answer to each of the following questions. *(All AICPA adapted)*

a. You are reviewing a write-up of internal control weaknesses in cash receipts and disbursements procedures. Which of the following weaknesses, standing alone, should cause you the least concern:

(1) Checks are signed by only one person.

(2) Signed checks are distributed by the controller to approved payees.

(3) Treasurer fails to establish bona fide names and addresses of check payees.

(4) Cash disbursements are made directly out of cash receipts.

b. Internal control over cash receipts is weakened when an employee who receives customer mail receipts also:

(1) Prepares initial cash receipts records.

(2) Records credits to individual accounts receivable.

(3) Maintains a petty cash fund.

c. Which of the following is an effective internal accounting control over cash payments:

(1) Signed checks should be mailed under the supervision of the check signer.

(2) Spoiled checks that have been voided should be disposed of immediately.

(3) Checks should be prepared only by persons responsible for cash receipts and cash disbursements.

(4) A check-signing machine with two signatures should be utilized.

d. An effective internal accounting control measure that protects against the preparation of improper or inaccurate disbursements would be to require that all checks be:

(1) Signed by an officer after necessary supporting evidence has been examined

(2) Reviewed by the treasurer before mailing

(3) Sequentially numbered and accounted for by internal auditors

(4) Perforated or otherwise effectively canceled when they are returned with the bank statement

e. Which of the following is a standard internal accounting control for cash disbursements:

(1) Checks should be signed by the controller and at least one other employee of the company.

(2) Checks should be sequentially numbered and the numerical sequence should be accounted for by the person preparing bank reconciliations.

   (3) Checks and supporting documents should be marked "Paid" immediately after the check is returned with the bank statement.

   (4) Checks should be sent directly to the payee by the employee who prepares documents that authorize check preparation.

 f. An internal management tool that aids in the control of the financial management function is a cash budget. The principal aim of a cash budget is to:

   (1) Ensure that sufficient funds are available at all times to satisfy maturing liabilities

   (2) Measure adherence to company budgetary procedures

   (3) Prevent the posting of cash receipts and disbursements to incorrect accounts

   (4) Assure that the accounting for cash receipts and disbursements is consistent from year to year

 g. Which of the following internal accounting control procedures is effective in preventing duplicate payment of vendors' invoices:

   (1) The invoices should be stamped, perforated, or otherwise effectively canceled before submission for approval of the voucher.

   (2) Unused voucher forms should be prenumbered and accounted for.

   (3) Canceled checks should be sent to persons other than the cashier or accounting department personnel.

   (4) Properly authorized and approved vouchers with appropriate documentation should be the basis for check preparation.

 h. For good internal control, the person who should sign checks is the:

   (1) Person preparing the checks

   (2) Purchasing agent

   (3) Accounts payable clerk

   (4) Treasurer

 i. For good internal control, the monthly bank statements should be reconciled by someone under the direction of the:

   (1) Credit manager

   (2) Controller

   (3) Cashier

   (4) Treasurer

 j. Operating control over the check signature plate normally should be the responsibility of the:

   (1) Secretary

   (2) Chief accountant

   (3) Vice-president of finance

   (4) Treasurer

CASES

32. Design Cash Management System

Cash control is a critical system in any company. In the Apogee Company (Appendix C), the function is discharged almost casually. The company has just borrowed $700,000 on a long-term note and is about to engage in a significant expansion of operations, including an aggressive selling campaign. The tempo can be expected to increase dramatically in both the cash receipts and cash disbursements flows.

Design a well-documented and controlled information system for cash management. Include in your proposal the important relationships with accounts payable, accounts receivable, banks, auditing, and payroll.

33. Cash Control

Cash inflows come from three sources in Bubbling Stone Beverage Company. Comment on the control procedures of each and on the controls surrounding cash in general.

CHAPTER EIGHTEEN

The Property and
General Ledger Systems

This chapter examines two important functions of the administrative cycle, the property system and the general ledger system. These systems are the responsibility of the accounting department, which is in charge of the maintenance of records and appropriate related controls.

Because the dollar value of fixed assets is usually large relative to total assets, there should be proper planning and control over these expenditures. To maintain controls, the property system should interface with the purchasing, accounts payable, and cash systems. If a company constructs its own fixed assets, materials, labor, and overhead costs from the production system will interlock with the property system. Upon disposal of the fixed assets, the cash receipts system will be utilized.

Accountants attempt to match the cost of the property "consumed" with related revenues through depreciation. The property system should be designed to accommodate this procedure. Because depreciation of manufacturing machinery represents an overhead charge, the property system relating to depreciation must include consideration of the company's production and cost accounting systems.

The general ledger system, on the other hand, includes the accounts from all the various accounting information subsystems. Thus the various accounting subsystems described in detail in prior chapters provide inputs, either directly or indirectly, into the general ledger. As a consequence, the general ledger system may be viewed as an umbrella system (see Figure 18.1) that draws upon the various subsystems that impact on its many component accounts.

FUNCTIONS AND OBJECTIVES

A primary objective of any accounting system is to generate reliable and relevant information. Specifically, the general ledger system must record and summarize all financial transactions promptly and accurately so that timely and useful financial reports may be generated. Since the general ledger system depends on the proper functioning of the various subsystems, it must be designed with recognition of these important interlocking relationships. Functions of the general ledger system, listed in order of consideration, are

GENERAL LEDGER SYSTEM.

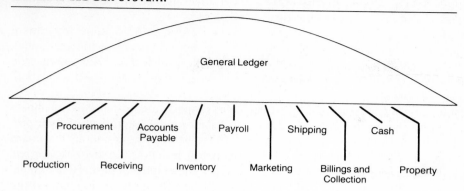

General Ledger

Procurement
Accounts Payable
Payroll
Shipping
Cash

Production
Receiving
Inventory
Marketing
Billings and Collection
Property

Figure 18.1

proper organization and procedures, record maintenance, report generation, and internal controls.

The objectives of the property system should be to ensure that:

1. The company has physical custody of the assets.
2. The assets are properly safeguarded.
3. Acquisitions and deletions are properly planned and approved with supporting documentation.
4. Capital acquisitions are properly recorded.
5. Deletions are removed with an appropriate removal of accumulated depreciation.
6. Depreciation expense is properly recorded.

Organization and Procedures

The chief officer in the financial function cycle of an organization is usually the treasurer or financial vice-president. The treasurer is often positioned at the functional level of financial vice-president and serves as chairman of the company's finance committee.

The treasurer, of course, must administer the functions under his or her authority. The role of the treasurer, however, is much broader than administration. The treasurer also participates in top-level management decision making through the exercise of special skills and familiarity with the finance function. For example, the treasurer often makes recommendations regarding investments, dividend policy, and capital budgeting.

The controller (or comptroller) who reports directly to the treasurer, has the responsibility for the company's accounting function. As the top-level accounting information systems manager, the controller supervises the collection and processing of data and the preparation of reports from such data.

This distinction in roles between the treasurer and controller represents the traditional organizational structure for the financial function. Organizational structures may vary between companies: In small companies the functions of treasurer and controller are often combined; in others the treasurer and controller may be on the same organizational level and report to a vice-president of finance.

The general ledger function is usually performed within an accounting department under the supervision of the controller. A typical organization chart for the accounting function is shown in Figure 18.2. In this chart the general ledger comes under the auspices of general accounting along with accounts payable, billings and collection, payroll, and property.

Although the accounting department maintains property records, it does not initiate the acquisition of property. Typically, for large dollar amounts, approval of such purchases must come from top management (e.g., the president, the treasurer, the board of directors), and should relate directly to the budgetary process. The level of approval for property acquisitions often depends on the dollar value of the purchase. For example, the president of the company may have the authority to approve purchases from $50,000 to $100,000, but the Board of Directors may be required to approve purchases of more than $100,000.

Record Maintenance

The general ledger, composed of its myriad component accounts, must be maintained and updated continually. As a consequence, the general ledger should be the appropriate source of documentation and audit trails.

General ledger accounts are updated by recording transactions in the journals. Whereas journals record financial *activity,* ledgers reflect financial *balances.* Thus journals may be thought of as "transaction files" that record all economic activity. Since ledgers represent files of current data, they may be considered "master files." Because

ORGANIZATION CHART FOR THE ACCOUNTING FUNCTION.

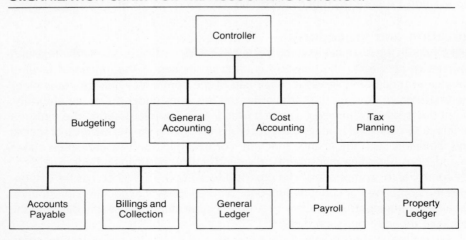

Figure 18.2

these master files or ledgers represent current balances, they must be updated frequently. To update a master file or ledger, financial activities recorded in the transaction files or journals must be posted to the ledger accounts. In a system context, the process of posting is often referred to as *file maintenance.*

Companies typically maintain a transaction file (or general journal) to record economic activity. Some companies, however, have developed several specialized journals to record certain types of economic activity. For example, a company may have a cash receipts journal to record all cash inflow and a cash disbursements journal to record all cash outflow. In this situation, the general journal would contain all economic activity except cash receipts and cash disbursements. Other special journals frequently utilized are sales journals and purchases journals.

Since these journals provide original entry for all economic activity, they represent the foundation of all financial information generated in the accounting information system and provide the evidence for posting in the ledgers. Consequently, all journals and related documentation should become part of a company's permanent records. Maintenance of these files is essential for reporting purposes and providing audit trails.

If the general ledger is considered the *master* file of all company accounts, the subsidiary ledgers then represent detail listings of balances *within* a given general ledger account. As an example, the accounts receivable subsidiary ledger is composed of all the individual customer's account balances. The total of these individual balances in the subsidiary ledger should agree with the accounts receivable balance in the general ledger. In fact, the sum of the balances of the individual accounts in any subsidiary ledger should agree with the balance of the control account in the general ledger. A schematic diagram of the recording of financial activity and the resulting financial balances is shown in Figure 18.3. To facilitate the maintenance of these master file accounts, and the posting procedures for updating the accounts, companies generally develop a chart of accounts (see Chapter Four for a detailed discussion).

Property records should be maintained on the property master file. This file contains all necessary information on property for financial reporting and managerial control. In addition, the file often contains information relating to tax requirements and tax filings. The typical property master file reflects the following:

1. Asset control number
2. Location code
3. Asset class code
4. Description
5. Date acquired
6. Cost
7. Accumulated depreciation
8. Current-year depreciation
9. Depreciation method
10. Estimated life
11. Estimated salvage value
12. Budget vendor number

RECORDING OF FINANCIAL ACTIVITY.

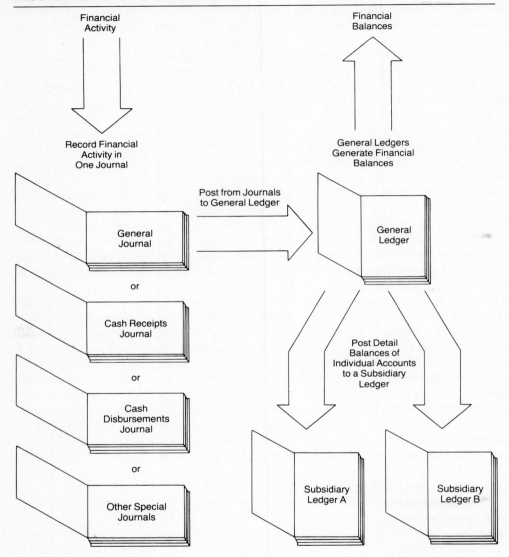

Figure 18.3

13. Compliance restriction Code
14. Tax—cost
15. Tax—accumulated depreciation
16. Tax—current-year depreciation

17. Tax—depreciation method
18. Tax—bonus depreciation
19. Investment tax credit

Figure 18.4 illustrates a portion of such a property master file.

The asset control number is a unique number assigned to identify the asset. A tag with this same number is generally affixed to the asset. The location code indicates the specific plant, building, and department in which the asset may be found. The asset class code represents the major classification by asset group. In Figure 18.4, Code 02 refers to vehicles. The budget vendor number represents the specific vendor from whom the asset was purchased, and is useful for repairs, maintenance, and replacement purposes. The compliance restriction code refers to any restrictions placed on the property. For example, in Figure 18.4 a restriction code of 01 indicates that the property had been pledged as collateral in a borrowing agreement.

Depreciation

Depreciation is the matching of the cost of a fixed asset with the revenues derived from the utilization of the asset over time. As such, depreciation impacts on both the balance sheet and the income statement and represents an important component of the property system.

Companies often use a different depreciation method (e.g., accelerated cost recovery system) for tax purposes from that used for financial reporting, an approach that requires the maintenance of separate depreciation records for tax and financial reporting purposes. Although the estimated life and estimated salvage value may remain the same, cost and depreciation methods often differ between the two reporting requirements. As a consequence, such items as the tax basis, depreciation method, additional first-year bonus depreciation, current depreciation expense, and accumulated depreciation should be maintained separately on the property master file as shown in Figure 18.4.

Internal Controls

One of the most important functions of any system is the observance of reliable internal controls. Controls are necessary to safeguard the assets and provide reasonable assurance that the accounting transactions are being properly recorded.

The safeguarding function is especially critical for fixed assets, considering their large dollar values and wide dispersion of location. Internal controls for fixed assets do not differ appreciably from traditional internal control features. Such attributes as segregation of duties, proper procedures for authorization, adequate documents and records, physical control over assets and records, and independent checks on performance are necessary in a well-designed property system.

As a result of the strong dependence of the general ledger system on the other accounting subsystems, the internal controls are naturally interrelated directly with these subsystems. A primary objective of the internal controls incorporated in the general ledger system is to provide an independent check and verification for accounting information processed in other accounting information subsystems. For example, the general ledger provides a control total of the balance in accounts receivable that can be utilized

PROPERTY MASTER FILE DECEMBER 31, 198X

Asset Control Number	Location Code	Asset Class Code	Description	Date Acquired	Cost	Accum. Deprec.	Current Year Deprec.	Deprec. Method.
101050	0142	02	1981 Ford Pickup	0182	5412	3126	1042	SL
492260	2740	04	1983 John Deere Tractor	0384	31613	15556	3111	SL
071052	1638	02	1986 Olds 98	1286	18112	3582	3582	SL
081277	0844	09	IBM Electric Typewriter	0784	614	102	102	SL

Figure 18.4

in an analysis of the propriety of the subsidiary accounts receivable records maintained by billings and collections.

Internal controls in the general ledger system are also designed to serve other purposes. Another objective of the system is to ensure that all transactions are recorded and that *only* valid transactions enter the system. Internal controls in the general ledger system are also concerned with posting the correct amounts to appropriate accounts and balancing the general ledger.

PROPERTY SOURCE DOCUMENTS

The design of source documents for the property system may vary significantly among companies as a result of differences in organizational structures, type of business, equipment, location, and tax requirements. However, although the design may differ, there are certain types of source documents that are common to most property systems.

Property documents must necessarily reflect the design of the property system and the accounting controls integrated into the system. Purchase of fixed assets should include proper authorization and approval from an appropriate company executive. Budgeting considerations must also be taken into account during this stage. In addition, for certain types of assets the engineering department may be utilized to determine the appropriate specifications of the asset. Typically, *a property expenditure request* is completed to initiate a purchase of a fixed asset. This request, shown in Figure 18.5, should include a description and specifications of the asset, proper approval by appropriate officials, an indication of any review by the engineering department, and appropriate detail information for input in the property master file.

Transfer of a fixed asset from one operating department to another should be properly documented by a change in location code, and entered on the property master file. To facilitate this type of transaction, *a property transfer request form,* as shown in Figure 18.6, is often prepared.

							Tax			
Est. Life	Est. Salvage	Budget Vendor Number	Restr. Code	Cost	Accum. Deprec.	Current Year Deprec.	Deprec. Method	Bonus Deprec.	Investment Credit
5	200.00	017641	00	5412	4243	779	ACRS	0	360
10	500.00	069130	01	31613	16556	2911	SL	2000	0
5	200.00	001041	00	18112	7244	7244	DDB	0	540
3	0.00	017477	00	614	204	204	ACRS	0	20

Figure 18.4 (cont'd)

Disposition of a fixed asset may take one of several forms: a sale, a trade, scrapping, or donation. Such dispositions should be properly approved to prevent unauthorized dispositions. In addition to approval, other information relating to the disposition is needed. This includes factors such as cost, asset number, accumulated depreciation, any unearned investment tax credit, other tax information, and justification for the disposal. Many companies utilize a fixed asset disposition form similar to the one shown in Figure 18.7 to record disposition of fixed assets. This form should contain all necessary information relating to the disposal, including the approval of the appropriate executive.

GENERAL LEDGER SOURCE DOCUMENTS

Accounting subsystems discussed in preceding chapters included diverse source documents from a relatively limited number of sources. For example, in payroll the primary source documents were various personnel action forms, time cards, payroll deduction forms, and payroll adjustment forms. All these documents were generated by payroll or personnel or the production shops.

In the general ledger system, however, there is generally only one primary source document—the journal voucher specifying the details of the journal entry. This form, as illustrated in Figure 18.8, includes the accounts and respective account numbers to be debited and credited, an explanation of the entry, source of the entry, and who approved the entry.

Once recorded in a journal, these entries must also be posted to the general ledger. Instead of physically rewriting journal voucher information in a journal, some companies simply file journal vouchers in a binder that represents the general journal. Also, when a company utilizes special journals, the journal voucher system may be slightly altered. For example, the cash receipts journal may be summarized only at periodic intervals, with a journal voucher prepared at that time for direct posting to the general ledger.

RUSSELL CORPORATION **AUTHORITY FOR EXPENDITURE**

DIVISION	PLANT/FACILITY	DEPARTMENT	DATE	PAGE	EXPENDITURE NUMBER
				1 OF	

SUMMARY

DESCRIPTION ☐ NEW ☐ USED

REASON ☐ ADDITION ☐ IMPROVEMENT ☐ REPLACEMENT ☐ SAFETY

DELIVERY	ESTIMATED DATE COMPLETION	ESTIMATED USEFUL LIFE	INVESTMENT CREDIT	ANNUAL SAVINGS	RATE OF RETURN
		YRS.			%
NET TO CAPITALIZE	ADD RELATED EXPENSES	TOTAL BUDGETED EXPENDITURE	ADD SALES/USE TAX	LESS TOTAL DEDUCTIONS	NET COST OF AUTHORIZATION

APPROVAL

FINAL APPROVAL BY	PLANT/FACILITY MANAGER	DATE	VICE PRESIDENT	DATE
BOARD OF DIRECTORS ☐ EXECUTIVE COMMITTEE ☐ DATE APPROVED	GENERAL MANAGER AND/OR OTHER APPROVAL	DATE	DIVISION PRESIDENT	DATE
		DATE	CORPORATE APPROVAL	DATE

DIVISION REVIEW				CORPORATE REVIEW		
PLANT CONTROLLER	ACCOUNTING	INDUSTRIAL ENGINEERING	ACCOUNTING	INDUSTRIAL ENGINEERING	PURCHASING

DETAIL

CAPITAL DETAIL				SUMMARY CALCULATIONS		
GUIDELINE CLASS NAME						
NUMBER					RELATED EXPENSE DETAIL	
USEFUL LIFE						
PURCHASE PRICE						
MILL LABOR						
MILL SUPPLIES						
OTHER - INCL. FRT.						
SUB-TOTAL					▼	
LESS TRADE-IN ALLOWANCE				NET TO CAPITALIZE	TOTAL RELATED EXPENSES	TOTAL BUDGETED EXPENDITURE
NET TOTAL						

Computation of Investment Credit as applicable by Law

					DISPOSAL NO. OF ITEMS	SALES/USE TAX
BOOK VALUE OF TRADE-IN *					TRADED-IN SCRAPPED	▼
AMOUNT SUBJECT TO INVESTMENT CREDIT						
INVESTMENT CREDIT RATE ‡	%	%	%	* Obtain from Property Accountant		
INVESTMENT CREDIT AMOUNT				‡ Refer to Rate for each Guideline Class No. in the Fixed Assets Manual.		
LESS UNEARNED INVESTMENT CREDIT *				**DEDUCTIONS**		
NET INVESTMENT CREDIT				TOTAL NET INVESTMENT CREDIT	SCRAP VALUE OF ITEMS MADE USELESS	TOTAL DEDUCTIONS
COMMENTS:				NET COST OF AUTHORIZATION ▶		

WP-84778

01387

Figure 18.5

548 The Administrative Cycle

USP&FCO.
STD. 98 REV. 12-65

REQUEST FOR PROPERTY TRANSFERS

TRANSFER NO. _____
DATE . . . _____
ORIGINAL COST _____

Property Transfer From_____To_____

Reasons:_____

_____

_____

_____

_____

_____

_____

_____

_____

_____

ITEM NO. OR P.I. No.	CLASS	DESCRIPTION OF ITEM	ORIGINAL COST	ACCRUED DEPR.	SALVAGE	
		TOTAL				

DISTRIBUTION APPROVED_____
                          VICE PRESIDENT & TREASURER

RECOMMENDED_____ APPROVED_____

                          APPROVED_____

Figure 18.6

RUSSELL CORPORATION

ALEXANDER CITY, ALABAMA 35010 • (205) 234-4251

AUTHORITY FOR DISPOSAL
OF FIXED ASSETS

DIVISION	PLANT/ORGANIZATION	DEPARTMENT	DATE	PAGE O F	DISPOSAL NUMBER

PROPOSED METHOD OF DISPOSAL					UNEARNED INVESTMENT CREDIT	REFERENCE AUTHORITY FOR EXPENDITURE NO. (IF ANY)	ESTIMATED VALUE ON SALE/TRADE-IN
SELL	SCRAP	TRADE-IN	DONATE	TRANSFER			

DESCRIPTION OF ITEM(S)

REASON FOR DISPOSAL

ANALY-SIS NO.	COST CTR.	ASSET NO.	DETAILED ITEM DESCRIPTION	GUIDE LINE CODE	F/Y ADD.	TAX BASE COST	OBTAIN FROM PROPERTY ACCOUNTANT		AMOUNT RECEIVED IF SOLD OR TRADED IN
							ACCUMULATED DEPRECIATION	BOOK VALUE	

APPROVALS					
	PLANT MANAGER			TOTAL TAX BASE COST	
	VICE PRESIDENT			TOTAL ACCUMULATED DEPR'N	
	VICE PRESIDENT			TOTAL BOOK VALUE	
	DIVISION PRESIDENT				IF SOLD SHOW
	CORPORATE PRESIDENT		DISPOSITION	SOLD SCRAPPED TRADED DONATED TRANSFERRED	AMOUNT RECEIVED
	FINAL APPROVAL DATE			TO	DISPOSITION BY
	PURCHASING	ACCOUNTING		CITY & STATE	DATE COMPLETED

#P-84779

Figure 18.7

▬▬ **550** The Administrative Cycle

JOURNAL ENTRY

DIVISION NO. _____

DATE ⬚ | | | ⬚   J E No. ⬚ | | | ⬚

1   6   7   12

| LOC **1** 43 | A/B 44 | SOURCE 55   60 | 61 ENTRY DESCRIPTION 79 | S/R 80 |

Page _____ of _____

		ACCOUNT DESC.	ACCOUNT NO.			DEBIT	CREDIT	X
			13		24	45 54	45 54	
				TOTALS				

EXPLANATION OF ENTRY

PREPARED BY:

APPROVED:

08544

Figure 18.8

Although other subsystems generally receive their source documents from a limited number of sources, the general ledger system receives its source documents from a variety of sources. Almost every subsystem generates a journal voucher that must be entered into the general ledger. Consequently, the general ledger directly interfaces most other subsystems through the journal voucher.

These factors also suggest another difference between the general ledger system and other accounting subsystems. The general ledger impacts on all company accounts, whereas the other subsystems, and even their larger representation, the cycle, impact on significantly fewer accounts. Figure 18.9 compares the impact of the various cycles on the accounts with the impact of the general ledger system.

THE GENERAL LEDGER INTERFACE

An analysis of the general ledger system centers around the journal voucher, the only source document providing input to the general ledger system. Whereas the specific entry on the journal voucher is dependent on the accounting subsystem, the format of the journal voucher and its impact on the general ledger need not vary.

As indicated in Figure 18.10, journal vouchers are initiated by various accounting systems in all the cycles: expenditure, conversion, revenue, and administration. A brief description of these journal vouchers and their impact on the general ledger follows. The numerical sequence of the discussions do not necessarily indicate the chronological flow of journal vouchers into the general ledger system. Clearly, the flow of journal vouchers into the general ledger represents a vibrant, random, and continual process from these related subsystems; thus, an assumption regarding the chronology of such a flow does not reflect the dynamic nature of systems interrelationships.

1. When accounts payable matches the purchase order, receiving report, and vendor invoice, a journal voucher to book accounts payable is prepared. Representative journal entries on this voucher that would impact on the general ledger include:

Manufacturing Overhead	XXX	
General and Administrative Expenses	XXX	
Fixed Assets	XXX	
Various Inventory Accounts (Separate)	XXX	
Accounts Payable		XXX

2. Whereas property purchases are entered through the accounts payable system, the property control system must prepare journal vouchers for routine depreciation and retirement disposals. A typical journal voucher from the property system might be:

Accumulated Depreciation—Automobiles	XXX	
Loss on Disposition of Automobiles	XXX	
Automobiles		XXX
Depreciation Expense—Machinery	XXX	
Accumulated Depreciation—Machinery		XXX

FINANCIAL STATEMENT CAPTIONS AFFECTED BY CYCLE

Account Usually Affected (X)	Cycle				
	Administrative (Other Than General Ledger)	Spending	Conversion	Revenue	General Ledger
Assets:					
Cash	X	X		X	X
Receivables				X	X
Investments (temporary)	X				X
Inventories—					
Raw Materials		X	X		X
Work in Process			X		X
Finished Goods			X	X	X
Prepaid Expenses		X	X		X
Property, Plant, and Equipment	X	X	X		X
Investments (long-term)	X				X
Liabilities:					
Notes and Loans	X				X
Trade Payables		X			X
Accruals Other Than Income Taxes			X	X	X
Income Taxes—Current	X	X	X	X	X
Income Taxes—Deferred	X	X	X	X	X
Contingencies	X				X
Equity:					
Common Stock	X				X
Preferred Stock	X				X
Additional Paid-in Capital	X				X
Retained Earnings	X				X
Treasury Stock	X				X
Income/Expense:					
Revenue				X	X
Revenue Deductions				X	X
Cost of Revenue		X	X	X	X
Selling Expenses		X		X	X
General and Administrative Expenses		X			X
Other—Interest, etc.	X				X
Unusual Items	X	X			X

SOURCE Adapted from Arthur Andersen and Company, *A Guide for Studying and Evaluating Internal Controls* (Chicago: Arthur Andersen and Company, 1978). By permission.

Figure 18.9

JOURNAL VOUCHER FLOW IN GENERAL LEDGER SYSTEM.

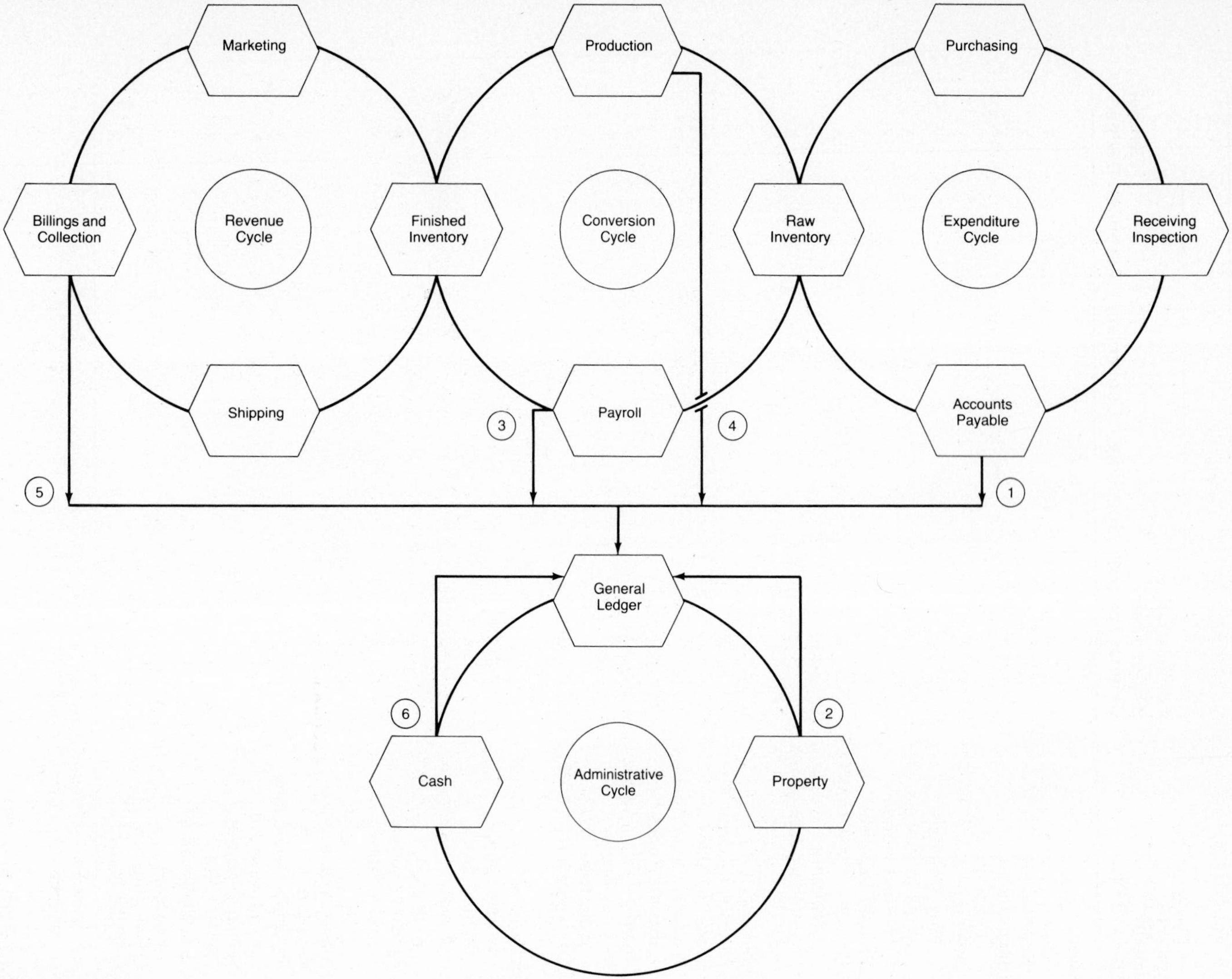

Figure 18.10

3. The payroll function handles all payroll liabilities. Thus, upon receipt of the journal voucher for payroll, this entry would be made:

Direct Labor	XXX	
Salaries—General and Administrative Expense	XXX	
Wages Payable (Net)		XXX
Federal Income Tax Payable		XXX
FICA Payable		XXX
Other Payroll Deductions Payable		XXX

4. In production, raw materials, direct labor, and manufacturing overhead come together to produce a finished product for inventory. The following journal vouchers are prepared:

Work-in-Process Inventory	XXX	
Direct Labor		XXX
Materials Inventory		XXX
Factory Overhead Applied		XXX
Finished Goods Inventory	XXX	
Work-in-Process Inventory		XXX

5. Upon completion of the revenue cycle, the billings and collections cycle records the accounts receivable in the accounts receivable subsidiary ledger and prepares a journal voucher that is forwarded to the general ledger system. Upon receipt of the voucher, the following entry is made:

Accounts Receivable	XXX	
Sales		XXX
Cost of Goods Sold	XXX	
Inventory of Finished Goods		XXX

6. A variety of transactions are generated by the cashier's office that represent the culmination of both revenue and expenditure cycle activities.

Preparation of vouchers for transactions from the cash control system may be categorized as either cash receipts or cash disbursements. The typical journal voucher for cash receipts generated by the cash receipts journal would be:

Cash	XXX	
Accounts Receivable		XXX
Sales (for Cash)		XXX
Other Sources (Specified)		XXX

Journal vouchers for cash disbursements also necessitate entries in the general ledger, as shown in the sample entries here.

Accounts Payable	XXX	
Cash		XXX
Wages Payable	XXX	
Cash		XXX

For the reports generated by the general ledger system to be accurate, certain other journal entries must be prepared. These entries may be broadly labeled as either special transactions or recurring adjusting entries. A master file of recurring adjusting entries is often maintained to facilitate the periodic posting of these entries. To record and control these transactions properly, the general ledger system must receive special journal vouchers from authorized sources.

Such special journal vouchers are often generated by the treasurer's office. To illustrate, the declaration of a dividend would not enter any of the major subsystems described in preceding chapters, primarily because of its uniqueness and infrequency. It must therefore be introduced by special journal vouchers submitted by the treasurer's office and would affect the following entries:

Retained Earnings	XXX	
Dividends Payable		XXX

Adhering to the matching principle requires the generation of adjusting entries for certain accruals or deferrals. In such cases, the general ledger system would receive and record entries from general accounting as shown in the following examples:

Insurance Expense	XXX	
Prepaid Insurance		XXX
Rent Receivable	XXX	
Accrued Rental Revenue		XXX

GENERAL LEDGER ACCOUNTING CONTROLS

Accounting controls in the general ledger system serve a dual purpose: (1) They provide auxiliary controls for the various related accounting subsystems, and (2) they provide controls over the general ledger system itself. Controls utilized in the general ledger system that apply to other related subsystems have been discussed in appropriate prior chapters, and include such features as (1) comparison of journal vouchers to batch or listing amounts, (2) reconciliation of totals per general ledger control accounts to totals in the subsidiary ledgers maintained by these subsystems, and (3) separation of the recording function in the general ledger from the collection and payment functions performed by other systems.

Other accounting and processing controls related to the general ledger function emphasize procedures regarding journal vouchers, journal entries, and ledger postings. Such accounting controls are:

1. Journal vouchers should be sequentially prenumbered.
2. Journal vouchers should be authorized by a responsible official.
3. Limited access to prenumbered journal voucher forms and accountability for the forms should be maintained.
4. Journal vouchers and journal entries should be properly filed.
5. A register of recurring entries should be maintained (e.g., accruals, eliminations).
6. Period-to-period comparisons of amounts of recurring entries should be made.
7. Periodic comparison of journal entry amounts with source data should be performed.

8. A supervisory review and approval of each nonstandard journal entry should be performed.
9. Internal audits of compliance of journal voucher and entry procedures should be performed.

These controls apply to inputs of the general ledger system. A primary control over the output of the general ledger system is the preparation of a trial balance. Clearly, when the debits do not equal the credits in the trial balance, an error has occurred in some phase of the recording system. Thus, a periodic trial balance provides an outstanding control procedure for the general ledger system. Because of the importance of the trial balance, control procedures should be established to:

1. Require the preparation of a periodic trial balance
2. Have adequate written procedures for the investigation of differences disclosed by the trial balance
3. Have the trial balance prepared and checked by persons other than those that post entries to the general ledger
4. Have someone investigate the differences disclosed by the trial balance

PROPERTY ACCOUNTING CONTROLS

A well-designed property system includes appropriate control features to safeguard fixed assets and ensure that the fixed asset transactions are properly recorded. Segregating the property accounting function from the operating departments is a primary control for most companies and an important factor in maintaining good internal accounting controls.

The property master file also facilitates the achievement of the accounting control objectives. The asset control number and location code provide controls over fixed assets. The asset control number (stamped on the corresponding asset) provides a means for property control to verify periodically the continued existence of each asset. The location code not only provides information regarding the specific location of the asset, but also establishes responsibility with the various operating departments for the physical safeguarding of the asset.

Proper documentation and required authorizations for fixed asset transactions add to the controls that the company has over its fixed assets. Documentation and authorizations aid in both the safeguarding of fixed assets and proper recording of such transactions.

To provide some assurance of the property master file's validity, the balances for the cost of these assets, related accumulated depreciation accounts, and depreciation expense should be checked against the corresponding general ledger accounts. Any discrepancies should be investigated, reconciled, and corrected.

MANAGEMENT INFORMATION REQUIREMENTS

The most important reports generated by the accounting information system are the company's financial statements. These financial statements are a product of the general ledger system and are often required by governmental agencies (the Securities and Exchange Commission), owners (shareholders), and creditors (bankers). Often reproduced in the company's annual report, these statements consist of an Income Statement, a Balance Sheet, and a Statement of Changes in Financial Position. Such financial statements summarize many accounts and divisions into singular lines on the statements. For internal purposes, more detailed financial statements are often needed, and the general ledger system should be able to produce detailed information by individual account, division, or department.

The general ledger system should be designed to assist the tax accountant in preparing the company's tax returns. Other management information requirements from the general ledger system are the production of cash flow statements and statements comparing budgeted amounts to actual amounts. An example of a budget performance report generated by the general ledger system is shown in Figure 18.11.

For the property system perhaps the most common report is the *Balance Sheet report,* shown in Figure 18.12. This report presents the cost of each asset, its related accumulated depreciation, and the resultant net book value. Assets in the report may be grouped by class or location to aid the reader. Various totals included in this report, of course, tie in to corresponding balances shown on the company's Balance Sheet.

A *location report* that details asset listings by location is one of the most frequent reports generated in a property system. As shown in Figure 18.13, this report lists all fixed assets by location, along with detailed information regarding asset control numbers and descriptions of assets. Typically, it serves as a guide when physical inventories of fixed assets need to be taken.

BUDGET PERFORMANCE REPORT
10/31/8X

Division: Towel
Department: Bleaching
Foreman: Mark Beasley

Account Code	Account	Year to Date			Month Ending October 31, 198X		
		Budget	Actual	Over (Under) Budget	Budget	Actual	Over (Under) Budget
Overhead							
631-00-3-20	Indirect Labor	14,030	13,860	(170)	1,200	1,150	(50)
632-00-3-20	Supplies and Tools	3,100	2,340	(760)	310	155	(155)
634-00-3-20	Heat, Light & Power	4,600	4,892	292	460	495	35
636-00-3-20	Maintenance	2,070	1,922	(148)	207	185	(22)
Direct Materials (610)		156,708	162,681	5,973	14,324	15,376	1,052
Direct Labor (620)		181,303	176,501	(4,802)	16,708	15,781	(927)

Figure 18.11

**BALANCE SHEET REPORT
BY MAJOR ASSET CLASS
DECEMBER 31, 198X**

CLASS: Automobiles

Asset Control Number	Description	Cost	Accumulated Depreciation	Net Book Value
101050	1981 Ford Pickup	$ 5412	$ 3126	$ 2286
071052	1980 Oldsmobile	18112	3582	14530
	TOTALS	$ 23524	$ 6708	$ 16816

Figure 18.12

**LOCATION REPORT
DECEMBER 31, 198X**

PLANT: Auburn Plant No. 2

Asset Control Number	Description	Building	Department
061923	Lathe	Machine Shop	Maintenance
120723	Loom	Weave Shop	Production

Figure 18.13

Detailed reports on fixed asset activity may also be generated in the property system. As previously stated, such activity may result from acquisitions, transfers, and retirements or disposals. These reports provide a hard copy that supplements the property master file, and are often useful in the budgeting and auditing processes.

Management also requires information on fixed assets for income tax purposes. When a company claims depreciation expense, a detailed listing that includes a description of the property, date the property was acquired, cost or other basis, accumulated depreciation, depreciation method, estimated life, and current-year depreciation must be attached to the tax return. A property system should have the capability of producing schedules in the same format as required by the tax agency.

Other reports may also be produced by the property system, such as depreciation expense schedules, documents for use in determining payments of *ad valorem* taxes, replacement cost information for Securities and Exchange Commission filings, and reports for determining the appropriateness of current insurance policies and any need for expanded insurance coverage. These often provide very useful information for management.

GENERAL LEDGER SYSTEM CONFIGURATION

The primary function of the general ledger system is to record journal vouchers and post them to the various general ledger accounts. The physical arrangements for handling these data depend, to a great degree, on whether the system is manual or electronic. Systems configuration for each type of system will be briefly discussed.

Manual System

In a manual system, journal vouchers are received by the various accounting subsystems, checked for approval and equality of debits and credits, and verified against other documentation when available. An entry is subsequently made in the proper journal and appropriately posted to the correct general ledger accounts. The general ledger system also posts various accrual and adjusting entries and compares totals between control accounts and various subsidiary ledgers.

Computerized Systems

Although the functions of the general ledger system are the same in an EDP or a manual system, the specific procedures used with each are different. In an EDP system, subsidiary ledgers are often integrated with the general ledger. Thus, entries are posted simultaneously by the computer to both the control account and the individual account in the subsidiary ledger.

An EDP application for the general ledger includes a series of updating processes that occur over time as a result of inputs from other accounting subsystems. For example, when fixed asset transactions are entered through the property system, they are also entered in the general ledger. Regardless of the systems configuration used, the basic objective and functions of the general ledger system remain the same.

An overview of an EDP general ledger system that incorporates entries from the several accounting information subsystems is shown in Figure 18.14. Journal entries that have recorded economic activity are generated from a variety of subsystems, as shown by the eight tapes in Figure 18.14.

Whichever source generates the journal entry, all entries must be posted to the general ledger. This procedure is accomplished by the general ledger processing run that generates an updated general ledger and a general ledger listing. This listing represents a hard copy of the general ledger that allows the accounting department to use general ledger information without rerunning the general ledger tape. Once the updated general ledger tape is produced, it may be used along with the budget tape of detailed budgeted data to generate a variety of reports, such as budget performance reports, financial statements, and special project reports.

PROPERTY SYSTEMS CONFIGURATION

As activity occurs that relates to the company's property, the property system is programmed to make the appropriate adjustments to the property master file and the general ledger. The systems configuration is illustrated in Figure 18.15. Activities relating to most acquisitions (i.e., property expenditure request, purchase order, invoice, and necessary

OVERVIEW OF EDP GENERAL LEDGER SYSTEM.

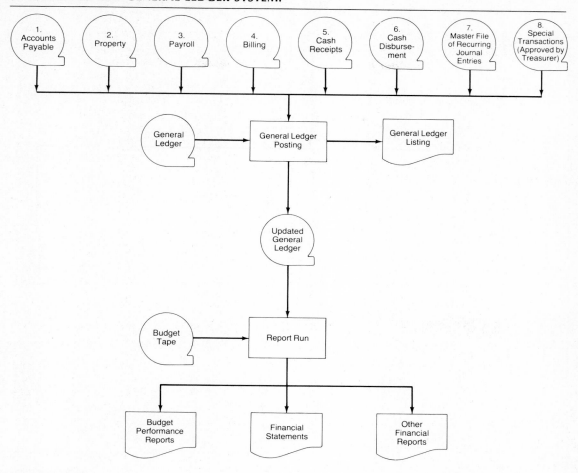

Figure 18.14

receiving reports) originate outside the property system. These documents should be matched and comparisons made regarding quantities, descriptions, cost, and location. The system generates and assigns the unique property identification number, and a property master file record is created. Subsequent activities (transactions) are used to update this master and keep it current.

The system must also be capable of producing management reports and making year-end adjustments. The management reports described in the preceding section are relatively easy to produce from a properly designed property master file.

Year-end adjustments for the property system focus on computation of current-year depreciation expense and updating of accumulated depreciation. These computations,

SYSTEMS CONFIGURATION—PROPERTY.

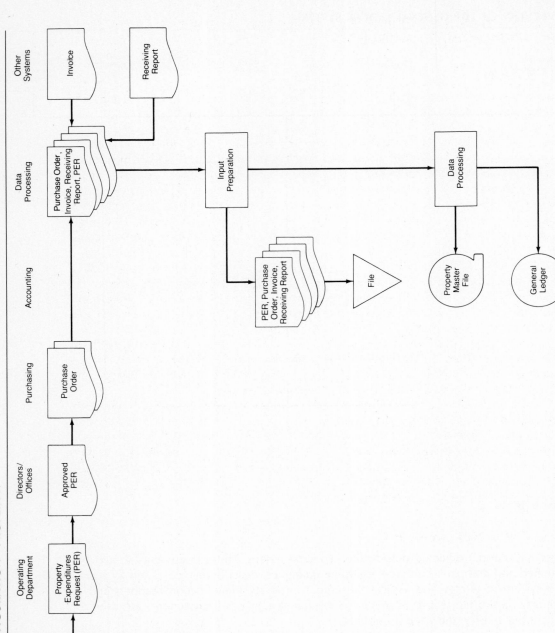

Figure 18.15

of course, depend on the depreciation method used for each asset. Further, separate computations are often made for financial reporting and income tax purposes.

SUMMARY

This chapter has discussed the property system and the general ledger system. The general ledger system is the accounting information subsystem that provides basic financial reports for both internal and external users. As a consequence, the general ledger system should be designed to function accurately, efficiently, and promptly while providing necessary and effective accounting controls. Differing from most other accounting information subsystems, the general ledger system has only one major source document, the journal voucher. Further, these journal vouchers represent the necessary vehicle that links the general ledger system with the many other accounting information subsystems. Recognition of these characteristics in relationship to the importance of the reports generated by this system must be considered in a well-designed general ledger system.

The property system generally centers around the property master file, a subsidiary ledger that supports the fixed asset accounts on the general ledger. This master file includes all necessary information for the property system—asset control numbers, descriptions, location codes, and cost and depreciation information for both financial reporting and tax purposes.

The primary objectives of the property system are to ensure that these assets exist and are properly safeguarded, to determine that all activity relating to fixed assets is properly recorded, and to determine that all accounting treatments and presentations are in accordance with generally accepted accounting principles.

To achieve these objectives, most systems require various source documents with related approvals and other internal control procedures. These internal accounting control procedures provide reasonable assurance that the system is functioning properly and that reports generated by the system are reliable. Reliability of data is an important requirement of the property system since numerous reports from the system are needed by management and other parties. These reports include Balance Sheet reports, location reports, activity reports, and depreciation reports.

SELECTED REFERENCES

Anthony, Robert N., and John Dearden. *Management Control Systems,* 3rd. ed. Homewood, Ill: Richard D. Irwin, Inc., 1976.

Arthur Andersen & Company, *A Guide for Studying and Evaluating Internal Controls.* Chicago: Arthur Andersen & Company, 1978.

Beaton, J. W. "What Value Fixed Assets?" *CAMagazine* (July 1979): 29–34.

Bodnar, George H. *Accounting Information Systems,* 2nd ed. Boston: Allyn & Bacon, 1983.

Commercial BMS 11 General Ledger Module—Capabilities Manual. Detroit: Burroughs Corp., 1976.

General Ledger and Responsibility Reporting—Users Manual. Chicago: Arthur Andersen & Company, 1978.

Grollman, William K. and Robert W. Cally, "Internal Control for Small Business," *Journal of Accountancy* (December 1978): 64–67.

Hill, Dan J., and Garold L. Rutherford. "Computerized Financial Data Reporting System," *Management Accounting* (July 1976): 57–60.

Horngren, Charles T. *Cost Accounting: A Managerial Emphasis,* 5th ed. Englewood Cliffs, N.J.: Prentice-Hall, Inc., 1982.

Kitchen, J. "Fixed Asset Values: Ideas on Depreciation," *Accounting and Business Research* (Autumn 1979): 79–88.

Leitch, Robert A. and K. Roscoe Davis. *Accounting Information Systems,* Englewood Cliffs, N.J.: Prentice-Hall, Inc., 1983.

Lubas, Daniel P. "Developing a Computerized General Ledger System," *Management Accounting* (May 1976): 53–56.

Management Science America, *Fixed Assets Accounting,* Atlanta, 1981.

Moscov, Stephen A., and Monk G. Simkin, *Accounting Information Systems,* 2nd ed., New York: John Wiley & Sons, 1984.

Quarnby, C. "Fixed Assets—The Inflation 2 Problem," *Accountant* (February 7, 1980): 18–23.

QUESTIONS

1. Explain why the general ledger system acts as an umbrella system to the other accounting information systems.
2. Explain the difference in responsibilities between the treasurer and the controller.
3. Discuss the impact of the separation of property record keeping in the accounting department from custody of property by the various operating departments.
4. What is the difference between a journal and a ledger?
5. Why is the general ledger considered a "master file," whereas journals are considered "transaction files"?
6. How does a subsidiary ledger interlock to the general ledger?
7. List three types of special journals.
8. Describe the typical organizational arrangement for approval of property purchases.
9. Describe and discuss the importance of the inclusion of each of the following items in the property master file:
   a. Asset control number
   b. Location code
   c. Asset class code
   d. Description
   e. Acquisition date
   f. Cost
   g. Accumulated depreciation
   h. Current-year depreciation
   i. Depreciation method
   j. Budget vendor number
   k. Compliance restriction code
   l. Tax information
10. What is the purpose of the chart of accounts?
11. Why do many companies code accounts by division? By department?
12. List and discuss the various types of changes in the status of property that may occur.
13. Why do source documents for property often vary significantly among companies?
14. How does a capital budget interact with the property system?
15. Describe the items that should be included in a property expenditure request.

16. How does the general ledger system provide internal controls over the various accounting information subsystems?
17. How does a property master file act as an internal control?
18. What information should be included on a journal voucher?
19. Discuss the difference in the number of source documents in a general ledger system as compared to other accounting subsystems.
20. Why are journal vouchers sometimes filed in a binder to represent the general journal?
21. Cite some examples of recurring adjusting entries.
22. List and describe at least four different types of management reports that might be generated from the property system.
23. List five accounting controls for the general ledger, and state how they improve internal controls.
24. Why is the trial balance a control over the general ledger system?
25. What control procedures should be established over the trial balance?
26. Cite three external users of reports generated by the general ledger system.
27. How does a properly designed general ledger system aid in the generation of budget performance reports?
28. Briefly describe the systems configuration of a manual general ledger system.
29. Briefly describe the systems configuration of an EDP general ledger system.
30. In a computerized system, why does data processing update the property master file and the general ledger concurrently? How do the property master file and the general ledger interface?

PROBLEMS

31. General Ledger Controls—Control Applications

For each of the following situations, describe a general ledger internal control feature that, if implemented, would prevent or detect the situation. Consider each situation independently.

a. A transposition in the posting of the debit portion of a journal voucher
b. A transposition in the posting of the debit and credit of a journal voucher to record a credit sale
c. Failure to post a journal voucher representing cash receipts for a day
d. Posting a journal voucher twice
e. A nonstandard journal voucher entered in the general ledger that was prepared by the cashier to hide an embezzlement
f. Failure to adjust prepaid expenses each month

32. Property Control Applications

For each of the following situations describe a property internal control feature that, if implemented, would prevent or detect the situation. Consider each situation independently:

a. Theft of a fixed asset at a remote plant location
b. Computation of depreciation expense that exceeds the cost of the asset
c. Loss on the destruction of property not properly insured

d. Theft of property by an employee who reports that the property has been scrapped

e. Acquisition of a fixed asset by a plant manager that seriously impairs the company's capital budgeting plans.

f. Acquisition of a fixed asset that provides no benefits to the company

g. Inability to determine who is the manufacturer of a fixed asset that desperately needs maintenance and repairs

h. Failure to take bonus depreciation for tax purposes

33. Controls over Trial Balance Applications

You have been engaged to audit Rover College, a small private college with 1,500 students. The college's accounting department consists of a financial vice-president, a bookkeeper, and a cashier. The bookkeeper, Pauline Plainsman, has only a limited knowledge of accounting. Although all entries prepared by her have an equality of debits and credits, the journal entries are sometimes incorrect.

As the first step of your audit, you pull a trial balance. During this procedure you observe the following:

a. Total debits do not equal total credits in the trial balance.

b. The automobile account has a credit balance.

c. Miscellaneous accounts receivable exceed all other receivable balances (accounts receivable, student receivables). There is no subsidiary ledger for miscellaneous accounts receivable.

You know from prior experience that the college never prepares a trial balance. You also know that the financial vice-president is capable of preparing and/or reviewing a trial balance, but she believes she is too busy to do such a menial and unproductive task. You believe, however, that the periodic preparation and review of a trial balance would be an effective internal control for the college general ledger.

Required:

a. Explain what arguments you would give the financial vice-president to encourage the preparation of a periodic trial balance for the college.

b. Explain specifically how the preparation and review of a trial balance by the financial vice-president might have impacted upon the errors you uncovered.

34. General Ledger Systems Review

Tidy Tiger Company maintains a manual general ledger system with subsidiary ledgers for accounts receivable, property, and accounts payable. As credit sales are made, the sale is entered in the sales journal along with the customer name and number. At the end of each week, a duplicate copy of the sales journal is forwarded to the accounts receivable clerk for posting to the accounts receivable subsidiary ledger.

Cash receipts for credit sales come into the mail room, where a remittance listing is prepared detailing the customer name, customer number, and amount. The remittance listing is forwarded to the accounts receivable clerk each day, and is posted to the accounts receivable subsidiary ledger. Remittances consisting of cash and checks are forwarded to the cashier, who enters the total amount in the cash receipts journal daily.

At the end of each week, the salesclerk writes a journal voucher for total credit sales and forwards the voucher to the general ledger. Likewise, the cashier prepares a weekly journal voucher for cash receipts and forwards the voucher to the general ledger personnel. All vouchers received by the general ledger system are manually entered in the general ledger upon receipt. Due to a lack of personnel, the accounts receivable control total is not compared to the total per the accounts receivable subsidiary ledger.

Required:

a. Cite weaknesses in the company's general ledger system as it relates to accounts receivable.

b. How might these weaknesses hurt the company?

c. What improvements would you suggest?

35. General Control Features

XYZ Construction Hauling Company recently signed the largest contract in its 5 years of existence. Because of the large workload involved in the project, several new trucks and pieces of machinery will be needed. Bill Sharp, the company's purchasing supervisor, has decided to purchase the trucks from a regional dealer. He has based his decision on the fact that the trucks were lower in cost and that a salesman at the dealership is a long-time friend. As he explained to the budget committee, "the trucks are not the best in the world, but they can get this job done." The committee accepted Mr. Sharp's proposal and okayed the purchase. After about 12 months on the new jobs, the trucks and several pieces of machinery began to malfunction quite regularly. Mr. Sharp contacted his friend at the dealership about the problems, but the friend could only say, "Your warranty is up. I wish I could help, but policies are policies." It was obvious the majority of the equipment being used was the old equipment, and new equipment was needed badly. So Mr. Sharp decided to go to the board again and ask for additional funds to "complete the project." Again the board accepted his proposal and rendered the funds. With these funds he completed the project.

Required:

Explain some of the control features that should be implemented by the company.

36. Systems Flowcharting and Control Review

The Wolfe Manufacturing Company has recently hired a new controller, Mr. Amos Thomas. Mr. Thomas has decided to make a few changes that will ensure better control over fixed assets. His major concern is fixed asset purchases, which are currently under the control of Mrs. John Doe.

In the past, Mrs. Doe has made purchase requisitions for all major assets to be purchased. She would, on instruction from the controller, select the type and model of the asset she thought best. She would then call different suppliers and decide who could give her the best deal. After making her decision, she would order the asset and prepare the check for the controller to sign.

On arrival of the asset, Mrs. Doe would check to make sure it was the right item, and then enter it on the appropriate asset account in the general ledger.

Next, she would take the invoice to the controller, who would review and initial it. She would then file the invoice and send a check to the vendor.

Mr. Thomas doesn't like this system, and has decided to handle all purchases in a different way. Each purchase must now be started by a two-part requisition. The requisition must be approved by a certain individual in each department. One requisition is sent to the purchasing department, the other filed. The purchasing department then prepares a purchase order form that comes in five copies. One is kept on file in that department, two are sent to the vendor. The fourth copy is sent to the receiving department, and the fifth to the accounting department. All these documents are in some way matched when the goods arrive from the vendor.

All forms are prenumbered and all equipment is tagged for identification. Periodic checks are made to ensure that all equipment is accounted for.

Payment for the goods is handled in the accounting department, where all checks over $1,000 are signed by the controller. Any transfers are done by property transfer request, and disposals are also handled by request forms. All the books and accounts are reconciled periodically to ensure their accuracy.

Required:

Flowchart the new system. Explain why the old system was changed and identify strengths of the new system.

37. Flowchart Evaluation and Internal Control Weaknesses

You were recently appointed the internal auditor for a private college. Your first assignment is to appraise the adequacy and effectiveness of the student registration procedures. You have completed your preliminary survey. Based on your interviews and a walkthrough of the student registration operation, you prepared an informal description outline.

Required:

Examine the following informal outline and list five internal control weaknesses (such as omissions of certain steps or measures) in the student registration procedures. *(IIA adapted)*

ADMISSION—PROCESSING OF REGISTRATIONS

1. *Mail Room*

Opens all mail, prepares remittance advices, and remittance listings.
Sends copies of advices and listings to:
a. Cashier (with cash and checks)
b. Accounts receivable clerk
c. General bookkeeper
Destroys other copies of advices and listings.

2. *Registration Clerk*

Receives three copies of completed registration forms from students.

Checks for counselor's or similar approval.

Records appropriate fee from official class catalog.

If completed properly, approves forms and sends students with registration forms to cashier.

If not completed properly, returns forms to student for follow-up and reapplication.

3. *Cashier*

Collects funds or forwards two copies of registration forms to billing clerk.

Records cash receipts in daily receipts record.

Prepares and makes daily deposits.

Forwards duplicate receipted deposit slips and daily receipts records to general bookkeeper.

Destroys copies of daily receipts records.

4. *Billing Clerk*

Receives two copies of registration form, prepares bill, and makes entries in registration (sales) journal.

Forwards copies of billings and registration forms to accounts receivable clerk and forwards copies of bill to general bookkeeper.

5. *Accounts Receivable Clerk*

Posts accounts receivable subsidiary ledger detailed accounts from remittance listings.

Matches billings and registration forms and posts accounts receivable subsidiary ledger detailed accounts.

6. *General Bookkeeper*

Journalizes and posts cash receipts and applicable registrations to general ledger.

Enters registration (sales) journal data in general ledger.

38. General Ledger Systems Design

The city of Opp recently established a city building maintenance department that provides services to other departments. Because this department charges for services based on the cost of providing the services, it computes depreciation on all machinery. Different methods are used to determine the depreciation of the machinery. For example, those assets used evenly throughout their life are depreciated using the straight-line method. Others are depreciated using accelerated methods. Opp has recently computerized their entire accounting system and would like your advice relating to property accounts.

Required:

  a. List information needed to account accurately for (1) acquisition, (2) depreciation, and (3) retirement of fixed assets.

  b. Recommend for Opp any procedures and controls that are characteristic of a strong asset acquisition system.

39. Subsidiary Ledgers

You have just been engaged to audit the financial statements of Phillips Broadcasting Station (PBS), founded recently by Anna Phillips. Ms. Phillips has experienced cash flow problems and several bills have become past due. Because Phillips feels "more pressure" from some vendors than from others, she has paid some in full, leaving entire balances to others unpaid. These vendors are becoming very angry and Phillips runs the risk of losing her credit privileges. Unfortunately, she has kept neither an accounts receivable nor an accounts payable subsidiary ledger, and thus is unsure how many vendors she owes and the balance of each.

Required:

    a. Explain to Phillips the need for accounts payable subsidiary ledgers.

    b. Assuming Phillips is installing a computerized system and would like to know the (1) balance due and (2) the due date for each vendor, identify the information needed.

40. General Ledger Controls

You have been engaged to audit College Bookstore, a bookstore located at State College. Having limited funds, the manager of the store hires beginning accounting students to handle this aspect of the operations. Because they are still learning accounting, many mistakes are made. For instance, when posting to the general ledger, one student credited notes payable for a purchase made on credit. In another instance, several transactions were posted twice, while a few were never posted. This resulted in accounts receivable being overstated and several expenses not being recognized.

    When performing the audit of accounts receivable, you note that it is overstated.

Required:

Explain to the manager several control procedures to ensure that all items are entered into the books, and also that transactions are entered only once.

41. Property Controls

Carter Mize has recently opened a corporation specializing in golf-related services. The corporation, Mize Inc., has a division that manufacturers golf equipment such as clubs, balls, and bags. Another division operates in a service industry specializing in golf lessons and golf camps.

    Mize Inc. recently purchased a plant and machinery for the manufacture of golf balls. Because the machinery was used, a major overhaul was needed. Mize also employs a maintenance staff for the practice of preventive maintenance.

Required:

Assume you are a systems analyst, describe to Mize the information needed to ensure that all items are either properly capitalized or properly expensed.

42. Property and General Ledger Controls

Select the best answer to each of the following questions. *(AICPA adapted)*

a. To achieve effective internal accounting control over fixed asset additions, a company should establish procedures that require:

(1) Capitalization of the cost of fixed asset additions in excess of a specific dollar amount

(2) Performance of recurring fixed asset maintenance work solely by maintenance department employees

(3) Classification as investments, those fixed asset additions that are not used in the business

(4) Authorization and approval of major fixed asset additions.

b. Which of the following is an internal accounting control weakness related to factory equipment:

(1) A policy exists requiring all purchases of factory equipment to be made by the department in need of the equipment.

(2) Checks issued in payment of purchases of equipment are not signed by the controller.

(3) Factory equipment replacements are generally made when estimated useful lives, as indicated in depreciation schedules, have expired.

(4) Proceeds from sales of fully depreciated equipment are credited to other income.

c. Which of the following is the most important internal control procedure over acquisitions of property, plant, and equipment:

(1) Establishing a written company policy distinguishing between capital and revenue expenditures

(2) Using a budget to forecast and control acquisitions and retirements

(3) Analyzing monthly variances between authorized expenditures and actual costs

(4) Requiring acquisitions to be made by user departments

d. Which of the following policies is an internal accounting control weakness related to the acquisition of factory equipment?

(1) Acquisitions are to be made through and approved by the department in need of the equipment.

(2) Advance executive approvals are required for equipment acquisitions.

(3) Variances between authorized equipment expenditures and actual costs are to be immediately reported to management.

(4) Depreciation policies are reviewed only once a year.

e. A company holds bearer bonds as a short-term investment. Custody of these bonds and submission of coupons for interest payments is normally the responsibility of the:

(1) Treasury function

(2) Legal counsel

(3) General accounting function

(4) Internal audit function

f. Operating control of the check-signing machine normally should be the responsibility of the:

(1) General accounting function
(2) Treasury function
(3) Legal counsel
(4) Internal audit function

g. Matching the supplier's invoice, the purchase order, and the receiving report normally should be the responsibility of the:

(1) Warehouse receiving function
(2) Purchasing function
(3) General accounting function
(4) Treasury function

CASES

43. From your study of the Apogee Company case (Appendix C), you no doubt observed that the company has no property control system and maintains very poor general ledger records. This is inexcusable, of course, particularly for a company of Apogee's size, which is on the threshold of tremendous physical growth and expansion.

Design a complete system for property control, making provision for the automatic generation of straight-line and accelerated depreciation for both internal reporting and tax purposes. Consider matters such as acquisition, costing, maintenance, location, and disposal of company-owned properties.

Also, develop a general ledger system designed to bring together all the accounting entries emanating from the several "operating" systems, along with special journalizations of nonroutine financial transactions.

44. Bubbling Stone does not have a formal property accounting system. Since the president's secretary monitors property accounts, comment on the possible problems of accuracy as related to calculating depreciation and property taxes.

SECTION

APPENDIXES

Banking Information Systems

When designing any accounting information system, one should examine a variety of factors. A properly designed system must recognize the objectives of the entity and incorporate them in the design of the system. Recognition of management information requirements, an understanding of the operating departments within the entity, an understanding of any unique industry accounting practices, and a determination of appropriate internal accounting controls constitute factors that should be taken into consideration when designing or analyzing the accounting information system of any organization.

To illustrate the importance of these factors in systems design and analysis, we present a brief discussion of their impact on the accounting information system. As stated previously, the first requirement of any valid accounting information system is a recognition of the objectives of the entity as they relate to the accounting information system.

The text emphasized the importance of internal controls on any well-designed accounting information system and the interrelationship between internal controls and the entity's structure. Obviously, these factors should also be recognized in the systems design of financial and public sector organizations as well as for-profit enterprises. The concept of internal control and its emphasis on safeguarding assets and properly recording transactions remain constant, regardless of the type of organization.

A SYSTEMS OVERVIEW FOR BANKING

Financial institutions have unique characteristics that impact on the systems design. Banks and other service institutions are a vital part of our economic system. In the United States, banks are generally profit-oriented. However, the banking environment includes certain restrictions and regulations imposed by state and federal regulatory authorities. A bank's accounting information system must not only aid in achieving its basic objectives but also incorporate those features necessary to comply with regulatory requirements.

ORGANIZATION

The organization of a bank depends on its functions and services. Most banks are divided into an operating division, a loan division, a business development division, and a financial division. If the bank offers trust services, a trust division is often established. A typical bank organization is shown in Figure A.1.

BANK ORGANIZATION.

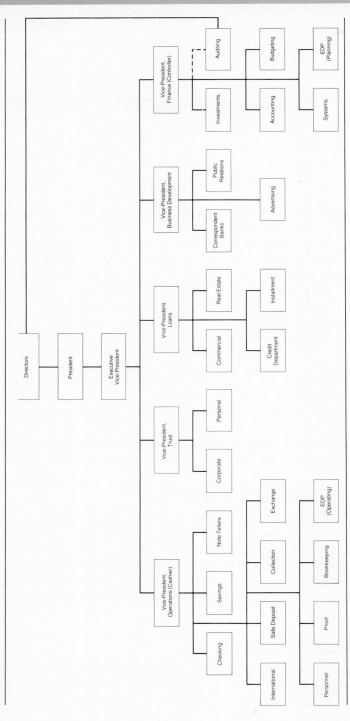

Source: *Introduction to Banks* (Cleveland, Ohio: Ernst and Whinney, 1976). By permission.

Figure A.1

The operating division directs the bank's operating methods and procedures and supervises the clerical personnel. Included in the operating division would be the tellers, the bookkeeping department, and the proof department. The proof department, unique to banks, represents the heart of the bank's operation. All paperwork flows through a properly planned proof department. By providing control totals the proof department allows the bank's other departments to balance daily. The flow of documents through the proof department is shown in Figure A.2.

The loan department invests the bank's funds in loans according to bank policy and supervises the lending activities of the bank. The business development division includes the functions of marketing, customer relations, and relations with other banks. The financial division maintains and supervises the bank's accounting and budgeting functions.

UNIQUE ACCOUNTING PRACTICES

Banks must comply with certain regulatory requirements and reporting practices. Those that are members of the Federal Reserve System are restricted as to the types of securities they may purchase and own. Other areas of unique accounting practice for banks include the computation of the reserve for loan losses, income tax requirements, capital debentures, reserves for contingencies, and classifications of certain Balance Sheet and Income Statement items.

MANAGEMENT INFORMATION REQUIREMENTS

Bank management needs a variety of reports and information for both external and internal purposes. Financial statements are often required by stockholders, the Securities and Exchange Commission, the Comptroller of the Currency, the Federal Reserve System, the Federal Deposit Insurance Corporation, and various state bank regulatory agencies.

For internal purposes, management needs a variety of reports to monitor and plan bank activities. In addition to the traditional reporting requirements of reliability and timeliness, reports for bank management must be quite frequent. The need for frequency is generated by the unique nature of bank activities, that is, frequent and often erratic activity by both depositors and loan customers.

Internal reports should include a variety of information reports on loan activity, demand deposit activity, interest rate fluctuations, average cash on hand, and average account size. Other management information requirements may include typical operational reports on payroll, property, and the general ledger as discussed in preceding chapters.

ACCOUNTING CONTROLS

Many aspects of bank accounting controls are unique. For example, almost every piece of paper utilized by a bank becomes a source document for the accounting entry. Such papers include checks, deposit slips, debit and credit memos, and notes.

DOCUMENT FLOW IN PROOF DEPARTMENT.

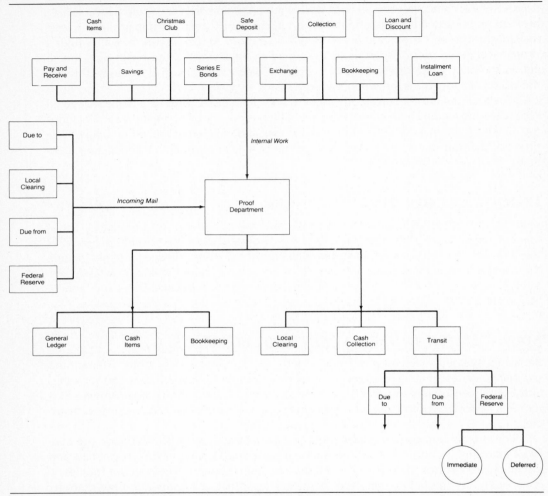

Source: *Introduction to Banks* (Cleveland, Ohio: Ernst and Whinney, 1976). By permission.

Figure A.2

These same pieces of paper generate another unique aspect of bank accounting. Banks process literally thousands of source documents each day. These same source documents often leave the bank in a few days. As a consequence, it is imperative that banks balance their books each day. If this procedure is not performed, it may be impossible to balance the books as a result of the thousands of transactions, many of which no longer remain as source documents.

Many of the assets of a bank are negotiable, including cash, bearer bonds, consigned travelers checks, consigned U.S. Savings Bonds, and collateral on secured loans. One of the most important accounting controls is the safeguarding of these many negotiable assets. The primary objectives of a bank's internal controls should be to promote dual controls over such negotiable assets and to fix responsibilities for recording transactions and maintaining assets.

A well-designed bank accounting information system should contain a variety of control elements. Important control features for banking include:

1. Segregating duties among personnel handling assets, recording transactions, and supervision
2. Rotating duties among employees
3. Requiring that every officer and employee of the bank take full, uninterrupted vacations so that transactions under the control of any one individual may clear
4. Exercising dual control over negotiable assets by requiring the authorization, approval, or action of two individuals to complete a transaction.
5. Establishing and maintaining a strong, well-staffed, and independent internal audit department.

SYSTEMS CONFIGURATION

Principles of systems analysis, design, and configuration do not vary significantly across types of business entities. Many of the procedures and systems configurations presented in earlier chapters are applicable to banking. Nonetheless, certain differences do exist between banking and business organizations.

These differences, of course, do have an impact on systems configuration. In the design and analysis of any system, the reader should apply the concepts presented in prior chapters but recognize the unique aspects of the organization under examination. To illustrate the application of these concepts, a review of the systems configurations in a manual system for one aspect of a bank's operations, commercial loans, is presented.

As illustrated in Figure A.3, the customer presents the approved note to the teller upon the issue date. The customer receives cash for the note and assigns the collateral to the bank. A receipt is issued for the collateral, the collateral is entered in the collateral register, and dual control over the collateral is maintained.

The note is filed in the vault, and a copy of the note goes to bookkeeping for posting in the note register and general ledger. The teller also prepares a maturity tickler. The maturity tickler includes all information on the note and is filed by due date. Thus, the tickler file indicates which notes and what amounts mature each day.

When the note is paid, the customer receives the "paid" note and collateral release in exchange for the note payment and collateral receipt. This transaction is also recorded in bookkeeping by postings to the note register and the general ledger.

Whether the system for commercial loans is manual or computerized, it is nonetheless a relatively straightforward systems application adopting basic systems principles in the unique environment of banking. Although other systems in banking may be somewhat more complex, the principles involved do not significantly differ.

COMMERCIAL LOAN SYSTEM.

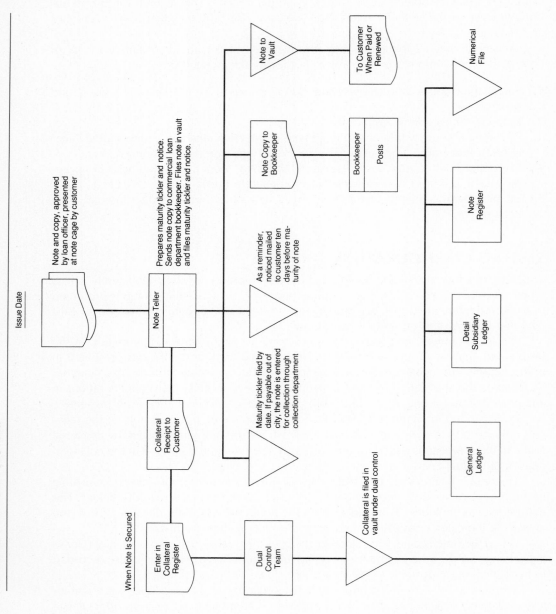

Issue Date

Note and copy, approved by loan officer, presented at note cage by customer

Note Teller

Prepares maturity tickler and notice. Sends note copy to commercial loan department bookkeeper. Files note in vault and files maturity tickler and notice.

Collateral Receipt to Customer

When Note Is Secured

Enter in Collateral Register

Dual Control Team

Collateral is filed in vault under dual control

Maturity tickler filed by date. If payable out of city, the note is entered for collection through collection department

As a reminder, noticed mailed to customer ten days before maturity of note

Note to Vault

To Customer When Paid or Renewed

Note Copy to Bookkeeper

Bookkeeper

Posts

General Ledger

Detail Subsidiary Ledger

Note Register

Numerical File

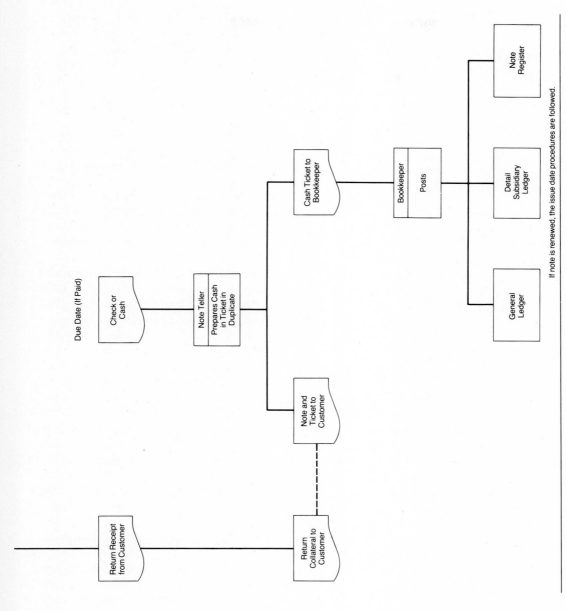

Due Date (If Paid)

Check or Cash

Note Teller Prepares Cash in Ticket in Duplicate

Cash Ticket to Bookkeeper

Bookkeeper Posts

Note Register

Detail Subsidiary Ledger

General Ledger

Note and Ticket to Customer

Return Collateral to Customer

Return Receipt from Customer

If note is renewed, the issue date procedures are followed.

Source: *Introduction to Banks* (Cleveland, Ohio, Ernst and Whinney, 1976).

Figure A.3

SUMMARY

This appendix has presented an overview of accounting information systems for banking. *Any* accounting system should be designed to meet management needs and accounting information requirements while recognizing any unique aspects of the company. Consequently, the unique characteristics of banks impact on their system's design. This appendix only skimmed the surface for banking accounting systems. However, the presentation should illustrate one salient point. Regardless of the type of industry, the need for accounting information systems and the principles underlying those systems still apply.

PROBLEMS

1. Dan Matt, a junior auditor for Kramp and Company, was assigned the responsibility of conducting a preliminary application review of a client bank's loan department operations.

    Dan had completed his flowchart and explanation of the loan process and turned it over to his senior. He was writing up his assessment of the process from his notes when his senior interrupted and asked what happened to the collateral received on loans. Dan recognized the significance of this omission and agreed to check it out right away.

    Collateral can be anything of value acceptable to the bank, but is typically some type of security. Dan found that customers turn over any collateral to their loan officer, who prepares and signs the next in sequence of a prenumbered four-part form, which describes the collateral and serves as a receipt. Each copy of the form is a different color to facilitate identification. The customer receives the original of the collateral receipt form, which is pink. The second or white copy of the form is sent directly to the collateral records clerk who logs it in. The loan officer takes the blue or third copy to the vault custodian along with the collateral. The final or yellow copy is canceled and discarded. The vault custodian compares the blue copy of the receipt with the collateral in the loan officer's presence. If they are in agreement, the vault custodian signs the blue copy. He then attaches a tag to the collateral, and carries it and the blue copy of the collateral receipt to the vault attendant. The vault attendant also compares the description on the blue copy with the tagged collateral. If they match, the vault attendant opens the vault and jointly with the vault custodian deposits the collateral therein. The vault attendant notes the location on the blue copy and signs it. The completed blue copy is then taken by the vault attendant to the collateral clerk. Until the blue copy is received, the collateral clerk keeps the unmatched white copy, filed numerically in a suspense file as a reminder for follow-up purposes.

    Upon receipt of the blue copy from the vault attendant, the collateral clerk compares it to the white copy that has been previously received directly from the loan officer. If the blue and white copies are in agreement, the collateral clerk completes the entry in the collateral register in numerical order. The white copy and the blue copy of the collateral receipt are placed in a permanent file by name. Any differences are resolved with the loan officer's assistance. *(Adapted from Touche Ross Foundation)*

Required:

a. Prepare a flowchart of the collateral receipt process and cross-reference it to the following list of procedures.

b. List any apparent weaknesses noted in the description of the collateral receipt process.

List of Procedures

CUSTOMER

1. Brings in collateral to loan officer
2. Receives receipt for collateral

LOAN OFFICER

3. Receives collateral from customer
4. Removes prenumbered four-part form from file
5. Completes form describing collateral and signs it
6. Gives pink copy to customer
7. Sends white copy to collateral clerk
8. Takes blue copy to vault custodian
9. Cancels and discards yellow copy
10. Takes collateral in sealed bag to vault custodian

VAULT CUSTODIAN

11. Receives blue copy of collateral receipt from loan officer
12. Receives collateral from loan officer
13. Reads description and instructions regarding collateral on blue copy
14. Compares collateral with blue copy
15. Signs blue copy
16. Gives blue copy to vault attendant
17. Opens vault jointly with vault attendant
18. Deposits collateral in vault

VAULT ATTENDANT

19. Receives blue copy from vault custodian
20. Compares blue copy to collateral being deposited
21. Assists vault custodian in opening vault
22. Signs blue copy upon witnessing deposit of collateral
23. Takes blue copy to collateral clerk

COLLATERAL CLERK

24. Receives white copy from loan officer
25. Makes entry in numerical sequence in log book
26. Holds white copy until later receipt of blue copy
27. Matches blue copy when received to white copy and notes appropriate signatures
28. Records deposit of collateral in collateral register
29. Files collateral receipt copies in permanent file

2. Dan Matt drew up a flowchart for the depositing of collateral (assignment 1) and turned it over to his senior. The senior inquired if collateral were only deposited and never withdrawn. Dan realized that he had not followed the collateral process through to its completion. He still had to investigate the withdrawal of collateral that resulted when the loan was paid.

Dan found that the customer initiates the withdrawal of collateral by presenting the pink receipt copy to the loan officer. The loan officer forwards the customer's request for return of his or her collateral to the collateral clerk, who prepares a prenumbered, four-part withdrawal form. Each copy of the form is a different color to facilitate its distribution. The original (pink) of the request is sent back to the loan officer, the second (blue) copy is sent to the vault custodian, and the third (white) copy is filed by the collateral clerk with the deposit form. Again, the yellow or fourth copy is discarded. The vault custodian takes the blue copy of the request to the vault attendant, and together they remove the collateral and match it against the request. If they match, both the vault custodian and the vault attendant sign the blue copy of the request. If they are not in agreement, the vault custodian contacts the loan officer to iron out the discrepancy. The signed blue copy is sent back to the loan officer accompanied by the collateral. The loan officer verifies that everything is proper and then signs the blue copy and turns the collateral over to the customer. The customer, after verifying that the collateral is correct, signs the pink copy of the request which had been on file with the loan officer. Then both the blue and the pink copies are returned to the collateral clerk. The collateral clerk matches the two copies of the request to the white copy in his file. If they are all in agreement, he or she then records the return of the collateral in the log, staples the copies together, and files them in the completed file by number. *(Adapted from Touche Ross Foundation)*

Required:

a. Prepare a flowchart of the collateral withdrawal process using the description given in the case.
b. List any apparent weaknesses in the collateral withdrawal process as described.

Hospital Information Systems

Another service type of organization that has been receiving increasing attention in recent years is hospitals. Like banking, discussed in Appendix A, hospitals require a different type of information system. In these organizations, information must be supplied continuously and all services must be kept up-to-date.

All information systems must necessarily reflect the characteristics of the organization. As noted in Chapter Nine, the macrosystem perspective for a service concern differs appreciably from that of a manufacturing organization. Systems should recognize the specific and unique attributes of the entity and be designed to aid in the achievement of entity objectives. Clearly, the objectives and environment in which a publicly owned hospital operates differ significantly from the objectives and environment of a steel manufacturer. Although such factors indicate that differences in systems design will emerge as a result of differences in organizations, certain common systems characteristics nonetheless exist.

The text has presented accounting information systems from the broad perspective. This appendix discusses systems in the context of a unique entity, and is an application of the broad foundations of accounting information systems presented in the text.

The first requirement of any valid accounting information system is a recognition of the objectives of the entity as they relate to the accounting information system. For government and nonprofit entities, the basic objective of accounting is the production of timely, accurate, pertinent, and fairly presented financial statements and reports for use by management, legislative officials, the general public, and others having the need for public financial information.[1] Management information requirements for such entities are often broad and varied. In addition to traditional external reporting requirements, there may be statutory requirements for these entities to publish certain other types of reports in newspapers.

Systems design for a governmental entity (many hospitals are in this category) must incorporate the special features unique to governmental accounting. The concepts of funds, budgets, and encumbrances must therefore be an integral part of the accounting information system for a governmental unit.

Regardless of organizational structure, many hospitals have difficulty defining their goals and objectives. Whereas the professional goal is probably to improve a person's health, other goals may be anomalous. The concept of making a profit is taboo in many types of hospitals, although they are constantly seeking outside funds. Most hospitals also need a goal more definite than just "trying to break even." Measures of efficiency and effectiveness need to be established. This can be accomplished by measuring the cost of specific services, such as pediatrics, evaluating statistics, such as the nurse-to-patient ratio, and controlling labor costs by minimizing overtime hours. Hospital administrators need to be aware of the possibilities that accounting information systems can provide and be willing to commit to measuring and evaluating both financial and nonfinancial information.

A SYSTEMS OVERVIEW FOR HOSPITALS

Hospitals are the most significant component of health care facilities in our society. Although hospitals have medical care as their main purpose, they often serve as educational institutions for training nurses and physicians. The American Hospital Association has defined a hospital as

> [a]n establishment that provides—through an organized medical or professional staff, permanent facilities that include inpatient beds, medical services, and continuous nursing services—diagnosis and treatment for patients.[2]

Hospitals may be divided into two classifications on the basis of ownership: governmental and nongovernmental. Governmental hospitals include those operated by the federal, state, and local governments. Nongovernmental hospitals may be further categorized as either profit or not-for-profit facilities. Many not-for-profit hospitals are owned and operated by religious groups. Profit hospitals, often called proprietary or investor-owned hospitals, have been traditionally owned by the physicians who staff them. There has been a recent trend, however, toward hospital ownership by publicly held companies. Like other profit institutions, proprietary hospitals are subject to federal and state income taxes.

Hospital systems requirements vary according to ownership. For example, since proprietary hospitals must file reports with their shareholders and possibly the Securities and Exchange Commission, their accounting systems must be designed to meet these particular reporting requirements. Alternatively, a city-owned hospital must have an accounting system that produces reports that are compatible with the city's accounting report format and with certain federal requirements.

Regardless of the type of ownership, all hospitals have certain unique accounting problems and follow a specific set of accounting principles. To facilitate presentation, a not-for-profit hospital is assessed in the following discussion.

Hospitals must provide reports to a variety of constituencies. The accounting system must provide reports for management, the owners (in this case, the religious organization), federal and state governments (for Medicare, Medicaid, etc.), and private third-party payers (e.g. Blue Cross/Blue Shield). Thus, hospitals are highly complex organizations that must not only perform vital health services, but must also interact with a variety of other private and public entities. As a consequence, the hospital is an appropriate vehicle for presentation of a systems overview for an organization in the public sector.

ORGANIZATION

The organization of a hospital is to some degree dependent on the extent of services provided by the hospital. Some hospitals are primarily clinic-type operations; others offer a full range of services from operating therapy and laboratory services through radiology, nurseries, and electrocardiology. The presentation in this section assumes that the hospital offers a wide range of medical services.

An organization chart for such a hospital is shown in Figure B.1. In this chart, the hospital is divided into numerous divisions. Nursing services represent the administrative units for the supervision of the various nursing units: operating rooms, recovery rooms, delivery rooms, surgical units, and newborn nursery. The general services office represents the administrative unit for hospital ancillary functions: dietary services, cafeterias, housekeeping, laundry and linen, and medical records. Fiscal services supervises such functions as accounting and admitting. Other divisions of the hospital include pharmacy, personnel, and purchasing.

UNIQUE ACCOUNTING PRACTICES

Hospitals have traditionally utilized a fund accounting approach for recording transactions. Although similar to accounting for various governmental units, hospital accounting differs substantially from accounting for the vast array of manufacturing, retail, and service companies. To analyze or design an accounting information system for any organization, a person must understand the accounting techniques and procedures that apply to that organization.

One special characteristic of hospital accounting is the classification of revenues. Most hospitals receive three types of revenues: *patient service revenue, other operating revenue, and nonoperating revenue.* Patient service revenue is the largest component of hospital revenue, and is discussed in the next paragraph. Other operating revenue is derived from day-to-day activities indirectly related to patient care and includes sources such as tuition and student fees from hospital educational programs, rental revenue from hospital properties, proceeds from cafeteria sales, and revenues from shops, newsstands, parking lots, and other service facilities. Nonoperating revenue is unrelated to day-to-day activities and includes revenue such as unrestricted gifts, income from endowment funds, and other miscellaneous revenues.

Patient service revenues fall into two categories: routine service and ancillary services. Routine patient services, also referred to as general or daily patient care, include items such as patient rooms, patients meals, and regular nursing care. Ancillary or special nursing services include items such as the operating room, delivery room, recovery room, laboratory tests, and radiology tests. These services are unique in that they originate by a written order from the patient's physician.

Ancillary services may be further classified as either inpatient or outpatient services.

HOSPITAL ORGANIZATION CHART.

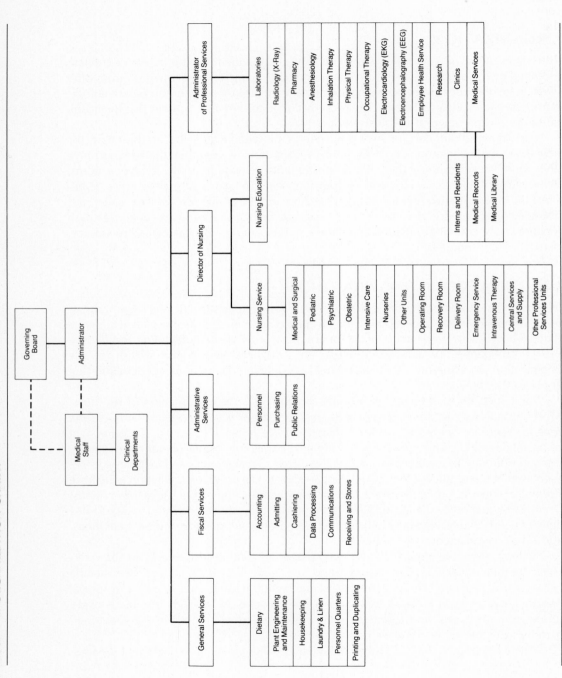

Source: *Introduction to Hospitals* (Cleveland, Ohio: Ernst and Whinney, 1978). By permission.

Figure B.1

Inpatients are those who are given lodging while receiving hospital services: Outpatients are those who receive hospital services but are not lodged in the hospital. The ancillary services to outpatients include emergency room (note that a patient may be admitted to the hospital later as an inpatient) and clinical services.

Hospital accounting represents a subclassification of fund accounting. However, hospital accounting recognizes only two basic types of funds: unrestricted and restricted. These funds are self-contained accounting entities that account for a specific activity or project. Unrestricted funds include all assets and related liabilities over which the hospital governing authority has discretionary power. Restricted funds are those on which the donor has placed limitations on the use of the principal or income or both.

Owing to the nature of hospital services, they must make claims to various third-party payers for services. Specifically, most patients do not pay directly for the services they receive. Rather, their insurance company (e.g., Blue Cross/Blue Shield), or some other organization (e.g., Medicare or Medicaid), reimburses the hospital for these charges. Since these third-party payers generally are the major component of hospital receipts, it is imperative that the accounting system be designed to handle these billings and payments properly and promptly.

The reporting requirements of these third-party payers usually influence the hospital's record-keeping procedures. For example, some third-party payers pay on the basis of costs, not charges. Using these cost-based formulas requires significant amounts of underlying cost data. Data typically needed in these cost-based formulas are occupancy rates, type of patients, average length of confinement, and costs of providing services to particular groups of patients.

Hospitals may use different accounting methods for third-party payer cost reimbursement purposes and financial reporting purposes (e.g., depreciation methods). This procedure is similar to an industrial concern using different accounting methods for income tax purposes and financial reporting purposes. The accounting entries relating to these timing differences are parallel. When items are accounted for in different periods for reimbursement and financial reporting purposes, the effect of the resultant timing differences must be recognized in the financial statements.

Another unique situation with most hospitals, and other service-oriented organizations, is the inability to measure the quality, and often quantity, of output with some standard. Outputs from a hospital could be defined as patients being (1) in a worse condition than when they entered, (2) in the same condition as when they entered, and (3) in a better condition than when they entered. From these alternatives it would be difficult to set standards and measure the variances. Without standards measurement, a primary evaluation tool of the accounting information system is missing, and in the case of hospitals, the professional medical staff must evaluate the outputs by using other measures.

MANAGEMENT INFORMATION REQUIREMENTS

Hospitals require a wide variety of internal and external reports. Management needs a variety of internal reports to manage the hospital effectively and efficiently. These could include data on patient days, occupancy rates, revenue by special service centers, and nurse-to-patient ratios. Such reports can show cost and revenue analyses that have been generated through the accounting system. Patient days typically represent one of the most important hospital statistics. This statistic is used for internal reporting and control purposes, and often plays a critical role in cost determination for cost reports to third-party payers.

ACCOUNTING CONTROLS

Accounting controls for hospitals do not differ significantly from accounting controls for other types of organizations as discussed in the text. Certainly, the concepts behind these controls remain constant. Of course, controls over any system should recognize the unique characteristics of the organization. Appropriately designed accounting controls for hospital accounting systems possess the characteristics that are basic to all sound systems of internal control while recognizing the unique accounting attributes. These characteristics are proper segregation of duties, clear lines of authority and responsibility, proper documentation and authorization, and competent personnel.

Because of the significant impact of third-party payers, it is important that the hospital account for expenses on a departmental basis. Thus accounting controls for hospitals as compared with those for a manufacturer are designed with a greater emphasis on proper departmental cost accounting.

Accounting controls for hospitals also place a heavy emphasis on controlling costs. Since most hospital rate structures are based on budgeted costs, these budgeted costs should be maintained. The rising costs of health care and the resultant government threat of "cost controls" provide further evidence of the need for accounting controls over costs.

The primary costs incurred by hospitals are payroll expenses, fees to doctors and other professionals, and supplies expense. Many hospitals also have severe problems with bad debts, which are especially difficult to control with outpatients for whom the hospital must frequently provide service on an emergency basis. As a consequence, accounting controls over these aspects of a hospital's operations are most important. Although hospitals emphasize controls over these areas, the principles supporting these controls do not significantly differ from those in institutions other than hospitals. Although the control environment and areas emphasized may differ by industry, good control principles do not vary.

SYSTEMS CONFIGURATION

Concepts supporting systems design, analysis, and configuration do not vary between types of organizations. However, the environment in which these systems operate does vary, as noted in the discussions on accounting practice and management information requirements.

Several companies that specialize in health care information systems have developed computer applications for hospitals. Because of the size of most hospitals, these systems have been primarily for minicomputer and microcomputer configurations. The patient accounting applications of these computerized information systems typically are:

1. *Daily account management.* This includes a daily operating summary of each patient, updates accounts receivable, and provides an aging analysis of account.
2. *Insurance control.* A subsystem that provides each patient's payment method, amount of third-party coverage, and insurance and medicare claim forms preparation.
3. *Revenue analysis.* This subsystem provides daily revenues earned by category, patient, doctor, or other predetermined classification.
4. *General accounting.* All necessary reports are provided including general ledger balances, income statements, accounts payable ledgers, payroll, and inventory.
5. *Statistical reports.* Standard and special reports are prepared on vital statistics of the hospital, including items such as patient days per month, nurses-to-patients ratio, average stay per patient, and average revenue generated per patient.

To illustrate the application of accounting systems concepts to a unique hospital situation, Figure B.2 characterizes a design for hospital admissions. As shown in the chart, hospital admissions are initiated by the patient, usually through a doctor's referral. The admissions office has the patient complete a registration history form, which includes patient personal and financial data and information on insurance and billings.

A copy of this form is sent to the proper department for credit approval and should be returned to admissions prior to formal admission of the patient. Admissions also completes forms on billings and assigns accommodations and patient numbers. After all forms have been completed and credit has been approved, the patient is admitted to the hospital. The admissions office also prepares daily census reports regarding admissions, discharges, and transfers. This report is forwarded to accounting, where it is used in the reconciliation of the daily census from nursing services and in the compilation of various management reports as discussed previously.

The admissions systems represents only one aspect of the accounting information system for hospitals. The principles and concepts involving other systems do not differ significantly. Although other systems such as billings and collection, cash control, pharmacy, purchases, and personnel are not discussed, design and analysis of these systems are similar to the systems presentation in earlier chapters.

NOTES

[1]National Committee on Governmental Accounting, *Governmental Accounting, Auditing, and Financial Reporting* (Chicago: Municipal Finance Officers Association, 1968), p. 14.

[2]*Classification of Health Care Institutions,* American Hospital Association, (Chicago: American Hospital Association, 1976), p. 5.

PROBLEMS

1. An analysis of the patient accounts function reveals that, under the current billing system, accounts are held for 3 days after discharge so that late charges and credits may be posted. The analysis also indicates that the unbilled accounts are broken down in the following manner:

	Number of Accounts Unbilled			
Principal Payer	**Awaiting Diagnosis**	**Benefits Missing**	**Ready to Bill**	**Other**
Medicare	40	83	285	24
Blue Cross	52	76	141	27
Welfare	36	82	115	28
Commercial Insurance	38	26	197	22
Self-pay	—	—	53	27
	166	267	791	128
Average number of days behind on billing (at 40 discharges per day)	4	7	20	3

(FHFMA adapted)

Required:

    a. Prepare a brief description of the situation for the administration.

    b. Establish a list of priorities to handle the problem areas in the accounts receivable section.

    c. Outline the corrective actions to be taken, giving particular attention to (1) the number of accounts ready to bill and (2) the normal billing activities.

    d. Explain the steps you feel should be taken to prevent a recurrence of this situation.

2. Even though not-for-profit organizations do not have profit-oriented goals and objectives, they do have incentives for efficient and effective operations. Discuss some of the characteristics of profit-oriented organizations that should be found in not-for-profit organizations.

Required:

Which characteristic would you rank as the most important for a not-for-profit organization? Why?

3. St. Mary's Hospital has just been bought by a group of investors who intend to convert it from a religious to a proprietary hospital. The hospital currently operates with a manual accounting information system although it has 500 beds and averages 400 patients per day. The religious order is selling the hospital because of the tremendous losses that it had been incurring in recent years, even though it had reduced to a minimum the number of patients it admitted who could make no or only partial payments on their accounts.

    The investor group hired a consulting firm to evaluate the hospital before the purchase and several important facts were found that led them to their decision. The hospital had an excellent location in a growing city and was supported by several large medical associations with good reputations. The billing system was

FLOWCHART OF HOSPITAL ADMISSIONS.

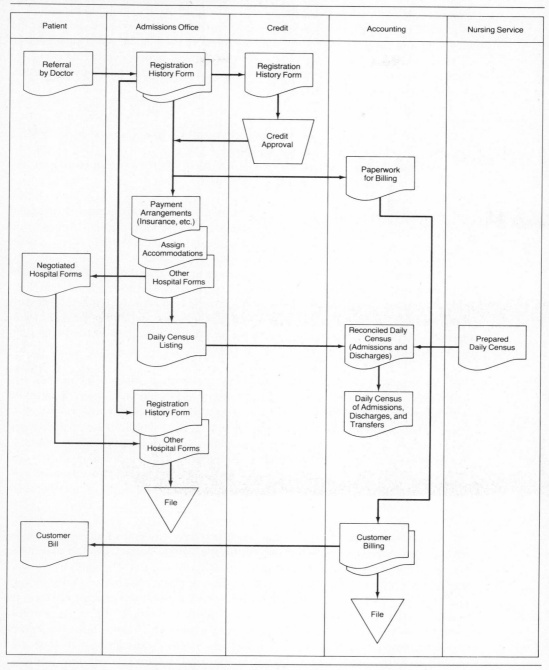

Source: *Introduction to Hospitals* (Cleveland, Ohio: Ernst and Whinney, 1978). By permission.

Figure B.2

always several weeks late in sending statements to third-party insurers, with an average collection period of 86 days from the date of patient discharge. The personnel management system was found to have inefficient managers who did little planning, resulting in considerable overtime for the nursing staff. The inventory system was also found to be weak with few controls over anything but drugs. At the date of purchase the inventory was very large because the previous administrator never wanted to be out of anything.

Required:

a. What should be the goals and objectives of the new owners? State specific items that they could use for objectives.

b. List several steps the new owners can take to improve the operating procedures in the accounting information system.

4. The Aaron County Hospital is located in a popular summer resort area. The population of the area doubles during the summer months (May through August) and hospital activity more than doubles. Although the hospital is small, it has a well-trained medical staff and support of the local physicians.

An administrator was employed a year ago to improve the business operations of the hospital. Among the new activities he started was responsibility accounting. This program was introduced along with quarterly cost reports supplied to department heads. Previously, cost data were presented to department heads infrequently. Excerpts from the announcement and the report received by the laundry supervisor follow.

The hospital has adopted a responsibility accounting system. From now on you will receive quarterly reports comparing the costs of operating your department with budgeted costs. The reports will highlight the differences (variations) so that you can zero in on the departures from budgeted costs. (This is called management by exception.) Responsibility accounting means you are accountable for keeping the costs in your department within the budget. The variations from the budget will help you identify what costs are out of line, and the size of the variations will indicate which ones are the most important. Your first such report accompanies this announcement.

The annual budget for 19X8 was constructed by the new administrator. Quarterly budgets were computed as one fourth the annual budget. The administrator compiled the budget from analysis of the prior 3 years' costs. The analysis showed that all costs increased each year, with more rapid increases between the second and third years. He considered establishing the budget at an average of the prior 3 year's costs, hoping that the installation of the system would reduce costs to this level. However, in view of the rapidly increasing prices, he finally chose 19X5 costs less 3 percent for the 19X8 budget. The activity level measured by patient days and pounds of laundry processed was set at the 19X5 volume, which was approximately equal to the volume of each of the past 3 years. *(IMA adapted)*

PERFORMANCE REPORT—LAUNDRY DEPARTMENT
JULY—SEPTEMBER 19X8

	Budget	Actual	(Over) Under Budget	Percentage (Over) Under Budget
Patient days	9,500	11,900	(2,400)	(25)
Pounds of laundry	125,000	156,000	(31,000)	(25)
Costs				
Laundry labor	$ 9,000	$12,500	$(3,500)	(39)
Supplies	1,100	1,875	(775)	(70)
Water	1,700	2,500	(800)	(47)
Maintenance	1,400	2,200	(800)	(57)
Supervisor's salary	3,150	3,750	(600)	(19)
Allocated costs	4,000	5,000	(1,000)	(25)
Equipment depreciation	1,200	1,250	(50)	(4)
	$21,550	$29,075	$(7,525)	(35)

Required:
- **a.** Comment on the method used to construct the budget.
- **b.** What information should be communicated by variations from budgets?
- **c.** Recast the budget to reflect responsibility accounting, assuming the following:
  - **(1)** Laundry labor, supplies, water, and maintenance are variable costs. The remaining costs are fixed.
  - **(2)** Actual prices are expected to be approximately 20 percent above the levels in the budget prepared by the hospital administrator.

Case Study: Apogee Equipment Company

The facts, figures, and circumstances reflected in the following case are based on an actual situation. All names and quantitative data have been sufficiently camouflaged to preclude any possible identification or association with any existing company, past or present.

The Apogee case provides an excellent opportunity for students to visualize a large and growing industrial complex, perhaps similar to one in their own hometown, that has outgrown its beginnings and stands desperately in need of both organizational and systems development assistance. As is usually the case, unfortunately, such assistance must come from outside the company.

Accountants are consistently engaged in situations like Apogee, and are expected to somehow diagnose all the problems, identify critical information, cast it in an understandable form, and make helpful criticisms, comments, and suggestions to management. Clearly, in the Apogee case, an accountant would have much to say about the inadequacy of current operating procedures in the light of impending large-scale growth.

Amidst all the operational and systemic disarray inherent in Apogee, an accountant should be able to visualize the individual centers of voluminous business activity called *systems.* His or her training should suggest the necessary documents (called objective, verifiable evidence), the information flows, the controls, and perhaps even the technology (equipment and methods) for processing vital data into refined management information. Finally, the accountant should be able to prescribe an orderly arrangement of the elements of the systems so that ordinary operators, following specific procedures, could operate the systems effectively and efficiently.

We feel that the best use can be made of the case by requiring students to design specific information systems for Apogee as they are discussed in the text. That is, beginning with Chapter Ten, members of the class should be prepared to create an adequately sophisticated *procurement* system to handle Apogee's current and growth problems in purchasing. Intelligent assumptions concerning computers and other systems equipment will of course be necessary.

In subsequent chapters, systems to handle receiving, accounts payable, inventory, and other functional areas can be designed for Apogee as they are discussed. In the end, the student will have achieved an in-depth understanding of all the major systems functions in a company, and, perhaps more importantly, will have simulated hands-on experience in designing solutions to real-life systems problems.

The case question at the end of later chapters directs the student to apply what he or she has learned in that chapter to solving Apogee's problem.

As a general assignment the case can be used for any of the following requirements.

Possible Requirements

I. Analyze each function of the company and describe its strengths and weaknesses.
II. Flowchart the following functions as they currently exist:
  A. Purchasing
  B. Accounts payable
III. Develop the following systems for Apogee (manual or computerized):
  A. Procurement
  B. Raw materials (receiving, inspection, storage, and disbursement)
  C. Accounts payable
  D. Production control
  E. Payroll
  F. Marketing and shipping
  G. Sales and accounts receivable
  H. Cash
IV. Develop an integrated computer system for the company including as a minimum the following functions:
  A. Purchasing
  B. Accounts payable
  C. Payroll
  D. Sales and accounts receivable
V. Design or redesign the necessary documents for the various functions of the company.

FIRM HISTORY

The Apogee Equipment Company was formed in the mid-1960s at a time when the nation was engaged in the most massive road construction project ever undertaken—the national network of interstate highways. The company was the brainchild of Worth A. Wadd, an innovative mechanical engineering genius whose experience and interest in road construction, surfacing, and resurfacing problems drove him relentlessly toward the discovery of better methods.

As any good scientist might do, he kept a list (in priority sequence) of problems that begged for solutions. He recalled his own queuing problems associated with keeping the pavers continuously supplied. Limited-capacity dump trucks had to be scheduled in a sort of reverse queue to permit backing up and dumping their load into the pavers. The line could not be too long or the temperature of the hot mix would fall below the critical point. Driver time wasted while waiting in line always rankled Mr. Wadd. But the most frustrating problems came when trucks disgorged their hot and messy burdens into the asphalt spreaders, spilling generous quantities on road shoulders and adjacent completed lanes and requiring removal by manual methods. Also fresh in Wadd's memory were the steeply inclined curves in mountainous terrain where top-heavy trucks often overturned during the dumping process, causing considerable waste, delay, damage to equipment, and risk to personnel.

Wadd was determined to design and build a line of more effective and efficient road-surfacing equipment. His fertile mind envisioned a vehicle with a lower center of gravity, which would carry about three times the payload of the ordinary dump truck. It would be independent of the power unit (cab) and would have an easy coupling device to facilitate maneuvering. As an integral part of the system, he designed a portable heating unit to keep the hot mix at precisely the right temperature for spreading and rolling. The problems in dumping were overcome by a built-in conveyer system to disembark the material in metered quantities, thus eliminating costly overspills.

Most important, Mr. Wadd felt he could manufacture his vehicle for about one third the cost of a new dump truck. Using one power unit to transport the three carrying units, contractors could move *nine* times the quantity of asphalt normally moved by three dump trucks. This procedure would not only produce a better road surface, but would allow contractors to reduce investment in equipment by one third while cutting operating expenses by about one half.

Mr. Wadd carefully designed his model and selectively explored his ideas with influential friends in the concrete, sand, gravel, and asphalt businesses. They were impressed and enthusiastic. It was not difficult for Wadd to promote, organize, and arrange financial backing for the company. As president and majority stockholder, he immediately began production of the prototype, which had become affectionately known as the Spread-Man.

Spread-Man was demonstrated successfully in several regions of the country and encountered immediate market demand. Mr. Wadd rented an abandoned warehouse complex near a rail spur in a large midwestern city. He employed a small group of skilled metal workers and began handcrafting Spread-Man for specific orders on a first-come first-served basis.

In the meantime, Wadd continued to experiment with other ideas, paramount among which is a "street renewer," with which he expects to revolutionize the maintenance of potholed city streets. Apogee Company is given an excellent rating in consumer testimonials and expects to grow rapidly in the years ahead.

ORGANIZATION AND OPERATION

After 10 years of operations beginning in 1976, Apogee was producing at the rate of 147 units of Spread-Man per year. Although the company had grown considerably in terms of capital investment and number of employees, its basic modus operandi had not changed perceptibly by 1986. Mr. Wadd continued to manage most aspects of the company personally, occasionally to the dismay of two bright young men he hired to help him in the production and marketing areas. Although he was a charming and considerate man with a capacious mind and an insatiable appetite for work, many employees felt that his interests were so strongly focused on experimentation and invention that he seriously delayed the production process with his incessant "tinkering." His occasional incursions into the shop area to divert labor, parts, and materials to his experimental operations kept the shop in some distress and imposed on the labor force a considerable amount of unpopular weekend overtime.

Officially, the structure of the company's organization is quite simple, as shown in Figure C.1. The office operation consists of a conglomerate of loosely coordinated but vital functions including customer accounts management, supplier accounts management, payroll and timekeeping, cash handling and recording, general bookkeeping, and warranty service. Persons in appointed and/or assumed leadership positions constantly flow in and out of the office area. Office personnel summon employees to the telephone by yelling the message or relaying it through someone nearby. Persons on the phone casually leaf through stacks of papers and company documents in search of needed information to respond to telephone inquiries.

In general, the impression is one of hectic, sincere, responsible, but uncoordinated activity. All the accounting functions are performed by two employees. One is a fairly young, intelligent (though untrained), and personable woman who demonstrates a "take charge" attitude. She manages to create a measure of order out of what would otherwise be chaos. The other is a middle-aged, somewhat experienced but self-trained, "bookkeeper-type" man. Although he is responsible and hardworking, his grasp of fundamental accounting principles and controls is shallow at best. Together, they perform the payroll, keep employee time, order the production and office materials, prepare the supplier invoices for payment (usually *after* discounts are lost), compute the taxes, respond to

**APOGEE EQUIPMENT COMPANY
ORGANIZATION CHART.**

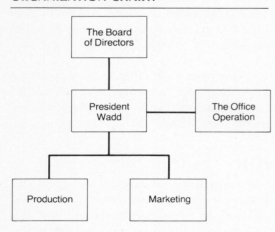

Figure C.1

telephone inquiries, and put together information such as Mr. Wadd and his two managers need for decision making.

Production and marketing, although distinct operations, appear to function homogeneously. Very little of the business communications, even on technical matters, is put into writing. The company uses no preprinted forms other than for shipping and invoicing. There is no production paperwork and no evidence of formal inventory records.

FINANCIAL STATUS

At July 31, 1986, the company's financial statements reflected a current-period loss of $24,000 and an accumulated retained earnings deficit of about $345,000. The company has no long-term debt. Rather, it operates largely through borrowing on short-term notes. The working capital ratio had improved by mid-1986 to a respectable 1-to-1, but the acid-test analysis reflected an alarming 1-to-3 ratio. Understandably, this condition of not being able to meet maturing debt requirements occasioned the decision to employ a management consulting firm to study the company's operations and recommend financial solutions.

The company followed the practice of calling in a local CPA once a year to help prepare financial statements. Since the engagement required no audit work, the auditor did not express any professional opinions concerning the statement contents. The statements therefore reflected the best information the office personnel could provide at the time. Although they reflected numerous inconsistencies in accounting procedures and principles, the statements were believed to be reasonably complete and accurate.

Copies of the comparative Balance Sheets for 1985 and the first seven months of 1986 are presented in Figure C.2. Also shown in the following pages are the Income Statement, Statement of Changes in Financial Position, and other related schedules (see Figures C.3 through C.8). These statements have all been reconstructed by the consulting firm.

PRODUCTION OPERATIONS

The production operation, although seemingly organized and effective in a physical sense, follows absolutely no systematic cost accumulation pattern. In fact, when asked what a Spread-Man cost to build, Mr. Wadd responded, "I don't know, but you can get that from our purchase contracts and payroll."

The production process flows in somewhat the pattern illustrated in Figure C.9. The major phases are:

1. Wheel and axle parts and assemblies are subcontracted. Reasonable quantities are stored in an area adjacent to the initial production line position. The carriage assembly originates at this point. Very little cutting or welding is required in this operation, and no waste results except in cases where defective materials and parts are detected. These are promptly returned to suppliers for modification, replacement, or credit. The major emphasis here is quite naturally on strength and alignment.

APOGEE EQUIPMENT COMPANY
COMPARATIVE BALANCE SHEETS
OCTOBER 31, 1985 AND JULY 31, 1986

	Oct. 31, 1985	July 31, 1986	Changes (9 Months)
Assets			
Current Assets:			
Cash	$ 2,336	$ 3,603	$ 1,267 +
Accounts Receivable	2,468	88,091	85,623 +
Inventories	119,368	336,287	216,919 +
Prepaid Expenses	11,249	11,517	268 +
Property and Equipment:			
Total per Statements (Net)	55,943	158,385	102,442 +
Other Assets:			
Project Development Costs	39,737	39,737	-0-
Patents	201,106	185,543	15,563 —
Distributorship	-0-	20,000	20,000 +
Deposits	10	1,871	1,861 +
Total Assets	$ 432,217	$ 845,034	$ 412,817 +
Liabilities			
Current Liabilities:			
Notes Payable	$ 214,279	$ 360,954	$ 146,675 +
Accounts Payable	70,999	231,171	160,172 +
Advances from Officers	-0-	2,179	2,179 +
Accrued Expenses	33,601	22,664	10,937 —
Other Liabilities:			
Advances on Stock Purchases	25,000	-0-	25,000 —
Long-Term Debt:			
None	-0-	-0-	-0-
Total Liabilities	$ 343,879	$ 616,968	$ 273,089 +
Stockholders' Equity			
Common Stock	$ 341,500	$ 441,500	$ 100,000 +
Less Treasury Stock	(137,700)	(23,480)	(114,220) —
Donated Capital	205,013	154,908	50,105 —
Total Capital Contributed	$ 408,813	$ 572,928	$ 164,115 +
Retained Earnings (Deficit)	(320,475)	(344,862)	(24,387) +
Total Equity	$ 88,338	$ 228,066	$ 139,728 +
Total Liabilities and Equity	$ 432,217	$ 845,034	$ 412,817 +

Figure C.2

2. The second operation is the most visible, and perhaps the most critical since it involves the cutting, forming, and welding of very heavy and expensive sheet metal stock. Use of acetylene cutting torches makes the operation dangerous and seemingly inefficient. Waste metal scraps and other assorted debris litter the area. The

APOGEE EQUIPMENT COMPANY
INCOME STATEMENT
FOR PERIOD ENDED JULY 31, 1986

Sales (94 Units)	$ 1,078,504		100.0%
Less Sales Returns & Allowances (2 Units)	22,759		2.0%
Net Sales		$ 1,055,745	98.0%
Less Cost of Goods Sold (Schedule A)		$ 797,319	73.9%
Gross Profit on Sales		$ 258,426	23.9%
Less Operating Expenses:			
Selling Expenses (detailed elsewhere)	121,000		11.2%
Administrative Expenses (detailed elsewhere)	93,636		8.7%
Total Operating Expenses		214,636	19.9%
Net Income from Operations		$ 43,790	4.0%
Other Income and Expenses:			
Interest Expense	(15,745)		(1.4%)
Royalties	(52,432)		(4.8%)
Net Increase or (Decrease)		(68,177)	(6.3%)
Net Income (Loss) Before Estimated Income Tax		(24,387)	(2.2%)
Less Estimated Income Tax		NONE	
Net Income After Income Tax		($24,387)	(2.2%)

Figure C.3

workmen in this shop area are the highest paid among the production employees—and appear to be the most temperamental and dissatisfied. Emerging from this area is the completed superstructure of the vehicle, prepared in every dimension to receive the more complicated accoutrements essential to its purpose.
3. The third stop on the assembly line facilitates the mounting and installation of special fittings, hydraulics, sprockets, conveyor belts, heating elements, and the like. Although rather precise engineering measurements and techniques are practiced, some special "tailoring" is occasionally required at this point.
4. The last stage of the manufacturing process is the finishing, testing, and painting operations. The company uses a standard one-color finish but will apply decals and other special markings upon specific instructions of the customer. From this point the Spread-Man exits the production area and is temporarily stored near a railroad siding for periodic loading and shipping.

Apogee is a quality-oriented company. However, complaints inevitably come from field operations where construction companies experiment with the units beyond their design capability. Such complaints have focused on the need for more thickness and

SCHEDULE A
STATEMENT OF COST OF GOODS SOLD
FOR PERIOD ENDED JULY 31, 1986

Direct Materials:			
Raw Materials Inventory (Beginning)		$ 19,896	
(1) Purchases and Freight-in	652,947		
Less Returns and Allowances (Discount)	1,716	651,231	
Materials Available for Use		671,127	
Less Materials Inventory (Ending)		121,267	
Direct Materials Consumed			$549,860
(2) **Direct Labor:**			54,032
Factory Overhead:			
Factory Supplies		25,442	
Patent Amortization		15,562	
Vacation and Holidays		1,429	
Payroll Taxes (Factory)		9,389	
Overtime Premium		5,532	
Indirect Materials		8,482	
Indirect (Variable) Labor		1,168	
Freight-out		1,550	
Shipping Supplies		53	
Warranty Expense		7,625	
Rework Expense		2,762	
Factory Supervision		25,371	
Storeroom and Shipping		8,888	
Other Factory Payroll Benefits		24,814	
Bonus Expense		29,788	
Rent—Factory		6,708	
Telephone—Factory		1,048	
Utilities—Factory		2,184	
Depreciation—Factory		5,411	
Machine Repair and Rental		2,379	
Janitorial Services		3,455	
Expendable Tools		5,241	
Other Factory Expenses		4,148	
Total Factory Overhead		198,429	
(3) Less Decrease in Finished Goods Inventory			
Attributable to Factory Overhead		24,505	173,924
Total Manufacturing Costs			777,816
Add Work-in-Process Inventory (Beginning) (Units)		None	
(4) Add Inventory Costs Transferred by Inventory			
Adjustment		135,051	135,051
Total			912,867
Less Work-in-Process Inventory (Ending) (12 Units)			79,968
Cost of Goods Manufactured—Completed			832,899
Add Finished Goods Inventory (Beginning) (11 Units)			99,471
Total			932,370
Less Finished Goods Inventory (Ending) (18 Units)			135,051
Cost of Goods Sold (Income Statement)			$797,319

Figure C.4

EXPLANATION OF COST OF GOODS SOLD CALCULATIONS

(1) Purchases and Freight-In: Direct Materials $540,488
Freight-in   3,669
      544,157

Inventory Adjustments by Client:
Raw Materials Inventory Increase   +$101,371
Finished Goods Inventory Increase
   Materials (Difference in WIP)
   Balances (Mat'l.), Begin. & End.   +   7,419   108,790
Purchases and Freight-In Before Inventory Adjustment   652,947

(2) Direct Labor: Before Inventory Adjustment   56,449
Inventory Adjustment by Client:
   Finished Goods Inventory Decrease Direct Labor (Difference in WIP
   Balances [Labor], Beginning and Ending)   2,417
Direct Labor Before Inventory Adjustment $ 54,032

(3) Factory Overhead reflected in finished goods inventory (beginning) improperly included in current factory costs. See statement of CPA at October 31, 1985.

(4) Since inventory adjustments have already been made in the accounts, it is necessary to add back transfers to finished goods in order to determine true total cost of goods manufactured.

Figure C.5

APOGEE EQUIPMENT COMPANY
STATEMENT OF CHANGES IN FINANCIAL POSITION
9-MONTH PERIOD ENDED JULY 31, 1986

Sources of Funds

Sale of Common Stock	$100,000	
Disposal of Treasury Stock	114,220	
Operating Expenses Not Requiring Funds:		
a. Depreciation of Fixed Assets	5,400	
b. Amortization of Patent	15,563	
Total Funds Provided		$ 235,183

Application of Funds

Purchase of Property (Exclusive of Depreciation)	$107,842	
Distributorships	20,000	
Increase in Customer Deposits	1,861	
Reduction in Advances on Stock Purchases	25,000	
Decreases in Stockholders Equity		
a. Net Operating Loss to Date	24,387	
b. Decline in Donated Capital	50,105	
Total Funds Applied		(229,195)

Net Increase in Working Capital $ 5,988

Figure C.6

APOGEE EQUIPMENT COMPANY
SCHEDULE OF CHANGES IN WORKING CAPITAL

	Oct. 31, 1985	July 31, 1986	Increase (Decrease)
Current Assets			
Cash	$ 2,336	$ 3,603	$ 1,267
Accounts Receivable	2,468	88,091	85,623
Inventories	119,368	336,287	216,919
Prepaid Expenses	11,249	11,517	268
			$ 304,077
Current Liabilities			
Short-term Notes Payable	$ 214,279	$ 360,954	($146,675)
Accounts Payable	70,999	231,171	(160,172)
Advances from Officers		2,179	(2,179)
Accrued Expenses	33,601	22,664	10,937
			$ 298,089
Net Increase in Working Capital			$ 5,988

Figure C.7

APOGEE EQUIPMENT COMPANY
COMPUTATION OF EQUIVALENT UNITS OF FINISHED PRODUCTION

November 1, 1985	July 1986	October 31, 1986
	111 Units Started	
11 Units Finished Inventory	18 Units Finished Inventory	

Projected Production

Started in Production 1986	111 Units
Deduct Gross Work-in-Process 7/31/86	12
Units Started and Completed	99 Units
Add Back Percentage Completion WIP (90%)	11
Equivalent Finished Units to 7/31/86	110*
Inventory (Finished) at 7/31/86**	18
Units Sold to Date	92

12-Month Estimate:

$$\frac{110}{9} \times 12 = 147 \text{ Equivalent Production}$$

*Nine-month production = 110
**Sales calculation on a cash basis. Purchase orders on hand are not included as sales.

Figure C.8

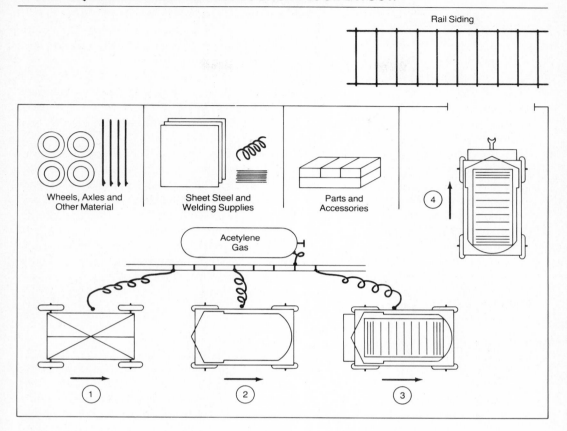

Figure C.9

durability of the inner side plates, and greater dependability of the chain sprockets. Operators in Salt Lake City requested modification for salt hauling, and others experienced minor difficulties when hauling gravel, rock, and bituminous materials.

PRODUCT PRICING

As was suggested in Mr. Wadd's comment about production costs, the manfuacturing process operates under absolutely no financial controls or guidelines. Budgets, standards, cost analyses, and other typical management control features have never been considered. Although each customer's order is started and completed without major interruption, suggesting the application of a job order standard costing system, the actual approach tends to approximate a sort of clumsy "process cost" method. To estimate the costs absorbed in a Spread-Man, one would have to summarize all manufacturing-related costs for a period (from scratch) and divide by the number of equivalent finished units. Obviously, the method would produce a homogenized result, causing all customers to share in the cost of "extras" required by some, and offering no help in discerning the impact of raw material price and labor rate fluctuations. Moreover, there is no method of judging the efficiency and effectiveness of the production crews.

Mr. Wadd's pricing policy, of which he often boasts, involves the establishment of a price that he believes will (1) discourage "meddling" by the larger heavy equipment manufacturers and (2) give his company time to become firmly established as the leader in the field during the life of his patents. Although he may intuitively consider his own rough estimate of costs, his price bears no direct relation to it.

Confronted with the large and growing deficit, and a revenue from operations obviously insufficient to cover operating costs, debt service, royalties and other "extraordinary" expenses, an increase in price was essential. Evidence reveals that each Spread-Man is currently averaging $7,572 ($832,899 ÷ 110 equivalent units) of fixed and variable manufacturing costs. Mr. Wadd was pressed into accepting a suggested retail price of $15,750 for each unit effective in 1986. After deducting excise taxes and a 20 percent dealer discount, the net yield will be increased to $11,512. On that basis, a modest profit of $138,000 can be projected for 1987 at current operating levels. See the break-even analysis (Figure C.10) and pro forma statements for the ensuing year based on sales of 300 units projected (Figure C.11) and 500 units targeted (Figure C.12) resulting from a recent market study.

MARKETING OPERATIONS

The Apogee Company markets Spread-Man through a network of distributorships established across the country. The company employs an extremely effective salesperson/demonstrator, who, by appointment, transports the demo rig into any part of the country for demonstrations. These demonstrations are usually arranged through the state highway officials and staged at a central location where road construction company representatives attend by invitation. Problems have arisen in at least one state, where state laws limit the overall tonnage a vehicle can move on the highway systems to 73,280 pounds. This reduces the pay load of a Spread-Man to only 21 tons, making it only marginally effective compared to traditional dump trucks in that state.

A forecast of Spread-Man sales for the 10 months beginning November 1986 is presented in Figure C.13.

Interestingly perhaps, but not surprising, the market for road construction equipment has proved to be highly seasonal. This fact might suggest to the company the need to produce "for inventory" during the off-season to bring a leveling effect to the production schedule, thus reducing overtime and cutting costs. Normally, the shops accelerate and slow down to fit the current demand pattern.

Hot mix (asphalt) production in the United States in 1980 was 310 million tons. For 1987 the projection is 380 million tons. Five percent penetration of the 1987 hot mix hauling market would produce sales of 418 Spread-Man units. Accordingly, the management consulting firm established a 1987 sales "goal" of 500 units based on *realistic* expectations.

APOGEE EQUIPMENT COMPANY 1987-OPERATING PROJECTION.

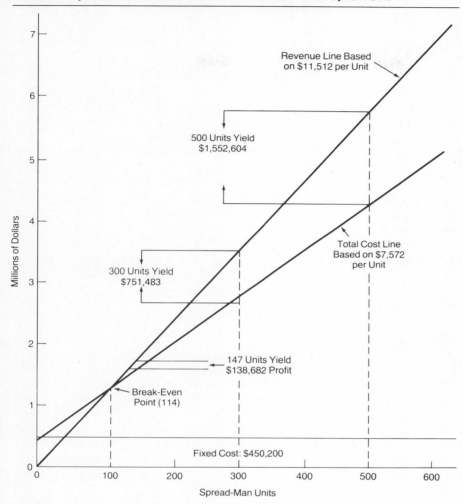

Figure C.10

Responses to a market study just completed strongly indicate the need for at least one additional demonstrator and the employment of a suitable crew to show it. Mr. Wadd agreed to engage the new personnel and to pull a new Spread-Man off the production line to be capitalized for this purpose. The question of capitalization value and method of depreciation are under discussion, since the company currently has no formal depreciation philosophy.

Invoices to customers are prepared and mailed by the office manager on the basis

APOGEE EQUIPMENT COMPANY
PRO FORMA OPERATING STATEMENT
(BASED ON SALES OF 300 UNITS)

Sales at Dealer Price*		$ 3,453,600
Less Manufacturing Costs:		
Variable [($981,000/147) − $480] × 300	$ 1,858,041	
Fixed (Total)	116,300	
Total Estimated Cost of Sales		1,974,341
Contribution Margin		$ 1,479,259
Operating Expenses:		
Variable:		
Selling Expenses (174,000/147 × 300)	$ 355,102	
Administrative Exp. (18,000/147 × 300)	36,734	
R & D Expense (1,000/147 × 300)	2,040	
Total	$ 393,876	
Fixed:		
Selling Expenses	$ 123,700	
Administrative Expenses	174,800	
R & D Expenses	35,400	
Total	$ 333,900	
Total Operating Expenses		$ 727,776
Pretax Net Profit		$ 751,483

*$11,512 (excludes excise tax)

Figure C.11

APOGEE EQUIPMENT COMPANY
PRO FORMA OPERATING STATEMENT
(BASED ON SALES OF 500 UNITS)

Sales at Dealer Price*		$ 5,756,000
Less Manufacturing Costs:		
Variable [($981,000/147) − $480] × 500	$ 3,096,734	
Fixed (Total)	116,300	
Total Estimated Cost of Sales		3,213,034
Contribution Margin		$ 2,542,966
Operating Expenses:		
Variable:		
Selling Expenses (174,000/147 × 500)	$ 591,837	
Administrative Exp. (18,000/147 × 500)	61,224	
R & D Expense (1,000/147 × 500)	3,401	
Total	$ 656,462	
Fixed Expenses:		
Selling Expenses	$ 123,700	
Administrative Expenses	174,800	
R & D Expense	35,400	
Total	$ 333,900	
Total Operating Expenses		$ 990,362
Pretax Net Profit		$ 1,552,604

*$11,512 (excludes excise tax)

Figure C.12

APOGEE EQUIPMENT COMPANY
SPREAD-MAN SALES FORECAST

Dealer Forecasts* (Survey Attached)	1986		1987								Total
	Nov.	Dec.	Jan.	Feb.	Mar.	Apr.	May	June	July	Aug.	
Central States Machinery	2	3	3	3	2	2					15
Phillup Space Equipment	1	1		6	7	7					22
Grand Falls Equipment	1	1			4	4	4	4	4		22
Horizon Equipment						2	2	2			6
Comet Line Equipment					4	4	4				12
McNaughton Machinery	1	1				7	8	8	7		32
Ace Tractor Company						3	4	3			10
Cook and Bake Equipment				2	3	3	2				10
Hercules Heavy Equipment	2	2				5	10	10	10	5	44
Dobbs Motors	1	1					20	10	10	10	52
Tiger Equipment	No comment—not enough experience										—
Gulf States Equipment	1	1				2	2				6
Smith Equipment	1					1	1	1	1	1	6
Total	10	10	3	11	20	40	57	38	32	16	237
1983 Sales (New Dealer Performance)				4	16	20	22	20	9	4	95
Projection	10	10	3	15	36	60	79	58	41	20	332

*Based on survey replies from 13 of 17 dealers. Projections are low estimates of sales from the 13 reporting dealers.

Figure C.13

of the shipping document. Copies are kept in an alphabetical file awaiting receipt of payment. The size of this task is not overwhelming at the present time, since only a few dozen customers are involved in the 1986 volume of 147 units sold. Projected sales for 1987, however, are expected to be 332 units, a full third of which will come from new accounts (see Figure C.14). With a sales goal of 500 units, one can easily visualize a growing problem in the management of accounts receivable from dealerships.

PURCHASING PRACTICES

In spite of the almost casual manner in which purchasing transactions are initiated, the production line has never been seriously delayed by a shortage or "stock-out" condition in any of the raw material or assembly parts inventories. Typically, someone from the production floor will wander into the office and say, "Mac says you-all better get some more ⅜-inch sheet stock and some welding rods." The office manager promptly takes whatever procurement action is customary or expedient. One wonders what the status of inventory items should be if the production employees were not instinctively aware of their upcoming needs.

Reference to the Income Statement for the 9-month period just ended reveals net purchases and freight of over $650,000—an average of over $18,000 per week. Raw materials of over $121,000 are currently on hand and kept under no special physical or financial controls. This represents a 500 percent increase in inventory over the past year.

Payment of suppliers' invoices is accomplished periodically by the two accountants as their busy routines permit—usually about mid-month. Some of the suppliers allow cash discounts to be taken regardless of payment date, whereas others demand payment in full when the due date is passed. The accounting staff quickly learned the difference and groups the invoices payable into two stacks accordingly. Some of the invoices in each stack might not yet be due, and some might represent shipments not yet received. In fact, confirmation of delivery of purchased materials appears as casual as the ordering process. The accountants simply do not have the time, the ability, or the means to track down every delivery transaction. Unfortunately, the receipted shipping tickets arriving with the shipment are not always retained and are seldom given systematic handling.

Neither Mr. Wadd nor his production manager envisage anything alarming about this procedure—either in the ordering, storing, or receiving area. The plant is kept under security lock when not in operation, and at least one member of the management group is always present during normal working hours. Mr. Wadd has complete confidence in the office manager and bristles at the suggestion that the system could easily be manipulated by an unscrupulous person.

The processing of vendor invoices for payment results in a charge to "raw material," and perhaps lesser charges to various other accounts as appropriate, and a single credit to cash. Accounts payable is accrued at statement time by totaling unpaid invoices and adjusting assets and expense accounts accordingly. Care, but no special *control,* is exercised to ensure against double handling of these invoices. No formal adjusting and reversing entries are made.

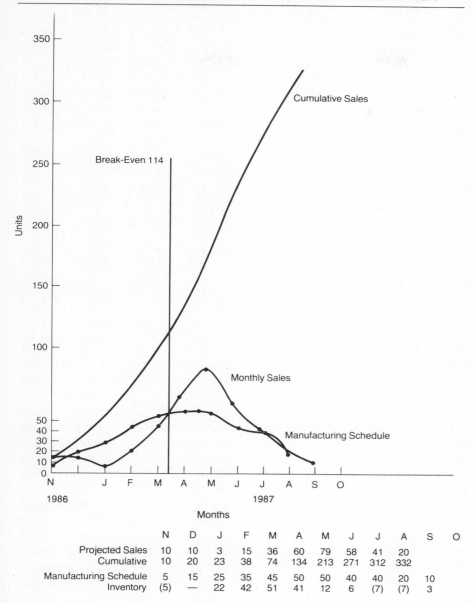

	N	D	J	F	M	A	M	J	J	A	S	O
Projected Sales	10	10	3	15	36	60	79	58	41	20		
Cumulative	10	20	23	38	74	134	213	271	312	332		
Manufacturing Schedule	5	15	25	35	45	50	50	40	40	20	10	
Inventory	(5)	—	22	42	51	41	12	6	(7)	(7)	3	

Figure C.14

INVENTORY MANAGEMENT

Up to the present, the somewhat limited variety of raw stock needs has not presented serious planning problems for the intuitive buying practices of Mac and the other production leaders. With the development of the "Street Renewer" and the almost certain quadrupling of Spread-Man production, however, problems loom on the horizon.

The management consulting team made some general recommendations that included the adoption of a formal bid procedure aimed at obtaining the best prices for raw materials. It was also suggested to Mr. Wadd and his production manager that they establish minimum stock levels for each item carried in inventory, and investigate with their suppliers the possibility of receiving price breaks for quantity buying.

Mr. Wadd anticipates a time in the not-too-distant future when he will be forced to consider expanding the present facility, which he occupies under a 10-year lease expiring in 1987. Alternatively, he will be forced to search for larger plant space. The company holds an option to renew the present lease at a 20 percent increase in rent. The lessor would agree to a leasehold improvement such as the Apogee Company would require.

Included in such plans, currently existent only in Mr. Wadd's mind, is the construction of a more efficient inventory storage area equipped with overhead conveyer systems to facilitate movement of heavy materials into the production area. This idea would replace the dollies and forklifts presently being used. This idea would have the effect of moving inventory out of the constant observation range of the production crews and place the burden of a physical inventory control on someone else. It would also require the employment of special personnel to service the production operations.

ADMINISTRATION

The culmination of financial events that has brought Apogee and Mr. Wadd to this point of decision has made a lasting impression on all of the Apogee Company management. It has become obvious that the company's product is capturing the interest of state and federal highway officials and heavy construction companies across the country. Consumer demand is on the verge of geometric growth.

On the other hand, it is equally obvious that the company's present administrative, manufacturing, and marketing practices simply cannot accommodate more growth. Although the management consulting firm was engaged primarily to help the company work its way out of the present financial bind and chart a course for profit improvement for the immediate future, almost daily conferences with the team are held to consider ways to prepare for almost certain expansion. One salient point pervades all such discussions. The company's organization structure must be streamlined to handle such growth!

Mr. Wadd has begun thinking along the lines of creating three distinct functional operations within the company, with divisions of authority along the following lines.

Manufacturing Branch Functions

Procurement
Inventory
Production
Quality Control
Receiving

Marketing Branch Functions

Sales
Customer Relations
Shipping and Invoicing
Warranty Service
Research and Development

Finance Branch Functions

Payroll and Agency Funds
General Bookkeeping
Customer Accounts Management
Supplier Accounts Management
Cashier Operations
Property Control
Systems and Procedures

The consulting team has convinced Mr. Wadd that the need for more formality of operations in all areas is imperative. Some of the matters under consideration are:

1. The development of a set of company forms to provide hard evidence of company activities and transactions in production, inventory, receiving, purchasing, shipping, invoicing, personnel, property, payroll, cash receipts and payments, and the like.
2. The development of labor, material, and overhead standards for production, and the adoption of a production costing system to facilitate the measurement of performance against those standards.
3. The development of formal accounting systems and controls over all value transactions, transformations, and flows within the company. This could be accomplished by the systems and procedures department to be located in the finance branch. A concomitant of this action is the eventual addition of a small computer.
4. The clear delegation of authority and the assignment of responsibility for specific company operations, including the budgeting of company costs along these lines.

Selected information from the report of the management consulting firm gives some insight into the objectives and activities of the company during the coming year (see Figures C.15 and C.16). On the basis of this rather optimistic (but realistic) report, a large bank has agreed to lend Apogee Company $700,000 on a 5-year, 10 percent note.

APOGEE EQUIPMENT COMPANY
GOALS AND OBJECTIVES FOR 1987

Manufacturing
Budget
   Fixed Costs $116,300.00
   Variable Costs   6,196.00/unit
   Capital Investment   50,000.00
Objectives
   Install shear and press break and effect $480/unit reduction in material costs
   Maintain production in accordance with manufacturing schedule

Sales
Budget
   Fixed Costs $123,700.00
   Variable Costs   1,184.00/unit
Objectives
   Establish dealers in all states by February 1987 (approximately 17 new dealers)
   Sell 500 units: sales goal
       332 units: conservative projection
       147 units: pessimistic projection (based on same performance as 1986)
   Implement advertising program
   Add: 2 salespersons
       1 demonstration driver
       1 serviceman
       (1 demonstration unit was added in August, 1986)
   Collect size and weight data from every state
   Collect construction and resurfacing program data from every state
   Analyze Street Renewer market
   Develop dealer sales aids
   Collect information for development of future Apogee products

Administrative
Budget
   Fixed Costs $147,800.00
   Variable Costs   119.00/unit
Objectives
   Add accounting capability in administrative office
   Add clerical capacity to support sales and manufacturing volume
   Install revised management information system
   Evaluate and refine compensation plan

Research and Development
Budget
   Fixed Costs $ 35,400.00
   Variable Costs   6.80/unit
Objectives
   Develop Tow Boy prototype
   Evaluate and implement Spread-Man improvements
   Begin Street Renewer refinement
   Add draftsman—to share with manufacturing

Figure C.15

Profit Goals

If 1987 performance equals the 1986 performance rate of 147 units, profits of $138,682 will result.

300 units will produce $751,482 profit.

332 units will produce $879,792 profit (projection).

500 units will produce $1,552,604 profit (sales goal).

Financing Needs

In order to purchase the equipment needed to reduce material costs by $480/unit and maintain an inventory of finished goods to meet peak season demands, financing arrangements must be made for $364,374. The $50,000 capital investment will be needed at once. Need for the remaining funds will arise in December or January, peak in February, and be retired by April or May.

This need is based on a projection of 332 Spread-Man sales between November 1986 and October 1987. If sales exceed this projection, sufficient income will be generated to finance increased production requirements. In the event sales do not follow projected patterns, manufacturing schedules can be adjusted to effect a corresponding reduction in financing needs.

All 1987 costs will be met at the breakeven point of 113 units. Sale of 113 units represents 77 percent of 1986 equivalent performance and 34 percent of the projected 332 sales in 1987.

Figure C.15 (cont'd)

APOGEE EQUIPMENT COMPANY
KNOWN OR ANTICIPATED 1987 ACTIVITIES

1. $50,000 additional capital investment. Additional fabrication capacity will reduce costs by $480 per unit.
2. $30,000 new advertising program.
3. Additional personnel (sales):
   Two salespersons @ $600 per month (+ 2½% sales commission)
   One demonstration driver @ $700 per month (+ $200 per trailer sold)
   One serviceman @ $650 per month (+ $150 per trailer sold)
4. Additional personnel (research and development):
   One draftsman at about $700 per month (+ $120 per trailer sold)
5. Additional personnel (office), based on increased volume of information:
   Accountant and clerk @ $2,400 per month

Figure C.16

Case Study: Bubbling Stone Beverage Company

The following narrative, financial data, and pictorial accounts are based on an actual real-world business operation, although information is thoroughly disguised to conceal any possible identity. The case portrays a strong, efficiently run company, successfully managed by *one* dominant majority stockholder. The owner is a gentleman of impeccable character and personal charm, who, over the years of his leadership, has earned the respect and admiration of an entire metropolitan community. The company remains one of the few large "paternalistic" enterprises in the country. No union exists because employee satisfaction, loyalty, and esprit de corps generally prevail.

What benefits accrue to students from studying the information systems of a well-managed business organization, as opposed to, say, those of a struggling company in desperate need of systems solutions? The authors feel that students need to observe, and can learn a great deal from analyzing well-designed and effective procurement, production, inventory, marketing, and cash systems. In this way they are able to make informed comparisons and intelligent judgments. Even in the most idealistic systems environments there can often exist control weaknesses; redundancies in document handling, processing, and filing; and risks in data base management techniques. Seeking out these probably well-camouflaged deficiencies tends to refine one's perceptions and understanding in a systems environment characterized by infinite variability in design, nature of the business, and organizational syntality.

This case can be best utilized by analyzing the various subsystems as they are discussed in class. See the case assignments at the end of Chapters 10 through 18. Additional analyses might include the following approaches:

1. Describe the apparent objectives of the various subsystems as stated and implied in the case.
2. Identify the foundation documents representing financial transactions, their points of origin, and their roles in the decision-making processes of the company.
3. Transcribe the functions of the individual subsystems in flowchart form (systems flowchart), and trace the flow of documents and information through the several related departments (document flowchart) en route to their ultimate resting place in the company's permanent records.

4. Critique the company's control procedures and assess any related risks.
5. Comment on any aspect of the company's operations that might be improved.

COMPANY BACKGROUND

The Bubbling Stone Beverage Company began bottling its soft drink, Sassafras Ale, in 1895. The drink quickly began to enjoy strong local demand as a refreshing, tangy, thirst quencher, and gradually grew in popularity as a mixer for a variety of more libatious beverages. The company was then, and continues to be until this day, a tightly controlled family business. The vast majority of the equity shares are held by Mr. Hamm R. Locke, the only son of the founder. Lesser numbers of shares are held by Mrs. Locke and three children. The company has always been led by a single strong personality (father and son) who, fortunately, exemplified the personal attributes essential to successful leadership.

In the beginning, Bubbling Stone bottled its single product and distributed it through Associated Grociers, Inc. When Mr. Hamm R. Locke assumed control in 1950, the company entered a prolonged period of sustained growth. Home-based in a large southern city, the company gradually expanded its operations to the 18 surrounding states. Mr. Locke first acquired the Popsi Cola franchise in his home city, followed in 1960 by the acquisition of the 6-UP and Dr. Peeper franchises. Company growth continued throughout the decades of the 1960s and 1970s through the acquisition of bottling and distributing operations in strategic locations in other states.

Today, all drinks are bottled exclusively in the home-based bottling facility and shipped to remote areas for distribution by other retailers and bottlers, and in an increasing number of instances by the company's own retail operations. This philosophy of centralized manufacturing and decentralized marketing has made the company one of the most cost-efficient bottling companies in the industry. The completely computerized high-speed production processes not only assure highest standards of product quality, but it also permits distribution at retail prices significantly lower than competing colas and other brand-name soft drinks. Its line of products now includes Popsi, Diet Popsi, Popsi Free, Mountain Frost, 6-UP, Diet 6-UP, Dr. Peeper, Diet Dr. Peeper, A & Z Root Beer, Sunpict, Fruitrite, and its own patented Bubbling Rock Sassafras Ale. The company maintains separate records (by division) for its own local retail sales and sales to outside distributors.

ORGANIZATION

As might be expected in a family company, all functions and operations fall under the personal supervision of the owner, Mr. Locke. The organization chart shown in Figure D.1 depicts a structure consisting of nine "departments" under the direct control of the President. The Executive Secretary to the President manages the flow of corporate information in and out of that office. Each department is headed by an executive of vice-presidential rank, to whom certain specific functions and responsibilities are delegated.

The vice-president of manufacturing and operations is responsible for procurement,

BUBBLING STONE BEVERAGE COMPANY: ORGANIZATION CHART.

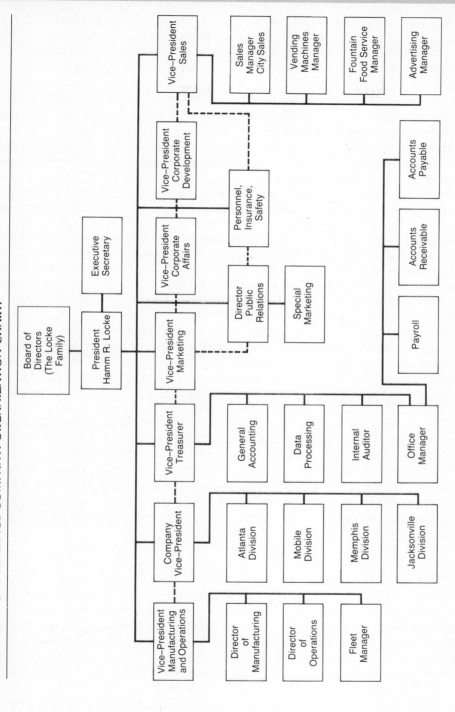

Figure D.1

manufacturing, and distribution of the product. Reporting to him are the director of operations, director of manufacturing, and the fleet manager.

The company vice-president manages the four retail divisions of the corporation. He has subordinates in charge of operations in Memphis, Atlanta, Mobile, and Jacksonville.

The vice-president/treasurer holds direct responsibility for all financial affairs of the company. His departmental operations are subdivided into general accounting, data processing, internal auditing, and office management.

The vice-president of marketing works directly with the public relations department and a special marketing unit to create and implement an overall marketing strategy for the company.

The vice-president of corporate development coordinates and tests new product lines, whereas the vice-president of corporate affairs works within and outside the company to develop corporate goodwill and monitor the public image of the company.

Finally, the vice-president of sales holds direct responsibility for maintaining and monitoring the activities of the sales force.

Mr. Locke often humorously alludes to his "horizontal" organization, referring, of course, to the broad span of control at the executive level. He insists, however, that he is quite capable and comfortable with these diverse and challenging responsibilities. In a speech to a local professional accounting meeting one evening, he stated that he personally "handled" every dollar that came into and went out of his business. He has set as his primary goal the acquisition of all major franchises for his company's products in his home state and contiguous states.

SYSTEMS LOGIC (REVENUE CYCLE SUBSYSTEMS)

In order to accomplish the corporation's objectives, the President and his key officials have structured an effective network of transaction processing subsystems to handle, control, process, and report vital financial information. These subsystems are linked in an interdependent chain of information flows illustrated in Figure D.2. Although this chart portrays the company's *overall* information systems philosophy, as described by the newly appointed Director of Internal Auditing, specific operations may appear to fit only clumsily into the pattern. The following subsystems descriptions evolved from lengthy discussions with lower management and "line" personnel.

Sales

Bubbling Stone operates two separate sales systems: a "route," or city, sales system and an "outside" sales system in distinctly separate streams.

City Sales System   This system originates through the activities of route salespersons, each traveling an established itinerary with a truckload of company products and calling on predesignated established customers. At the beginning of each workday the route salesperson's truck is stocked with the products from inventory by the shipping department. He or she is then given a list of approved customers on whom to call. Sales are made exclusively from the stock on the truck and may be made either for cash or on

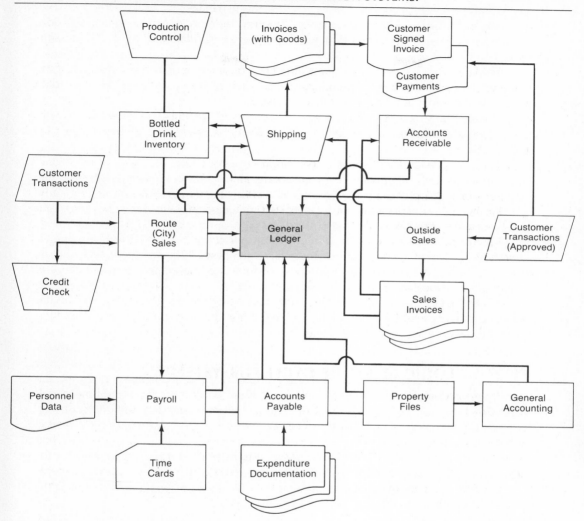

Figure D.2

account. The salesperson is authorized to pay for certain miscellaneous company expenses out of collected cash.

Check-in procedures at the end of the day require the salesperson to turn in all cash and unsold inventory and to account for all of the day's transactions. A physical count of both returned inventory and cash is made at once. The salesperson is required to reconcile total sales for the day with (1) cash turned in, (2) charge sales, and (3) out-of-pocket expenses. Discrepancies, if any, are identified and corrected before financial data are allowed to enter the system.

When all route salespersons have "cleared" the check-in procedure, a master reconciliation is performed by a designated sales office clerk, and all sales-related financial data enter the *route sales systems.* Data are processed to the general ledger system (master data base). Interfacing systems such as accounts receivable and inventory-shipping are provided all information that is critical to their operation by the route sales system.

Outside Sales System   This system handles all sales to nonlocal bottlers and distributors. Orders are routinely taken by telephone, filled from finished goods inventory, and shipped via company fleet vehicles to remote locations.

Upon receipt of the telephone order, and before confirmation of the sale, inventories are verified and the customer's credit is checked. Confirmation is immediately followed by the creation of a four-part invoice by the person handling the sale. One copy is sent to accounts receivable. The remaining three copies go to shipping where one is filed and the other two travel with the product to the customer. The customer acknowledges receipt by signing and returning a copy of the invoice to accounts receivable via the truck driver. Accounts receivable then transmits sales data and customer account information to the general ledger system.

Accounts Receivable

The division of the sales function into route sales and outside sales subsystems has resulted in the maintenance of two separate accounts receivable subsystems. Customer account changes are independently transmitted to the general ledger system by each of the accounts receivable systems, and each acts as a subsidary ledger supporting the general ledger control account. Payments on account received in the central mail room are divided according to type of account (route or outside), and distributed intact to the appropriate accounts receivable systems. Cash handling is discussed under the section of cash control.

Shipping

The shipping function varies slightly in its service to route sales and outside sales.

Route Sales   Each route salesperson provides a "stocking form" to shipping at the end of each day, specifying the goods he or she wants on the truck the following day. Each evening the shipping personnel withdraw the drinks from inventory and load the salesperson's truck in accordance with the stocking form. The route sales system is then advised by an "executed" copy of the stocking form of the exact amount of inventory on the truck, which must be accounted for at the end of the following day.

Outside Sales   Shipping is notified of outside sales by the three-copy invoice set—a copy of the form as an inventory withdrawal document and, as indicated earlier, two copies accompany the shipment to the customer. Shipping is responsible for obtaining a receipted (signed) copy of the invoice from the customer and returning it to accounts receivable—outside sales. This "turnaround" document then provides completed transaction evidence for inventory and general ledger system updating.

Inventory

When bottled products are transferred to finished goods storage by production, the inventory and general ledger subsystems are notified and updated by production reports from production control. Although inventory withdrawals are made on the basis of (1) a stocking list for route sales, and (2) copies of invoices for outside customer sales, it is incumbent on the two separate accounts receivable systems to provide transactional data to support the inventory subsystem and general ledger entries. The only direct link between inventory and the general ledger system occurs when reconciliations or manual adjustments are necessary.

SYSTEMS LOGIC (EXPENDITURE CYCLE SUBSYSTEM)

As indicated in Figure D.1, Bubbling Stone Company has no separate purchasing department. The procurement function is performed by each department according to its own needs. Although all purchases must be executed on the company's standard purchase order form, they are not serially prenumbered, and no attempt is made to control their use. Control is exercised in each division by requiring the approval signature of the vice-president in charge of the function.

Authority to receive purchased goods and services is also exercised by the organization making the purchase. A standard receipt form is used, to which all shipping documents (bills of lading, packing lists, and freight bills) are attached to support subsequent payment.

Accounts Payable

Authority to make expenditures may originate in any of the company's several departmental units. Proper documentation for such expenditures is clearly understood and observed by all units as a prerequisite to the disbursement of cash. Accounts payable plays a normal role in the cycle by reconciling vendor invoices with internally generated support documents. Discrepancies are resolved through the use of accounts payable debit and credit memoranda as necessary. The sequence of events in the purchasing/receiving/payment cycle are outlined as follows and can be visualized in Figure D.3.

1. Each department, operating within its scope, negotiates with suppliers and executes its own purchase contracts. Purchase orders are not recorded in the company's records, and all relationships with vendors are conducted by designated individuals in each department.
2. Receipt of a vendor's shipment is acknowledged by the ordering department, and a receiving memorandum is prepared in duplicate. The preparer retains a copy for the files.
3. All transaction support documents (purchase order, receiving memorandum, shipping documents) are sent to the accounts payable system.

DOCUMENT FLOW: PURCHASING AND RECEIVING.

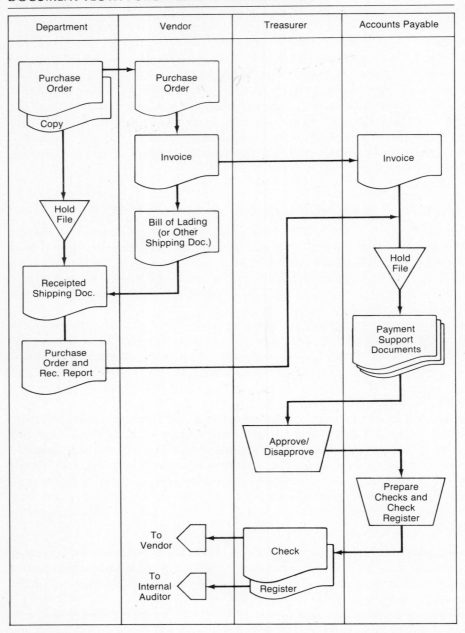

Figure D.3

4. Accounts payable holds all transaction support documents in an alphabetical file, by vendor, until an invoice is received.
5. Liability is recognized by transmitting invoice data to the general ledger. All documents are then refiled by due date.
6. On the due date, accounts payable forwards all payment document sets to the treasurer for approval or disapproval.
7. Upon approval, a check is manually prepared by the accounts payable clerk, signed by both the treasurer and the president, and mailed to the vendor.
8. All supporting documents are punched "paid" by a perforating machine and sent to the internal auditor for review.
9. At the end of each day, a recap of payments (check register) is prepared and copies are distributed to the treasurer, general accounting, and internal auditor.
10. All supporting documents are permanently filed in accounts payable.

Although accounting distributions (expense, inventory, and other property acquisitions) are effected in step 9, certain information regarding capitalizations of fixed assets purchased is provided to departmental vice-presidents. The property control system is discussed later.

Payroll

Payroll is considered a component of the expenditure cycle in Bubbling Stone, primarily because the production process is so highly automated that very little direct labor is involved. The payroll system is supported by input data from the personnel/insurance/safety department (employee status), the various operating departments (time cards), and the sales department (sales commissions). The normal payroll functions are performed (such as computation of gross pay, salaries, and commissions, and the calculation of all withholding data and payroll taxes).

Payroll system output consists of employee checks, payroll register, employee master file, withholding data for the various federal and state agencies, and payroll account distribution. Copies of the payroll register are provided to accounts payable for use in transferring funds to an imprest payroll account at a specified bank, and to the internal auditor who audits the payroll account. Other matters relating to payroll checks are discussed in the section on cash control.

General Accounting

Certain miscellaneous functions involving short-term debt are performed periodically as required by the accounting department. These matters include all accruals, reversals, taxes, interest paid and received, and profit distribution. The company has no significant long-term debt and only a minimum of short-term debt, mainly related to insuring loans to employees. Acquisitions of other franchises are totally financed through the owner. The company maintains a very attractive profit-sharing plan. Since these data are not generated in other subsystems, they are routinely journalized by general accounting to update the general ledger.

SYSTEMS LOGIC (CASH, PROPERTY, AND GENERAL LEDGER SUBSYSTEMS)

This cycle of company activities is naturally dominated by the cash control system. As previously stated, Mr. Hamm prides himself that he, or a highly trusted delegate (the treasurer), personally monitors all cash flows. Not surprisingly, therefore, all cash disbursements are made, and all incoming cash is received and accounted for, at the corporate headquarters.

The pattern of cash inflows naturally follows the company's method of distributing its products. Fleet truck drivers are not authorized to handle cash. Consequently, *all* out-of-town deliveries are charge sales. Most local (route) sales are cash transactions, however, and must be tightly controlled at the check-in reconciliation point. The system is designed to control both types: cash and mail receipts. It should be noted that mail receipts far exceed local collections.

Cash Receipts from Route Sales

Each route salesperson is provided a NORAND "route commander" computer on which each sale must be recorded. The memory of this small, hand size, computer will have been preloaded with the description and amount of inventory loaded on the salesperson's truck at the start of the day. As the type and amount of inventory sold is entered in the computer, the driver must also indicate the nature of the sale (cash or credit). Credit customers, of course, must be approved in advance by Bubbling Stone Company. The computer's printer produces a two-part sales ticket. The customer is given a copy and the other is retained to aid in reconciling the day's activities at check-in time.

When the salesperson returns to the company, a designated (bonded) clerk in the "city salesroom" is given the cash, sales tapes, and the NORAND computer. The data stored in the computer is processed, and a summary tape is produced. The summary tape, the sales tickets, the remaining physical inventory, the cash, and charge sales *must* agree. Any discrepancies are resolved at this time.

The cash is kept in a locked vault in the city salesroom where it remains until picked up by a Wells Fargo courier precisely at 5:30 PM and carried to the bank. A cash-for-deposit form (summary) is prepared in the city salesroom for each salesperson's cash transactions. These summaries are batched and sent to the office manager. At the end of the day the office manager prepares a master deposit slip for the entire day's cash receipts, including those received through the mail (discussed below).

The office manager makes copies of the master deposit slip and all the supporting deposit forms, which he retains on file in his office for a period of 3 years. The originals are placed in the city salesroom vault for 5:30 PM pickup by Wells Fargo. The bank does *not* return the "receipted" original deposit slips to the company but keeps them on file at the bank for the company.

The sales ticket and summary tape prepared by the NORAND computer at check-in point are then routed to accounts receivable where subsidiary customer accounts and the general ledger cash account are updated. Updating is accomplished by manually keying the information into the company's main computer. The hard-copy forms are then returned to the office manager for preparation of a "daily recap sheet" of all sales and cash receipts.

Mail Receipts

Most of the company's cash inflow arrives through the mail. The standard procedures for handling mail is as follows:

A designated secretary opens *all* incoming mail and separates those letters containing cash (checks). Checks and supporting documentation are then separated according to local and outside sales and routed to the appropriate accounts receivable clerk. Accounts receivable clerks in each sales system (1) endorse all checks "for deposit only," (2) prepare a list of checks by customers, (3) prepare the standard cash-for-deposit form, (4) update subsidiary accounts receivable and general ledger cash accounts by keying information into the main computer, and (5) route summary forms and endorsed checks to the office manager. The checklist is handled and filed in accounts receivable in the same manner as the summary form for local cash sales. The office manager's routine is similar to that for local cash sales, except that he is responsible for placing the endorsed checks along with the summary deposit slip in the Wells Fargo pickup vault before 5:30 PM each day. See Figures D.4 and D.5 for an abbreviated systems flowchart of each of these cash functions.

Cash Controls and Cash Management

The company treasurer exercises a great deal of power in Bubbling Stone's operation, particularly in matters relating to cash. His function is therefore closely scrutinized by Mr. Hamm R. Locke.

All checks are authorized and written at corporate headquarters. Accounts payable checks are manually prepared by an accounts payable clerk on the authority of an approved document set, signed by the treasurer and countersigned by the president, and mailed directly from the treasurer's office. Payroll checks are computer prepared, received and signed by the treasurer before being referred to Mr. Hamm for review and stamping with the signature plate. The signature plate and the blank check stocks are kept in separate safes under the singular control of the treasurer. Regular bank reconciliations of all company bank accounts are made *and* reviewed by the treasurer each month. Close monitoring of cash inflows and outflows make it possible for the company to forecast cash balances accurately, and to seek short-term investment opportunities for otherwise idle cash balances.

Petty cash funds are maintained at each division through the use of local bank checking accounts. All petty cash funds are reviewed and periodically replenished by the treasurer through normal accounts payable procedures.

Property Control

The company generally divides its fixed assets into two broad categories: (1) plant assets, which includes plant building, land, equipment, furniture, and fixtures, and (2) trucks and vending machines. Although the "system" is not *really* divided, a characteristic that distinguishes the latter grouping is an asset card file that is kept on each machine. Each card record carries a detailed description and control number of the individual asset. The

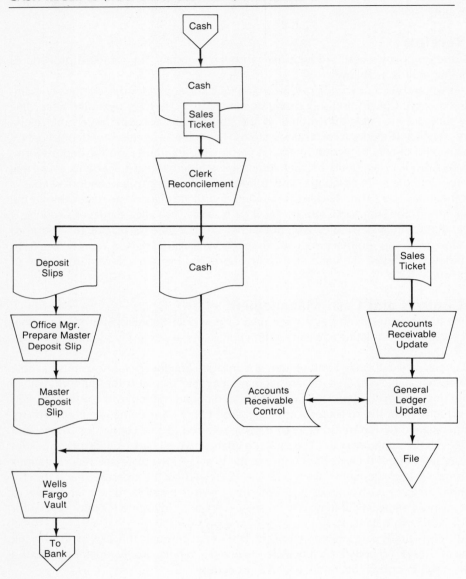

Figure D.4

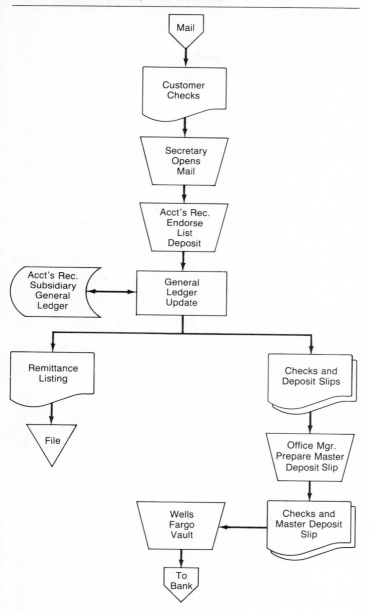

Figure D.5

location and condition of each machine is carefully monitored. Truck drivers are held responsible for the vending machines on their respective routes.

Designated company officers approve all large purchases and disposals of fixed assets. New purchases are entered into the general ledger through accounts payable. Titles to all properties owned by Bubbling Stone are kept in a safe by the president's secretary. The company has no written policy or procedure for periodic verification of asset inventories. See Figure D.6.

Property records, such as they are, serve mainly as the basis for determining depreciation. Assets acquired since 1981 are depreciated in accordance with federal accelerated depreciation procedures. The double-declining balance method was used prior to 1981. The straight-line method is uniformly used for book purposes. The expected useful life of equipment and machinery is 5 years, whereas vending machines have a 3-year book life.

General Ledger

Financial data are communicated to the general ledger system, directly or indirectly, by the sales, accounts receivable, shipping, inventory, accounts payable, payroll, property, and general accounting subsystems. General ledger accepts, stores, processes, and presents information in meaningful form for use by company management. The unique centrality of this system is illustrated in Figure D.2.

As can be seen, the general ledger is at the heart of the company's financial information flow, carefully linked to all related subsystems. The system maintains the current status of all the company's financial accounts. The current status of any or all accounts is available via trial balance printout upon request by authorized officers.

SYSTEMS LOGIC (PRODUCTION AND INVENTORY)

The inventory/production philosophy at Bubbling Stone is to maintain a minimal investment in inventories, both raw and finished, and to plan production so that customer orders can be filled within a maximum of 2 days from receipt of the orders. This often means that many of the raw material items such as syrup flavors and aluminum cans are not purchased until the day prior to production and delivery. Ready availability of cans from manufacturers in the area make it both illogical and expensive to unnecessarily consume limited warehouse space for empty can storage.

Inventory

Raw materials are usually transported in the company's own trucks by backhauling from a customer delivery. The materials are delivered to a designated receiving ramp at the home facility where a receiving slip is immediately prepared by the dock supervisor. A copy of the receiving slip is routed immediately to the production department where the shipment is recorded on a cardex file. Production planning also receives a copy of the receiving slip along with the bill of lading which are held in a suspense file until the supplier's invoice comes in. Upon receipt of the invoice, the receiving documents are attached and submitted to accounting where they are associated with the covering purchase order and processed for payment (see Accounts Payable).

CAPITAL ASSET ACQUISITION AND DISPOSAL.

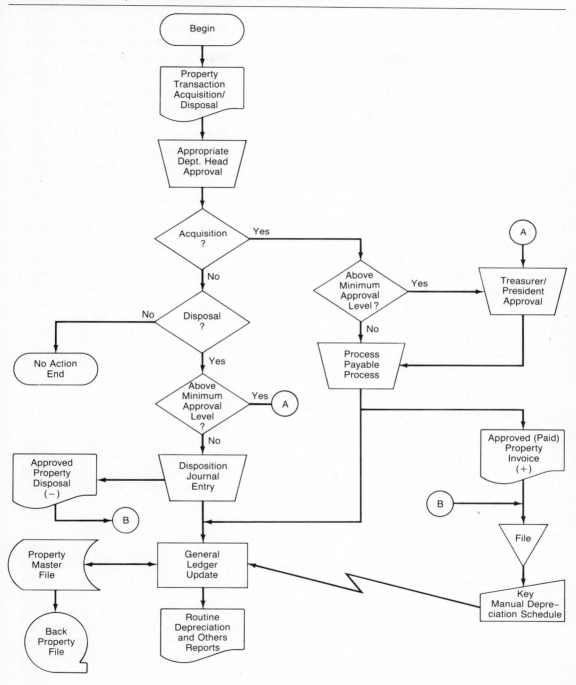

Figure D.6

Bubbling Stone has not automated its inventory control and record-keeping function. Many of the standard control features are practiced, however, albeit somewhat cumbersome and time-consuming. For example, a perpetual inventory of sorts is maintained for finished goods by adding production and subtracting sales from "running inventory balances" by flavor. The record itself is a simple handwritten worksheet.

Each morning between 4:00 AM and 7:00 AM a physical count is taken of all finished goods and raw material inventories. A copy of the daily physical inventory is sent to production planning, the production operations department, and top management. Operations personnel compare the physical inventory taken as of that morning to the production report for the previous day. The prior morning's inventory, less all sales of each product for the day, plus all production via the daily efficiency report, must correlate with the physical inventory, all of which is compared manually in production planning.

A similar procedure is used for raw materials. Actual purchase prices are charged to the cost of goods sold account in the general ledger. Since raw materials are purchased only a few days prior to actual use in production, a material usage report is prepared for processing by the accounting department.

A physical inventory is taken each month and costed at standard. All inventory transactions (purchases, usage, production, and sales) are transmitted to the computer where (1) variances are determined and (2) adjustments are made for inventory over and short. The offsetting debit or credit for these adjustments is carried in an account entitled "change in inventory."

Production

Two responsible individuals in production planning make the system work. Together they (1) place all purchase orders for raw materials, (2) prepare daily and weekly production schedules, (3) reconcile production reports to pallet tickets (for inventory updating), and (4) maintain perpetual inventories.

Based on the weekly production schedule, a third individual in production operations places orders for raw materials. In addition to production supervisors, copies of the production schedule are also routed to quality control, maintenance, and the warehouse department. Since Bubbling Stone's production processes run 24-hours a day, 7 days a week, maintenance personnel must perform routine and preventive maintenance during line downtime.

The daily production schedule, although bearing no signature of approval, serves as an authorization to release the equivalent quantity of syrup flavors to the filling room. The production process itself is totally automated from that point.

Production supervisors prepare a daily production report by shift, reflecting the (1) start and stop time, (2) types of products produced, (3) total production by cases, (4) actual run time, (5) downtime (if any) and reasons, and (6) problems encountered. Total production hours and total cases produced are keyed into the computer by one of the two production planning schedulers, from which processing a daily efficiency report emanates. The source for input regarding cases produced is the "pallet tickets" prepared by a production operator at the end of a 300-foot conveyor system far removed from the actual filling operation. Pallet tickets are prepared in triplicate, with special codes diffentiating the various container sizes. Two copies are attached to the pallet, and the original is sent to production planning for computer entry.

Any significant difference between production reports and pallet ticket summaries is immediately investigated by production planning personnel.

ELECTRONIC DATA PROCESSING

A Hewlett Packard 2000 series mainframe comprises the heart of Bubbling Stone's computer center. The company plans to replace this computer with an H/P 3000 series that is currently being test-operated in parallel with the 2000 series. At conversion time, the H/P 2000 will be given to a large university near the company's headquarters.

Plans are that the H/P 3000 will serve all the company's data processing and operational needs once management is confident that the new system can perform as expected. The system provides on-line, real-time capability, and the company's data bases are maintained on disk with back-up magnetic tapes created daily for disaster control. The back-up tapes are stored in the computer operations room. Access to the computer is controlled through the use of special passwords assigned to personnel who are authorized to perform their assigned duties.

The data bases generate a variety of sales and financial reports, usually on cue (monthly) but occasionally on request. Sales summarizes are produced on a daily basis for review and management decision making. The computer is programmed to generate periodic sales and cash forecasts. These reports are invaluable in production and inventory planning and serve the treasurer in the management of excess cash.

Computer programmers, who are responsible for systems design as well as for programming, have unrestricted access to tape and program libraries in addition to all computer center hardware. Program and systems changes are made by the programmers with the knowledge and approval of the treasurer and internal auditor.

Glossary

Access Time the time interval between a request for a transfer of data to or from a memory and when this operation is completed.

Accounting Control the plan of organization and the procedures and records that are concerned with the safeguarding of assets and the reliability of financial records.

Address the location of data contained in memory or electronic storage.

Alphanumeric a set of characters that includes alphabetic characters, numeric characters, and other characters such as commas, periods, and so forth.

American National Standard Code for Information Interchange (ASCII) a 7- or 8-bit American Standard code adopted to facilitate the interchange of data among various types of data processing and communication equipment. Also called ANSCII.

American National Standards Institute (ANSI) the organization that developed and standardized the flowcharting symbols used by systems analysts and programmers to create documents, systems, and program flowcharts.

Application Program a program that has been designed for a specific use such as inventory.

Assembly Language a special-purpose computer program or translator that converts symbolic instructions in programs into instructions that can be executed by the computer system.

Audit Trail a technique that makes it possible to retrace processing of data in order to change, add, or delete records in a file; done by documents or references that describe the action taken.

Auditing the examination of information by a third party to establish its reliability and the reporting of the results of such an examination.

Auditing Around the Computer an auditing technique in which no testing or sampling is done using the computer.

Auditing Through the Computer an auditing technique in which the computer is used for testing and sampling.

Auxiliary Storage storage that supplements a computer's primary internal storage, usually having a larger capacity but longer access time than the primary storage.

Backup files, equipment, and procedures available in case of failure or overloading in the normal course of work (includes parent and grandparent backup files).

BASIC a high-level compiler language that is algebraic in nature, usually found in time-sharing applications.

Batch Mode a computer processing philosophy in which programs are processed from beginning to end without interruption in processing.

Batch Processing. a form of processing in which items to be processed are periodically collected into groups to enable fast and efficient processing.

Batch Total a sum of a set of items that is used to check the accuracy of operations on a particular batch of records.

Bill of Materials the list of parts and/or materials required to manufacture a single unit or subassembly, or a batch of a given homogeneous product.

Binary a numbering system using only the digits 0 and 1 with positional values determined by the base 2 raised to successive powers. Most computers use some form of binary manipulation.

Bit abbreviation for binary digit; a digit, either 0 or 1, used in the binary representation of a number.

Blocking the combining of two or more records into one group for the purpose of increasing the speed and efficiency of input/output operations.

Boundary the separation between two elements, systems, or processes; a line of demarcation that separates and distinguishes two or more different entities.

Buffer (Memory) a storage area set aside as a temporary place of residence for data being transmitted (in either direction) between the central processor and a peripheral device.

Byte the equivalent of a character. A sequence of adjacent binary digits (8 bits) operated upon as a unit and usually shorter than a computer word.

Card Punch (verifier) an offline device used to punch cards, and verify the content of punched card media.

Card Reader an input device that can electronically read the holes in punched cards and transmit the data contained in them to the central processing unit.

Cathode-Ray Tube (CRT) an electronic vacuum tube, similar to a television picture tube, that is used in computer input/output terminals. The tube contains a screen on which information in any form can be displayed.

Central Processing Unit (CPU) the principal hardware component of a computer. The CPU consists of the main storage facility, the arithmetic and logic facility, and the control facility. Additionally, the CPU controls the input and output facilities.

Chain a group of records in a file logically linked together by means of pointers in such a way that all like records are connected.

Character a single element of a group of data such as a letter, number, or any special character.

Chart a graphical tool used to communicate qualitative information in a manner that is easily comprehended by the human reader.

Check Digit a digit associated with a word or group of words for the purpose of checking for the absence of certain classes of errors.

Closed (loop) System a system having no significant interaction with its environment, in contrast with an "open" system.

Coding   an ordered list or lists of successive instructions that will cause a computer to perform a particular process. Also, the act of preparing a program.

Common Business Oriented Language (COBOL)   a programming languange for business applications.

Compiler   a computer program that converts (compiles) a program written in a source language, such as COBOL, into machine language.

Completeness Tests   a type of program check designed to test input for the prescribed amount of data in the input fields.

Compliance Testing   audit testing designed to establish a degree of reliance that can be placed on internal controls.

Computer-assisted Audit Techniques   the tools and techniques, such as audit software and integrated test facility, used by auditors to audit through the computer.

Computer Program   a set of instructions or commands that guide the processing of data in a computer system.

Configuration   a specific set of equipment units that are interconnected and programmed to operate as a system.

Console   a device used as a communication link between an operator and the computer.

Control   the plan of organization and all the coordinate methods and procedures adopted within a business to safeguard its assets, check the accuracy and reliability of its accounting data, promote operational efficiency, and encourage adherence to prescribed managerial policies (AICPA definition).

Control Facility   the portion of the central processing unit that controls the other facilities by retrieving machine language instructions from main storage and then interpreting the instructions. Next, the control facility generates the signals and commands that cause the other facilities to perform their operations at the appropriate times.

Control Group   one or more persons responsible for verifying the authorization, completeness, and accuracy of input data, and for assuring that erroneous transactions are corrected and reentered.

Control Log   a record of control totals used by the control function in an EDP department to enable the reconciliation of control totals generated in related computer processing runs.

Control Totals   amounts that represent a certain point in processing to validate actions already taken.

Control Unit   a component of the central processor that controls the operations of the other CPU components and the peripheral devices on-line with it.

Core Storage   a storage device in which binary data are represented by positive or negative directions of magnetization of magnetic material.

Cost/Benefit Analysis   a technique of assessing the impact of information systems in organizations by identifying the costs and benefits of the system. Analysis of costs and benefits associated with the introduction of computer-based systems in organizations.

Credit Limit   the maximum dollar limit to which automatic credit may be extended without further credit screening.

Credit Rating   a customer's credit worthiness expressed by using an index or code.

Critical Path Method (CPM) an application of network theory to the scheduling of complex projects involving multiple component tasks.

Customer Master File a file (data base) containing relevant data on all (and each) active customers including, but not limited to, accounts receivable balances and associated summarized transaction data.

Data facts, ideas, or concepts that can be collected, communicated, or processed. The representation of facts, ideas, or concepts electronically in digital form.

Data Bank a general term for the entirety of data files in all subsystems comprising an entity's total information system.

Data Base a generalized, integrated collection of data structured to model the natural relationships in the data. A collection of files. A set of data processible by several different computer programs.

Data Base Management System (DBMS) a software system that allows access to stored data by providing an interface between users or programs and the stored data.

Data Entry Controls application controls designed to protect the system from entry of invalid or erroneous input data.

Data Filtering The process of eliminating erroneous and irrelevant data at the point of original input.

Data Processing a systematic sequence of operations performed upon data—for example, handling, computing, merging, sorting, or any other transportation or rearrangement whose object is to extract information, revise the data, or alter their representation.

Data Redundancy duplication of data in more than one file or more than one location.

Data Structure the manner in which data are represented and stored in a computer system or program.

Debug to detect and correct errors in a computer program. Synonymous with "troubleshoot."

Decentralized System a computer system configuration in which independent processing facilities are maintained at a number of separate geographical locations.

Decision Support System a functional subsystem of the management information system, responding to specific requests for information, and supporting the planning, control, and decision-making processes.

Decision Table a list of all contingencies being considered in defining and evaluating a problem.

Direct-access Storage Device a storage device, such as magnetic disk or drum, that enables data to be written or retrieved in a random manner.

Disk a direct-access storage device consisting of circular metal plates coated with magnetic oxide.

Diskette a term used alternatively with flexible (floppy) disk. A computer storage medium.

Distributed Processing System a type of system in which linked processing facilities are maintained at separate geographical locations.

Document a hard-copy medium on which data are recorded for human readability. It usually represents a business transaction such as an invoice, or time card, but may also represent a report.

Document Flowchart a graphic presentation of the flow of documents from one function (department) to another showing the source, flow, and final disposition of the various copies of all critical documents.

Documentation an accumulation of information pertaining to a given system as an aid to the people using the system.

Dump a process by which the contents of a set of storage locations are transmitted usually from an internal storage device such as core storage (primary) to an external storage medium such as magnetic disks, tape, or paper.

Echo Check a control in hardware that transmits data from an output device back to a source and compares the data to the original data.

Edit to change the form or format of data. To rearrange, or delete unwanted data.

Edit Check an application control ensuring that input data conform to certain expected characteristics.

Encoding the transformation of data into machine sensible form for subsequent computer processing.

Error-detecting Code a code to express the presence of errors that occur in processing of a program or system.

Error Log a list of errors detected by console operators during processing that should be reviewed by the control group.

Event Log a technique for assessing the impact of information systems by maintaining a list (i.e., a log) of significant events or occurrences related to the introduction and use of a system.

Exception Report a report that is produced only when certain events or circumstances are above or below prescribed standards or goals.

Executive Routine a program routine that controls the execution of other program routines.

External Auditor an accountant, usually a CPA, who renders an independent opinion on the reasonableness of an entity's financial reports.

External Labels a paper label attached to a magnetic tape or disk to identify its contents.

External Storage a facility or device, not an integral part of a computer, on which data usable by a computer is stored, such as off-line magnetic tape, disks, or punched card devices.

Feasibility Study examination of the technical, economic, and behavioral feasibility of an information system's project proposal. If the study indicates that the project can be done, it will be incorporated into a master plan for systems development.

Feedback data or information that are collected and returned to a system or process so that actual performance can be evaluated against expected performance and goals.

Feedback Loop the components and processes involved in correcting or controlling a system by using part of the output as input.

Field one or more characters representing a subdivision of a record.

File a collection of related records, such as a payroll file, arranged in sequence according to a key value contained within each record.

File Activity   the proportion of records actually affected by an updating run relative to the total number of records in the file.

File Label   a label that identifies a particular file, either internally or externally. An internal label is recorded directly onto the medium on which the file is stored as the first or last record and is machine-readable only. An external label is attached to the medium holder and is not machine-readable.

File Maintenance   adding, deleting, or changing the contents of records in a file. Reorganizing the structure of a file to improve access to records or to change the storage space required.

File Organization   a method for ordering data records stored as a file and providing a way to access the stored records.

Fixed-length Record   a record that always contains the same number of data items and the same number of characters in a particular data item.

Floppy Disk   a secondary storage medium similar in appearance to a 45-rpm record.

Flowchart   a pictorial representation of processes and procedures for operation on data. A diagram that describes documents, procedures, processes, and equipment used in processing data in a specific application.

Format   a predetermined arrangement of data, usually on a form or in a file.

FORTRAN   a high-level compiler language suitable for mathematical-type programming. Literally a "Formula Translator."

Generalized Audit Software   a computer program or group of programs that can perform certain data processing functions, such as reading computer files, performing calculations, printing reports, and selecting desired records. It is the most widely used computer-assisted audit technique for compliance and substantive testing.

General-purpose Computer   a computer designed to function in a wide variety of problem areas.

Gigabyte   one billion bytes.

Group Mark   a mark identifying the beginning or end of a set of data, including words and blocks of records.

Hard Copy   output prepared by a processing system and printed on paper or other relatively permanent forms as compared to output displayed on a cathode-ray tube terminal, which is generally temporary.

Hardware   the electrical and mechanical devices that make up a computer system. The equipment that is part of a computer system.

Hash Total   the sum of the numbers of a certain field in each record of a batch of records that is used as a processing control total.

Header Label   a machine-readable record at the beginning of a file containing data identifying the file and data used in file control.

Hierarchical Structure   a distributed system design or organization in which a superior/subordinate relationship exists between related installations.

Hollerith (card) code   a widely used system of encoding alphanumeric data into 80-column cards, developed around the turn of the century by Herman Hollerith. First used by the U.S. Bureau of the Census.

Information   the meaning that a human assigns to data by means of the known conventions used in their representation (International Standardization Organization).

Information Retrieval   methods or procedures used for recovering specific information from stored data.

Input   data entered into the system for the first time or data transfered from one system (output) to another system (input).

Input device   a device or combination of devices used to enter input data into a computer system.

Instruction   in a programming language, a meaningful expression that specifies an operation and identifies its operands, if any (International Standardization Organization).

Integrated Data Processing   a data processing system in which all relevant business data (orders, invoices, etc.) are processed in a coherent system.

Integrated Test Facility (ITF)   a computer-assisted audit technique in which a dummy entity is created (a fictitious customer, employee, store) through which test transactions are processed with regular transactions through the client's records to the general ledger, at which point they are reversed by journal entry.

Interface   a shared boundary at which point hardware components may be linked, or two or more systems may interact.

Internal Auditor   an auditor who is typically involved in appraising the accounting, financial, and operating controls within an organization in which he is employed and who renders the results of his appraisal to management.

Internal Label   a record magnetically recorded on tape to identify its contents as an integral part of the program function.

Internal Storage   addressable storage directly controlled by the central processing unit of a computer.

Inventory Management   the process of maintaining custody and control of goods in inventory in conformity with management's objectives.

Inverted File   a file whose sequence has been reversed, or is sorted by a key other than the one on which the main file is ordered.

Job Control Language   a language that programmers use to give the operating system the necessary instructions for handling a job.

Key   one or more characters within a set of data that contains information about the set that may be used to identify it, or control its use.

Keying   entry of data into a computer through a keyboard.

Keypunch   a keyboard-actuated card punch. The punching in each column is determined by the key depressed by the operator.

Kilobyte   one thousand bytes.

Label   one or more characters, within or attached to a set of data, containing information about the set, including its identification.

Labor Distribution Report   the output of a payroll system that reflects the accounting distribution of labor costs to jobs, products, projects, departments, cost centers, and other (general ledger) accounts.

Layout   see record layout. Schema.

Ledger   a compilation of accounts making up the chart of accounts together with their balances.

Librarian   a person who for security purposes is delegated the responsibility of controlling access to programs, files, and documentation in a computer installation.

Line Printer   an output device that has one print mechanism for each character position in a line of print, enabling the printing of one whole line at a time rather than one character at a time.

Lockbox   an arrangement under which customers of a company send payments directly to the company's bank, where they are credited to the company immediately.

Log   a record of the operations of data processing equipment, which lists each job or run, the time it required, operator actions, and other pertinent data.

Logical Error   a mistake in the problem-solving logic of a computer program. Unlike grammatical or data errors, most language compilers cannot alert the user to this type of error.

Loop   a sequence of instructions that can be executed repetitively, usually with modified addresses or modified data values. Each repetition is called a cycle.

Machine Language   a language that is used by the central processing unit of a computer to execute instructions and process data. Understandable by the CPU. Machine language instructions can be executed (processed) without any translation.

Magnetic Disk   a secondary storage device. A circular disk, similar in appearance to a phonograph record. Data can be recorded on the magnetic surface of the disk. Several disks can be mounted together as a stack to create a disk unit or disk pack. Data are written on or read from the surface as the unit revolves at high speeds.

Magnetic Drum   a large cylinder having a magnetic surface on which data can be stored by selective magnetization of portions of the surface.

Magnetic Ink Character Recognition (MICR)   a technique for "reading" characters printed in magnetic ink and translating them into computer-readable code.

Magnetic Tape   a tape that contains a magnetic surface on which data can be recorded by polarization of the magnetic particles.

Master File   a file that contains relatively permanent information used for reference and is updated periodically.

Microcomputer   a computer system that is functionally and structurally similar to a minicomputer. However, the microcomputer is less expensive, smaller, and has less computing power than the minicomputer.

Microsecond   one millionth of a second.

Minicomputer   a small programmable, general-purpose computer that generally has less memory than larger computers.

Mnemonic Code   a symbol designed to assist the human memory; for example, EDP for electronic data processing, MPY for multiply, and so on. Used primarily in assembly code programming.

Modem   a device for modulating and demodulating signals transmitted over communications facilities.

Monitoring Report a nondecision-oriented report that summarizes or describes events that have taken place, for example, a payroll expense report.

Multiplexor a device to regulate, interleaf, or simultaneously transmit two or more messages on a single channel.

Multiprocessing a term referring to a mode of operation of a computer system that uses two or more central processing units to execute instructions simultaneously. This approach provides better system organization by using a hierarchy of operations and control, greater system reliability, and more efficient use of processing time by permitting portions of each task to be executed on the processor that is best suited for that particular task.

Multiprogramming pertaining to the concurrent use of two or more programs by a computer.

Nanosecond one billionth of a second.

Network a system of data communication channels used for the transmission of data from one location to another.

Normalization the process of scaling. Generally, multiplying a variable by a numerical coefficient to create an integral of a variable.

Numeric Characters numerals, or representations by decimal numbers 0–9, or their equivalents (binary) digits.

Numeric Data data consisting of the numbers 0–9 on which arithmetic operations are performed.

Object Program a fully compiled (assembled) program expressed in machine (computer) sensible language.

Off-line computer equipment or devices that are not in direct contact with the central processing unit (CPU).

Off-page Connector a flowcharting symbol connecting the flow of logic in a flowchart, parts of which occur on separate pages.

On-line computer equipment or devices that are in direct contact with the central processing unit (CPU) of a computer system and usually under its direct control.

On-page Connector a flowcharting symbol that directs the reader's attention to another segment of the logic flow on the same page which cannot be connected by an unbroken line.

Operating System software that controls the execution of computer programs and the operation of a computer system.

Output data or information resulting from processing and made available to users. In a general systems sense, output is anything that is produced by a system and moved across the boundary into the environment.

Overflow in an arithmetic operation, the generation of a quantity beyond the capacity of the register or storage location that is to receive the result.

Paper Tape a strip of paper capable of recording and reusing data in the form of punched holes. Such data are capable of being read by computer-related devices in much the same fashion as punched cards.

Parallel Processing   concurrent or simultaneous execution of two or more processing units.

Parallel Simulation   the use of generalized audit software to perform functions essentially equivalent to those of the client's programs.

Parity Check   a method of self-checking data that tests whether the number of 1-bits in a binary coded array are even (even parity check) or odd (odd parity check). This is a control measure that helps to detect hardware malfunctions while transmitting data.

Payroll Register   a printed recapitulation of a company's payroll transactions with its employees including gross earnings, authorized deductions, and net pay.

Peripheral Equipment   all equipment or devices related to a computer system such as input/output units and secondary storage units but not including the central processor and its associated storage and control units.

Physical Record   a unit of data to be input or output, such as a punched card, record on a disk, or tape block. A physical record may contain several logical records; however, a logical record may require more than one physical record.

Picosecond   one-trillionth of a second.

Pointers   a field contained in one record pointing to the address of another.

Point-of-Sale Automation   devices and codes used in the retail trade (e.g., groceries, clothes) to improve the customer checkout procedure and inventory data collection procedures. The retail goods are labeled with machine-readable codes and are then read at the point of sale. Photoelectric devices transmit the machine-readable codes directly to a central computer.

Primary Storage   the component of the CPU that stores data and instructions as required during program execution; also known as main memory.

Production Cost System   a method of collecting and accumulating all costs associated with the manufacture of a product. Typically there are two: job order and process.

Production Cost Variance   the amount by which actual costs expended for the production cost elements (labor, material, and overhead) vary from predetermined cost standards.

Program   a sequence of instructions written in a computer language that directs a computer to perform a particular process.

Program Flowchart   a symbolic representation of the flow of logic, or sequence of operations, used by a programmer in developing computer programs.

Programmer   one who converts a sequence of logical steps leading to a problem's solution into a program written in a particular computer language. The person is usually involved in the writing, testing, and debugging of a computer program.

Punched Card   a secondary storage medium made of lightweight card stock. A standard-size card has 80 columns, each of which is capable of representing one character of information in the form of a rectangular punched hole.

Purchase Order   A legal document offering to buy goods at stated prices, usually with some type of time limit.

Purchase Requisition   an authorizing control document directing a purchasing agency to acquire materials and services from outside vendors.

Random Access   a method of locating records in a file in which a desired record can be found by going directly to that record location without first having to access all the preceding records. Same as Direct Access.

Raw Material   unprocessed materials, manufactured parts, and subassemblies used in the production of a finished product.

Real-time Processing   the processing of transactions as soon as they occur and in such a manner as to provide an immediate response to the user.

Receiving Memorandum   an official record or receipt of a shipment from an outside source. Generally it authenticates the order; confirms its acceptability; and verifies the quantity, measure, or weight.

Record   a collection of data fields treated as a unit.

Record Count   a count of the number of records in a file or the number of records processed by a program.

Record Layout   a diagram showing the nature, location, size, and format of fields within a record.

Remote Batch Processing   refers to the processing of jobs using special terminals with high-speed input/output capabilities from a location removed from the central processor.

Remote Terminal   usually an input/output computer device that is located at a distance from the main computing center.

Response Time   the amount of time that elapses between a request for data or processing and the receipt of the data or processing results.

Responsibility Accounting   a system of cost distribution in which all value flows (revenues, expenses, costs, and assets) are directed to the responsible cost centers.

Routing List   a sequence of production operations (steps) specified by manufacturing engineering to assure uniformity of product and efficiency of operations.

Run Manual   a manual containing documentation that describes the elements and procedures required for a computer run (e.g., processing system documentation, program logic, controls, program changes, and operating instructions).

Sales Discount   an incentive granted by the seller of merchandise to encourage prompt payment by the buyer. Example; 1/10, n/30. It is generally based on the total *amount* of the sale, and is focused on time, not price.

Sales Invoice   the culmination of a purchase/sale transaction requesting payment from the buyer.

Sales Order Processing   the execution of the purchase/sale agreement, encompassing the production, order assembly, and shipment of goods and services.

Schema   the arrangement of data fields within a record. Literally, the record layout. The description of a whole data base in terms of its component data elements and their various relationships.

Secondary Storage   a form of data storage that supplements a computer's primary storage. Data kept in secondary storage must first be read into primary storage before processing can be done. Examples of secondary storage media are magnetic tape, disk, and punched paper tape.

Sequential Access a method of locating records in a file in which each record is either read or processed one after another. If a desired record is located in the middle of a file, all previous records must first be processed in sequential order before the desired record can be accessed.

Sequential Processing same as Batch Processing.

Service Bureau an independent organization that specializes in providing the data processing needs of its customers for a fee.

Shipping Document an order, manifest, or bill of lading to accompany goods in transit. They specify the descriptions and quantities of goods shipped, and assign custodial responsibility while in transit.

Software the collection of programs and routines, such as compilers, operating systems, and utility programs, that facilitate the use of hardware.

Source Code instructions written in a higher-level programming language. Source code is translated into object code that can be executed by the central processing unit.

Source Document a document from which data are extracted—for example, a document that contains typed or handwritten data to be keypunched.

Source Program a computer program written in a symbolic language, later to be converted into a machine sensible "object program" by an assembler program, or compiler.

Standard Cost established cost expectations for the factors of production (material, labor, and overhead) against which actual cost experiences are compared for control purposes.

Symbolic Language a programming language using symbolic operations codes and addresses that are more understandable to humans than machine language equivalents.

System an organized entity characterized by a boundary that separates it from all other systems. A system may consist of other systems or components and may interact with its environment through input and output.

System Configuration the rules for interconnecting the available equipment units that collectively define the range of possible configurations for a particular computer system.

System Flowchart a diagram using symbols to depict the flow of work, documents, and operations in a data processing system.

Systems Analysis the examination of an activity, procedure, method, technique, or business to determine what needs to be done and how it can best be accomplished.

Systems Analyst one skilled in the analysis and design of information systems.

Teleprocessing a data processing system that employs a combination of computers and communications networks, thereby enabling the data collection points and the main computing installation to be separated from each other.

Terminal an on-line device through which data are entered using a typewriter keyboard or optical scanner.

Test Data a set of dummy records and transactions (including calculations where the results are known) used to determine whether a program or system is operating according to its design.

Time Sharing   a system that allows a communication link to multiple users and the computer simultaneously.

Track   the section of a data storage medium that is associated with each read/write head; for example, on a magnetic disk, one of several concentric rings in which data are stored, or on magnetic tape, one of several channels (usually seven or nine) that run parallel to the edges of the tape.

Trailer Label   a record that follows a group of records on a file and contains summary information related to those records.

Transactions File   a file containing detail records of temporary data that accumulated during a specific period of time.

Turnaround Document   an output document designed to stimulate a specific customer action and act as an input document upon completion of that action. Example, a remittance advice attached to an invoice that is returned with the payment.

Turnaround Time   the elapsed time between the initiation of a task (job, document, assignment) and its completion (availability of the output).

Uniform Chart of Accounts   an orderly arrangement of asset, liability, capital, revenues, and expense accounts making up the general ledger.

Utility Program   a standard program that performs routine tasks such as sorting or merging files.

Variable-length Record   a record that may contain a variable number of characters. Contrast with fixed-length record.

Verifier   a keypunch-like machine used to establish whether data that were keypunched onto a storage medium (e.g., punched card) were accurately punched. The check is made by rekeying the same data.

Virtual Storage   a strategy for increasing the effective size of working memory by automatically moving program segments and data back and forth between main memory and auxiliary storage.

Work-in-Process   the value of goods currently in various stages of production expressed in terms of equivalent units of the finished product, and reflecting the material, labor, and overhead costs accumulated against those units.

Work Order   a production authorization document.

Index